W9-CNL-271

A HISTORY OF

GEORGETOWN UNIVERSITY

VOLUME 2

Georgetown has really made itself a university, not just
an overgrown college or collection of colleges. . . .
[It] has brought into being a harmonious,
well articulated educational society.

MIDDLE STATES ASSOCIATION OF COLLEGES AND SECONDARY SCHOOLS REPORT, 1961

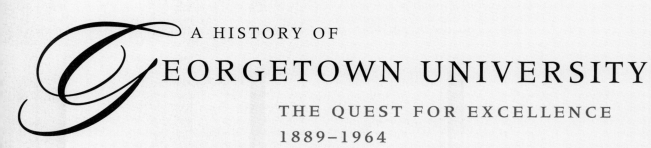

A HISTORY OF

GEORGETOWN UNIVERSITY

THE QUEST FOR EXCELLENCE
1889–1964

VOLUME 2

ROBERT EMMETT CURRAN

Foreword by John J. DeGioia

Georgetown University Press | *Washington, D.C.*

This text of this book is set using the Meridien typeface family with Myriad as the supporting sans serif typeface and Sloop for the script elements that appear in the front matter.

The ornamental images used in the chapter opening pages are details of the stained glass window in Healy Hall (photographed by James Schaefer).

The book is printed on 70# Somerset matte paper by R.R. Donnelly and Sons, Willard, Ohio.

Cover and interior design and composition by Naylor Design, Inc., Washington, DC.

Library of Congress Cataloging-in-Publication Data

Curran, Robert Emmett.
    A history of Georgetown University / Robert Emmett Curran ; foreword by John J. DeGioia.
        v. cm.
    Includes bibliographical references and index.
    Contents: v. 1. From academy to university, 1789-1889— v. 2. The quest for excellence, 1889-1964—v. 3. The rise to prominence, 1964-1989.
      ISBN 978-1-58901-688-0 (v. 1 : cloth : alk. paper)—ISBN 978-1-58901-689-7 (v. 2 : cloth : alk. paper)—ISBN 978-1-58901-690-3 (v. 3 : cloth : alk. paper)— ISBN 978-1-58901-691-0 (set : alk. paper)
    1. Georgetown University--History. I. Title.
      LD1961.G52C88 2010
      378.753--dc22
                                                                    2009030489

∞ This book is printed on acid-free paper meeting the requirements of the American National Standard for Permanence in Paper for Printed Library Materials.

15 14 13 12 11 10   9 8 7 6 5 4 3 2
First printing

Printed in the United States of America

FSC
Mixed Sources
Product group from well-managed forests, controlled sources and recycled wood or fiber

Cert no. SCS-COC-000648
www.fsc.org
© 1996 Forest Stewardship Council

Lord, teach me to number my days aright that I may gain wisdom of heart.

PSALM 90

In memory of Michael Foley and all his heart-wise companions through Georgetown's two centuries.

TITLES IN THIS SERIES

CONTENTS

Appendices

FOREWORD

From the Jesuit tradition of education and the American spirit of independence, Georgetown has grown from the Catholic academy founded by Archbishop John Carroll that first educated six students, into a global research university with more than 1,300 faculty members that today welcomes 15,000 students from more than 130 countries to our campuses each year. *A History of Georgetown University,* volumes 1–3, captures the compelling narrative of the people and the traditions that have made this remarkable transformation possible.

Georgetown's first hundred years saw great change in Archbishop Carroll's academy. From the very start, we had assets of incalculable value: the extraordinary vision of our founder, and a commitment to pluralism, inclusiveness, and support for the highest ambitions of this country. In the decades leading to the Civil War, Georgetown transformed itself from something not much more than a high school—our first student, William Gaston, was only thirteen years old when he entered—to a full college. In 1851, Georgetown established the nation's first Catholic medical school. And at the close of Georgetown's first century, the leadership and extraordinary vision of Patrick Healy, SJ, laid the foundation for our emergence as a university. Perhaps the most symbolically significant step was Father Healy's decision to construct the building that would bear his name, and to reorient the college to have it positioned away from the river and directly facing the city of Washington, DC, thereby permanently linking our campus and community. Over the next hundred years, Georgetown expanded in enriching ways by becoming a more diverse community committed to educational excellence in each of our nine schools. In the early twentieth century, as a direct response to the tragedy of World War I, Georgetown opened the nation's first school dedicated to the study of international affairs and to the preparation of a new type of public servant. After World War II, in response to the nation's new, international economy, we founded a school of business.

Georgetown has seen immense growth and change in the size and diversity of our community, in the breadth of scholarship, and in the physical expansion of our campus. We have seen the university grow from an outstanding regional university that is recognized for superior undergraduate teaching and highly regarded for our schools of medicine and law, to an exceptional national research university, and now as an aspiring global university. Yet we know that the Georgetown University of today is only possible because we move forward in the traditions espoused by John Carroll and animated by our identity as a Catholic and Jesuit university. The commitment to education, service, and academic freedom that brought the first Georgetown community together in 1789 continues to inspire and motivate our faculty, students, and alumni today.

In over two centuries, our university has become something that John Carroll and our other early leaders could never have imagined. Sometimes, when I see the Gilbert Stuart portrait of John Carroll that hangs on the wall in my office, I wonder what he would think of his little "Academy." I suspect that he would marvel at how far we have come, how much we have accomplished, and how much we have contributed to the educational and social landscape of our city and our nation. I also think that he would remind us of our continuing responsibility to fulfill our promise and potential and to strive to become the university we are called to be.

We are deeply grateful to Robert Emmett Curran for creating this wonderful record of our work as a community to fulfill this mission over the past two centuries. In the words of the 28th Superior General of the Society of Jesus, Father Pedro Arrupe, we seek to foster a community of "women and men for others"—individuals who are committed not only to intellectual inquiry, but to advancing human knowledge in service to others and, in turn, advancing the common good.

—John J. DeGioia
President, Georgetown University

PREFACE

When the first volume of this history, titled *The Bicentennial History of Georgetown University: From Academy to University, 1789–1889,* was published in 1993, I noted that it was appearing much later than the bicentenary of the university that had originally occasioned it. Little did I realize that it would not be until the end of the first decade of a new century before the companion volumes would be in print, two decades removed from the event it was supposed to commemorate. Lateness, however, can bring some benefits.

Father Timothy Healy had envisioned a bicentennial history that would carry Georgetown's story up to 1964, with the retirement of Father Edward Bunn, who is commonly considered to be the university's second founder. To go beyond that, Father Healy reckoned, would be to plunge into historical waters that were still making their way to shore and carrying along many persons still very much part of the Georgetown scene. Even in the 1980s that constricted coverage of the university's past made little sense to me. Ending Georgetown's history in the middle of the 1960s was to miss a great, if not the greatest, part of the narrative that was the university's by the end of its second century. My intention early on was to carry the history to 1989. From the prespective of another fifteen years I decided finally to bring it—through an epilogue—as close to the present as I could, knowing that recent history is always quite different from the older kind to which there is paradoxically greater access with less of a tendency to bring presuppositions to the weighing of people and events. Georgetown as a vital institution should have a living history that tries as best as it can to tie past to present. However realized, that has been my aim.

This edition consists of three volumes. Volume 1 is a revision of the 1993 volume that covers Georgetown's initial century. The second volume traces Georgetown's history through its next seventy-five years, from 1889 to 1964. Two very strong presidents bookended its second hundred years: Joseph Havens Richards and Edward Bunn. Richards, in his ten-year tenure

(1888–98), renewed Patrick Healy's aspirations to make Georgetown a full-fledged American Catholic university in the nation's capital. "Situated as we are at the nation's Capital, and enjoying an exceptionally fine reputation," he wrote in September 1894, "we have an admirable field for development into one of the greatest, perhaps the greatest institutions of the country." Richards's efforts to create a broad cadre of academic specialists to direct advanced studies, do research in the arts and sciences, as well as develop the facilities and funding to support them, failed in great part but they set the standard for Georgetown's quest to become an elite research university over the course of its second century.

With Richards's departure, that quest was essentially put on hold for the next twenty years while his successors concentrated their attention on the college, and the professional schools of law and medicine reverted to their separate spheres. In that interim the configuration of the university changed as the professional schools of dentistry, nursing, and foreign service were added piecemeal, and the preparatory school, which had been the heart of Georgetown during its first century, was finally unlinked from the university and relocated in Maryland. In the 1920s "The Greater Georgetown" campaign was a formal attempt by a new president, John Creeden, to create an endowment to enable the university to develop the centralized facilities and faculty that would make it a bona fide comprehensive institution of higher education. That campaign proved to be a crushing disappointment and Creeden's successor had little interest in pursuing his plans. The Depression, however, ironically proved to be a catalyst for the effective resumption of "The Greater Georgetown" as the next president, Coleman Nevils, took advantage of the favorable building conditions to construct a new home for the medical and dental schools, a classroom building, and a student residence.

The second "Great War" of the twentieth century transformed the main campus of Georgetown into a testing center for the Army; most of the medical, dental, and nursing students became members of the training corps of the various services. To compensate for the loss of male students, females were admitted to the graduate school and the school of foreign service for the first time. In the immediate postwar era enrollment nearly doubled as the GI Bill opened the university's doors to many who earlier could not have considered such an education.

Edward Bunn (1952–64) brought the university into the modern world of higher education by centralizing the administration of its schools, introducing planning as a mechanism for shaping the development of the university, by recruiting, particularly in the medical center, a faculty who was more committed to research and publication, and by overseeing an unprecedentedly ambitious building program largely funded by the federal government. By the time he stepped down as president at the end of 1964, "Doc" Bunn had earned the title of "founder of the modern Georgetown."

The third volume, with the exception of the epilogue, covers the shortest part of Georgetown's history, barely a quarter of a century, yet arguably its most important one in terms of its development as a university. Edward Bunn's immediate successor, Gerard Campbell, completed the modernization of the university in the 1960s and brought it into the mainstream of American university life by restructuring the governance of Georgetown and allowing, for the first time, participation of faculty in the process; establishing the first comprehensive capital development campaign; and completing the democratization of student enrollment by admitting African Americans and women into all the schools of the university.

The last three decades of the twentieth century have proved to be the most dynamic in Georgetown's history as the institution acquired national and international stature. Its enrollment at both the undergraduate and professional levels not only doubled but the diversity and quality of the student body increased dramatically as well. The caliber of the faculty improved impressively across the three campuses. Strong administrative leadership in those decades developed the institution's academic and financial strengths. No one was more responsible for Georgetown's rise to prominence as a university than Timothy Stafford Healy, who as president from 1976 to 1989, gave the university an unprecedentedly national voice as he became one of the most influential leaders in higher education by articulating its ideals and challenges, as well as defining the unique Catholic and Jesuit traditions that inform Georgetown. Healy personally led the university in becoming more diverse in both the student body and faculty, and he was highly instrumental in sextupling the institution's endowment during his tenure. By the time he stepped down from office at the end of Georgetown's second century, he had brought the university to the brink of becoming a truly great institution.

The organization of the three volumes is partly chronological, partly thematic. Volume 1 follows a broadly chronological pattern, with the exception of chapters 7 and 8, which deal with student culture and education, respectively, during the antebellum era. In volume 2 the chronological approach prevails, aside from chapter 4, which covers the development of intercollegiate sports at Georgetown from the 1890s through the 1920s. Volume 3 employs a topical approach within the larger timelines of the period we have come to know as "The Sixties," as well as that of the fifteen years following the "Sixties" that has yet to receive a distinguishing label. In organizing the volumes in this way, I have tried to minimize the repetition inherent in such a treatment.

ACKNOWLEDGMENTS

In the course of nearly a quarter century of work on this history, I have amassed many debts. The board of advisors that Father Healy established to supervise the project were very helpful in the early planning. Several members were especially invaluable: John Rose was an unfailing resource for the history of the medical center; Father Brian McGrath generously shared with me over the course of many hours his extensive knowledge of Georgetown's history from the 1930s to the 1980s; and Dorothy Brown, Paul Mattingly, and James Scanlon read all three manuscripts. The published text has profited immensely from their critiques. When the bicentennial volume was published in 1993, I said that had they themselves been the authors, Georgetown's history would have been the richer. Having benefited from their comments on the second and third volumes, I can repeat that with even more assurance. Georgette Dorn provided great help by translating documents in Italian and Spanish. Hubert Cloke, John Hirsh, John Farina, Christopher Kauffman, Dolores Liptak, Timothy Meagher, and Paul Robichaud, CSP, also generously read and responded to various chapters.

I would like to thank also the following archivists and historians for their assistance: Sister Felicitas Powers, RSM, the Reverend Paul Thomas, and Tricia Pyne of the Archives of the Archdiocese of Baltimore; Francis Edwards, SJ, of the English Province Archives of the Society of Jesus; Edmond Lamalle, SJ, of the Roman Archives of the Society of Jesus; Henry Bertels, SJ, librarian at the Roman Curia of the Society of Jesus; John Bowen, SS, of the Sulpician Archives of Baltimore; Hugh Kennedy, SJ, and John Lamartina, SJ, of the Maryland Province Archives of the Society of Jesus at Roland Park, Baltimore; and Paul Nelligan, SJ, of the Archives of the College of the Holy Cross.

The university has been consistently generous in its support of this project. A university leave from 1985 to 1987 allowed me to begin the research in Europe and in this country. The university also provided research assistants for the project: Keith Allen, Mark Andrews, Anne Christensen, Katherine

Early, Tracy Fitzgerald, Bruce Fort, Patricia Jones, Ellen Kern, James Miller, Mark Sullivan, and Yang Wen put in countless hours, largely in the tedious task of compiling and entering information for the student-faculty databanks. Sally Irvine and Barbara Shuttleworth, my two original assistants, were marvels at organizing the research and setting high standards in coordinating it. Anna Sam, my research associate for several years, was virtually a coauthor of the bicentennial volume. Grants from the graduate school in recent years assisted me significantly in bringing the project to a close.

At the Joseph Mark Lauinger Library, several persons have been especially instrumental in the preparation of these three volumes: Artemis Kirk, university librarian; John Buchtel, head of special collections; Jon Reynolds, university archivist from 1970 to 2000; Lynn Conway, his successor; Lynn's assistant, Ann Galloway; and David Hagen, of the Gelardin New Media Center. Patrick J. McArdle, associate athletic director, was a rich source of information for the history of Georgetown sports. At Georgetown University Press, director Richard Brown has shown a steady, not to mention resourceful, hand in shepherding this edition through its long and twisting path toward publication. Rebecca Viser was invaluable as photo editor in locating and securing permissions for the many illustrations in the three volumes.

It is with added pleasure that I acknowledge the photography of James Schaefer, associate dean for academic affairs and financial aid in the Graduate School of Arts and Sciences. Jim has photographed the campus over many years and we acknowledge with gratitude his permission to use many of his photographs throughout the three volumes.

Finally, to my wife, Eileen, whose patience and support have meant more than she can ever realize, I give heartfelt appreciation.

ABBREVIATIONS

ARSI	Archivum Romanum Societatis Jesu
AVP	Academic Vice President
B	School of Business Administration Alumnus
C	College of Arts and Sciences Alumnus
CAS	College of Arts and Sciences
CJ	*Georgetown College Journal*
D	Dental School Alumnus
F	School of Foreign Service Alumnus
G	Graduate School Alumnus
GUA	Georgetown University Archives
I	School of Languages and Linguistics Alumnus
L	Law School Alumnus
M	Medical School Alumnus
MD	Marylandia
MPA	Maryland Province Archives
MPARP	Maryland Province Archives at Roland Park
N	Nursing School Alumna
SBA	School of Business Administration
SFS	School of Foreign Service
SLL	School of Languages and Linguistics
WL	*Woodstock Letters*
x	This designation, preceding a date and school classification, indicates an alumnus who did not graduate but was a member of that class.

Aerial View of GREATER GEORGE Town

PART ONE

TOWARD A GREATER GEORGETOWN, 1889–1928

CHAPTER 1

Joseph Havens Richards and the Emergence of the University

We stand tonight on the threshold, between the first and second centuries of organized Catholic teaching. . . . An almost incredible expansion & multiplication of organized and growing, but still incomplete universities, has taken place. . . . What is wanted is to bring together these able men, to concentrate our forces in some few really great institutions, and leave the larger number of our Catholic Colleges to the field that really belongs to them—that of intermediate education. . . . And what spot so suitable for this . . . focus of light and learning, as our own city of Washington, the nation's capital.

JOSEPH HAVENS RICHARDS, 1889

Joseph Havens Richards and the Quest for Excellence

In the spring of 1889, less than a year after becoming president of Georgetown, Joseph Havens Richards gave an address of welcome to Bishop John J. Keane, who had recently returned from Rome to become the first rector of the Catholic University of America. "We stand tonight," Father Richards told his audience at Walker's Hotel in Washington, D.C., "on the threshold, between the first and second centuries of organized Catholic teaching. . . . [V]ery much has been done. An almost incredible expansion & multiplication of institutions, schools, academies, and colleges, with half a dozen organized and growing, but still incomplete universities, has taken place." In truth, Richards went on, many, if not most, of the Catholic institutions of higher education were really high schools. There was no uniformity in curriculum or standards. Scientific education was "almost entirely lacking." Specialists in any branch were virtually unknown.

"If we analyze closely the confusion existing at present in our Catholic educational system," the fault, he suggested, lay in two areas: "want of concentration and want of organization." The Catholic community was not lacking talented and able scholars and educators, he contended. They were simply fragmented among too many colleges in too many isolated places. "What is wanted," he proposed, "is to bring together these able men, to concentrate our forces in some few really great institutions, and leave the larger number of our Catholic Colleges to the field that really belongs to them— that of intermediate education." And so he welcomed the new university as a provider of such an intellectual center and a measure of academic excellence. "Concentration she will supply—because by bringing here a nucleus of able and admirable men, as she has already done in the persons of the Professors who are ready to open her classes, she will attract others. . . . And what spot so suitable for this collection of eminent men, for the focus of light and learning, as our own city of Washington, the nation's capital. Here the Science, the wit, the literature, the art of our country is slowly but surely concentrating."[1]

At the conclusion of Richards's remarks, Keane told Richards that they were the "best utterance he had heard on the Cath[olic]. University."[2] In 1889 the idea of the university, including a Catholic one, was still very much in germination in America, an idea with variable, if not competing, meanings. Whether the primary function of the institution was chiefly or even exclusively graduate, as opposed to undergraduate, education; whether research and specialization were to be integral to the mission of the university; whether the university ideally should encompass undergraduate, graduate, and professional training—these and other considerations were still unsettled both in Catholic intellectual circles and in the larger world of higher learning. The episcopal leaders who had founded the Catholic University of America clearly had a vision of the institution as primarily a higher seminary for the training of clergy. Bishop Keane had in mind more of a Catholic version of Johns Hopkins, the research university that had been established a decade before in Baltimore.[3] However close Richards had come to Keane's vision in delineating his idea of a university, the potentially great university the Georgetown president had in mind was not so much the one so recently given a pontifical charter but his own institution that had secured such a charter more than a half century before. As Richards confided to a Canadian Jesuit, "I know . . . the Society possesses very few Universities properly so-called in the world. But I cannot read the fourth part of the constitutions without perceiving that St. Ignatius was anxious to have us eminent in that field as in others, for the glory and service of God."[4]

In Richards, Georgetown did have a second Patrick Healy—a man with the vision and determination to make Georgetown a first-rate American Catholic university. Healy had clearly influenced Richards deeply during the latter's five-year stint teaching mathematics and physics at Georgetown from 1878 to 1883. Healy had been the one responsible for sending Richards to Harvard for scientific studies. Once he became president of Georgetown in 1888, Richards continued to rely on Healy for advice and support. Indeed there was much about Richards that suggested a younger and more intense Healy.

Like Healy, Richards was something of an outsider, the son not of a slave but of a former Protestant clergyman. The angular and ascetical-mannered Richards, even more than Healy, struck many as an austere man, aloof in his personal relationships and rigid in his principles, the residue, some thought, of his Protestant background. As a superior general summed up the appraisals of Richards, "Neither the community nor the students care much for him."[5] Like Healy, he was a man of enormous energy, a prodigious administrator concerned with, if not involved in seemingly everything about, the university, from the composition of the medical faculty to the recipients of scholarships for the various athletic teams. Unlike Healy, he began taking small but meaningful steps to build up the administrative bureaucracy to match the realities of the expanding university. But the work of development fell overwhelmingly to him, as it had Healy, and, like his predecessor, Richards paid the price in periodic collapses of his health and eventual forced retirement. As with Healy, he was considered too ambitious in his goals for Georgetown, spending more than the university and the province could afford in order to realize his dreams of institutional glory.

Richards brought to the office not only the intention to complete Healy's ambitious designs for Georgetown but a broader, more contemporary notion of what a university at the close of the nineteenth century needed to be: a comprehensive institution that would bring together all the arts and sciences; provide a broad but elastic liberal education for undergraduates; attract and develop specialists to do research, especially in the sciences and medical profession; and serve as an intellectual center for the community, church, and nation. Richards, from virtually his first month as president, boldly attempted to make Georgetown a modern university with advanced study in all the arts and sciences and with the facilities, experts, and financial support to realize them. He intended to revive the observatory as a research facility to demonstrate dramatically the university's commitment to scientific development. The centerpiece of that commitment was to be a scientific school, where work and training would be done in physics, chemistry, and the other natural sciences, as well as in engineering. The medical and law departments needed more adequate facilities, especially the former. As early as 1890, Richards was pressing to construct a hospital that would provide the facility for assembling a first-rate clinical staff and the means for providing superior clinical training and research. He also determined to bring back to Georgetown the Jesuit theologate, or divinity school, that had moved to Woodstock in 1869.[6] Like Carroll, Richards's ambition for Georgetown was nothing short of audacious. "Situated as we are at the nation's Capital, and enjoying an exceptionally fine reputation," he once wrote, "we have an admirable field for development into one of the greatest, perhaps the greatest institution of the country."[7]

Riggs Library

One of the first things Richards did as president was to complete the library portion of the new college building (Healy) that had stood unfinished for over a decade. He seized upon the dismay expressed by a prominent Washington Catholic, the banker Elisha Francis Riggs, at the pathetic condition of Georgetown's old library to approach him about funding the completion of the projected library in the new building or as a separate structure.[8] Riggs agreed to fund the former, and Paul Pelz, one of the architects for the building, did the design for the library. The four-story library opened in early 1890 in the south wing. The *Georgetown College Journal* noted the elegance of the new facility but pointed out that the "many vacant places" on the wrought-iron shelves was a testament to the embarrassingly small size of the university's actual holdings.[9]

In fact Richards had been appalled at the state of the library since serving as librarian in the early 1880s. "Even in theology and Philosophy," he wrote to a local woman who was the lone regular contributor, "there exist not merely gaps, but chasms everywhere." She embraced his suggestion to use her donations to develop a core of classical Catholic texts to "build up our library from the bottom and make it what the library of the oldest Catholic College in the United States ought to be—a representation and comprehensive Catholic collection."[10] Through her support and that of others, Richards was able to acquire, among other things, the 387-volume Migne edition of Greek and Latin patrology as well as a complete set of the works of Aquinas.[11] The president also had Georgetown designated as a depository of U.S. government documents beginning in 1894.[12]

In the following year Richards purchased the ten-thousand-volume library of John Gilmary Shea, the eminent Catholic historian. When Richards in 1889 had approached Shea about writing a history of the university for its centenary, he had broached the possibility of Shea's leaving his library to Georgetown. Two years later, when the president heard that Shea was being solicited by New York interests for the seminary there, Richards offered to buy the library. In fact, the historian's failing health and concern for his family's security had led him to put it up for sale. By year's end Richards had raised enough pledges from Riggs, John Dahlgren, and others to obtain Shea's library in exchange for the purchase of five hundred sets of his four-volume history of the Catholic Church in the United States, at a total cost of $10,000.[13] This brought the total number of volumes in the new Riggs Memorial Library to a reported 70,616 by 1895.[14] This ranked the university well behind Harvard (450,000 volumes), Chicago (250,000), and Yale (180,000) but ahead of Amherst (61,000) and Johns Hopkins (60,000).[15] Use of the library by students was highly restricted. By decree of the provincial superior, students could read only texts that had been assigned by teachers; no books could be withdrawn from the library.[16]

Seeking a Specialized Faculty

Securing a core of specialists in the rapidly proliferating disciplines of knowledge in the late nineteenth century was central to Richards's quest to make Georgetown a true university. "I hope," he wrote his provincial superior within the first year of his appointment as president,

you will remember the very great need we have here of *able men*. . . . We are constantly under public observation; scientific men of the government technical departments &c. are anxious to fraternize with us and give us all the assistance in their power. . . . Soon we shall be placed in comparison with the Catholic University. . . . It is a matter of the very greatest importance, not only to this college, but to the reputation and success of the whole Society in this country, that we should have, *during the coming year,* able men, *specialists,* who can be called upon in an emergency to do something handsome in their respective lines,

in philosophy, physics, mechanics, geology, mathematics, French, and German. He meant scholars who were accomplished in their field, who in the humanities had command of their literature and were no mere grammarians and who in the sciences had the experience or potential to make contributions to that rapidly expanding world of knowledge.[17]

On the Georgetown college faculty itself, Richards could point to only five individuals who were fit to teach subjects at the higher level.[18] The problem was that few Jesuits in the region—the traditional source of Georgetown's faculty—possessed such specialized training or competence. As the provincial superior pointed out somewhat sardonically to Richards in response to his plea for specialists, "I haven't got a limitless supply of great men on tap." Georgetown was already getting more than its share of the limited number of "able" men available for the needs of the seven colleges that the order was staffing on the East Coast.[19] Richards indeed was looking well beyond the horizons of the eastern United States in his search for Jesuit specialists, appealing to Rome itself for "men of knowledge" who could enable the university to gain a place in the higher academic world.[20]

John Hagen and the Georgetown Observatory

John Hagen, an Austrian Jesuit astronomer, was Richards's first great acquisition. If Georgetown was to develop as a center for science, the observatory was a long-neglected but standing asset upon which to build. The well-published and highly regarded Hagen, then doing research in America, was the best qualified Jesuit to give it instant recognition and respect. Less than a month after taking over as president, Richards was urging the superior general for permission to persuade Hagen's German provincial not to recall him to Europe, as he planned to do, but allow him to revive Georgetown's observatory as its director.[21] Immediate action was vital, the new president added, as the Catholic University of America was talking of beginning their own astronomical observatory. To delay would risk the charge that Georgetown was simply trying to compete with the new institution in advanced studies. Richards's campaign was an instant success. By the middle of October 1888, Hagen was appointed director of the Georgetown College observatory, a post he held for nearly twenty years until being appointed director of the Vatican Observatory in 1906. Richards welcomed him with the announcement that he had set aside $1,000 for Hagen to "make a beginning" in renovating the observatory and pledged to raise "a considerable sum" to enable Hagen to secure equipment and anything else needed to make the facility a major scientific center.[22] Richards set out immediately, using the services of his two predecessors, Patrick Healy and James Doonan, to raise at least $10,000 to enable Hagen to conduct the observatory "in first class style."[23] Within two years he nearly realized his goal.

The forty-one-year-old Hagen, a native of Bregenz, Austria, had done intensive studies in mathematics and astronomy at the universities of Münster and Bonn. Exiled from Germany because of the anticlerical laws of the Kulturkampf, Hagen had been sent first to Austria, then to England, and finally to America, where he taught the sciences, alternating between two of the colleges then being conducted by German Jesuits in the United States, Canisius in Buffalo and Sacred Heart in Prairie du Chien, Wisconsin. At the latter college he built a small observatory where he began the research on the variable stars that would give him a notable place in international astronomy.[24]

At Georgetown, Hagen quickly took up Richards's challenge to make the Georgetown observatory a major research facility. With a $5,000 gift secured by the president from an anonymous donor, in 1890 Hagen purchased a twelve-inch equatorial telescope for the large dome. Other costs, including those for raising the dome

Title page and interior page (opposite) of German edition of the first volume of John Hagen's *Synopsis of Higher Mathematics* (1891). Hagan subsequently produced three additional volumes. (Image courtesy of Woodstock Theological Library)

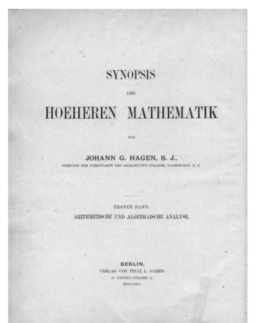

SYNOPSIS

DER

HOEHEREN MATHEMATIK

VON

JOHANN G. HAGEN, S. J.
DIRECTOR DER STERNWARTE DES GEORGETOWN COLLEGE, WASHINGTON, D. C.

ERSTER BAND.
ARITHMETISCHE UND ALGEBRAISCHE ANALYSE.

BERLIN.
VERLAG VON FELIX L. DAMES.
25 TAUBEN-STRASSE 27
MDCCCXCI.

B. Entwickelung nach Produktreihen.

Vorbemerkung (1). Unendliche Faktorenfolgen eignen sich besonders zur Darstellung von Funktionen mit unendlich vielen Wurzeln, also der algebraischen Funktionen von unendlich hohem Grade und der periodischen transcendenten Funktionen. *Euler* (no. 188) bemerkt aber von den zu seiner Zeit bekannten Produktreihen, dass sie sich, der schlechten Convergenz wegen, zur Berechnung der Funktionen wenig eignen.

Vorbemerkung (2). Die *Jacobi*'schen Produktreihen zur Darstellung der elliptischen Funktionen sind einem späteren Abschnitte vorbehalten.

3. Die Entwickelung der trigonometrischen Funktionen in unendliche Produktreihen lässt sich aus der Kenntniss der unendlich vielen Nullwerthe unmittelbar hinschreiben:

$$\frac{\sin x}{x} = \Pi\left[1 - \left(\frac{x}{r\pi}\right)^2\right], \quad \cos x = \Pi\left[1 - \left(\frac{x}{r\pi - \frac{1}{2}\pi}\right)^2\right], \ (r = 1, 2, \ldots \infty),$$

woraus man durch blosse Division die Entwickelungen der übrigen Funktionen: tg x, cotg x, sec x. cosec x erhält.

Zusatz (1). *Euler* (no. 184) setzt $x = \frac{m}{n}\frac{\pi}{2}$ und bringt die beiden Reihen in die Gestalt:

$$\sin\frac{m}{n}\frac{\pi}{2} = \frac{m}{n}\frac{\pi}{2}\frac{4n^2 - m^2}{4n^2}\cdots, \quad \cos\frac{m}{n}\frac{\pi}{2} = \frac{n^2 - m^2}{n^2}\frac{9n^2 - m^2}{9n^2}\cdots$$

und richtet (no. 185) die erstere zur Berechnung der Zahl π folgendermassen ein:

$$\frac{\pi}{2} = \frac{n}{m}\sin\frac{m\pi}{2n}\cdot\frac{2n}{2n-m}\frac{2n}{2n+m}\cdot\frac{4n}{4n-m}\frac{4n}{4n+m}\frac{6n}{6n-m}\cdots$$

indem er nacheinander setzt:

$$\frac{m}{n} = 1, = \frac{1}{2}, = \frac{1}{3}, \ldots \text{ also } \sin\frac{m\pi}{2n} = 1, = \sqrt{\frac{1}{2}}, = \frac{1}{2}, \ldots,$$

wovon der erste Fall die Formel von *Wallis* (1655) liefert:

$$\frac{\pi}{2} = \frac{2\cdot2\cdot4\cdot4\cdot6\cdot6\ldots}{1\cdot3\cdot3\cdot5\cdot5\cdot7\ldots}.$$

Viele andere Produktreihen für π, namentlich solche, die nach Primzahlen fortschreiten, gibt er im cap. 15. (Vergl. *Lacroix*, Traité, § 964). *Bessel* (Abhandl., II. S. 348) hat diese Produkte durch Fakultäten dargestellt.

Zusatz (2). Obige Reihen gelten zwar für jedes x, haben aber nur bedingte Convergenz. Schreibt man nämlich dieselben in der Form:

$$\Pi(1 - u_n^2) = (1 - u_1)(1 + u_1)(1 - u_2)(1 + u_2)\ldots = P\cdot Q,$$

so bilden die Glieder $u_1, u_2, u_3\ldots$ eine arithmetische Reihe erster Ordnung, und man hat (nach **2.**) $P = 0$ und $Q = \infty$.

Ordnet man die Faktoren so, dass auf je m Summen n Differenzen folgen, so hat die erste obiger Produktreihen, nach *Cayley*, den Werth:

$$\sqrt[\pi]{\left(\frac{m}{n}\right)^x}\cdot\frac{\sin x}{x}.$$

4. Die trigonometrischen Funktionen mit vielfachem Argumente lassen sich als endliche Produktreihen derselben Funktionen mit abnehmendem Argumente darstellen (*Euler*, no. 240—242):

15*

and a photographic corrector, put the university more than $1,500 in debt. An annex was built in 1891 to house a five-inch equatorial telescope for making latitude observations by photography. Three years later another anonymous donation of $1,000 made it possible to procure a nine-inch transit instrument and standard clock, which, Richards happily reported, would "entirely complete the equipment of the observatory."[25]

"Father Hagen," Richards reported to Doonan in 1890, "has already begun the preliminary work on his 'maps of the known variables,' which, with the aid of this large telescope, will be the classic work of reference in that branch for the next twenty-five or fifty years or more."[26] With a telegraphic linkup with the Naval Observatory, Hagen began to consult closely with Asaph Hall of that observatory, Samuel Pierpont Langley of the Smithsonian Institution, and Edward Pickering of the Harvard Observatory. In 1891 Georgetown published the first volume of Hagan's encyclopedic *Synopsis der Hoeheren Mathematik*. Three other volumes followed within the next several years. The work became a standard within the mathematical world. Meanwhile, Hagen continued the nightly observations of the fluctuations of the variable stars. In 1896, at the meeting of the Congress of Astronomers held in Bamberg, Bavaria, he made the first announcement of his mature findings. Three years after the Bamberg meeting Hagen issued the first volume of the *Atlas Stellarum Variabilium,* a work that eventually comprised eleven volumes (1899–1905).

Richards continued to attempt to establish a general endowment for the support of the work of the observatory, including annual publications. "It ought to have an endowment of about fifty thousand dollars, the interest of which would suffice to pay for running expenses, repair, annual publications, and the occasional purchase of instruments."[27] A sister of a Georgetown Jesuit agreed to provide a legacy in excess of $10,000 to the college for such an endowment.[28]

Under Hagen's direction, other Jesuits from both the United States and abroad began to train at Georgetown for astronomy. Notable among them was George A. Fargis, who developed the photochronograph, a special instrument that, utilized in both the transit and the zenith telescope, allowed for the determination of time, the variation of latitude, and the measurement of double stars. In 1891 he and Hagen published a monograph on the photochronograph, the first publication from the observatory in nearly a half century.[29]

That same month John Hedrick (**C** 1871) returned to Georgetown as assistant director of the observatory. Hedrick had trained at the Naval Observatory following his graduation and later studied with the distinguished astronomer Benjamin Gould in Argentina. He had entered the Society of Jesus in 1879 and had been teaching astronomy and mathematics at Woodstock College before his appointment as Hagen's assistant. Hedrick, a gifted mathematician, proved to be a highly valuable assistant over the next fifteen years before succeeding Hagen as director in 1906.

Throughout his decade as head of Georgetown, Richards's attempts to secure specialists, lay as well as Jesuit, native and foreign, brought mixed results. In 1889 he recruited Joseph Bayma, the Italian Jesuit mathematician then in residence at Santa Clara College in California, whose work on molecular mechanics had been published by Cambridge University, but failed to lure the émigré east, apparently because of his age (Bayma was then seventy-two). From the New Mexico mission he gained Aloysius Brucker for political economy and ethics. In 1895 he convinced a reluctant California provincial superior to assign Armand G. Forstall to teach science at Georgetown, with the argument that the provinces needed to concentrate their best scholars at "one School worthy of our times."[30] In 1896 he explored ways to bring Henry Pesch, a Jesuit political economist, from Germany to Washington, but Pesch remained in Germany.[31]

Beginnings of Graduate Education

Under Richards the university developed specialized programs in the arts and sciences for postgraduates. Postgraduate education at Georgetown dated back to 1855–56, when four students had been granted master's degrees for remaining to do a second year in philosophy. In the late 1860s and early 1870s a residential graduate program had been revived, with concentrations in the history of philosophy, natural law, and science, but the program was essentially a means to attract those who would be willing to teach preparatory students in exchange for the opportunity to earn a master's degree in addition to receiving room and board along with library privileges. Virtually the only requirement for the master's degree was a thesis.

In 1891 Richards introduced formal graduate studies with a postgraduate course, a year-long concentration in three of six fields (philosophy, literature, history, mathematics, physics, and chemistry). Students who possessed bachelor's degrees attended three hours of lectures weekly in each course. Chemistry involved unspecified laboratory work, and the second semester of history was conducted as a seminar with research projects.[32] Those who successfully completed the courses by writing satisfactory examination papers earned a master's degree. Within five years Richards had developed specialized studies, organized by departments, including language and literature (English, French, German); history; natural sciences (chemistry, physics, and mathematics); biology; and music. By 1895 he had twelve of the twenty-three faculty involved in graduate education. He brought in outside experts to offer certain courses.[33] An eminent zoologist, Charles W. Stiles, led a team of ten specialists who lectured and supervised laboratory work for the students in the Department of Biology. Clinton Hart Merriam, a naturalist at the Smithsonian Institution who headed the Biological Survey Division of the Department of Agriculture, also taught graduate biology at Georgetown, as did Merriam's fellow naturalist at the Smithsonian, Charles Torrey Simpson. "The new department of Biology has thus far proved a great success," Richards reported in 1896. "Twenty-five students, mostly graduates, are doing good work in that department under eight professors, all of whom are prominent specialists."[34]

A graduate library was established in Old North and 1,000 books were purchased especially for graduate studies.[35] A dean of graduate studies was appointed. A chair of ethics, political economy, and history of philosophy was established, held successively by two German Jesuits, Armand Forstall and Aloysius Brucker. By the 1892–93 school year, fifty-eight students were enrolled in graduate studies. The programs were not particularly demanding. Many of the students simultaneously pursued degrees in the medical or law departments; indeed, medical and law students were prime prospects for Richards's new graduate education.[36] The vast majority were from New England and the Midwest, and virtually all were Catholic. Many of them were graduates of Jesuit colleges, such as Marquette, Holy Cross, and Boston College, where Richards heavily recruited for graduate students. Each Jesuit college, in fact, could nominate one alumnus for a scholarship to the graduate school.

In 1896 graduate studies were extended to include the doctorate program. Students who held the master's degree could qualify for the doctorate by doing an additional year's work in a particular field and either writing a thesis or completing a successful experiment in the sciences.[37] There was little or no original research required. Candidates for the doctorate in philosophy, for example, were responsible to know the seven-volume Stonyhurst series of Catholic philosophy as well as a history of philosophy text. Besides writing a thesis, they needed to pass an hour-long oral examination on a syllabus of theses. Thus, in May 1897, a doctorate in physics was awarded to Edgar Kidwell for his work on the "Strength and Construction of Built Up Wooden Beams," and one was awarded in philosophy to Edward J. Tobin for his thirty-five-page thesis on "God: His Existence and Providence."[38] The quality of the courses was greatly uneven. As one knowledgeable Jesuit observed, "The courses of Philosophy, History & literature are really good. Much of the rest of the Programme is showy rather than real."[39]

Most of the dozen or so graduate faculty were Jesuits, although Richards increasingly brought in lecturers from the professional schools of the university or from government agencies. By 1896 the president was clearly frustrated in his attempts to secure Jesuit specialists through his own international recruiting. "The Graduate School is in serious danger in regard to its Faculty," Richards admitted privately. Jesuits were being transferred within the province or recalled to home provinces, and there were no replacements.[40] But Richards tended to see crises as opportunities and used this one as an occasion for a bold appeal to the superior general to make Georgetown in effect the center for higher studies within the Society of Jesus, with Jesuit scholars from various parts of the world sent there to teach and research their fields. Father General Luis Martín, however, was not about to give Georgetown such a designation. He clearly was nervous about developing such a university, at least in the United States, and especially in Washington where a university under the auspices of the pope and American hierarchy had just begun. The superior general informed Richards that each province should ideally provide its own specialists but left the Georgetown president free to approach provincials, within and beyond America, about securing a faculty for higher studies.[41] Subsequently, in that year Richards managed to get the province to petition Rome for permission to have those destined to teach at Georgetown and Woodstock undertake specialized studies at appropriate institutions.[42]

A top priority for Richards in his plans for Georgetown's development as a university was the establishment of a scientific school that would provide the necessary facilities for the natural sciences as well as for engineering. He had in mind a separate technological school such as those that had recently been established at Pennsylvania, Lehigh, and Cornell. "What nobler monument," he wrote a fellow Jesuit, "could any one desire to build for himself than a Catholic Scientific School, the effect of which would be felt in the world to the latest generation?"[43] Richards sought to raise from potential Catholic donors the $30,000 he felt was needed to build the structure but failed to attract support for the project. He continued to hope that the funds would materialize to allow him to realize his dream of a scientific school at Georgetown. By 1898 he had to settle for working out an agreement with several of the leading engineering schools in the country to allow Georgetown graduates to complete their program with an additional two years' work.[44]

For all of Richards's plans and efforts, Patrick Healy, now in virtual retirement in Providence, Rhode Island, had no illusions that Georgetown could become a centripetal university for the province and the Society of Jesus, drawing human resources from near and far as a designated magnet institution. "As far as my experience goes," he confided to Richards in 1897, "I do not find any pronounced disposition among Ours [Jesuits] to aid you in building up your Post Graduate course. Now, as years ago," he added, no doubt reflecting on his own earlier attempt to create a university, "Georgetown has to go it alone. It is slowly forging its way." The Medical and Law Schools, he added, had developed, gradually but surely, despite the indifference or even opposition outside of Georgetown. "It will be the same with the P[ost].G[raduate]. Bide your time."[45] In truth, many Jesuits, some even within Georgetown, thought that Richards was consumed by grand delusions about his institution's status and possibilities. "Many of our Fathers," one Jesuit who had taught at Georgetown in the 1890s wrote to Rome, "are indignant at Father Richards' efforts to make a university out of what is not a first class college." Most, he contended, thought that he had indeed neglected the college by concentrating so heavily on graduate and professional education. "We have neither the time nor the men to employ them in this university work, which besides is putting us in open opposition with the Catholic University of the Bishops."[46]

The Jesuit superiors in Rome needed little persuading that Richards was imperiling Georgetown by attempting to make it a university. "Unless we use a certain exquisite prudence," Superior General Martín chastised Richards in 1897, "the danger is that all the higher Faculties . . . will be taken away from you and the College reduced to lower studies only." To insist on converting the college into a university was foolhardy and historically uninformed of the Society's traditional emphasis on collegiate education. "You do not seem to appreciate this danger to the college," Martín cautioned Richards's provincial superior, William Pardow, but the jeopardy to the college's existence was very real.[47]

The Catholic University of America and Georgetown

Part of Martín's concern was triggered by his knowledge that Pope Leo XIII was bent on making the new Catholic University of America a complete one, with professional schools and advanced studies in the humanities and sciences —"all those faculties and schools which Georgetown College, especially in recent years has greatly promoted." Martín's fear, as he confessed to Pardow, was that "Georgetown College will be forced to lose all these faculties or schools, lest we seem to oppose the Catholic University and indeed the Supreme Pontiff himself."[48]

Indeed, Georgetown nearly lost its professional schools to the new university, and Richards initially was willing to let this happen. In 1893 the apostolic delegate, Francisco Satolli, the pope's representative in the United States, approached Dr. George Magruder, the dean of the Medical School, about the desire of the pontiff to have both of Georgetown's professional schools become part of the new Catholic University of America. The idea of incorporating the schools within the new university was Satolli's solution to the possible conflict between two Catholic institutions of higher education within the same city. Without professional schools Georgetown would no longer be a university.[49] The superior general of the Jesuits, gravely concerned about the likely papal suppression of the Society's institution of higher education in Washington precisely because it competed with the pontifical institution across town, had already indicated his approval of the proposed annexation. Better to give up those professional schools if need be, he no doubt thought, to save the college. When Magruder brought the news of the delegate's seemingly nonrefusable offer to Richards, the president was at first inclined to go along with it, as long as the new university paid Georgetown something in the neighborhood of $75,000–$150,000 and gave Georgetown top priority in reclaiming them should Catholic University fail to survive. That conveniently would have paid off Georgetown's diminished but still considerable debts. Richards was actually convinced that the Catholic University of America was going to fail for lack of support for its grandiose plans. Once that happened, Georgetown would have the opportunity to take over the entire university, including its old professional schools. As Richards put it, "Our consent would show a disinterested desire on our part to do whatever the Holy Father may think best for Catholic education in this country, and at the same time would open the way for the [Catholic] University itself to be transferred to us at some future time."[50]

Richards never had the opportunity to test this "Jesuitical" strategy. Dean Magruder and his faculty had absolutely no intention of becoming part of the Catholic University of America. The law and medical faculties both indignantly threatened to obtain a special charter from Congress and set up an independent university, free from any outside control. "None of them," Richards reported to Jesuit authorities in Rome, "are anxious to be incorporated into an institution so markedly, in its name, Catholic. Georgetown is known to be thoroughly Catholic; but its high reputation, long standing, and the esteem in which it is held by non-Catholics generally, many of whom have been educated here, relieve it of the odious features which anything Catholic ordinarily has in Protestant eyes."[51] That threat scuttled the plan. By May 1894 no one at Catholic University claimed to have favored the transfer, except the papal delegate. "The incident," Richards was happy to report, "is closed."[52]

Nonetheless, the specter of Catholic University continued to haunt Georgetown through the 1890s, particularly when the former opened departments in law, engineering, philosophy, and letters in the fall of 1895 and accepted students who had not yet earned a degree. Within a year the new university had more than 115 graduate students in the new departments. Quite likely to compete with its crosstown rival, which was offering scholarships to graduates of Catholic colleges, Georgetown also began to offer them. When the rector of Catholic University, Bishop Keane, began visiting Catholic colleges to recruit graduate students, Richards followed in his wake.[53] Despite Richards's hope to establish theology as a graduate subject at Georgetown, he finally bowed to the prudence of not waving red flags at Rome or anyone else on this side of the Atlantic. In 1897 the board of directors resolved "that under the present circumstances and for an indefinite period to come no theological degrees should be granted, even on examination."[54]

Reclaiming Woodstock

Richards believed that the very establishment of Woodstock in 1869 had been "a grave error of policy," a conviction he was not reticent about stating openly. "The Professors and students," he wrote in an 1897 issue of the *Woodstock Letters,* "were transported to a semi-wilderness, remote from libraries, from contact with the learned world, and from all those stimulating influences which affect intellectual life in large centres of population and culture." Georgetown in this one move had lost "her highest Faculty" and "from this separation" had been "reduced to a place of inferiority by the fact of the division of our resources."[55]

By the time Richards assumed office in the summer of 1888, there was a general recognition among Jesuit officials, from Rome to Washington, that removing the theologate from the city to the country had been a serious mistake. In response to the superior general's desire that it be relocated to an urban area, the provincial superior proposed to return it to Georgetown by converting the college into a day school. Of the three boarding colleges of the Society of Jesus in the East, the discipline among college students at Georgetown seemed by far the worst. A history of lax administration for many years had created, so regional superiors thought, a constantly deteriorating situation. Students had gained too much freedom in "wandering" through the city. Regular scandalous behavior was the inevitable result; this in turn had a grave effect on studies and produced a ruinous annual turnover (approaching 45%) of boarding students.[56] Replacing the boarding students with Jesuit scholastics studying theology would have two main effects, the provincial superior, Thomas Campbell, was convinced: "The college will be saved and a complete university will be established, that is worthy of the Society."[57]

Richards seized the opportunity to recapture the theologate for the university, but he had no intention of reducing Georgetown College to a school for locals. Instead of converting the college into a day school, he proposed abolishing the prep school, which would immediately make certain facilities available for the use of the theologate, and converting the private rooms of the college students into common sleeping quarters and study halls ("a return to ancient tradition"). A new building, to the north of the 1795 building (Old North), would meet the rest of their needs.

The superior general, however, decided that the matter of transferring the scholasticate should be submitted to the opinion of the officials and other senior members of the province before making any decision. If the common judgment of the province was in accord with Richards's proposal, the president was told, he could proceed to carry it out "at an opportune time and in a prudent fashion."[58] A large majority, it turned out, favored Fordham rather than Georgetown as the site of the school of divinity. The New York school was in poor shape and possessed no graduate schools and an undergraduate college that was declining in enrollment, discipline, and studies. In April 1891 the provincial and his consultors petitioned the superior general to allow them to convert Fordham into a day college, the first step toward making its facilities available for the transferred scholasticate.[59] New York, so the thinking went, was the cultural and intellectual center of the nation, as well as a Catholic stronghold, and the ecclesiastical authorities there looked favorably upon such a development. Georgetown was located in a city that was merely the political center of the country, with few Catholics, but was the home of the pontifical Catholic University of America, which, along with its ecclesiastical patrons in Rome and America, would surely resent the introduction of a competing institution in the higher studies of philosophy and theology.[60]

Almost alone among the Jesuit leaders, Richards argued that by virtually any measure—age, reputation, development, and site—Georgetown had the best claim as an urban home for the theologate. "This city," he wrote the general superior in March 1890, "daily grows as the center and sun of the entire intellectual life of this republic." There was a rapidly growing intellectual infrastructure in the form of museums and libraries, scientific institutes, and the Cosmos Club, and Georgetown was rapidly establishing working relationships with the people involved with these ventures. As for the Catholic University, its rector had expressed his hope that all the religious orders in the United States would locate their houses of studies in its vicinity. If Catholic University proceeded to flourish as an institution, it would be important to have Jesuit theologians and philosophers at Georgetown as a countervailing weight to the pontifical faculty across town. If it failed, "which already seems probable to many lay people—it behooves us to be here to take it over."[61] In brief, Richards argued, Georgetown in its present development was "far in advance of any other Catholic educational institution in the United States." With the addition of the theological and philosophical faculties, "we should *ipso facto* be possessed of *a fully developed University which could not be equalled in its present condition by any other institution, no matter how much money they might possess, for the next thirty or forty years.*"[62]

Richards's arguments, however, swayed few. Many found him far too generous in his estimation of Georgetown's status and too optimistic about the difference the scholasticate would make to its development as a university. The provincial, Thomas Campbell, who himself had initially favored Georgetown, advised the general superior in February 1892 that the scholasticate should be moved to Fordham. Nothing happened, however, even though there was a nearly universal judgment that the scholasticate should not remain at Woodstock. Cardinal James Gibbons foiled the move to Fordham by strenuously objecting to having it leave his archdiocese.[63] He was agreeable to a transfer to Georgetown, which was then part of the See of Baltimore, but Roman fears of the consequences of appearing to compete with the Catholic University doomed any such development. Richards's plan to bolster the university by reclaiming its school of divinity fell victim to provincial politics and Roman caution.[64]

A related Jesuit matter was the plan to begin a monthly review of religion, science, and intellectual life. This idea of beginning a Jesuit counterpart of the *North American Review* surfaced in the late 1880s, and Jesuit officials approved in 1889 its general concept. Richards was determined that, if Georgetown was to be the chief Jesuit university in the United States, "it is here the review should be begun."[65] He was well aware that universities had begun to be the base for scholarly publications in the 1880s, such as Johns Hopkins's *American Chemical Journal* (1879), Columbia's *Political Science Quarterly* (1886), and Harvard's *Quarterly Journal of Economics* (1886). "Concentration at Georgetown," Richards remarked to his predecessor, James Doonan, "is now the only watchword that will lead us to a high standing before the world. . . . The review will be the greatest engine for 'booming' a college, in the line of dignified and able intellectual work that has ever been in the possession of the province." And Washington itself was the natural home for such a journal. "What is most important to consider, all [Washington's] advantages in the line of scientific collections, libraries, &c. &c must always continue to increase with ever accelerating rapidity" as the government inevitably expanded its intellectual concentration and other academic institutions sprang up.[66]

The initial thought was indeed to locate the journal at Georgetown, and negotiations were begun with a local printer. But New York's centripetal forces within the Society soon prevailed, and by the end of 1890 a team of six editors, drawn from the provinces of the United States and Canada, had set up headquarters at St. Francis Xavier College in that city. Richards apparently made a final attempt to house the journal on campus in Washington. As the province was looking for the means to begin publication in the spring of 1891, Peter Collier, the New York publisher whose son, Robert, was at Georgetown and who had underwritten the university's centennial history, approached the regional provincial with an offer to publish the periodical, including the assumption of its costs. One can only surmise that Richards had alerted Collier to the project, presumably with the hope of using him as a lever to secure the journal for Georgetown. Whatever Collier's full intentions, the publisher and the province never reached an agreement, as the latter became frustrated over the former's growing specifications about the project and had second thoughts about its ability to provide enough articles for a monthly review. To Richards's dismay, in the late fall of 1891 the provincial superior reluctantly dropped the project.[67]

Richards had by 1890 begun to publish books by the faculty under the university's imprint. In that year Father Russo's *Lectures on Moral Philosophy* were printed, as were Hagen's *Synopsis of Higher Mathematics* and Edward Connolly's edition of De Cygne's *Rhetoric*.[68]

The College in the 1890s

By its centennial year the college had enrolled 231 students. Enrollments during the 1890s rose to nearly 300 before the hard times of the middle of the decade reduced them again. But a greater percentage was enrolling in the college proper, as apart from the preparatory school. The median age of entering students was now fifteen and a half. By 1894 college students made

up more than 46 percent of the 288 enrolled. Two years later they became a majority for the first time in the school's history. Nearly a fifth now earned degrees. Partly this represented a tightening of requirements for admission to the preparatory school, including the raising, in practice, of the minimum age to fourteen, and the completion of a grammar school course.[69] It also represented the success of recruitment efforts that Richards had begun in Pennsylvania, New York, and other northern states. Indeed, more students now came from the North—more than 36 percent—than from any other region. Maryland and the District of Columbia accounted for nearly one-third (32%), the Midwest accounted for more than 12 percent, and the West 7.33 percent. Only 11.7 percent were from the South, Georgetown's historic provider. An even sharper decline was seen in the number of international students, a mere .5 percent of the total. Richards was obviously uninterested in potential students from South and Central America, a traditional source for the college; in fact, he discouraged them from coming. He was convinced that they came merely to learn English before going elsewhere for engineering or commercial training.[70]

Football squad of 1898, the first year since the banning of football following the death of George Behan four years earlier. (Georgetown University Archives)

Nearly three-fourths of the students came from urban areas. And they were overwhelmingly Catholic, nearly 95 percent. Continuing a trend from the 1880s, Georgetown became increasingly a school for northern Catholics, particularly Irish Catholics. Almost half the students in the 1890s (45.5%) were Irish or partly Irish. Thirty percent had family connections with the university, such as Francis Joseph Semmes of Louisiana (AB 1890), the valedictorian in 1890. Virtually all were from solid middle-class, if not wealthy, families. Seventy-eight percent were boarders. The median length of stay was a year and a half.

The tuition and board, which had been $300 since 1879, Richards raised to $325 in 1892 because of the expenses he had incurred from the various improvements he had made since 1888. Total costs for an undergraduate, including room, medical care, laundry, and library fee, were $417. To a parent complaining in 1893 of the costs of maintaining a son at the college, Richards replied that Harvard, Yale, and other leading universities typically cost in the neighborhood of $1,200 to $1,500 while at Georgetown the comparable figure would not exceed $500.[71] Fifteen percent of the students received support from the college or outside sponsors, either as tuition waivers or scholarships, including athletic ones.

Richards tightened admission standards. He informed an applicant, "To enter Freshman class here, you should know your Latin, Greek and English Grammar well, and be able to translate Homer, Virgil, Sallust & Cicero with no great difficulty. An elementary knowledge of algebra is very desirable; though you can get on if you know Arithmetic thoroughly. Some acquaintance with French or German is also expected, and in those who come from our own preparatory department is rigorously exacted."[72] The expectation was that they were entering either from Georgetown's preparatory school or from some classical high school. Applicants had to pass examinations to demonstrate their knowledge of these subjects as well as ancient and modern history.

The curriculum continued to be the classical course, with few options for students. Students studied Latin and Greek grammar and literature for three years: they were required to have ten and a half hours each week of study in the former and four hours of study in the latter. English and mathematics were the other three-year components, with four hours of instruction for English and six hours for mathematics required weekly. French or German was the one option students had in their first year.[73] In their sophomore year students began a three-year program of natural science: general chemistry (with lab) in sophomore year; qualitative or quantitative chemistry in the junior year; and mechanics, physics, astronomy, and geology for ten hours in the senior year. The other major component of senior year was philosophy (logic, metaphysics, and ethics), which required an additional ten hours of instruction. The philosophy course included monthly "specimens" in which students defended theses and culminated in oral examinations on a comprehensive list of theses, such as "objective evidence is the supreme test of truth."

This curriculum, the 1894 catalogue maintained, "is based on the conviction that a complete liberal education should aim at developing all the powers of the mind, and should cultivate no one faculty to an exaggerated degree at the expense of the others." The liberal arts (the classics, mathematics, science) offered incomparable training of the various faculties of the mind: aesthetic appreciation, imagination, and critical analysis. "It serves," the catalogue concluded, "as a foundation for special training in any branch that the student . . . may decide to take up." Such comprehension could not suffer wide choice in the selection of courses. Yet Richards did allow certain electives during the last two years of the college course.[74]

This permission to choose electives may have reflected Richards's keen awareness that Georgetown was losing a growing number of affluent Catholics to schools like Harvard where electives flourished. Richards noted the tendency of "ambitious and rising Catholic laymen" to send their sons to Harvard on the assumption that it was "immeasurably superior." Richards was concerned that an astonishing number of Catholic students were being sent to Harvard and its like annually "for the sake of social advancement and worldly profit," which inevitably, he thought, led to their loss of faith.[75] Indeed, one contemporary survey of Catholic students in Catholic and non-Catholic colleges had concluded that a majority of them were now in the latter.[76]

Richards, whenever possible, confronted parents who intended to transfer their sons from Georgetown to a more prestigious non-Catholic institution. When Dr. Edward Keyes of New York indicated that he was withdrawing his son from Georgetown to complete his premedical training at the Sheffield Scientific School at Yale, Richards persuaded the father to allow the son to graduate from Georgetown. Edward Keyes Jr. did so in 1892 and went immediately to Columbia Medical School.[77] Keyes apparently represented one of Richards's few successes in preempting transfers for reasons of social and educational upscaling. He had seen at least a dozen Georgetown students depart before graduation for Harvard and her prestigious secular counterparts, a trend that would become even more pronounced in the next decade. The only antidote, Richards was convinced, was Catholic universities "where they may find opportunities and facilities for the highest special and professional training, without those extreme dangers to faith and morals which must beset them elsewhere."[78] In Georgetown, Catholics already had one such option. Richards confessed to being surprised to discover "from long observation that in the collegiate branches of study our instruction and training is already far more thorough and valuable than that to be had in the non-Catholic universities."[79]

One matter that did bother him about collegiate instruction at Georgetown was the transience of the faculty, including the Jesuits who constituted the large majority. For the most part, faculty—both Jesuit and lay—came and went in a blur. An exception was the Jesuit James Conway, who taught metaphysics for forty years, from 1874 to 1915. The median length of stay for the college faculty was scarcely two years, only marginally better than the meager one for students.

If Richards had convinced himself of the superiority of Jesuit higher education in the United States, he also wanted the outside educational world to recognize its merit. Thus, when the faculty of the Harvard Law School omitted Georgetown from the list of schools whose graduates it would receive automatically (without examination) by virtue of their degree, Richards protested the decision to President Charles W. Eliot. On the one hand, Richards may well have been troubled that there were scores of Catholics at Harvard, but on the other, he wanted Harvard authorities to acknowledge that Georgetown graduates were in no way inferior to those of the elite nonsectarian colleges. Having examined Georgetown's catalogue and standard examination questions, Eliot informed Georgetown's president that his college's graduates merited admission and would be on subsequent lists.[80]

Four years later, in 1898, the Harvard Law School dean had second thoughts about admitting the graduates of Jesuit schools. Holy Cross and Boston College were first to be eliminated, and eventually Georgetown. "I am inclined to believe," Richards wrote Timothy Brosnahan, the president of Boston College, "that there is a systematic and deliberate intention on the part of these gentlemen to discredit Catholic education, and to drive us from the field. They consider us enemies, and they are determined to secure Catholic patronage for their University."[81] When Brosnahan published a spirited reply to Eliot's article in *Atlantic Monthly* in October 1899 contrasting Harvard's liberal elective system unfavorably with the supposedly static and rigidly uniform Jesuit curriculum, Richards thought it well deserved. Brosnahan may have bested Eliot in the journals, but it was a Pyrrhic victory. Not only did Harvard continue to exclude Jesuit schools from its list of those whose graduates were automatically accepted at its law school, but also the decline in enrollment at Jesuit colleges continued through the first decade of the twentieth century and pressured Jesuit authorities to change the structure and content of its traditional curriculum.

Kathleen Mahoney, in her incisive study *Catholic Higher Education in Protestant America: The Jesuits and Harvard in the Age of the University,* argues that the controversy served as a wake-up call for Jesuit educators in America to confront the new academic order, epitomized by Harvard, that was severely challenging the relevance of the traditional Jesuit curriculum and discipline in the modern world. In Richards's case, the event may have crystallized his concerns about the Catholic exodus to non-Catholic colleges and the need to adapt the *Ratio Studiorum* more effectively to the sociointellectual conditions prevailing in the late nineteenth century, but those concerns antedated the Harvard Law School crisis. As early as 1890, Richards wanted to add to the curriculum an alternative scientific course to give students the opportunity to pursue something other than the mandatory program of Latin and Greek in order to earn a degree. Richards's scientific course would have excluded the classical languages entirely; students in the scientific course would receive a bachelor of science degree rather than the traditional bachelor of arts. His consultors unanimously opposed the change, and Richards dropped the idea.[82]

The introduction of academic garb was one means by which the school could project the ethos of a university. The initiative actually came from the senior class in 1891, who petitioned to be able to wear the cap and gown on campus, a tradition in the English universities and one being adopted on some American campuses by the 1890s. Permission was finally granted three years later; indeed, wearing the academic robes became mandatory for seniors on formal occasions, as it did for graduate students. For the commencement of 1896, cap, gowns, and hoods were worn by graduates and faculty: Blue and gray was adopted as the colors for the hood lining, and the intercollegiate code was followed for designating disciplines on the hood exterior.[83]

One nod to individuality and freedom in 1896 was to allow students to leave meals as they finished rather than processing out in order. In a sense this marked the beginning of the end of the traditional practice of ranks, or the practice of marching in assigned order to and from chapel, meals, and the like. But the organization of the day still remained highly controlled, with assigned times for virtually everything, including recreation and required attendance at daily Mass, reinstated by Richards after Healy had discontinued it. Students continued to march in the quadrennial presidential inaugurations, although no longer in uniform as in antebellum days. Mardi Gras remained an annual event, including dinner, play, and a grand march of masked students in grotesque costumes.

At the initiative of Patrick O'Gorman, later a Jesuit, the college began a mandolin and banjo club in 1893. The group gave concerts in the middle nineties in New York and Philadelphia as well as in Washington. A glee club was also started in that decade, with a large number of the upperclassmen participating. The *College Journal,* in its twenty-fifth year in 1897, converted its format to that of a magazine, which had become popular among university publications.

Debating remained popular, though distinctly less so than sports. Besides monthly public debates held by both the Philodemic and Philonomesian societies, the Merrick Debate, traditionally held on February 22, continued to mark the high point of the Philodemic Debating Society's year. Four students elected by the society debated chosen topics, with three lawyers or government officials serving as judges before crowds of five hundred or more in Alumni (Gaston) Hall. The subjects were typically very topical, such as the one for 1890, the year of the Sherman Antitrust Act: "Should a law be en-

acted prohibiting those combinations commonly called trusts, in which capital or property, belonging to several parties is placed under control of one
body for the purpose of advancing the price or limiting production of certain
articles of commerce?" Richards encouraged Georgetown's entry into intercollegiate debating ("a more intellectual form of conflict") in the wake of the
cancellation of football in 1894 after a fatal injury to a Georgetown player
and the extraordinary growth of the forensic activity across the nation.[84]
Debates were held with Columbian College and with Boston College, where
in May 1895 Georgetown took the negative side of the topic: "Resolved that
the present Income Tax is equitable."[85] Georgetown, in a very close decision,
was the victor.[86] That, however, ended Georgetown's intercollegiate debating
until the next decade.

Among the notable graduates of the college during the decade were a
surprising number who stayed at Georgetown to earn a law degree (or in
the case of one graduate—William Franklin Sands—to earn it simultaneously with his AB) at a time when relatively few lawyers had college degrees. Daniel William O'Donoghue (AB 1897, MA 1898, LLB 1899, LLM
1900) joined the law faculty in 1904 and taught common law pleading and
equity jurisprudence at the school over the next three decades. O'Donoghue
was made a justice of the D.C. Supreme Court in 1930. Charles Edward
Roach (AB 1895, LLB 1897), the son of Senator William Nathaniel Roach
(C 1857–59) of North Dakota, practiced law in the city and also became a
regular faculty member at the law school in 1905. Patrick Henry O'Donnell
(AB 1892, AM 1893, LLB 1894) became a practicing criminal attorney in
Chicago and established a firm there with another Georgetown alumnus,
James T. Brady (LLB 1892).

A well-known political and courtroom orator, O'Donnell became known
as "the Bourke Cockran of the West," a reference to the famous Tammany
politician. Charles Edward Roach (AB 1895, LLB 1897, LLM 1898), the son
of William Nathaniel Roach, the governor of North Dakota and a senator
from that state, also became a member of the law faculty; he taught conflict
law at Georgetown Law from 1899 to 1928. His brother, William (AB 1896,
LLB 1898), was chief of the patent division of the ordnance department of
the War Department. William Franklin Sands (AB 1896, LLB 1896), the son
of Adm. James Hoban Sands (C 1853–57), entered the foreign service upon
graduation and served for a decade in Asia and Latin America before entering private business. James Aloysius O'Shea (AB 1899, LLB 1902) became a
noted criminal lawyer in the District of Columbia.

One notable graduate who did not practice law was Charles Patrick Neill
(AB 1891), who pursued doctoral studies in economics at the Johns Hopkins
University before organizing the Department of Economics at the Catholic
University of America in 1896. From 1905 to 1913, as U.S. commissioner of
labor, he mediated labor-management disputes and investigated the meat-
packing industry. His report on the latter contributed to the enactment of the

federal inspection law of 1906. Matthew Denver (AB 1892), an Ohio banker, served three terms in the U.S. House of Representatives. Edward Loughborough Keyes Jr. (AB 1891), after earning his MD at Columbia Medical in 1895, became professor and eventually dean of Cornell Medical School.

Four graduates made important contributions to the publishing world. Robert J. Collier (AB 1894), the son of the publisher, did postgraduate studies at Harvard and Oxford before inheriting the family publishing business and editing *Collier's Weekly*. His classmate, Condé Nast (AB 1894, MA 1895), first president of student government ("the Yard") in 1891, went on to singular success as a publisher in New York City, where, after serving as business manager of *Collier's Weekly*, he published *Vanity Fair, Vogue, Glamour,* and *House and Garden*. Thomas Walsh (PhB 1892) became a writer. He was a regular contributor to *Harper's Magazine, Atlantic Monthly, The Bookman,* and *Ave Maria,* as well as the author of several volumes of poetry. Edward James Tobin (AB 1895) became one of the founders of *Commonweal*, a Catholic journal of opinion. One notable alumnus who did not graduate was John E. Sheridan, whose illustrations had graced the *Georgetown College Journal* from 1898 until he left Georgetown in 1900 to join the Outing Publishing Company in New York as an illustrator; during his career he produced cover art and other drawings for the *Saturday Evening Post, Collier's, the American Magazine,* and other journals.

The Medical School and Georgetown Hospital

For Richards, a first-rate medical education was an integral part of a modern university. Richards had considerable training in science. He had been one of the first Jesuits sent for special studies in the field (at Harvard) and had taught both mathematics and physics at Georgetown a decade before being named president at thirty-six. To secure his plans for the medical department, Richards quickly moved to change the relationship of the school with the university from that of proprietary associate to one of full integration. In his first month as president he assumed the debt (nearly $10,000) of the medical corporation and acquired its building for the university.[87] With permission secured from Rome, Richards was able to finance the expansion of facilities at the medical school in the 1890s, a change from the policy of incurring no expense on behalf of that school. With the university assuming financial responsibility, a substantial wing designed by Paul Pelz that nearly doubled the space with new laboratories and dissecting room was added to the building on H Street in 1893 for $13,809, and the entire space was electrified.[88] A year later the medical faculty dissolved its corporation, thus putting the legal and financial aspects of the school directly under the university.[89]

Richards was also instrumental in terminating the Medical School's tradition as a "sundown college." Convinced that medical education confined

to the evening hours was inherently unable to provide the proper amount of instruction, laboratory, and clinical training, he "from time to time encouraged the doctors" to consider "the question of the feasability [sic] of a change" to day classes. By 1895 the faculty were ready to make the change, persuaded that it was pedagogically better and that, if they continued as an evening school, some other institution would establish a day medical school that would sooner or later replace them in the District. Richards was prepared to suffer the financial loss, a temporary one he estimated, in order to make the change.[90] The thinking of Richards, Dean Magruder, and the others proved right as general enrollment fell off sharply the next year, but the number of first-year students ("of much higher quality than has been the rule heretofore," Richards thought) was large—more than thirty—and within two years the school was realizing more than $5,000 from tuition for faculty salaries and more.[91] By 1900 it was reporting its largest incoming class in history, more than forty students from across the country, including four from Puerto Rico.[92]

George Lloyd Magruder, dean of the medical department from 1888 to 1901. (Image from the *History of the Medical Society of the District of Columbia, 1817–1909*)

Richards was also primarily responsible for the establishment of Georgetown Hospital. There were several reasons that he wanted the university to add a hospital. At a time when hospitals were moving from the periphery to the center of medical education, he grasped the importance of Georgetown's having a hospital for the clinical practice of its faculty and the clinical instruction of its students. At the same time, as hospitals changed from being warehouses of the sickly poor to laboratories of medical care and healing for all segments of society, Richards saw the contribution that Georgetown could provide to the general community through such a facility. He hoped that an annual appropriation could be obtained from Congress to maintain it, along with the revenue from "a few private rooms."[93] Accordingly, the structure of the Georgetown hospital would reflect the changing patient profile in hospitals by providing both traditional wards for charity patients and modern private rooms for paying ones.[94]

But the construction of a hospital was not among the top priorities for Richards in his early planning for Georgetown. A scientific school, a gymnasium, and a separate preparatory school were all higher on his agenda when Dean Magruder persuaded him that a hospital was a pressing necessity.[95] Once persuaded, Richards took the initiative in making the hospital a reality. Having found an order of nuns, the Sisters of Saint Francis of Philadelphia, to staff it, Richards secured the approval of the board of directors in October 1894 to begin the hospital. It took another year and a half to convince the faculty to move on the matter by choosing a site.[96] The loss of their chief surgeon seems to have been a catalyst for their belated action. Dr. James Kerr, who practiced at the Emergency Hospital, had just withdrawn from the faculty in a dispute over charging private fees for his instruction to medical students at the hospital. Kerr's departure left the school with no surgical clinic to which they had access. If they intended to attract

Initial section of Georgetown Hospital, which opened in 1898. (Georgetown University Archives)

a first-rate surgeon to the school to hold the chair in surgery, a hospital controlled by the institution seemed essential. The growing scope and volume of surgery within hospitals, along with the revenue it produced, was also making surgically equipped hospitals both an indispensable part of medical education and research and a rich source of revenue.[97]

Richards persuaded the faculty of the advantage of having all of the departments of the university "close together" and offered a site at the corner of N and 35th streets, two blocks from the college campus, then occupied by black tenants in the former parish residence and school.[98] A fund-raising drive was begun, with Richards leading, and within two weeks more than half of the $10,000 was raised from E. Francis Riggs, the eminent local banker who had built the college library; Christian Heurich, a local brewer; Mrs. Thomas Fortune Ryan; and other benefactors. C. B. Keferstein designed the four-story brick structure, with a central portion and two wings, along N Street, with accommodations for 100 patients. Given the still-depressed economy, the university was only able to raise one-third of the estimated $50,000 needed to construct the hospital; hence only the central portion of Keferstein's design was initially built. It opened in July 1898.[99]

In 1897 Richards boasted that "the Medical School has kept pace with the growth of Medical Science in the country . . . and at the present time its standing among like institutions is high. Its course comprises four years; there are fifty-five Professors and Instructors, with one hundred students, a large portion of the latter entering only after graduation at some College."[100]

The dean of the school was George Lloyd Magruder (1848–1914), a graduate of the school (1870) and a member of the faculty since 1871. Elected dean during Richards's first year in office, he served until his resignation in 1901. Frank Baker continued as professor of anatomy. Baker became president of the Association of American Anatomists in 1897. During that decade he edited the *American Anthropologist* (1891–98). John Brown Hamilton, who had acquired an international reputation as supervising surgeon general of the U.S. Public Health Service before his appointment to Georgetown in 1883, was professor of surgery. During his eight years at the school he performed (at Providence Hospital) one of the first successful operations for a gunshot wound of the abdomen.[101] In 1887 he created the National Laboratory of Hygiene, the first facility devoted to bacteriological research in the United States.[102] When Hamilton resigned to accept a position at his alma mater, Rush Medical College, in 1891, James Kerr succeeded him. Kerr, as senior surgeon at Providence Hospital, Garfield Hospital, and the Emergency Hospital, became noted for his advocacy and practice of aseptic surgery, which involved scrubbing and clean gowns as well as a sterile operating room. When Kerr resigned from the faculty, George Tully Vaughan took his place as chief surgeon, a position he held for the next thirty-six years. Vaughan was a pioneer in performing surgery on the heart and blood vessels.

James Kinyoun, director of the National Laboratory, served as professor of pathology and bacteriology at Georgetown. Kinyoun became the first physician in the United States to experiment with diphtheria antitoxin and subsequently was recognized as a leader in the development of fin-de-siècle American science. Professor of hygiene was George M. Kober (MD 1873). He had joined the faculty in 1888 after serving for twenty years as an army surgeon. Samuel Shugert Adams (MD 1879) was professor of the diseases of infancy and childhood and then professor of the theory and practice of medicine. Professor of obstetrics was Henry Davidson Fry, who published extensively on typhoid fever and infectious inflammation of the heart and presented papers at Harvard, Cornell, and other medical centers. He was one of the founders of the American Pediatric Society, serving as president in 1916.[103] William Creighton Woodward (MD 1889) taught medical jurisprudence as well as anatomy. As the health officer of the District of Columbia, Woodward gained a national reputation for his efforts to improve sanitation and eradicate disease within the city. Hugh McCormick Smith (MD 1888) taught histology at the school but became internationally famous for his other occupation, as ichthyologist for the U.S. Fish Commission. Charles Wardell Stiles was professor of medical zoology at Georgetown. In 1902 he discovered the species of hookworm responsible for the widespread anemia in the southern states. His efforts eventually secured support from the Rockefeller Foundation, which began the eradication of the disease in the region.

It was a highly stable faculty, the median length of employment being eleven and a half years, and young (the median age was twenty-eight). More than half (56%) were alumni. By the middle nineties the faculty was reaching out to obtain faculty to improve or begin new fields. In 1894 the school sought and secured T. Morris Murray as chair of laryngology and physical diagnosis and so increased the school's clinical facilities in this field.[104] The following year Walter Augustus Wells, who had trained at both the University of Vienna and the University of Chicago, was brought in to become professor of laryngology and otology. William Henry Forwood, a noted botanist and mineralogist, joined the faculty in 1895 to teach medical surgery. In 1902 Theodore Roosevelt named him surgeon general. It was a distinguished faculty.

In 1893 the school increased the course of studies from three to four years, something the Association of Medical Colleges mandated two years later.[105] The course of instruction comprised two years of anatomy, physiology, chemistry, the practice of medicine, surgery, obstetrics, gynecology, and pathology, as well as courses and/or clinics in materia medica, histology, therapeutics, minor surgery, embryology, therapeutics, diseases of infancy and childhood, urinalysis, hygiene, special pathology, bacteriology, perinatology and physical diagnosis, ophthalmology and otology, animal parasites, toxicology, hygiene, and medical jurisprudence.

During the decade the faculty, particularly Frank Baker, took measures to regulate the quality of instruction and the standards of assessing the academic progress of students. In the fall of 1894 a standing committee on curriculum was created to evaluate all "didactic, clinical and lab instruction" and to recommend improvements to ensure a high standard. In the future every professor and instructor was required to provide a syllabus of his course to the committee.[106] The following year the passing of formal examinations was made a requirement for the fulfillment of the major portions of the curriculum, including the six clinics.

The student population dropped from 124 in 1893 to 75 in 1895, following the change to day classes that compounded the attrition that the economic hard times of the decade were having on student enrollment. To encourage college graduates to enroll, the faculty established tuition scholarships, an undetermined number to be awarded by the faculty and twenty-five to be given by the president of the university to college graduates. Most of the latter went to graduates of Jesuit colleges.[107] They also began to distribute thousands of catalogues, first regionally from Virginia to lower Pennsylvania; by 1899 ten thousand catalogues were being sent to sixty colleges, as well as to pastors of churches from Maine to Texas, physicians in all the New England states, and alumni.[108]

With the change to full-time students, applicants increasingly came from the Northeast and Midwest, and most held bachelor's degrees. The median age at entry by the end of the century was twenty-two. True to Richards's prediction, enrollment, along with the economy, eventually recovered, reaching 123 in 1900. Two classes of applicants not admitted to the school, no matter what their credentials, were blacks and females. An African American graduate of Howard, James A. Wormly, seeking to do further work at Georgetown in 1892 was informed that it was "inexpedient" to admit him.[109] Richards acknowledged in a letter that "it is a fact that our college has not as yet opened its doors to colored people. The rule of all the departments of our University restrict the attendance to white males."[110] As for women, there was apparently some support for allowing them to matriculate in the school in 1889 (two female students apparently took classes in 1888). Since the beginning of the decade, medical schools had begun to admit women in significant numbers. By 1893 they would represent 10 percent of the student population at the nineteen medical schools, including Johns Hopkins, that accepted them as candidates for degrees.[111] Richards, however, declined to have Georgetown become one of the coeducational schools.[112]

Students organized themselves during the decade by establishing an Association of Medical Students in the fall of 1890. In its first year of existence, the association successfully lobbied to have the valedictorian at graduation selected by students rather than by the faculty. The association was also responsible for certain changes in the examination protocol, such as the scheduling of examinations in subjects immediately following the completion of the respective courses and for the granting of options in fulfilling their clinical observation requirements. The association apparently became moribund after the 1897–98 academic year.[113]

Among the school's students during this decade were Walter Wheeler Alleger, Bailey Kelley Ashford, Fielding H. Garrison, Theodore Sherman Palmer, Charles O'Connor, Edwin Behrend, and Joseph Milton Heller. Alleger (MD 1890) became chief of the medical division of the U.S. Pension Bureau. Garrison became one of the country's leading historians of medicine. Edwin Behrend (MD 1891), the son of Dr. Adajah Behrend, after postgraduate studies in Europe, returned to Georgetown in 1898 to establish a clinical laboratory. For thirty-seven years he taught as a professor of pathology and bacteriology until his retirement in 1954. Joseph Heller (MD 1896) practiced surgery in the U.S. Army during two wars as well as in private practice in the District where he taught at the George Washington University School of Medicine. Ashford (MD 1896), whose father had been dean of the school from 1878 to 1883, joined the U.S. Army Medical Corps upon his graduation. Stationed in Puerto Rico following the Spanish-American War, Ashford diagnosed the hookworm (*ancylostoma duodenale*) as the cause of thousands of deaths annually on the island and organized the first attempt in the Western Hemisphere to eradicate the disease. Subsequently he founded the Institute of Tropical Medicine in 1911, which eventually became part of the University of Puerto Rico. By 1910 Ashford and his teams had treated about three hundred thousand patients and reduced the death rate from "the Deadly Hookworm" in the island by 90 percent. His success encouraged the Rockefeller Institute to begin a worldwide crusade to eliminate hookworm disease.[114]

Law School

The 1890s witnessed an enormous growth, in both numbers and size, of law schools throughout the nation. As a growing and increasingly complex society found itself needing more lawyers and as states began to require formal legal education in order to practice law, new law schools were founded and existing ones enlarged to meet the need.[115] Particularly in the ascendancy in this development were evening or part-time schools such as Georgetown. Richards inherited a law school that was becoming one of the largest in the country. By 1891 it was the third largest. It was also considered the best in the city, but it needed a permanent home. Since its beginning in 1870, the school had moved through a succession of rented spaces. During the 1880s it had been forced to move twice.[116] The rented space on F Street was inadequate for a school of nearly two hundred students. Students were standing in the aisles to attend lectures. Richards immediately

Law School building, 1891.

(Georgetown University Archives)

responded to the law faculty's plea to build but had difficulty securing the provincial superior's approval to take on the additional financial burden for a university already with a debt of nearly $100,000. After several attempted plans of financing, Richards finally was given the go-ahead to purchase property law at 506 E Street Northwest. The university assumed the expenses, with the understanding that the school would offset them through increasing tuition. At a cost just slightly over $30,000, the school constructed in 1891 a three-story, red brick, Romanesque building running 52 feet wide and 95 feet deep.[117] It had three lecture halls, with the largest accommodating four hundred students.[118]

Martin Morris, one of the founders of the school, was dean. Among the faculty was Joseph James Darlington, general counsel of the Riggs National Bank and author of *The Law of Personal Property,* who taught property law at the school. The chief justice of the United States Court of Claims, William A. Richardson, taught statutory law. Henry Billings Brown, the associate justice of the U.S. Supreme Court, also taught at Georgetown. In 1892 George E. Hamilton (AB 1872, LLB 1874) of the firm Morris and Merrick was appointed to teach torts and testamentary law. Hamilton succeeded Morris as dean in 1900 and remained in that post for more than four decades. Justice Henry R. Brown of the Supreme Court lectured on admiralty in 1891–92. Louis E. McComas, justice of the Supreme Court of the District of Columbia and later a senator from Maryland (1899–1905), taught international law from 1896 to 1899. Also Judges Tallmadge Lambert and Edmund F. Dunne were part of the faculty during this decade. The school's faculty represented a select circle of Washington lawyers and judges, nearly 60 percent (57.1%) of whom were alumni of the school.[119] President Richards preferred to have more Catholic representation on the faculty (Catholics constituted about one-quarter of the members). He secured René Holaind from Woodstock College to teach natural and canon law as well as a course in ethics.[120] But few other Catholics joined the faculty during Richards's decade-long tenure.

Martin Morris, dean of the Law School. (Georgetown University Archives)

Of course all the faculty, including Morris, were part time, being practicing attorneys or judges. Richards wanted to change this, at least to the extent of having a full-time dean. In 1896 he attempted to persuade the noted lawyer and former congressman Bellamy Storer to become a full-time professor in the school with the intent of making him its chief executive in the near future. Storer evidently declined, and Georgetown remained a night school with part-time faculty and students.

Class began regularly at 6:30 PM. The students were all employed full time, either as clerks in the government or as congressional aides. Although the leading law schools in the nation had become day schools with full-time students by the late 1890s, Georgetown opted to continue its night school tradition. There were no admission requirements—no high school diploma, much less a college degree. As the university catalogue stated, "Students desiring to become members of the School enter their names upon the Secretary's register, at or before the opening of the term."[121] As a later historian of the school noted, a faculty of adjuncts tended to produce a legal education that lacked consistency and comprehension.[122] Too often the curriculum depended on who was available to teach and on what they chose to lecture.

Students were more than half Catholic (52%). Very few had previous degrees. For incoming students the median age was twenty. There were 152 students in the regular course in 1889–90, and 50 were enrolled in the graduate course. With the new building, enrollments soared, providing the revenue to retire the building debt. Throughout the nineties, average enrollment, including master's candidates, was 275, with a top figure of 313 in 1897–98.[123] In 1896 alone, 93 bachelor of law degrees and 65 master of law degrees were awarded.

The school followed a two-year curriculum. The standard form of instruction comprised lectures that commented on matter assigned from a text, such as Darlington's *Law of Personal Property,* and questions eliciting the students' understanding of the text. Georgetown was self-consciously resisting the case method that Harvard had introduced, which was rapidly setting the standard for teaching in the leading law schools by the 1890s.[124] The year had three terms, with written examinations completing each. In second, or junior, year students studied personal property, torts, domestic relations and criminal law, real estate, contracts, and bills and notes. In senior year they repeated several of their first-year courses plus pleading, practice, evidence, realty, and moot court, which had begun in 1890.

Richards was also intent on extending the course from two to three years. The American Bar Association was moving toward recommending this as a norm (it would do so in 1897).[125] By 1896 Columbian College was attempting to persuade Georgetown to join them in making the transition. Dean Morris agreed with Richards: "I suppose we must come to it for it is simply impossible under our circumstances for students to get any adequate knowledge of law in less than three years." Yet there was a reluctance to do so without the assurance that the other law schools of the city (the new Columbus School of Law at the Catholic University of America and the National Law University) would follow suit and not drain off students seeking a quicker degree. Finally, in 1897, the law faculty decided that they were in a sufficiently strong position to take the step in conjunction with Columbian College, and the three-year program became mandatory the following academic year, making Georgetown one of the first law schools to do so.[126]

The Law School's debating team, organized in 1894, engaged in regular contests against other law schools in the 1890s, including debates against the Columbian College, New York University, and Wisconsin debating societies. Over a five-year span in the later nineties, they were highly successful with but one loss (to NYU) in 1897. The Law School debating team continued to debate intercollegiate rivals such as Columbian College, Boston University, and others well into the next decade.

A substantial number of the graduates during this decade entered government service at the local, state, or national levels. William J. Hughes (LLB 1891) served in the Department of Justice for more than three decades. A specialist on jurisdiction and procedure within the federal courts, Hughes taught this subject at the Law School from 1914 to 1938 and eventually published a sixteen-volume treatment of the matter in 1931. Frank H. Norcross (LLB 1894) was appointed to the Nevada State Supreme Court and later as a judge of the Circuit Court of Appeals of the United States. William B. Bankhead (LLB 1895) won election to Congress from Alabama in 1916. His brother, John Hollis Bankhead Jr. (LLB 1893), succeeded his father in the Senate in 1931 and served there until his death in 1946. John Patrick O'Brien (LLB 1897), the son of an immigrant, joined the New York City government in 1901 as assistant corporation counsel. He held several city posts, including that of surrogate, before becoming mayor of the city as the Democratic candidate in a special election in 1932 to fill out the term of James J. Walker, who had been forced to resign from office.[127] Francis Asbury Lever (LLB 1899) became a South Carolina representative in Congress in 1901. His most notable accomplishment there was as cosponsor of the Smith-Lever Act of 1914 to improve American agriculture. William Hitz (LLB 1898) became associate justice of the U.S. Court of Appeals for the District of Columbia. Robert M. Douglas (LLB 1897) became an associate justice of the Supreme Court of the State of North Carolina.

Building an Endowment

Richards had inherited a debt of slightly less than $100,000, far less than the $400,000 burden that his predecessor had acquired but a considerable drag on his ambitious plans for the university.[128] With new facilities for the law and medical schools the debt increased to $152,171.16 by 1895. Despite the hard times brought on by the depression of the mid-1890s, Richards was initially hopeful that the university, if it only increased or even simply maintained its present enrollment in the several schools, could within the next few years liquidate the entire debt on the college and most of it on the other schools. Others did not share his optimism. "Everyone anxious about our prospects," the official Jesuit diary of the college recorded in September 1894. "The financial crisis and general stringency in money matters which have been affecting the country for the last year are feared with reason. They certainly will keep many students from attending."[129] They did.

Even wealthy families were badly shaken by the depression. New Yorker Horace Kelly's investments had suffered so badly by the fall of 1892 that the Park Avenue resident could not afford for his two sons to return to the college.[130] And the attrition jumped sharply as the depression deepened to become the worst the country had ever experienced. Enrollments dropped drastically across the university between 1894 and 1898; the college fell from 296 students to 241, the Medical School from 125 to 86, and the Law School from 304 to 280. The consequent decline in tuition revenue precipitated a financial crisis during the 1896–97 school year. The Medical School alone had a shortfall of nearly $4,000 in the autumn of 1897.[131] Salary reductions in all the schools became a necessary financial measure. "People who have no money cannot spend it," Richards told George Hamilton, the dean of the Law School. "That the Professors are underpaid is no doubt true. . . . But in fact they are paid more at present than the School can afford. . . . The hard times are pressing us in every direction, and it would be very imprudent for us to suppose that we can keep up the scale of expenditures which was adopted when business was prosperous and the school decidedly larger."[132] A year later the situation was no better. "We are at present feeling very deeply the effect of the financial stress," Richards wrote an alumnus. "From New York, Boston and all the West we hear that business is improving rapidly; but here in Washington the effect is not visible. Indeed, I have never known such distress to exist among people of respectable classes as is at present prevalent in Washington."[133]

The greatly depressed economy proved a grave obstacle for the success of the first organized fund-raising campaign that Richards began in the early nineties. The president realized all too well that financial resources were a prerequisite for the development of any real university. Major universities had endowments in 1899 that ranged from Stanford's $18 million to Princeton's $2 million.[134] "Money, Money!" he lamented to a fellow Jesuit in 1890, "the root of evil and the instrument of good!"[135] It would take hundreds of thousands of dollars, and more, to construct the facilities, establish the endowments, fund the chairs, and support the programs that he envisioned for Georgetown. The only obstacle standing in the way of Georgetown's becoming a first-rate university, he was convinced, was money—indeed a lot of it. As the *College Journal* noted in 1897, "To be able to compete on anything like equal terms with the great non-Catholic institutions of learning, she should . . . have a permanent endowment of a million dollars."[136] Richards was sure that men and women of wealth, within and beyond the Catholic community, could be persuaded to support Georgetown's development on the merits of its present achievements and future promise.

In this first systematic effort at fund-raising for the university, Richards established goals with priorities and utilized agents to solicit donors and earmarked gifts. His first priority was to complete the new building (Healy): the classrooms, auditorium, library, laboratories, and porches that were still unfinished nearly a decade after the building had opened. Within three months of assuming office, he had persuaded Francis Riggs to contribute $10,000 to furnish the library (a sum that Riggs nearly tripled before the facility was completed).[137] At the conclusion of the centennial celebration, a half-dozen alumni, having listened during the past three days to Richards and others speak directly and indirectly of Georgetown's need for the financial means to fulfill her incomparable potential, pledged to do whatever they could "to assist her financially." They pledged to raise the more than $50,000 needed "to make this noble building, unsurpassed on this continent, fully available for educational purposes."[138] The initial building fund drive netted only several thousand dollars, although Richards appealed personally to virtually every alumnus of wealth and many other persons that he calculated to have some, at least potential, interest in the university.

The alumni continued to hold annual banquets in the 1890s in Washington, but these proved to be mainly social events rather than occasions for fund-raising. Richards encouraged the formation of regional alumni clubs in Philadelphia (1893) and New York (1896) and endeavored to replicate that development in all cities in which the university counted a large contingent of former students, obviously in the hope that such groups would be a natural base for encouraging alumni financial support.[139] Yale's New York alumni had instituted an alumni fund in 1890 that annually contributed more than $10,000.[140] Richards was no doubt aware of this initiative but was unable to inspire a similar movement from the organized Georgetown alumni or to increase the number of regional alumni organizations beyond New York and Philadelphia.

Richards attempted to raise an endowment of $50,000 for the perpetual support of the observatory, $100,000 for the construction of a scientific school, and nearly $80,000 for a gymnasium (which he considered crucial to Georgetown's ability to compete fully with other universities in America's growing stress on physical culture and sports). Unfortunately, the funds raised fell far short of his targets. But half the endowment intended for the observatory was raised, which was largely from an unanticipated legacy. In addition, $5,000 was raised for a new science school.[141] All told, approximately $150,000 was raised through Richards's labors, nearly triple the amount Patrick Healy had managed to gain during his continental fund-raising efforts two decades earlier, but far less than Richards had hoped and needed to raise to make his plans a reality.[142]

Richards summed up his frustration over the disappointing results of his ten-year effort to endow Georgetown when he wrote a benefactor of the university at the end of 1897, "Your interest and sympathy . . . [is] so different from the coldness of many whom we might perhaps expect to be our friends. . . . We have a very great work here, a work the importance of which becomes more evident to me every year, and we have also every means of accomplishing it to the honor and service of God and the good of humanity— a fine situation, a venerable and glorious history, an excellent staff of professors, well organized and regulated courses, everything in fact except money."[143] His only hope was that a rising level of cultivation would match the growing wealth among the Catholic elite and bring them to have "a more active interest in higher educational work, and consequently in more liberal financial support."[144]

One such Catholic whom Richards cultivated strenuously was John Vinton Dahlgren (**C** 1889, AB). Dahlgren, the son of Adm. John Adolph Dahlgren and the half-brother of Col. Ulrich Dahlgren, whose ill-fated cavalry raid on Richmond in the spring of 1864 had set in motion the train of events that led to Lincoln's assassination (see chapter 9 of volume 1 of this history), had been excited by Richards's vision for Georgetown as a "great Catholic university" and pledged to put much of his fortune, at least $100,000 or more, at the president's disposal for the development of the institution, as well as raising money from others. By 1896 Dahlgren was having second thoughts about

Richards's ability to translate vision into reality. Other Jesuits, he found, shared little of Richards's intentions to "make Georgetown a great university." Without that common commitment, he had little hope that Richards could succeed. Meanwhile, the Catholic University, with its own energetic and ambitious president in John Keane, seemed to be well about the business of becoming what its name professed. Richards was able to make Dahlgren reconsider transferring his support from Georgetown to Catholic University. Unfortunately, Dahlgren's premature death in 1899 prevented either institution from receiving such a major benefaction.[145]

Dahlgren Memorial Chapel of the Sacred Heart

The chief benefactor of the university in the 1890s was Dahlgren's wife, the former Elizabeth Drexel, a wealthy heiress of the Philadelphia banking family. She and her husband provided the funds to build a chapel for the university in 1892. Richards's ambitious plans for augmenting the facilities of the institution as part of a commitment to make it a Catholic university of the first order had not included a chapel. Indeed, since its founding the university had had only a private chapel for students. For much of Georgetown's first century, Trinity Church, a block from campus, had been the university church.[146] The only visible sign of Georgetown's Catholicity as late as 1890 was the statue of St. Joseph in the garden outside the student infirmary (Gervase). In the summer of 1891 an opportunity unexpectedly arose, however, for putting in the heart of the campus a house of worship that would palpably declare Georgetown's religious character.

The occasion was the sudden death, from pneumonia, of the Dahlgrens' sixteen-month-old child. When their firstborn died in July 1891, they asked permission to bury him in the college grounds in a mortuary chapel to be erected somewhere on the college walks. The child was interred temporarily in the college cemetery, but Richards suggested that his permanent resting place be not a small memorial chapel but one large enough to serve as a devotional center for the university. They agreed to give the university $30,000 over five years to erect a chapel that would accommodate four hundred students.[147]

That estimate proved an unrealistic one. The architect, Henry Simpson, submitted plans for an English Gothic chapel. The projected cost was nearly $45,000. Richards attempted to secure the permission of Jesuit officials, first in America and then in Rome, to allow the college to go into debt for the additional money, with the virtual assurance that the Dahlgrens would ultimately redeem the entire sum. "We already have 250 persons, counting students and community, who attend services in the chapel simultaneously, and our number is increasing steadily, the advance this year being 40 to 50 students. We shall need more room very soon, probably next year."[148] Neither the Jesuit officials in New York nor those in Rome were moved by Richards's arguments. In the end the grand stone chapel became a more modest brick one, with seating for 350 students. In December 1891 excavation work began in the area behind Healy Hall. The courtyard was lowered by some five feet to bring it to the level of the first floors of Healy Hall and the buildings on the south side of the campus. Construction of the chapel began in early April 1892. The red-brick, cruciform-shaped Dahlgren Memorial Chapel of the Sacred Heart was consecrated a year later on June 9, the titular feast day. With the new chapel, Richards introduced the practice of celebrating the Mass of the Holy Ghost as a formal inauguration of the school year in 1893.[149] For seniors and graduate students, Richards began the practice in 1895 of a voluntary senior retreat off campus at St. Inigoes. It apparently lasted only two years because of poor response.[150]

Dahlgren Chapel
Old store shoe shop and bakery at left hand side.

The Campus and the Neighborhood

The deterioration in the neighborhood that had begun with the influx of poor blacks and Irish during the Civil War continued into the last decade of the century as shantytowns of blacks around Reservoir Road and of Irish below the canal closed in on the university.[151] The establishment of a day security force for the university in 1894 was one effect of this change, but the immediate need for a day watchman, in addition to a night one, was because of the threat of "Coxey's army" invading Georgetown as well as the Capitol. The college had long been attempting in vain to get special protection from the District to guard against young neighbors, "men of loose and lawless habits" who persisted in trespassing to steal chickens and fruit for food and trees and fences for kindling.[152]

The college continued to maintain a farm. In the spring of 1895, a suggestion from one of the black campus workers from Arkansas led to the experimental planting of cotton, which, thanks to a very warm and sunny autumn,

Dahlgren Chapel of the Sacred Heart. (Georgetown University Archives)

proved to be a bumper crop of fine quality.[153] It did not, however, become a staple of the farm.

Accommodations for students were single rooms in the Healy Building for those who desired and could afford them. Others, including all the preparatory students, slept in common areas in the North Building or preparatory building (Maguire). Double rooms in the North Building were reserved for graduate students, who could also live off campus. Indoor plumbing was introduced in the 1890s. In 1893 the Jesuit Community, which had been dispersed about the quadrangle, took over the second, third, and fourth floors of the South Building (Mulledy), previously serving as the auditorium and chapel, which Gaston Hall and Dahlgren Chapel, respectively, replaced.

In 1897 Richards finally realized his intention of completing the Healy Building, not only the Riggs Library but also the embellishment of the central and north porches, the refinishing of the basement as a chemistry lab, and the outfitting of Gaston Hall (named for Georgetown's first student) with stage, galleries, and seating for eight hundred, in 1897. To adorn the walls of the completed building, Richards purchased or solicited eighty-four portraits of Jesuit cardinals, superiors general, past presidents of the institution, and distinguished graduates. The crowning touch was Gilbert Stuart's portrait of John Carroll, which Richards, through the generosity of Judge Placidus Ord (**C** 1835–37), purchased for $1,000 in 1895 and unveiled at the commencement exercises in June. Earlier, at the time of the centennial, Richards had hoped to place a statue of the founder outside the main entrance of the new building and had a model designed by a leading Washington sculptor but was unable to raise the $12,500 needed to execute it. Electricity, which had first been used temporarily for the centennial celebration, came permanently to campus in the fall of 1892, first to the observatory, then to the Dahlgren Chapel and the Riggs Library, with the other buildings awaiting the funds to allow the electrification of the entire campus.

Richards was also looking to physically expand the university toward the city, to encompass all the property between 37th Street on the west, P Street on the north, 35th Street on the east (excepting Holy Trinity's grounds), and Prospect Street on the south. "I think we shall gradually get a great portion of these two squares into our hands," he wrote his predecessor, James Doonan, in 1890.[154] Over the next eight years Richards managed to acquire most of the property facing the college on 37th Street, but the total acquisition of the two squares eluded him. At the same time, he held at bay an attempt of the Georgetown Citizens' Association to force the university to open access to the streets (N, O, and P streets) that theoretically ran through its grounds and reached a compromise that enabled the city to extend Prospect Street to 38th Street while it respected the college's claim to this property.[155] No sooner had this agreement been reached when the Washington and Great Falls

Electric Railway won a court order in 1894 condemning the property on Prospect between 37th and 38th streets so that they could extend their line toward their intended eastern destination at the new station being built at Prospect and 36th streets. The university received $3,000 for the property, with the stipulation that the land would be resold to the university should the rail line cease to operate.[156] For Georgetown, the extension of the Georgetown and Washington Street trolley line to the edge of campus, plus the new Washington and Great Falls line and the Washington and Arlington line all converging at the same station, meant much better transportation to and from the university.

War with Spain

Tensions with Spain over the independence of its Cuban colony that had been building among the American public erupted in mid-February 1898 when the U.S. battleship *Maine* mysteriously exploded in Havana harbor, causing the deaths of 266 American crewmen. Public opinion, led by the yellow journalism of William Hearst and Joseph Pulitzer, screamed for war. Men across the nation clamored to volunteer for service against Spain. At Georgetown, students formed a battalion of cadets in reaction to the crisis. A week after the *Maine* sunk, they marched around campus setting bonfires as they went. The next morning, newspapers in Washington and New York reported that at Georgetown College a student "insurrection" had taken place against the Jesuit authorities of the institution, presumably because of the historic Spanish connection of the Jesuits (and indeed the superior general of the order at the time was a Spaniard). A Spanish flag had reportedly been destroyed, and oil paintings of Spanish cardinals had been vandalized. Students were telling reporters that their next target was the adjoining Western High School, where they intended to appropriate the arms and equipment of its cadet corps, seize some fast craft in the Potomac, and begin their own filibustering expedition to Cuba.[157] When Richards, who was in New York at the time, telegraphed to find out what was happening, he was assured that the story was bogus, the concoction of some students in junior year who had fed the tale to the local press.[158] A few days later, however, portraits of the Spanish Jesuit cardinals that hung in Gaston Hall were indeed defaced by students.[159]

When war finally came in mid-April, George Tully Vaughan took leave from the Medical School to return to the army as brigade surgeon of the Seventh U.S. Army Corps. Few students went off to enlist. One was Raphael Burke Durfee (MD 1900); another was William O. O'Neill (LLB 1899), who became a member of the First U.S. Volunteer Cavalry ("Rough Riders"). At least twenty-three alumni, most of them very recent ones, joined the American forces. Joseph Heller (MD 1896) was the first volunteer accepted after

Bailey Kelley Ashford, **M** 1896, served as a surgeon during the Spanish-American War. (Georgetown University Archives)

the formal declaration of war in April 1898. J. Malin Craig (**C** 1892–94), a newly commissioned graduate from West Point, joined the Fourth U.S. Infantry as a second lieutenant and saw action in both Cuba and later the Philippines. Martin F. Crimmins (**C** 1891–95) joined the Rough Riders. At the outbreak of the war, Robert Francis Wynne (LLB 1897), a member of the District National Guard, was ordered to Cuba and saw action in the eastern theater. W. E. Horton (LLB 1892), another member of the District National Guard, participated in the charge of San Juan Hill and received a Silver Star for gallantry in action. Maximilliano Luna (AB 1889) of the New Mexico territory recruited his own troop of Rough Riders in the southwest and took part in the battles at San Juan Hill, Las Guasimas, and Santiago. Capt. Edward B. Ives (x**C** 1874), on the staff of Gen. Fitzhugh Lee, played a prominent role in the battle of Pinar del Rio. Brig. Gen. Joseph O'Connell (LLB 1887) was the highest-ranking alumnus to serve in the war. Bailey Ashford (MD 1896) served with the military expedition to Puerto Rico as chief surgeon. Another alumnus, Thomas Sherman, SJ, the son of William Tecumseh Sherman, served as a chaplain in Puerto Rico.

Several, including Raphael Edmonston, Heller, Horton, Luna, O'Connell, Louis W. Mohun, and Wynne, subsequently saw service in the dirty guerilla war that followed the United States's acquisition of the Philippines. Major Heller took part as a surgeon in the expedition through Luzon, during which he earned a Silver Star for his care of the wounded while under fire. Maximilliano Luna, now a lieutenant in the regular army, went to the Philippines in the fall of 1899 and drowned in a river crossing shortly after his arrival. Edmonston also died as a result of service there. Louis W. Mohun (x**C** 1989), a member of the Ninth U.S. Infantry, was killed in action at Manila in November 1899, one of many American casualties during the protracted conflict. But the Americans eventually subdued the guerillas, and Georgetown alumni helped establish the territorial government of the Philippines. Richard Campbell (LLB 1899) was appointed by President Roosevelt as assistant to the attorney general of the islands in 1902, where he continued to serve in various executive and judicial capacities for several years. Amasa S. Crossfield (LLB 1883) also became a judge of the territorial administration, as did James J. Tracey (AB 1874), who became a justice of the Supreme Court of the Philippines.

The End of the Richards Era

In March 1898 Richards became seriously ill. It was not the first time he had been so during his decade as president. In the fall of 1891 he suffered fainting spells and weakness of the heart, a condition that continued off and on for the next year, forcing him to spend much time away attempting to recuperate. The diagnosis was a nervous condition from overwork. By the end of 1892 he fully expected to be replaced because of his health, and a list of candidates was sent to Rome for a new appointment. But his health revived and he remained in office. The revival was, alas, short lived. By early 1895 he was pleading to be relieved, claiming that he was "getting old and forgetting all I once knew."[160] His pleas went unheeded.

A year and a half later his health was breaking again, and he manifested the same symptoms he had in the early nineties and evoked the same diagnosis: nervous disorder from overwork.[161] "My head is not right," he wrote his superior in August 1896. "A single morning's work disables me entirely. . . . The doctor says the trouble is a nervous one, that I must take some rest, but that I need not apprehend any serious danger."[162] That confession apparently spared him appointment as the next provincial superior (he had been the current provincial's choice), but he still remained at Georgetown. When the new provincial superior made his visit in December 1897, Richards, pleading that he was utterly worn out (he was forty-six at the time), virtually begged him to relieve him of office. The provincial agreed that, after a decade, a change seemed best for all.[163] Three months later Richards collapsed again. In late March he was so weak that his brother was summoned. Then he rallied and in May went to the Ramapo Mountains in New York to convalesce at the villa of Mrs. Thomas Fortune Ryan.[164] He never returned to Georgetown as president. On July 3, John Whitney succeeded him.[165]

It was remarkable that he had done so much under such nearly constant strain. But he had proven in his decade as president to be the most imaginative and far-sighted leader Georgetown had had in its history. If he had failed to achieve much of his vision for the university, circumstances were as much, if not more, responsible than any failings of character.

CHAPTER 2

Georgetown in the Early Twentieth Century

[May the day come when] not only a broad and liberal-minded President would name a son of Georgetown to the high dignity of Chief Justice of the United States, but that an equally broad, liberal and noble people would be willing to select a son of Georgetown to be the Chief Executive of this great country of the United States.

ALPHONSUS DONLON, SJ, May 1912

The Presidents of the Period

In the quarter century between 1873 and 1898 Georgetown had three presidents. In the next two decades it would have five. The lack of both stability and strong leadership in the period had its impact on the institution. The innovations that Richards introduced at Georgetown were either not pursued or discontinued. Any systematic planning and vision of the institution as a university departed with Richards. His successors, unlike Richards, were little aware of, or concerned about, developments in the broader world of higher education. Indeed provincial superiors often made presidential appointments more with an eye to their appointees' aptitude to serve as a religious superior of the Jesuit Community at Georgetown than any ability to lead the university. Not surprisingly, in this period presidents tended to have a very limited focus that did not reach beyond the college. The rest of the university reverted to their traditional separate spheres.

John Whitney, SJ, Richards's successor, was another New Englander and convert to Catholicism who had entered the Jesuits' New Orleans Province.

He had been sent to England for his training, where he caught the eye of Edward Purbrick, the Englishman who subsequently had been appointed superior of the Maryland–New York Province in 1897. Whitney had taught at Jesuit schools in England, Alabama, and Louisiana, as well as at Fordham College, before being named president in 1898. He was noted for his personal touch with people, whether students or others, something notably lacking in his predecessor. At Georgetown he did not change. Students honored at the monthly reading of marks, for instance, were taken to dinner at Cabin John by President Whitney. He also daily visited the sick in the new university hospital and reached out to assist the charitable organizations in the city.[1] Within six months of naming Whitney president, his superior was clearly happy about the choice: "It is early, of course, as yet to judge of the government of Fr. Rector. But one thing is very evident—his wonderful influence over boys. They are enthusiastic about him. . . . As far as can be judged as yet there is much improvement in their general conduct & the tone of morality, candour and good feeling of most. . . . Fr. Rector is frank, kindly but can be very firm, but he wins the affection, respect and confidence of boys."[2]

By the spring of 1900, however, the superior general was warning Whitney that his priorities were all wrong. In his dealing with others, his first concern had to be their "spiritual formation, then their intellectual formation, and only last those matters that pertain to food, games, and all other such matters."[3] A year later, Whitney, health poor and growing increasingly despondent, wrote plaintively to Richards, "Will you be ready to come and take up the reins again this summer? I shall be very glad if your health is such that you will be able to become Rector again; I am about tired of the fight."[4] Richards was not ready, but the Jesuit superiors by this time had long become disillusioned about Whitney's capacity to govern. His indulgence of students, obsession with sports, and spendthrift ways (the university had sustained an imbalance of $10,000 the previous year) had convinced superiors not to renew his tenure when his first term ended in 1901.[5]

Whitney's successor was Jerome Daugherty, SJ. The fifty-two-year-old Daugherty was a Baltimore native of Irish and German immigrant parents. He had taught briefly at Georgetown in the early 1870s, but, as his obituary hinted, had felt out of place among the higher class students at Georgetown. He had returned to the college again in 1889, serving as Richards's director of physical operations for seven years. But he had little academic experience, and even less vision, and his administration tended to be perfunctory. He survived a year longer than Whitney. When his health began to suffer in the late winter of 1905, superiors sent him on a cruise to recuperate, but, back in Georgetown, he collapsed, like Richards, from nervous exhaustion (neurasthenia), and he was forced to give up his office.[6] David Hillhouse Buel, SJ, the administrator of the university, succeeded him.

The forty-three-year-old Buel, the son of a general, had converted to Catholicism as a sophomore at Yale. Buel entered the Society of Jesus after graduation and had taught physics, mathematics, Latin, and Greek at several Jesuit colleges including Georgetown. Buel, with his balding forehead and rimless glasses, projected the image of an academic but brought to his office a concern for order, efficiency, and a proper balance between studies and the extracurriculum. He immediately put intercollegiate athletics under tight restraint and effectively deprofessionalized football, baseball, and track (see chapter 4). He reinstituted a rigid order for attendance not only of class but also of study hall, meals, and daily religious exercises (Mass, night prayers, and benediction) and enacted a strict demerit system for absences. His norms were unwavering. Absences from class were simply inexcusable, no matter what the reason or who the petitioner. When one parent requested that his son, a freshman, be allowed to come home to New York in January 1906 to attend the wedding of his sister and the baptism of his niece, Buel refused. The son went home anyway and was dismissed for his absence. The case ended in court, with the court upholding Buel's right, as president of a private university, to establish his own rules for the conduct of students.[7] Another parent, a congressman from Maryland with long ties to the university, fared no better with Buel later that year in attempting to gain permission for his son to attend the Democratic state convention that was nominating him for Congress. The parent, an alumnus with three sons at the college, was outraged. "You are trying to make of the college a cloistered institution," Sydney Mudd wrote Buel. "You are treating young men as infants; you are treating their parents with disrespect; you are proceeding onward to a course which will do no good, and naught but harm, to the College."[8]

Students from time to time protested such rigidity by breaking crockery or marching en masse from campus, for example on the occasion of Buel's refusing to grant a holiday on St. Patrick's Day. Others voted with their feet more permanently by withdrawing. After Buel's first year there were only seventy-seven collegians enrolled. By 1908, Buel's provincial superior had seen enough of the president's "indiscreet zeal," "fault-finding character," and "legal righteousness." "There is an armed neutrality" between the president and the students, he reported to Rome. Buel had alienated students, faculty, alumni, and benefactors alike by his rigidity and coldness.[9] "If you wish to rescue Georgetown College from certain impending ruin," a faculty member pleaded, "a substitute for Fr. Buel as President must be found as soon as possible. Three more years of the present administration will leave little of Georgetown to be cared for."[10] The superior general instructed his provincial representative to send a *terna* (a slate of three nominees) to Rome to replace Buel if the provincial and his consultors concluded that it would do grave harm to leave him as president for another three-year term, due to begin that summer.[11] The provincial sent the *terna*, and Joseph Himmel, SJ, was chosen to succeed Buel in August 1908.[12] He was the fourth president the university had had in seven years.

A native of Annapolis, Himmel had entered the Redemptorist order before joining the Jesuits. He had taught at Georgetown for several years as a scholastic but, following his ordination, had spent most of his career on the mission band, where he had been extremely effective at securing gifts; in two decades he had brought in more than $400,000.[13] The fifty-three-year-old Himmel brought to his post an imposing figure—he was bearded and six feet tall—an eloquent, if seldom-used, voice (at least at Georgetown), and a sense for administration. "A man of few words and many deeds," as one faculty member recalled.[14] After a year and a half in office Richards congratulated him on "the great progress made by the College" since his appointment. "Wonderful opportunities are before you," Richards wrote, "if you can only be enabled to grasp them."[15] But Himmel's deteriorating health was already undermining his work. "Sickness [arterial sclerosis] has prematurely aged me," he wrote the superior general in the summer of 1910. "The urgent need of this college," he pleaded, "is a younger and more active Rector."[16] By the end of the 1911 academic year, Himmel was ordered to take a leave of absence to rest. He returned only to suffer recurring bouts of vertigo and vomiting, one so acute in January 1912 that he was hospitalized for five months. By that time Rome had named Alphonsus Donlon, SJ, to succeed him.[17]

Donlon, forty-four years old, had been a star athlete at the college, starting on the baseball team for four years. After graduating in 1888, he had spent a year at the Massachusetts Institute of Technology before joining the Jesuits. As a scholastic he had been faculty director of athletics in the late nineties, as well as a teacher of physics, mechanics, geology, and astronomy. He had been an assistant to the provincial superior in New York City when he was appointed to head Georgetown in late January 1912. A retiring man, despite his athletic background, Donlon was a minimal administrator, delegating responsibility freely, some thought excessively. As a friend later put it, "He lacked the drive and power necessary for dealing directly with present-day educational questions, and with the business arrangements of a growing institution like Georgetown."[18] Indeed, after two years in office, Donlon was pleading with superiors to be relieved, claiming that "the whole thing is beyond me and I feel like a boy trying to do a man's work."[19] His pleas fell on deaf ears; he was the first Georgetown president to serve two terms since Richards, 1912 to 1918.

The College

These years represented a drastic growth in the university and college proper. In 1898 there were 634 students in the various schools of the university. By 1917 there were more than that in the Law School alone and 1,500 in the university in all. In 1898 there were 106 students in the upper classes of the college. By 1917 that number had more than doubled to 241. In the process, the college had finally enrolled more collegians (beginning in 1909) than prep schoolers. The northern regional dominance of enrollment patterns that had begun in the late nineteenth century continued to grow. Nearly half the students (45%) now came from the North, one-quarter from New York and Pennsylvania alone.

Interestingly, there was a revival of students from Central America. Whitney rescinded the tacit ban that Richards had established; for the period, more than 9 percent came from that area, including large numbers from Puerto Rico and Cuba.[20] In 1900, President Whitney admitted a half-dozen Puerto Ricans as scholarship students at the request of the commissioner of education in San Juan.[21] There were also a dozen or so students from the newly acquired Philippines, most of them sent by the United States Philippine Commission. The first academic year of the new century (1900–1901) saw the admission of the first student from Japan, Shogaburo Yoshino. The Irish remained the largest ethnic group, comprising about one-third of the students. By the first decade of the century the college had become almost exclusively populated by Catholics—97 percent.

The length of stay was remarkably short, a mean of one year. A small minority not only graduated from the college but also earned a professional degree from Georgetown, such as John A. Foote (AB 1902, MD 1906), who became a well-published authority on pediatrics and a faculty member (and later dean) of the Medical School, where his father had long taught, and the grandnephew of Dr. Samuel Mudd, Sidney Emanuel Mudd Jr. (AB 1906, LLB 1909), who later became a U.S. representative from Maryland.

The notable increase in enrollment began in 1910 when the college overtly turned to alumni, an untapped instrument, for the recruitment of students, not only for the college, but also for the whole university. As the 1911–12 catalogue advertised, thanks to the cooperation of loyal alumni, "there has been a notable increase in all the Departments of the University during the past year. The total enrollment for the year is 1293." In addition, a dozen alumni clubs throughout the country established scholarships for prospective students in their areas.[22]

Ryan Hall (1902), on the site of the original building demolished the previous year. (Georgetown University Archives)

The increase in enrollment heightened the need for additional student housing. In 1902 Ida Ryan, the wife of the industrialist Thomas Fortune Ryan, who had two sons at Georgetown, agreed to fund a dormitory on the site of the South Building to provide student rooms and a dining hall. She wanted an imposing building to replace the decrepit original structure and to provide a counterpart on the riverfront to Healy Hall on the east. The result was a four-story, brick hall with classical portico, completed in late 1904 at the cost of $113,500.[23] A counterpoint to Healy it was not. As the official chronicler of the college diplomatically noted in his report to Rome for 1904, "The new building is noted more for its utility than its beauty."[24] Ryan Hall housed more than one hundred students, but within three years it proved inadequate to meet the needs of a growing population, and officials looked for other sources for still another residence hall.[25] A serious fire in the North Building in 1909 underscored the poor state of that building and the need for additional facilities, but no solution was at hand.

There were now fifteen Jesuit and five lay instructors in 1911 for the college proper. But faculty turnover continued to be extremely high. More than half the faculty (55%) stayed two years or less. Among those who were there more than five years were the Jesuits John A. Conway, a Scotsman who taught religion and philosophy at both the college and the Law School; John Thompson Hedrick, the son of Benjamin Hedrick, who had taught chemistry at Georgetown in the 1870s, and a trained astronomer who became director of the observatory in 1906; and Peter V. Masterson, who taught history and government.

J. Havens Richards had first signaled the need to modify the traditional curriculum in order to "adjust our colleges to the altered circumstances of the times." In an 1896 article circulated among Jesuits in the *Woodstock Letters*, Richards argued that this meant changing both the order and content of the courses "in order to conform to the government requirements."[26] Richards was referring to the rise of regional accrediting agencies that were establishing criteria for defining secondary education, for setting collegiate entrance requirements, and for determining and structuring the collegiate curriculum, which was fundamentally different from the seven-year program of classical studies that the *Ratio Studiorum* specified for a "collegiate education" that actually combined secondary and postsecondary education.[27] Richards was prepared to make substantial changes to accommodate realities. Most of his fellow Jesuit educators in the East were not. Four years later the provincial superior issued a new schedule of courses for the high school and collegiate programs, which made modest adjustments to the traditional order of studies to satisfy, at least nominally, the wider educational world's definition of secondary education and college. The new schedule transposed what had been freshman year to the fourth year of high school and added a year to college in which seniors would continue the study of philosophy begun in junior year, as well as Latin, English, physiology, political economy, and an elective.

There were also changes in the curriculum, which, on the whole, separated Jesuit colleges even more sharply from their secular counterparts. Latin (four years) and Greek (three years) were still at the center of the curriculum, although less classroom time was given to the classical languages and more to English and the sciences. Electives were formally included, another nod to modernization.[28] For the first time, theology, or "Christian doctrine," became an integral part of the four-year curriculum. But the most significant change was the great increase in the time devoted to the study of philosophy. There were five hours per week devoted to philosophy in junior year (cosmology, general metaphysics, epistemology) and ten hours devoted in senior year (psychology, natural theology, ethics), plus two hours dedicated to the philosophy of history and two to the history of philosophy in junior and senior years, respectively. Immediately, there were widespread complaints from the Georgetown faculty and elsewhere, ranging from the de-emphasis on Latin to the inability to offer certain traditional subjects (e.g., political economy).[29] A revised schedule followed in 1906 that restored additional time for Latin and increased the electives in senior year. But the confusion and unrest continued. In 1908 a new provincial, Joseph Hanselman, citing a "crisis in studies," created a general committee on studies to examine the curriculum anew.[30] The committee confirmed the basic changes since 1900 while allotting ten hours (from five) to philosophy in junior year, two hours for religious instruction (from one) for all years, and terminating the study of Latin at the end of sophomore year.[31]

As the place of the classics moved from centering the curriculum, educators searched for a new force of intellectual coherence. Protestant and secular schoolmen increasingly found it in the "humanities," which combined history, literature, and philosophy in a study of culture.[32] For Jesuit and Catholic educators, it was the newly recovered Thomistic tradition of philosophy. The 1908 reform of the curriculum marked the full emergence of neoscholastic philosophy as the capstone of the unity of knowledge that was the fundamental premise of the Catholic philosophy of education, although this would not become clearly articulated until the postwar period. If the changes in the curriculum were effectively reducing, if not eliminating, the role of the classics as the undergirding element of a Jesuit education, they had made philosophy the new synthesizing force in the course of studies. For the next six decades, philosophy retained its hegemonic place in the curriculum of the college.[33]

Whether the classical course, including five or six years of Latin and Greek, should remain the sole program of study at Georgetown and other Jesuit colleges was a deeply contested question by 1910, when the committee issued its report. By that time most private universities, including Yale and Harvard, had dropped Greek as a requirement for the bachelor of arts degree. More and more Georgetown administrators became convinced that the particular requirement of Greek to earn a bachelor's degree was badly hurting enrollment. "I am fully convinced," one Jesuit official at Georgetown wrote to Rome in 1913, "that we cannot hope to get to Georgetown the sons of wealthy Catholics, if we insist on Greek. The people of America do not want Greek. I do not see how we are going to force it on them."[34] Alphonsus Donlon was pleading for permission to introduce a scientific course as an alternate degree program to change the ebb tide of enrollments, driven by the alienating impact of Greek within the curriculum. "Students who are now going to non-Catholic colleges are driven away because of their unwillingness to take Greek for which they have no training and no inclination—. . . [The retention of] Greek [as a curricular requisite] . . . keeps us from reaching many of the best young men in the country, who are to be the prominent men of the future and who would otherwise come under our influence."[35]

Description of the new scientific course in the catalog of 1915–16.
(Georgetown University Archives)

"To insist on it will be to sound the death knell of Georgetown."[36] Although everyone in authority, from the provincial superior to the prefect of studies at Georgetown, was urging the superior general to grant Donlon's request, Wernz was unmoved by arguments of popular demand ("people should not be *followed* but *taught*") and denied the move.[37] Six months later Wernz was dead, and Donlon renewed his plea, a virtual begging, with Wernz's vicar general: "Daily we find the need of greater elasticity in our curriculum and the most essential thing is to have a course without Greek. I wish I could make your Paternity realize this."[38] Finally, his arguments hit home, and permission came in 1915 to institute the scientific course.[39] Immediately, enrollment increased dramatically, with 210 students enrolled in the college for the 1915–16 academic year, the largest number so far in Georgetown's history, and more applicants than the college could accommodate.[40]

94   GEORGETOWN UNIVERSITY.   [1915-1916

COURSE 3.—Descriptive Geometry and Mechanical Drawing. B. S. Sophomore; Optional for Junior and Senior A. B.—Three hours a week.
COURSE 4.—Calculus—Differential and Integral. B. S. Sophomore; Optional for Junior and Senior A. B.—Three hours a week.

PHYSICS.

COURSE 1.—Mechanics—Lecture Course. Kinematics and Dynamics. The lectures are supplemented by work in problems which involve the topics discussed in class. The application of these subjects to every-day life is brought out by illustrative examples. Two hours a week.
COURSE 2.—Lecture course the same as Course 1, but laboratory work, according to a Standard Laboratory Manual, is added. B. S. Sophomore.
COURSE 3.—Physics—Lecture Course in Mechanics of Fluids, Sound, Light, Heat, Magnetism, and Electricity. In each subject practical problems are given in class to impress the student with the necessity of a knowledge of the theory. Five hours a week. Junior Year.
COURSE 4.—Lecture course as in Course III together with five hours of laboratory work. In this course observation and accuracy of execution are insisted on. The student is prepared for the more advanced work of the professional schools. B. S. Junior; Optional for A. B. Junior.

EVIDENCE OF RELIGION.

COURSE 1.—Freshman Year—One hour a week. Text-book, Wilmer's Hand-book of the Christian Religion.

Roman authority, a distinctive feature of Jesuit higher education, also affected the personal freedom of the students. A persistent source of Roman censure was the college's practice of allowing students to visit the city at night. Superiors general thought it an abuse and a grave temptation for students to go into Washington several nights a week and return at midnight or later. American Jesuit administrators defended the practice as a pragmatic necessity. To insist, as the general did, that students return no later than 10 PM was, in one provincial superior's judgment, impossible to execute and tantamount to closing the college. "You cannot restrain so much the liberty of our American College students."[41] "If the . . . plan suggested by your Paternity is adopted I have good reason to fear," David Buel wrote, "that the number of students would so fall off as to make it impossible to carry on the College."[42] To assuage Rome, Buel's successor, Himmel, began in 1909 to eliminate, class by class, town permissions, until only the upper three classes enjoyed them. Still, the superior general, now Wernz, insisted that they be further curtailed. Finally, in 1914, despite continuing protests from Georgetown administrators, he decreed that the rector restrict town visits to case-by-case concessions that he or his delegate could alone grant.[43] The decree apparently resulted in the rector's simply granting permissions to virtually all senior students who asked. Roman opposition notwithstanding, presidents at Georgetown and other Jesuit institutions continued to seek ways to liberalize student discipline as a recognition of the liberty-loving culture of America.[44]

In the second decade of the century, students of the college initiated two scientific clubs. In 1912, with the encouragement of the biology professor, Francis Tondorf, students started the Georgetown Biological Club. The club held weekly meetings during which local biologists or medical doctors gave lectures on biological topics. The series of lectures, given by such prominent scientists as Joseph Hall of the Smithsonian Institution, soon attracted an audience beyond the walls of the university, and by 1914 it became necessary to hold the sessions in Gaston Hall to accommodate the growing crowds. In 1915 a chemistry academy was organized to study "the industrial applications of the principles of chemistry." Members made visits to industrial plants in the area to "study more closely the subjects discussed" in papers delivered by students at the academy's weekly meetings, such as the making of glass or gunpowder and explosives.[45] A chemical museum was established, made possible by the contributions of various companies throughout the country of their products, such as minerals from the Bon Ami Company, or of exhibits illustrating the making of various products, from beer to glass.

In 1911 there was a revival of the mandolin and glee clubs, defunct since 1903. The Dramatic Association had revived in the 1890s. Among the highlight performances of that decade was *The Merchant of Venice,* with Robert Collier playing the role of Shylock. In the 1900s the Dramatic Association moved its productions from campus to various Washington theaters. Plays included *Richelieu, The Rivals, All the Comforts of Home, The Last of the Gladiators,* and *The Dream of Gerontius*. Students began to publish yearbooks in the first decade of the century. In 1908 the annual publication first appeared under the name *Ye Domesday Booke*.

The traditional conservative leanings of the upper-middle-class college students continued in the Progressive Era. A common target in articles in the *Georgetown College Journal* was socialism, denounced as a pathway to atheism, free love, the confiscation of property, and despotism. Fear of socialism as an alien force seeking inroads into America also caused Georgetown students, few of whom were even the sons of immigrants, much less immigrants themselves, to favor literacy tests and other forms of immigration restriction. "It is time for the people of these United States to arouse themselves to the fact," one student wrote in 1911, "that the evils of immigration are poisoning the very life blood of their boasted liberty."[46] The literacy test was a major topic for the debating societies by 1915–16, and the affirmative invariably won. Attitudes toward the organization of labor, pace *Rerum novarum,* were also critical, opposing the notion of a closed shop and calling for compulsory arbitration to avoid strikes. In another debate, the negative won the argument that government had an obligation to solve the unemployment problem.[47]

Women's suffrage had little if any support at the college. An editorial in 1910 suggested that Christian ideals and women's suffrage were mutually exclusive. "The wild agitations of the suffragettes are in marked contrast to the serenity, the simplicity and the gentleness which Christian art has idealized as the perfection of true womanhood," it noted.[48] Five years later another editorial expressed the hope that the suffrage issue would suffer defeat at the polls.[49] When the Philodemic Debating Society in 1917 debated the proposition that "Congress should pass a law conferring on women the power of suffrage," to no one's surprise the negative prevailed.[50]

There was also opposition to a progressive income tax. "Instead of being able to reap the full harvest of [a man's] endeavor," a 1914 editorial commented, "his reward always falls a little short of his deserts."[51] And Georgetown students, despite the decline in southerners among their ranks, were full supporters of the Jim Crow system that had come to prevail in the South, even in Washington, by the turn of the century. When the Harvard baseball team played Georgetown on the Hilltop in the spring of 1903, Georgetown students were outraged that Harvard insisted on starting a black player at shortstop. Harvard, they felt, had insulted Georgetown by failing to respect its southern tradition of segregation of social intercourse, including sports. "No intelligent person," the *College Journal* lectured, "can be blind to the fact that Southern gentlemen refuse absolutely to receive the negro into their parlors or into their sports." What made it particularly offensive, the author added, was that the captain of the Georgetown nine came from the same hometown in Alabama, indeed the same street in Montgomery, as the Harvard shortstop. Harvard had been specifically asked not to play him in Washington but insisted on treating "the people of Washington . . . to the unwonted spectacle of a negro mingling in the sports of white men."[52]

Graduate Education

Superior General Martín was patently clear in his directions to Whitney at the outset of his administration that, unlike Richards, Whitney should focus his energies not on "the schools of the University," meaning law, medicine, and graduate studies, but on the college, which Martín plainly felt was the proper work of the Society.[53] Graduate education survived Richards's departure but was under continual questioning about its place, costs, and impact on the university. The provincial superior in 1899, William Purbrick, confessed to Rome that his inclination was to terminate the program to eliminate the expense as well as the offense it gave to the Catholic University and its sponsors in Rome. That action, he admitted, would antagonize most local Jesuits, so the best he could hope to do was rein in the program by getting the administration to concentrate on certain fields of learning—philosophy, history, literature—in which they were strong and drop the rest. He charged John Whitney to discuss the whole matter with his advisors.[54]

This was but the first of several internal evaluations of graduate studies over the next fifteen years. The status quo prevailed in 1899. Two years later, the rector of the Catholic University of America, Thomas Conaty, complained to the succeeding provincial superior about Georgetown's pretentious and competitive graduate program. The new superior, Thomas Gannon, who regarded Georgetown as a college masquerading as a university, assured Conaty that he would do all he could to allay their concerns. Gannon was of a mind to suppress graduate education entirely at Georgetown, but the superior general insisted that they basically keep doing what they had been doing, but as quietly as possible.[55]

Ironically, the provincial's chief assistant, James P. Fagan, SJ, who had progressive ideas about higher education and the Jesuit place within it, thought that the province was making a serious mistake in not putting sufficient resources, either human or material, into Georgetown. Fagan, in a report to Rome on the condition of Jesuit higher education in the eastern United States, clearly regarded Georgetown as the most important institution in the province, an estimation that he assured Roman superiors was held by the wider educational community. Indeed, Georgetown's reputation among outsiders, he told Roman officials, sadly did not reflect reality. But there was little hope that the situation would change, he reported, owing to the deep jealousy and resentment toward Georgetown on the part of eastern Jesuits outside of Georgetown itself, particularly in the New York–New England region, that prevented provincial superiors from investing in a special way in the institution.[56]

Fagan's report brought no pressure from Rome to change the provincial attitude toward Georgetown and to begin treating it as the special Jesuit institution in which public opinion held it. Gradually there was a downscaling of the graduate program at Georgetown. The number of students doing graduate work unsurprisingly plummeted with Richards's departure, from 41 in 1897 to 14 in 1901. In 1905, David Buel dropped all graduate scholarships. By 1906 seven students registered for courses. The following year the president's advisors recommended that the program be limited to a few courses supplementing "Senior work in the College."[57] That same year a new superior general, Franz Wernz, advised that they simply discontinue graduate studies.[58] Wernz had a vision of establishing one great Jesuit university in the United States, to rank with Jesuit institutions in Rome and Louvain. Unfortunately for Georgetown, Wernz thought that this major university should be, not in its political but its intellectual center, which meant New York—thus not Georgetown but Fordham. Wernz wanted Fordham to become "a great center of studies and publications," housing the Society's periodicals in the United States as well as a full range of graduate faculties, including the theologate.[59] Fordham, which had been struggling to survive as a college since the late nineteenth century, had only incorporated itself as a university a few years earlier when it had begun law and medical schools. Under Wernz's prodding, steps were taken to fulfill his vision. The *Messenger of the Sacred Heart* was relocated to Fordham in 1907; *America,* the weekly journal of opinion that the Society began in 1909, had its offices in New York. The Society purchased land to bring the theologate from Maryland to Yonkers. Wernz's death in 1914 prevented all the steps he had envisioned from being taken, but from 1905 on, resources began to be concentrated slowly but surely at Fordham rather than at Georgetown, a trend that would continue for decades, to the great detriment of Georgetown's development of higher studies.

Francis Tondorf, SJ, at the Observatory. (Georgetown University Archives)

From 1907 to 1914, there was no graduate education at Georgetown. When a fire in the North Building in 1909 destroyed the postgraduate library, it seemed to seal the fate of graduate education. There was a tacit recognition, even by Georgetown administrators, that the Catholic University was indeed a reality. In 1910 President Himmel, at the urging of Thomas Conaty, petitioned Jesuit authorities in Rome to send a German Jesuit biologist to teach at the Catholic University.[60] In 1914, however, the graduate program at Georgetown was revived but attracted only a handful of students over the next several years.

Georgetown's locus of scientific research, the observatory, also declined during this period. John Hagen continued to do original work, train other astronomers, and

Seismological station under the quadrangle. (Georgetown University Archives. Photo by Harris and Ewing)

publish the series on the observations of variable stars. In 1906, Hagen was called to Rome to assume the directorship of the Vatican Observatory. In his place at Georgetown the provincial superior appointed a Maryland Jesuit astronomer, John Hedrick. Hedrick proved a disappointment, failing to keep up the publishing that Hagen had established and refusing to train other astronomers. Officials continued to seek in vain for the endowment for the observatory that Richards had first tried to establish a generation earlier.

Through the grant of an alumnus, Patrick H. O'Donnell (**C** 1892), the university in 1909 established a seismological station on campus, initially in the south end of the Healy Building, then under the quadrangle. The station was part of an effort of a midwestern Jesuit, Frederick L. Odenbach of John Carroll University in Cleveland, to create a network of seismographic stations at Jesuits institutions throughout North America.[61] Directed by Francis Tondorf, SJ, the Georgetown station, with its two astatic horizontal seismographs and two Bosch-Omori pendulums as well as two conical pendulums, registered motions of earthquakes around the world. Over the next fifteen years it became the most active in the country in reporting observations of quakes on land and at sea and made Tondorf a leading figure within the seismological community.[62] In 1918, at the request of the government of Honduras, Georgetown established a seismographic substation in that country.[63]

Law School

No school grew more during the period than the Law School. Legal education across the country was booming, with a rapid increase in institutions and students. Georgetown, with its virtual lack of requirements, took full advantage of the booming market. The largest school in the university in 1898 with 280 students, the Law School enrollment increased to 730 by 1910 and, with a new building the following year to accommodate even more, reached a prewar high of more than 1,000 students in 1913, leading President Donlon to boast that the university now had the largest law school in the country.[64]

The part-time faculty grew apace, more than doubling from 18 to 46 between 1900 and 1917. Despite the increase in size, there was, unlike the college, remarkable continuity in the composition of the faculty at the Law School from year to year. Three-fourths of the professors taught for more than five years at the school. The federal or judicial bureaucracy was a major source for such faculty as Judge Harry M. Clabaugh, chief justice of the Supreme Court of the District of Columbia, who served as dean of the school between Hamilton's two stints (1903–14); Seth Shephard, chief justice of the Court of Appeals of the District of Columbia, who taught equity and constitutional law; J. Harry Covington, Clabaugh's successor as chief justice, who taught corporations and common law pleading; Ashley Mulgrave Gould (LLB 1884), an associate justice of the Supreme Court of the District, who taught contracts at the school for two decades; Daniel Thew Wright, associate justice of the Supreme Court of the District, who taught several subjects at the school from 1903 to 1914; and John Ellsworth Laskey, U.S. district attorney, who was professor of criminal law for thirty-five years beginning in 1910. Other notable faculty included former U.S. senator (Maryland) Louis E. McComas, who lectured on international law and foreign relations; former solicitor general of the United States Holmes Conrad, who lectured on the history and development of law and comparative jurisprudence from 1901 to 1915; Charles Edward Roach (AB 1895, LLB 1897), the son of Senator William Nathaniel Roach of North Dakota, who taught conflict of laws for thirty years from 1906; and Thomas Ewing Jr., patent commissioner, who taught patent law for eighteen years (1914–32).

Since the Law School remained a night school, nearly all its students had daytime positions, most with the government. As a result, unlike the collegiate population that was predominantly from the northeast, significant portions of the law students came from a wide range of areas. About three-fifths were from either the local area (D.C. and Maryland, 30%) or the East (29%), 17 percent each were from the Midwest and the South, and 7 percent were from the West. About two-thirds (64%) were from urban areas, with one-fifth having a rural origin. About 58 percent were Catholics. In 1901, Roman

J. Lacson (LLB 1904) was the first Filipino student to enter the school. Three years later a group of Filipino students were sent by the United States government to the school. Five graduated in 1907, including Delphin Jaranilla, who rose to the position of attorney general in his homeland.[65]

Attempts by the profession to enact a minimal set of standards for the training of lawyers affected the school in this period. In 1897 the American Bar Association (ABA) set three years of formal training as a prerequisite for admission to the bar.[66] The following year, Georgetown lengthened its program accordingly. When, however, the Association of American Law Schools in 1905 established a standard of graduation from a high school or its equivalent for admission, the school withdrew from the association rather than implement the requirement that would have reduced enrollment.[67] The only prerequisite remained a personal interview.

Uncontrolled enrollment quickly taxed facilities built to accommodate far fewer than the 635 students of 1910. Indeed, the anticipated continuing increase in enrollment led school authorities to double the size of their quarters. An addition extending the school west on E Street was constructed in 1910–11 for $100,000, after George Hamilton, the former dean of the school,

George Hamilton, dean of the Law School, 1900–1903 and 1914–41. (Georgetown University Archives)

Law School annex on E Street NW, 1911. (Georgetown University Archives)

persuaded the administration that the addition could be funded out of the growing revenue from the soaring enrollment. The three-story wing, with lecture halls, library, and faculty room, opened on Washington's birthday in 1911. A year later enrollment exceeded 1,000, and in 1913 it was necessary to attach a second addition to the 1891 building.[68]

Curricular development at the school reflected a modest recognition of the case method that was sweeping law schools across the nation. The most popular textbook utilizing the case method, James Barr Ames's *Selection of Cases on Pleading at Common Law,* had been required reading for third-year students since 1894. In 1910 casebooks were made part of the assignments for three upper-level classes.[69] Still, the treatise method of legal education, teaching by definition and rule rather than analysis of appellate court decisions, continued to dominate. Professors assigned students thirty to forty pages of a text such as Ames's *Cases on Pleading or Darlington on Personal Property.* In class the instructor explained the text and then orally quizzed students on the same matter. By 1910 "quizmasters" substituted for professors in doing the testing.

This period marked the introduction of honor fraternities into the Law School. By 1908 students belonged to local chapters of Delta Chi, Phi Alpha Delta, and Sigma Nu Phi, and each chapter comprised eight to thirty members, plus honorary ones from the faculty and government. The 1910s also saw the establishment of three law clubs—the Morris Club, the John Carroll Club, and the Edward Douglass White Club—in which members pursued their particular legal interests. Political clubs also made their first appearance at the school, the Georgetown University Democratic Club forming in 1911 as a member of the College Men's Democratic League. Five years later, for the 1916 presidential campaign, the Hughes Republican Club was organized and, under the auspices of the Republican National Committee, sent speakers throughout Maryland to work for Charles Evans Hughes during the month prior to the election. In a straw vote conducted among the students by the two political clubs, Woodrow Wilson won convincingly, 335 to 231. As the president of the Hughes Club observed, the results were unsurprising given the southern composition of Georgetown's student body and the fact that so many of them were employed by a Democratic administration.[70]

Prestigious law schools such as Harvard, Yale, Pennsylvania, and Columbia had since the 1880s been establishing reviews that carried learned articles by faculty and other legal scholars. In 1912 Georgetown students put the school on the law review map by starting the *Georgetown Law Journal,* which not only published legal articles by faculty and alumni but also functioned as a record of student club and related activities. Competitive ambition was clearly a motivation for the students. "Realizing the great strides made by Georgetown Law School in the past two years," a newspaper reported, the student founders of the review felt confident in providing this new medium for promoting the school.[71]

Among the graduates of the school during the two decades before the country's entry into World War I, Carl B. Rix (LLB 1903) became one of the founders of Marquette University's Law School, where he taught from 1908 until 1946. In the latter year he was elected president of the ABA. Two graduates of the period became governors of Rhode Island, James Higgins (LLB 1999) and William Flynn (LLB 1910). Eleven law students of the period later served in the House of Representatives, including Butler Black Hare (LLB 1913) of South Carolina, James V. McClintic (x 1917) of Oklahoma, Francis B. Condon (LLB 1916) of Rhode Island, William P. Connery Jr. (LLB 1916) of Massachusetts, Francis E. Walter (LLB 1919) of Pennsylvania (co-sponsor of the McCarren-Walter Act of 1952), and William R. Thom (LLB 1916) of Ohio. John Ignatius Cosgrove (LLB 1913) became associate justice of the Supreme Court of South Carolina in 1929. Jesse Corcoran Adkins (LLB 1899) became assistant attorney general in the District before being named to the U.S. District Court. Adkins also taught at the school for more than three decades, beginning in 1906.

William Witthaft Bride (LLB 1904) became corporation counsel of the District of Columbia. Frank J. Hogan (LLB 1902) became a highly successful lawyer in the District, a founder of the firm of Hogan and Hart, and president of the ABA in 1938. Robert T. Scott (LLB 1916) became an assistant attorney general of the United States during the Hoover administration. William F. X. Geoghan (LLB 1906) went into law practice in New York City, where he served as a district attorney for Brooklyn in the 1930s. Hugh Joseph Fegan Jr. (AB 1901, LLB 1907) joined the faculty after his graduation and remained for forty-three years, serving as secretary-treasurer and then as dean. Martin Conboy (1908) became a U.S. attorney during the 1930s and the president of the alumni association in 1940. William Edward Leahy (1912) became a noted trial lawyer in the District and dean of the Columbus School of Law at the Catholic University of America from 1932 to 1954.

Medical School

The Medical School experienced a stretch of growth in the last years of the nineteenth century and the first years of the twentieth and then suffered a brief decline during the mid-1900s, principally due to higher entrance requirements.[72] It thereafter climbed to a record enrollment of nearly 160 in 1911 before reforms and heightened standards occasioned by an unfavorable report on the school sponsored by the American Medical Association (AMA) in 1910 caused far fewer students to be admitted and cut enrollment by more than half. The demographic pattern was remarkably like that of the college, with 47 percent of the students coming from the Northeast, more than one-third of that from Massachusetts. It was heavily Catholic (75%), with the

Irish (37%) and Germans (19%) dominating the ethnic ranks. Virtually all were full-time students.

The school joined the university in supporting a recruiter working the region (Maryland, Pennsylvania, Virginia, and West Virginia) to secure students and paid a commission of ten dollars for each student obtained.[73] One remarkable recruit was John Ambrose Foote, a twenty-five-year-old druggist in Archbald, Pennsylvania, who received a scholarship to Georgetown in 1900, earned his MD in 1906, and did postgraduate work at the University of Berlin, where he specialized in children's diseases, a field in which he gained an international reputation. He returned to Georgetown as professor of pediatrics for a quarter of a century while maintaining a prolific scholarly output in books and journal articles.[74] In 1908, bedeviled by a continuing decline in enrollment, the faculty authorized the dean to purchase lists of high school graduates from New England and Middle Atlantic states at five dollars for one thousand names.[75] When the school began requiring two years of college for admission in 1911, the lists switched to college graduates at double the rate.[76]

Besides Foote, notable graduates of the school in this period included Loren Bascom Johnson (MD 1900), who taught pediatrics and then child psychiatry at Georgetown for nearly four decades following his graduation, and Thomas Parran (MD 1915) from southern Maryland, who established the precursor to the Centers for Disease Control as U.S. surgeon general (1936–48). J. Winthrop Peabody (MD 1914) became a pioneer in the treatment of tuberculosis and other respiratory diseases. Leo Henry Bartemeier (**M** 1920) became a psychiatrist and medical director of Seton Psychiatric

George Kober, dean of the Medical School, 1901–28. (Georgetown University Archives)

Institute in 1954. Robert Emmett Moran (MD 1920) went on to be a fellow at the Mayo Clinic in 1921 in medicine and surgery. In 1940 he returned to Georgetown to become associate professor of surgery. He was later (1958) elected president of the American Association of Plastic Surgeons. William Parker Herbst Jr. (MD 1915), George Kober's nephew, went on to become a fellow in surgery at the Mayo Clinic. In 1933 he returned as a professor of clinical urology to Georgetown where he made many contributions in that field, particularly his introduction of estrogen therapy in the treatment of prostate cancer. Ralph M. LeComte (MD 1910) became a specialist in urology, and he taught that subject for many years on the school faculty. Maurice Arthur Selinger (**M** 1915), a D.C. practitioner, became one of the first physicians to support enthusiastically the utilization of blood banks.

The faculty of the school was nearly as stable as that of the Law School, with more than half of the members remaining more than four years. In 1901, George Magruder resigned after thirteen years as dean. George Kober succeeded him in June 1901. Kober brought to the office national standing as a leader in medical education. He became president of the American Association of Medical Colleges in 1906 and secretary to the Association of American Physicians from 1909 to 1916. Since his appointment to Georgetown in 1888, Kober had promoted sanitary reform and public health in the area. He had been the first to postulate that the polluted Potomac River and flies were the sources of typhoid fever in the city. Later he discovered the role that tainted milk could play in the transmission of disease, particularly to infants. He was a major partner in the Washington Sanitary Improvement Company established in 1897 to make available to workers sanitary homes at reasonable rental rates. He was a prominent member of presidential commissions in the first decade of the century that examined the causes and prevention of industrial diseases such as tuberculosis, pneumonia, and typhoid fever. He became a leader in the study of tuberculosis and its treatment; he was responsible for the design of the Tuberculosis Hospital in Washington, which opened in 1908. In all, he published some two hundred articles on hygiene, disease prevention, and philanthropy.[77] At his death in 1931, the *New York Times* noted, "Few men have been more prominently identified than Dr. Kober with the promotion of public health in the District of Columbia and throughout the country."[78]

A key addition to the faculty was George Tully Vaughan, who finally provided the school with the eminent surgeon it had been seeking for the new hospital. His well-received book, *Principles and Practice of Surgery,* had been published in 1903. Tully was one of the earliest American surgeons to do successful suturing of the heart.[79] Another major appointment was William Holland Wilmer in 1905 as professor of ophthalmology. Wilmer, during his two decades on the Georgetown faculty, established a reputation as the leading American ophthalmologist of his generation in treating diseases of the eye. Among his patients were several presidents of the United States, J. P. Morgan, Booth Tarkington, Charles Lindbergh, and James H. Doolittle.[80] Other prominent members of the faculty included Ralph Alexander Hamilton (MD 1904), professor of pathology; Robert Young (MD 1905), professor of gynecology; William Gerry Morgan, professor of gastroenterology; John B. S. Dunlap, professor of orthopedic surgery; Thomas Sim Lee (the great-grand-nephew of Charles Carroll), who had studied at both Johns Hopkins University and the University of Vienna, professor of cardiology; and William Mercer Sprigg, professor of obstetrics. Sprigg had performed the first successful Cesarean section in the city in the 1890s.

An addition to the hospital was completed in 1904, including a four-story wing, thirty feet by ninety-five feet, which increased the capacity of the hospital to one hundred beds, and an enlarged dispensary. Francis Riggs provided the approximately $5,000 in funds needed for the addition.[81] In 1908 a second addition on N Street, thirty feet by sixty feet, made possible by the benefaction of local merchant Abraham Lisner, provided more operating rooms, wards, and a laboratory at the cost of approximately $19,000.[82] In 1911, Riggs's widow agreed to fund a building in memory of her husband. The E. Francis Riggs Memorial Building for Children's and Maternity Service, at a cost of $60,000, opened in May 1912.[83] It brought the capacity of the hospital to two hundred beds. In 1913 a final extension brought the hospital complex to 36th Street. Financed by Kober's own funds and named the Kober-Leclerc Memorial Wing (in honor of his parents), it provided forty-eight additional beds as well as a pharmacological laboratory and lecture room. President Donlon was convinced that it would give the university the best-equipped hospital in the city.[84]

George Kober remarked at this time that the university had taken on an indebtedness of more than $200,000 for the development and expansion of the school and hospital.[85] Nonetheless the school's paltry operating budget of $11,000, exclusively dependent as it was upon tuition income, paled against that of other schools. (Harvard's was more than $250,000; Cornell's was $209,888. Even George Washington's budget of $23,779 was more than twice that of Georgetown.)[86] Left unsaid was the negative impact that George-town's minuscule budget was having upon the development of the school.

Kober established a committee in 1905 to maximize the use of the hospital as a means of medical education, "the main purpose for which it was erected."[87] The committee later noted that the "Hospital should be to the practical branches what the lab is to the scientific" but found it "questionable whether the existence of the hospital has been of any estimable value to the med student." It recommended that fourth-year students spend more time in the hospital.[88] Utilizing the hospital for teaching purposes proved more difficult in practice. A committee of the faculty in 1909 reported that "in its present disorganized condition the utilization of the dispensary for teaching purposes is next to impossible." There was need of a director to supervise groups of seniors assigned there for terms of two months, and more modern equipment.[89] There were relatively few charity cases, the traditional patients for students' clinical practice. The key to increasing the number of charity cases was to secure more paying patients to offset the costs of the former.[90] That eventually happened with the establishment of the Riggs Memorial Building in 1912, after which time juniors and seniors did all their work at the hospital.

By the 1900s, private hospitals across the country were increasingly re-lying on volunteers, usually women, to sponsor fairs, dinners, and other events to raise funds. In 1907 a former patient at the hospital, Mrs. Milton Ailes, started the Ladies Auxiliary to assist the hospital through their ser-vice and fund-raising. By the 1920s there were more than one hundred members who had raised scores of thousands of dollars for the hospital and nurses' home.

Standardization and the Flexner Report

As an important member of the Association of American Medical Colleges (AAMC), George Kober chaired the Committee on National Uniformity of Curricula in 1905, which established standards of hours for course work leading to a degree. That same year the AAMC adopted a standard of two years of college as a prerequisite for admission to a medical school. Georgetown, under Kober's lead, immediately instituted the change, resulting in a drop in enrollment from 133 to 90. After two years the school reverted to its former requirement of a high school degree, and enrollment increased, countering a national trend of declining medical school rolls.[91] It did adopt the standard of the National Confederation of State Licensing and Examining Boards of the AMA in 1906 that required four years of high school plus one year each of chemistry, physics, biology, and language, to take effect January 1, 1910.[92]

That year President Himmel reported to the superior general that "the Medical School is passing through a crisis and we may have a hard struggle for a couple of years—so that it may become a financial burden to the college—However the movement will improve the standing of the School in the eyes of the profession."[93] The crisis was the issuing of a report by the Carnegie Foundation on the state of medical education in the country. Abraham Flexner, a professional educator, had visited every medical school in the country in 1909 to assess its facilities and programs. His report concluded that the country needed to reduce the number of schools on the basis of their quality in forming doctors. Among the candidates he proposed for elimination was Georgetown. The school, Flexner evaluated, was, as constituted, not "equal to the task of training physicians of modern type"; it was a "University Department in name only." Its entrance requirements, at least in practice, were inadequate, admitting persons with less than a high school degree; its faculty, being part time, could neither do research nor teach adequately. Its laboratories were insufficiently equipped, it lacked a proper library and museum, and there was insufficient clinical training.[94]

Georgetown was in good company in the list of candidates for suppression (George Washington, among others). In the wake of the report, nearly half the medical schools in the nation closed over the next fifteen years, leaving seventy survivors, including Georgetown.[95] Georgetown had arguably been underrated because Flexner did not take into account its great strength, the teaching faculty, many of whom, although part time, were well-regarded, contributing members of the profession.[96] Dean Kober protested a number of the criticisms as unfair but advised the faculty that the critique of their institution could not be ignored, particularly given the poor performance of Georgetown graduates in recent years.[97] In the first decade of the century, a disturbingly high proportion of Georgetown graduates failed the state board exams. In 1900, for instance, one in three graduates failed in Massachusetts; in 1901, one in two graduates failed in Virginia.[98] One symptom of the poor preparation was the persistent cheating that plagued the school, climaxing in 1905 when eleven of the twenty-five seniors failed to graduate because of cheating.

Subsequently, Dean Kober, along with President Himmel and several members of the faculty, met with the Carnegie Foundation in April to discuss Georgetown's situation.[99] The next month the faculty instituted several changes to improve their standing, including the appointment of standing examiners or quizmasters, who were charged with monitoring the progress of students throughout their courses, and the creation of the position of curator, who would be responsible for forming a "proper museum both of patheologi-cal & anatomical specimens, and the call for a librarian to enlarge the library holdings."[100] A special lab was also set up for pharmacological work.[101]

A year later the faculty determined that the entrance requirements of the school needed to be raised in order to keep pace with the leading medical schools and revived the two-year college prerequisite. As in 1905, admissions plummeted, with only nine in the freshman class of 1912. But the school was determined to endure the transition. To ensure a steady pool of qualified candidates, the school and the college established in 1912 a joint six-year program in which students at the college did basic work in the sciences (biology, chemistry, mathematics, and physics) and humanities (philosophy, English, theology, modern languages) during their first two years and received a combined MD and BS. "By offering the degree," President Donlon explained to Rome, "we can lead them from the college to our own Medical school and thus build it up. Without something like this the school will hardly survive."[102] By the 1914–15 academic year, there were more than forty students enrolled in the program.[103]

In the fall of 1911 there was a new crisis. The New York State Board of Regents had decreed that within the year all schools seeking recognition by the board would have to have, among other things, at least six full-time salaried faculty.[104] The faculty's initial reaction was to conclude that the regents were "determined to suppress all schools that do not possess an ample endowment for teaching." It was folly, they thought, to expect Georgetown to provide such a faculty from its annual income of slightly more than $7,000. But Kober pleaded that it would be possible to provide six modest salaries to professors teaching basic courses. All the others teaching practical or clinical medicine would forgo all financial compensation to make this possible.[105] Kober eventually persuaded the faculty to adopt this solution, and the full-time posts were created in the departments of chemistry, anatomy, histology and embryology, bacteriology and pathology, physiology, and experimental pharmacology.[106] The following summer the regents added Georgetown to their list.

Keeping their standing in New York State was one matter. Doing so on a national level was another order of magnitude. That crisis occurred the very next year (1912) with the new rating of medical schools by the Council on Medical Education and Hospitals (CME). For basically the same reasons (lack of full-time faculty, inadequate facilities, lax admission standards, etc.) that Flexner had judged Georgetown unsatisfactory, plus the finding of the great distance between the school and its clinical facilities at the hospital, the CME now placed the Medical School on its B list.[107] The root of the problem was lack of money. "If Georgetown University," the secretary of the CME advised the dean, "is going to have a medical school bear its name it cannot afford to let it be conducted on fees of medical students alone."[108] Kober pleaded his case, listing the improvements that Georgetown had made since Colwell's inspection.[109] Kober's pleas did not convince Colwell to change Georgetown's status, but he did agree to another visit as soon as the new academic year began.[110] Colwell and his colleagues, more impressed this time, noted the school's "unusual opportunities . . . to develop a high-grade university school," particularly should the school be relocated to the vicinity of the hospital.[111] Acting on Colwell's subsequent recommendations, the school was able to upgrade its status to A level by the end of the year.

The faculty had already been considering moving the school to the same square as the hospital and had put their downtown property in the hands of real estate dealers to attract a suitable buyer, but the effort failed. One reform occasioned by the CME rating controversy was the creation of distinct departments, headed by respective chairs, within the school in 1912.[112] Raising an endowment was another matter. President Donlon expressed the hope that the university would target alumni to create one. In the next decade, a very modest endowment of $155,000 was developed, with the faculty themselves contributing most of it from their share of fees at the school.[113]

The Origin of the Dental School

In 1901 the proprietary Washington Dental College became the dental department of the Georgetown University Medical School. It capped a three-decade attempt by one Washington dentist to make dentistry a part of professional education at Georgetown. In 1870, W. Warrington Evans, the college dentist, had first approached the medical faculty about sponsoring a dental college that he was organizing. The faculty informed him that they "were more or less committed" to establishing such a college but could not do so at present. In all likelihood he made other such proposals over the years, but in 1891 he took the matter to President J. Havens Richards, who assured him that he was "extremely anxious to have a good department of dentistry connected with the University." He encouraged him to begin his own institution; if successful, Richards was sure that the university would be happy to incorporate it and give it the support necessary to develop.[114]

Original facility of the dental
department, 1901. (Georgetown
University Archives)

Five years later, in late August 1897, Evans announced the opening of the
Washington Dental College and returned to Richards with yet another request for the university to let him begin the dental college under the university's auspices. Despite his earlier provision that Evans first establish the school
on a sound footing before approaching the university, Richards was favorably
disposed to have the university sponsor it. The Jesuit provincial superior,
however, cognizant of Evans's history of financial failure in his undertakings
and aware that a group of leading dentists in the city were about to launch
their own dental school, refused to allow Richards to authorize the acquisition.[115] Four years later, Evans offered the Medical School his college, but they
declined.[116] As it happened, Evans had also approached the university president, now John Whitney, and convinced him of the distinct advantage of
adding dentistry to the professional divisions of the university. The president

urged the medical faculty to reconsider. They quickly did so at a special meeting in mid-May and agreed to accept the school as a department within the Medical School but left the formal legal arrangements to university authorities. Apparently someone at the university's end, probably the provincial superior, made Evans's disaffiliation with the school a sine qua non condition for the merger. In early July, Evans submitted his resignation from the faculty and board of directors of the school. Later that month the formal agreement between the Dental School and the university was signed, and the Washington Dental College incorporated into the school as the dental department.[117]

That summer construction began on a dental facility contiguous to the Medical School, and the two-story building, with its two laboratories and clinic, was ready within three months for the 1901–2 academic year.[118] Twenty-nine students, including one from Japan, were in the first class. Tuition was $100 for the academic year. Among the faculty were William Neal Cogan, one of the original founders of the Washington Dental College, and Alexander Graham Bell, who taught speech cleft anatomy.[119] Cogan became the first dean of the department, holding that position until he entered the Naval Dental Corps in 1912; his successor was Shirley W. Bowles, who in 1916 was elected president of the American Institute of Dental Teachers.

Students needed minimal education, not even a high school degree, to enter. Some had only an elementary education. But more typical were those who had a year or two of business college or a commercial high school background. In three 32-week sessions students studied operative dentistry, prosthetic dentistry, oral surgery, orthodontics, dental pathology, histology, anatomy, physiology, materia medica and therapeutics, physics, chemistry and toxicology, and the practice of dental medicine. The school's graduates tended to do poorly on their state board examinations. Over a period from 1910 to 1921, the failure rate of Georgetown Dental School graduates was nearly one-fourth, much above the national rate of 15 percent.[120]

Enrollment at the new school declined from the original twenty-nine in 1901 to eighteen by 1903–4. The school's finances were further weakened when the registrar of the school absconded with one-quarter of the revenue during its second year of operation.[121] When enrollments in the three-year program continued below the minimal twenty-five to thirty students needed to survive, the faculty first proposed to make the school coeducational to increase the pool of applicants, but when the university board of directors found this "unadvisable," it switched its classes to evenings, a move that cost the school its membership in the National Association of Dental Faculties, which recognized only schools with exclusively day classes.[122] Enrollment more than doubled to fifty-three in 1908. Three years later it tripled to 125.[123] That increase encouraged the faculty to begin both an evening and a day school in 1913, with students divided almost equally between the two. At the same time, there was a growing conviction among the dean and faculty that they should increase the length of the course of study from three to four years. Fear that such a change would result in a loss of students to the Dental School at George Washington, which was giving no indication of abandoning its three-year program, prevented the faculty from taking any action. But the web of standardization soon touched the Dental School. Under pressure from the New York Board of Regents, and with the assurance that George Washington was now also committed to requiring four years of study for its doctor of dental surgery degree, the school voted in October 1916 to adopt a four-year day program.[124] Two months later they eliminated the evening program.[125]

Nursing School

For a highly pragmatic reason—the need to provide assistance for the professional nurses at the hospital—in 1903 the Medical School established the Georgetown University Hospital Training School for Nurses under the supervision of the Sisters of St. Francis, who conducted the hospital. The three-year program accepted those young women who could present a certificate of their physical "fitness" from their family physician. Those in the program received room and board and a monthly stipend ($5). The curriculum, taught by Medical School faculty, consisted of certain basic courses in anatomy and physiology, materia medica, bacteriology, hygiene, symptoms of disease, obstetrics, eye and ear nursing, gynecology, surgery, and the practice of medicine, but most of the education was not in the classroom but in the ward—in practical nursing. Indeed, as soon the student was accepted into the program after a two-week probation, she wore the floor-length, blue-and-white-striped uniform with bib and white apron that marked her for hospital duty.

Eight students enrolled the first year. At the first commencement in 1906, eight received their diplomas as well as gold medals from George Kober.[126] The program grew steadily in its first decade, with fifteen students in 1906 and thirty-two in 1910. The vast majority were from the Baltimore-Washington area. Facilities were constructed contiguous to the hospital in 1908 to house twenty-four students, and more were constructed in 1920 to double the accommodations.

Development

The lack of an endowment plagued not only the Medical School but the university in general. Besides individual benefactors for specific needs, such as Francis Riggs and Ida Ryan, the only significant income beyond tuition the university realized were unsolicited legacies and gifts. But they were hardly of a scale large enough to provide the basis for an endowment. For instance, from 1899 to 1906, the university received legacies and bequests of some $60,000, an average of barely $7,500 a year. The largest individual legacy left

The administrator of the hospital, Sister Pauline, OSF, and the first graduating class of the Nursing School, 1906. (Georgetown University Archives)

to the university during this period was less than $30,000.[127] This was at a time when leading institutions across the country were building endowments from $500,000 to $5,000,000. Indeed, the college endowment, minuscule as it was, actually shrank during the period. The $20,000 endowment of 1898 contracted to $11,000 by 1917, the victim of deficit budgets in nine of the nineteen years.[128] By 1915 the university debt was $153,000.[129]

To promote the material development of the university through the commitment of a group of prominent alumni and others, David Buel in 1907 created an alumni advisory committee for the university, composed of ten members chosen by the president from lists of recommendations sent by alumni from regions of the country where there were heavy concentrations of graduates. The committee's purpose, according to its founding statement, was "to obtain the benefits of [alumni] counsel in matters of business direction, and to encourage cooperation in the upbuilding of the University in all of its Departments."[130] It represented the university's first and comparatively late attempt to broaden its governance beyond the small circle of Jesuit faculty directors, a trend that had long characterized public institutions and, more recently, their elite private counterparts. George E. Hamilton, Justice Edward D. White, Robert Collier, Condé B. Pallen, Ernest LaPlace, and Senator Thomas Carter of Montana (not a graduate, but granted an LLD by Buel in 1908) were among the group of Georgetown alumni chosen for the committee, which was to meet twice yearly. The group, so Buel intended, would incorporate itself to act as a receiver (and presumably a giver) of funds for the institution, as well as begin a quarterly bulletin to awaken interest in the university. The committee met only once before Buel's sudden removal in 1908, and his successor let it die.[131] Four years later Donlon established a Board of Regents of Georgetown College, which consisted of the president and directors as well as twelve "regents" elected by the university alumni. Like its predecessor, the board's aim was clearly to aid in the raising of funds for the institution as well as to help determine how the money raised would be used or invested. The regents also were to function as a board of visitors, making recommendations "concerning the administration of the University in all its departments."[132] Many of the same individuals (George Hamilton, John Agar, etc.) that had composed the advisory board made up the first board of regents. A by-product of the creation of the board was the publication, in 1916, of the first directory of living and deceased alumni.

One Hundred and Twenty-Fifth Celebration

In 1901 the university began an annual Founder's Day celebration to commemorate the founding of the university. Each January an alumni banquet would be held in a Washington hotel to mark John Carroll's purchase in 1789 of the deed to the property on which the institution had begun. In 1911 the guest of honor at the banquet at the Willard was alumnus Edward D. White, whom in the previous month President Taft had named chief justice of the Supreme Court. A former senator from Louisiana, White had first been appointed to the court by President Grover Cleveland in 1894. Although he had left college before graduation in 1860, White remained a loyal alumnus, even serving as president of the alumni association.

In 1912 the alumni raised money to realize a dream envisioned by J. Havens Richards of a centerpiece for the main entrance to the university: a statue of John Carroll. The statue was dedicated on May 4 before a throng of students, alumni, and guests from the government and hierarchy, including Richards, Cardinal Gibbons, Attorney General Wickersham, and Chief Justice White. In his address to the gathering, President Donlon noted how pleased Carroll would have been that Georgetown had produced congressional representatives, governors, and now even a chief justice of the Supreme Court. He hoped the day would come when "not only a broad and liberal-minded President would name a son of Georgetown to the high dignity of Chief Justice of the United States, but that an equally broad, lib-

Dedication of the John Carroll statue, 1912. (Georgetown University Archives)

eral and noble people would be willing to select a son of Georgetown to be the Chief Executive of this great country of the United States."[133] "The celebration," President Donlon reported to Rome, "was a great success & has brought the members of the [Alumni] Society into much closer relations to the college than ever before."[134]

Beginning in 1904, commencement became a weeklong affair, including school banquets, games, baccalaureate mass, alumni reunion, and graduation exercises, the latter held separately for all schools for the first time (the college, the Law School, and the Medical/Dental Schools) on Healy lawn. In 1914, in conjunction with commencement, the university celebrated its 125th anniversary. Five hundred and fifty alumni packed the Ryan dining hall to hear speeches by Martin Conboy and others. The next morning graduates from the college, law, and medical schools, all in cap and gown, joined alumni in processing from campus to Holy Trinity Church, a block beyond the front gate, for the baccalaureate mass. The following evening the alumni gathered on the porch of the North Building and sang "the old songs." At commencement on Healy lawn before 417 graduates and 4,000 spectators, Governor Martin Glyn of New York delivered the address. At week's end, the official diarist noted that the celebration had been a huge success and had done much to strengthen the bonds of the alumni to the university.[135]

CHAPTER 3

Over Here
World War I and the 1920s

To live up to her splendid possibilities, and to develop along the lines of growth, which are so clearly marked out for her, she needs help from her alumni and friends. . . . In our own day, gifts to education are many and notable. . . . Without [such] gifts Harvard, Yale, Princeton, Chicago, Stanford . . . would have remained in swaddling clothes. State universities are likewise endowed institutions inasmuch as they are supported by state funds.

What Georgetown has achieved without endowment and through the self-sacrifice of her faculty is a record to be proud of and marvel at. But she must not be allowed to lag behind or stand still.

GEORGETOWN ENDOWMENT ASSOCIATION [1922]

The Onset of War

Since the summer of 1914, war in Europe had threatened the American horizon. Most Americans, particularly those not of German or Irish origin, initially sided with the Allies against the Central Powers. Some, including a few alumni, joined the Allied armies or ambulance units. Denis Dowd (AB 1908) went to France during the first month of the war to fight for the

French foreign legion. He survived a wound at the front in October 1915 only to be killed nine months later in a plane crash.[1] Arthur Morris Zinckhan (MD 1912), who had gone to Russia in 1913 with a Red Cross group, joined the Russian army in the medical corps when war broke out; he eventually transferred to the U.S. Army Medical Corps in 1917. William Linden (LLB 1922) joined an American ambulance unit with the French army in 1914. Fred L. Bawlf (**C** 1920), a Canadian, joined the Royal Canadian Air Force and was killed in an air battle in France in April 1918.

For most at Georgetown during the war's first two years, the conflict "over there" was more than an ocean away, a fight in which the country had no vital interest. As an editorial in the *Georgetown College Journal* declared in February 1915, the wisdom of George Washington's advice against entangling foreign alliances still held. The United States, it concluded, must remain "absolutely neutral," despite the "many disturbing elements at large seeking to involve us in the European conflict."[2] Nine months later one of the college's debating societies took up the topic "Resolved, that Germany's submarine warfare is justifiable," and the affirmative prevailed.[3] Nonetheless, when President Wilson delivered his war message to Congress on April 2, 1917, the university community, like institutions of higher learning across the country, responded with enthusiastic patriotism.[4]

On the evening of April 18, twelve days after Congress declared war, students from all three campuses gathered in the flag-festooned quadrangle for a "grand war demonstration" of speeches and songs.[5] The following day, officially designated Flag Day, students hung the American flag from every window of the Healy Building.[6] The administration canceled the remaining spring schedule of intercollegiate athletic events so that the students could concentrate on drilling as members of the newly created Georgetown unit of the Reserve Officers' Training Corps (ROTC).[7] Congress had created the corps in the summer of 1916 to provide military training for undergraduates as part of the nation's preparedness campaign. By the spring of 1917, 115 institutions, including Georgetown, had been authorized to form units of the ROTC. "The bugle sounds the reveille & the taps," a faculty member wrote to Donlon. "We have some 60 applicants—College, Medical & Law—for the Officers Reserve Corps at Fort Myer."[8] On Memorial Day, the university took a prominent part in the Knights-of-Columbus-sponsored demonstration of Catholic loyalty at the Columbus Monument at Union Station. "A large number of our students, at least of the two upper classes," Donlon wrote to the superior general at the end of April, "will, I think, enter one of the camps that have been established for the Officers' Reserve Corps, so that . . . there is a great question in my mind as to whether we shall have a public commencement or not, and I know not what next fall will bring us."[9] Indeed, a great many joined the camp at Fort Myer, across the Potomac.

The commencement did take place, on a rainy June 11, with ceremonies moved indoors to Gaston Hall. Secretary of War Newton Baker was the com-

Hanging outside of
Gaston Hall, the flag sewn
by Visitation students portrays
Georgetown alumni in U.S.
service. (Georgetown University
Archives. Photo taken for the
College Journal, January 1918.)

mencement speaker for the thirty-seven graduates. When classes resumed in
September, surprisingly, more students registered at the college, including
more than 100 for first year, than at any time since before the Civil War, so
many that 50 applicants were refused because of lack of space.[10] Despite the
war and the raising of tuition (from $425 to $474), there were 241 students
in the highest four classes alone, although members of the senior class continued to leave through enlistment or the draft.[11] There were no exemptions
from service for those who reached the age of twenty-one. Thus many left
school in order to enlist in the service of their choice before being drafted. As
at other East Coast institutions of higher education, where enrollment
dropped sharply from 27 to 40 percent during the first year of the war,
Georgetown College eventually saw a steep decline in upperclassmen.[12]

At the Medical School, enrollment increased from 60 to 71. Medical students, as long as they maintained a certain academic standard in their work, received a deferment. Enrollment dropped sharply in both the dental and law schools. The Dental School drop-off had more to do with the change from night to day classes and from a three-year to four-year program than with the war itself. Law School enrollment fell from 850 to 690, despite the largest first-year class in school history. Nearly 100 of the students enrolled the previous year were now servicemen. Nearly half of the senior class had been drafted or enlisted, "doing their bit," as the *College Journal* noted, "either in this country or 'over there.'"[13] By the end of the academic year there were scarcely more than 400 students in the school. All in all, well over 700 students and alumni were in the country's service.

The Challenge of Patriotism

Unlike the situation in prior wars, Georgetown officials felt acute pressure to manifest the institution's support for the war effort. If, at the outbreak of the Civil War, officials had feared the ominous consequences that could befall a Catholic institution in the United States for taking a stand on any political question, even that of secession, in the spring of 1917 the fear was that the university would not demonstrate resoundingly enough its total commitment to the intervention of the country into the world conflict. The German-born dean of the Medical School, George Kober, worrying about the stigma that his origins would put upon the university, felt compelled to submit his resignation to the university's president in the spring of 1917, only to have it refused.[14] Donlon wrote his provincial superior in the late fall of 1917, "I have met many who are asking what the Jesuits are doing in the war. . . . I fear that if we do not make a better showing that we shall lose credit in the country."[15] The provincial agreed that in these "abnormal times, . . . one must give external manifestation of his patriotism, in order that he may avoid suspicion of lacking this virtue."[16]

The previous May, just two weeks after the declaration of war, 150 representatives of higher education meeting in Washington had attested, "In the supreme crisis that confronts the nation the colleges and universities of America have the single-minded thought and desire to summon to the country's service every resource at their command, to offer to the Nation their full strength without reservation."[17] Georgetown, whether it was aware of the group's commitment, in practice certainly lived up to this open-ended determination to support the war effort. Well before the United States entered the war, the Medical School in January 1917 had agreed to cooperate with the Commission for National Defense by authorizing for senior students instruction by army medical officers on military tactics and medicine.[18]

A few days after Congress declared war, the school placed 150 beds of its hospital at the disposal of the surgeon general of the U.S. Navy, a number that doubled by the next year. At the same time, the medical faculty at their monthly meeting resolved to make every effort to encourage all graduates of recent years to enlist in the medical service.[19] By the 1917–18 academic year, all medical students had been inducted into the army reserves. By August 1918 no fewer than sixteen of the faculty themselves had enlisted or been drafted. George Tully Vaughan, head of surgery; John Ryan Devereaux, the head of materia medica; and twelve others resigned to join various branches of the military in the months following the United States's declaration of war. Tully, now fifty eight, for most of the war was senior surgeon on a troop transport that was attacked five times by U-boats.[20] The professor of ophthalmology, William Wilmer, became chief surgeon of the Medical Research Laboratories at Issoudunin, France, where he trained the first flight surgeons and developed means for combating the high altitude effects on pilots.[21] Brothers John Joseph (MD 1909) and Patrick Sarsfield Madigan (MD 1912) left the faculty to join the First and Seventh Divisions, respectively, in France as surgeons.

George Tully Vaughan, professor of surgery in the Medical School. (Image taken from *Journey's End*, 1942)

At the outbreak of war, the dental faculty committed itself to putting its personnel at the disposal of the military, including offering dental service to any enlistees in need of it. They also approved candidates to take the examination for the Army and Naval Dental Corps.[22] Dean Shirley Bowles of the school resigned in 1918 to accept a commission in the army. Three members of the law faculty were called to active duty, including James Easby-Smith (LLB 1891), who won a Distinguished Service Medal for his administration of the selective service law in the office of the judge advocate general of the army.[23] The new law building was requisitioned by the government for the quartermaster corps. Several Georgetown faculty were utilized by the government as consultants in managing the war effort.[24]

Besides establishing mandatory military drill for the students, the college subscribed over $35,000 to the Liberty Loan, created special courses in aviation, navigation, and military French and proudly advertised how many of its students and alumni were serving in the armed forces.[25] In early December 1917 there was a ceremonial raising in Gaston Hall of a service flag sewn by Visitation Academy students, with 761 stars marking the known number of former Georgetown students serving in the various branches of the military. In attendance were the vice president of the United States, Thomas R. Marshall; Chief Justice White; several senators; and other government officials. President Donlon in gold cope blessed the flag before the solemn crowd, some in tears, and those gathered sung the alma mater, "Sons of Georgetown." The vice president and Father Donlon addressed the crowd. Condé Pallen read a patriotic poem.[26] "No college," Georgetown's correspondent to the Jesuit periodical, *Woodstock Letters,* reported, "has done more to adopt the life and energy of its educational forces to the insistent war demands of the government than Georgetown."[27]

That dedication to meet any and all demands of the government in promoting the war included the suppression of academic freedom. As Caroline Gruber has noted, "Academic freedom was a precarious ideal in the best of times; it was rendered more precarious still when the United States entered the war."[28] The Committee of Academic Freedom of the recently founded American Association of University Professors in a report in March 1918 made it perfectly clear that the normal respect for faculty members' freedom of speech no longer applied in wartime. The committee recommended that colleges and universities dismiss any faculty member found to have engaged, intentionally or not, in any "propaganda" that had the consequence of encouraging or aiding others in resisting service in the war.[29] President Nicholas Murray Butler of Columbia was even more expansive in his understanding of the limits of academic freedom when the nation was at war. He warned his faculty that dismissal would be the fate of any professor who was not "with whole heart and mind and strength committed to fight with us to make the world safe for democracy."[30] Two professors at Columbia paid this price for their failure to meet Butler's standard of academic patriotism. In fact, major universities terminated at least a score of faculty members for their lack, or suspected lack, of enthusiasm for the Allied cause.

Georgetown, too, dismissed a faculty member for actions deemed unsupportive of the war effort. In the spring of 1918, a distinguished member of the Law School, Hannis Taylor, former ambassador to Spain and professor of constitutional law, represented a Missouri draftee who claimed that the government had no constitutional right to send him abroad for military service. That spring the case had reached the Supreme Court. By that time the objecting draftee, Cox, had already been shipped overseas. In remarks to the court, Taylor characterized this peremptory treatment "as the most outrageous insult and indignity ever put upon the court in the history of English and American law."[31] The court ruled against Cox and censured Taylor for his remarks and ordered them stricken from the record.[32] Within a week of the court's decision, the executive committee of the law faculty determined that his statements on the initiation and conduct of the war by the government "represented an attitude of mind, incompatible with that which the Professor of Constitutional government and International Law ought to have in an American Law School" and asked for his resignation. When Taylor refused, he was immediately terminated as a member of the faculty.[33] Taylor was a victim of the 100 percent Americanism that all professors on campuses were expected to display with enthusiasm; given the university's sensitivity about demonstrating its patriotism, Taylor's dismissal was a foregone conclusion.

By February 1918 Donlon could report that "we have about a thousand Georgetown men in the Service and others are going every few days."[34] Eventually more than 2,630 alumni(ae), including fourteen graduates of the Hospital Training School for Nurses, were among the 4.3 million to serve in the United States forces. Fifty-six died.[35] Five earned the Croix de Guerre (Cross of War), one the British Victorian Cross, and one the Medal of Honor.

Bailey Ashford rejoined the army (he had been a surgeon in the Spanish-American War). He eventually earned a Distinguished Service Medal for his work as chief surgeon of the Sixth Army Corps in France. Henry Warren (**C** 1912) won the Croix de Guerre for driving his ambulance for more than two days under constant enemy fire in the summer of 1918. Another winner of the cross was Floyd P. Gibbons (**C** 1905–6), a war correspondent for the *Chicago Tribune* who at Belleau Woods in July 1918 was hit in the eye and shoulder by German fire while attempting to rescue a marine major. Charles T. Buckley (x**L** 1919), an American flier, was the third alumnus recipient of the cross for his valor during a massive air fight.

When the Germans mounted their spring offensive in March 1918 along the Somme River, some American troops, including K. W. Kindelberger (**L** 1914) were diverted to the breaking French lines. For two nights in mid-April, "the Germans threw gas at us, and we carried many victims for some forty or fifty hours." Kindelberger himself was gassed and hospitalized for two months before returning to his sector.[36] When the Germans mounted a second offensive across the Marne in May and were threatening to take Paris, Nelson Shephard (x**C** 1913) and Richard Sanderson (AB 1913) were in the marine brigade that, along with three American infantry divisions, was diverted to the French sector to stem the tide. "We were ordered to hold our positions at all costs," Shepherd wrote home. "For four days our marine brigade stopped that German advance like a stone wall along our sector." Then Shephard and his machine gun crew counterattacked, taking the German headquarters at Chateau-Thierry and more than one thousand prisoners. "We had twenty-one days of it, before we were relieved—it's a wonder," he concluded, "any of us were left to write home at all."[37]

At the Second Battle of the Marne in July 1918, which proved the crucial turning point of the war, Malin Craig, now brigadier general, was chief of staff of the First Army Corps, which successfully repulsed the German attack near Vaux. Charles E. McFadden was on the front lines when the final German offensive began. For nearly a month, McFadden's company held their position, despite withering artillery barrages and gas attacks. By August the company had shrunk from 260 to 18. Finally the Germans broke through. McFadden found himself cut off from his unit but managed to fight his way back, taking bullets and shells through his sleeve, gas mask, canteen, and helmet, finally using his undershirt as a white flag to avoid the fire of his fellow troops. Then the battle turned and McFadden found himself chasing the Germans. "We were pretty badly used up," he wrote home in August, "I can't understand how I ever pulled through without a scratch." For nearly a month he had survived shelling, gas, snipers, machine guns, and bayonet combat.[38]

The Allies began their final counteroffensive in September. In early October, Brigadier General Craig planned the attack of the 82nd Division on

German forces at Flexill.[39] Lt. Robert E. Purcell (AB 1911) was among the first companies to lead the assault over the top. Over open ground and through woods they went for three days, with great success, as they created a salient in the German lines. On the fourth day they found themselves facing German machine guns, snipers, and artillery on three sides but pushed forward in three waves. "The firing was intense," he remembered. "But we pushed on and gained the first hill [as] . . . all kinds of shells, shrapnel and gas was thrown into us. . . . Our boys were falling right and left, but we had the Huns on the run. . . . As I was standing up shooting something hit me on the right shoulder. It felt like a sledge hammer. Down I went, but got up again, and made for a trench."[40]

Other Georgetown alumni in that final offensive were less fortunate. Ralph E. Donnelly (LLB 1914), a former end on the football team and a lieutenant in command of a company of the 101st Infantry, was killed attempting to capture his second machine gun during the drive at Saint-Mihiel.[41] Lt. Francis M. Tracy (LLB 1904) died near the end of the war leading his platoon of the 363rd Infantry in a charge. Another platoon leader, Lt. William A. Sheehan (LLB 1913), was killed in action at the end of September from machine gun fire. Two weeks later Capt. Melvin M. Augenstein (**D** 1912) of the 313th Infantry was killed in action. A week before the armistice, Lt. Douglas G. Cameron (x**C** 1910) died west of the Meuse.

The Student Army Training Corps

Wartime inflation and shortages strained the university's finances. The United States government proved its financial savior. In July 1917 President Woodrow Wilson, himself a former president of Princeton, authorized the establishment of the Student Army Training Corps (SATC), in which participating colleges would train cadets to become officers, in return for which the institutions would receive government compensation. Approximately 500 colleges and universities across the country qualified (having a minimum of 100 students eighteen or older) for the program, which eventually involved more than 125,000 students.[42] Georgetown was one of them. With the establishment of the SATC, the government became essentially responsible for the university's expenses, beginning in the fall of 1918. Under the SATC arrangement, students from the college as well as the professional schools could apply for acceptance (or "voluntary induction," as it was officially labeled). Upon acceptance they became members of the United States Army with a private's pay.

At the beginning of the 1918–19 academic year, the campus became a military training camp for the student soldiers. Formal inauguration of the SATC took place in October at Georgetown and the other 515 participating institutions. Maj. E. V. Bookmiller, a retired officer who was already serving

Student Army Training Corps in Ryan Gymnasium, 1918.
(Georgetown University Archives)

as a professor of military science and tactics at the college, was appointed by the U.S. government as commander of the unit, with eleven officers assisting. In addition, a 100-man naval section of the corps was established at the university. So long as they remained in the SATC, students would be exempt from the draft. But it was presumed that those reaching the age of twenty-one would be inducted as officers of the army or navy.[43] In all, the Georgetown SATC unit had approximately 500 members.[44] Besides the returnees from the college and professional schools, 65 students arrived from Loyola College in Baltimore, which had suspended classes because of the war, to join the Georgetown SATC. Others soon arrived from Gonzaga, which had closed as well. Classrooms were converted into temporary dormitories to accommodate the influx of students. Old Trinity Church became the barracks of the medical students in SATC and the naval unit. The commanding officers of the SATC and the naval unit took over the front parlors of the Healy Building. The billiard room in the Healy basement became the quartermaster's supply room.[45]

The War Department determined the curriculum, which consisted of three-month, six-month, and nine-month courses, depending on the age of the students. Training included ten hours of military instruction a week, including six for drill and rifle practice. Special courses in navigation and aviation were also begun. All students took required courses on War Aims, Military French and English, and Military Instruction. The War Aims course consisted of lectures on civil society, authority, the rights and obligations of citizens, the legitimate authority of the republic to call its citizens to arms, as well as the historic and economic causes of the war. A major aim of the course was to demonstrate the German belief in the supremacy of the state, such as the subordination of religion to the government and the use of law to make citizens dependent on the state; another was to show Germany's imperialistic designs.[46] In addition, twenty-year-olds took trigonometry, logarithms, military map making, and reading and surveying. Electives ranged from aviation and navigation to mechanics, physics, chemistry, and biology as major subjects to English literature, history, and geology as minor ones. The Greek-Latin core was a war victim.[47]

Seniors were an endangered species. "I was the only senior on campus that September," remembered John Brunin. "So for the balance of that year, I held all Philodemic offices . . . and all on the Hilltop were in uniform."[48] As enlistees, students were subject to military order and discipline, including set times for rising and retiring as well as marching to and from classes and meals. Students also replaced much of the university staff in kitchen and dining room duty, as well as cleaning dormitories and maintaining the grounds. At least one Jesuit appreciated the new regime. "Is it possible," he wondered, "that in our methods of discipline we are to return to some of the . . . practices of the old school and the college student of the near future will not be the pampered individual he has been during the last three decades?"[49] This was one bonus, he thought, of college life mirroring the larger world beyond the walls.

The Flu Pandemic of 1918

When the SATC began at Georgetown in September 1918, the deadly pandemic known as the Spanish influenza was sweeping the world from Europe to Asia, killing anywhere from 20 million to 100 million persons in its wake. With the end of summer it reached America, where it eventually affected more than one-quarter of the population and killed more than a half million.[50] By the middle of September the monster flu, with its unprecedented death rate, reached Washington. Within weeks there were more than 10,000 cases in the city alone. The Law, Medical, and Dental Schools suspended operations when the city ordered all schools within the District closed at the beginning of October. Because of its status as a military unit, Georgetown College was allowed to continue classes.

The first cases showed up at the college in late September, a week after the resumption of classes. Victims experienced chills, fever, and muscle aches; in advanced cases the lungs would fill with fluid and pneumonia would set in. By October 2, seventeen students were afflicted. The stricken were quarantined in the infirmary. As their numbers grew, they quickly filled all the beds and were on mattresses borrowed from the hospital. Five nurses attended the sick. Despite the efforts to minimize the spreading of the disease (outsiders were barred from campus; masses were held on the baseball field), maintaining a community of approximately 500 persons in the prime of life in close quarters during an epidemic proved costly. Ironically, those between the ages of twenty and forty were most vulnerable to contracting the disease. Those in confined quarters like military camps and colleges were especially at risk. Nearly 40 percent of the United States Army and Navy forces contracted the flu.[51] Eventually 200 students and faculty, approximately half of the Georgetown community, were felled by the flu. Twelve cases were complicated by pneumonia, and one student seemed mortally stricken.

In the middle of the month the Jesuits made a triduum to St. Joseph, as the institution's patron of health, with special prayers for a time of pestilence. The saint had proven a beneficiary of the community during an earlier epidemic in the 1870s. "It is hoped," read the announcement to the Jesuits, "that the fervor of the Community during the Triduum will secure the protection of the Saint during the time of the present epidemic."[52] Miraculously, there was but one death, that of one of the nurses, Sister Augusta of the Order of Bon Secour.[53] Georgetown servicemen on active duty fared much worse. At least six alumni died of flu-related causes in camps or in the trenches.

With influenza finally abating, the army dispatched forty of the oldest students to Camp Zachary Taylor in Kentucky at the end of October to go on active duty. Eleven days later the war was suddenly over, an armistice declared. On November 26 the War Department demobilized the SATC. The official discharge of all students in the program took place the following month. The program continued for the remainder of the academic year on a voluntary basis, but "army rule" had ended and the regular curriculum returned.

Peace and Remembrance

The 1919 commencement became a welcome-home celebration for Georgetown veterans and a memorial service for the dead. On the eve of graduation, the Marine Band led a procession of students, faculty, distinguished guests, and relatives of those who had died in the war to the valley beyond the Jesuit cemetery, where they dedicated an open-air amphitheater and, surrounding it, fifty-four newly planted Lombardy poplars in honor of the fifty-four known Georgetown war dead, including four members of the class of 1919. Dr. Ernest LaPlace (**C** 1880) in his dedicatory remarks looked to the League of Nations as the only means "through which . . . we can reap the fruits of the war," which the blood of fallen patriots such as those they were honoring had made possible.[54] That evening in Gaston Hall the service flag was raised a final time, now a Gold Star Service flag, with fifty-four stars for the known war dead from Georgetown. Plans were announced for a memorial student building to honor the fallen.

At class-day exercises for the law and college graduates, there was a historical pageant depicting the war roles played by "The Boys of '61" and "The Boys of '17." The highlight of the evening's activities was the inauguration of the Cohonguroton Oration, given by a senior, Louis A. Langie, who emerged in full Indian dress from a tepee erected in the portico on Second Healy overlooking the quadrangle.[55] At the commencement itself, with the largest number (234) of graduates in the school's history, honorary degrees were given to Gen. William Nichelson (AB 1871), who had won the Distinguished Service Cross in France as commander of the 157th Infantry Brigade, and to George Tully Vaughan and William Holland Wilmer of the medical faculty, both of whom had served during the war.

A New President

John B. Creeden, SJ, president of Georgetown, 1918–24. (Georgetown University Archives. Photo by Harris and Ewing)

In May 1918 Georgetown suddenly had a new president. Changing presidents during wartime was unprecedented but, in this case, Rome apparently felt the need for change, despite the extraordinary conditions. Alphonsus Donlon had served seven years, the longest since Richards. The previous summer he had pleaded that the superior general relieve him, for purposes of health and the good of the institution. It had been a mistake, he wrote Wlodimir Ledochowski, the new superior general of the society, to appoint him to a position that needed a man of greater power and presence than he had to deal with Washington society. "We are losing much of the old prestige that once was ours because of this mistake. . . . Moreover I am pretty well worn out. . . . My head is bothering me and my energy and initiative is gone."[56] Nine months later Ledochowski appointed John Creeden, SJ, the dean of the college, to succeed Donlon. The forty-seven-year-old Creeden, the son of Irish immigrants, was a Massachusetts native who knew Georgetown well. He had taught there as a regent for five years at the turn of the century and then returned in 1909 to become prefect of studies, or dean.

The Separation of the Preparatory School

At the 1919 commencement President Creeden announced that "a long de-sired change" was about to take place. The following September a new Georgetown Preparatory School would open at Garrett Park in Montgomery County, Maryland, nine miles north of the university campus. The reason for the move, Creeden explained, was to restore "real boyhood into the lives of the students." The new school, "far removed from contact with the fascina-tions of the city," would provide young men with the opportunity for "the real sports of boyhood and intense study . . . uninterrupted by the distraction of moving picture houses and parties."[57]

The establishment of a separate boarding school for the precollege stu-dents was actually the result of more than the desire to provide a rural refuge from the dissipating temptations of the city. For two decades the bureau-cratic rationalization of modern education, image problems, and the deleteri-ous effects of mixing students together of widely differing ages (from fourteen to twenty-two) had been increasing pressure for separating the preparatory school from the college.[58] The emerging standardization of high school units and requisite qualifications for college admission within educational circles had led the Jesuit colleges, including Georgetown, to establish a four-four system (i.e., four years for high school and four years for college) in place of the traditional seven-year program of studies. But reorganizing the curricu-lum proved inadequate for meeting the problem of a college and preparatory school within the same institution. The bias against such mixed enterprises continued within the educational establishment. The American Association

Dedication of the unfinished Georgetown Preparatory School building in Garrett Park, MD, 1918. (Georgetown University Archives)

of Universities refused to accept into its ranks any institution that contained a high school. Some states, such as New York, were considering legislation that would deny recognition to any college with a preparatory school.[59] In addition, a mixed high school–college setting was harming the image of the university in the eyes of both perspective collegians who did not care to share space with boys and parents who did not want their teenage sons marginalized within a collegiate structure.[60]

One Jesuit college, Holy Cross, simply eliminated its preparatory department. Georgetown never considered closing its lower school. By 1901 the university was making plans to establish a separate campus for the preparatory school that would rival those of prestigious secular preparatory schools, such as Groton or Andover.[61] In 1912 the university approached Jesuit superiors for permission to secure a site and build a preparatory school.[62] Having finally secured enough money from alumni, particularly from the Baltimore railroad magnate and philanthropist, alumnus Henry Walters (AB 1869), in the spring of 1915, the university acquired ninety-two acres of rolling meadowlands on Rockville Pike.[63] Difficulty in fund-raising caused Jesuit officials to defer approval at the beginning of construction.[64] Ground was broken a year and a half later for a building to house more than one hundred boarders plus day students. Initial plans were to open the school for the academic year 1917–18, but poor weather, strikes, and war-induced labor and material shortages delayed completion of the building until the spring of 1918. By then the administration had decided to lease the new building to the government as part of the university's war effort.[65] Finally, in September 1919, classes opened for thirty-one freshmen at the new site. For its first four years the new school remained under the jurisdiction of the university, but in 1923, with all preparatory classes now at Garrett Park, the high school at last became truly separate from the university.

The School of Foreign Service

A month after the Armistice the provincial superior, Joseph Rockwell, wrote the presidents of the Jesuit colleges and universities on the East Coast, "With the advent of Peace . . . we are facing a new period, one of reconstruction in our field of education. The present and the future are of vital import to us. . . . Jesuit education in this Province has not borne the results our talents, our labor, our time and our equipment seemed justified in demanding. In a sense, we have been ostracized in the educational world and as educational factors we have been either entirely overlooked or purposely set aside as antiquated and of narrow vision by men who are the recognized leaders and spokesmen in educational movements." The fine record compiled by Jesuit colleges during the war, he went on, in responding to the nation's need for military training, had given them an unprecedented prominence among government and educators. What was now needed was a revolution in Jesuit relations with the larger world of education and intellectual enterprise. Jesuit faculty and administrators needed to become actively involved with the larger scholarly community: to become members of academic associations, to give papers at scholarly meetings, and to contribute articles to scholarly journals. Institutions needed to spread their energies from concentrating on a strictly classical curriculum to widen "our scope of intellectual endeavor" by attracting a larger number of students through "offering them more practical, career-related studies." He promised to pursue this matter further.[66]

This remarkably candid appraisal of the status of Jesuit higher education was a challenging critique of the insular, complacent mentality that had continued to confine Jesuit education within narrowly understood traditional ways. Rockwell, as provincial superior, did indeed pursue the matter further, among other things by sending Jesuits to higher studies, in recognition of the specialists that the division of intellectual labor within separate disciplines was now making an essential part of the world of higher education. As for widening the "scope of intellectual endeavor," in its way, Georgetown had already taken steps to do this as a response to the crisis and opportunity that the end of the war represented. Another announcement at the 1919 commencement concerned the most important result of the war for Georgetown, the establishment of the School of Foreign Service, the first such institution in the country. President Creeden noted that the regents of the university, in the summer of 1918, had recommended such an undertaking in this "period of reconstruction by training men to represent the United States and business houses in foreign countries. These representatives require culture, technical knowledge and tact, and it was felt that the traditions of the University, its location in the Capital, the depository of knowledge and experience, and its wide sphere of influence gave the University exceptional facilities for the development of these qualities."[67] The *College Journal* elaborated on the rationale for the opening of the school. In the context of America's growing participation in international affairs and commercial expansion, dramatically highlighted during the war, both government and the business community had voiced the need to develop "a well-trained group of men for efficient and successful service in all branches of foreign representation, diplomatic, official, commercial, financial and industrial" in institutions such as those found in France and Germany.[68]

Even before the war broke out in Europe, former president Donlon, citing the "great demand," had been considering the establishment of a "School of Diplomacy."[69] Donlon's plan came to naught, but his successor, John Creeden, revived it five years later. "I have been impressed," he wrote the superior general, "by the arguments of alumni and government officials in favor of establishing at Georgetown a school for Foreign Service—i.e. for training men for the Diplomatic and Consular Service and for business in Foreign

Countries. The Government wants such a school and a high official has stated that the school should be under private control. It is quite clear that no city can equal Washington for such courses. We can call on the experts of the Government and on the Representatives of foreign countries."[70]

The immediate catalyst for Creeden's decision to start such a school was Constantine McGuire, a twenty-eight-year-old Harvard-trained PhD in economics, who since 1916 had been assistant secretary to the Inter-American High Commission in the Treasury Department under William McAdoo. In that position he had become convinced of the need for an institution to prepare individuals for foreign service as well as international commerce. McGuire had previously attempted to interest authorities at Harvard and Columbia in sponsoring such a school in Washington, but without success. In May 1918, a Jesuit friend of McGuire's brought to Creeden's attention the proposal that McGuire had previously prepared for the establishment of a school for diplomatic and consular service.[71]

McGuire noted in his proposal that the establishment of a school for the diplomatic and consular service had long been a topic of interest among those concerned with improving the quality of foreign service within the United States but that no one to date had taken the steps to make one a reality. Washington, he argued, was the ideal location for such a school, given the presence of the State Department, whose library, archives, and staff would be invaluable sources, as well as the presence of the international diplomatic corps, whose members could be tapped as lecturers for certain courses within the school's curriculum. Maguire was sure that a working agreement could be arranged with the State Department whereby a student at the school, after completing a year of the two-year program, could do an internship for one or two years either at the department or in an embassy or consulate in a nearby country. Finally the student would return to Georgetown to do his second year of the academic program. "In this way," McGuire reasoned, "not only would the men receive a practical insight into the work of the Department of State, but the department itself would mold the character of the instruction in the school." He was sure that similar arrangements could be made with the Department of Commerce or with international business firms such as United States Steel, which annually sent hundreds of young men abroad. McGuire had little hope that the government, unlike its counterparts in Europe, would take the initiative in establishing such a school. The endeavor would have to be undertaken by a private institution of higher learning. But he was confident that "the institution inaugurating such a school would not only strengthen its own prestige but would perform a genuine service to the country."[72]

Creeden subsequently agreed to provide the institutional sponsorship that McGuire sought, but on two conditions: that adequate funds be raised before launching the school and that a group of distinguished faculty be recruited.

McGuire promised to do both, and Creeden established a provisional committee headed by McGuire to plan the curriculum and raise the necessary endowment.[73] The committee subsequently determined that a sum of at least a half-million dollars was necessary as an endowment to set the school on a proper footing.[74] In short order, Maguire had persuaded James A. Farrell, president of the United States Steel Corporation, to make a major donation to the creation of the school's endowment. He also began to recruit a faculty from government agencies and embassies within the city.[75]

To complete the organization and head up the school, Creeden chose Edmund Walsh, SJ. The thirty-four-year-old Walsh was indeed just the man. Walsh had succeeded Creeden as dean of the college in 1918 but a few months later had been called to military service as a regional inspector of the SATC. In overseeing the program of study for the SATC program, Walsh came to appreciate the need for the creation of a similar elite group for the promotion of peace rather than war, "the West Point for Foreign Service and a national clearing-house of foreign trade information," as he put it in an address in 1919.[76] As Walsh explained to the National Foreign Trade Council, "America must train her young men to the demands of the foreign trade fields. . . . It is a new and a very promising profession. . . . [I]f American boys are to meet and successfully cope with the men of other nations, they must be prepared in schools designed for such preparation."[77] Although Edmund Walsh is commonly considered the founder of the school, he publicly acknowledged Creeden as the one who had conceived the school. "I have been," he said in 1920, "an executor and too much credit cannot be given to the President of the University, the man who dared."[78] In reality, the man who had conceived the school was Constantine McGuire, but, if anyone is to be designated the founder, it should be Creeden, who, as J. de S. Coutinho, a close friend of both McGuire and Walsh, pointed out, was the one who had accepted McGuire's plan and made the decision to start the school. That said, Coutinho added that what Walsh had accomplished in leading the school from its inception for more than three decades was without precedent.[79]

Walsh immediately began building upon McGuire's success in soliciting support and funding from U.S. officials and business leaders. The United States Shipping Board was one of the first supporters of the new school. Roy MacElwee, of the Bureau of Foreign and Domestic Commerce of the Department of Commerce, was an early backer. Within six months Walsh had secured the pledges of an endowment of a half-million dollars to support the school, about four times the endowment of the university itself.[80]

Edmund Walsh, SJ, dean and regent of the School of Foreign Service, 1919–56. (Georgetown University Archives)

The initial announcement of the school at the end of 1918 drew more than 350 applications, many of them from army and navy officers. A provisional four-month semester of classes was held in the late winter and early spring of 1919, with the U.S. Shipping Board supplying and subsidizing a majority of the 70 students, ranging in age from twenty-five to forty-five.[81] The official inauguration of the school took place the following November, with the beginning of the first two-year program of studies. There were approximately 300 students enrolled during the first full year, selected from nearly 700 applications. Students could seek either a certificate or a diploma. Those seeking the latter needed to have two years of college. The curriculum drew heavily from programs devised by government agencies to train those who would be engaged in foreign trade.[82] Many of the early students were employed by the Department of Commerce, especially the U.S. Shipping Board.

Students typically took six courses a semester. The ninety-minutes-per-week courses focused heavily on commerce and trade (e.g., Staple Commodities of World Trade, Ocean Transportation, Ports and Terminal Facilities, and Marine Geography). In addition, there were courses in economics, history, political science, and languages (Spanish, French, Portuguese, Russian, Chinese, Japanese, and Arabic). R. S. MacElwee, director of the Bureau of Foreign and Domestic Commerce and a PhD from the University of Halle–Berlin, served as the dean of the school and was responsible for the publication of faculty lectures given during courses to serve as texts for the emerging field of studies.[83]

Much of the twenty-six-man faculty had originally been employed by the U.S. Shipping Board, the Department of Commerce, or the Federal Trade Commission. In 1920 James Brown Scott, secretary of the Carnegie Endowment and editor of the *American Journal of International Law,* joined the faculty to teach international law. Guillermo Antonio Sherwell, secretary general of the Inter-American High Commission; John Holladay Latane, the chair of the history department of Johns Hopkins University; Arnold Werner Spanhoofd, a PhD from the University of Bonn; William Smith Culbertson, a PhD in economics from Yale; Leo Stanton Rowe, director general of the Pan American Union; and William F. Notz, a PhD in economics from the University of Wisconsin and the chief of the Export Trade Division of the Federal Trade Commission, were among the original faculty. William Franklin Sands, a member of the State Department; John Waldron, the first English professor at the school; William Gordon Buchanan, who established the accounting division in the school; Leo J. Schaben, chief economist for the Department of Agriculture; and William Manger, of the Pan American Union, all joined the faculty of the school during its first years and consistently taught there for at least two decades.

Since both faculty and students had daytime occupations, classes were held in the evenings. The third floor of the new law building at Sixth and

E streets was the "temporary" home of the school until a permanent one could be built. That location proved to be the school's home for the next dozen years.

Eighteen students received the first degrees in Foreign Service (BSFS) in June 1921. More than half immediately gained positions in American or foreign corporations. Six entered the diplomatic and consular service.[84] One, Willard L. Beaulac, became a career State Department official and ambassador to several Latin American countries. Many graduates obtained international positions within government or commerce. Of the initial 121 alumni of the school, 70 were employed in government service, either that of the United States or that of a foreign country. Some continued their careers with the Shipping Board or Department of Commerce, such as Roy H. Flamm and James R. Mood. Emmett Chapman became chief of the publications division of the department during his thirty-five years of service. Others joined different departments of the government, such as Vivian Raymond Craley (BSFS 1925) with the State Department and Manuel Cambouri (BSFS 1927) with the Department of Labor. Donald M. Flynn became the first member of the school to enter the diplomatic service in 1921 when he accepted an appointment as secretary of the American legation in Bucharest, Romania. Other early graduates who became career foreign service officers were Willard Leon Beulac (BSFS 1921), who became ambassador to several Latin American countries, including Chile and Argentina; Glenn Allan Abbey (BSFS 1925); Robert Joseph Cavanaugh (BSFS 1928); Jack Kirkham McFaul (BSFS 1929); and Raymond Clendenin Miller (MSFS 1922), who eventually became inspector general of the Foreign Service during the 1950s. By 1925 a large map at the school depicted with red pins the more than one hundred locations around the world where alumni were in the foreign service of the government.[85]

William Manger (BSFS 1921) served as assistant secretary general of the Organization of American States, as well as teaching at the School of Foreign Service and founding its Latin American Studies program. Richard R. McNulty (BSFS 1922) became a rear admiral in the merchant marine and founded Kings Point, the federal academy for the merchant marine. Oscar Glenn Iden (BSFS 1924) continued for many years the career he had begun in 1914 in the Internal Revenue Service.

By 1924 enrollment in the school had climbed to five hundred, with students from nearly every state and twenty-one foreign countries. Three years later it surpassed six hundred, with students from every state and thirty foreign countries. In 1926 day classes began for full-time students, and a four-year program of studies was initiated. A master's program was also inaugurated in the middle 1920s.

Walsh was extraordinarily adept at promoting the school with his urbane mien, regal manner, and general ability to make connections within government, diplomatic, and business circles. During the second school year of

1920–21, he organized a series of public lectures in the auditorium of the National Museum on "The History and Nature of International Relations." Carlton J. H. Hayes, John Bassett Moore, and William A. Dunning of Columbia University; James Brown Scott; Michael Rostovtseff of the University of Wisconsin; James Laurence Laughlin and Roscoe Pound of Harvard; Edwin Borchard of Yale University; and L. S. Rowe, president of the American Academy of Political and Social Sciences, were among the lecturers. Walsh also staged grand receptions for the diplomatic community, such as the Honorary Degree Ceremony in April 1921 for the foreign minister of Venezuela. Walsh gave an annual series of talks, from 1924 to 1942, first at the Smithsonian Institution, then at Constitution Hall, to accommodate the growing crowds. Out of these series came two books, *The Fall of the Russian Empire* (1926) and *The Last Stand* (1931).

Concerned that the education of the school be practical rather than simply academic, cosmopolitan rather than insular, Walsh, fulfilling in a way Maguire's vision of internships as an integral component of the curriculum, was also responsible for sending students abroad for study and related projects from the very beginning of the school. The first group of Georgetown students went to Venezuela in the summer of 1920 to survey the economic resources, commercial usages, and facilities for transportation and distribution.[86] Other groups subsequently went to Mexico, Spain, Germany, Poland, Portugal, the Netherlands (The Hague), Czechoslovakia, Hungary, and Romania.[87] Scholarships for students to do graduate studies in London, Venice, Buenos Aires, and other places were instituted in 1920. In addition, affiliations (exchange programs) were formed with Jesuit and Catholic universities around the globe, from Japan to Chile, in which Georgetown students went abroad to study and foreign faculty came to Georgetown to teach. Students of the school also established, in 1920, the first fraternity associated with the university, Delta Phi Epsilon, which was intended to be a sponsor of lectures on foreign relations and trade and other academic supplements. Kappa Alpha Phi and Delta Sigma Pi followed shortly thereafter.

Walsh was abroad for three years, 1921–24. After completing his Jesuit course of training in France, the Vatican appointed him director general of the Papal Relief Mission to the famine- and war-ravaged Soviet Union and its representative to the Soviet government. His experience in the Soviet Union engendered a deep antipathy to the new Communist state. Upon his return to the United States, he began a campaign to enlighten people about the inherent dangers of Marxism and its Russian propagator. Over the next two decades, Walsh gained a national reputation as a Soviet critic, particularly in his Washington talks and subsequent books. His concern over the rise of totalitarianism, not only in the Soviet Union, but also in Germany, led to his later interest in geopolitics, the study of the relationship between political economy and geography. Geopolitical study became an integral part of the School of Foreign Service's curriculum.[88]

Expansion, Endowment, and Building

The postwar period ushered in a remarkable expansion of American higher education that saw the percentage of Americans attending colleges and universities double from 4 percent to 8 percent.[89] At Georgetown enrollment boomed in all schools following the war. In 1919 the college registered 326 students, the largest in school history. A year later, it enrolled 447 students, nearly double its number in 1917; the following year enrollment surpassed 500. "So many are annually rejected because of the lack of dormitories and professors," Creeden reported to the superior general. "It certainly would be possible to increase the enrollment [within the college] to 1200 within three years" with more facilities and faculty.[90] The Law School reached a new high in its student population, 1,153; the Medical School saw the largest increase, 172, as compared with its 71 students three years earlier; and the Dental School doubled its numbers from 80 to 163.

The enormous increase in enrollment underscored the limited facilities of the university and added pressures for acquiring the means to address its physical shortcomings. The Medical and Dental Schools had badly outgrown their ancient quarters. Medical School enrollment leapt from 172 in 1920 to more than 400 by 1927. By 1928 the school had more than 700 applicants for its first-year class but had room to admit only 170.[91] Third- and fourth-year medical classes had to be shifted to the hospital for lack of space. Foundations such as Carnegie and Rockefeller were refusing to support either school until adequate permanent facilities were secured. The School of Foreign Service, of course, had no building of its own, but was perforce aggravating the already strained quarters of the Law School, symbolized by the tiny room that was obliged to house the libraries of both schools. At the college there were fewer than 150 rooms for a student body approaching 500. Even with four students in some rooms, the college could not accommodate nearly 100 qualified applicants each year. Classrooms were lacking, especially for the sciences. The basement of Healy continued to house most of the laboratories. A shed behind the infirmary served as the biology lab. The athletic facilities, as a 1922 summary of the university's needs put it, "are woefully lacking." The one field for intercollegiate sports was "makeshift"; the track itself was improvised by the students. The gymnasium, although only twenty years old, had been hopelessly outgrown by the student body.[92]

Beyond the physical needs of the schools were the developmental needs of the faculty. Lacking an endowment, the salaries of the professional schools, particularly those of the School of Foreign Service, were shockingly low. Language teachers, for instance, received only $450 a year. At the college, it was necessary to hire laymen because the rapid expansion of Jesuit institutions of higher education across the country had greatly outstripped the number of available Jesuits to fill positions in the arts and especially in the sciences. In addition, the absence of an endowment was impairing the standing of the Medical and Dental Schools with the Council on Medical Education and Hospitals (CME) of the AMA.

The long-range plan toward meeting the physical needs of the university was to locate all the schools on an extended main campus running from Reservoir Road on the north, 35th Street on the east, Glover Park on the west, and Prospect Street on the south. The scattering of the schools throughout the city, with the hospital miles from the Medical School itself, was a detriment to the development and realization of the potentialities of the university. Creeden renewed the policy, begun by Richards, of acquiring any property that became available in the area bounded by 35th, P, N, and 37th streets. The board of directors noted in 1923 that such a policy "of gradually acquiring all the adjacent property" was an absolute necessity for expansion.[93] Later, in the 1920s, when the C & O Canal ceased operations, the college purchased several hundred thousand square feet of ground previously owned by the company in the gulch west of the campus barn. It also acquired adjoining property south of the observatory.[94]

To advertise the university regionally and nationally, Creeden established in 1920 a Georgetown Publicity Bureau, a student operation charged with promoting its interests, largely by distributing news of the university to newspapers across the United States.[95] Earlier, Creeden had hired a publicity agent to gain national exposure for the university.[96]

What was needed ultimately, of course, was an endowment to make these plans realizable. The current university's investments amounted to no more than $150,000, a pitiable sum compared to the nearly $3 million endowment of the Catholic University of America, much less to Harvard's $70 million. This sad state led to the creation of the Georgetown Endowment Association in 1922, the first formally organized fund-raising operation in the school's history, with the goal of raising $5 million for the foundation of what was called the "Greater Georgetown"—so that the university might "fulfill its greater destiny in the future."[97]

Almost immediately following the war, President Creeden had initiated plans to raise money. In the spring of 1919 he approached the medical faculty for advice about the best means to build up an endowment fund for the school.[98] He began to assess a certain portion of income from the Medical and Dental Schools toward the accumulation of an endowment for their operation. By 1923 he had accumulated some $156,000 from those sources. "In a short time," he confidently assured the superior general, "these schools should have a sufficient endowment that we can operate them without anxiety" and free the faculty there from working, in essence, pro bono for the university.[99] Finally, in the closing days of 1921, he called a meeting of the university's regents in New York City to organize a drive for an endowment for the university. The following June the board of regents passed a resolution to secure an endowment fund and develop a master plan for the future loca-

tion of all the schools on the main campus of the university.[100] One member of the board, James Farrell, who had played such a vital role in the creation of the School of Foreign Service, especially encouraged the undertaking and promised to ensure its success. Condé Pallen (AB 1880) agreed to be the national chairman and devote his full attention to the work. A goal of $5 million was set. Gift categories included members ($100), patrons ($1,000), builders ($5,000), and founders ($10,000). As the promotional brochure explained,

> To live up to her splendid possibilities, and to develop along the lines of growth, which are so clearly marked out for her, she needs help from her alumni and friends. . . . In our own day, gifts to education are many and notable. . . . Without [such] gifts Harvard, Yale, Princeton, Chicago, Stanford . . . would have remained in swaddling clothes. State universities are likewise endowed institutions inasmuch as they are supported by state funds.
>
> What Georgetown has achieved without endowment and through the self-sacrifice of her faculty is a record to be proud of and marvel at. But she must not be allowed to lag behind or stand still.[101]

A major element of the "Greater Georgetown" was a quadrangle that would replace the athletic field to the north of Healy. The plan for the main campus was obviously inspired by the monastic quadrangle movement that had developed in academic architectural circles in the early twentieth cen-

Sketch of the planned first stage of "The Greater Georgetown," the Edward Douglas White Quadrangle. (Georgetown University Archives)

tury as the perfect embodiment of the residential college. Modeled after the medieval English college, the completely enclosed or nearly enclosed quadrangle featured neo-Gothic buildings that promoted a symmetrical, ordered environment and an intimate community of faculty and students.[102] The quadrangle at Georgetown, which would be known as the Edward Douglas White Quadrangle, would be formed by a memorial student dormitory in the center on the north, with a science building and classroom building flanking it.[103] The Medical and Dental Schools would have a new home adjacent to the hospital with endowed chairs for professors and fellowships for postgraduates.[104] A twenty-thousand-seat, coliseum-type stadium, similar to those being built at Yale and Harvard, was projected for the northwestern edge of campus.

The depression that struck the business and financial communities in 1921 forced the postponement of the drive until the following year, but, once begun, it experienced early success. The association appointed chairmen in communities across the country; the chairmen in turn selected captains who were to organize bands of fund-raisers within their region. The chairmen were to convene meetings of interested alumni, students, and friends in the area who in turn were to prepare lists of potential donors to be sent to the national office. Possible contributors who were thought to be willing to make large donations were to be approached with specific proposals for designated gifts ranging from $5,000 to $1 million.[105] Within a year the association had received pledges of nearly $700,000 and collected $225,000. Creeden was delighted that the alumni response had "exceeded our fondest hopes. At least half of the benefactors are Protestants and Jews." The president was sure that "we will obtain a great sum of money."[106] Coleman Nevils, the dean of the college, became national secretary of the association and, after Pallen withdrew in 1922 due to poor health, its director. With Pallen's departure, Nevils scaled down expenses (Pallen had been on a yearly salary of $20,000 and had been renting a downtown office for himself; Nevils took no salary and moved the office to campus), formed an endowment committee, and began to hold meetings of potential donors across the country in 1923 and 1924. By the summer of 1923, Nevils had organized the alumni in thirty-three cities from Boston to Los Angeles and received pledges of nearly $600,000. Through the drive and internal taxing of revenue, the university built up its endowment from $175,000 to nearly $3 million by 1925.

But the drive failed to approach the $5 million envisioned by its planners. In the summer of 1923 an attack of phlebitis essentially made Creeden an invalid for the remainder of his presidency. By the winter of 1924 Creeden was looking forward to shedding "the burdens of . . . handling the truly enormous challenges of this office."[107] Nevils continued his fund-raising efforts into 1924, but, with a new president expected to be appointed in the summer, it was decided to scale back operations to the New York and Washington areas until the new president was in office.[108] Charles Lyons, SJ, was finally appointed president in late October.

He proved to be a good deal less than Creeden had hoped his successor would be. The fifty-six-year-old Jesuit, another Boston native, had been president of St. Joseph's College and of Boston College. He was known as a "builder." At both colleges he had carried out significant building additions for faculty housing. But once at Georgetown he exhibited no interest in the fund-raising operation begun by Creeden, and the drive ended far short of its goal. A popular preacher, Lyons, like James Ryder had earlier, spent much of his time away from Georgetown on the retreat and preaching circuit, and even when at home gave minimal attention to the university.[109]

There was construction under Lyons but no systematic pursuit of the master plan. The initial action envisioned in the plan was the building of a stone-faced memorial dormitory to match the facade of Healy Hall. This had been a centerpiece in the projected White Quadrangle. Plans for an

New North Building, 1925.

(Georgetown University Archives)

$800,000 building on the athletic field had been developed and land had been filled near Reservoir Road for a new sports venue. By the late spring of 1924, the expected cost of the building on the proposed quadrangle had risen to $1 million, nearly three times what the university had so far raised. Replacing the athletic field would add another $100,000. Creeden was inclined to build on a more modest scale—in brick, not stone—on ground westward from the North Building.[110] Once Lyons arrived, he concurred with his predecessor that they did not have the wherewithal to begin the proposed quadrangle and to relocate the athletic field, and so he adopted the site contiguous to the North Building, at less than half the projected cost of the memorial dormitory, which would provide more than 120 rooms as well as classrooms and a central heating plant.[111] The George A. Fuller Company of New York began construction in the spring of 1925. The building, named New North, delayed for nearly three months by a bricklayers' strike, was completed in June 1926. The 49-foot-by-224-foot colonial structure designed by the architectural firm of Marsh and Peter of Washington featured four floors of student rooms and four lecture rooms, including a large, tiered hall, named for George McNeir (LLB 1881), a regent of the university. In the basement were the central heating plant and the drill hall and rifle range for the ROTC. Once New North was completed, the interior of Old North was gutted and thoroughly renovated for classrooms, individual student rooms, and student services.[112]

The College

With New North nearly doubling the available housing, the college population grew to more than eight hundred students by the 1926–27 academic year, nearly six times its size before the war. The introduction of an alternate course to the classical one, the increase of electives, and the limited specialization that majors offered upperclassmen proved to be effective adjustments, if reluctantly made, to the demands of modern education that began to reclaim for Georgetown portions of the Catholic middle class that had been deserting Catholic institutions for their more modern private and public counterparts. The great increase in students necessitated the hiring of lay faculty, particularly in the sciences. In 1920 the faculty had comprised twenty-four Jesuits and six laymen, two of the latter officers of the ROTC unit. By 1927 the lay faculty outnumbered the Jesuit members, twenty-seven to twenty-five. Among the new laity were Tibor Kerekes (PhD 1921, University of Budapest) teaching history and German, Herbert Francis Wright (AB 1911, PhD 1916, Catholic University) teaching political science, Walter O'Connor (PhD 1938) teaching economics, Joseph Arthur Muldoon (PhD 1923, Fordham University) teaching chemistry, and James Ruby (AB 1927, PhD 1930) teaching English. All except O'Connor (who moved to the Catholic University of

America in 1930) would be at Georgetown for at least the next quarter of a century. These lay additions, who received salaries (unlike the Jesuits), in turn led to a substantial increase in tuition. By 1928 tuition and board had risen by nearly 30 percent to $1,000.

The increase in students did not change the northeastern and Catholic student profile, but only strengthened it. By 1925, 64 percent of college students were coming from that area. Of 302 freshmen entering in 1925, exactly half were from four northeastern states: Massachusetts, New York, New Jersey, and Pennsylvania. This northeastern increase tended to strengthen the upper-middle-class profile of the Georgetown College student, as the overwhelming proportion of students from the Northeast were from that cohort of the social spectrum.[113] Notable students of the decade were Alfred F. Benziger (AB 1920), from New York, son of the Catholic publisher; James C. McCann (AB 1921), from Bangor, Maine, who went from Georgetown to Harvard Medical School and then to the Mayo Clinic in Minnesota with a fellowship in surgery; William E. Cleary Jr. (1925–27) who, as vice president of the New York Port Authority, played a key role in the construction of bridges for the Hutchison River Parkway in the 1950s; Edward Francis Cavanagh Jr. (AB 1929), who became fire commissioner and deputy mayor of New York during the 1950s and 1960s; Charles T. Fisher (AB 1928) of Detroit, who later became an executive in the family auto manufacturing firm; and John Saul (AB 1918), son of the prominent Washington realtor, B. F. Saul, who succeeded his father as president of the firm until becoming executive vice president of American Security and Trust Company in 1939.

A large proportion of the graduates went on to study law in the 1920s. Baker Lowndes (AB 1923), son of the medical director of Georgetown Hospital, earned his LLB from Harvard in 1926 and then joined the faculty of the Law School until the mid-thirties. Frank J. Murray (AB 1925, LLB 1929) became judge of the U.S. District Court in Boston before being appointed to the Superior Court of Massachusetts. In the graduating class of 1926, at least a dozen of the graduates enrolled in law school immediately following commencement. Philip C. Lauinger (AB 1922), president of the Yard, became a publisher in Tulsa, Oklahoma. His classmate, James Johnson Sweeney, became director of several New York museums, including the Museum of Modern Art and the Guggenheim. Cyril Clemens (AB 1925), a descendent of Samuel Clemens, became an author and the publisher of the *Mark Twain Journal,* a semiannual periodical. Joseph D. Ahern (AB 1923) joined the Society of Jesus and taught Latin at Holy Cross College for thirty-five years. Louis Joseph Twomey (x 1927) joined the Southern Province of the Society of Jesus in 1926 and founded the Institute of Industrial Relations at Loyola University in New Orleans. Jeremiah F. Minihan (AB 1925) became a priest of the Archdiocese of Boston in 1929 and was eventually elevated to auxiliary bishop there. Thomas Mattingly (AB 1928, MD 1930) made his career in the U.S. Army Medical Corps and became a noted cardiologist in the Washington area as chief of the Department of Medicine at Walter Reed Hospital. Nevins McBride (BS 1929) combined skills of engineering, planning, and real estate brokerage to enjoy extraordinary success as a contractor.

Robert Parsons, SJ, succeeded Louis Gallagher as dean in 1926 and promptly instituted the departmental system for the college. Parsons also reinstituted the PhB degree as an alternate to the AB to accommodate the large number of applicants for the college, particularly those seeking a prelegal course who did not have the requisite Latin background to qualify for the bachelor of arts program. The new program substituted courses in the social sciences (economics, political science, sociology, and education) for the classics core of the AB.[114] Thus not only was it now possible to receive an arts degree without Greek, but it was possible to receive one without Latin as well, which ended the dominance of classics within the arts curriculum.

Nevils introduced a number of elective courses, including one in journalism that featured guest lectures by prominent local journalists. Out of the journalism course sprang the first college newspaper, the *Hilltopper*, in the spring of 1919. As a class exercise, a twelve-page typed paper posted on a bulletin board in March was the initial issue. The subsequent monthly issues were four-page pamphlets. The following fall, the *Hilltopper* took the shape and size of a regular newspaper. In January 1920 its name was changed to the *Hoya*.

Despite the leap in the size of the college classes, monthly reading of marks in Gaston Hall for each student persisted. Daily Mass for all students also continued to be obligatory; compulsory attendance at benediction on Sunday and holiday evenings was introduced as well. Intercollegiate debates resumed following the war. In the spring of 1920 representatives of the Philodemic Debating Society defeated debaters from Yale, and two days later the Princeton debate team, in the process defending both sides of the issue of the open shop in industry.[115] A year later they repeated their success against Yale in a debate at Georgetown. The twin triumphs over the powerful Yale team, Creeden reported to Rome, had given the debaters "widespread fame" in collegiate forensic circles.[116] In the postwar period the dramatic association reorganized under a new name, the Mask and Bauble Dramatic Society. Beginning in 1922 it staged Shakespearean and original dramas as well as one-act plays that attracted crowds from beyond the gates of Gaston Hall. An occasional social event of the period was the "Hum," a gathering of the students ranked according to classes in the quadrangle in the evening. The classes took turns, seniors to freshmen, chanting cheers and class songs with interludes of silence. The finale was always the singing of the alma mater, set to the Welsh song "Men of Harlech," Robert Collier's gift to the school.

Hazing made a postwar appearance at the college. At the beginning of the 1920–21 school year, the *Hoya* printed a set of freshman rules that called for a distinctive cap to be worn by freshmen, restrictions on where first-year students might walk, and the need for freshmen to yield the right of way to all upperclassmen.[117] The highlight of hazing was "the postmaster campaign," a series of stunts that upperclassmen, usually sophomores, required freshmen to perform. A connected annual event was the so-called Battle of the Caps, in which a team of sophomores would compete against one of freshmen in a football game in early December. If the freshmen prevailed, they were able to shed their skullcaps and acquire regular upper-class privileges for the remainder of the year. Jesuit authorities were quick to denounce these imports from secular institutions. "This is wrong . . . ," the provincial superior wrote to President Creeden in 1920, "and should be stamped out— There should be equality and perfect fellowship among all of our boys."[118] Despite the superior's edict, hazing continued at Georgetown for the next four decades.

The ROTC continued after the war on a voluntary basis for members of the college and Law School. The army supplied two officers, two noncommissioned officers, and equipment. One noncommissioned officer, M.Sgt. Ernest Alexander, was an instructor with the unit from 1926 until World War II, and then he rejoined the Georgetown battalion in 1946. The university partly subsidized the operation. In 1923 school authorities debated whether to abolish the unit but decided that, all things considered, including financial, patriotic, and academic concerns, the ROTC should be retained.[119] By that time the army had rated Georgetown's program as among the best in the nation and granted it a First Class Institution designation, which permitted the university each year to have one of its students commissioned in the regular army at the completion of his training.[120] By 1924 there were 265 cadets in the corps. During this decade the Georgetown battalion annually staged mock battles on campus, complete with tanks, infantry attacks, machine guns, mortars, and airplanes. The unit regularly held reviews, for example during Marshal Ferdinand Foch's visit in November 1921, and marched at special events both in the city and beyond.[121]

Film became a staple of popular culture for the Georgetown community in the 1920s. Moviegoing to one of the large theaters constructed during the decade was a favorite recreation of the postwar period. It was to one of these show palaces, the Knickerbocker Theater, at 18th Street and Columbia Road, that ten Georgetown students went on a snowy Saturday evening in late January 1922. Despite the storm that had been blanketing the area with more than 30 inches of snow since the evening before, there were hundreds in the theater for the evening show. Shortly after 9 PM, as the orchestra played during an intermission, the roof collapsed under the weight of the snow and killed nearly 100 inside, including 5 students from Georgetown (2 from the School of Foreign Service, 2 from the Medical School, and 1 from the Law School). A sixth student just escaped their fate; he had purchased his ticket and was preparing to enter the theater when the roof collapsed.[122] Four other Georgetown students were among the 146 injured.[123]

When Warren G. Harding died suddenly in the summer of 1923, several Jesuits from the college, including Creeden, were in the funeral procession. The Georgetown contingent had brought a large wreath to leave at the Capitol, but when they saw that so many in line intended to do the same, they brought the wreath back to campus and displayed it in front of the Carroll statue as Georgetown's official tribute. The following year, at Creeden's invitation, Harding's successor, Calvin Coolidge, spoke at the 1924 commencement; he was the first president to do so since Theodore Roosevelt spoke in 1906. At Coolidge's subsequent inauguration in 1925, he invited Creeden's successor, Charles Lyons, to his swearing-in on the Capitol steps and to sit among the cabinet on the reviewing stand for the inaugural parade. President Lyons dined with Coolidge at the White House nine days later. Three years later, Lyons's successor, Coleman Nevils, also dined at the White House.[124]

The Law School

On December 4, 1920, the school marked its golden jubilee. The occasion chosen was the opening of the new law library that would house its 15,000 volumes, the gift of Dean George Hamilton. With Chief Justice White among the guests, along with faculty, students, and alumni, James Brown Scott, secretary of the Carnegie Endowment for International Peace, gave the address. The university conferred eight doctor of law degrees on distinguished alumni. A banquet followed at the Willard Hotel. As the school began its second half century, it ranked as one of the largest law schools in the country, if not the largest, with an enrollment of more than 1,100 students and a faculty of thirty-five. It remained, however, strictly an evening school, with part-time students and faculty, an absentee dean, and minimal requirements for admission. The Association of American Law Schools (AALS) had accordingly rated Georgetown in its B category. To upgrade its standing to an A, the school would have to make its admission standards more rigorous (by 1921 the association required that law students have a minimum of two years of college education before beginning legal studies) and establish a day division with full-time faculty.[125]

The structure and operations of the school were a concern for President Creeden. In the spring of 1920, with the backing of the university regents, he had persuaded Dean Hamilton to reorganize the government of the school, effectively ending its existence as a proprietary school and putting control directly in the hands of the university administration. This change was part of Creeden's general goal to centralize authority within the university and ensure that each school within the institution was conforming to the tradition and mission of the university. Within the decade Creeden and his successor, Coleman Nevils, would appoint Jesuits as regents of the various professional schools, as had been the case in the School of Foreign Service from its beginnings. These regents effectively became the chief authorities within the respective schools. As a Jesuit Roman official responded approvingly to the news of Creeden's plan to make himself, through the regents, the chief authority in all the schools of the university, this was particularly important, given the high percentage of non-Catholics teaching in the professional schools.[126] Under the plan for the Law School, the executive faculty would consist of the president, a dean, an assistant dean, and no more than six professors, all appointed by the president and board of directors.[127] This school faculty would be responsible for setting policy, recommending appointments, determining the curriculum, and setting tuition.[128]

In the new by-laws adopted as part of the reorganization, four years of high school were set as the minimum requirement for admission. The question of admitting women, something a growing number of law schools, including Fordham, had done, was raised, but authorities decided that maleness would remain a prerequisite for admission. In practice, the admission criteria of the school in the early part of the postwar decade proved to be minimal, to say the least. Louis Fine (LLB 1925) arrived unannounced from Norfolk in 1922 and was accepted on the spot, on the strength his acceptance to the University of Virginia.[129] Many students, such as Leonard W. Hall (LLB 1920), had only a high school education or less. Dennis Chavez (LLB 1920), an eighth-grade dropout, was allowed to enter because he had passed a special examination. In the early 1920s, most students continued to be part-timers employed in government or private business. Leonard Hall worked for the Potomac Electric Power Company. Dennis Chavez, the son of a dirt farmer-laborer in New Mexico, worked as a clerk in the United States Senate.

A mere reorganization of the school did not satisfy President Creeden. Nor was he alone among school officials in seeing the need for radical change.

1870   1920

The Dean and Professors of the Faculty of Law
unite with
The Rector of Georgetown University
in requesting
the honor of your presence
on the fourth, fifth and sixth of December
at the ceremonies commemorating
the completion of the Fiftieth Year
of the School of Law
of
Georgetown University

Invitation to the celebration of the fiftieth anniversary of the School of Law, 1920.
(*The First 125 Years: An Illustrated History of the Georgetown University Law Center*)

Hugh Fegan, the assistant dean of the school, in the summer of 1920 read clearly how the winds were blowing in legal education:

The struggle is on between attorneys who have been trained under the older methods in law schools where the type of instruction has been similar to ours, namely a Faculty made up, in large part, of practicing attorneys. But the majority of the American Bar in the next five or six years will have been trained in law schools where the Faculty is made up of full-time law professors. . . . No one can doubt what the effect will be. The Association of American Law Schools will be given an autocratic control over all law schools, just as the Association of American Medical Schools now has. It would seem that what the Law School must do is clear,—husband its financial resources which good fortune has given us this past year, and obtain the requirements prescribed of law schools in the Association of American Law Schools.[130]

In December 1920 Creeden proposed to the new executive faculty that they adopt "rigid entrance requirements," presumably the collegiate educational background that the ABA and AALS were calling for, and that they seriously consider the adoption of morning classes. Hamilton supported the latter suggestion, adding that he favored the appointment of three, full-time professors to teach the day division.[131] In the spring the faculty decided to institute day classes, beginning in October 1921, which would follow the identical curriculum of the evening classes.[132] Two full-time professors, Charles W. Tooke and Charles A. Keigwin, were hired to teach torts and contracts, respectively, in the new division. Both were eminently qualified. Tooke was the former head of the Department of Public Law and Administration at the University of Illinois. Keigwin, former assistant to the attorney general of the United States, had authored textbooks on common law pleading and torts while teaching law at National University.[133]

In 1923 the faculty established a year of college as a prerequisite for admission; in 1925 this requirement was increased to two years, as Georgetown joined the one-quarter of law schools in the nation who maintained this prerequisite.[134] To promote the appropriate college preparation, the university instituted a two-year prelegal course embracing a liberal program consisting of history, economics, political science, ethics, logic, and rhetoric.[135] The evening division's program was also extended from three to four years.[136]

The changes had the desired effect upon the school's ranking. The ABA raised it to a class A school in 1925. That same year the school was admitted as a member of the AALS.[137] But the changes had devastating effects upon enrollment, the anticipation of which had made the faculty reluctant to make them. They knew that only one-third of their present students had the college background the AALS set as the standard.[138] The initial drop in enrollment was slight. "Despite our fears," Creeden happily reported in 1924, "the number of entering students has scarcely decreased.[139] But within a few years, particularly after the addition of a second year of college as a prerequisite, the toll on admission from the changes proved to be a steep one. From an enrollment of nearly 1,200 in the fall of 1921, enrollment predictably shrunk by nearly two-thirds to 453 in 1928. The day division accounted for more than half of the students. Clearly the college prerequisite, combined with the lengthening of the program, had eliminated many of the traditional applicants for the evening division. Revenue from tuition had dropped from more than $105,000 in 1920 to $89,200 in 1928, while expenses had spiked from $86,864 to $97,367, most of that increase going to faculty salaries. From a high of 51 members in 1916, the faculty had shrunk to 31 by 1927. For the first time, a majority (19) of the faculty were Catholic.[140] From 1926 on, when the new changes went completely into effect, the school suffered losses ranging from $8,000 to $18,800 and needed to make up the difference by selling securities.[141] Despite a reduction in part-time faculty and in the salaries of those adjuncts retained, and despite having established, through the benefaction of alumni and faculty, its first chair, the Gould Chair of Contracts (for Tooke), faculty salaries had risen from $45,000 in 1920 to $75,000 in 1926, while total income had shrunk to $125,000.[142]

A large number of Georgetown Law School graduates continued to attain national political office. In 1933, Joseph C. O'Mahoney (LLB 1920) was appointed to the Senate by the governor of Wyoming to complete an unfulfilled term and then was elected in his own right the following year. Dennis Chavez of the same class entered the House of Representatives from New Mexico in 1932. He subsequently represented New Mexico as a senator through five consecutive terms, with his major achievement being the crafting of the Interstate Highway Bill in 1950. Leonard W. Hall (LLB 1920) became a Republican congressman from New York and eventually chairman of the Republican National Committee. Francis E. Walter (LLB 1919) became a representative from Pennsylvania. Edward J. Hart (LLB 1924) became a representative from New Jersey in Congress in 1934. William P. Connery (LLB 1926) was a representative from Massachusetts in Congress and championed farm relief and union rights during the Depression. Ellsworth Foote (LLB 1923) was a Connecticut congressman in the 1940s. Charles F. Risk (LLB 1922), a veteran from Rhode Island, was chosen to replace another Georgetown alumnus, Francis B. Condon (LLB 1916), in Congress when the latter was appointed to the State Supreme Court of Rhode Island. A classmate of Risk's, Paul J. Kilday (LLB 1922), another veteran, represented his home district from Texas in the House of Representatives. Edward J. Hart (LLB 1924) became a House representative from New Jersey in 1934. Other alumni veterans who became congressional representatives were Clarence J. McLeod (LLB 1920) from Michigan and James A. S. Howell Jr. (LLB 1928) from Illinois.

Other Georgetown graduates joined the new Federal Bureau of Investigation under the Department of Justice, such as Herman E. Hollis (LLB 1927), who was killed by "Baby Face" Nelson in a shootout at Barrington, Illinois, in 1934; L. Clark Schilder (LLB 1924), who played a key role in organizing the FBI Crime Laboratory; and Thomas H. Sisk (LLB 1929), who led the investigation of the Lindbergh baby kidnapping. Henry Joseph Winters (LLB 1929) entered government service the year he graduated, first as an investigator for the Veterans Administration, then as a special agent for the Public Works Administration, and finally as a regional director of the National Labor Relations Board in 1937. Joseph Walsh Stewart (LLB 1923) worked for the Justice Department before becoming chief clerk to justices of the U.S. Court of Appeals until his retirement in 1963. John J. Sirica (LLB 1926), after establishing himself as a top trial lawyer in the firm of Hogan and Hartson, eventually became chief judge of the U.S. District Court in Washington, where in the mid-1970s he presided over arguably the most politically consequential trial in American history, that of the Watergate burglars.

Still other graduates of the school secured success outside the practice of the law. Wallace Groves (LLB 1923) went into banking. From the capital he amassed in that field, he was able to become a major developer in the 1950s and 1960s, with the founding of Freeport and Paradise Island in the Bahamas as a shipping port and resort, respectively. Stephen J. Barabas (LLB 1930) went into the clothing business and opened the Georgetown Shop initially to serve the university community by offering a complete line of men's clothing as well as dry cleaning services. Jaime Benitez-Rexach (LLB 1930) became president of Puerto Rico University.

The Medical School

In the fall of 1919, at the urging of Creeden, the medical faculty created the position of dean of studies and made Francis Tondorf, who taught physiology at the school, its first occupant.[143] This move reflected a desire of the Jesuit authorities to have a Jesuit administrator in the school who could exercise general supervision over its curriculum, finances, and policies.[144] Tondorf's most notable action as dean was to initiate an aggressive campaign against the antivivisection movement in the early 1920s that was threatening, through pending congressional legislation, animal research for medical purposes. Tondorf publicly debated a representative from the Society for the Prevention of Cruelty to Animals, and under his leadership the faculty sponsored nine public lectures on the importance of animal research, which he published and distributed to medical institutions and newspapers across the nation. As a result, Congress defeated the bill to outlaw experimentation, and the Medical School received credit for the turnabout.[145]

Among other things, the Jesuit used the office to function as a prefect of discipline. For years, the grave Jesuit, with his black skullcap and steel-rimmed spectacles, was known to prowl the bars and disreputable places in the vicinity of the school looking for wayward medical students. One student remembered him as "a slightly built man with thinning black hair, a beak of a nose, a stern mouth. He wore a small black skullcap and steel-rimmed spectacles through which his deepset brown eyes blazed at the world with piercing intensity. His expression was sombre. He seldom smiled and was never heard to laugh. . . . There were those who revered him and those who detested him, but no one ignored him."[146] That was true as well of his performance in the classroom as a professor of physiology. In the spring of 1920 the sophomore class threatened to boycott his class for his arbitrary and high-handed manner of conducting his course. Creeden and Kober defused that crisis, but feelings about the Jesuit grew so strong that the pair finally reluctantly had to remove him in 1924. Another Jesuit, Walter Summers, replaced Tondorf in the physiology classroom and, with the title of regent, assumed responsibility for the academic as well as moral order of the institution. Summers, who had previously taught physics and philosophy at the college, was bright and had broad interests in science (he would later found the Department of Psychology at Fordham and there invent an early lie detector, the pathometer). But he soon clashed with Kober over the priorities and planning of the school and hospital.

In the postwar period, expansion of the hospital resumed. In 1919 the hospital was extended to 36th and N streets with the completion of a building that included two wards and an x-ray laboratory. With the growth of the Medical School, however, even more clinical facilities were needed for the students, so Dean Kober argued, and there was a public demand for beds that the university could not satisfy.[147] The regent of the school, Walter Summers, and four of the nine members of the executive faculty vehemently disagreed. They felt strongly that a new medical school was a much more pressing priority than an enlargement of the hospital. They were particularly bothered that the funding of the extension was to come from the endowment that the school had acquired, much of it the benefaction of the faculty itself. "Our most urgent need is a new Medical School," Summers wrote in an appeal to the provincial superior to stop the pending expansion. He warned that he had inside knowledge that the AMA was intending to investigate the two "white" medical schools in the District within the next two years, with a high probability that they would recommend closing one. Should Georgetown defer building a new medical school in order to expand its hospital, Summers implied, it was nearly certain what the decision of the investigating committee would be.[148] Finally, all agreed to proceed with the building, on the condition that the loan from the endowment would be restored, with interest, when construction on a new medical/dental school commenced.[149] Two years later a final segment of the hospital, costing

Walter Summers, SJ, regent of the Medical School, 1924–29. (Georgetown University Archives)

$250,000, was added on the corner of 35th and Prospect streets, including, besides clinic rooms and three laboratories, thirty private rooms and six wards, bringing the capacity of the hospital to nearly three hundred beds.[150]

In 1920 the Riggs family had given the university $40,000 as an endowment for the hospital.[151] In that same year the school appointed Col. William Arthur as its first director "to secure co-ordination among the different forces in the Hospital."[152] This appointment meant, primarily, the routinization of record keeping and the supervision of interns. But it also initiated the bureaucratization of the hospital that would make possible its becoming an integral part of clinical medical education at the university as a teaching hospital, with its internships, clerkships, professors' rounds, and laboratory facilities.

During the decade the school lost an important opportunity to become the site of an ophthalmological institute. William Wilmer's work in ophthalmology at Georgetown was drawing patients beyond Washington, and even the United States, to Georgetown. In 1922 one of his successes, a society woman, Mrs. Root Breckinridge, began a campaign to establish an institute under Wilmer that would be a center for research and treatment of eye disease. Wilmer and Kober both wanted the institute to be located at Georgetown, but Abraham Flexner of the Rockefeller Foundation made it a condition of matching the $1.5 million that Mrs. Breckinridge was raising that the institute be part of the medical center at Johns Hopkins University and that Wilmer move to Baltimore to head it. In March 1925 Wilmer reluctantly resigned his chair at Georgetown and headed north to direct the Wilmer Institute for Ophthalmology.[153]

Among the notable graduates of the school during the 1920s was Thomas William Brockbank (MD 1924), who became a pioneer in the early diagnosis and treatment of mental and emotional illness in children. A classmate, Richard Maurice Rosenberg, became renowned as the deputy coroner for the District of Columbia, where his command of traumatic pathology earned him a national reputation as "the crime doctor." His assistance was frequently sought throughout the region to solve murder cases. Raymond T. Holden (MD 1928) practiced as an obstetrician and gynecologist in Washington for more than four decades. From 1975 to 1977 he was board chairman of the AMA.

The Dental School

Like its professional counterparts at the university during the postwar period, the Dental School confronted the challenges brought on by standardization and bureaucratic rationalization within dental education. In 1918 the Dental Educational Council of America rated Georgetown among its B schools according to its criteria of full-time faculty ratios and the quality of faculty, facilities, curriculum, and entrance requirements. In response the school introduced a new requirement for admission: a year of predental education. Unfortunately it did not enforce it. It also considered the appointment of some full-time faculty but made no appointments.[154] In 1921 the Carnegie Foundation sponsored a national review of dental schools that confirmed the earlier criticism of the Dental Educational Council: deficiencies in classrooms and laboratories, equipment for teaching, and the caliber of teachers due to an inability to pay adequate salaries.[155] It also bluntly called for "the President and Regents of the University to take over the direction of the school in order to meet more effectively the requirements of modern dental education."[156] The new report lowered the school's rating to B-minus.

The Dental School, like the Medical School, was caught in a bind that restricted improvement. To improve facilities, it needed an endowment; yet a chief source of such a financial infrastructure, foundations such as Carnegie and Rockefeller, tended to confine their benefactions to institutions that already were excellent. To attract first-rate teachers, the school needed to have the A rating that in part was based on having such a faculty.

The university could and did take some steps to address the problems identified in the report. In 1924 it became one of the charter members of the American Association of Dental Schools, which would become the chief organization governing dental education in the United States. In the summer of 1924 Walter Summers, SJ, was named regent of the Dental School as well as of the Medical School, thus putting the school directly under the university in the setting of policy and management. In the year following Summers's appointment, several changes occurred in the academic program of the school. The school hired two full-time, clinical faculty members, one in operative dentistry and one in prosthodontics.[157] The school announced that beginning in the academic year 1925–26 it would require one year of predental college work for admission. At the same time, the college introduced a predental program to accommodate this requirement.

When the Dental Educational Council issued a new report in 1926 that put Georgetown in the class B category, both Summers and Lyons disputed its critical findings about Georgetown.[158] Summers noted the many positive changes the school had instituted over the past two years: the thoroughgoing replacement of equipment in the laboratories, the complete reorganization of the faculty, a full-time superintendent of the dental infirmary, all this in close consultation with officials of the Dental Educational Council. He also pointed out that Georgetown graduates had improved immensely in the past several years in their success rate in state examinations. Whereas one-third on average had failed these exams in the decade before 1920, since 1921 only five Georgetown graduates had failed to pass an examination before any state board.[159] For all the changes and pleadings, the Dental Educational Council continued to rate Georgetown as a B school.[160]

Another of Summers's goals for the school was a reorganization of the faculty as well as the inclusion of a full-time dean. In the spring of 1926 he was able to achieve both, but not without incident. In June 1926 Summers persuaded William Cogan, one of the founders of the original Washington School of Dentistry, who was retiring from the Navy, to return as dean of the school. When word appeared in a local newspaper in late May that Lt. Comdr. William Neal Cogan was retiring from active duty to become the first, full-time dean of the school, there was universal consternation among the clinical faculty of the school that they had not been consulted about the appointment and that Georgetown officials were bypassing both the acting and assistant deans in order to bring back Cogan. It was also the first confirmation of the reorganization that the faculty had been hearing rumors about for months. Cogan's appointment, acting dean W. B. Hoofnagle told the *Washington Star,* came "out of a clear sky." Twenty-seven members of the faculty, including Hoofnagle, promptly resigned—this in the midst of examinations—in protest. Regent Summers, who had been responsible for Cogan's return, called a meeting of the executive faculty of the school, which consisted of the president, the regent, and several members of the medical faculty holding joint appointments. The executive faculty proceeded to accept the resignations and to elect Cogan dean.[161] It ignored the offer of the protesting faculty to administer the examinations and had the remaining faculty members, along with local alumni dentists, give them. The following fall the school had not only a full-time dean but also five full-time professors and virtually a new faculty, as only six of the twenty-seven strikers returned to the school, a winnowing process that the regent had occasion to implement as he sought to secure "the better dentists of Washington" for the school staff, in a city where there were no longer any competing schools for the white community (George Washington's Dental School had closed in 1920).[162]

The school in the postwar period attracted many students but produced far fewer graduates. Of the fifty-plus first-year students in the 1919–24 period, fewer than one-half graduated. The change in admission requirements had a drastic effect upon enrollment, but the proportion of graduates increased. Before 1925 the number of students in the postwar, first-year class had averaged more than fifty. In 1925, there were only sixteen first-year students, but gradually, in large part through the predental course at the college, numbers returned to nearly the pre-1925 figures by the end of the decade.

Toward a Greater Georgetown

The period from the entry of the United States into World War I in the spring of 1917 through the "roaring years" of the 1920s had been one of great change for the university. The college had survived the war by converting itself into a military training school and then experienced a huge increase in students in the postwar period that necessitated the hiring of many lay faculty, who for the first time in the university's history became a majority among the teaching staff in the school. The pressure to expand also led to curricular changes, most significantly the introduction of a nonclassical arts degree, which seriously weakened the hegemony that the classics had long enjoyed. The postwar student and faculty expansion also made more pressing the need for academic and residential facilities, which led to the first comprehensive planning in the university's history and the creation of its first formal capital fund campaign—the development campaign for a Greater Georgetown. Although, in the end, that campaign fell far short of realizing its goals, it nonetheless established the model for later, and more successful, drives. The immediate postwar period also saw the university separate from the preparatory school, which, in sheer numbers, had been the mainstay of Georgetown since its inception. And, as the most striking institutional consequence of the war, Georgetown radically departed from its liberal arts undergraduate tradition by establishing the avowedly career-oriented School of Foreign Service.

At the professional level, the Law School underwent a series of reforms, including the raising of admission standards, the institution of day classes, and the introduction of full-time faculty, which, as a result, secured an A rating for the school and membership in the AALS. But reform also greatly depressed the enrollment in the school. The Medical School, by contrast, expanded its enrollment and hospital facilities during the period, but its academic facilities, or lack of them, constituted a grave impediment for the school's advancement. The Dental School became a founding member of the American Association of Dental Schools; made changes in its requirements (modest), curriculum (significant), and faculty (sweeping); but still failed to raise its rating above the B level. The three schools, as well as the new School of Foreign Service, were for the first time put under Jesuit direction, in the form of regents appointed to represent their schools on the university's highest authoritative body, the board of directors. As the decade neared its end, Georgetown, while able to point to many positive developments over the past eleven years, still seemed in need of some stimulus to move it forward along the several fronts that comprised its educational mission. That stimulus would come, unexpectedly and with pain, before the decade's close.

CHAPTER 4

"Hoya Saxa"
Georgetown Athletics from the 1890s to the 1920s

That Georgetown has accomplished remarkable results in late years with rather limited means cannot be gainsaid—In baseball[,] in field and track athletics[,] in tennis she is doing splendid work—. . .

   Among the larger universities—(Yale, Harvard, Penn, Princeton, Cornell and Columbia)[—]Georgetown has in recent years won a high rank—We do not understand why she is not honored accordingly.

JOHN CONWAY to WALTER CAMP, 1897

Georgetown and the Rise of "Prolegiate" Sports

By the 1890s intercollegiate sports were rapidly becoming a business involving professional coaches, the recruitment of semiprofessional athletes with scholarships and other rewards for their services, the charging of admission to games, the keeping of regional and even intersectional schedules, and the rabid support and involvement of alumni. Organized sports had emerged as the preeminent builder of character and virility among America's prestigious institutions of higher education. In an urban, middle-class society concerned about the decline of the strenuous life among young males, sports, especially in the form of the newly devised, bone-crushing American football, became an almost ideal "moral equivalent to war." Success at the highest level of athletic competition, no matter what the cost to academic integrity, became an almost irresistible quest for virtually every college, major or minor.[1] Indeed, athletics became one way in which undersized, underfinanced institutions could hold their own with the more elite colleges and universities.

Georgetown was very much a part of the culture of "prolegiate" athleticism in the decade, despite misgivings about the recruitment of mature, semiprofessional athletes and about the claim that such perennial student athletes were legitimate candidates for college or professional degrees. The growing prominence of intercollegiate sports led the college to change its class schedule and weekly holidays. The altered daily schedule of classes permitted the teams to have practice time in the afternoon. Wednesdays and Saturdays replaced Tuesdays and Thursdays as the weekly half-holidays in order to accommodate the football and baseball teams, which scheduled games with regional and even intersectional opponents on those days.[2] The Athletic Association, the student organization responsible for the management of intercollegiate sports at Georgetown, instituted an advisory board composed of faculty, alumni, and students both to supervise and to raise money for Georgetown teams. The university began to employ professional coaches, and this was often made possible by the financial assistance of interested alumni. In 1891 John Brisben Walker (C 1863–65), then an editor for *Cosmopolitan* magazine, sent a coach, Tommy Dowd of Brown, to Georgetown to prepare the football team for its upcoming season. Dowd was the first of five part-time coaches during the decade and a precursor to the hiring of a professional coach for baseball, Joe Kelly, in 1897.[3]

The university also began to charge admission to athletic events. In 1889 the playing field north of Healy was enclosed. That fall Georgetown played its initial, intercollegiate football game against visiting Virginia. The Blue and Gray won decisively, 34–0, the first round of what would become a very heated rivalry over the next two decades.[4] Football games by the early 1890s, especially the Virginia game and the Thanksgiving Day contest against a local opponent, drew thousands of spectators, many of them alumni not only from the area but from as far away as New York and New England. In 1895 a small, wooden grandstand that provided seating for two hundred persons was erected, and season tickets were sold to alumni and others.[5] Three years later a much larger grandstand that accommodated several thousand people, made possible by pledges from ten alumni, replaced it.[6]

President J. Havens Richards was also intent upon adding a modern gymnasium to the university's campus, calling it "the most pressing" need the institution had in 1894. "Our students have been for some years past," he wrote to a prospective donor, "deeply interested in the athletic movement which has taken place in the great colleges of the country, and though want-

Tallyho carrying fans to football game at the turn of the century. (Georgetown University Archives)

ing in means they have, by their energy and pluck, achieved a place in the first rank beside Yale, Harvard, Princeton and University of Pennsylvania. . . . They recently desired a fine gymnasium, provided with swimming baths and all the modern form of apparatus."[7] "Every great college except ourselves has [one]," he pointed out to another potential sponsor.[8] Spurred by several alumni, Richards attempted to raise the $50,000–$100,000 he thought was necessary to construct a facility housing gymnastics, swimming pool, billiards, and reading rooms. The depression of the mid-nineties made it an inauspicious time to find outside money; by 1897 Richards had scaled back his plans for the building by half but still failed to raise more than a few thousand dollars toward the gymnasium. Meanwhile, a temporary gym including a track and batting cage was set up in the basement of Healy in 1896.[9]

As a school whose college students still numbered fewer than 150, Georgetown was hard-pressed to compete with universities such as Yale or Virginia whose enrollments had passed the one-thousand mark. One avenue that many institutions had already pursued was the use of students in the graduate or professional schools to make up their sports teams. By the end of 1890, the *Georgetown College Journal* was urging that the Athletic Association secure "the participation of the Law and Medical students in the sports of the University" as the final link to ensure athletic success for Georgetown, by thus quadrupling the pool of potential athletes.[10] (The football team had just completed a mediocre season [4-4] in which their losses had included a 70–4 drubbing at the hands of the Naval Academy.)

Within the year, presumably at the initiation of the Athletic Association, representatives of the college, Medical School, and Law School approved the participation of students from every department in the university's athletic teams. Medical and law students were soon members of the football, track, and baseball teams. Half of the 1892 baseball squad was from the two professional departments. A year later there were virtually none but medical, law, and graduate students on that team. By the middle of the decade professional and graduate students were dominating all sports at Georgetown. Sports became an unprecedented integrator for the three departments of the university. By 1892 blocs of medical, law, and college students were supporting the fortunes of the Blue and Gray. At the Thanksgiving Day game at the National Park on Seventh Street, students from the law, medicine, and college departments of the university arrived as units in hired coaches and carriages and "paraded about the grounds wild with enthusiasm," splitting the air with "Hoo-rah!" "Hickey! Hickey!" and "Hoyah! Hoyah! Saxah!"[11] For the next three decades, Georgetown athletes would come substantially from the Law, Medical, and (after 1901) Dental Schools.

Distinctive institutional yells became an integral part of collegiate athletics in the 1890s, closely connected with football. At Georgetown, "Hoya Saxa" emerged as the official cheer by the latter part of that decade. As William McFadden has shown, "Hoya Saxa," along with its variants, was but one of several chants that emerged around 1890 in support of Georgetown teams, then known as the Blue and Gray. By 1894 it had become *the* college yell, an honor it has maintained ever since. As for its meaning, all the evidence points to nothing more than "hickey! hickey!" or "hooray!"[12]

Georgetown, like most schools in intercollegiate competition, acquired fight songs and alma maters to be sung during contests. The 1890s was the period during which the school's two major songs, the fight song ("Lie Down, Forever, Lie Down") and the alma mater ("Sons of Georgetown") were written and performed. They were both written for football. The occasion for the composition of the fight song was the game with the University of Virginia, a staple of the football season in the period from 1889 to 1905. Indeed, the original lyrics were "Lie down, Virginia, lie down." Robert Collier (AB 1894) composed "Sons of Georgetown" initially as a fight song. The original words were

> Sons of Georgetown, on to battle, hearken to our thundering rattle;
> 'Gainst the foeman show your mettle; win for us the day.
> Burst their line asunder, hurl the foeman under.
> When they've the ball, stand like a wall.

In 1906 the familiar words penned by Collier first appeared in a football program (Georgetown vs. Virginia)—"Sons of Georgetown, Alma Mater"—but the melody from the Welsh ballad "Men of Harlech" was sung fittingly at a fast, fight-song pace. Only in the post–World War II era was the singing of "Sons" slowed to a statelier tempo and the song made the school's alma mater.[13]

Football in the Richards Era

Although Georgetown's poor performance in intercollegiate football had been the catalyst for transforming athletics at Georgetown, Blue and Gray teams enjoyed only moderate success during the decade before tragedy brought a ban on intercollegiate play in the sport to the campus. With students drawn from all three departments for the 1891 season, the team still managed only a break-even season (2-2), beating Gallaudet and Washington and Lee while losing closely to Navy (12–4) and to their archrival, Columbia Athletic Club, on Thanksgiving Day, before five thousand fans at the Seventh Street grounds. The following year proved to be the high-water mark for Georgetown football in the decade. The team compiled a 4-2-1 record, but it was largely at the expense of such nonpowers as the Media Academy of Pennsylvania (32–5) and the Neptune Boat Club of Maryland (96–0). The best part of the season was a 12–0 victory over the Columbia Athletic Club, with a roster featuring former college players, on Thanksgiving for the silver trophy (awarded to the champion of the District), again before an estimated crowd of five thousand at National Park on Seventh Street, which included much of the faculty from the three campuses and many alumni from near and far. During the next two seasons the team struggled against more difficult competition (Virginia, Pennsylvania, the Naval Academy, North Carolina), and the results were predictably mediocre.

Football in the 1890s had become an increasingly dangerous and brutal sport. Innovations of mass formations such as the flying wedge and the lack of equipment, including helmets, led to an escalating number of serious injuries that affected one-fifth of the players, according to one study in 1894.[14] The provincial superior of the Jesuits on the East Coast, disturbed by these developments, decreed that Georgetown should no longer participate in university football. President Richards chose to interpret this interdiction in a broad fashion: that Georgetown would no longer play any games outside of Washington and drop the "larger universities" from its schedule.[15] The student manager of football agreed to the restrictions but ignored them in scheduling games against Pennsylvania, Navy, and North Carolina, the first two in away games. Richards may not have liked it but nonetheless let the schedule stand. Georgetown lost to all three. The team entered the 1894 Thanksgiving game on November 29 against Columbia Athletic Club, needing a victory to achieve a winning season. Ten thousand people turned out for the contest at National Park. "Play had not been on five minutes before it was seen that it was to be a game for blood," the

Washington Post reported.[16] The Columbia quarterback came out of a pile of bodies with his collarbone broken. Moments later George "Shorty" Bahen, the Georgetown captain and a running back, crumbled while attempting a block and was carried off. Three other Georgetown players were also disabled in the 20–0 loss.[17] Bahen suffered fatal spinal injuries from which he died several months later.

The week following the game the university's board of directors unanimously decided to discontinue intercollegiate football "until the character and rules of the games shall have been so radically modified as to preclude with reasonable certainty all danger of serious casualties."[18] Richards did not think that possible and expected the ban to be permanent.[19]

Baseball's Return to Supremacy on the Hilltop

By the time football was suspended, baseball, temporarily eclipsed by football as the leading sport at Georgetown in the late 1880s, had already achieved the success that had eluded the Blue and Gray teams on the gridiron in the 1890s. By 1894 the "base ballists" had become one of the elite teams in the country, more than holding their own against Princeton, Yale, Harvard, Dartmouth, Pennsylvania, and other powers. In late May 1893 the team made its first northern tour—a weeklong trip—in order to play some of the best college nines. The team, restricted to law and medical students who had already completed their academic year, won three out of seven games against Brown, Harvard, Holy Cross, Princeton, and Wesleyan. When they returned to Washington in early June following a final victory against Princeton, the students were granted a holiday to greet the team at the station as conquering heroes and parade with them in triumph in coaches along Pennsylvania Avenue, with "great rejoicing and greater noise—yells and shouts, fishhorns and cymbal, . . . 'Hoia, Hoia'" cutting the sultry air of the city.[20] The following season they were 12–2 (the two losses coming against Yale and Virginia), climaxed by a highly successful northern trip made at the end of May by the entire team.

In 1895 the superior general of the Jesuits, moved by protests from some Jesuits at Georgetown and elsewhere that the extended tour was inimical to the education and morals of the young men involved, refused permission for the team to make a third northern trip. Richards pleaded in vain that playing Harvard, Yale, Princeton, and some of the other leading schools on their home turf was a great morale booster for Georgetown students and an opportunity to replicate the same tours these schools were accustomed to have their teams make. "The freedom that non-Catholic universities allow students," he wrote the general, "proves very attractive, even to Catholic youth. . . . For us to put rigid limits on athletics will be to tempt many students to leave us and go to non-Catholic universities. Indeed this is already happening."[21] The superior general eventually agreed to allow one weeklong trip a year to cities where the team could stay at a Jesuit college (i.e., Philadelphia, New York, Boston, Worcester).[22]

Whatever the immediate effect of the modified ban on the team's morale, the subsequent season, 1895, was a distinct success. Yale and Princeton came to Georgetown, and the latter won two out of three games (including a 20–5 routing of the Eli) before an average of slightly fewer than 1,000 people at its new diamond and grandstand north of Healy. The Blue and Gray split a pair of home and away games with both Pennsylvania and Virginia, two eastern powers. For the home game against Virginia, the reigning champion, more than 1,500 persons turned out, including a large contingent of females from the Visitation Academy. The glee club provided fight songs, including one composed for the game ("Old Virginia's doomed to fall . . . we'll change the blue and gold to black and blue").[23] And so they did. The final score was 16–2 in favor of Georgetown. Two weeks later an even larger crowd, more than 2,500, was on hand to see Georgetown avenge its loss to Pennsylvania with another decisive win, 8–2.

John Sheridan poster for Yale-Georgetown baseball series, 1899. (From the art collection of the Lauinger Library)

With one game to go in the season, they were 12–2. Several stars had emerged: George Mahoney had proven to be a dominating pitcher, and captain Edward Mahoney, Robert Carmody, Dan McCarthy, Bernard McGrath, and Pat Sullivan were the other leading players. By June the Blue and Gray were laying claim to the college baseball championship.[24] All that remained was a final rematch with Princeton in New Jersey for the college championship. But Princeton, despite several key injuries, spoiled Georgetown's dreams, 8–3, as George Mahoney was uncharacteristically hittable.

With the graduation of five seniors from the 1895 team and a curtailment of scholarships by Richards due to financial exigencies and concern about professionalism, the team struggled during the next three seasons, despite the reinstatement of the northern tour in 1896 and the hiring of a coach, Joe Kelly, in 1897.

Tennis, Golf, and Track

Three other intercollegiate sports in which Georgetown began to compete in the 1890s were tennis, golf, and track. By 1891 cement courts had been built on the southern part of the campus, and the tennis team, led by Condé Nast and Richard Walsh, had joined the Southern Association. In 1895 it was admitted to the Intercollegiate Tennis Association and took part in their games in New Haven, Connecticut, in October. By 1900 there were thirty-three members on the team. Golf was another team sport to begin at Georgetown in the 1890s. The 1901 yearbook, *Hodge Podge,* listed eighteen students on the golf team.

The annual athletic sports festival, a three-week, November event featuring an intramural track and field competition that had begun in 1875, continued to be a highlight of the fall semester into the 1890s. In 1891 a quarter-mile running track was laid out around the baseball field. A year later the festival served as the trials for the selection of a team to represent Georgetown at the Intercollegiate Athletic Meet, Mott Haven, in New York City. The Georgetowners finished eighth out of twenty-two college teams.[25] In 1895 William Foley, who had attained a national reputation as a coach in making Brown a track power, was hired as the full-time track coach. Along with him came a Massachusetts sprinter, twenty-two-year-old Bernard Wefers, who had already distinguished himself as a runner for the New York Athletic Club, as well as his brother, James.

In November the school hosted an invitational meet. Led by the two Weferses, Georgetown stunned the University of Pennsylvania, considered to be the best squad in the nation, by winning the main relay race.[26] In January, Bernie Wefers equaled the world mark for the 75-yard dash with his time of 7.6 seconds. In May, Georgetown, for the first time, had high hopes of success at the New York intercollegiate meet. "Great things are expected of Wefers," the official diarist reported.[27] Wefers exceeded expectations, equaling the world mark for 100 yards (9.8 seconds) and setting a world record for the 220-yard dash—21.2 seconds, which had the stands, filled with Yale, Harvard, Columbia, and other supporters, cheering wildly in recognition of Wefers's achievement.[28] Then in September, in Ireland, he set a world record for the 300-yard race (30.6 seconds). By November, at the Georgetown invitational meet, Bernie Wefers, "moving like a magnificent piece of machinery" (he was 6 feet tall and weighed 185 pounds), set two more world marks (although unofficial), in the 300-yard race (30.4 seconds) and the 100-yard race (9.6 seconds).[29] The following year he lowered his own record in the 220 to 21 seconds.

Prolegiate Sports at Georgetown at the Turn of the Century

The appointment of John Whitney as president in 1898 brought a reemphasis on sports at Georgetown. Whitney, an avid sports fan, immediately revived football, increased scholarships, and revised the daily academic schedule to allow three hours of afternoon training or games for the intercollegiate teams. He actively involved himself in the recruitment of athletes. In 1900 he persuaded Samuel Logan Owens, an outstanding halfback and relay racer, to return to Georgetown on scholarship after he had transferred to Tulane in 1899. Later Whitney appointed the first graduate manager of athletics to supervise and coordinate intercollegiate sports. "The Rector himself has little use for books and libraries," one Jesuit critic remarked, "but he will sit for hours on a bench of the base-ball or foot-ball field like a big school boy."[30] The high point during the team's northern trip in 1899, another Jesuit remembered, was the rector's reading of the telegram relating the latest victory to the thunderous applause of the students. "Now is baseball queen of studies," he wryly concluded.[31] The students, however, recognized what a difference Whitney had made for Georgetown's intercollegiate status. "The Athletic Association," the *College Journal* noted in 1901, "has prospered gloriously under his supervision."[32]

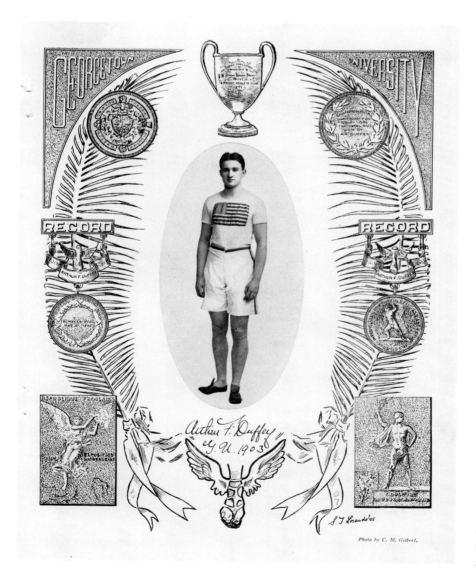

Arthur Duffey, Olympian sprinter. (Georgetown University Archives. Photo by C. M. Gilbert.)

Georgetown track continued in the national spotlight, largely through the exploits of another sprinter from Massachusetts, Arthur Duffey, who followed Wefers to Georgetown. Duffey became even more celebrated for his speed, becoming known as the "world's fastest man." Duffey, who had been attending Worcester College, already had a national reputation, having beaten Wefers in Boston in 1898. It was likely Foley who convinced Duffey to transfer to Georgetown by enrolling in the law department. In his first year with the Blue and Gray, the diminutive Duffey (he was barely 5'7") equaled the world's mark for the 60-yard dash (6.4 seconds) in an indoor meet at Madison Square Garden. Described as a glider who seemed to touch the ground only "in high places," Duffey had "a beautiful stride, and when under full headway is the very poetry of motion."[33] In 1901 he set a new world's record for the 50-yard indoor dash— 5.0 seconds. He won the 100-yard dash three years in a row (1900–1902) at the English championships. In 1902, at the New York Intercollegiate Athletic Meet, Duffey equaled Wefers's mark for 100 yards at 9.6 seconds. In the summer of 1900, Duffey was part of a contingent of three (W. J. Holland, a quarter miler, and Edward Minahan, another sprinter, were the others), along with Foley, that Georgetown sent to the second modern Olympic games held in Paris. Foley by then was the best-known track coach in the country, having developed more record breakers than any other coach. Duffey, a favorite in the 100-meters, unfortunately fell in the finals of the race while leading at the halfway point, but both Holland and Minahan medaled at the games.

By 1901 there was a track squad of thirty-nine, and Georgetown began to host indoor meets at Convention Hall. In 1903 Joe Reilly set a new world's record (52.4 seconds) for the 440. At the same site a year later, the relay team set the world mark for the mile (2:28.8). By 1904 Georgetown students or alumni held the indoors records in the 50-, 100-, 220-, and 440-yard races and the 1,280-yard relay record.

With Bill Donovan of Brown as coach, the Blue and Gray's return to the gridiron in 1898 proved quickly successful as they went 7-3. Led by John Casey, the team defeated Virginia Military Institute and Columbian College (on Thanksgiving Day) and split home and away games with Virginia. In the home game against Virginia, a 12–0 loss, Casey was seriously injured, but unlike George Bahen four years earlier, his injuries did not prove fatal. The following season, under Coach Bill Church of Princeton, promised even better results but saw the team manage only a 5-2-1 record, the tie coming in a scoreless contest with the University of Virginia before a great throng on the Hilltop in late November. Under the third coach in three seasons, A. E. Bull of Pennsylvania, the team, led by Art Devlin, a fullback and punter, as well as tackle Moran Barry and halfback Joe Reilly, managed virtually a repeat of its previous season, going 5-1-3 in 1900, with wins over Virginia and the Virginia Military Institute, and ties against North Carolina, Swarthmore, and

Georgetown University–University of Virginia football game, November 17, 1901, won by Georgetown 17–16. (Georgetown University Archives)

Gallaudet, which enabled Georgetown to claim the football championship of the South.

Bill Church returned as coach in 1901, but the team managed only three victories and a tie in seven games. One was a stirring comeback victory against Virginia, 17–16, at Georgetown Field in late November. Down 16–6 halfway through the second half (when touchdowns still counted but five points), Georgetown rallied, and Halfback James "Hub" Hart scored the winning touchdown as time expired. It was a sign of things to come over the next three years, in which the team went 21-7, with four of the losses coming to national powers Princeton and the Carlisle Institute, the Indian school coached by Glenn "Pop" Warner. Crowds of two thousand or more paid $1.00 to $1.50 to watch one of the rising teams in the East. The 1904 team (7-1) had only fourteen points scored against them and completed the year with a 62–0 trouncing of George Washington before three thousand fans.

The 1899–1900 academic year marked the revival of crew at Georgetown. Alumni supplied rowing machines on which members began training in the basement of Healy. C. R. Zappone, of the Potomac Boat Club and president of the National Association of American Oarsmen, was hired as a coach. The crew surpassed itself in the first year by defeating Navy in Annapolis in its first intercollegiate race. The following year Whitney acquired the Columbia Athletic Club boathouse, with all its shells and equipment, at the bottom of 32nd Street for the team's use. In its second season, the crew, competing in the Poughkeepsie Regatta for the second time (they came in last in their first outing), finished fourth behind Cornell, Columbia, and Wisconsin but, in so doing, bettered the existing world record for a four-mile race.[34] With four sophomores in the starting eight, the immediate future for crew seemed very bright. The next year, 1901–2, seemed initially to confirm that promise, when, under its new coach, Patrick Dempsey, the crew defeated the Naval Academy in Annapolis but came in last at the championship regatta in Poughkeepsie. Then, in 1903, Georgetown announced its arrival on the crew scene when its eight, with Murray Russel as captain, finished second behind Cornell at Poughkeepsie. With the support of alumnus Robert Collier, who provided equipment for the team, including a coaching launch, the crew continued to compete intercollegiately and to participate at Poughkeepsie until 1907, when it finished sixth out of seven entries. At the end of that season the university decided to drop the sport because of its expense, re-vived it briefly three years later with Dempsey again as coach, but following that season discontinued it again due to prohibitive costs.

In baseball in 1899, Georgetown, with essentially the same team as the previous year, surprised the baseball world by attaining the very pinnacle of the collegiate competition, that is, winning seventeen out of nineteen inter-

Baseball championship squad, 1899. (Georgetown University Archives)

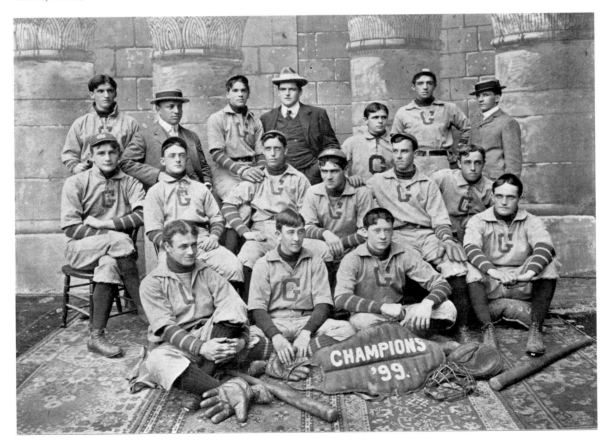

collegiate games, including three wins each over Princeton, Virginia, and Yale. Under new coach Philip King, a trio of pitchers (Edmund Bach, Guy Harris White, and Edward Kenna) led the team to its unprecedented success. After the team completed its season by sweeping through the North with only one defeat (to Holy Cross), the *Boston Herald* unofficially crowned Georgetown as the intercollegiate champion. The team, it judged, "has certainly made the most wonderful record achieved by any college team in recent years."[35] Others thought that Georgetown had taken advantage of its milder climate in getting into midseason form ahead of its northern rivals. But even they had to admit that no college team could match Georgetown's record for 1899.[36] When the team returned to Washington on the evening of May 31, virtually the entire university met them at the Baltimore & Ohio station. A carriage carrying the university officials (President Whitney and Deans Hamilton and Magruder) led through town a torchlight parade consisting of a band of mounted students called "the Rough Riders," representatives of the alumni, the team in a blue and gray coach, the college band, and the students in the three schools. As they reached campus they were greeted by fireworks.[37]

The view from the top was a very brief one for Georgetown, though over the next three years it remained a contender for the unofficial national title. Only three of the starters, as it turned out, returned the following season. Among the missing was the entire pitching corps. Nonetheless, the 1900 team managed to win 16 of its 21 intercollegiate contests and the following year went 12-4-1, losing only to Princeton (twice), Brown, and Pennsylvania. The next year (1902) was even better. Led by their catcher, Louis Drill, Georgetown went 20-5, beating the Washington Senators twice, as well as Pennsylvania, Princeton (twice), and Yale. But this success was followed by two disappointing years (13-11-1 and 13-8).

Reform and Retrenchment

The domination of sports at Georgetown during this period by graduate and professional students was no accident and, in fact, was the result of the introduction of recruiting and athletic scholarships for accomplished athletes throughout the Northeast. Although at most colleges in the 1890s students controlled and financed campus athletics, at Georgetown there was more university supervision. The Athletic Association, re-formed in 1889, was governed by an executive committee headed by a Jesuit faculty member and elected student managers of the various sports. The managers were responsible for the team's schedule, equipment, travel arrangements, and all other off-field matters, although final authority was exercised by the faculty member acting for the president. Finances for each sport were the responsibility of the Athletic Association.[38]

By the 1890s student managers were intensely involved in the recruitment of star players, often graduates of other colleges, for the football, baseball, and track squads. Since there were as yet few, if any, standards established for intercollegiate sports, including eligibility, it was possible to enroll athletes in medical or law or graduate schools who had already competed in college sports for several years. Most of Georgetown's recruited athletes in the 1890s were veterans of intercollegiate play elsewhere. At Georgetown they were most often enrolled either in the professional schools or in the newly established postgraduate program. Even with the best of intentions, it was obviously very difficult, if not impossible, for athletes to attend classes regularly at the dental, law, and medical schools, which were all located across town and began classes in the early evening, when the athletes would still be at practice.

Theoretically, the Athletic Association should have been responsible for providing the scholarships from their own funds. In actuality, the university, through the president, provided them, beginning apparently in 1892, with the student manager as the recruiting agent and awarder of scholarships. President Richards was uneasy with the arrangement. Richards clearly did not want the university to be identified publicly with the practice of subsidizing athletes but felt bound to do it, given the extraordinary importance that organized sport had assumed in the world of higher education. In the summer of 1893 he authorized the student manager, John B. Ryan, to give scholarships in the four departments of the university (college, graduate, law, medicine) to those he deemed to be "men of good character and conduct and otherwise acceptable." Richards urged him not to give scholarships automatically to everyone he recruited. "This tends to destroy the student spirit," Richards noted, "and to make a business of the game." The goal should be to have teams composed of as many legitimate students as possible. Scholarships, he directed, should only be used if the manager was sure that the individuals being recruited would improve the quality of Georgetown's teams, something any manager would invariably assume. At any rate, no one was to know that the university, and not the Athletic Association, was providing the support.[39]

Such a system unsurprisingly produced abuses that Richards tried to curtail. At least some of the recruited stars obviously considered Georgetown as nothing more than a place to gain athletic glory and its other, more tangible prizes. In explaining to the mother of the track star Bernard Wefers why her son was not being promoted to senior year, Richards noted with exasperation, "He shows no interest at all in his studies and his mind is taken up entirely with athletics. Both years of his stay at Georgetown have been begun by his remaining away until the 15th of October, the date on which he is absolutely obliged by the rules of the intercollegiate athletic association, to be present in the college." Once there Wefers attended classes infrequently. And he had failed all his examinations in 1897.[40]

Still, Richards did not withdraw his scholarship (something the university did not publicly admit, anyway). Wefers subsequently transferred to the medical department, along with his brother, James, also on scholarship. He thus was able to run track for another year before the school finally dropped him in the fall of 1898 after another year of class absences and failure to take examinations.[41]

Such transfers were fairly common among the scholarship athletes, no doubt because it was far easier to be simply "on the books" at the professional schools than in the college, where there was constant supervision both in and out of the classroom and regular testing. Neither Wefers was particularly qualified to study medicine: Their examinations "showed great deficiency in preliminary education," the dean reported, who admitted that they had been allowed to matriculate without his knowledge.[42] But athletic scholarships continued to be awarded by the university, including in the Medical School. In 1899, for instance, five of the nine medical school scholarships went to athletes. Subsequently, three of the five either failed to attend classes or to appear for examination.[43] Richards did come to insist that those recruited actually have a financial need for support, but most could certainly qualify by that measure. Indeed he disagreed with the emerging definition of "pure amateurism" as the standard of college sport, a standard he recognized as a design to protect the wealthy from competing with the poor. Richards himself saw no inherent reason why college athletes should not be paid, at least during vacation, for playing sports, if they needed the money. Still, he enforced the unwritten rule set by the elite institutions of refusing to allow Georgetown players to play summer ball for municipal teams.[44] But he thought it a hypocritical measure on the part of those setting such a "gentleman's" standard for collegiate sport.[45]

It should also be said that at least a strong minority of the scholarship athletes on the books of the Medical, Dental, and Law schools actually graduated. That may say more about the rigor (or lack thereof) of the academic programs at the professional schools at the time, particularly the Dental and Law schools, than about the educational commitment of the athletes. Some athlete graduates from the Medical School, such as Edward Mahoney (MD 1895), Bernard McGrath (MD 1895), and Samuel Logan Owens (MD 1803), the outstanding athlete that President Whitney coaxed back to Georgetown from Tulane, went on to distinguished careers in medicine. But the pattern of academic abuse and exploitation was clear enough.

By the middle of the decade Georgetown was acquiring a certain notoriety for its success in intercollegiate sports. When the baseball team defeated Yale 20–5 during the 1895 season, there were complaints in the papers by Yale players about the disadvantages of playing a school who pursued such "a semi-professional game." At the end of the 1894–95 academic year, the board of directors, presumably at Richards's instigation, began a discussion of the presence and desirability of "semi-professional athletes" within the university but apparently concluded that there was no need to take action.[46] Two years later, when a very negative article about Georgetown's professionalism in athletics, including the alleged paying of Wefers to attend the university, appeared in *Harper's Weekly,* the board considered responding but decided it would be useless to attempt to vindicate the university "until challenged by legitimate authority."[47] When challenge eventually came a decade later, it was not from any external authority but the highest internal one—the university's president. For the rest of the 1890s and beyond, Georgetown teams, especially in baseball and track, continued to be national powers.

The allegations that Georgetown used professionals grew even louder in the new century. In 1904 the Athletic Association briefly suspended S. V. "Tate" Crumley, a star freshman pitcher in 1904, when newspapers reported that he had played for the Indianapolis professional team the previous year, but Crumley was reinstated when the professional club maintained that he had played without pay.[48] The issue resurfaced in the spring of 1905. Virginia, which had not played Georgetown since 1901, refused to renew play until Georgetown agreed to restrict eligibility to those who were bona fide students (i.e., attending classes), had been in residence for at least a year (if they had transferred from another college), had participated for fewer than four years of intercollegiate sports, and had not played on a professional team.[49] Georgetown's Athletic Association initially refused to agree to all the conditions (the residence clause being the apparent stickler), but eventually the two schools reached a formal agreement about their academic standards for athletes.

The temporarily aborted agreement became the occasion for an open letter to the students by a recent graduate of the college, Francis M. Foy (AB 1904). Foy charged that most of the players on the baseball team were professionals and that the university was winking at the fact. In football, a majority were either professionals (in baseball) or "students" who were retained even though they had failed exams or never attended classes. This, Foy maintained, summed up much of the university's recent athletic success. "Such a reputation as we have made in baseball and football would be something to be proud of if it were honest [but] it has been earned by hypocrisy and double-faced dealing."[50] "The common opinion among the faculty and students," the keeper of the Jesuit Community diary noted, is that the facts alleged are true—at least in the main."[51]

Two months later, in July 1905, President Daugherty announced that the university was effectively divorcing itself from student athletics. In the future the students would be solely responsible for financing the various sports. The university would still appoint a faculty director of athletics, the president added, but his duty would be "to make sure that none but bona fide students take part in athletic sports."[52] The university would allow free use of Georgetown Field. Beyond that, athletics would now basically be in the students' hands. But there would be no carte blanche for achieving athletic success. In the future no athletic official or manager would have authority to make contracts with players that involved giving board, room, or money. By eliminating athletic scholarships, Daugherty wrote to the Georgetown athletic community, "Georgetown will be kept clear from that professional taint . . . more or less rife in many of our schools and colleges," by having teams "composed of *bona fide* students who come to Georgetown primarily to acquire its intellectual training and engage in sport solely for sport's sake."[53]

To Daugherty's successor, David Hillhouse Buel, fell the task of implementing the new order. Buel, a Yale graduate who had no sufferance for prolegiate sports, was more than happy to execute the general purge of athletes that ensued. The administration, led by Buel, considered the abolition of football in the late fall of 1905, as a number of institutions, such as Columbia, New York University, and Stanford had done in a year in which deaths (twenty-five in 1905 alone) and brutal play had brought the game to a crisis.[54] Perhaps the enactment of new rules for football, including a set scrimmage line, the requirement to make ten yards in four downs, and the introduction of the forward pass, persuaded Georgetown authorities to continue to play under the reformed structure.[55] Buel furthered the restrictions on athletics, setting severe limits on travel by the various intercollegiate teams (two away meets for track, two away races for crew, two away games for football, and four for baseball, with all away games to be held on Saturdays or holidays).[56] This necessarily shortened the schedules for the various teams.

Sports, 1905–10

The fallout on football was immediate. The 1905 team, decimated by the new restrictions, went 2-7, with lopsided losses to Princeton (0–34), Pittsburgh (0–27), Swarthmore (0–34), North Carolina (0–36), and Carlisle (0–76). From 1905 to 1908, the team won only two games in three of the four seasons. The next season, 1909, the team won three of its first five games and tied Fordham on their home field in a game that featured the first extensive use of the forward pass by the Georgetown quarterback, H. Clifton (Curly) Byrd. In the key game of the season against Virginia, the latter won 21–0, but its star halfback, Archer Christian, suffered a fatal brain hemorrhage, apparently while attempting one of his distinctive backward swan dives over a Georgetown tackler.[57] When Christian died the next morning at Georgetown Hospital, Georgetown, along with Virginia, canceled the remaining games on its schedule, and President Himmel announced in December that football would be banned until the game could be reformed to prevent such tragedies.[58] Himmel's decision to abolish football was part of a general reaction by presidents of eastern colleges to a series of highly publicized maimings and fatalities that had struck the sport during that 1909 season. Most, however, simply wanted to extend the reforms that had been introduced in 1905.[59]

In baseball, the downside was less severe and more short lived. In the 1906 season, with only three members of the previous year's team now eligible, the Blue and Gray baseball squadron, after a surprisingly fast start, endured a losing season, going 9-11. The new standards notwithstanding, the team, led by the center fielder Gerhard Simon and infielder Sidney Emanuel Mudd Jr., over the next two years had winning seasons, going 12-9 in 1907 and 17-7-1 in 1908, including wins over Cornell, Pennsylvania, and Virginia (two). The winning pattern continued through 1909 when the team compiled a 15-11-1 record. The 1910 season was a disappointing 11-15-1, with two losses to the Catholic University of America, but wins over eastern powers Harvard, Virginia, and Cornell provided distinct consolation.

If Buel saw no place for intercollegiate sports as they had evolved in America, he had a high regard for intramural games and student fitness in general. One result was the building of the gymnasium for which J. Havens Richards had in vain courted prospective donors. Buel found a benefactress in Mrs. Thomas Fortune Ryan, who had just built the new student residence hall and dining facility. Ground was broken for the Ryan Gymnasium in late December 1905, and the building, equipped with gymnastic equipment, elevated indoor running track, arc lights, and lockers for the athletic teams, opened the following October. The total cost was approximately $60,000.[60]

In accordance with his accent on general student fitness, Buel appointed the first instructor in physical education in September 1906 at the princely (for Georgetown) salary of $1,200 to give "athletic instruction" to the students for two hours each day.[61] The new gym provided a setting for indoor

Ryan Gymnasium, 1906.

(Georgetown University Archives)

track meets as well as for the introduction, at Georgetown, of a new American sport, basketball.

Students had been playing basketball since 1904, on campus and at the Carroll Institute gymnasium downtown. There a treasury agent, Maurice Joyce, was refining the game that James Naismith had invented (including reducing the number of players from nine to five per side). Several Georgetown students persuaded Joyce in the winter of 1907 to coach the team they had formed on campus. In February the team played Virginia in their first intercollegiate game at Carroll Hall and won 22–11.[62] Later that month they lost to George Washington at Convention Hall, 18–16, then beat them the following week, 15–13. The next season Georgetown played a four-game schedule, beating Columbia (22–18), William and Mary (68–8), and Virginia (64–12), while losing to Fordham (25–14). The following year, 1908–9, Georgetown went 9-5, with wins over Virginia, Navy, and Pennsylvania State. That team was led by two law students, Fred Rice and Frank Schosser. In 1910–11, Schlosser averaged 13 points a game as the team went 13-7. His final year, 1911–12, the team went 11-6, during which Schlosser scored more than half of the points the team averaged (20.2). By 1916 the team was playing a fifteen-game schedule, including a northern tour of four games. The team, with Robert Olone starring, went 9-6, with wins over George Washington, Gallaudet, and Brooklyn Polytechnic.

During its first nineteen seasons of competition, the team had but one losing season, in 1909–10, when it went 5-7. Between 1919 and 1920, the team, led by Fred Fees and Andrew Zazzali, won twenty-one out of twenty-three games.

Blue and Gray Resurgence, 1910–16

The 1909 ban on football died before the next season. President Himmel was apparently persuaded by other Jesuits that the reforms passed by the Intercollegiate Athletic Association in the spring of 1910 that eliminated mass formations and flying tackles were sufficient to justify Georgetown's continuing to field a team. The university resumed financing sports. Football was again emphasized and scholarships were revived under Himmel's successor, Alphonsus Donlon, who had been a star baseball player at Georgetown. As President Donlon saw it, a football program competitive with the finest teams in the country was essential for the institution's spirit, student morale, alumni financial support, and institutional reputation.[63] President Donlon also wanted to build a (presumably giant) stadium for the game, something many elite universities were beginning to do.[64]

The football eleven went 7-1-1 in both 1910 and 1911, losing only to national powers Carlisle and Pittsburgh. The highlight of both seasons was the defeat of Virginia, in 1911, before an estimated crowd of ten thousand at

Georgetown Field, including high officials of the government and diplomatic corps, with the Blue and Gray's star halfback, Harry Costello, kicking three field goals in the 15–0 win.[65] In 1911, Georgetown also managed a tie at West Point against the military academy. In 1912, the team went to 8 and 1, with the sole loss to Carlisle by a relatively close score, 34–20. For three seasons, 1910, 1911, and 1912, the Blue and Gray reigned as champions of the South Atlantic region. The following year, 1913, was a bitterly disappointing one as Georgetown fell to 4-4, including shutouts by Carlisle, North Carolina A & M (State), and Navy.

Having lost to Carlisle six straight times, the university turned to a Carlisle alumnus, Albert Exendine, who, as head coach for the 1914 season, installed the Pop Warner system that put a heavy emphasis on deception and complicated passes. His Blue and Gray charges were slow to make it work, going 2-4-2 his first year, but the losses were close, and even the Pittsburgh score (21–0) did not reflect the closeness of the contest. "Playing such elevens as Navy, Pittsburgh, and Washington and Jefferson," commented the graduate manager, Charlie Cox, "means that Georgetown in a year or two will be classed with the strongest teams in the North."[66] Cox was prescient as Georgetown under Exendine went 7-2 the next year and 9-1 in 1916. The sole losses were to Princeton, Army, and Navy.

The 1916 team, basically the same as the previous year's, featured Jack Maloney, the quarterback, punter, and field-goal kicker, and Johnny Gilroy, the halfback, whose long and accurate passes became Georgetown's chief offensive weapon, which made him the leading scorer. The Blue and Gray ran up a total of 474 points and allowed only 33. For the season, Gilroy scored 160 points, top in the nation. Georgetown had become a national power, one whose very success caused potential opponents to shun the Blue and Gray. In the spring of 1917 the graduate manager reported that "all of the large institutions, including Yale, Harvard, Dartmouth, Princeton, Cornell and Brown" had refused to add Georgetown to their schedules because "they could not take on another strong team next year."[67] Despite this cold shoulder, Georgetown put together a credible schedule that included Navy, Lehigh, Fordham, and Virginia Tech and went 7-1 (the loss to Navy), even though virtually all of its upper-class players were unavailable because they had joined the war effort. That proved to be the last collegiate football at Georgetown for the next two years.

Sports in the 1920s

During the war, intercollegiate sports continued at the request of the government, but on a curtailed basis (in 1918 the football team had a five-game season, four against Marine and Navy squads). In the postwar period Georgetown resumed big-time athletics in its major sports of football, baseball, and track. The university petitioned for membership in the National Collegiate Athletic Association in 1925, two decades after its founding, and gained membership in December of that year. The Georgetown Athletic Association was reorganized with a nine-member board of directors, composed of faculty, alumni, and students, which was responsible for setting policy, naming student managers of the several sports, and establishing a budget. The association was to be solely responsible for the revenues raised and the expenses incurred by the athletic teams. Student managers were to plan the schedules of the respective teams and be responsible for the players' meeting the eligibility codes set by the university. One of the faculty, designated by the president of the university, would serve as faculty director of athletics.

Vincent McDonough, SJ, the prefect of discipline and moderator of athletics since 1916, became, in effect, the chief operating officer of athletics at Georgetown. "Father Mac," stooped and caped, seemed forever to be roaming the campus, particularly on the sidelines of athletic contests, where his booming voice and relentless pacing became an integral part of Georgetown's sports culture during the 1920s. His confidante and chief assistant was John D. O'Reilly, the physical director, who was also coach of track, baseball, and basketball. McDonough and O'Reilly made up the schedules, selected the athletes, and secured their admission on scholarship to the various schools within the university by negotiating a quota system by which each school (medical, foreign service, law, etc.) would accept a certain number of athletes each year.

By 1927 there were nearly 140 scholarship athletes at the college. The Athletic Association was supposed to pay for their tuition and board but was continually in debt. In 1927 it had accumulated a deficit of nearly $80,000.[68] Some Georgetown officials, such as Robert Parsons, SJ, and Edmund Walsh, felt that athletics had assumed a disproportionate place within the university and was seriously compromising the institution's academic integrity and finances. Dean Parsons complained in 1927 about "the hold that the Athletic Association has on the College. Some athletes were admitted to the college last year against [my] express orders." Courses were instituted at midyear simply to accommodate freshly arriving athletes. Athletes were routinely "shipped around the University" to keep them eligible after they failed out of a particular school. And they were having a ruinous effect on the finances. "If you consider just the cost of maintaining these boys [athletes] at the college by the Athletic Association," he went on, "the sum must come to close on to thirty thousand dollars."[69]

These academic scandals and financial costs were part of the price Georgetown officials were willing to pay for athletic success. During this decade,

Vincent McDonough, SJ, moderator of athletics, 1916–30. (Georgetown University Archives)

Georgetown enjoyed arguably its best success in any period across the spectrum of sports. The school won or claimed national intercollegiate championships in indoor track, baseball, and rifle and achieved unprecedented national status in football.

In the postwar period, track at Georgetown experienced a revival. John O'Reilly had come to Georgetown in 1914 as a renowned coach in New England, but it was not until after the war that his teams regained national prominence. In 1921 Georgetown hosted the track and field championships of the South Atlantic Intercollegiate Athletic Association that included George Washington, Virginia Tech, North Carolina, Georgia Tech, Virginia Military Institute, and seven other schools. Georgetown easily bested the field, scoring 75 points to Virginia Military Institute's next best of 41 points. Captain Robert Legendre alone scored nearly as many points (28) as the second-place team, setting three South Atlantic records in the javelin, discus, and broad jump; in addition, he won the 100-yard dash and placed second in the 220 hurdles and shot put. Legendre had won the American Pentathlon Championship at the Penn Relays in 1919 and the same event in Paris that summer in the Interallied meet. His best event was the long jump, at which he set a world record of 25 feet, 5 inches in 1924. Twice he represented the United States in the Olympics in the pentathlon, finishing fourth in 1920 and winning a bronze medal in Paris in 1924.

Georgetown sent four others to Paris: James Connolly, a world class miler, in the 3,000-meters; Emerson Norton, in the decathlon, in which he won a silver medal; Jim Burgess in the 400-meters; and William Dowding in the long jump. In that 1923–24 season Anthony Plansky (BSFS 1926) won the national decathlon championship as a freshman. The following two years he won the event at the Penn Relays. Plansky was also a top 100-yard-dash performer and high jumper for Georgetown from 1924 to 1927.

The team won the intercollegiate indoor championship on March 7, 1925, in New York. Bill Dowding set an intercollegiate record with his long jump of more than 23 feet. The relay teams also won their events, to put Georgetown on the top of the intercollegiate indoor track world. The mile team, led by captain George Kinally, set an intercollegiate record in the championship meet with a time of 3 minutes 21.8 seconds. The two-mile relay team in the same meet broke their own world record by running the distance in 7 minutes and 41.6 seconds.[70] In 1925–26, Georgetown relay teams set four world records in the 1,280 yard run, the 1,600 meter, and the 1- and 2-mile events.[71] Another member of the 1925 team, Andy Gaffey (PhB 1925), set the world record for the 150-yard dash, an event that was discontinued shortly afterward. In 1928, David Adelman twice broke the world indoor record for the shot with marks of 50 feet 6 inches and 49 feet 7.25 inches, unfortunately at meets unsanctioned by the Intercollegiate Association of Amateur Athletes of America (IC4A), at Georgetown and Annapolis, respectively.[72]

JEUX OLYMPIQUES DE 1924
LEGENDRE BAT LE RECORD DU SAUT EN LONGUEUR AVEC 7.765

Robert Legendre, the world record holder for the long jump (25 feet, 5 inches) in the 1920 Olympics. (Georgetown University Archives)

Golf reorganized as a varsity sport in 1926. In its first intercollegiate match, with Lafayette, the newest Georgetown team scored its first victory. In its third year of intercollegiate competition, Maurice McCarthy won the national singles title in 1928. In tennis Gregory Mangin reached the semifinals of the U.S. Open tennis championship in 1928, an event he would win a year after graduation. The 1923 rifle team won the national intercollegiate title. A year earlier, the baseball team, led by pitchers Art Reynolds and Sam Hyman and first baseman Del Bissonette, reeled off twenty-five consecutive wins to claim the national championship. The basketball team, coached by Elmer Ripley and led by freshman Fred Mesmer, went 12-1 in the 1927 season, which was its best record in eight years.

All of this achievement in other sports notwithstanding, the dominant one at Georgetown in the 1920s was football, when Blue and Gray teams reached a level of success that Georgetown football had never known. Albert Exendine, who had come to Georgetown from Carlisle in 1914, continued as football coach through the war and for four years beyond it. His teams of 1919 through 1922 went 27-11-1, but he left after the 1922 season when business interests in Oklahoma prevented him from meeting the new requirement of the Athletic Association that coaches be employed for the full

Lou Little (left), football coach, 1924–29. (Georgetown University Archives)

year. His assistant, John Maloney, a former Georgetown quarterback, succeeded him but lasted for only one season, during which the team went 3-6. The one notable event of the 1923 season was the first appearance of a bull terrier as a regular mascot at the games. "Stubby," in truth of very mixed pedigree, had become renowned throughout the Western world by the time he first nudged a football around the field, to the delight of the crowd, during half times at Georgetown games. A war hero decorated by both the American and French governments for his valorous service with the 102nd Infantry in Europe, Stubby performed for two seasons before being followed by a series of authentic Boston bull terriers who roamed the sidelines with "Father Mac."

After a national search for a football coach, the board of the Athletic Association chose Lou Little (Luigi Piccolo), a two-time, All-American tackle at Pennsylvania, and the coach of the Frankfort Yellowjackets, at that time the dominant team of the National Football League, at a salary of 10 percent of the net profits from football. Little also had five assistants (no previous coach had had more than one). One of his first acts was to establish a preseason camp in nearby Virginia to provide a month's training before the school year began. A year after arriving, the thirty-one-year-old Little was named athletic director and given a three-year contract, with McDonough becoming the moderator of athletics. Little quickly restored Georgetown to football prominence. In Little's second season, Georgetown went 9-1, with impressive wins over Detroit, Lehigh, and Fordham. The single loss was to Bucknell, 3–2, on a quagmire field. The team was a defensive giant, shutting out seven of its opponents. The offense scored 281 points, fifth highest in the nation. Backs Jack Hagerty, Lou Metzer, and Tony Plansky, along with 275-pound tackle Harry Aloysius "Babe" Connaughton, were the core of the team. The team was the fall obsession for students, faculty, and alumni. For the Fordham game in late November, three busloads of students, which comprised the majority of the college, made the trip to New York, while most of those who remained on campus packed the gymnasium to "watch" the game on "Grid-graph," a giant board depicting a gridiron upon which a telegrapher recorded the progress of play.[73] The upset of eastern power Fordham by 27–0 marked the highlight of the season.

The following two years solidified Georgetown's position as a national power, with records of 7-2-1 in 1926 and 8-1 in 1927. In 1928, Georgetown gained wide attention with its startling upset of one of the top teams in

the country, New York University
(NYU), 7–2, before fifty thousand,
at Yankee Stadium. Georgetown
scored on a fumble recovery and a
run of 85 yards in the second period. That seemed hardly enough to
defeat NYU, who in the second half
began a constant series of threats to
score. Five times the Violets pene-
trated within the Georgetown five-
yard line to begin a set of downs but
never crossed the goal. Finally, in
the waning minutes, Georgetown
took an intentional safety and Jim
Mooney punted deep into NYU territory.[74] With its win over NYU the
team was 6-0. A week later, how-

The Hoyas (on defense)
in the 1928 season.
(*Ye Domesday Booke*, 1929)

ever, the Blue and Gray could not duplicate its success when it lost to another
national powerhouse, Carnegie Tech; a key factor in that setback was the loss
of the team's captain, guard Jerry Carroll, due to a broken leg. Further injuries
led to a second loss to Detroit, and the team record for the season was 8-2.

The team received several bids for postseason games, notably from Southern Methodist and St. Mary's of California. Coach Little expressed great interest in making the trip as the extension of the regular season that ended in
Detroit, but, for whatever reasons—perhaps the mounting injuries on the
team—Georgetown did not go west for its first postseason game. By that
time McDonough, who might have backed Little's desires, had been replaced
as faculty moderator. Little left Georgetown a year later, and a radical change
in Georgetown athletics shortly followed his departure.

De-emphasis and the End of an Era

By the end of the 1928 season there were growing rumors that Little was
unhappy with the changes at Georgetown and would return to the University of Pennsylvania, his alma mater, to become head coach. The promised
$350,000, twenty-thousand-seat stadium had failed to materialize. The new
president of Georgetown, Coleman Nevils, had reduced the number of athletic scholarships to 100. He also refused to continue the practice of paying
Little 10 percent of the profits from football (Little also had a base salary of
$5,000, far more than any faculty member was making at the time). In the
spring of 1929, Little requested a contract extension of seven or eight years
at $12,000 (his six-year contract ended in 1929), but Nevils failed to grant
it.[75] Little, with a record of 41-12-3 at Georgetown, left for Columbia after

the 1929 season, where he became an institution over the next thirty-seven years, although not nearly as successful as he had been on the Hilltop.[76]

Nevils saw no place for big-time athletics at Georgetown, and from his first year in office he began to de-emphasize sports. If athletics had any part in higher education, for Nevils it was in the form of intramurals rather than intercollegiate competition, which was expensive and required subsidized athletes who were, at best, marginal students. Nevils eliminated the position of athletic director, the position Little had held, as well as that of coach and made John Kehoe, SJ, the effective head of athletics as faculty moderator of sports. The "supplementary support," or cash, that scholarship athletes had traditionally been given for their expenses was discontinued.[77] In the spring of 1932, Nevils announced that Georgetown was eliminating athletic scholarships entirely, effective for the 1934–35 academic year.

Three things likely provided Nevils with the rationale for taking this dramatic step in de-professionalizing athletics at Georgetown. First was the report on college athletics that the Carnegie Foundation released in the fall of 1929. The report castigated the professionalism that characterized intercollegiate athletics, particularly in football, especially the "widespread practice of recruiting and subsidizing athletes." The report specifically cited Georgetown as one of many schools that "unequivocally award athletic scholarships" and charged that the university also provided financial assistance to needy athletes beyond tuition and board.[78] The second factor was an action taken by the Middle States Association of Colleges and Secondary Schools, in the spring of 1932, that outlawed athletic scholarships for its members, of which Georgetown was one.[79] The third factor was the directive issued by the Jesuit superior general that same spring to Jesuit colleges in the United States to discontinue athletic scholarships. Nevils immediately put it into effect. There was to be no spring practice or summer camp for football and no new scholarship players.

That fall the football team quickly began to feel the effects of the new policy. After opening wins against weak competition, Georgetown went winless for the rest of the season, including crushing losses to NYU and Carnegie Tech of 39–0 and 51–0, respectively. Tommy Mills, the former assistant to Knute Rockne at Notre Dame who had succeeded Little in 1930, resigned as coach in the middle of the 1932 season. Georgetown finished the year 2-6-1. With basically the same schedule the following season (1933), Georgetown won one game.

De-emphasis was the order of the day for other major sports at Georgetown as well. In the spring of 1930, Nevils forced the resignation of the vaunted track coach, John O'Reilly, by reducing his salary. When new buildings north of the Healy Building supplanted the old athletic field, the baseball and track teams found themselves without a home field. The former had to play its games thereafter at a field on the grounds of the Army War College at Fort McNair. The track team piled into a pick-up truck daily to practice at a cross-town high school track. By the fall of 1934, the student paper was pronouncing that track at Georgetown had "fallen to such a state that it is just about one degree above oblivion."[80] By the end of the 1932–33 year, the entire sports budget had been reduced to $29,000, less than half of what it had been three years earlier.

Facilities and monies shifted to intramurals. Two playing fields were constructed on landfill south of the Medical School and in the hollow southwest of New North. Ten tennis courts were built on the Old Freshman field on the southeast edge of campus, and four handball courts were added shortly thereafter. In the fall students competed in interclass competition in tackle and touch football as well as in a handball tournament and in field hockey, which proved attractive especially to students from the North who had played hockey and those from Latin America, where the game was a staple. In the winter, interclass and intramural basketball games were played; in the spring, class and intramural teams played baseball as well as engaged in swim meets at the outdoor pool. Volleyball, fist-ball, and quoit-pitching were other sports on the intramural calendar. In 1931 an Intramural Athletic Association was established that conducted football, basketball, and baseball leagues (organized among residence floors), as well as fall and spring tennis and handball tournaments and a boxing tournament. By the end of the first year, the association reported that more than two-thirds of the students were participants.[81] Unfortunately, the student commitment to intramurals proved short lived.

The *Hoya*, in an editorial in the fall of 1933, summed up the state of sports at Georgetown: "Whether we like it or not, major sports are on the decline at Georgetown and have been for several years. . . . For the immediate future, the paper argued, minor sports were providing the occasion for the university to rebuild its reputation in sports. "In the meantime," it concluded, "there is no reason for hanging to ancient history and living on our past reputation; declining in the old fields we should embrace new ones to prove our worth—especially when the old ones prove much too expensive to maintain at the old standards."[82] If the editorial was naïve in its expectation of what credit minor sports could bring to Georgetown, it was a fitting commentary on the passing of an era of Georgetown athletics in which the major varsity teams had achieved prominence over several decades in the world of intercollegiate sports. In that forty-year period, the prolegiate character of Georgetown sports, epitomized by football, had waxed and waned according to the determination of individual presidents about the place that sports should occupy within the university's academic order. Under Coleman Nevils it had shrunk to its smallest stature since sports had first emerged in the 1890s as a major part, if not the dominant part, of student culture. But as with earlier attempts to eliminate prolegiate athletics at Georgetown, its demise would prove to be a very temporary one.

PART TWO

KEEPING THE DREAM ALIVE, 1928–45

CHAPTER 5

Depression, Centralization, and Expansion, 1928–35

[Under Father Nevils] the University has assumed at Washington, throughout the Nation, and in foreign countries a position which it has not hitherto enjoyed . . . it has become known in foreign countries more certainly, perhaps, than any other American institution of learning.

RAYMOND H. REISS, June 1934

A Visibility in Official Washington

In late October 1928, representatives of ninety-three colleges and universities from the United States and abroad, delegates of twenty-six learned societies, officials of the United States, and members of the diplomatic corps gathered in Gaston Hall to inaugurate William Coleman Nevils as the thirty-ninth president of Georgetown University. Representatives in academic dress of institutions ranging from Louvain University to Harvard, Yale, and Princeton to the Catholic University of America, along with delegates from learned societies, followed an ROTC honor guard carrying the American and Georgetown flags into Gaston Hall. The board of regents and the various faculties of the university followed. It was, as the new president noted, "the largest gathering of educators from universities, colleges and learned societies that has been held by any Catholic college in the United States."[1] It also marked the first formal inauguration of a president in the history of the institution. Following the intoning of the *Veni Creator* by the college glee club, James A. Farrell, president of the United States Steel Company and a member of the board of regents, introduced Nevils and presented him with a doctoral degree in divinity, as well as the charter and seal of the university—symbols of university authority.

Holding the charter and seal, the new president proclaimed, "With these symbols of the University authority I take office as President of Georgetown University, and I promise that loyalty to our country and our Constitution will guide my every aspiration and action, and the charter granted by the Congress of the United States will be preserved intact."[2] The new president then delivered an inaugural address in which he proclaimed anew the perennial superiority of the *Ratio Studiorum* as the foundation for a liberal education, which recognized the need to impart a core of knowledge, "the sine qua non of a degree," as well as to cultivate the power to acquire more understanding and make rational judgments in a changing world.[3] At his conclusion, the glee club sang the alma mater, "Sons of Georgetown," after which honorary degrees were awarded to several faculty members and alumni. The singing of the "Magnificat" and the soon-to-be national anthem, "The Star Spangled Banner," closed the pomp- and symbol-laced program.[4]

The new president was a fifty-year-old Philadelphian who had served as dean of the college and academic vice president of Georgetown from 1918 to

Inauguration of W. Coleman Nevils, SJ, as thirty-ninth president of Georgetown, 1928. (Georgetown University Archives)

1924. Distinguished by his steel-gray hair and magnetic presence, Nevils, as many remembered, projected gravity and engagement to all he met. The inauguration was an early indication of Nevils's ambition for the university and of his intent to give it a presence within the political and diplomatic circles of Washington that it had never known. It was a statement about the special status that Georgetown had, or aspired to, as an institution of higher learning in the capital city of a growing world power.

One of Nevils's initial acts was to revive the board of regents, dormant since the early 1920s, and make it an effective instrument for fund-raising and the sanctioning of policy. Significantly, he reached beyond Georgetown's alumni to invite leaders in the business world to join the board, including James Farrell; George McNeir, a leading New York City businessman; John S. Drum, a San Francisco banker who had been president of the American Bankers Association; and Richmond Dean, vice president of the Pullman Corporation.

From his inauguration onward Nevils reached out to the political, diplomatic, ecclesiastical, and intellectual communities of Washington in an unprecedented manner. He became a fourth degree member of the Knights of Columbus, eventually serving as faithful friar of its assembly in the District. He was also elected to the Cosmos Club. Exploiting the connections that Edmund Walsh had made within the diplomatic community in Washington, Nevils regularly entertained and honored ambassadors from various countries. Walsh had been responsible for a reception at Georgetown in the winter of 1928 to honor French ambassador Paul Claudel, to which some six hundred members of the international community and other dignitaries were invited. Once in office, Nevils made such events a regular part of his efforts to promote the university's presence in the capital. As one student remembered, "There seemed to be a never-ending series of diplomatic receptions. Something was always being celebrated."[5] Nevils had truly given Georgetown a visibility in official Washington it had never before known.

Founders' Day, the event that Nevils revived in 1930, became a great medium for international outreach. The day, as noted in chapter 2, originally commemorated John Carroll's acquisition of the deed that marked the beginnings of the university in 1789. Nevils changed the date of celebration from January 23 to March 25 to honor the "founders" of Georgetown, by tracing the origins of the university to the beginnings of the Maryland colony in 1634, thus implicitly making Georgetown the oldest institution of higher education in the United States. As Nevils explained in a Baltimore newspaper in 1934, "Though the University was established on its present site in 1789, it was in the '30s of the seventeenth century that Georgetown was really born [, that] . . . the seed was planted which eventually grew into the university as we know it today."[6]

On March 25, 1930, the anniversary of the landing of the Maryland colonists on St. Clement's Island, the first Founders' Day reflecting the new vision of Georgetown's genesis was held in Gaston Hall, attracting there, one observer noted, "the biggest number of Diplomats that could be gather[ed] anywhere in D.C. outside the White House."[7] As the *Georgetown College Journal* reported, "The celebration took place amid great pomp and ceremony, with the red and purple cassocks of the hierarc monsignori, the braid and uniforms of the army and naval officers, the ribbons and decorations of the diplomats and others, and the many-colored glitter of evening gowns all forming an environment that spoke of something akin to pageantry."[8] The roll call of the founders was read by the auxiliary bishop of Baltimore. The bell from the first church in Maryland was tolled six times to honor key Jesuits in the colonial history of Maryland, including Andrew White, Thomas Copley, and John Carroll. Academies were established for the occasion to award honors to outstanding persons in the worlds of art, science, and philosophy. Among the initial honorees were Ambassador Paul Claudel of France and Maestro Arturo Toscanini of the New York Philharmonic. In subsequent years the John Carroll Academy of Diplomacy and Foreign Service as well as the William Gaston Academy of Law were created to bestow honors on persons in diplomacy and government service.

The largest such Founders' Day was in 1934, termed the Tercentennial Celebration, to mark the alleged three hundredth anniversary of the founding of Georgetown. The celebration began in November of the previous year to mark the anniversary of the sailing of Andrew White and his companions from the Isle of Wight to the new world. Ambassadors and ministers from Germany, Japan, Italy, China, and several other countries were present for the occasion. The tercentennial Founders' Day exercises took place in April 1934. Thirty-two ambassadors and foreign ministers, along with Supreme Court justices, members of the cabinet, members of Congress and the government, and bishops and archbishops joined a packed throng in Gaston Hall for the ceremonies, during which the apostolic delegate, Amieto Giovanni Cicognani; the governor of Maryland, Albert Ritchie; and the gynecologist and former medical faculty member, Sophie Nordhoff-Jung, received academy honors, while the benefactress, Genevieve Brady, received an honorary degree.[9] During Nevils's six years in office, several European and Latin American countries, including Chile, Belgium, Czechoslovakia, France, Italy, Romania, and Yugoslavia, awarded him honors in recognition of his educational achievements and promotion of international relations. When Herbert Hoover received the official notification of his renomination in August 1932 at Constitution Hall, Nevils gave the invocation.[10] Two years later, Hoover's successor, Franklin Delano Roosevelt, invited Nevils to be a delegate of the United States to the 15th International Conference of the Red Cross in Japan. In that same year President Roosevelt appointed him to the board of visitors of the United States Naval Academy.

The Greater Georgetown Plan Revived

A vital part of giving the university a greater presence in the Washington area was purely physical. The very first thing that Coleman Nevils did upon becoming president in 1928 was to revive the Greater Georgetown plan, the ambitious consolidation and expansion program of the schools that the university had drawn up in the early part of the decade to provide living and academic facilities for a growing undergraduate and professional population. Nevils had effectively headed the fund-raising for the plan before Lyons, his predecessor as president, had chosen to curtail the drive and suspend the plan. On the day that the board of directors officially elected him president, August 27, 1928, Nevils made his first move toward the reimplementation of the plan—by modifying it. The previous administration had been on the brink of breaking ground for a new medical school just outside the front gate on 37th Street. Nevils had the board transfer the site to the northwestern edge of the campus on Reservoir Road.[11] Construction of the Medical-Dental Building began scarcely four months after Nevils took office on January 3, 1929. An H-shaped, five-story, brick structure with wood columns very similar to the new preparatory school building at Garrett Park, the new home for the two schools, cost nearly $1 million including equipment, about five times what the university had intended to spend for the 37th Street building.[12] It formally opened sixteen months later in May 1930.

The central piece of the Greater Georgetown plan had been the English quadrangle to be formed by the Healy Building and four new collegiate Gothic structures to the north and east of it. There would be a dormitory, two science buildings, and a classroom facility, with a total cost of $2.5 million. Under Nevils's hand, the complex, originally to be named the Edward D. White Quadrangle in honor of the alumnus chief justice, now became the Andrew White Memorial Quadrangle, to honor the first Jesuit in Maryland and the purported first founder of the university. The initial phase of construction was to be a 220-bed dormitory. With applications to the college and School of Foreign Service continuing to increase, there was still a pressing need for housing, even though New North had been added just three years earlier.

At the beginning of 1929, Nevils engaged architect Emile G. Perrot of Philadelphia to do the general design for the quadrangle. Official approval came from Rome in the beginning of 1930, with a ceiling of $660,000 set by superiors for the cost of the dormitory.[13] By that time the president and his directors had accepted not only Perrot's plan for the dormitory, which consisted of two- and three-person suites, but also the builder's contract to erect a building for $662,955, not including the costs for pilings and steel, which were estimated at an additional $80,000.[14] In the late winter, construction began on Copley Hall, named for another of the earliest Maryland Jesuits. Nevils was hoping that anticipated savings in construction and promised contributions from the architect and contractor would bring the project

Medical-Dental Building, 1930. (Georgetown University Archives)

within the lines superiors had set. The president, building on the connections he had made as head of the endowment fund earlier in the decade, through letters and personal appeals quickly raised most of the needed money for Copley Hall within months of announcing the plan. This was achieved despite the onset of the business downturn that would become the Great Depression. Indeed, the depressed state of the economy meant lower building costs, and the project came in more than $125,000 under budget.[15] The five-story building, containing 148 suites, a chapel with seating for 200, and a spacious reading lounge, was acclaimed as the equal of any college dormitory in the country.[16] It opened for 221 seniors on Monday, February 16, 1931, with 350 guests, including many from the diplomatic corps, attending the formal dedication.[17]

Spurred by his success in the funding of Copley Hall, Nevils turned to the next unit of the quadrangle, originally planned as a home for chemistry laboratories and lecture halls. Perhaps realizing that the hard times would put ultimate limits on the complete fulfillment of the original plan, the president had the new building designed as a combination science laboratory, classroom, and administrative building. Nonetheless, he felt confident that in the current economic climate they could continue to build for a minimal cost, as the construction of Copley had proven. With a projected price of a half-million dollars for the building, Rome was wary of having the university take on such a large debt in such uncertain times and stipulated that Nevils raise half the cost of the building before breaking ground. With this conditional approval, Nevils proceeded to seek new funding.

The Depression became a motivator for fund-raising as Nevils appealed to the patriotism of potential donors to aid the nation's recovery by contributing to the Georgetown building project and thus to the creation of jobs. As he wrote to President Hoover in March 1932, they were starting the new building as their part in the national attempt to revive the economy.[18] By June 1932 Nevils had enough money in hand to sign a contract for a new building, to be named White-Gravenor after Andrew White and still another early Maryland Jesuit, John Gravenor, on the site of Susan Decatur's cottage on the northeast edge of campus. The four-story structure, also collegiate Gothic in style, employed the same stone mixture for its exterior as did Copley, granite stone from a quarry in northern Maryland interspersed with gray stone cut from a recently dismantled bridge over Rock Creek. The building, which housed 20 classrooms, 5 chemistry laboratories, and 2 large lecture halls to accommodate 350 students, and offices for faculty, dean, and registrar of the college, measures 190 feet in length and 90 feet in width, with a fronting 40-foot esplanade guarded by a balustrade of carved stone 3 feet high.

Both Copley and White-Gravenor were "sermons in stone," with broad utilization of carved symbols over doorways, windows, and gables of Jesuit and Georgetown history. Flanking the main entrance to White-Gravenor, for instance, are shields depicting artifacts of the early Maryland colony and the coat of arms of Archbishop Carroll. Over the entrance itself are five carvings depicting the emergence of Georgetown from the Indian school at St. Mary's City in 1634 to the academy on Georgetown Heights in 1789.

White-Gravenor opened in November 1933, eleven months after the beginning of construction. Final cost of the building was a little more than $400,000. Once again hard times had made it possible for a major construction project to be completed at a significantly lower cost than anticipated.[19] Remarkably, in the course of four and a half years, Nevils had constructed three major buildings, and, as he informed the regents in 1933, "will be able to finish without any debt."[20] This was achieved during the depths of the Depression, with banks and businesses failing daily across the country, cities declaring bankruptcy, and one-quarter of the working force unemployed. The *College Journal* understandably marveled at what Nevils had achieved in his first few years as president, "some of the most important improvements and most indisputable marks of progress in the history of the University."[21] Nor was the praise strictly intramural. The *American Business Journal* was equally impressed by Nevils's "outstandingly efficient management," which, the journal judged, had made him a recognized "leader of exceptional attainments in the education world" through his extraordinary building record.[22]

White-Gravenor Building, 1933. (Georgetown University Archives)

This was hardly the end of Nevils's plans for the Greater Georgetown. He intended to complete the quadrangle on the east side with another class-room-science building that would be called the Poulton Building in honor of the Jesuit who in the mid-eighteenth century had founded the precursor of Georgetown at Bohemia on the eastern shore of Maryland. He thought it imperative to build a new hospital contiguous with the Medical-Dental Building on Reservoir Road. The old hospital buildings on N and 35th streets could then be converted into housing for the professional students (Nevils calculated some 700 professional boarders within the old quarters).[23] He also anticipated moving the other two professional schools, law and foreign service, to the main campus to a site on 37th Street, between O and P streets, occupied by houses that the university had acquired over the previous forty years. Where the Medical School had been initially slated to be transferred, on 37th Street, between O and N streets, Nevils envisioned a 4,000-seat gymnasium built to accommodate intercollegiate and intramural sports as well as academic convocations. All this was part of the Greater Georgetown vision that would integrate and centralize the facilities of the three campuses.

In 1931 Nevils had begun the process of securing permission to build the gymnasium and talked at the 1932 commencement of laying the cornerstone for the new Law School home. He was sure that the money secured by the sale of the old law building in its downtown location would nearly cover the cost of the new one. At commencement the following year the president was still hoping to find the means to move the Law School to the main campus. The reality of the Depression must have burst the balloon of his building ambitions soon afterward (there was hardly a market for real estate, even in a central spot of the city, by the summer of 1931). By 1934 Nevils had to admit that given the persistent bad economic conditions, it was probably prudent to defer the gymnasium project until there was a better climate for raising the money among interested alumni.[24] A persistent depression and a new president with different priorities effectively ended the Greater Georgetown program. Nevils's successor attempted to begin a new fund-raising drive among the alumni in 1938 to build the gymnasium, but in six months he managed to raise less than $12,000 (and that was mostly in pledges).[25]

Hard Times

For most of Nevils's term, since the stock market crash in October 1929 the country had been in the worst economic crisis of its history. As unemployment mounted alarmingly and businesses and banks failed, the collapse initially seemed to little affect higher education across the nation. Enrollments actually showed a national increase in the 1930–31 school year, and Georgetown was no exception. Indeed, if universities and colleges were slow to feel the effects of the Depression, Georgetown was even slower, because it was located in the capital where the impact was not felt until the summer of 1932, when the federal government began to drastically cut spending and its work force. Unemployment in the area suddenly rose to the 200,000 mark.[26] At Christmas 1930 the editorialist of the *College Journal* warned his readers of the unprecedented scenes they could expect to encounter in this holiday season when they returned home: "Hundreds of beggars . . . on the streets . . . at every corner, in front of theatres and restaurants, many of them cold and shivering, most starving for food, all looking for work."[27]

As late as June 1931, the *College Journal* was still sympathetic to, if not supportive of, President Hoover, and it decried the media's tendency to mock Hoover rather than appreciate his earnest attempts to lead the nation to recovery. During the 1931 football season, in response to a national appeal from the president's Committee on Mobilization of Unemployment Relief Resources, the university donated the proceeds from one of its home games to unemployment relief. In December the university team also participated in a Depression Bowl at Griffith Stadium, a double-header matching Georgetown against Catholic University and George Washington against Alabama, for the benefit of public relief in the District of Columbia. In a speech on campus, the conductor of the recently established National Symphony Orchestra made a personal appeal to the student body to support the fund-starved orchestra by attending their concerts at Constitution Hall.[28]

In April 1932, the college paper, the *Hoya,* managed to see the Depression, which was devastating business and ruining old-line institutions, as a "golden opportunity" for the college graduate to start his career "at rock bottom" with the confidence that things could only get better. Still, as one editorialist suggested, if one had the means, it would be better "for a year or two" to take advantage of graduate school or foreign travel, presumably until the corporate world had truly bottomed out. The presumption was that many, if not most, of his readers had that option.[29] Indeed, two weeks later another editorial advised students not to waste their time seeking a summer job in a jobless market but to take advantage of the lowest rates since 1904 and travel abroad.[30] Nor were they much impressed by the most dramatic symbol of the upheaval created by the Depression, the more than 20,000 "bonus marchers" who set up camps in various abandoned buildings and mud flats along the Anacostia River of the District in the spring and summer of 1932 seeking early delivery of their promised bonus for their service in World War I. An editorial in the *Hoya* the following fall dismissed "the moronic turmoil" that the marchers had created during the previous summer as "amusing and pitiful" and observed that the violent conclusion to their march (when troops under Gen. Douglas MacArthur had routed them from their camps) was sadly inevitable.[31]

By the late fall of 1932, the attitude toward Hoover and the Republican Congress had changed. The topic of the White Debating Society for the fall term, "Resolved, that the relief measures undertaken by President Hoover have been too conservative for the best interests of the country," summed up the change.[32] The student journals welcomed the Democrats' sweep of government in the November elections and called on Roosevelt and the Democrats to "rise to the demands of the crisis" and "rebuild . . . the American Dream on a new basis."[33] "It is the President's duty, in this hour, to act quickly to save the country from calamity—for banks and businesses cannot forever fall and the nation continue to exist."[34] That same week the *College Journal,* in an editorial, opined that "no President of this nation was ever inducted in the face of more tremendous problems. . . . If the President is able . . . to initiate steps that will lead toward recovery, he will verily be hailed as a great man."[35]

When the new president closed the nation's banking system in his first week in office—university officials had been warned of the impending action, apparently by someone at Riggs Bank—the university withdrew $200,000 to the rooms of Edmund Walsh and the college treasurer for safekeeping.[36] The banks were reopened a week later, and the new administration began to spend, not cut, and to add personnel, not reduce them. Thirty thousand positions were added to the government payroll over the next year and a half; for the rest of the decade the number of new positions would total 66,000, nearly one-third of the District's entire work force at the start of the decade.[37] By the end of the new administration's first month in office, a writer in the *Hoya* proclaimed that "we, the people of the United States," have been witnessing the working out of a great miracle. . . . Franklin D. Roosevelt in the short time in which he has been in office has made the New Deal a living thing. . . . The destiny of America is in good hands."[38] At the end of 1933, the student paper was enthusing that "the objectives are plain: to win back the land where prosperity formerly waved and to thrust beyond the frontiers of civilization the Three Horsemen of Want, Famine, and Fear."[39]

Five months later, the same writer, under the headline "Excelsior," was sure that "when the history of the New Era comes to be written, among the names that will stand out in colors as bright as those that enshrine the name of Abraham Lincoln the emancipator, will be that of the thirty-seventh president of these United States."[40] When Roosevelt ran for reelection in 1936, the student press heartily supported him. After Roosevelt's crushing defeat of Alf Landon, Georgetown's weekly paper declared that the president's next objective had to be the reform of the Supreme Court, which continued to undermine the New Deal programs through its rulings on their constitutionality. The paper supported the administration's proposal to enlarge the Supreme Court as the only way to curb the resistance of "the Nine Old Men."[41]

At the university overall enrollment shrank modestly, from 2,148 in 1928 to a low of 1,998 in 1933. At the professional schools, registration either increased slightly, as in medicine, dentistry, and nursing, or remained steady, as in law, throughout the early years of the Depression. But at the undergraduate levels there was a dramatic drop in enrollment, evidence of the toll that the economic crisis was taking, even for affluent Catholics. At the college, student numbers declined nearly 50 percent, from nearly 1,000 in 1928 to 526 five years later. In the fall of 1931 a recent graduate was shocked to discover "scores of empty dormitory rooms in New North and Copley."[42] Several lay instructors were let go. The School of Foreign Service lost one-quarter of its enrollment, from 476 to 313, in the same period, as the federal government halved its work force in the Department of Foreign and Domestic Commerce, a traditional source of employment for foreign service students as well as for faculty.[43] In the spring of 1933, to meet its debts, the school was forced to sell 10,000 Liberty Bonds and reduce the salaries of faculty.[44] The Law School, fearing lower enrollments in the fall of 1932, increased the teaching schedule and also cut the salaries of their full-time faculty to conserve costs.

The following year enrollment did indeed dip, though not as badly as feared. Enrollment rebounded in 1933, but officials found it "harder to collect tuition fees this year."[45] Despite this difficulty, the school managed to meet its expenses. The other schools of the university were much less sol-vent. During the 1934–35 academic year, all schools, with the exception of the Law School, suffered serious financial losses.[46] By the winter of 1934–35, with student enrollment dropping below 300 and despite concerns about potential strings, the School of Foreign Service accepted subsidies from the Federal Emergency Relief Administration, on the condition that the aid go directly to students and not through the school itself.[47] Enrollment subse-quently increased for the first time since 1929 and continued to grow for the remainder of the decade, peaking at 628 in 1940.

By 1932 the college adopted a practice of allowing persons to pay on a deferred schedule. The college treasurer boasted that "no one has been sent away from Georgetown on account of being in arrears."[48] For the 1933–34 academic year, college officials reduced tuition in order to sustain enroll-ment, but the latter continued to decline until 1934. There was a small in-crease over the next three years, but, despite a virtually open admissions policy, enrollments continued to fall below the level needed to meet ex-penses, and the college continued to experience mounting debts.[49] By 1938 its total debt was just short of $90,000 and growing, thanks to the lingering economic depression, faculty salaries for the expanded graduate program, and the high proportion of students (one in six) on athletic scholarships.[50] All departments were under strict orders to spend monies only for what was "absolutely necessary."[51] Nevils discontinued giving contracts to lay faculty, in effect hiring them from month to month, as a measure of financial pru-dence.[52] Attempts to economize in the midpart of the decade by greatly re-ducing the number of workmen at the university provided little relief to its financial stress.

College Life in the 1930s

In 1931 President Nevils instituted the position of dean of the college. This represented only one move on Nevils's part to professionalize the administra-tion and faculty of the university's oldest division. He also was responsible for hiring several established academicians, all with PhDs, such as Anton J. Lang, a German immigrant with a doctorate from the University of Göttinger, who chaired the modern languages department from 1932 to 1960; Emeran Jo-seph Kolkmeyer, who chaired the physics department in 1929; and Theodore Maynard of the English department. During his first year he added two prom-ising Jesuits, Paul McNally, SJ, a physicist and astronomer (PhD 1928, Ford-ham University), to head the Georgetown Observatory, and Frederick Wyatt Sohon, SJ, who had had extensive training in astronomy in Europe, to teach mathematics and astronomy and eventually to take over the Seismological Observatory after Tondorf's death. Nevils especially was drawn to George-town alumni or those working toward degrees at Georgetown in his faculty

Joseph Solterer, professor of economics. (Georgetown University Archives)

appointments. George Francis Harbin (AB 1902) was appointed instructor in mathematics in 1929; Joseph Solterer (PhD 1932) became an instructor in economics in 1928 and eventually chair of the department; Bernard M. Wagner (PhB 1924), with a master of arts from Harvard, returned to Georgetown as a member of the English department in 1931; James Ruby (AB 1928) also received an appointment as a faculty member of English and eventually chaired the department.

The College of Arts and Sciences had three degree programs in its curriculum by the 1930s: a bachelor of arts, a bachelor of science, and a bachelor of philosophy (for students preparing for legal studies or business; in 1933 a bachelor of science in social science [BSSS] replaced the PhB). The Nevils administration had discontinued, in 1929, the two-year premedical course.

All students preparing to enter Medical School at Georgetown were now required to take the four-year bachelor of science program. The traditional required courses in classical languages, literature, philosophy, and theology still dominated the curriculum, especially in the arts program. As President Arthur O'Leary noted in his inaugural address in 1935, "Our aim is to provide an education adapted to the integral man. Education is a progressive and harmonious development of all the higher faculties—principally of the intellect and the will." To do that required the imposition of a carefully constructed core curriculum that had proven its worth over the four centuries of Jesuit involvement in higher education. Beyond that prerequisite, some choice in subjects could be permitted the student.[53] Indeed, since 1923 a modest number of electives had been introduced for those seeking an AB or PhB in junior and senior years in order for students to concentrate on a major field of studies (philosophy, English, education, economics, political science, sociology, history, French, German, Spanish, Latin, and Greek). Six courses in each field were required to fulfill the major. In 1938 comprehensive examinations in the major field were made a requirement for all seniors.

There was some student concern about the makeup of the curriculum. Too much of the junior and senior years, they felt, were devoted to philosophy (twenty-four hours, more than half of one's courses in senior year) and not enough time devoted to science for nonscience majors or to the major fields for all students. And the lockstep concentration on Latin and Greek during the first two years, which treated alike those with classical background and those lacking it but seeking the bachelor of arts degree, seemed to some student critics both wasteful and nonproductive.[54] There was also much dissatisfaction with the scholastic format of theology that presented religion as a series of abstract propositions, watered-down versions of seminary courses. Such unhappiness with theology was not confined to Georgetown students but was widespread within Jesuit colleges in the region. In 1940, Jesuit educational directors asked John Courtney Murray, a professor of theology at Woodstock College, to develop a new approach to teaching theology at the college level. The following year, as a result of Murray's reconceptualization, the college introduced a new syllabus in theology that stressed not the rational structure of Catholicism and the apologetical approach but the faith-based commitment that led believers to engage the world within the social apostolate of the church, that is, by "Catholic Action." The importance of theology within the curriculum was recognized by the increase of credits for its combined required courses from eight to twelve.[55]

Extracurricular organizations and activities, heavily promoted by Nevils and the deans of the college, boomed during the period. By 1929 there were at least twenty-three such clubs, including three debating societies, three musical groups (band, glee club, and orchestra), two religious societies (Sodality and John Berchmans), language clubs (French and German), the Literary Society, the Chemistry Academy, Mask and Bauble, the journal, a newspaper, a yearbook (*Ye Domesday Booke*), the Current Events Club, and the Pathfinders Club (a career opportunities organization). The *Hoya* noted already at the close of 1929 how actively the student body was becoming involved in the various activities as both members and the number of organizations continued to grow.[56] During the subsequent decade, other clubs were introduced, including a classics society (the Horace Academy) and a poetry society (Vergilian Academy, later Gerard Manley Hopkins Society).

Georgetown's second oldest club, the Philodemic Debating Society, was in the midst of its golden age. Georgetown's greatest success in intercollegiate competition during the decade came in debating. Under the direction of John J. Toohey, SJ, professor of logic, who moderated debating at Georgetown from 1912 to 1943, the Philodemic Debating Society gained national prominence for its unequaled success. By 1930, when the society celebrated its centennial, it had compiled a remarkable record of thirty-one victories out of thirty-six intercollegiate contests. Indeed, for seventeen years, from 1921 to 1938, Georgetown debaters went undefeated in intercollegiate competition. The Georgetown debaters stressed eloquence and style as much as argumentation in compiling their string of victories over such schools as Yale,

The Debating Society, Georgetown's most successful team in intercollegiate competition in the interwar years. (Georgetown University Archives. Photo by Stewart Brothers)

Dartmouth, Columbia, Princeton, Harvard, the University of Pennsylvania, the University of Pittsburgh, Johns Hopkins, William and Mary, and Williams. Despite its success, the Philodemic usually drew scant audiences for its home debates in Gaston Hall.

Mask and Bauble, the venerable acting company within the college, enjoyed its own revival during the decade. In 1931, for the first time in several years, it staged a major play, "If I Were King." Thereafter Mask and Bauble put on one major production annually, usually for a run of several days. In 1934, in an attempt to reach the general public, it presented "The Tavern" at the Belasco Theater. A notable innovation in the casting was the use of Trinity College students in the female roles. The play drew positive reviews from the city's papers, but the disappointing attendance forced subsequent productions back onto campus in following years. Two years later, "In the Fool's Bauble" played for four February nights at Gaston Hall before pitiably small audiences, despite heavy advertising. Rain and sleet plagued the region during the run, but the college producers sadly concluded that the weather was not the culprit behind the paltry crowds. "We have come to the conclusion," one observed, "that the people of Washington are not interested in college plays."[57] The following year brought some small improvement in public response when the Mask and Bauble presented "Loyalties." Gaston Hall was half filled for Patron's Night, a benefit performance for the indigent sick of Georgetown Hospital, but saw far smaller gatherings for the following performances. "A college play," the Jesuit diarist lamented, "does not seem to appeal to the people who find their pleasure in professional acting, operas or movies."[58]

The ROTC remained the largest extracurricular activity within the university, with a majority of the students enrolled in the voluntary program, many of them for two additional years beyond the required two. The annual drill and review on the athletic field was a highlight of the spring semester. A six-week summer camp for corps members followed. It enjoyed huge popularity and support on campus. There was little sympathy on the Hilltop for the antiwar mood spreading across college campuses in the early 1930s.

The glee club continued to have a limited schedule of concerts during the year. In January 1932, for the first time, it performed over the air, on a nationwide hookup as part of the Sunday program, "The Church of the Air."[59] The university band, outfitted in uniforms of blue and gray, had become the ROTC band by the 1930s. It regularly performed in military and civic parades, including the inauguration of Franklin Delano Roosevelt in 1933. Together with the Collegians, a twelve-piece orchestra, it gave occasional concerts on campus, including the annual military concert in May on the White-Gravenor esplanade.

Religious exercises continued to be a prominent part of Georgetown student life. Daily mass for resident students was still a requirement. In the fall, three-day preached retreats were held for residents and commuters, respectively. On Sunday evenings in Dahlgren Chapel there was benediction. During May there were daily devotions to Mary in Dahlgren, which drew a majority of the students to recite the Litany of Our Lady and to hear a short talk by a sodalist about a particular virtue of Mary. In May 1933, to mark the Holy Year proclaimed by Pope Pius XI, the university held a special holy hour, during which President Coleman Nevils preached, students recited the Litany of the Sacred Heart, and solemn benediction was given, concluding with the hymn, "Heart of Jesus, May Thy Reign, O'er the World Its Power Regain."[60] On Thanksgiving Day there was a formal procession of the students, according to classes, to the athletic field, where the student body president read the president's Thanksgiving Day proclamation and a member of the faculty addressed the students about the religious significance of the day.

In October 1936 the university welcomed the papal secretary of state, Eugenio Cardinal Pacelli (later Pope Pius XII), to campus. Greeted by a double line of Georgetown students in ROTC uniforms or cap and gown that extended from the gates of the university to Healy Hall, the cardinal was escorted to Gaston Hall, where an honorary degree of Juris Utriusque Doctor was conferred upon him. "It was an event unprecedented in the history of the University," the *College Journal* reported, "for never before had Georgetown been given the honor of greeting one who occupied so high a position in the affairs of the Church."[61] The cardinal saluted Georgetown as "the Alma Mater of all Catholic Colleges in the United States" and noted the "signal service" the university had given to church and country over the past century and a half. At the conclusion of the cardinal's address, the student president rose to his feet in the audience and, waving his fist, shouted, "OK, fellows, hit it!" The entire student body stood and thundered throughout the hall, "Hoya, Hoya, Saxa! Hoya Georgetown! Pacelli, Pacelli, Pacelli!" and broke into deafening applause. The cardinal, at first perplexed, if not somewhat unnerved by the strange proceedings, ended up immensely pleased by the singular tribute.[62]

For its first century and a half, officials at the institution had maintained discipline basically through an unwritten tradition. For the most part there was a regimenting of daily student life, from mandatory chapel at seven, through room checks by prefects, to lights-out at eleven. "It was a life," one alumnus remembered, "regulated by bells and prefects on campus and of getting permission from the Prefect of Discipline for almost any activity other than chapel, classes, or a walk on the Mile Path."[63] "The whole college," another recalled, "had an atmosphere like one of the Jesuit seminaries."[64]

By 1939 life at Georgetown, authorities seemed to recognize, had become too complex to be any longer governed by common custom and oral tradition. This recognition may have been quickened by a student protest during the previous year. In March 1938 an open letter from the Georgetown undergraduates to the administration appeared in the local newspapers; it expressed their grievances regarding the level of tuition, the quality of the dining hall food, and the numbing discipline under which they were constantly forced to live.[65] That evening the students organized a parade in the quadrangle with torches and firecrackers to underscore their demands. Subsequently the student council (the governing body of the college) and administration officials reached an agreement by which the students promised no further protests in return for the administration's agreeing to improve the food service and to take their other grievances under consideration. As a result the woman who had been in charge of student food services for the previous sixteen years was dismissed, and the students' dining room was converted into a cafeteria by the following school year.[66] In the spring of 1939, there was a codification of custom with the first *Student Regulation Manual.* Two years later all forms of hazing, violent or otherwise, were officially banned after a particularly bloody interclass brawl involving fire hoses, fisticuffs, and other forms of mayhem.

Georgetown entered the electronic age in 1941 when the college, with equipment provided by Edmund Walsh, established a student-run broadcasting station, WGTB. The range of the station was restricted by the Federal Communications Commission to the area of the main campus. Initially operating in the afternoons and evenings, WGTB featured music and news.

The vast majority of Georgetown college graduates in the 1930s continued to seek careers in law, medicine, and business, with a growing number entering the seminary to study for the priesthood. Of the class of 1933, thirty-nine went on to study law, nineteen to study medicine, five to study business, and twelve entered business directly. Three graduates began studies for the priesthood. By the end of the decade, a majority of graduates were still choosing to pursue the law, but the number choosing medical school had dropped sharply, as had those entering business, while those entering the seminary had increased. In fact, the number of alumni studying for the priesthood more than doubled from the 1920s to the 1930s (from seventeen to forty-one).

Hard times and social crisis were bad for business opportunities but apparently conducive to fostering vocations. Joseph Brunini (AB 1930) and George H. Guilfoyle (AB 1935) eventually became bishops of Jackson (Mississippi) and Camden (New Jersey), respectively. Among those who did achieve success in business were Walter Owen Briggs Jr. (BS 1934), Howard Gunlocke (AB 1934), John James Powers Jr. (AB 1934), Daniel F. Reeves (AB 1933), Henry deCastro (BS 1931), and William Sullivan (AB 1931). Briggs, the son of the Detroit automaker and owner of the Detroit Tigers, went on to inherit both. Gunlocke started a furniture business in upstate New York. Dan Reeves, with his family inheritance, purchased a seat on the New York Stock Exchange and became owner of the Cleveland Rams in the National Football League in 1941. Powers, after practicing law for a few years, joined the Pfizer Company in 1940 and played a key role in transforming it from a small specialty chemical house to a worldwide giant in pharmaceuticals and hospital supplies. Henry deCastro defied the economic climate of the 1930s to achieve

Philip A. Hart (center), **C** 1934, future U.S. senator. Joseph G. Smith, left; Jerome J. Downey, right. (Georgetown University Archives)

success as a salesman, entrepreneur, and inventor (lemon- and lime-shaped juice squeezers, fabric dyes, etc.). William Sullivan became head of the Metropolitan Life Insurance Company.

Of those going on to study law, Philip Hart (AB 1934) received his LLB from the University of Michigan in 1937. In 1951 he left the practice of law to enter government service, first at the state level in Michigan, then as a U.S. senator from that state for three terms beginning in 1958. In the Senate he was a leader in promoting civil rights legislation, consumer protection bills, and gun control, for which he earned the title "conscience of the Senate" in the 1960s and 1970s.

Some graduates went into journalism or higher education. Jack Spalding (AB 1936) eventually became editor in chief of the *Atlanta Journal.* Martin Quigley Jr. (AB 1939) went into film journalism and headed up Quigley Publications, publishers of *The Motion Picture Herald* and the *Motion Picture Almanac.* William Wimsatt (AB 1928) earned a PhD in English literature at Yale University, where he joined the faculty and became a leader in the critical theory known as New Criticism.

The Medical School: Division and Sanction

In September 1928, George Kober resigned as dean of the Medical School, a post he had held for twenty-seven years. The seventy-eight-year-old Kober had been increasingly frustrated by the interference of the regent, Walter Summers, SJ, in the administration of the school. The final straw was the decision to build the Medical School on the Reservoir Road site. Kober had for more than a decade been pursuing the vision of a medical center that would develop outward from the existing hospital and embrace a six-block area between the borders of 35th, P, 37th, and Prospect streets. This would unite, for the first time, hospital and school, whose separation the accrediting agencies (the AMA and AAMC) had over the years cited as a shortcoming. To place the new school a mile from the hospital would be to continue the old situation. Conversely, to relocate the hospital eventually to the new school site, as was now planned, would be to dishonor the benefactors who had made the old hospital possible, a process in which Kober had played a large role. Building the school on the new site, at a much greater cost than the projected one on the 37th Street site, would also leave the university saddled with millions of dollars in debt that it had little capacity to retire.[67] That the decision had been made, seemingly so suddenly, in August when Kober was out of town on vacation, only compounded the pain. Whether Walter Summers played a role in persuading Nevils to change the site at such a late moment is unknown, but Kober probably suspected Summers's hand in the switch. At any rate, Kober resigned and was named dean emeritus.

The construction of the new medical-dental complex at a cost of $1 million left the university with a debt of approximately $800,000, which it attempted to retire by greatly increasing the size of the student body at the school. From an enrollment of 344 in 1926, the school numbered nearly 600 students five years later, making Georgetown Medical School the largest in the nation, more than twice the size of the average school, and putting enormous stress on the teaching staff, which was forced to carry teaching loads two to three times higher than normal in medical education.[68]

If the new building led to a greatly augmented student enrollment that strained both faculty and facilities, it also provided the occasion for the beginning of serious medical research at Georgetown. Government funding and, particularly, foundation support were making research a major component of medical education institutions by the second quarter of the twentieth century. By the 1920s nearly thirty foundations, led by the Rockefeller-financed General Education Board, were providing funding for medical research, often to clinical professors at prestigious medical schools for work on specific diseases.[69] Georgetown, however, with its largely part-time faculty and lack of facilities, had no active researchers and had realized no such funding. When Walter Summers became regent in 1924, Georgetown sought to be part of this research enterprise. The catalyst was George L. Coyle, SJ, a member of the chemistry department. Coyle, who had earned his doctorate in organic chemistry at the University of Göttingen in Germany and was a fellow of the American Association for the Advancement of Science, was actively involved in chemical research, and he had published many papers and several books on chemistry and chemical education. Acting on a report to the American Chemical Society that cited the need for a center that could concentrate on chemo-medical research to alleviate suffering from cancer and related diseases, Coyle persuaded Summers and then-president Lyons in 1924 to establish at Georgetown an endowed institute of fundamental chemical research, devoted to the study of important problems in the field of chemotherapy treatment for cancer.[70]

Over the next several years Coyle attempted to raise the $4 million estimated as a minimum for the construction of the building and facilities for the intended research. By 1928 he had secured pledges of nearly $3 million for the institute from foundations and individuals. When the Depression struck, many of the pledges went unredeemed. Still, Coyle, along with a former member of the United States Public Health Department, was able to begin some research by 1931 in quarters provided in the new medical building. "The research work . . . is progressing favorably," he reported in late 1931, "and we hope in six months to announce an early diagnostic test for cancer. . . . We have also discovered the mother substance produced by cancer and hope later to be able to stop its formation."[71] Tragically, Coyle, sixty-two, died suddenly of a cerebral hemorrhage at the beginning of 1932. The cancer research continued for a while under Dr. M. X. Sullivan, now within the chemistry department of the college and with very modest support ($1,000) from the university.[72] It would be nearly another half century before Georgetown realized a cancer research and treatment center.

By the 1920s not only were clinical professors in medical schools becoming full-time, as their preclinical colleagues had become a generation before, but also the laboratory rather than the case report was becoming the key instrument of their research.[73] In 1929, Georgetown appointed its first full-time clinical professor, Wallace Mason Yater (MD 1921), who had been a fellow at the Mayo Clinic and a disciple of Henry A. Christian, the clinical physician who stressed the importance of combining patient observation with laboratory pathological studies for effective clinical research. Yater's appointment marked the beginning of modern clinical research at the school and hospital. Walter Summers was responsible for persuading Yater to leave the Mayo Clinic to return to his alma mater as professor of medicine with the promise of becoming chair of the department upon the retirement of its incumbent.[74] Yater became one of the school's most prolific researchers, publishing more than 145 papers and two textbooks during his sixteen years at Georgetown.

When Yater succeeded to the chair of medicine in the spring of 1930 upon the sudden death of Wilfred Barton, he brought in a former colleague from the Mayo Clinic, Jacob Markowitz, to chair the Department of Physiology and to provide another top-flight researcher to the faculty, in this case the first Georgetown professor to specialize in animal research. Markowitz's wife, Cecile, was also an experienced research

Wallace Mason Yater, **M** 1921, first full-time clinical professor. (*Ye Domesday Booke*)

scientist who continued her experiments as an independent researcher at Georgetown.[75] In his first year at Georgetown, before a national audience of visiting doctors, Jacob Markowitz teamed with Yater in a pathbreaking experiment in transplanting a dog's heart into the neck of another, a success that made possible later developments in cardiovascular surgery and organ transplants.[76] Yater was also responsible for recruiting Theodore Koppanyi from the University of Chicago in the fall of 1930. Koppanyi, a pharmacist trained in Vienna, became the school's most productive researcher during the 1930s. During his four decades at the school, he wrote more than eight hundred papers on pharmacology, particularly on the study of barbiturates, which earned national recognition.[77] In 1933 Owen Stanley Gibbs, a British graduate from the University of Edinburgh and an accomplished experimental scientist, became head of the Department of Physics at the school.

The following year two other researchers, Charles J. Stucky and Joseph L. Schwind, joined the Medical School. Stucky, a biochemist, came from the New York State Psychiatric Institute, where he had conducted research on the applicability of biochemistry to psychiatry. Schwind had been a member of the anatomy department of the Cornell Medical School and had authored numerous papers on biological subjects. Other researchers were brought in from Harvard, Johns Hopkins, Rochester, Pennsylvania, and Yale. By 1934 an inspector for the Commission for Higher Education in New York reported that Georgetown's buildup of its medical faculty for research over the past year and a half had been "phenomenal." Practically every department, he noted, was engaged in productive medical research.[78] This revitalization of the faculty had taken place through a combination of deaths, resignations, and recruitment. Yater replaced Barton as chair of medicine in 1930. In 1933 George Tully Vaughan agreed to step down as head of surgery and was succeeded by James Augustine Cahill (MD 1915), Fellow of the College of Surgeons.

In part this changeover reflected an attempt to Catholicize the faculty. During the decade there was a very conscious effort to make the school as Catholic as possible in its administration, faculty, and students. In 1928 the superior general of the Jesuits had issued a letter to regional superiors that insisted that every school in every Jesuit institution have a Catholic administration and faculty.[79] By 1933 the president reported to the provincial superior that the university had fully complied with the directive of the superior general regarding department heads. He noted that James Augustine Cahill and Joseph Mundell, both Catholics, had been named heads of the important departments of surgery and obstetrics, respectively, previously occupied by non-Catholics.[80] On at least one occasion the board of directors denied the dean and regent permission to appoint a professor to the school on the grounds that he was not Catholic.[81]

But the selection of Catholics to head departments, or even the school itself, was limited, usually, by available choices. When the deanship became vacant in 1931, William Gerry Morgan, a non-Catholic, had been chosen as the strongest candidate, largely through faculty pressure. Other chairs had been filled by non-Catholics, such as Yater or Markowitz, because of previous commitments or other circumstances. In 1934 complaints were finding their way to the provincial superior about the large number of non-Catholics and those of no religion holding faculty positions and making Georgetown Medical School known, one Catholic critic wrote, as "the Godless School."[82] When the provincial made his annual visitation of Georgetown in the fall of 1934, in his report on the Medical School he reiterated the "ideal of having an all-Catholic Staff" and the "mandatory regulation" that the dean be Catholic.[83] Despite official policy and commitment, the school's Catholic faculty remained a distinct minority, about one-third of the total teaching and research staff.

The school's student composition was heavily Catholic at the beginning of the 1930s and remained so throughout, constituting nearly 90 percent of the student population. Most had in fact done their undergraduate work in Catholic colleges; nearly 40 percent of the students had done their collegiate studies at Georgetown. Most of the students were from the Middle Atlantic region; three states—Pennsylvania, New Jersey, and New York—often accounted for more than 60 percent of the school's students in any given year. A quota was established for Jews in 1934—with a maximum of five to be admitted.[84] This was not to correct a heavy Jewish influx, as many prestigious institutions such as Harvard and Cornell were experiencing, but was seemingly a proactive move. Previously there had been no more than a handful of Jewish students at Georgetown in any one year. As Nevils wrote in that year, "We don't want to build up our Medical and Dental School with the foreign element, particularly with a large number of the Semitic element."[85]

A new constitution was drawn up as part of the reorganization, clearly in part to put more authority in the hands of the president and regent and less in the hands of the executive faculty. A superior council was created, which consisted of the president, the regent, and the dean of the school, which took over some powers formerly held by the executive faculty.[86]

The resignation of Kober in the fall of 1928 was the beginning of six years of administrative turmoil for the Medical School. After several months of fruitless searches for an outside dean by Nevils and Kober, the appointment went to an insider, John Ambrose Foote (MD 1906), who had been professor of pediatrics at the school since 1921. Foote was in poor health and served in the position barely more than a year. In the meantime Jesuit authorities removed Walter Summers in the summer of 1929, just after the cornerstone laying of the new Medical-Dental Building, whose construction Summers had played such a large role in bringing about. Summers had been the point man in persuading the Jesuit authorities of the urgent need to build. They had badly outgrown their existing facilities downtown, and their obsolete facilities were endangering their class A ranking. "We must begin a new building—to be ready for occupancy not later than September 1929," Summers had written to the provincial superior in the late winter of 1928.[87] Now, despite his resistance, he was transferred to St. Joseph's College in Philadelphia.

Summers had been regent for five years, virtually a dean of both the Medical and Dental schools. On his watch there had been the mass resignation of dental faculty three years earlier. That had led to talk of removing him, but Summers had successfully pleaded his case with the provincial. Summers had alienated many of the medical faculty as well by attempting to remove those he deemed wanting. Then there was his ongoing dispute with the Franciscan nuns on their operation of the hospital, which led the sisters to threaten to leave if Summers remained.[88] Administration officials sustained the authority of the nuns and ordered Summers to stay away from the hospital in June 1929.[89] The new president, Coleman Nevils, had finally written in exasperation in June 1929, "I haven't the physical strength to stand the constant upheavals. . . . Hospital, Medical School, and Dental School are constant worries, in fact beyond me if Fr. Summers remains." The provincial superior made a personal investigation of the situation, found that many of Summers's complaints about the hospital's administration and school faculty were justified, but faulted him for the rash manner in which he attempted to address them.[90] He removed him two months later in August. In his place the provincial appointed John Gipprich, SJ, chairman of the physics department at the college, who had also taught in the Medical School.

Gipprich proved to be an even more disruptive regent than Summers had been. Within a year his actions had fractured the faculty into two blocs, roughly the basic science faculty versus the clinical faculty. Gipprich very much opposed the turn toward faculty research as a central goal for the school. Teaching, not research, had to be the top priority. Consequently, he promoted the interests of the basic sciences rather than those of the clinicians. (Ironically, the buildup of research faculty came during his tenure, despite his opposition.) His rigid, high-handed manner and vindictiveness alienated dean, faculty, and students alike. By the summer of 1931, Nevils and his consultants wanted to replace him, but the provincial superior, a friend of Gipprich, refused to act on their request.[91] A controversy had occurred in 1931 when Dean Foote had died suddenly in April. The faculty, with virtual unanimity, thought they had an excellent candidate in their own ranks to succeed Foote. William Gerry Morgan was a noted gastroenterologist who had been elected president of the AMA in 1929. Gipprich, however, wanted to appoint one of his basic science colleagues as Foote's successor. The senior faculty, getting word of this, revolted. In a secret meeting the department chairmen and other senior professors resolved to resign in a body should Gipprich's choice become dean. Informed of the senior faculty's intention, Nevils persuaded the provincial to disregard Gipprich's advice and acquiesce in the appointment of Morgan.[92]

In the summer of 1932, a New York doctor wrote Nevils that he had been asked by the president of the AAMC to act as an informal investigator of a critical situation at Georgetown Medical School that had come to the association's attention. According to information that the AAMC had received, there was "serious dissension in the faculty as to the integrity of two principal men in the Department of Anatomy." The chair of the department, Joseph Madigan, was accused of accepting money from failing students in return for passing grades. A professor of histology, George A. Bennett, had falsified his credentials by claiming to have a medical degree and passing off as his own papers that had been written by a man with the same last name.[93]

Neither of these charges was new, as Nevils informed the New York doctor. Rumors of Madigan's questionable, if not venal, practices had been circulating for years: that he forced his students to buy his notes; that he invited failing students to his home to read, for a price, notes about a particular course; and that he passed students for money. In 1928 a fellow faculty member brought these charges to the executive faculty, but the latter defended Madigan by claiming that he was justified in securing a reasonable return for the cost of producing the notes and by dismissing as baseless the charges that he accepted bribes for passing grades. The then regent, Walter Summers, had led the defense for Madigan, and Summers's successor, Gipprich, supported him as well. But the rumors persisted, and the faculty was increasingly divided over whether Madigan should be dismissed. Nevils suspected that the charges of bribery were true ("it is so universally spoken of") but pointed out that no solid proof had been found on the previous two occasions in which charges had been raised against Madigan: "I have never been able to get such a statement as could be defended in court in case we were sued for libel."[94]

Bennett was an even more divisive force within the faculty. In 1930 Gipprich had appointed the twenty-eight-year-old Bennett, whom he had known as an instructor in the physics department of the college, to the histology department without consulting anyone on the medical faculty. Gipprich then charged Bennett with revising the curriculum of the first two years of courses. When Bennett began acting on this commission, several faculty members, including Wallace Yater, found it intolerably intrusive. Through his own investigation, Yater discovered that Bennett had received no medical degree at the University of Heidelberg as he claimed (his highest degree was an AB from Wabash College) and that the publications he advertised as his own were really the work of a C. A. Bennett at Harvard, where George A. Bennett had been a teaching fellow for three years. Yater and Markowitz publicly accused Bennett of being an imposter.

Bennett's defense was that he never pretended to have a medical degree and that he had not imagined that anyone would think the imprints were his own.[95] The issue split the executive faculty broadly between the basic science professors and the clinicians, led by Yater, Markowitz, and acting dean Prentiss Willson. Willson had hesitated to bring the matter up, precisely because he feared that it would provoke a fatal split between the preclinical and clinical faculty, out of which would come a reorganization of the faculty by the victorious group, which Willson feared would be the preclinical faculty, as Gipprich was in their camp.[96] As it turned out, Gipprich strongly backed Bennett and no action was taken. Instead, Willson's fears about a purge were realized within the next year when both Markowitz and Willson were forced out, Markowitz on grounds of a lack of collegiality and Willson for teaching therapeutic abortion, although colleagues thought that the stated reasons were pretexts for the real cause of dissent from the regent's administration.

Nevils suspected that Markowitz and/or Willson were the sources of the complaints that had reached the Association's ear. Nonetheless, he admitted that there was no defense for Bennett and that he should indeed be terminated. The provincial, whose ear Gipprich had, was convinced that the present complaints were part of "a blackmail affair" of the former faculty dissidents.[97] But Dean Morgan was more impressed with the charges, at least those against Madigan, than was the provincial. A recent graduate of the school who was a current intern at the hospital had come forward to provide the direct evidence that authorities had sought in vain for over a decade. He testified that he had paid $100 (he claimed Madigan had initially demanded $250) in order to pass an anatomy exam and that he had acted as an agent for other students who had paid Madigan $100 to $500 for passing grades. The dean called a special meeting of the executive faculty to report the charges, hear the evidence of the intern, and warn the faculty that the school could not afford an investigation of this matter. Despite Gipprich's opposition, the faculty agreed that Madigan must go, and two days later the university told him that his contract would not be renewed.[98] Bennett remained, apparently protected by Gipprich.

In the summer of 1933, James A. Gannon, associate professor of surgery, submitted his resignation from the school in protest of the school's policies under Gipprich. The immediate issue, Gannon informed Nevils, was the forced resignation of George Tully Vaughan, but the underlying ones were the admission policy that was accepting far more students than could be effectively taught, the subsequent growing number of failures of graduates in state examinations (in 1932 no fewer than one-fifth had failed, the highest failure rate in the country), the dismissal of Willson for his purported abortion views, and above all the dictatorial governance of Gipprich, who had seized power that "properly belongs to the Faculty and the Staff," as he had come to control absolutely all faculty appointments and to make the dean his "tool." Gannon thought that the university urgently needed to take four steps regarding the school: (a) the number of students in any class should be reduced to fifty, (b) the Supreme Council should be abolished, (c) the duties of the regent should be explicitly defined, and (d) due authority needed to be restored to faculty and staff.[99]

When Gannon subsequently laid his evaluation of the school's problems and needs before the provincial superior, the latter, apparently taken aback by the charges against Gipprich, wanted to know from Nevils whether the school really had become a "one-man affair" and was deteriorating, as Gannon believed.[100] Nevils assured him that Gannon was wildly exaggerating about Gipprich's control and that his comments on the deplorable state of the school were "unfounded." Gannon, Nevils informed Phillips, was simply embittered that he had not been chosen to succeed Vaughan as chair of surgery.[101] Despite his disavowal of Gannon's charges, the friction between Gipprich and much of the Medical School faculty was a concern for Nevils. Nine months later, in the spring of 1934, Nevils and his consultors concluded that although "things have improved at the Medical School in some respects," there was still "an attitude of dislike and distrust" on the part of the faculty toward the regent. Dean Morgan had indicated that it would be wise to replace Gipprich. The president and consultors concurred. The provincial was apparently reluctant to make the change but after "long consideration and consultation" replaced Gipprich with David V. McCauley, SJ, a biologist and professor of empirical psychology at Woodstock College, in the summer of 1934.[102] One of McCauley's first actions was a revision of the school's constitution that made clear the president's final authority over the Supreme Council and executive faculty and his singular power to make all appointments.

The following winter in New York the secretary of the AMA, William Cutter, requested a meeting with the provincial superior, Edward Phillips. When Phillips arrived at the secretary's office, Cutter startled him by asking whether he had any fundamental reason for continuing the Medical School at Georgetown; if not, Cutter thought it a prudent time for the school to close, before it was forced to do so by outside accrediting agencies. If Phillips chose to continue it, the school, despite the progress it had shown over the past few years (reduction of students, faculty additions), had much to do to satisfy the required high standards. It could no longer depend exclusively on tuition but needed a minimum endowment that would provide $500 per student. The admission of students had to be much more selective; too many currently were from New York, all too often rejects of New York medical schools. The secretary pledged that the association stood ready to assist the school in every possible way to overcome its problems.[103] It is likely that either Wallace Yater or Morgan was behind Cutter's intervention. Yater had close friends within the hierarchy of the AMA and kept them apprised of the state of things at the Medical School; Morgan was a good friend of Cutter's.[104] In any event, Phillips accepted Cutter's offer and over the next year was in consultation with him about the school.

Within a month of Cutter's meeting with Phillips, the AMA's Council on Medical Education and Hospitals conducted a scheduled inspection of the school and placed it on confidential probation "because of manifest deficiencies." The deficiencies were ones that previous inspection groups had reported but tolerated in the precarious years of the early Depression. There were too many students, many of them not meeting the minimum academic standards for admission to an approved medical school. This, the team implied, was perhaps a result of the obvious preference given to Catholics for admission. There was virtually no endowment. The library was below standard in its holdings of journals and volumes (fewer than 11,000). Some departments, notably anatomy and histology, were not sufficiently or ably staffed. "Most of the Preclinical Departments were not alone understaffed, but certain of the Department Heads were apparently incompetent," they judged. In short, there were too many unqualified students; too few full-time, qualified faculty; no endowment; and a confused organization, particularly between the regent and the dean.[105]

David V. McCauley, SJ, regent and dean of the Medical School, 1934–46. (Georgetown University Archives)

In light of the criticism of the division of authority between dean and regent, William Morgan resigned in June 1935. In his last months in office, President Nevils attempted to secure for the school a full-time dean for the first time, but his successor, Arthur O'Leary, on the advice of the provincial in consultation with Cutter, decided to amalgamate, for at least the time being, the two positions of regent and dean.[106] This meant, of course, since the regent by definition had to be a Jesuit, that the regent would become dean. McCauley was consequently appointed Medical School dean shortly before the new academic year began in 1935. It was a move the executive faculty unanimously endorsed, so effectively had McCauley won the respect and support of the faculty through his energetic, irenic administration as regent during the previous year. As dean, one of his first actions was to raise admission standards and sharply reduce the size of the incoming medical class for 1936 to 100. Enrollment dropped from 507 in 1934–35 to 337 by 1938–39. He also eliminated most of the teaching fellows who had previously handled much prebasic teaching and several incompetent faculty members, including department heads.

Despite these actions, the school received a further accreditation threat from the AAMC in the spring of 1938 when its team of inspectors found the university still short of meeting the expected standards regarding admissions (sixty, not one hundred, should be the maximum for any class), the staffing of preclinical departments, and opportunities for clinical instruction. The team recommended that Georgetown be put on probation.[107] McCauley and the executive faculty suspected some anti-Catholic bias at play. The dean pointed out that, of the forty-three schools originally scheduled for AAMC visits during the year, only three Jesuit medical schools were actually inspected and all three recommended for probation.[108] The executive faculty reported to the president and directors that there apparently was "a movement on foot in certain quarters to force Jesuit-run medical schools out of existence by reducing their rating through the gross exaggeration of minor deficiencies."[109] Nonetheless, the faculty recognized that the lack of an endowment was a fatal weakness of the school. "Without an endowment of at least $3 million the school can not continue to exist," they told the board. An endowment, they argued, was desperately needed to obtain an adequate preclinical staff and to attract and retain experienced clinical professors. The university simply had to make a major effort to procure an adequate endowment as soon as possible.[110]

The board in response authorized McCauley to begin a private fund-raising campaign among selected potential benefactors, as well as to pursue the possibility of securing government funds to construct a new hospital, which would greatly improve clinical education at the school.[111] At the school itself, admissions became more selective, and enrollment continued to fall. The curriculum for clinical education was completely revised, with the elimination of much didactic instruction and with the increase of hospital experience through an agreement reached with Gallinger Hospital, which provided Georgetown students with the opportunity of regular clinical training in wards.[112] The examination of senior students was also made much more rigorous. In 1939 more than one-third of the senior class failed final examinations, an unprecedentedly high rate. When the AAMC revisited the school in November 1939, its team was "agreeably surprised to find so much had been accomplished since our former visit." Its one criticism was that the dean of the school was not a doctor, but overall, as the secretary of the association reported to McCauley, it had given the school "a clean bill of health."[113] Despite this favorable evaluation, the association did not see fit to lift the confidential probation it had imposed on the school a year previously.

Class A Dental School

The decade saw the Dental School acquire national recognition as a top-flight dental institution. With the move into its new facilities in 1929, officials had hoped that this would enable the school to gain a class A rating from the American Dental Association (ADA). But new facilities could not cancel out incompetent faculty and ineffective administration. In the summer of 1930, students had written a collective letter to Regent Gipprich to warn him that "something is wrong with our school." They were failing to get proper instruction in many of their courses, they reported. Student morale was "almost broken." There were, they admitted, some "very fine men" on the faculty, such as John Brezinsky and John Burke. There were also "some awful dead-heads." Unless radical changes were made, students on a massive scale would soon begin voting with their feet.[114] Gipprich needed no warning. As he admitted to Nevils, the "saddest part of the story is that everything" they said "is absolutely true." Something "drastic must be done and the only way it can be done is for you and me to take the matter in our hands and do it."[115]

Less than a year later, the Dental Educational Council of America sent a representative to Georgetown to lay out to President Nevils and Regent Gipprich the council's concerns about the school. They involved central elements of the school's character: Cogan's leadership, the competence of the faculty, admission standards, the curriculum, and the library.[116] Nevils was ready to replace the dean, William Cogan, who had held that office since 1901, except for a period of naval service, with another member of the faculty, Sterling Meade, who was then vice president of the ADA, as a way to gain the association's top ranking. "He would give us a standing that we could not obtain in any other way," Nevils assured Phillips.[117] The provincial, however, advised that Nevils seek an outsider, who, unlike Meade, would be a Catholic.[118] Nothing apparently came of this search (Cogan would finally become dean emeritus in 1938). In the meantime, in 1933 the school raised the entrance requirements to include two years of predental college preparation, a prerequisite that many state accrediting agencies insisted upon.[119] New faculty were appointed, including George Edward Emig, Clemens V. Rault, Charles Murto, and William Brown Ingersoll.

Finally, the school received its long-sought A classification in the summer of 1933. Nevils was sure that, with this new ranking, the school would quickly gain official recognition from all states, including New York, and the potential pool for applicants would become truly national.[120] The following year the New York Commission for Higher Education officially recognized the Dental School for the first time, meaning that Georgetown dental graduates would thereafter be able to practice in New York.[121] That same year a Georgetown graduate, George F. Kopf of New Jersey, led the country in his scores in the national dental boards.[122] By 1936 every state in the country had given the school official recognition, making Georgetown one of the few dental schools to enjoy such national accrediting.

Enrollment grew as Nevils had anticipated. The school had set a limit of 75 for class size in the 1920s, although it had never realized that ceiling. In 1933, with the higher admission standards in place, enrollment plummeted to 14 for the incoming class. By 1935 total school enrollment had rebounded to 165, from a total of 100 the previous year. Enrollments

Dental students in lab in the 1930s. (Photo provided by the author)

continued to grow for the remainder of the decade. By 1941, with more than 200 in the school, there was also a greater distribution from states throughout the East. Previously, a near majority had come from the District of Columbia, with the rest largely from New York and New Jersey. By the end of the decade, relatively few students were from the District. New York and New Jersey still provided large numbers, but the rest of the students came from a broad distribution of states, particularly in the Middle Atlantic and New England regions. One New Yorker, Gustav Otto Kruger (DDS 1939), joined the faculty as professor of oral surgery and eventually chaired that department in the school.

In the spring of 1933 the school began a student-edited journal, the *Georgetown Dental Journal,* which included scientific papers delivered by dental students at meetings of the Dean Cogan Society as well as general articles on dentistry and school news. The journal, one of the few of its kind among dental educational institutions, gained national recognition and lasted, with only a few interruptions, until 1964.[123] Omicron Kappa Upsilon, the national dental honor society, also established a chapter at Georgetown in 1934. In 1929 the school formed an alumni organization specifically to raise money for the new building. The organization survived the building campaign and, beginning in 1937, began holding annual alumni clinics at the school. The first attracted nearly three hundred dentists in February 1937 for a series of seminars, a dinner, and class reunions.

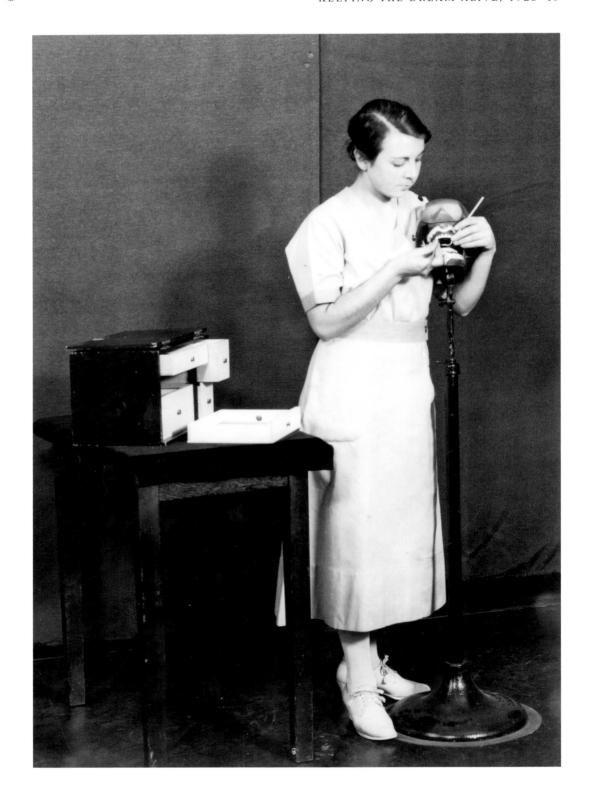

During the early Depression, when enrollments were beginning to decline, a woman's organization approached the university about opening the school to women. "It seems a pity," the chair of the National Women's Party wrote to President Nevils in 1932, "that you have empty chairs when there are women in Washington desiring to take up dentistry as a profession. . . . We hope Georgetown University may be one of the pioneers in this forward-looking moment." The university, however, would not budge on its anticoeducational tradition. The board of directors, Nevils tersely replied, "have felt obliged to refuse any change."[124] In fact the school did, by that time, have gender-integrated classes. In 1929, in response to a growing interest in public health, the school started a dental hygiene program, a one-year course for women with a high school education to become dental assistants and/or public lecturers on hygiene. Students in the program took most of their courses—including anatomy, bacteriology, dental pathology, histology, and chemistry—with the dental students and paid the same tuition—$250—as their male classmates. Lillian Cain, as supervisor of dental hygienists, became the first woman faculty member at the school. But the program failed to attract many candidates, usually ten or fewer, despite the lowering of tuition by one-third after the first couple of years, and the school discontinued the program in 1937. In its eight years it had graduated fifty hygienists.

"His Work['s] Not Yet Finished"

Jesuit rector-presidents normally served two 3-year terms. When Coleman Nevils was nearing the end of his second term in the late spring of 1934, a group of forty-three faculty, alumni, and political dignitaries petitioned the superior general in Rome to extend Nevils's tenure as president. In "a time of universal unrest," it was absolutely essential, they pleaded, that Nevils be allowed to continue his leadership of such an important educational institution. "Confronted by this nation-wide social, moral and industrial disorder, Father Nevils, with a vision and ability that few men possess, . . . from the beginning of his Rectorship has labored successfully to meet them." His work, they pointed out, was not yet finished. "The building program, the location of the professional schools [outside the main gate], . . . broadening the graduate and undergraduate curricula, the creation of a spirit becoming a University, and the bringing of every department to a higher degree of efficiency has not yet reached the stage where Father Nevils can be spared."[125] Thanks to Nevils, the distinguished petitioners pointed out, "the University has assumed at Washington, throughout the Nation, and in foreign countries a position which it has not hitherto enjoyed . . . it has become known in foreign countries more certainly, perhaps, than any other American institution of learning."[126] Within

Georgetown dental hygiene student in the 1930s.
(Georgetown University Archives)

the month, the superior general decided to keep Nevils in office for one more year in order to prepare a successor. Nevils had someone in mind who was already on campus—Arthur O'Leary, who had been on the faculty in the department of philosophy for the past fourteen years and had been the university librarian for the last four.[127] Rome agreed, and the following October O'Leary served as acting president during Nevils's three-month trip to Japan as a representative of the American Red Cross at the international conference.

In his seven years as president of Georgetown, Nevils had left marks both transient and permanent on the life of the university. In a world in which image was becoming more and more a determinant of one's status, Nevils skillfully promoted the university's image, largely through the elaborate ceremonies he staged. His unprecedented extramural outreach to the various segments of public Washington gave the university on an unprecedented scale a presence in the larger society, even if it did not long survive his departure. His deflation of intercollegiate sports proved even more ephemeral than Georgetown's new civic presence, as sports returned to their big-time status by the latter part of the decade. His positioning of Georgetown at the very root of the American Catholic experience, whose ancient history his buildings on the Andrew White Quadrangle symbolized, was an audacious effort to privilege the institution historically in a rather blatant appeal to status-minded Catholics.

His accomplishments as a builder dwarfed those of any of his predecessors, and the new facilities dramatically changed the landscape of the campus. Except for the hard times of the 1930s, he would undoubtedly have changed it much more through the addition of academic and athletic facilities as well as a new law school and hospital on campus, all part of his grand plan to physically integrate and centralize the schools of the university. As it was, he proved a remarkably efficient fund-raiser in the worst of economic times and began to make fund-raising an institutional part of the university through his reactivation of the board of regents, only to have his successor allow the board to lapse once again.

For the oldest school of the university, the College of Arts and Sciences, Nevins took important steps to professionalize its administration and faculty, not the least of which was the unprecedented number of PhDs he appointed to the various departments of the college. He heavily promoted the extracurriculum, which during the 1930s grew to include no fewer than twenty-three clubs that focused on everything from arts, language, and religion to rhetoric, literature, and current events. At the professional level, Nevils brought the administration of the Medical, Dental, and Law Schools more under central authority through the appointment of Jesuit regents for those schools. Also, following the directive of superiors, the president attempted, wherever possible, to Catholicize the faculties, including putting Catholics into the leadership positions of deans and department heads. During Nevils's

presidency the Medical School also joined the modern world of clinical research through the appointment of distinguished clinicians who quickly
made Georgetown a productive medical research center. On his watch, reform of the Dental School took place as well, which involved the raising of
entrance standards and the appointment of faculty, which in turn resulted in
the school's being one of the few in the country to be fully accredited by both
the Dental Educational Council of America and every state in the country.
Nevils's seven years of leadership had proven to be significant ones for
Georgetown—in the final analysis, ones marked more by substantial achievement than mere showmanship, although there were always ample amounts
of the latter.

CHAPTER 6

Renaissance and the "Clouds of War," 1935–41

Mindful of the fact that in the year 1789 Georgetown College was founded, thus beginning its service to the Nation simultaneously with the congress of the United States . . . [we] pledge ourselves anew to the defense of the civil and religious liberties enumerated in that document, under which both the nation and the University have subsisted for the past one hundred and fifty years.

PRESIDENT and DIRECTORS OF GEORGETOWN UNIVERSITY to the Congress of the United States, February 19, 1939

Arthur O'Leary as President

Arthur O'Leary, SJ, officially succeeded Coleman Nevils as president in July 1935. The first native Washingtonian to head Georgetown, O'Leary, the son of a Baltimore & Ohio Railroad worker, was in many ways Nevils's opposite—lanky (well over six feet tall), reticent, psychologically conservative, and wary of the public eye. He was more at home in the library than in Gaston Hall or Embassy Row. The *Washington Post* hailed O'Leary as an excellent choice to follow such "a great and able leader" as Coleman Nevils, who had set the university on such a distinguished path over the past seven years.[1] Certainly his inauguration paralleled Nevils's in grandeur, with a Supreme Court justice, cabinet officers, diplomats, and hundreds of college and university representatives from around the world filling Gaston Hall in late November. In his inaugural address O'Leary affirmed the public purpose of Georgetown's existence:

Arthur O'Leary, SJ, president of Georgetown, 1935–42.
(Georgetown University Archives)

to train men to an understanding of the rights and duties of citizenship . . . a citizenship [not divorced] from religion but founded on a philosophy of life which is balanced and equitable because derived from an unchanging revelation of an unchanging God. If the acknowledgment of a First Cause is the alpha of the physical sciences, reason itself conducts the honest thinker to the omega of moral obligation. . . . That stern logic has continued to be the tradition of Georgetown during the century and a half since Carroll's day. From its foundation the University has continued to link Science and Religion in a training equal to the best in the land.[2]

The public square itself was not part of O'Leary's natural habitat. As one Jesuit who served under him observed, "He was not a great [ambassador to society but] he knew what this university was about and what they needed; he knew and did it."[3] As librarian he had already made one major contribution to the university. Beginning in 1935, O'Leary had comprehensively catalogued the university's holdings of approximately 177,000 volumes according to the Library of Congress classification. It marked the first time that all the holdings of the several undergraduate and graduate libraries (in English, the social sciences, and the sciences) were integrated into one professional system of organization, an arduous task that O'Leary oversaw to its successful completion after becoming president.[4] As president he appointed the first professionally trained staff and greatly increased the library budget to enable the university for the first time to make substantial acquisitions in both books and journals to enhance its collections.[5]

Arthur O'Leary's major accomplishments during his six-year tenure were the modernization of graduate studies, the reorganization of the alumni association, and the revival of major collegiate athletics. Two things besides his introverted personality seriously deterred O'Leary as president, however: the effects of continuing depression and his health. Debilitating kidney stones forced him to undergo an operation in the spring of 1937 that nearly killed him. In June, a month after his operation, O'Leary suffered a relapse that left him fighting for his life for over a week. He eventually recovered but spent several months recuperating in New England and Jamaica before returning to campus in late October 1937.[6]

The Renaissance of the Graduate School

Graduate education at Georgetown had, since the early part of the century, been decentralized, ephemeral, and followed minimal standards. The college as well as the professional schools (law, medicine, and foreign service) all had graduate departments that awarded master's degrees and doctorates for the fulfillment of very limited requirements. In the college, one earned a PhD through a 1-year's residence, 48 hours of course work, passing an oral exam on 60 theses in scholastic philosophy, and completing a 10,000-word dissertation. This reflected the intellectual rigor mortis within Jesuit higher education that could lead the dean of the graduate school at Fordham to conclude that "research cannot be the primary object of a Catholic graduate school, because it is at war with the whole Catholic life of the mind."[7] Small wonder that little scholarship could be found in such an isolated, complacent ghetto of learning. When the American Council on Education in 1934 issued a report ranking graduate programs in various fields, Georgetown unsurprisingly received approval for none of its graduate programs (only two Catholic institutions—the Catholic University of America and Notre Dame—were included).

Concern about the lack of distinction that characterized Jesuit advanced education in the United States had led the superior general of the Society of Jesus, Wlodimir Ledochowski, to appoint a commission on higher studies in 1931. The following year the commission issued a report that called for Jesuit institutions of higher education to do what their secular and religious counterparts had been doing since the beginning of the century: create a national association for the purpose of unifying standards, professionalizing the preparation of Jesuits for the academy, reforming graduate programs, and gaining academic recognition.[8] Two years later the superior general issued an instruction on studies and teaching in which he called for Jesuit academic programs that would receive "due recognition and rightful standing among other groups of a similar rank and grade." Teachers in higher education should henceforth have appropriate degrees to teach at the advanced level, publish in the community of scholars, and be active in the world of the academy. As an instrument toward reaching this goal, he created the Association of Jesuit Universities, Colleges, and High Schools of the United States and named a secretary with powers to carry into effect the superior general's directives.[9]

Although Coleman Nevils had made some gestures toward strengthening graduate education (creating, among other things, several fellowships for graduate students in 1930), the new emphasis on graduate education at Georgetown had its beginnings in 1932, the year the commission issued its report. When Francis Connell, the provincial official in charge of studies, made his annual visit to the campus, he showed particular interest in the condition of graduate studies at Georgetown and urged its development.[10] Shortly afterward Nevils created a separate position of dean of the Graduate School (previously the dean of the college had held this position as well) and appointed Miles O'Malia, SJ, a sociologist who had formerly been dean of the graduate school at Fordham, to the new position. O'Malia apparently solicited the advice of Thomas H. Healy—assistant dean of the School of Foreign Service, a publishing scholar, and a highly active professional in the academic world—about the possibilities and problems regarding graduate education at Georgetown. In a seventeen-page memorandum, Healy surveyed the state of graduate education at Georgetown and its potential.[11] As it happened, Healy was very aware of the landscape of higher education in the area. "There is probably no city in the entire western hemisphere," he wrote, "with better facilities and more adapted for first-class post-graduate work than is the city of Washington."[12] As it was, "the soil has been barely scratched." No institution in the region had a graduate program that remotely approached the area's potential.[13]

Still, he felt that Georgetown was in an excellent position to "occupy an almost virgin field in Washington by establishing a really first class post-graduate department commensurate with the unique facilities available in Washington."[14] It would mean building a faculty "of unusual training, ability and distinction." Fortunately, there were already present in Washington many such persons at federal or private institutions who could staff a graduate program, but it would take money to attract them and effective administration to keep them. Admission standards had to be rigorous. The university had to consider the establishment of fellowships for graduate students. Classes should be small (ideally fifteen or fewer students) and limited to graduate students. A board of graduate studies should be created to govern the program. As for fields of study, Healy thought that Georgetown was best prepared to offer advanced degrees in history, political science, mathematics, and the applied sciences of astronomy and seismology.[15] Only through such steps, Healy was sure, would Georgetown be able to establish the kind of strong postgraduate program that would warrant full membership in the American Association of Universities (AAU), the highest status that a university could have.[16]

Nothing much immediately came of Healy's memorandum, although Nevils did make a few special appointments to the Graduate School over the next two years. The paper passed into the hands of Arthur O'Leary, who succeeded Nevils as acting president in the fall of 1934. When the head of the Jesuit Education Association, Daniel O'Connell, SJ, made his visit to Georgetown in January 1935, he found O'Leary "eager" to meet the AAU's standards by strengthening the university's graduate program through the addition of faculty, the radical improvement of its library holdings, and the quality and number of its graduate students.

Upon leaving O'Connell issued a directive calling for the reorganization of graduate studies that implemented many of Healy's recommendations. Subsequently, all graduate education hitherto conducted separately at the individual schools of the university would be under the jurisdiction of a graduate dean, with the assistance of an advisory graduate council. Five to six new professors should be appointed in the fields of biology, chemistry, economics, history, and mathematics. All available fellowships and scholarships should be given to graduate students. For the present only the master's degree should be awarded, while each department conducted a self-study of its resources, including faculty, and its needs. By the spring of 1937, the president, acting upon the advice of the graduate dean and graduate council, would decide which departments would grant the doctorate.[17]

In the fall of 1936 the provincial superior appointed Aloysius Hogan, SJ, dean of the Graduate School, with a mandate to reorganize graduate education. Hogan, forty-five, had just completed six years as president of Fordham University. With a doctorate from Cambridge University and having been dean of the graduate school at Fordham, Hogan was an ideal administrator to reform graduate education at Georgetown. He hit the ground running; within the first three months he had conducted the self-study of departments for which O'Connell had called and submitted a plan for "building up" the Graduate School. For the immediate future, graduate work would be limited to the departments of biology, chemistry, mathematics and seismology, physics, economics, history, and political science. New faculty appointments and library acquisitions would be concentrated on these departments.[18] In the late winter of 1937, O'Leary gave Hogan the go-ahead to proceed with his plan of reorganization.[19]

Goertz A. Briefs, professor of economics in the Graduate School. (Georgetown University Archives)

For the academic year 1937–38 seven new appointments were made to the faculty of the Graduate School. Goetz A. Briefs, a distinguished economist who had fled from the Berlin Institute of Technology in 1934 to escape Nazi persecution of dissident intellectuals, joined the economics department, as did two others, including Erik T. H. Kjellstrom, who had been an economic advisor to the Royal Economic Planning Commission of Sweden.[20] Four faculty members were also added to the history and political science departments, including the historian Bernard Mayo (PhD, Johns Hopkins University) and the Harvard-trained medievalist Olgerd P. Sherbowitz-Wetzor. The following year five additional appointments were made, four of them in physics (including Henry M. O'Bryan and Robert Lee Mooney, with doctorates from Johns Hopkins and Brown, respectively) and extensive improvements made in the laboratory facilities of that department. Michael X. Sullivan (PhD 1903, Brown), who had headed Georgetown's Chemo-Medical Research Institute since 1932 and was acquiring an international reputation, was made research professor and the chair of the graduate chemistry faculty.

Graduate faculty were given special offices and minimal teaching schedules to free them for scholarly work. Five fellowships and three scholarships were awarded to graduate students. Departments organized their book holdings into libraries and, in some instances, created them. In 1937–38 the libraries of the main campus added 10,000 volumes, mostly journals, to their approximately 200,000 holdings.[21] The dean limited enrollment in the school to fifty for the 1937–38 year, with twice as many applicants rejected. Thirty-six of the fifty students were full time. Nearly one-third of the full-time stu-

Paul McNally, SJ, astronomer.
(Georgetown University Archives)

dents held fellowships or scholarships worth from $1,000 to $1,200.[22] Classes were held throughout the day rather than in the evening, as they had previously. Oral examinations for doctoral candidates were now comprehensive ones, and the dissertation was expected to be worthy of publication and to contribute something original to its field.

Ironically, astronomy, which had originally been the centerpiece of Georgetown's commitment to advanced studies, was not made a part of the revitalization of post-graduate education, despite its revival as a research center. Since the second decade of the century the observatory effectively had been abandoned. In 1925 Edward Phillips, SJ, became the first director since John Hedrick had left in 1918. He found the equipment in such disrepair that he estimated it would take perhaps a decade to restore it to working order but began the process during his three years as director. Paul McNally, SJ, who came east in 1928 from the University of California, where he had been working at the Mount Hamilton Observatory to succeed Phillips, had grand plans for the observatory. He hoped to make it the astronomical center for the Society of Jesus in the United States, staffed by Jesuit astronomers from around the country.[23] McNally managed to attract several Jesuits from the United States and Canada to train under him at Georgetown as the nucleus of a national staff for the observatory. They took part in the first scientific field trip organized from the observatory in 1932 to observe a solar eclipse in Maine. McNally's photographs of that eclipse brought him international recognition and membership in the International Astronomical Union. He was subsequently chosen to lead or take part in expeditions to the Soviet Union, the South Pacific, and Brazil to observe total eclipses between 1936 and 1940.[24] Under McNally, Georgetown was also one of the observatories participating in the International Longitudinal Determination that studied changes in the Earth's surface in 1933.

Aloysius Hogan had served as dean of the Graduate School for only a year and a half when illness unfortunately forced him to step down in February 1938. Wilfred Parsons, SJ, replaced him. By 1939–40 there were ninety-eight students in the school, with fifteen fellowships and scholarships. Most were in history and political science (thirty-one), biochemistry (twenty-six), and economics (twenty-three). At commencement in 1941, six doctorates were awarded: five in biochemistry and one in history. Nine students earned master's degrees—in biochemistry, history, economics, and political science. Despite the investment of resources into physics, that department failed to attract many students. By 1940 Professor Mooney, who had been recruited from Johns Hopkins University in 1938 as the major research professor of the program, had left the university due to the lack of students. The school also lost its second dean in two years when Wilfred Parsons left to accept the chair of social economics at Catholic University, despite the efforts of O'Leary and other Georgetown officials to block the move on the grounds that it would "be patently injurious to the reputation and standing of Georgetown."[25]

The Law School

One of Coleman Nevils's first acts as president was to appoint a Jesuit, Thomas Chetwood, as regent of the Law School. This was apparently a move made not only to secure more control of the school but also to Catholicize it, as the superior general of the Society had directed presidents of Jesuit universities to do at all their schools. Chetwood, who had taught philosophy and psychology at Georgetown College, began to carry out this directive by pressing for more Catholic faculty and students and insisting on a more Catholic curriculum, such as canon law courses. Chetwood's heavy-handed efforts alienated much of the faculty and administration there. Less than two years later he was replaced by Francis Lucey. The thirty-nine-year-old Lucey, the son of Irish immigrants from Malden, Massachusetts, had been teaching ethics at the school for the previous two years. He would be regent and dean of the school for the next three decades.

Francis Lucey, SJ, Law School regent, 1930–61. (Georgetown University Archives)

When the committee of the AALS made its periodic visitation of the school in the fall of 1931, it found many aspects of its facilities to be inadequate, including the run-down condition of the buildings, poor lighting, lack of library space, and so on. When Lucey sought the president's approval for extensive renovations, Nevils was loath to commit large sums to improve the old building when he was planning to erect a new one for the school on the main campus in the immediate future. Despite the president's reluctance, Lucey began preparations for a thorough overhaul of the place. When Nevils's plans for a new law school were put on hold, the renovations began. The library was enlarged; classrooms were painted and paneled; new seats were installed; new, fully equipped offices for faculty and staff were created; new lighting was added; and a cool water system was installed. When the AALS returned for its next inspection five years later (1937), it found "a well equipped" facility that met "the expectations of the Association in every way."[26]

During its 1932 visit, the AALS had expressed concern about the extremely few academic failures among the school's students on an annual basis, "a number so small as to appear to be out of proportion to the normal experience in Association Schools."[27] Whereas twenty-five association schools annually dropped 9 percent of their students for academic failures, Georgetown's rate was 4 percent. For first-year students, the disparity in the drop rate was even worse, 10.8 percent among the association schools to Georgetown's 2 percent.[28] In response, the school empowered its committee on studies to have final jurisdiction over grades, including the ability to reduce grades in any course in which they were disproportionately high. It also eliminated the quizmaster system, by which recent graduates facilitated the major testing of students in classes and that was thought to be a serious factor in the prevalence of high grades and virtual absence of failures.[29] By 1936, Lucey reported that more than 80 percent of the graduates taking the D.C. bar exam over the past two years had passed, to him no doubt a confirmation of the school's academic improvement.[30] Despite these developments, when the AALS made its return visitation in 1937, it still found an abnormally small percentage of students eliminated for poor academic performance and cited a need for the school to put into effect better standards for testing and grading its students.[31]

The reduction in faculty in 1932–33 provided an occasion for curricular reform by which overlapping courses were eliminated and a more rational schedule of courses was created, including the transformation of several required subjects into electives, in conformance with modern law school practice. The case system was also integrated into the teaching method to complement the traditional textbook approach. At the same time, overall teaching loads of full-time faculty (there were eight in 1932) were reduced to three courses, with professors encouraged, if not expected, to "direct their attention to research and writing."[32] Five years later the administration introduced sabbaticals at half pay for full-time faculty. In 1932 the school also changed its starting time for evening classes to 4:30 PM, thus enabling them to be designated as "afternoon classes," which were approved by the AALS, unlike their night counterparts. In effect, this enabled the school to maintain its evening school under the pretext that it was an extension of its day division.[33] A much more important innovation was the institution in 1936 of clinical education, and classes were initially taken on a voluntary basis. The executive faculty urged students in senior year to devote an hour a week to working with the Legal Aid Society. The practice became obligatory the following academic year.[34]

In 1930 the school began, for the first time, to register the religious affiliation of students, which was an indication of the effort to increase the number of Catholics. It succeeded to the extent that Catholics remained a strong majority of the student body during the decade, but that majority actually declined, falling from 72 percent in 1930 to 60 percent in 1937. From 1931 to 1935, enrollment increased by more than 50 percent, from 499 to 714 students. In 1936 the school instituted a prerequisite for entrance that it had been considering for much of the past decade: a college degree. By 1936 more than two-thirds of those entering were college graduates. Still, some faculty feared that this requirement would lead to a drop in enrollment, as least in the short run, but for the overall status of the school and in the conviction that such a move would do more than anything else to improve academic standards at the school, Georgetown became one of a mere seven law schools in the country to require a bachelor's degree. The *Washington Post* hailed it as "Georgetown's Step Forward . . . to place the . . . Law School on a par with America's foremost institutions of legal training," presumably thinking of the other six—Harvard, Yale, Northwestern, California, Pittsburgh, and Pennsylvania—who already had the requirement in place.[35] Despite the new prerequisite, there was only an incidental decline in regular enrollment the following fall.

Notable graduates of the school during the decade included William Shea (LLB 1931), a New Yorker who returned to his native city to become partner in an important corporate law firm and to head up the municipal committee that successfully brought back a National League baseball franchise to New York in 1961. Henry Carter (LLB 1939) worked for the U.S. Maritime Administration during the 1940s before joining the Avondale Marine Ways of New Orleans, of which he became president in 1961. Louis Frick, James Bennett Howe, and Robert Hogan also went into government service, Frick (LLB 1931) with the General Services Administration; Howe (LLB 1933) first with the Public Roads Administration, then with the legal staff of the White House, and finally with the General Services Administration; and Hogan (LLB 1941) with the Central Intelligence Agency. Michael V. DiSalle (LLB 1931) became mayor of Toledo and later governor of Ohio. Alan Bible (LLB 1934) and Joseph Montoya (LLB 1938) represented Nevada and New Mexico, respectively, in the United States Senate.

In 1933, at Lucey's urging, the school decided to expand its graduate programs, partly to increase the prestige of the school and partly to strengthen enrollment.[36] A director of graduate research, Walter H. Jaeger, a recent juris doctor recipient from Georgetown, was hired in 1934. Special faculty appointments were made to offer advanced courses, such as that made to James Scott Brown for international law. By 1940 the school was awarding approximately twenty master of law and ten juris doctor degrees a year.

The faculty began to produce the legal scholarship these changes had facilitated and made part of the expected culture. In 1936, Lucey was proud to report that five members of the faculty had published texts or had them in press during the previous year. Under the imprint of the Georgetown University Law Press, James Scott Brown published *The Catholic Conception of International Law* in 1935. Walter H. E. Jaeger authored several works on the law and corporations. During this same period Charles A. Keigwin produced important casebooks on mortgages, common law pleading, and equity jurisprudence.[37] The *Georgetown Law Journal* became a major forum for scholars, including Georgetown faculty members such as Robert A. Maurer and others, which addressed the constitutionality of New Deal legislation of the Hundred Days and beyond.

To build alumni support for the school, Lucey revived the alumni association of the District and began an alumni publication, the *Law School Hoya* (later *Res Ipsa Loquitur*).[38] The initial event of the association was a banquet at the Mayflower Hotel in 1934 on the occasion of Dean Hamilton's sixtieth anniversary of his graduation from the school. More than nine hundred alumni and others gathered to honor the oldest living graduate of Georgetown Law and member of the faculty for nearly a half century, as well as to elect him president of the alumni association.[39] A related development aimed at the alumni in Washington and beyond was the establishment of a legal institute in 1935 to provide a public forum for the discussion of legal issues and the promotion of ethical standards in the profession.

School of Foreign Service on the Hill

The second decade of the School of Foreign Service proved to be an extremely challenging one; by the early 1930s, its continuing existence was in doubt. By decade's end, however, the school was larger, with a major new division and a much firmer financial foundation.

In 1932 the school moved from its quarters in the Law School to new ones in the Healy Building. As part of the Greater Georgetown plan to relocate the professional schools to the main campus, the move was also an indication of the school's troubled condition and its identity as a separate institution within the university. By 1932 the school had lost one-quarter of its enrollment in three years and was experiencing, so university officials were convinced, growing indebtedness. Unlike the other schools of the university, the School of Foreign Service had its own treasurer (Edmund Walsh) and thus controlled its own finances. By 1933 Nevils was predicting, "This department is . . . doomed to dwindle to rather small numbers. Foreign trade is shot to pieces and the diplomatic and consular services reduced abnormally."[40] In order to find a new student population, Walsh proposed adding a business program to the school's curriculum, but Nevils had no intention of presiding over the development of "a school of Commerce and Finance," which the president thought had no place at Georgetown. In Nevils's quest to make the university more Catholic, the School of Foreign Service posed his "biggest difficulty" in terms of its curriculum, faculty (heavily non-Catholic), and student body (40% Catholic).[41] Nevils expected the school to become a part of the college within the near future; the move to Healy made sense as a preparation for that eventual integration, which presumably would eliminate its financial independence and greatly diminish, if not end, its non-Catholic character.

The school, through financial tightening and government aid, weathered the crisis. Thomas Healy (AB 1914, LLB 1917) succeeded William Notz as dean upon the latter's death in the summer of 1935. With federal subsidies for students, enrollment increased in 1935 for the first time since the Depression began. The following year, with a new president in office, the school inaugurated a new Division of Business and Public Administration, an undergraduate program that, for students with two years of college, would require three years of additional course work. As officials explained, the new division was created to "meet the growing need for coordinated training for business and public administration, and is designed to give adequate preparation for a wide range of positions in business, accounting, and Government service."[42] As the school paper noted, "At a time when government is exerting such a direct influence on business and business on government, an acute demand for such a course was evident."[43] Enrollment accordingly nearly doubled from 1935 to 1940. By the end of the decade, nearly 40 percent of the School of Foreign Service's graduates were receiving degrees in business and public administration. Interestingly, during the same interval there was a dramatic increase in the number of Catholic students in the schools. From composing a minority in the early 1930s, Catholics by 1939 constituted a large majority (60%) of the student body. As the school prepared to celebrate its twentieth anniversary in 1939, the *Hoya* could confidently boast that it had established itself as the leader in the field of preparation for commerce and public service.[44]

Among those to join the faculty during the decade were two refugee scholars, Leonid Ivanovitch Stakhovsky and Edgar Leo G. Prochnik. Stakhovsky had met Walsh at the University of Louvain where the Russian émigré was earning a doctorate in history. Walsh apparently invited Stakhovsky to Georgetown to assist him in the preparation of a book on the Russian Revolution and to teach European history. Stakhovsky published *The Origins of American Intervention in North Russia* in 1937. Edgar Prochnik, the Austrian minister to the United States when Hitler annexed his country in 1938, received an appointment to the school one month after the Anschluss to teach diplomatic history. Charles Moser, chief of the Commerce Department's Far East division, taught Far Eastern economics. Joseph C. Rocca, an internationally known statistical expert who was a member of the Cuban embassy, taught statistics at the school from 1931 to 1943. Carroll Quigley, a PhD from

Carroll Quigley, professor of history and School of Foreign Service faculty. (Georgetown University Archives)

Harvard, joined the faculty in 1941, where during the next thirty-five years he became an outstanding teacher and scholar, whose development of civilization course for freshmen became an institutional hallmark, and whose interdisciplinary books *Evolution of Civilization* and *Tragedy and Hope: The World in Our Time* became influential works in the 1960s.

There were notable developments in student activities during the decade, including the organization of the current events club, the formation of an honor society for the social sciences, and the establishment of annual student economic conferences. At its first meeting in the fall of 1931, members of the current events club discussed disarmament and reparations. Subsequently, there were guest speakers on various topics as well as discussions at the monthly meetings. In February 1933 the chapter Phi Gamma Mu of the National Social Science Honor Society was organized at Georgetown. The chapter held regular roundtables with invited speakers from the government, labor unions, and other institutions. In that same year the school inaugurated its student economic conference. In February students gathered to hear Senator David I. Walsh of Massachusetts, who regularly taught a seminar on American government at the school, and Dr. William Culbertson, former ambassador to Chile, discuss various issues, ranging from the fiscal policy of the government and national defense policies to the Platt amendment and the Far East policy.

Notably, relatively few of the graduates of the school during this period went into foreign service. U. Alexis Johnson (BSFS 1932) and Jacques Reinstein (BSFS 1933) were two who made their careers in the State Department. The swelling bureaucracy of the federal government initiated by the Roosevelt administration absorbed many alumni, such as Joseph F. Santiana (BSFS 1931) in the Federal Bureau of Investigation, George N. Belie (BSFS 1936) later in the Central Intelligence Agency, and Thomas J. Radzevich (BSFS 1938) in the Department of Commerce. Chester Charles Ward (BSFS 1931) enlisted in the Navy in 1941 as a lawyer and eventually rose to the rank of rear admiral in his position as judge advocate general of the Navy. A surprisingly large number went into private business. James E. Jones Jr. (BSFS 1931) was an executive with the *Washington Post* between stints with the Reconstruction Finance Corporation. James W. Pearson (BSFS 1932) became an executive with the Home Builders Association of Washington. Dennison Mitchell (BSFS 1932) became a partner in the certified public accountant firm of Councilor, Buchanan, and Mitchell. Van Manning Hoffman (BSFS 1929) became a highly successful businessman in Washington. Aaron Goldman (BSFS 1934) became chief executive of the Macke Corporation. John W. Stadtler (BSFS 1939) became president of the National Permanent Savings and Loan Association. Frank Fadner (BSFS 1932) joined the Society of Jesus, earned a doctorate in history at the University of London, and returned to the school to teach Russian history and eventually succeed Edmund Walsh as regent.

Current Events Club, School of Foreign Service, in the 1930s. (*Ye Domesday Booke,* 1933)

Nursing: "In the University but Not of It"

In the 1930s the Student Nurses' Training Program moved toward an academic status with the establishment of a curriculum that culminated in a degree. The National League of Nursing Education had taken over accreditation of nursing schools and programs in the early 1930s; indications were growing that the agency would soon require schools to offer academic degrees in order to have a top, or class A, ranking. In 1935 David McCauley, as regent of the program, proposed that as an alternative to the traditional three-year program a five-year program be introduced, including two years of collegiate studies that would combine nursing and liberal arts courses and the regular three years of specialized training. McCauley wanted the nursing students to take their collegiate studies in regular classes at the college, but other Jesuit administrators opposed this breaking of the single-sex tradition of collegiate education at Georgetown.[45]

The school began a pilot program of sorts in the 1938–39 academic year, but with graduates of the training program or nurses employed at Georgetown Hospital who took extension courses taught by Georgetown College faculty for one year in order to obtain a degree in nursing science.[46] A year later the university sought approval from the provincial superior to inaugurate a formal course of nurse training that would lead to the bachelor of science degree. Georgetown was taking this step in response, not only to the growing pressure from the accrediting agency to provide a degree program, but also to the decision of Providence Hospital, which was Georgetown's chief local competitor in nursing education, to begin such a program in affiliation with Catholic University. The new course would include two years of academic work in one of the local Catholic junior colleges for women that was conducted by nuns. The provincial approved the request, and the academic program began in 1941 as an option for nursing students. Nursing at Georgetown was now, as the school's historian has put it, "in the university but not of it."[47]

The Alumni Revived

In the latter 1930s the Alumni Association had become a paper organization that met once a year at graduation and reelected the same people year after year to do nothing. Actual alumni participation was virtually nonexistent. From at least 1932, voices in the student press had been calling for the creation of an alumni bureau or office with a full-time secretary to direct and coordinate alumni organizations throughout the country.[48] By 1935 grassroots movements by graduates, particularly of the Law School, had organized or revitalized alumni clubs in several cities and states, including Washington, D.C.; Providence, Rhode Island; Pittsburgh, Pennsylvania; Chicago, Illinois; Los Angeles, California; Connecticut; Florida; and Utah.[49] In his

James Ruby, secretary of the
Alumni Association.
(Georgetown University Archives;
Reny Newsphoto Service)

first month in office, President Arthur O'Leary announced his intention to
establish a national office for the purpose of organizing and coordinating the
alumni, but other pressing matters, including his own health, prevented him
from taking any action.[50]

In the summer of 1937 Edmund Walsh suggested to President O'Leary
that a revitalization of the alumni was absolutely essential. Walsh was looking ahead to the sesquicentennial of the university in 1939 and was envi-
sioning a reorganized alumni as a prerequisite for any broad-based celebration
(there were an estimated 11,000 living alumni at that time).[51] O'Leary saw
the wisdom of Walsh's rationale and sensed the opportunity to secure an
instrument for building an endowment for the institution as well. During the
spring of 1938, O'Leary toured the country, making stops in Chicago, Illinois;
Los Angeles and San Francisco, California; Salt Lake City, Utah; Denver, Col-
orado; Kansas City and St. Louis, Missouri; Cincinnati and Cleveland, Ohio;
and Pittsburgh, Pennsylvania, to establish contact with alumni and reorganize the local clubs.[52] In the winter of 1938, O'Leary asked James Ruby of the
English department to become secretary of the association, with the specific
task of locating and organizing alumni across the country in preparation for
the celebration of the sesquicentennial in 1939. In the fall of 1938, with the
support of the board of regents, O'Leary established a national alumni organization and named Frank Hogan as president until national elections could
be held. An alumni office was created with an initial budget of $10,000.[53]
Ruby's efforts to identify and locate alumni resulted in the publication of
the first alumni directory since 1924. A monthly publication, the *Georgetown*

Alumni Bulletin, a four-page newsletter, was initiated. At O'Leary's invitation, the presidents of the twenty-five alumni clubs across the country met on campus in the fall of 1939 to form the Georgetown Alumni Association, to draw up a constitution, and to establish an alumni board of governors to serve as directors of the association.[54]

A "New Deal" for Georgetown Athletics

When Jack Hagerty, at the age of twenty-nine and six years out of Georgetown, took over in the middle of the 1932 football season as head coach of a team that had seen its fortunes plummet since President Nevils had de-emphasized big-time sports, he expressed confidence that things would improve with "Georgetown men in charge." Hagerty brought in George Murtaugh (xC 1926) as his end coach and Maurice "Mush" Dubofsky (PhD 1932, LLB 1935) as his line coach. Georgetown returned to a Pop Warner, power style of single- and double-wing offense rather than the Notre Dame system employed by his predecessor, Tommy Mills.[55] For the next season and a half things did not improve, as the team won only one game in that stretch. Despite mounting criticism from alumni and others, Nevils was unfazed by the team's dismal performance. In January 1934, Nevils pointed out that "in many schools the game had deteriorated into nothing more than a money-making scheme." He suggested that if all schools followed the policy adapted by Georgetown and some others in the Middle Atlantic states (no scholarships, limited resources for football, etc.), the sport "would be a pleasant but profitable pasttime."[56]

Nevils's assertion notwithstanding, Georgetown's policy toward athletics had already changed by 1934. In the summer of 1933 the board of directors, presumably at the urging of the moderator of athletics, John Kehoe, SJ, had authorized partial scholarships for athletes (but not as athletes) who were academically capable.[57] When Arthur O'Leary, SJ, who was much more interested in intercollegiate athletics than Nevils, took over as acting president in the fall of 1934 (and subsequently as president), he needed little urging from Kehoe to greatly expand the modest scholarship program that had been revived in 1933. By 1938, O'Leary was effectively allowing the major sports (football, track, basketball, and baseball) to set their own scholarship needs.[58]

For the 1934 season Georgetown resumed its summer camp training at Point Lookout in Southern Maryland. In early October, before the game against Manhattan College, the students staged a gigantic rally in the quadrangle. After the rally, hundreds of students snake-danced behind the marching band down Pennsylvania Avenue to the White House and the Ellipse. That Friday night, at a dinner for alumni in New York, acting president O'Leary announced "that Georgetown was ready to throw off the mask— that the time had come for the new deal" in Georgetown football.[59] The next

Football coaching staff (from left to right): Maurice Dubofsky, Jack Hagerty, and George Murtaugh. (Georgetown University Archives)

day Georgetown beat Manhattan 9–0. When the team returned that night to Union Station, a throng of more than one thousand students and supporters greeted them with banners proclaiming "Our New Deal" and paraded them home in a six-block-long, two-abreast caravan of cars. "All the pent up feelings that its supporters here have been harboring since Lou Little left . . . burst forth," the *Washington Herald* judged.[60] Georgetown went on to win two and tie one (NYU) of its next four games. Unfortunately, the team closed the season with losses against Maryland and Western Maryland to finish at 4-3-1, but it was the first winning season since 1929.

The following fall of 1935, the Hoyas, as the newspapers had begun to refer to Georgetown teams, had the nucleus of a very good team, not incidentally a core of sophomores brought in under the revised policy—Al Snyder, John Cavadine, Johnny Frank, Al Vaccaro, and Larry Hardy along the line and Tommy Keating and Bob Ferrara in the backfield.[61] The defensively minded team went 4-4. Three of its four losses—to NYU, Maryland, and Western Maryland—were by a total of eleven points. The next year, with the addition of promising sophomores Clem Stralka, Joe Frank, and Lou Shuker, local sportswriters were predicting that this "smart, workmanlike" team, "barring a few injuries," could match any team in the area and go undefeated. Georgetown's hopes for such a season died in mid-November when, indeed decimated by injuries, they lost to Manhattan, 13–0. Nonetheless, the team improved to 6-2-1, with highlight victories over West Virginia, Miami (Florida), and Maryland, and a tie with NYU at Yankee Stadium.

Georgetown football celebrated its fiftieth anniversary in 1937. With nine regulars returning from the previous season and Joe Mellendick, a triple threat in the backfield, and Joe McFadden, a quarterback, joining the team as sophomores, the team, even with a tougher schedule that added Holy Cross, Lafayette, and Pennsylvania, looked strong enough, as one local paper forecast, "to raise the hopes . . . that the road back to football fame and fortune has finally started."[62] The early season proved that forecast as too premature when the offensively challenged team, suffering from a rash of early season injuries, scored only six points and lost two of its first three games to Holy Cross and Lafayette. It then held Pennsylvania to a scoreless tie in Philadelphia before twenty thousand fans, and two weeks later tied West Virginia as well. The following week Georgetown went to New York to play NYU. Hagerty unveiled a new offense for the game, involving multiple options. Despite a steady, heavy rain that reduced the Polo Grounds to a swamp, Georgetown ran its new system with quarterback Tommy Keating repeatedly lateraling to halfbacks Joe Mellendick and Charlie Wychunas or faking the lateral and handing off to Myron Darmohray or keeping it himself. With this revitalized "spread" offense, which Georgetown would perfect over the next three years, the Hoyas vastly outgained the Violets but managed to score only after NYU fumbled a punt on its 2-yard line. Georgetown won

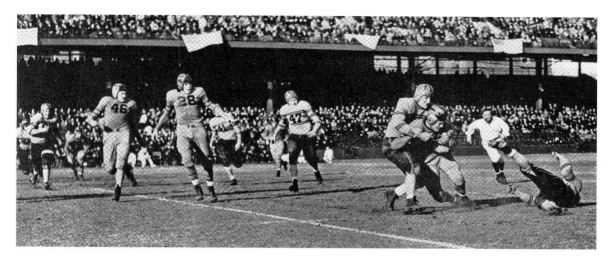

6–0. It ended the season a week later with a loss to Maryland to complete its record at a very disappointing 2-4-2.

With an easier schedule and some outstanding additions from the freshman class of 1937 for the 1938 season, particularly Jim Castiglia, Jules Koshlap, and Lou Ghecas in the backfield and Robert Kercher, Augie Lio, and Paul McArdle on the line, Georgetown achieved what many had predicted the previous year. Facing Maryland in its last game in late November, the Georgetown community knew that something special was at stake. As the Jesuit diarist recorded on the eve of the game, "Great excitement . . . on account of the Georgetown Maryland game. A victory to-day for Georgetown will leave the team untied and unbeaten this year, the greatest achievement in Georgetown Football history since 1874."[63] With its defeat of Maryland 14–7 the next day, the Hoyas completed a perfect season for the first time. Joe Mellendick won honorable mention as an All American but ended his career prematurely with a dislocated knee in the Maryland game.

The next season Georgetown, with its nucleus of players returning plus notable sophomore additions in Lou Falcone, a back, and Al Blozis, a 6-foot-6, 245-pound tackle, nearly equaled its success of the previous season. It opened its schedule by beating Temple in Philadelphia, 3–2, on a last-minute field goal, "a wobbly, humpbacked" kick by Augie Lio from 32 yards out. In the third game at Syracuse, halfback Lou Ghecas, with barely a minute left, ran 70 yards for a score, and Joe McFadden kicked the extra point that allowed Georgetown to tie Syracuse 13–13. A week later at Bucknell, the Hoyas again scored a late fourth-quarter touchdown, this on a run by Jim Castiglia, to beat the hosts 13–6. The next Friday night, before 18,000 fans at Griffith Stadium, Georgetown renewed its rivalry with George Washington after a hiatus of sixteen years. Despite being outplayed by the Colonials for most of the game, Georgetown won on a blocked punt that Lou Kopcik, the left end, recovered and ran back 13 yards to score the

Georgetown University versus University of Maryland at Griffith Stadium during the undefeated 1938 season. (*Ye Domesday Booke,* 1938)

Al Blozis, All-American in football and track and field.
(Georgetown University Archives)

only touchdown of the game. After beating West Virginia at Griffith the following week, Georgetown returned to beat Maryland 20–0. A week later the Hoyas ended their season with a 14–0 victory over NYU at Yankee Stadium before 19,000 fans. The opposition had been held to 22 points for the season, while Georgetown scored 109. They finished the year ranked sixteenth in the Associated Press poll. Bob Considine, after the NYU game, wrote in the *New York News* that one "could not find a better club to represent the East than Georgetown," but the team received no bids from major bowls and ended the season 7-0-1.

Hagerty regarded the 1940 team as the best he had coached. Utilizing an extremely complex offense that employed both a balanced and an unbalanced line, the single wing, and a spread formation, the Hoyas began the year in powerful fashion, reeling off seven consecutive wins in which they outscored the opposition, including Syracuse, NYU, Temple, and Maryland, 247–16. By the end of October they were ranked tenth in the nation. When they went to Boston in mid-November to play Boston College before 41,000 fans at Fenway Park, both teams were unbeaten. Boston College, ranked ninth in the country and coached by Frank Leahy, a former assistant at Georgetown under Lou Little, was a slight favorite. On a damp, chilly, windy day, the Hoyas jumped to a 10–0 lead in the first five minutes of the game on a Lio field goal and a Koshlap touchdown following a blocked kick. Boston College, led by its All-American quarterback Charlie O'Rourke, rebounded

Cartoon depicting the upcoming game between unbeaten powers Georgetown and Boston College, November 1940. (*Boston Post*, November 16, 1940; drawing by Bob Coyne.)

to take a 13–10 lead in the third quarter. Then Georgetown marched deep into Boston territory and scored on a double reverse from Koshlap to Ghecas to McFadden to retake the lead, but Lio's extra point attempt was tipped wide. Boston College responded with a 43-yard touchdown pass from O'Rourke to put the Eagles ahead 19–16. Georgetown staged a late drive that took them to the Boston College 31-yard line but could not attempt a tying field goal because Lio, their kicker, had been injured shortly before and, under the limited substitution rule, could not return. Boston College then ran down the clock with O'Rourke taking a safety in his end zone after avoiding Georgetown tacklers for sixteen seconds. There was less than fifty seconds left when Boston College free-kicked from its 20-yard line and the game ended, Boston College 19, Georgetown 18. For many observers the game transcended the outcome. Grantland Rice called it "an American football classic. . . . In many ways it was probably the greatest football game ever played by colleges or by pros. . . . It was the greatest all-around exhibition of power, skill, deception and flaming spirit that I have ever seen on a football field for over 40 years."[64]

When the team returned to Washington the next day, with its three-year unbeaten streak broken at last, a large contingent of students greeted them at Union Station with signs that proclaimed, "Still the Greatest Football Team in the World."[65] The team ranked ninth in the country in the final poll. The week after Georgetown's final game, which was an 8–0 win over George

Elmer Ripley, basketball coach, 1926–29, 1938–43, and 1946–50. (Georgetown University Archives)

Washington, they were invited to the Orange Bowl in Miami on New Year's Day 1941. Georgetown's opponent was Mississippi State. Before a crowd of 38,000 in the Orange Bowl, the Maroons beat the Hoyas, 14–7, on a blocked punt that resulted in a touchdown.

In basketball Georgetown was a member of the powerful Eastern Intercollegiate League, along with Carnegie Tech, Pittsburgh, Temple, West Virginia, and Pennsylvania State. In 1932, when the university decided to employ only Georgetown alumni as coaches as part of its reform of the intercollegiate program, Fred Messmer, a graduate of 1930, was brought in to coach. During his tenure Georgetown boasted some very talented players, notably Ed Hargaden, the slick All-Eastern floor leader from 1932 to 1935 and the first Hoya to play professionally, and shooting guard Harry Bassin. There were bright moments, such as Georgetown's upset of NYU in 1936 and its defeat of Temple, the national champion, the following season. In seven seasons Messmer's teams had two winning ones, going 12-11 in 1933–34 and 9-8 in 1936–37. Finally, in 1938, Elmer Ripley returned as coach after a nine-year absence. In Ripley's first season of his second term as coach, Georgetown, led by Joe Murphy and Edward Jurtyka, became Eastern Conference co-champions. Three years later, with Francis (Buddy) O'Grady, Irving Rizzi, and George Pajak, Georgetown had its best record since Ripley's first tour in the 1920s, as it went 16-4 for the season.

In baseball Georgetown started the decade as one of the most powerful teams in the country. Three of its players, Del Bissonette, Clyde Sukeforth, and Paul Florence, had gone on to play in the National League. But baseball, like its fall and winter counterparts, suffered during the period of de-emphasis, only to return to its former position in the late 1930s. In 1930 Georgetown went 22-6 with victories over perennial foes Dartmouth, Yale, and Princeton (twice). John Evers, son of the Chicago Cubs second baseman; catcher Frank Orefice; and third baseman Dick King were leading members of the squad. The following year at Georgetown the sport was reduced to a twelve-game schedule, and for the next five years, with no scholarship athletes, the team's record was mediocre or worse. Then, in 1937, the "new deal" arrived for Georgetown baseball. Joe Judge, the former Washington Senator, was named coach. In a season of thirteen games, the Hoyas, with Tony Barabas (outfield), Joe Keegin (catcher), Mike Petrosky (pitcher), Joe Mellendick (outfield), Tommy Keating (shortstop), and John Cavadine (third base), the team went undefeated, with the key win coming over Harvard, 16–15, in eleven innings. With essentially the same team the following year, the Hoyas went 16-4. Over the next three seasons the Hoyas continued to compete with and (mostly) defeat the top teams in the East, including Harvard, Cornell, Princeton, Temple, and Yale.

Track, where Georgetown had become a perennial power, experienced the same pattern during the decade that the other major sports teams had known—a decline in the early 1930s and a revival in the latter part of the decade. Jimmy Mulligan, another ex-Hoya, returned to coach in 1932, but his teams did not enjoy success until the 1936–37 season, and success was largely held to one event, the mile relay. In the indoor season of 1937, the mile-relay team prevailed in five meets, and it established a Madison Square Garden record of 3:21.3. The following year, the mile unit, now comprised of Vin Healy, Stuart Reeves, John Motzenbacker, and Vin Braun, was again one of the top relay teams in the East: They won at the Millrose, Southern Conference, and Penn Athletic Club games before losing Motzenbacker to injury in midseason. In 1938–39, the mile-relay team was among the best in the country, with Al Frey and Morton Alnwick now complementing Healy and Braun. The next year, under a new coach, Elmer "Hap" Hardell, the mile team of Braun, Alnwick, Ken Lyden, and George Tucknott won the collegiate championship in Baltimore. At the Millrose games they set a record of 3:21.6. The quartet went undefeated for the season and was named the top relay team in the East. Two years later, in 1941–42, the Georgetown relay team had six victories in indoor meets and set a world record of 3:17.2 in the Naval Relief meet with a time of 3:17.2.

Georgetown had lacked an outstanding performer in field events since its Olympic gold medalist in the shot put, Leo Sexton, graduated in 1930. In 1939 a freshman, Al Blozis, made Georgetown a force again in field competition when he set a new world indoor record in the sixteen-pound shot at the NYAC games in Madison Square Garden with a throw of 53 feet 8.5 inches. By the end of his junior year, Blozis had set world indoor and outdoor records in the eight-pound shot (78' 1/8") and twelve-pound shot (65') and the world indoor record for the sixteen-pound shot (57' 3/4"). He was named an All American in track and field for three years, 1940–42.

Golf shared in the athletic success of Georgetown teams in the late 1930s, highlighted by John Burke's (**C** 1940) becoming the second Hoya to win the intercollegiate championship. In 1939 a sailing club was established, with the Hoya sailors participating in their first regatta in Boston, the Dinghy Challenge Cup. The next year another intercollegiate sport was added: hockey. In its second season, 1941–42, the team went undefeated in nine games.

The Sesquicentennial

Edmund Walsh was the key mover of the sesquicentennial celebration. In the summer of 1937 he proposed to begin organizing the alumni as a preparation for their broad participation in the 1939 event. The more than 1,500 graduates who returned for the sesquicentennial festivities represented the largest such alumni reunion in the history of the school.[66] The theme of the week-long celebration was Georgetown's contribution to church and nation for over a century and a half. Walsh, who had suggested the theme, decorated a special classroom in Healy that he called the Constitution Room and brought together paintings, engravings, and artifacts of "Georgetown, the Carrolls, [and] Washington" as a permanent illustration.[67] To underscore the connection between school and nation, when in March 1939 the country celebrated the sesquicentennial of the first session of Congress, Georgetown officials presented a formal message to Congress through the Speaker of the House, William Bankhead, a Georgetown alumnus. The message declared, "Mindful of the fact that in the year 1789 Georgetown College was founded, thus beginning its service to the Nation simultaneously with the congress of the United States . . . [we] pledge ourselves anew to the defense of the civil and religious liberties enumerated in that document, under which both the nation and the University have subsisted for the past one hundred and fifty years."[68]

When the festivities began on Sunday, May 28, visitors found a transformed campus. Flags and banners bedecked the houses on O Street from 36th Street to the front gates. Inside the gates Copley and Healy displayed streamers from roof to ground; floodlights illuminated every building as well as the Carroll statue. That evening the annual celebration of Founders' Day inaugurated the commemoration. Academic forums sponsored by the several schools occupied the next three days. The sesquicentennial ball drew more than one thousand couples to the Grand Ballroom of the Willard Hotel on Thursday evening.

The sesquicentennial pageant, "Sons of Georgetown," held on the next evening at the nearby Western High School auditorium on 35th Street, was a highlight of the week. A cast of 150 students, faculty, and alumni presented 18 tableaux that depicted snapshots of Georgetown's growth from its imagined origins in the settlement of Maryland in the 1630s to its accomplishments of the 1920s. Individual scenes underscored the theme of the interconnection between school and nation. These included depictions of John Carroll opening his academy in 1791, George Washington visiting the college, William Gaston securing the federal charter in 1815, the Civil War dividing the college, the college serving as a garrison and hospital for federal troops, Teddy Roosevelt's commencement address in 1906 with his advice for success in life and sports ("don't flinch, don't foul, and hit the line hard"), and the university's response, 1,600 strong, to the nation's call during the

Healy Hall illuminated for the university's sesquicentennial celebration, 1939. (Georgetown University Archives)

Great War. The pageant concluded with a grand march of all the participants, as well as university officials, to center stage, where before a replica of the Carroll statue they sang a Te Deum in gratitude for the blessings the institution had enjoyed over its first century and a half.[69]

On Saturday, a special convocation was held on campus that closed the weeklong events. Thirteen honorary degrees were awarded to mark the occasion, and Speaker William Bankhead, Governor Herbert O'Connor of Maryland, and J. Edgar Hoover, the head of the Federal Bureau of Investigation, were among the recipients.

Race and Morality, War and Peace

The 1930s saw the rise of student political activism on campuses across the country.[70] Students at scores of colleges and universities, led by leftist organizations such as the National Student League, the League for Industrial Democracy, and the American Student Union (ASU), organized around issues ranging from economic justice, racial discrimination, free speech, and, above all, war and its surrogate on campus, the ROTC. Beginning in April 1934, the Student Strike against War became an annual one-hour walkout from classes that, by 1937, involved more than half of the nation's collegiate population in a physical affirmation of the Oxford Pledge that they would under no circumstances fight in any future war in which their country found itself.

The right of free speech—to advocate such politically adversarial positions as abolishing the ROTC and protesting war measures—often became the catalyst for mass student demonstrations that tore apart university communities at the City College of New York, the University of California at Los Angeles, Harvard University, Johns Hopkins University, and elsewhere. In the spring of 1935, as free speech controversies were plaguing more than fifty campuses in the nation, the president of Georgetown University, Coleman Nevils, asked by the *New York Times* what his institution's policy was concerning the issue, replied, "As far as possible we exclude all political activities among the student bodies and faculties. While of course each one is independent in the view he wishes to take, it is not the custom of the university to allow any propaganda for one side or the other."[71] The *New York Times* applauded the "direct and simple policy" of Nevils as a model for all institutions to follow.

Nevils seems to have applied this policy of avoiding any action that might be interpreted as being politically influenced all too well to his own administration. When, for instance, the Rockefeller Institute asked Georgetown to give an appointment to a Jewish refugee from Nazi Germany in the fall of 1933, with his salary to be paid by the institute, the university declined the offer on the grounds that "an appointment at this time would be very undiplomatic."[72] There was little, however, that Nevils or his successor, Arthur O'Leary, did to suppress political advocacy on the part of faculty or students. Edmund Walsh was prominently outspoken in opposing the establishment of diplomatic relations with the Soviet Union. Joseph Thorning supported munitions embargo legislation at public meetings. With other faculty members, they took public stands against the Roosevelt administration's policy toward Mexico, the Spanish Civil War, and other issues. In 1937 President O'Leary asked the provincial superior of the Jesuit order to appoint a censor to examine the speeches of any Jesuits intended to be given in a public forum in order to avoid anything "which might be adversely understood or interpreted" during this period of "political stress."[73] The provincial apparently did not see fit to impose such censorship, and Walsh and the others continued their public advocacy with impunity.

Among Georgetown students, organized political activity was largely absent during the decade. A rarity was the formation of a small group of School of Foreign Service students during the 1932–33 school year that supported the establishment of relations with the Soviet Union. Despite public demonstrations and press releases by the student group, Edmund Walsh, probably the country's most recognized opponent of recognition, made no attempt to suppress their actions.[74] The School of Foreign Service students' position was clearly against the current of campus opinion in 1933, which was generally conservative and highly anticommunist.

The student press at Georgetown, in the wet Catholic tradition, did promote repeal of Prohibition. In the spring of 1932 the *Hoya* issued a call for action: "If all the young men in the colleges throughout the country worked together to remove the disgraces which have grown out of the Eighteenth Amendment, the puffing, blow hard, would-be statesmen must act honestly and straightforwardly and finally do something that would be in full accord with the wishes of the entire people."[75] With Roosevelt's landslide victory in the presidential election of 1932, the paper saw a definitive referendum for repeal and the subsequent repeal legislation by Congress as a victory for states' rights at the expense of the unconstitutional federal usurpation of power that the Volstead Act had represented.[76]

In 1934 the film industry became the focus for marshaling student reform energies. Georgetown students formed a branch of the Legion of Decency on campus to promote morality in the movies through public pressure, particularly the boycotting of offensive films and the establishment of effective censorship to serve the common good.[77] On racial justice the student press was relatively silent, but it generally supported the status quo Jim Crow relations. "There is a distinct line between the two races. This always has existed, and probably will exist as long as human nature remains what it is. There is an inherent tendency in white people," the *Hoya* reflected in 1937, "to exclude colored people from the social circle, and similarly in the converse. It is understandable and frequently to be desired. . . . There is a physical distinction as well as a mental, or psychological. It is practically impossible to assimilate and weld both into one unified type. . . . On the other hand," it recognized, "all men have the same inalienable rights. To own property, be respected, enjoy freedom, and conduct their lives as they see fit is ordained by God for all men."[78] This separate but quasi-equal philosophy went virtually unchallenged.

In 1939 the Daughters of the American Revolution (DAR) denied the distinguished black opera singer, Marian Anderson, the use of Constitution Hall for a concert. When the local school board also put its auditoriums off-limits to Anderson, the *Hoya* pronounced it a "sorry page" in the history of DAR and the city to exclude a person "simply because she is colored."[79] If the student press had been privy to the deliberations of university officials, it could have included them in its condemnation. That previous week, university officials had been approached about inviting Anderson to sing in Gaston Hall, since all the other halls of the city had been denied to her. They unanimously rejected the proposal.[80]

Georgetown was not among the many campuses that embraced the antiwar movement of the mid-1930s. On the eve of the second Student Strike for Peace in the spring of 1935, the Georgetown student paper denounced the movement as a Communist front to erode American security and democracy under the false promotion of the abolition of the ROTC and of war as a national policy. In a series of articles titled "Un-American Activities" in the spring of 1935, the *Hoya* castigated the National Student League and their allies for being duped into becoming part of this subversion.[81] In its last two installments, the editors did admit that the Communist sponsors of the movement were exploiting the legitimate grievances about the "unjustified bloody slaughters, such perhaps as we have had in the past," as well as those stemming from "the present condition of the rich becoming richer, and the poor becoming poorer" that was clearly building a climate for class warfare.[82] The series concluded by calling for a crusade of Catholic collegians to promote the Catholic Church's principles concerning peace and economic justice on campuses across the nation, religious and secular.[83] The series was subsequently republished as a pamphlet. Ten thousand copies were sent to colleges and universities, newspapers, government agencies, and various organizations.

When the annual demonstrations persisted over the next two years, the *Hoya* reiterated that such demonstrations for peace were Communist manipulations. It was time, the editors insisted, for Catholics to present a ritual rebuttal to the annual ASU theater.[84] A year later Georgetown's student government took the initiative of organizing a national counterdemonstration for peace. The student body president, James Hickey, wrote to deans of Catholic colleges and universities, in which he urged fellow Catholic institutions to join with Georgetown in holding campus rallies on April 27, 1938, the day the Student Strike against War was scheduled that year.[85] At Georgetown on the eve of the twenty-seventh, hundreds of students from Catholic institutions in the area gathered on the esplanade of the White-Gravenor Building for the first National Catholic Students Peace Day, a one-hour exercise of speeches followed by the celebration of solemn benediction.[86] The event, the *College Journal* observed, had shown that Catholic students were active citizens opposing the false principles of Communism by promoting the authentic principles of the church concerning peace.[87] Over the next two years Peace Days were observed in similar fashion at Georgetown. Eventually 225 other Catholic universities and colleges across the country participated in the annual demonstration.[88]

To many student activists across the nation, the Spanish Civil War, which raged from 1936 to 1939, was a crisis about the spread of fascism in Europe and stark evidence of the baleful effects of the American neutrality policy that the student movement had earlier embraced. The ASU and other college activist groups began to promote collective security as an antidote to the expansion of fascism; more than five hundred college students made their own personal commitment by trekking to the Iberian Peninsula to join the Abraham Lincoln Brigade of American Volunteers for the Republican Forces.[89] Georgetown's students saw the war not as a crusade of fascists but a legitimate revolution against the spread of Communism. That two fascist powers, Germany and Italy, were supporting Generalissimo Franco's rebellion against the Republican government was, to the *College Journal*, merely these countries' natural response in light of their own bitter experience with

Communism. "These are the countries that wish the Spanish people freed from being state slaves."[90]

Nor was the spread of Communism merely a European danger. In October 1935, President O'Leary warned the Law School alumni that Communism was "rampant" in the United States and spoke of their "solemn obligation to help to stem the tide."[91] By 1936 the Georgetown student press saw alarming signs of its growth in the United States alone. The *Hoya* reported that the Communist Party had now grown to such proportions in the country—more than 50,000 members, not to mention the more than 100,000 in popular front affiliations—"that the American people could no longer ignore it."[92] The growth "of the teaching of these Reds can be likened to a disease," a *Hoya* editorial commented in October 1936. "It is malignant. It . . . has invaded our schools through the medium of half-crazed professors. It has trod into our factories. . . . It is not striking our older gentry as much as it is our youth. . . . A menace—RED PROPAGANDA—is running rampant through America."[93] The government's need to suppress organized Communism in this country was the unstated conclusion.

Given this fixation on Communism, international and domestic, Georgetown students understandably did not significantly share the concern of so many of their fellow students in the nation about German aggression and its persecution of its Jewish citizens. In an editorial of February 1939 titled "Justice towards All Nations," the *Hoya,* viewing the trail of German acquisitions over the past three years, commented that, at least in part, Germany was merely correcting the injustice that had been dealt it by the punitive Versailles settlement. As for the treatment of the Jews, the paper acknowledged the "disgraceful" persecution of this group but maintained that such an internal problem could only be settled internally and not through external intervention, especially war. The best thing the United States could do, the editorial concluded, was to work to ensure a peaceful restoration of the German rights denied it in 1919.[94] That same month the *College Journal* echoed this sentiment about nonintervention:

Public speeches and the influence of the Jewish controlled press and radio have whipped America into almost war-time fury against Germany. We repeat: we sympathize with the Jews and believe the refugees should be taken care of. But we can not forget that the press and radio took little note of other persecutions, of bloody persecutions. Little enough was said about the persecution in Russia, less about that in Mexico, and the whole picture of the Spanish situation has been distorted. There has been no wholesale massacres of the Jews in Germany as there was of the Catholics in Russia, Mexico, and Spain. Our government did not intervene, by word or act, in those cases and it should not in this situation.[95]

In a poll taken a month later by the student paper, Georgetown students were asked whether Hitler's latest seizures in central Europe were justified, whether action should be taken to halt Germany's "drive to the East," whether war was imminent, whether the United States should enter into an alliance with European powers to stop Hitler, and whether Georgetown students were willing to fight in such an alliance.[96] The results were unsurprising. Most respondents found Hitler's seizure of Moravia and Slovakia to be without justification, but very few favored the United States's joining any anti-Hitler alliance or were willing to fight under such an alliance. "It was evident," the paper concluded from the results, "that should the Federal Government form an alliance against the will of the people, the people would feel no compulsion to back the same alliance with force." Nonetheless, a majority thought that war was imminent.[97]

Five months later Europe was indeed at war, and antiwar sentiment, if not isolationism, faded at Georgetown. When the draft was reinstituted in October 1940, Georgetown students and their counterparts across the nation (by that time a majority of students nationwide supported the draft) fully cooperated by registering. The *Hoya* noted that "prudence demands that we build up our resources to meet any blow which may come." The best way to do that was to distribute the burden democratically, as a draft did by its nature.[98]

Georgetown students, however, still opposed any United States involvement in Europe's war. The *Hoya* instructed its readers that the country should "preserve inviolate her traditional neutrality."[99] Another editorial concluded, "This war is not America's; we want no part of it!"[100] In November, Georgetown undergraduates overwhelmingly chose Wendell Wilkie as their presidential candidate. Partly this reflected their dissent with Roosevelt's intention to break the two-term tradition for presidents; partly it reflected their conviction that the New Deal had by 1940 resulted in a fracturing of the constitutional balance of power between the federal government and the states; but partly they feared that Roosevelt, through the Lend-Lease agreement and other actions designed to support Great Britain, was leading the country on a path to war. Even those who favored Roosevelt did so because of their trust that his experience could best keep the country out of war.[101] When Roosevelt won an unprecedented third term, the student press at Georgetown continued to oppose his actions to aid the allies, sure that they would provoke German attacks on U.S. shipping that would force the country to war just as earlier attacks had done in 1917. As late as Armistice Day (November 11) 1941, the *Hoya* was pleading that the nation's task was to make home defenses "impregnable . . . ; our men should stay at home."[102]

The war had generated a new outpouring of refugees, some of them students. At Georgetown, in the fall of 1940, there were refugees from Germany, Great Britain, the Netherlands, France, China, and the Philippines. By the fall of 1941, Washington, in an ominous sign of impending war, began to swell with scores of thousands of defense personnel brought in to aid the country's war preparations. Georgetown's campus was a site for naval reserve training during the summer of 1940 and for both the navy and army the following summer. By the summer of 1941, war seemed inevitable. As the *Hoya* remarked in its parting editorial for the academic year 1940–41, those graduating faced a seemingly dismal future: "The pressure of mobilization is taking away men's liberties, and the clouds of war have blacked out peace. . . . The immediate prospect . . . is first the draft board and then the army."[103]

The first Sunday in December 1941 was Georgetown Day at Griffith Stadium. A crowd of 27,000 gathered for the Redskins' final game of the season against the Philadelphia Eagles, three of whom were Georgetown alumni. Before the game, gifts were presented by the university to Jim Castiglia, Augie Lio, and Joe Frank. The game was barely under way when the public address announcer began to issue calls for various generals, admirals, and diplomats to report to duty. Then he began to page several newsmen and radio announcers. Finally, word began to seep through the stadium, as a few individuals with portable radios heard the news that the stadium authority had refused to make public: "The Japanese had attacked Pearl Harbor in Hawaii."[104] "Everyone seems dejected and confused," the Jesuit diarist noted that evening, "due to reports of many killed and wounded.—'This means WAR.'"[105]

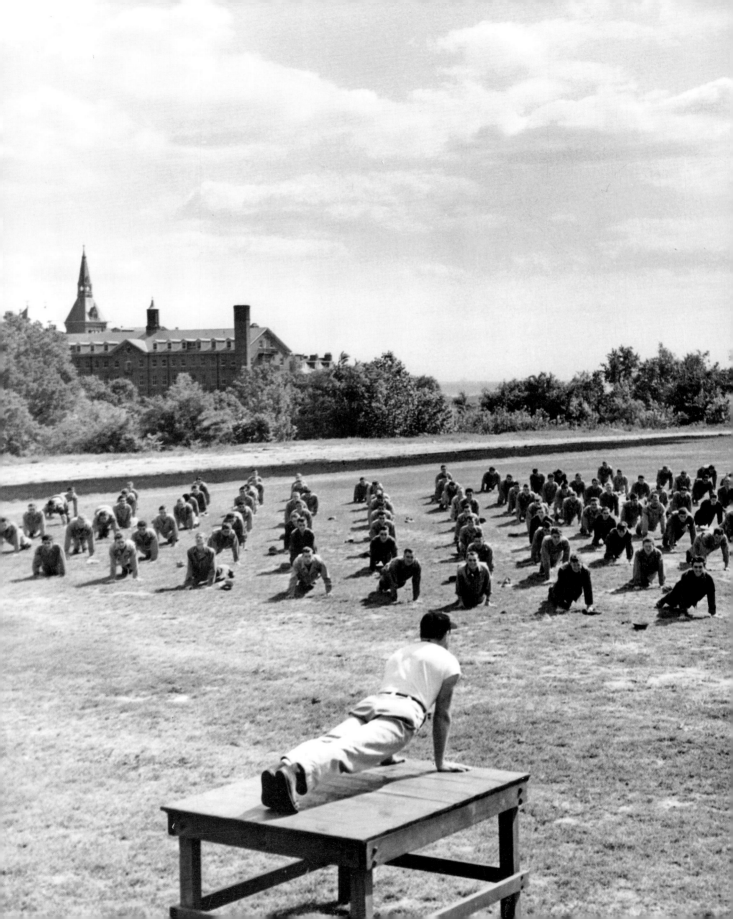

CHAPTER 7

"We Are Eager to Render Service"
The University and the Second World War

Lamenting the unparalleled attack made upon our national well-being and security, we are eager to render service to our beloved nation to the very best of our ability. RESOLVED: That the appeal to help our government in retrieving our honor as a nation and in securing safety for ourselves and all free peoples, will find us one and all ready to do our part with all possible generosity.

PRESIDENT and DIRECTORS OF GEORGETOWN UNIVERSITY to the President of the United States, December 15, 1941

"Remember Pearl Harbor!"

The shocking attack on American soil by the Japanese instantly changed the sentiment of the university community from determined noninvolvement in Europe's business to aggressive patriotism in response to the infamous transgression in Hawaii by an Axis power. The anti-Communist filter that had framed attitudes about foreign policy for the Catholic community over the past dozen years suddenly was useless in interpreting what the nation, including the university, needed to do. One horrible morning had rendered obsolete the ability of the old ideology to shape policy. A week following Pearl Harbor the president and directors issued the following proclamation in the name of the entire university: "Recognizing the emergency into which our beloved country has been thrust through the treacherous attack of the Japanese government with the connivance and assistance of the Axis nations . . . [w]hereas in every similar emergency of our country since the foundation of our University . . . the Directors and Faculties and Alumni and students have been unsurpassed in loyalty and self-sacrificing patriotism . . . BE IT RESOLVED: That lamenting the unparalleled attack made upon our national well-being and security, we are eager to render service to our beloved nation to the very best of our ability."[1] A week after Pearl Harbor, the student body president read aloud this historically challenged pledge to students and faculty gathered in Gaston Hall to observe the 150th anniversary of the enactment of the Bill of Rights, to which the crowd shouted a chorus of "Ayes" and gave a shattering "Hoya" for President Roosevelt.[2]

As in the nation's entry into World War I, Georgetown responded with a committed patriotism, albeit with more restraint than the unabashed enthusiasm that had swept the campus in 1917. As the *Hoya,* which had been so isolationist throughout 1941, editorialized ten days after Pearl Harbor, the nation was now in a total war in which everyone in the nation had a job to do. "We know what our job is; our duty is to keep at it, in the spirit of the times." At the bottom of the editorial was the slogan: "REMEMBER PEARL HARBOR!"[3]

The impact of the war was quickly felt on campus. A week after Pearl Harbor, the United States Army, without any notification, set up a searchlight crew

Joe Gardiner leading students in physical training, 1942–43.
(Georgetown University Archives)

on the football field behind the Medical School as a warning device against feared air raids.[4] The city had its first air raid drill a week later; a blackout test followed at the end of December at 8 PM. The university formed its own civilian defense council to prepare the campus for any emergency. The university, along with the rest of the nation, changed to "war time," where clocks were set one hour ahead for the duration of the conflict. Physical training was introduced for all students. A physical instructor, Joe Gardiner (**C** 1930), was hired to lead students in compulsory calisthenics on Copley lawn and in navigating an obstacle course set up on the hillside below the observatory, including a twelve-foot-high platform ("Gardiner's Gibbet") from which dangled ropes that students had to climb and then scramble back down to the ground below.[5] Gardiner eventually had a staff of several other former athletes and coaches to conduct physical training for Georgetown students and later for the army units stationed on campus. "Most everyone here . . . expects to be called into the Army or Navy sooner or later," the *Hoya* observed. That expectation carried with it an obligation to be in the best possible physical condition, the paper argued, and Georgetown students were fortunate to have "one of the finest physical training programs in the country."[6]

As at colleges across the nation, Georgetown students formed organizations to assist the war effort in various ways. In the winter of 1942 they formed the Victory Commission to sponsor various drives to conserve paper, salvage metals and other useful materials, buy war bonds and defense stamps, and participate in civilian defense. Georgetown students took the lead in forming a coalition of similar committees on Catholic campuses nationally "to vitalize the cause of America to the Catholic Students . . . to solidify the home front."[7]

A large portion of the faculty served in the military during the war. Soon after the attack on Pearl Harbor, Edmund Walsh was appointed a special lecturer by the army and was partly responsible for the War Department's establishing a geopolitical section of the military intelligence division that was a precursor to the Office of Strategic Services. By 1944 seven Georgetown Jesuits, including the chairs of the history and religion departments, Daniel Power and Martin O'Gara, respectively, held commissions as chaplains. Fourteen other faculty and administrators from the college were also in service. James Ruby, the alumni secretary, was a major in the army; Walter W. Wilkinson, instructor in history, was a second lieutenant; Rome Schwagel, the athletic director, as well as Jack Hagerty and his assistant coach Morris Dubofsky, were all in the navy. Twenty-six members of the School of Foreign Service were in uniform, including Leon Dostert, a lieutenant colonel who served as attaché to the supreme French commander, and John Parr, who was a lieutenant junior grade in the navy. A professor of English from the school, John Waldron, was one of many academics in the Office of Strategic Services. From the Law School, ten faculty were called to active duty, although a number, like Francis Nash, a navy commander, were subsequently stationed in the

Left: Leon Dostert, one of the SFS faculty in service during World War II. (Georgetown University Archives)

Right: Walter Wilkinson, one of the college faculty in service during World War II. (Georgetown University Archives)

Washington area and were able to continue teaching at the school, in Nash's case, his outstanding course in equity and taxation. The school with the largest contingent of faculty in service was the Medical School, which had no fewer than sixty-five members on duty with the army or navy.

The first response the university formally took toward aiding the war effort was to create an accelerated schedule of classes. This was one of the recommendations that came out of a specially called conference of the American Council on Education in the beginning of January 1942 to determine how colleges and universities could best serve the nation in wartime.[8] Georgetown had been among the participants, and university authorities immediately began taking steps to implement such a schedule. Beginning in July 1942, Georgetown schools went on a year-round, three-term schedule; first-year students entered at the beginning of each term and first-term schedules were available throughout all three terms. Thus an undergraduate could complete his program in fewer than three years; one who entered in September 1941 could expect to graduate in May 1944. In mid-February 1942 the dean of the College of Arts and Sciences informed parents that "Georgetown has been glad to accede to the request of the National Government and adapt its courses of study to the needs of the nation." Acceleration meant meeting these needs more quickly.[9]

That really "changed our life a great deal," Royden Davis, then a freshman, recalled. "[There was] a new tempo in the place," a tempo that reflected the institution's involvement in the nation's war.[10] "Everything is done in a hurry these days," another student reflected. "The war has changed the atmosphere on the campus. All faces are tense waiting to hear the latest war news, whether it be good or bad."[11] That sense of involvement in the war became more obvious as more and more members of the university

began "to disappear . . . by the early spring" of 1942, as the draft began to reach farther and farther into the nation's colleges.[12] By the spring of 1942, enrollments were down more than 15 percent in colleges across the nation; Georgetown was no exception. In April, university directors approved the awarding of academic degrees in absentia to candidates who had been called away to military service.[13]

The draft itself initially affected relatively few undergraduates. With the draft restricted initially to those aged twenty-one and over, college males were given a one year's deferment, which meant that ordinarily a college student could expect to graduate. In the spring of 1942 each of the services created reserve programs specifically for college students that would enable them to continue in college until graduation unless there was a pressing need for their manpower. Government authorities encouraged students under the age of twenty-one to enlist in the reserves of the army, navy, and marines to ensure graduation. Many at Georgetown did so.

The undergraduate schools inaugurated their first summer session in July 1942 and attempted to preserve as much of the rhythm of normal

The 1942–43 basketball squad, runners-up in the NCAA tournament. (Georgetown University Archives)

college life as possible. There were weekly band concerts in the quadrangle, barbecues outside of Ryan, and revues in Gaston Hall. The baseball team played a summer schedule of fifteen games against local colleges and military bases. In the fall the football team, despite returning only fourteen members of the 1941 squad (the rest were drafted), went 5-3-1, with notable victories over Temple, Mississippi, and North Carolina State. Basketball, with Elmer Ripley still coaching, had even better fortunes, despite losing two of its starters, including Andrew Kostecka, one of its top scorers, to the draft during the season. The starting five were John Mahnken, Robert (Miggs) Riley, Dan Gabbianelli, Danny Kraus, and Bill Hassett (Henry Hyde was the major reserve). They went 22-5 for the season and were ranked tenth in the nation. Qualifying for the eight-team NCAA tournament, Georgetown swept to the Final Four, where it proceeded to upset DePaul in the semifinals by neutralizing DePaul's intimidating giant center, George Mikan, by having its own center, Mahnken, draw Mikan constantly outside. In the NCAA final, Georgetown led Wyoming for most of the game and were up by 5 points with four minutes to play before Wyoming, behind Kenny Sailors and his pathbreaking jump shot, defeated the Hoyas 46–34.

By the late fall of 1942 the demands of a nation at war began to cut the remaining ribbons of normal collegiate life, and the student body shrank to a few hundred within the next several months. When Congress lowered the draft age to eighteen in October 1942, the reserves began to be activated. By the spring of 1943, all those in the reserves at Georgetown had been called away to active duty. Meanwhile, all those eighteen and over and not in the reserves began to receive "Selective Service greeting cards" in their mailboxes. As April 1943 began, a large majority of Georgetown's undergraduates had gone off to war. By the autumn of 1943 the total undergraduate population that had numbered 1,300 in 1941 had been reduced to 344, and most of them were freshman under draft age. By the end of the year there were only 140 resident students. The relatively few who remained on campus were housed on two floors of Copley.

Student activities began to contract or shut down. As 1942 ended, students realized that they were witnessing the end of an era of normal college life and the beginning of a military one at Georgetown. "In short," the *Hoya* declared in December, "the time has come when the social life of Georgetown is about to fall victim to the irresistible demands of war." The editors thought it fitting that the white-tie Victory Ball, scheduled for mid-December in a downtown hotel, should serve as a symbol of the change, marking the last of Georgetown's great social events for the foreseeable future.[14] It proved so. The junior prom for 1943 was canceled. The student council adjourned sine die. The *Hoya*, ending two decades of weekly editions, began publishing intermittently in the late spring of 1943. *Ye Domesday Booke* of 1943 proved to be the last edition of the war years.

The virtual pick-up baseball team suffered through a disastrous season. The graduate manager of athletics, Joe Gardiner, announced over the summer that Georgetown was abandoning all major intercollegiate sports for the duration of the war. (Gardiner himself left shortly afterward to join the navy.) About the only student organizations that remained active were the Sodality; the *College Journal*, which continued to appear monthly; and the international relations club, which cut against the current by being revived in the fall of 1943 with Professor Tibor Kerekes as moderator.

The Law School suffered an even more precipitous drop. From an enrollment of more than 500 in 1941–42, the school had shrunk to 132 by April 1943. Its only consolation was that top law schools such as Harvard and Yale had suffered even worse reductions.[15] With suddenly much more space than was needed, and as a way to secure income no longer provided through tuition, the school leased more than half of its space, about 12,500 square feet, to the War Production Board in January 1943.[16]

The school had attempted to take some steps, nearly a year before Pearl Harbor, to offset the anticipated losses that a wartime draft would quickly bring. In January 1941 it had established two new positions in military law and government procedures/contracts. It hoped that such courses as admiralty law, military law, and government contracts would attract military and government personnel to replace some of the drafted students. School officials knew that in order to attract government workers such courses had to be scheduled as evening classes, which in the past decade had become a minor part of the school's operations. By the fall of 1942 that projection had proven all too accurate. Of the 160 registered students, more than 130 were enrolled in the evening division, and nearly all of them were military or government personnel.[17] The twenty or so day students were military rejects, such as Edward Bennett Williams; those who had become disabled in service, such as Paul Dean; or a few military personnel whose work schedule allowed them to take morning classes.[18]

The school, while refusing to lower its standards for admitting students in this depressed market, nonetheless was determined to do whatever was necessary to maintain at least a skeletal day operation. When Philip Feldman, an army translator stationed in Arlington and employed in the secret army operation of breaking the Japanese code language, approached Lucey in the summer of 1943 about the possibility of coming to Georgetown on a scholarship, Lucey, apparently on the spot, replied that they had been thinking of starting a scholarship program, and if Feldman would have a copy of his Harvard transcript sent, he would be considered. A week later, Feldman received news of his admission and found himself with Williams, Dean, and the score of other students constituting the Georgetown Law day school. So small was the operation that a daily prepared lunch was made available for faculty and students in the basement of the building. Faculty, including Lucey, would regularly sit around the rectangular table eating the hot lunch with a dozen or so students and engage in legal shop talk, with Lucey directing the conversation.[19]

Camp Georgetown

Georgetown educators, like their counterparts across the country, had realized early on the devastating impact the draft would have on enrollment. In March 1942, Jesuit administrators held a special session to consider how to maintain a large-enough student population to keep the institution afloat during the war. They had no idea how many students would be there for the next year. One pool of potential applicants that the draft would not touch, of course, was women. Women had not been a traditional client of Jesuit education beyond those in nursing schools. Some Jesuit universities had begun to admit women for programs other than nursing by the 1940s. By the end of 1943 the graduate school at Georgetown began admitting women to its programs on a regular basis. Ironically, the first woman enrolled, Rita Lenihan, was a member of the WAVES (women's contingent of the U.S. Navy). By 1945 women constituted more than 40 percent of the 167 graduate students. The School of Foreign Service began to admit women working for the government to its evening courses in 1944.[20] The college and Law School never seriously considered such an option.

Lawrence Gorman, SJ, president of Georgetown, 1942–49. (Georgetown University Archives)

One nebulous idea for bolstering enrollment that Georgetown officials pondered during the late winter of 1942, perhaps drawing from the university's experience as a site for the SATC during World War I, was having the school designated as a site for the special training of soldiers.[21] As it happened, that was exactly the recommendation that came out of the Committee on Relationships of Higher Education to the Federal Government established by the American Council on Education in August 1942. The committee recommended that a college training corps be established on as many campuses as possible where trainees would receive technical education that they could put to immediate use in the service.[22] In December 1942 the army and navy, consciously aware of their lack of personnel with education in engineering, medicine, language, and other technical skills, established military training programs for implementation in colleges and universities across the country to be selected.[23] Eventually 227 institutions were chosen to host the Army Special Training Program (ASTP), the Navy V-12 Program, and the Army Air Forces College Training Program. At their peak, the programs enrolled nearly 145,000 special students on the selected campuses.

At the end of December Georgetown had a new president, forty-four-year-old Lawrence Gorman, SJ, who quietly took over from Arthur O'Leary (whose increasingly precarious health had forced Jesuit authorities to make the change during wartime). Once the army and navy had announced their intentions about the programs, Gorman, in one of his first acts in office, formed a war advisory committee that consisted of university administrators and faculty, as well as Frank Folson, the assistant secretary of the navy, as a liaison to the government. The committee thought that Georgetown had excellent prospects in securing programs, especially with its School of Foreign Service. Their optimism proved well founded. As a school that already had an army ROTC unit, Georgetown was selected to host an ASTP program beginning in June 1943, which would concentrate on intensive instruction in engineering as well as languages and area studies. It was also chosen as one of the thirty-two colleges with which the army contracted to serve as Specialized Assignment and Reclassification (STAR) units, to determine how applicants for the various programs would be tested and distributed to appropriate training programs.[24] Whereas the SATC during World War I had effectively inducted the Georgetown student body as a reserve unit to be prepared on campus for service, the ASTP and STAR programs involved the importation of soldiers for language and area studies training and for testing to determine future deployment.

The Nursing School also benefited from the establishment of a special training program. When the government created the cadet nursing corps in 1943 to provide more nurses for war service, Georgetown qualified as one of the sites for their subsidized training. The U.S. Public Health Service covered the cost of tuition, room and board, books, and uniforms of the nurse cadets and provided a monthly stipend. By the summer of 1943, more than 40 percent (thirty-nine of ninety-six) of the school's nurses were members of the corps.[25] The school's involvement in the program precipitated the government's construction of a new home for the school's nurses on Prospect Street.[26] When the new home was completed in the fall of 1944, the seventy-five nurse cadets, who by that time represented half the student body, were the first to occupy it. For the first time, college faculty taught the science and humanities courses of the Nursing School's curriculum.

So, too, the Medical and Dental Schools were able to take advantage of army and navy programs for training doctors and dentists for the respective services. In effect, those medical and dental students who were already members of reserve units—a large majority of the student body of the two schools—became members of the ASTP or the Navy V-12 program. One of these was William Walsh (MD 1943), who later served in the Pacific. His discovery of the atrocious health conditions under which the indigenous people lived led him to establish Project HOPE after the war.[27] In July 1943, about 475 medical and dental students at Georgetown resigned their reserve commissions to become privates first class or reserve midshipmen. The government subsequently paid the tuition, books, and other fees for the students who continued their normal medical or dental training—now in

Cadet Nursing Corps, 1943–45. (Georgetown *College Journal*)

uniform—with weekly drills and military lectures being the only change in their normal schedule. By the fall of 1943 all but 50 or so of the 524 medical-dental students were in one of these programs.

For the STAR and ASTP programs, the university was prepared to house 600 men, but the army intended to send more than twice that number. Three hundred wooden bunk beds were secured to accommodate the excess. Single rooms were turned into doubles, doubles into triples, and large rooms into dormitories.[28] Dining halls added 40 tables and 350 chairs and went on double shifts. In late April 1943, about 400 servicemen arrived at Georgetown. To the few remaining civilian students, their appearance was something of a shock. "The war," one student wrote, "had finally come to the sheltered Hilltop. It seemed as if the very heart of Georgetown had been cut out." Georgetown, he concluded, "is back again on active duty for its country."[29]

About 1,200 STAR participants were at Georgetown at any one time over the next year. The STAR participants typically stayed less than two weeks at Georgetown before receiving their assignments, most to engineering. They took over most of the residence halls—Old and New North, Ryan, Healy, and Maguire. During their stay at Georgetown they would go to orientation lectures and endure a series of tests and personal interviews by the STAR classification board, which would make the final decision about placement. The program, which lasted from April to September, became a model for other screening programs that the military services set up on campuses around the country. When inspectors visited Georgetown in September 1943 they told

Camp Georgetown, 1944.
(Georgetown *College Journal*)

school authorities that Georgetown's STAR program was the most outstand-ing in the nation in its efficiency and success in classifying individuals.[30]

The first ASTP men arrived in mid-June: 250 were assigned to language and special area studies, about 220 to medicine, and about 130 to dentistry. The medical and dental cadets lived off-campus, the others lived in the upper floors of Copley. Later in the summer 850 others arrived for the course in basic engineering. And until September 1943 there were always several hundred STAR participants in residence. At the height of the program, Georgetown had more than 1,800 military personnel on campus, which was the largest program for any Catholic institution in the country.[31]

By the summer of 1943 Georgetown had become "a military compound," as one returning student described it: "a factory of education" in the war ef-for.[32] At the front gate, manned by sentries, large signs on either side warned that this was a "Military Reservation—Restricted." The military students marched in units everywhere, often in cadence ("Hut, two, three, four"): to physical training at dawn, to and from classes, to meals, for roll calls. In the classrooms, platoon leaders would call them to attention at the entrance of professors. The bugle calls of reveille, taps, and other commands sounding throughout the day became, as one civilian student put it, "as familiar on the Georgetown Campus as the chimes of Healy tower."[33] In front of Copley a large flagpole had been erected around which at least 1,400 soldiers gathered each evening in ranks for the lowering of the flag and a formal parade (retreat), led by their band, back to their quarters. There were regular reviews of the troops, as well as grand reviews for special visitors such as the British ambassador, Lord Halifax, and the commander in chief of the French forces in North Africa, Gen. Henri Giraud. After reviewing Georgetown's companies of soldiers on July 10 to the strains of the "Marseillaise," Giraud proceeded to the steps of Old North, where like his fellow countrymen, the Marquis de Lafayette and Marshal Foch, he addressed the students (in French).[34]

The ASTP programs in basic engineering and language/area studies involved three terms of approximately three months each, during which students received intensive training that normally took two years in college, with a minimum of thirty hours a week spent in classroom and laboratory. The curriculum for the engineers included engineering, drawing, chemistry, mathematics, physics, geography, history, and English. Those in area studies and languages focused on becoming fluent in at least one language (French, Spanish, German, Italian, Russian, Japanese, Chinese), as well as studying related history, geography, and government. Faculty from the college and the School of Foreign Service taught the engineering and language/areas programs, respectively. Unlike the college, the School of Foreign Service brought in many outsiders from embassies and government agencies to teach the seven languages and area studies. Two émigrés that Edmund Walsh engaged in the program were the Belgian Jesuit Alphonse Verhoosel, who taught French and served as a special lecturer for the War Department on Africa, where Verhoosel had been a missionary; and the Austrian refugee Peter Berger, who was appointed by Walsh in 1943 to teach international relations, German, and Italian. Tatsao Arthur Miyakawa, a Nisei from California who was employed in the Office of War Information, taught Japanese, as did Harold Felsecker, a Maryknoll priest. The Japanese program at Georgetown was considered one of the finest, if not the finest, of those connected with ASTP.[35]

The curricular changes necessitated by the ASTP had effects beyond the program itself. With a depleted college faculty (six Jesuits and four laymen were serving in the war) stretched by the need to teach far more students than they had ever known in peacetime (there were fewer than fifty available faculty in the college, where most of the trainees studied), the range of offerings to civilian students was understandably greatly reduced. Even before the government established the ASTP and other training programs, it had been sending signals to the academic community that radical changes in curriculum needed to be made to prepare students for the war effort. In October 1942, Dean Stephen McNamee, SJ, reported that a government advisor had bluntly told him that traditional "education for the duration is out." What he suggested in its place was, to McNamee, "utilitarian courses calculated to produce a host of glorified mechanics to operate machines of war." When the draft age was lowered to eighteen, he concluded, the government would allow eighteen-year-olds to remain in colleges only if they were tak-

Edmund Walsh, SJ, lecturing
an area studies class in 1943.
(Georgetown *College Journal*)

ing an approved course comprising mathematics, physics, basic English,
modern language, and American history. Dean McNamee may have ab-
horred the changes, but he quickly put in place a curriculum for the entering
freshman in the next term to begin in January 1943 that mirrored the suggested one, with the addition of religion and the substitution of the vaguer
American Heritage course for American history.[36] The classics were truly
"dead languages" for the duration, and liberal education was in hibernation.

If liberal education was a casualty of the army's program at Georgetown,
the program certainly provided the revenue for the institution to survive,
since its regular student population was virtually eliminated. The first government payment came in June for more than $62,000. Then nothing more
was received for more than two months. By September 1943 the university
discovered that its financial sources were nearly exhausted. It took pressure
from a well-connected Georgetown alumnus lawyer, Martin Conboy, to get
the army to meet its financial responsibilities.[37] The next day a check for
$214,000 arrived from the government. Three months later the university
received nearly $340,000 from the army for its services.[38] For the academic
year 1943–44 the college showed an income of $1,325,943.50, most of it
from the federal government, which was far greater than the tuition-driven
revenues of prewar years. All told, the university received more than $1.5
million for its wartime service from 1943 to 1945. The total revenue for the
university in 1941–42 had been $1,682,409.26. For the 1943–44 fiscal year,
income increased by more than $1 million ($2,723,196.00).[39]

During the summer and fall of 1943 social life at Georgetown took on a
distinct flavor. There were occasional socials for the soldiers on campus, such
as the open house held in mid-July when 450 WACs (Women's Army Corps),

WAVES, and women marines joined the Georgetown ASTP unit for a cook-out around the tennis courts, followed by a navy band concert and a dance on Copley lawn. Other service bands gave concerts in front of White-Graven-or. There were boxing contests and football games between the personnel of different companies. Vaudeville shows and other entertainment were staged in Gaston Hall. For Christmas 1943 there was a special concert at which one member of the ASTP unit, Carl Reiner, served as emcee. Reiner gave a foretaste of his comedic brilliance by doing interpretations of Adolf Hitler and local Jesuits that had the audience in convulsions, including the Jesuits gathered in the balcony whom Reiner feared would fall over, so hard were they laughing.[40]

The first graduation of the ASTP cadets took place in March 1944, with 220 soldier students receiving certificates for completing their courses in engineering and language/area studies. As it happened, it was the only such commencement. Most of those who entered Georgetown's ASTP program never had the chance to complete their studies. Two weeks before commencement the army announced that in April it would begin to phase out the program on the college campuses. With manpower shortages in the armed services, there was growing criticism of having nearly 150,000 men in college studies. As Gen. George Marshall concluded in February when he asked Secretary Stimson to liquidate ASTP, there was no justification for not using this untapped source to replace manpower on the two fronts of the war.[41] Ten days after the Georgetown commencement, in mid-March, 550 soldiers of the engineering program left campus in fourteen buses that took them to a train that in turn carried them to Texas, and for many, into infantry duty. One hundred and eighty students involved in language studies stayed on to complete their training and to take part in the general college commencement in June. That ended the ASTP at Georgetown.

Ghost Campus and Victory

For the remainder of the war, the main campus reverted to the nearly abandoned state it had reached by the early spring of 1943, before the arrival of the STAR unit. Enrollment in the college and School of Foreign Service averaged around three hundred students combined from the summer of 1944 to the beginning of 1945. Among the students were a few foreigners, specifically refugees from China and the Philippines, including Ramon Osmen, son of the president of the Philippine Islands.[42] The armed forces continued to house some personnel on campus until November, mainly a few hundred army officers who would stay for several weeks while they took classes at the Pentagon as part of the Army Industrial College. After that, the campus, until the end of the war, had the feel of being on permanent vacation. Indeed, in March, the Boston Braves used Georgetown as its spring training site for three weeks, from mid-March to early April, with the relatively few players (baseball teams also being depleted by the war) residing in New North and eating their meals in Maguire, along with the few score students.[43] A brief change came in late June 1945 when four hundred Chinese students arrived for a six-week stay in New North while they went through a program to introduce them to American culture and business production.[44]

In late April a merchant marine vessel was launched from the Bethlehem Steel dock in Sparrows Point, Baltimore. Paul McNally and other university officials on hand joined in christening the ship *Georgetown Victory.* A week later victory indeed began to emerge. On May 6 the campus heard initial reports that the war in Europe had ended. When the official announcement of victory in Europe came two days later, there was only the most muted celebration at Georgetown, as in the District itself. The students gathered in Dahlgren Chapel to recite the rosary and litanies of the Blessed Mother, then they assembled in Gaston Hall to hear a reading of the official proclamation by President Harry S. Truman. "Taps" was played and the national anthem was sung. Everyone then went back to Dahlgren where students participated in solemn benediction and sang the Te Deum.[45] At graduation in June the university conferred the degree of doctor of laws honoris causa on President Truman, the first sitting president to be so honored. Joseph O'Callaghan, SJ (**G** 1938), whose heroic work aboard the stricken carrier USS *Franklin* off the coast of Japan in March would earn him a Congressional Medal of Honor (the first for a chaplain), gave the commencement address. Less than two months later, after days of false reports, official word came from Truman that victory had come in Japan as well, and peace was finally at hand. This time there was no muting the celebration. The students who had gathered around their dorm radios in anticipation of the announcement streamed onto campus and immediately proceeded, like their predecessors of previous football seasons, downtown amid the blare of automobile horns and the clanging of streetcar bells to join the happy throngs in front of the White House. President Truman came out to greet them. One of the students had a trumpet and began to lead the celebrating Hoyas in singing Georgetown songs and giving raucous cheers.[46] They boomed the alma mater into the mike of a radio network reporter for the entire nation to hear.[47]

Georgetown Heroes

During the war Jim Castiglia recalled an Armistice Day commemoration that he had attended at Georgetown in 1940. As the bell tolled for the fifty-six alumni who had died during the Great War, Augie Lio leaned over to Castiglia and said, "Someday those bells will toll for some of us."[48] Lio's words, whether in jest (as Castiglia thought) or not, proved to be prophetic. More than 6,600 Georgetown students and alumni served during the war. One hundred and sixty-eight died in action, by accident, in internment camps, or on hospital ships.

George Anderson Wolf (BSFS 1939), killed at Pearl Harbor, was the first. Albert A. Vaccaro (BSSS 1937) died during the initial fighting in the Philippines. In April 1942 James Gallagher (AB 1936) was killed in action in the fall of Bataan. Charles Wychunas (BSSS 1939), the captain of the unbeaten 1939 football team, also a defender of Bataan, was presumed dead for a year and a half before his parents received a card from him at Christmas in 1943. Comm. Bartholomew William Hogan, on leave from the psychiatry department at the Medical School, sustained severe burns and several fractured ribs while caring for the injured aboard the USS *Wasp* when it was struck by a torpedo in the South Pacific in September 1942. Hogan, for his "conspicuous gallantry," was awarded the Silver Star.[49]

In August 1942, James C. Palms (BSFS 1939), a United States Ranger taking part in the British raid of Dieppe on the French coast, was among the many mortal casualties suffered in testing German strength. William J. Kelley (xSFS 1943) went down with his merchant ship when it was torpedoed off of Greenland in February 1943. Victor Wales (BSFS 1941) was killed in the invasion of North Africa in early November 1942. William F. Nealon (x**C** 1942) had been among the first to land in North Africa as a liaison officer with the Eighth British Army, then in the late summer of 1943 won the Silver Star for his valiant action at Salerno, in which he was mortally wounded. John Burke (BSSS 1940), the 1938 intercollegiate golf champion, also died of wounds suffered during the same campaign. Edward Raymond Stone Jr. (MD 1939), another alumnus serving with the British army, was killed in action in Egypt in November 1943. Hank Coakley (x**C** 1941) and Joseph Fischer (xSFS 1943) both died in air crashes in August 1943. Howard Rothman (xSFS 1936), a bombardier, was fatally shot down in the pre-invasion bombing of the Marshall Islands. James F. Kehoe (BSS 1943) of the Marine Corps was killed in action taking a beachhead of the Marshalls. William C. Waldo (BSFS 1938) died in an internment camp in the Philippines in February 1944. Henry Gibbins Jr. (xSFS 1940), a star on the football and track teams of the 1930s, was shot down over Burma while on a secret mission in January 1944. Eugene Haverty (**M** 1938) was killed in February 1944 on the Anzio beachhead. A month later his medical school classmate, Capt. Alfred Schroeder (**M** 1938) was killed in action in Italy. Francis A. Shizzi (xSFS 1941) of the army engineers died in the South Pacific at Bougainville in March 1944. That same month Richard F. Hoffman (x**C** 1943) of the army air force died when his plane was shot down over the South Pacific. In June, Richard J. Murphy Jr. (BSSS 1940) was among those marines killed on the beachhead of Saipan. In the July 1944 New Guinea campaign, Charles G. Reichley (xSFS 1943), a gunner on a Flying Fortress, and Robert J. Sullivan (BSFS 1941), a tackle on the 1940 Orange Bowl team, were killed in combat. Sullivan had been the first American to win the British Empire Medal for his valiant performance as a member of the American Field Service with the British army in North Africa a year earlier. In France, a month after D Day, John E. Sosier (xC 1944) was killed while on reconnaissance. The advance through France in July also took the lives of medical major Edmund S. Kanses (MD 1933), Robert F. Hanlon (xC 1944)—who had been overseas just a month—and Brand Kleashna (xSFS 1943). The following month, on the French front, James L. Mooney (xC 1930), the great punter on Lou Little's teams in the late 1920s, was killed in action.

As the Allied forces pushed into Germany and the Netherlands in October and November, John S. Reilly (xC 1941), Richard J. Leahy (xC 1944), Albert S. Altman (xC 1944), John Shanley (AB 1943), Francis Commiskey (BSFS 1941), Earle H. Dooley (xSFS 1944), and Robert A. Duffey (BSSS 1944) were all killed in action. Duffey, one of the last of the class of 1944 to be drafted (he had gotten his diploma in absentia) had written to Georgetown shortly before his death that his machine gun platoon was "constantly in battle . . . met the enemy in France, Belgium and now in Germany."[50] Robert J. Digby (xSFS 1943) was killed by German antiaircraft fire as he was piloting his crippled Flying Fortress back to England from a raid on Germany in late December. Charles Marion Musso Jr. (MD 1935), a major in the medical corps, died from gunshot wounds in France on Christmas Eve 1944. Among the victims of the Battle of the Bulge that raged in Belgium from Christmas 1944 to early January 1945 were two graduates, Carolan J. Walsh (LLM 1928) and Fred Motz (BSFS 1942). Lt. Col. Philip Hart (AB 1934), who had been wounded on Utah Beach on D Day, rejoined his Fourth Infantry Division just before the German counterattack in Belgium and received a Croix de Guerre for his valor. Also in January, Al Blozis (BS 1942), the record-holding shot putter and tackle on the 1940 football team, was killed in a mountainous area between Belgium and France. Blozis had gone out in a blinding snowstorm to look for four members of his command whom he had sent to probe the German lines. Just as he located one of them, he was struck down by a burst from a German machine gun. As the soldier he had just reached remembered nearly six decades later, "Blozis was a real American Hero who would never leave any of his men under any circumstances."[51]

In the final push against Germany in the late winter and early spring of 1945, George A. Sesso (MD 1941), William A. Burns III (xC 1945), and Vincent J. Mulvaney (AB 1944) died during the campaign. Bernard W. Lyons (AB 1942), Herman Heide (AB 1934), and Charles Hagan (xC 1944) were captured by the Germans during the advance. Heide, a chaplain with the 42nd (Rainbow) Division, had been apprehended when he went to the front of a fierce fight to aid wounded men. A fellow officer recalled that "Chaplain Heide was the only man I saw who seemed to be completely without fear. He was a living sermon of vital religion."[52] Hagan, captured during the last stages of the war when German collapse was imminent, persuaded the German garrison to which he was brought to surrender to his platoon before they were engulfed by the Americans advancing from Munich.[53]

In the aftermath of the recapture of the Philippines in the summer of 1944, three alumni—Edwin J. Laragay (MD 1929), James A. Connell (MD 1925), and Philip Devereux Johnston (LLB 1913)—died on Japanese prison ships in December when they were torpedoed or sunk on their way to Japan. In the bloody battle to take Iwo Jima in February and March 1945, Charles Carter Anderson (xSFS 1946), Francis P. Daly (BSS 1940), Amelio L. Patrucco (BSFS 1943), Aloysius S. Fennell Jr. (xC 1942), and Arthur W. Carley (BSFS 1941) all died in action or of wounds. Edward J. Agnew (BSSS 1943) was shot down and killed over Luzon in the Philippines in March. On Okinawa, in May, Wilford S. Alexander Jr. (xC 1943) died of wounds received during that campaign. Two other alumni pilots—Richard V. Southwell (xC 1944) and Nicholas M. Pavonetti (xC 1943)—lost their lives during the fighting in the Southwest Pacific and over Japan in the late spring of 1945. Thomas Stapleton (AB 1934, MD 1938), who participated as a naval surgeon in the invasions of the Marshall Islands, the Marianas, and Iwo Jima, was badly wounded during the latter action but survived to earn a Purple Heart, Bronze Star, and Navy Commendation Medal. Another naval medic, Harvey Kreuzburg (MD 1937), was one of the victims of a kamikaze attack on his destroyer in the South Pacific; Kreuzburg continued to treat wounded crewman until loss of blood forced him to confine his assistance to counseling others. He lived and was awarded the Silver Star as well as the Purple Heart. John F. O'Brien (MD 1943) died when a kamikaze crashed into his hospital ship that was bringing wounded from Okinawa in late April.

In November 1945 on the Georgetown campus a crowd of students, faculty, alumni, and relatives of some of the university's war dead gathered around the tree seat outside of Copley. A pavement of flagstone had been laid before the tree, and two, new, semicircular stone benches had been added to the two already there. At the center of the flagstone a brass plaque had been placed with an inscription:

TO THE MEMORY OF RICHARD F. HOFFMAN, A.A.F.

COLLEGE '43

KILLED IN ACTION, PACIFIC, MAR. 20, '44

AND ALL

GEORGETOWN HEROES OF WORLD WAR II

THIS COPLEY TREE SEAT

AFFECTIONATELY DEDICATED

BY HIS PARENTS, SEPTEMBER 10, 1945

Charles Hagen, who six months earlier had persuaded his German captors to surrender to him, gave a tribute to the fellow alumni being honored. The dean of men, Richard Law, SJ, who had corresponded with so many of Georgetown's servicemen during the war, read the list of the 144 alumni then known to have died during the war. The college bell chimed the De Profundis in the background. Two trumpeters sounded "Taps," and a party of ROTC cadets sent three volleys of shots into the air. The solemn crowd then sang the alma mater and the national anthem.

The Legacy of the War for Georgetown and Higher Education

Georgetown had more than met its promise to "render service" to the nation with "all possible generosity." More than 6,000 alumni and scores of faculty had served in the armed forces and government agencies in prosecuting the war. Nearly 170 of them had made the supreme sacrifice. The university itself had become a major training facility for thousands of inductees in preparing them for duty in engineering, language specialization, and area expertise. Georgetown had proven to be a major contributor among American institutions of higher education in providing expertise in then little-known languages, such as Russian and Chinese and Japanese, and in knowledge of critical regional geopolitics and culture, which greatly benefited the nation's war effort.

The war also was the occasion for the introduction of scientific research projects for defense, most notably the development of the atomic bomb at the University of Chicago. Georgetown shared very peripherally in such research, but it too marked the beginning of a partnership between the universities and the federal government that would become much larger in the postwar period, with transformative effects on the mission and funding of American higher education.[54] In the immediate future, the federal government would become highly dependent on civilian scientists in the universities for much of the basic and applied science that would become crucial to its national interests.[55] In that partnership Georgetown would be a significant player.

PART THREE

RECOVERING THE IDEA
OF A CATHOLIC UNIVERSITY,
1945–64

AMERICAN

CHAPTER 8

In a Hot and Cold War World, 1946–52

Man today after two world wars is again impatient and enterprising. Where the Israelites had one idol, modern man has many. . . . Georgetown University has been iconoclastic [to modern culture] in the past and with God's help will wield a heavier hammer in the future.

HUNTER GUTHRIE, SJ, Inaugural Address, May 1, 1949

"[The GI Bill] Certainly Changed Georgetown"

The postwar period proved to be a critical launching pad for mass education within the realms of higher learning in the United States. Colleges and universities across the country experienced dramatic increases in enrollment during the first few years following the end of the war that made the prewar college/university population seem minuscule in comparison. In 1940 total student enrollment in institutions of higher education in the nation fell just short of 1.5 million. By 1949 it had recovered from the collapse the war had brought to reach nearly 2.7 million, an increase of approximately 80 percent in the 1940s.[1]

At Georgetown the expansion was even greater than the national trend. In 1944 the aggregate enrollment in the university had fallen to about 1,600. By the spring of 1946 it had regained its prewar level (2,500 plus), then within a year and a half enrollment soared to a then all-time high of more than 5,800. Individual schools showed unprecedented leaps in enrollment. For the academic year 1947–48, the College of Arts and Sciences was simply swamped with applicants—more than 4,000 for its 600 spots, which was itself a raised ceiling. The college went from slightly more than 260 students in 1945 to nearly 1,700 by 1948; the School of Foreign Service showed an even greater increase (from 212 to more than 1,700); the Law School saw the greatest increase of all (from 162 to 917). The phenomenal jumps in enrollment were not simply the effects of peace and of the return of students from the war. At Georgetown and institutions across the nation, there was an extraordinary influx of veterans, most of whom were not returning to institutions they had left during the conflict; indeed, most of them were the first members of their families to attend college at all.

Fears of a new depression brought on by an economy unable to employ the millions of returning veterans led Congress to pass, in the summer of 1944, the Servicemen's Readjustment Act, or the GI Bill, which subsidized and provided a stipend for the higher education of veterans.[2] The response of veterans to the academic offer was far greater than anyone expected. By the fall of 1946 more than 1 million veterans enrolled on campuses across the country; over the next decade more than 2.2 million former servicemen attended college under the GI Bill.[3]

Among the private institutions that a majority of the veterans chose to attend, Georgetown had more than its share. Having already collaborated with the federal government to establish the wartime training programs, Georgetown was well conditioned to welcome this peacetime government initiative. In May 1945 the Veterans Administration established offices in Old North to set up the program at Georgetown. Of the nearly 2,600 students at Georgetown in the spring of 1946, 52 percent were veterans, nearly all of them attending on the GI Bill. Veterans particularly came to dominate enrollment in the School of Foreign Service and the college. By the spring of 1946 they made up more than four-fifths of the students in the School of Foreign Service and, a year and a half later, nearly 90 percent.[4] During the 1946–47 school year, Veterans Administration funds for veterans constituted more than 90 percent of the revenue received by the college for tuition, room, and board.[5]

The "greatest factor in the growth of Georgetown was the G.I. Bill. It certainly changed Georgetown," Royden Davis, who returned to Georgetown in 1946 to complete his education, recalled. You now "had people you never expected to find" at the traditional upscale Catholic institution.[6] It "really helped to democratize Georgetown," Daniel Degnan (BSSS 1950), a navy veteran, remembered. It broadened the college "beyond the white-shoe set." When Degnan ran for president of the Yard in 1949, it was largely the support of fellow veterans that enabled him to beat the white-shoe candidate.[7]

The tsunami of new students struck in the academic year 1946–47. There were two entering classes in 1946, one in July and another in October. The

Temporary housing on the lower campus, 1946-47.
(Georgetown University Archives)

ages of these freshmen ranged from eighteen to forty-four. Because of the presence of so many older-than-normal students, for four years after the war Georgetown remained on the accelerated schedule it had adopted in 1942. Classes went from 7:40 AM until late afternoon, six days a week. First-year students continued to enter three times a year.

To accommodate the enormous increase, the capacity of existing dormitories was maximized by maintaining the doubling and tripling of room accommodation that had occurred when the army had first moved in the STAR and ASTP units. Even that crowding could not handle the influx, so in the spring of 1946, two, one-story, wooden barracks were obtained gratis from the government under the veteran's housing plan and constructed on reclaimed grounds to the southwest of New North. The barracks, known to students as Lower Slobbobia, became the residence for many of the veterans. Through similar gifts of surplus buildings under the amended Lanham Act of 1945, which authorized the Federal Works Agency to transfer surplus military buildings to any institutions needing academic facilities for the education of veterans, four additional wooden structures were put up on the east side of 37th Street, between P and N streets, to serve as classrooms and offices for the college and the School of Foreign Service. The northern two were bricked over, eventually connected, and named Poulton Hall. In the fall of 1946, the barn behind Dahlgren was converted to a dormitory and named

O'Gara Hall to memorialize Martin O'Gara, SJ, former theology professor and chaplain who had died in a plane crash returning from India in the spring of 1946. When the new hospital on Reservoir Road opened in 1947, the old one on 35th Street was converted to additional undergraduate housing. By 1950 the university was able to house more than 1,000 students on campus, nearly double its prewar level. James Shannon, one of the relatively few eighteen-year-olds to enter Georgetown in October 1946, recalled that, with all the temporary buildings and conversions, the campus "just mushroomed . . . overnight." It looked, he remembered, like a new city, alive and bustling.[8]

In the postwar years Georgetown saw its first black students enter at least several of the schools of the university. Despite being situated in a neighborhood that since the late nineteenth century had become increasingly black in its demography, and having had a president (Patrick Healy) of mixed-race origins, the university had never enrolled an African American. In the spring of 1947, the provincial superior, learning from a staff member of a Senate committee that a "certain group" was threatening to contest the appropriation of federal funds for construction projects at the medical center of the university on the grounds that the center segregated its black patients and had no black students or physicians, inquired about the charges. The regent of the center, Paul McNally, dismissed the threat as the work of those with "communistic leanings" who were simply trying to embarrass the university. "They demand that we deny to all white people their freedom of not associating with colored people if they so choose," he argued in defense of the segregated facilities for black patients, while ignoring the issues of blacks in the student body and on the faculty and staff.[9] Georgetown's president, Lawrence Gorman, SJ, in response to a related inquiry, stated that Georgetown had "no policy in effect to deny admission to any students otherwise qualified, because of race. . . . Race or religion is by no mean an eliminating factor."[10]

A year later, Julian Reiss, a New York alumnus and activist in improving race relations, called on Gorman to accept a black student who had received a scholarship from a national organization. Gorman brought the matter to the board of directors, who decided that the university should first accept a qualified black and then seek the scholarship Reiss was offering to provide. Gorman in turn urged all the deans and regents of the various schools to seek at least one black student for the following year of 1948–49.[11] The Law School did much more than meet Gorman's quota; that September it admitted four African Americans.[12] The Graduate School admitted one (but that person withdrew before classes began). The following year, 1949–50, twelve black students were enrolled in the university—nine in the Law School, two in the School of Foreign Service, and one in the Graduate School.[13] The two School of Foreign Service students were in the evening division and went to classes, as one of them put it, "under cover of darkness."[14] The college was not one of the integrated schools. When the social activist Catherine De Hueck Doherty came to campus during that year to address the Sodality, in her remarks she condemned the Jesuits for not admitting any blacks to the college. This led a group of concerned college students, including Gerald Ryan and Paul Sigmund, to raise the issue with the college dean and other administrators, but nothing immediately came of their efforts.[15] It would be several more years before the College of Arts and Sciences had its first black student.

A Faculty Surge and Facilities Crisis

To meet the enormous increase in enrollment, there was a corresponding surge in faculty hiring throughout the schools. Across the nation's campuses the number of faculty members increased by 52 percent during the 1940s. The increase at Georgetown was far greater. Between 1947 and 1948, the university appointed 233 new faculty. The college added 35, including 7 Jesuits. It marked a sharp turn in the proportion of laypersons on the school faculty that had traditionally had a large Jesuit presence, if not a majority. From a faculty of fewer than 50 in 1941 (including 20 Jesuits), the college faculty grew to more than 100 by 1950, and the vast majority were laypersons. Among the new appointments in the college were Lev Dobriansky in economics; Stefan Possony, Karl Cerny, Brian McGrath, SJ, and James

Left: Jules Davids, professor of history in SFS. (Georgetown University Archives)

Right: William O'Brien, professor of government in SFS. (Georgetown University Archives)

Brian McGrath, SJ, dean
of the College of Arts and
Sciences, 1951–57; academic
vice president, 1955–70.
(Georgetown University Archives)

Horigan, SJ, in government; Pierre Maubrey in French; Paul Hume in fine arts; and Eric McDermott, SJ, and Donald Penn in history.

The School of Foreign Service experienced an even greater faculty increase than did the college—forty-three new members. The new appointees included Jules Davids (MSFS 1945, PhD 1947) and Frank Fadner, SJ (BSFS 1933), in history; Walter Giles Jr. (BSFS 1943), William V. O'Brien (BSFS 1946, MSFS 1948, PhD 1953), and Jan Karski in government; Jesse Mann in philosophy; and Riley Hughes and John Yoklavich in English. The Law School made ten new appointments, including Paul Dean (LLB 1946) and Edward Bennett Williams (LLB 1944). Dentistry brought on twenty-eight, including Harry B. Sheldon (DDS 1943), who became chair of the Department of Operative Dentistry; Joseph L. Bernier, who became chief of the dental corps in 1960; and Gustav O. Kruger Jr. (DDS1939), who chaired the Department of Oral Surgery for forty years. Nursing added eleven, among them Mary Catherine Wisler and Stella Warfield. The Medical School, with its new hospital opening in 1947 and a reorganization of its faculty in full swing, brought in nearly one hundred new faculty and clinicians in the two-year period.

Given this enormous expansion of students and faculty, growing pains soon became evident. "One of the serious handicaps under which Georgetown labors," the dean of the college, Brian McGrath, SJ, reported in 1950, "is the lack of essential physical facilities." Most lacking was a modern central library with appropriate cataloguing of books and adequate reading areas. Another urgent need, in the dean's opinion, was a modern science building to house the departments of biology, physics, and mathematics. (Chemistry was the one science department to move into White-Gravenor.) The physics department was scattered through the basements of Healy, Old North, and New North, "in rooms that could scarcely meet the test of modern educational requirements in the matter of light, air and ventilation." Beyond the academic facilities there was an "indispensable" need for a student center that would provide space for student organizations, study halls, and lounges.

"No college," McGrath continued, "will rise above the level to which its faculty is capable of taking it." The Georgetown college faculty, he found, was still undermanned, inbred, and disorganized. One of the first things McGrath had done as dean was to create an executive faculty for the college, consisting of the deans, librarian, registrar, and department heads. Committees under the executive faculty were created to oversee admissions, curriculum, and discipline. He also began a reform of the freshman curriculum, with particular attention given to the placement of students in language and English courses, and increased emphasis on written assignments in the latter. The dean made regular departmental meetings mandatory to improve communication, planning, and coordination within the various disciplines. To assist and encourage faculty scholarship, he established a publications fund. To provide the students with an opportunity to critique and make recommendations about faculty and administration, McGrath established a senior committee to prepare an annual report on the merits and defects of Georgetown in the students' experience. To improve the library, the staff was enlarged and cataloguing of recent acquisitions begun. A faculty committee was created to advise and assist the librarian in acquiring new books and journals.[16] To prepare the ground for Georgetown to secure a chapter of Phi Beta Kappa, a quest the university had pursued in vain for more than two decades, the university established the Gold Key Society, a scholastic honor group, in 1948.[17]

Student Life in the Postwar Period

Despite the presence of a large number of older students in the immediate postwar period, student life quickly resumed its traditional pattern of tightly regimented schedules. Mass attendance was compulsory three times a week, in addition to Sundays. Students who were not veterans were required to be in their rooms after dinner; prefects made nightly checks at 7, 9, 10, and 11 PM (lights out). The veterans, who lived in separate dormitories, were expected to be home by 10 PM and in bed by 11 PM. On weekends, students had to sign out at the prefect of discipline's office before 7 PM in order to go off campus until 11 PM to 1 AM, depending on one's class. To be away for the weekend, one needed a parent's written approval. At least in the first year or so following the war, the rule applied to veterans as well. One veteran who was married had to secure the approval of his wife in order to visit her on weekends.[18] But students, especially veterans, found ways to evade this system of constant control, such as going out after the 9 PM or 11 PM check for some nightly beers, or checking back in on a weekend at midnight, only to go back out to resume a Saturday night date.

In general, a pious ethos prevailed. After dinner, the vast majority of students would make a visit to Dahlgren Chapel and then sit around the quadrangle or Copley lawn before the first evening check. In May selected seniors would form a living rosary in the quadrangle as students gathered for a daily recitation. The gift from the class of 1950 was the statue of Our Lady of Fatima that still graces Copley lawn.

The glee club, under its longtime director (since 1919) Dr. Edward Donovan (AB 1911), revived in the academic year following the conclusion of the war. The glee club performed on campus for its annual Lenten Mi-Carême concert, which Donovan had inaugurated in 1922, and other occasions as

Georgetown Chimes performing at a barbershop competition. (Georgetown University Archives)

well as performing in New York and other cities. In January 1950 the glee club hosted Vaughan Monroe's orchestra in Gaston Hall, where Monroe, in a coast-to-coast radio broadcast, played Donovan's latest Georgetown composition, a march, "Here's to the Blue and Gray." Donovan had earlier written "Georgetown's Chimes," which became the signature piece of, and provided a name for, a vocal ensemble that began in the academic year 1946–47, as part of the glee club.[19] Frank Jones, a first-year law student, who had begun an a cappella group (the Barballads) as a Yale undergraduate, recruited two fellow law students, Jack Slater (BSSS 1946) and Paul Conway (LLB 1949), as lead singer and baritone, respectively, and Chuck Laiosa, a college sophomore, as bass. The vocal quartet began to perform as the Georgetown Quartet as part of the glee club. The following year Jones expanded the group to nine by adding Jack Farrell (BSFS 1950), Gerald McGettigan (BSSS 1951), Ray Lyddy (LLB 1950), and others to become the original Chimes. They continued to be part of the glee club but increasingly made appearances on their own at dances; basketball games; on Copley lawn, where by the early fifties they were singing thrice weekly; and from the steps of Old North for monthly concerts. In 1953 Gerard Yates, SJ, and Richard Law, SJ, joined them as the first Celestial Chimes.[20] Over the next half century the Chimes would become the most important and successful musical organization in the university's history.

One of Georgetown's oldest student organizations, the Mask and Bauble Society, revived in 1946–47 with shows in Trinity Theater and Poulton Hall. In 1949 nursing students became regular performers in plays staged by the society. Three years later the class of 1952 staged the first senior musical, *Kiss Me, Tondalayo,* at Trinity Theater in the spring of 1952.

Pep rallies before key football games were major events, with students from the local Catholic women's colleges often being invited to attend the rally and a dance that followed. Football and basketball games, particularly those against traditional rivals such as Fordham or Maryland, became occasions for raiding other campuses to steal mascots or paint statues. In return the home campus would be guarded against retaliatory raids. By 1949 the Jesuit prefect of discipline, Emory Ross, had made himself a kind of minister of defense, organizing students into a "palace guard" in which, armed with bullhorns, they would hide in bushes around campus or be sent off in cars to reconnoiter the surrounding area to intercept any caravan of raiders from other campuses.[21] In the fall of 1950 the guard detected five Maryland students trying to penetrate the campus after midnight. Ross called out two dormitories to seize the invaders and was preparing to shave their heads and "brand" them with a "GU" before the dean of the college, Brian McGrath, SJ, who had been awakened by the commotion, rushed down to put an end to the proceedings.

In this atmosphere hazing predictably also made a brief return to Georgetown. In the "G Book," or handbook for students, in 1950–51, there was a set of freshman rules that ranged from wearing a distinctive hat (beanie) on campus, yielding the right of way to upperclassmen, walking on the north side of O Street, and committing to memory all official songs and yells of the college. By 1950 the discipline office was actually orchestrating it, much to the dismay of the dean of the college, by having freshmen routed out in the middle of the night for such trials as calisthenics on Kehoe Field, where they would subsequently be locked until the morning, or being forced to walk the diving board into the outdoor swimming pool on a rainy night. McGrath secured Prefect Ross's removal by the end of the 1950–51 year.[22]

Among the notable graduates of the period were those who made careers in government or nongovernmental agencies. Viron P. Vaky (BSFS 1947) became a career foreign service officer, including service as ambassador to Colombia and as assistant secretary of state for inter-American affairs. Henry Hyde (BSSS 1947) became a lawyer and then for more than thirty years a representative of the Sixth Congressional District in Illinois. John William Stanton (BSFS 1949) became a Republican congressman from Ohio from

Daniel Degnan (seated, far end), president of the Yard and of the Student Council, 1949–50.

1965 to 1983. Samuel H. Butterfield (BSFS 1949) became a key executive in the Agency for International Development and other federal agencies over the next three decades. John Dingell (BS 1949, LLB 1952) in 1955 succeeded his father as the Democratic representative from the Fifteenth Michigan Congressional District in Congress where, over the next half century and beyond, he became one of its most powerful figures. Indeed, he served long enough to see the cause for which he had labored for decades, universal health care, finally become law in 2010. John Carroll Whitaker (BSSS 1949) earned a PhD in geology at Johns Hopkins University and became undersecretary of the Interior in the Nixon administration. Lane Kirkland (BSFS 1948), a veteran of the merchant marine, became president of the AFL-CIO. Shlomo Argov (BSFS 1952) had a distinguished career in the Israeli diplomatic corps, serving, among other positions, as ambassador to Great Britain and minister to the United States.

Law continued to draw many graduates, including Eugene Stewart (BSS 1948, LLB 1951), a veteran who joined the firm of Steptoe and Johnson after earning his law degree and who in 1967 established Sursum Corda, the first privately funded urban housing development in the District of Columbia. His classmate, Peter Mullen (AB 1948), became a leading lawyer in New York City. Richard Fruchterman Jr. (BSS 1951, LLB 1954) made a career in the navy as an expert in international law in the judge advocate's office.

Among those to pursue careers in medicine was John J. Ring (BS 1949, MD 1953), who became chair of the AMA's board of trustees. James L. Hughes (BSFS 1951) was a career officer with the Naval Medical Corps.

Donald J. Donahue (AB 1947) became a chief executive of the Continental Can Group and the first lay chair of Georgetown's board of directors. Another veteran of the merchant marine, Robert E. McDonough (BSFS 1949), left a very successful career as an oil executive to found an equally successful company that supplied temporary workers to businesses. John R. Kennedy (BSS 1952) built his own paperboard company in Connecticut into a multibillion dollar business.

A notable number of graduates made careers in the academy, including Joseph Jeffs (AB 1949), who became the head librarian at his alma mater in 1969, a post he held for more than two decades. Paul Sigmund (AB 1950) earned a doctorate in political science and became a professor at Princeton University. John A. Carroll

Joseph Jeffs, **C** 1949.

(Georgetown University Archives)

(BSFS 1950) became a professor of history at Troy State University in Alabama. His biography of George Washington won the Pulitzer Prize in 1975. Promod Chandra (BSFS 1951) became the holder of a chair on Indian and South Asian art at Harvard University. John Phillip Reid (BSSS 1952) became professor of law at New York University and the author of the multivolume series *Constitutional History of the American Revolution.* John Lucal (BSSS 1950) and Daniel Degnan (BSSS 1950) became Jesuits and held various important posts. Peter Blatty (AB 1950) became a novelist and playwright; his most famous work is *The Exorcist,* a 1971 novel set in Georgetown that two years later was made into a sensationally successful film.

A New Era for the Graduate School

When Hunter Guthrie, SJ, was appointed dean of the Graduate School in the summer of 1943, he inherited a program that the university administration in the late 1930s had revitalized through distinguished faculty appointments and a concentration on a small group of largely full-time students. By 1943 a significant core of the key faculty remained; the number of students had shrunk to scarcely more than forty. The forty-two-year-old Jesuit had been trained in several European universities, including Louvain, Berlin, and the Sorbonne, where he had earned a PhD in philosophy. During his years in

Hunter Guthrie, SJ, dean of the Graduate School, 1942–49; president of the university, 1949–52. (Georgetown University Archives. Photo by Del Ankers.)

Europe in the latter 1930s, he had come into contact with an extraordinary range of philosophers within the European intellectual community. He had studied under Martin Heidegger, Werner Jaeger, and Emile Brédier. Edith Stein, Simone Weil, Jacques Maritain, and Etienne Gilson were all his acquaintances. This network allowed Guthrie to grasp German existentialism, logical positivism, and the beginnings of analytic philosophy a full decade before these movements made any inroads in the United States.[23] He came to Georgetown from Fordham, where he had chaired the philosophy department in the graduate school. Guthrie brought with him the conviction that graduate education should hold top priority in any university. He knew all too well that in the world of Jesuit higher education the graduate school was "too often considered a dilettante's luxury or an unloved appendage at best tolerated in times of plenty and lopped off in times of stress."[24]

Despite the unfavorable climate that war brought for liberal graduate education, Guthrie immediately set out to restart the revitalization process that had showed such promise just a few years before by strengthening the three departments that were Georgetown's strongest in graduate studies—economics, history, and political science—and by attempting to create, *ab ovo,* a unique philosophy department. In 1943–44 he made several significant appointments to the faculty. From Harvard he brought in the historian Cyril L. H. Toumanoff. He appointed the former Austrian minister to the Netherlands, and a refugee to the United States, Georg von Alexich, to teach comparative government and international relations. In philosophy he brought in Herbert Thomas Schwartz from Columbia. In history also he added Charles Callan Tansill, who, by 1943, was the author of six books. In 1944 he appointed Joseph Durkin, SJ (PhD Fordham), to the history graduate faculty. That same year Francis J. Heyden, SJ, a PhD in astrophysics from Harvard, was appointed to run the observatory and to revive a graduate program in astronomy. In subsequent years the school appointed Otto Donner, who had taught economics at the University of Berlin; Stefan Possony, an Austrian political scientist who had as an émigré in 1940 joined the Institute for Advanced Study in Princeton; and the philosophers Louis Mercier, John Francis Callahan, and Rudolph Allers, the last an émigré from Vienna.

There was a heavy preponderance of faculty from Central Europe. Their refugee status made it possible for Georgetown to afford such top-quality professors. It would have been simply impossible, Guthrie admitted, to hire American professors of that caliber at salaries Georgetown could pay. Thanks largely to the Europeans, the graduate faculty published. Sixteen of the thirty-eight faculty had books to their credit by 1948; four others had books in preparation.[25] To facilitate faculty publication, the school established the Georgetown University Press in 1945. Joseph Durkin's *John Dooley, Confederate Soldier: His War Journal* was the press' first publication, followed by fellow historian Charles Tansill's *Congressional Career of Thomas Francis Bayard, 1865–1885*. With Edmund Walsh and the School of Foreign Service faculty in mind, the school also was anticipating that the press would issue a series of publications on geopolitical studies.

Guthrie particularly concentrated on developing the field of international relations within the department of political science, a field that the School of Foreign Service had effectively abandoned when it discontinued graduate studies at the outbreak of war. The Graduate School very successfully cultivated the armed forces for personnel to pursue degrees in the field. Guthrie secured contracts from both the air force and the army to train senior officers in international relations and diplomacy. In 1946 the head of the incipient Air War University, Col. Lloyd P. Hopwood, decided to send officers for graduate training to two universities, one of which was Georgetown.[26] The air force alone sent sixty-seven officers to Georgetown from 1946 to 1951 to concentrate in international relations; the army sent fourteen.

Stefan Possony, who was a full-time intelligence officer for the air force, was effectively the director of this precursor to national security studies, as he taught most of the relevant courses as well as directed scores of dissertations and theses. The Graduate School, at the behest of the air force, in 1948 developed a year-long program in psychological warfare for the service, with Rudolf Allers; Possony; Jan Karski; Constantine W. Boldyreff, a Russian émigré; and Francis Seidler, an Austrian refugee, among the faculty teaching the course, which included topics on propaganda, intelligence and public opinion, ideologies, social psychology and national characters, the geopolitico-economic-cultural aspects of key areas, and Communist and non-Communist techniques. With the outbreak of the Korean War in June 1950, this course was shortened to a one-term offering, with a usual enrollment of fifty or so from the three main services. These courses and programs became, in effect, the graduate branch of the Air War University, which had been established in 1946. Indeed, the first graduation of the university took place in September 1947 in Gaston Hall.

Guthrie also attempted to build up a department of graduate philosophy that would have an interdisciplinary focus, stressing the relationship between philosophy and theology, philosophy and the sciences, and philosophy and education. In 1944 he established the Institute of Christian Philosophy, which featured a three-year program culminating in the doctorate in philosophy. The program, taught by economists (Goetz Briefs), historians (Olger Sherbowitz-Wetzor), as well as philosophers, concentrated on the influence of Christian revelation on philosophy, or the consequences of its lack, on societies. It proposed to include in its analysis modern culture; economic, political, and social theories; education; and the sciences. Despite its ambitious designs, the institute failed to attract many students during its near decade of existence.

But the other programs revived by Guthrie proved to be quite successful in drawing students. As noted earlier, Guthrie opened up the school for women in 1943. By 1947 they comprised one-fifth of all students. Most of the rest were men from the military or government agencies. From an enrollment of forty-four when Guthrie arrived in 1943, the school topped 640 by 1951. Those receiving their PhDs grew from seven in 1947 to thirty-five three years later; those receiving their master of arts degrees increased from fourteen to fifty-five in the same period. Nearly three-fifths of the graduate students studied history and political science and accounted for most of the master's degrees and nearly half of the PhDs. Chemistry was the only other major producer of graduate students. Most students, even in the sciences, including astronomy, were now part-timers, employed largely in the military services and government agencies. In general, Hunter Guthrie found the graduate students, many of them veterans, of "remarkably high" quality in general, precisely because of their maturity and purposefulness in approaching graduate studies.[27]

The Middle States inspection team in 1951 did not share that assessment, due to the school's high acceptance rate (85% of applicants). The Middle States report hailed the first-rate quality of a minority of the professors, that is, mostly those émigrés with degrees from Vienna, Berlin, Paris, and other "great continental universities." It was much less impressed with the overall scholarship of the faculty, which it found "scarcely distinguished." Nonetheless its final judgment was that it was a good graduate school within the limited area it had staked out within certain disciplines. Modest infusions of money would make it considerably better.[28]

As a consequence of the U.S. government's experience during the recent conflict, in which federally funded university research had proven to be so crucial toward the securing of victory, in the postwar years the government embraced the responsibility of becoming the major permanent sponsor of research in universities, a role that private foundations had played before World War II. The armed services, along with the Atomic Energy Commission and the National Institutes of Health (NIH), became the chief government funders of scientific research. By the close of the 1940s, the air force alone had contracts with institutions amounting to at least $14 million; the Office of Naval Research was averaging $20 million in contracts annually.[29] In all, the federal government was contributing approximately $200 million annually by the century's midpoint to support the vast majority of advanced research being carried out by the nation's universities.[30]

Georgetown benefited significantly, if on a modest scale, from this transformation of government research policy. By 1947 the Graduate School had contracts from the air force and the army to conduct classified research. Several Georgetown personnel, including Guthrie, Possony, and Tibor Kerekes, were given clearance to access classified materials on the logistics of jet aircraft and arctic warfare. Two members of the physics department, a retired air force colonel and a Jesuit, were conducting research on ultrasonics for the air force.[31] The chemistry department had a contract to do special investigations for the Army Chemical Center at Fort Detrick in Frederick, Maryland. There was a mapping project for the army in which Guthrie seems to have been directly involved. Trained in photography, Guthrie, in his private room on campus, developed film of maps and other related matter that he had shot.[32] Frank Heyden and the observatory had funding from the air force and army to do long-distance measurement experiments during solar eclipses in the late 1940s and early 1950s. By 1952 the Graduate School was under contract with different defense agencies for projects that in that fiscal year alone brought the university approximately $200,000. Only the "appallingly limited facilities" that Georgetown had to offer prevented the school from securing many more such projects with their ample funding.[33]

Hunter Guthrie was known for his comprehensive views that perceived the links among philosophy, education, society, and politics, in particular the disastrous sociopolitical consequences that had followed in the totalitarian societies of Germany and Russia from the ideas instilled in their elitist and deterministic education. From the latter stages of World War II through the early Cold War period, he involved himself with various government projects to promote education as a key toward building a democratic society. In 1941 he was selected as a member of the U.S. Commission on Restructuring Education that met with British counterparts at Princeton to consider how best to develop an educational system based on democratic principles. Fluent in four languages and able to read several others, he was particularly invaluable as an international emissary for the State Department and other U.S. agencies. The department translated his inaugural presidential address at Georgetown in 1949 and distributed it to outlets in Germany, Austria, Italy, Japan, and Korea for publication.[34] Through his contacts with government intelligence agencies, Guthrie also apparently took trips in conjunction with the State Department and the United States Information Agency, beginning as early as 1947 and extending into the 1950s, to the Iberian Peninsula and Latin America.

Renaissance of the Medical Center

The great surge in population in the District of Columbia during the war led to the realization of a longtime university objective—the building of a new hospital. In 1942, with the government prepared to fund new facilities to increase hospital accommodations in the city, the university applied for federal money for major hospital construction but then declined to accept the $381,000 grant because it carried the stipulation that the university had to deed over to the government the land on which the building was to be constructed.[35] Two years later Senator Millard Tydings of Maryland introduced legislation to award grants without strings to George Washington University and Georgetown University for the construction of new hospitals. In September 1944 Georgetown was awarded $1.4 million for a new hospital estimated to cost $2 million, and construction by the John McShain Company began in December on Reservoir Road contiguous to the Medical-Dental Building. A year later, due to inflation and additions, the estimated cost nearly doubled to $3.5 million. The government subsequently increased its share to $2.75 million, with the university left to raise $750,000.[36] In a special fund-raising campaign for the project, the university raised more than its goal, but a continuing rise in costs made it necessary for Dean Paul McNally to borrow more than $60,000 to complete the building.[37] The seven-story, four-hundred-bed facility opened on July 31, 1947, under the direction of the Sisters of Charity of Nazareth, who replaced the Sisters of St. Francis who had managed the previous hospital for nearly a half century.

Wallace Yater, the chair of medicine and the individual chiefly responsible for the design of the hospital, was no longer at Georgetown when the hospital opened. In the summer of 1945 Yater had submitted his resignation to the university in which he listed ten points that the Medical School needed to address in order to become a first-rate institution—from building up a minimum endowment of $2 million to the need for a physician as dean of the school, from the avoidance of inbreeding in the selection of department chairs to the upgrade of salaries, stricter admission and grading standards, and the better integration of clinical and preclinical departments. It was actually a drastic attempt to bring about reforms that Yater thought were absolutely necessary to bring the school out of its doldrums. The basic science teaching was notoriously bad. The performance of Georgetown graduates in national and state boards was a national scandal. In 1943 Georgetown students' rate of failure was 11.4 percent; the national average was 2.4 percent.

The following year was far worse. Over one-fifth of the school's graduates who took state boards failed, including nine of ten in New York State. In 1945 nine of thirty-two Georgetown students who took the national boards failed.[38] Yater eventually met with President Gorman to discuss his ideas, but in the end Gorman accepted Yater's resignation in September 1945.[39] That same month Joseph Wall, the chair of pediatrics, resigned in support of Yater. The two resignations left a crisis of morale for faculty and students. The Georgetown Alumni Association sent President Gorman a petition signed by ninety-nine alumni, including seven department chairs, and twenty other faculty, that urged him to bring back both men. There was no response from Gorman.[40]

In retrospect, Yater's resignation did have the effect he hoped to achieve, although certainly not in the way he intended. In his stead as chief of medicine,

Dedication of the new hospital by President Truman in 1947. (Georgetown University Archives)

the executive faculty chose Harold Jeghers, professor of medicine at Boston University School of Medicine and chief of the Boston University medical service at Boston City Hospital. Jeghers had not sought the chair but had been recommended by two Georgetown faculty who had worked with Jeghers in Boston.[41] Jeghers, as chief of the medical service in Boston, had acquired a trove of experience in medical education. He had a remarkable grasp of the symbiotic relationship between medical education, particularly its clinical aspects, and research that he had witnessed and was part of in the medical schools and teaching hospitals in Boston and Cambridge, which were among the leaders in the nation.[42] He was probably uniquely equipped, by his experience and contacts, to lead Georgetown to the higher level that Yater had so desired for it.

Jeghers agreed to take the position, with the stipulation that he be allowed to reform Georgetown's medical curriculum and to integrate the hospital more effectively as a component of medical education. Barely had Jeghers arrived when McCauley announced his own retirement as dean in the late summer of 1946. As his successor, Gorman named Paul McNally, SJ, an internationally renowned astronomer who had headed Georgetown's observatory for the past eighteen years but who had no background in medical education. Although his appointment initially was a disappointment to the faculty who, like Yater, wanted the dean to be a medical person, McNally quickly proved to be the perfect complement to Jeghers in reforming the curriculum, standards, and staffing of the school.

McNally, realizing his own lack of experience, allowed Jeghers to educate him into the world of modern medicine. On a two-week trip to Boston, Jeghers shepherded McNally through an intensive tour of Boston's medical institutions and introduced him to many leading medical educators there.[43] The orientation had a profound effect on McNally, who upon his return to Georgetown began to reorganize the faculty and put into effect the reform of curriculum and the integration of hospital and school that rapidly enabled Georgetown to become a first-rate medical school. On the advice of Jeghers and others, McNally began to recruit full-time persons to replace the part-timers who had traditionally chaired the various departments of the school. The sudden replacement of the old chairs, many of whom had long held their positions, caused a good deal of turmoil in the school, but the autocratic McNally did not let sentiment get in the way of reform.[44]

Robert Coffey, professor of surgery. (Georgetown University Archives)

The new chairs gradually brought into their departments other full-timers, and the effect was a transformed faculty. The timing for the extensive hires was very opportune. So many young medical people returning from the war were open to the kind of opportunity that McNally and Jeghers were offering, such as Robert Coffey, a Georgetown medical graduate with a PhD in surgery from Minnesota, who was made the first full-time chair of surgery. Other newly appointed full-time chairs were more experienced, indeed distinguished, medical educators whom McNally persuaded to come to Georgetown. Willi Baensch, for instance, who in 1947 was brought in to chair radiology, was a recent immigrant who had worked with Marie Curie and William Konrad Roentgen in Munich, had taught at the University of Leipzig, and had been president of the Roentgen Congress in the 1930s. From the Mayo Clinic came another person in the same year with an international reputation, Edward B. Tuohy, as chair of anesthesiology. In 1946, Charles F. Geschickter, who had been the director of the Garvan Cancer Research Laboratory at Johns Hopkins, came as chairman of pathology. Geschickter's associate at Johns Hopkins, Murray Copeland, also a nationally known authority on cancer, was made the chair of a newly created Department of Oncology and Radiology. As the full-time chair of obstetrics, McNally brought in Andrew Marchetti, who at Cornell had, among other things, helped develop the Pap smear for the detection of cervical cancer.

Within the central Department of Medicine, Jeghers had inherited a core of excellent faculty: Hugh Hussey, Sol Katz, Thomas Kelliher, and others. But Jeghers, realizing that the explosion of medical technology since the beginning of the war made medical specialization the wave of the future, reorganized the department into several divisions and brought in specialists to head them. To do so he mined his Boston connections for young specialists. These Boston imports from 1948 to 1952 were indeed a remarkable group. From the Boston City Hospital came five persons who had previously worked with Jeghers. Laurence Kyle, who would gain renown for his research on metabolic diseases, became chief of the metabolic and renal service. Irving Brick, whose specialization was the digestive system, was made chief of gastroenterology. Edward Freis, who had already distinguished himself in cardiovascular research with his work on drugs for the control of hypertension, was brought into the Department of Medicine in 1949. John Curry was brought in from Boston to begin a pulmonary unit at the hospital. Elbert Taylor Phelps was named chief resident in 1949.[45]

From Peter Bent Brigham Hospital in Boston, Jeghers secured Charles Rath in 1949 as Georgetown's first full-time hematologist. A year later Proctor Harvey and Charles Hufnagel came from Brigham as the first full-time cardiologist and cardiovascular surgeon, respectively. Harvey was made director of the division of cardiology. In Hufnagel's first year at

Proctor Harvey, professor of cardiology. (Georgetown University Archives)

Georgetown he implanted the first heart valve in a patient, the forerunner of open heart surgery valve replacement.[46] From Jefferson Medical School in Philadelphia, Francis Michael Forster, whose publishing resume was already extensive, was made head of the neurology department in 1950. Finally, in 1952, George Schreiner, the Georgetown graduate who had originally recommended Jeghers, came from the Boston City Hospital to head up the renal division. Georgetown had acquired the second artificial kidney in 1950 and over the next decade, Schreiner and his associates developed hemodialysis as a lifesaving measure for renal disorders.

Jeghers thought that the faculty reconstruction that he oversaw at Georgetown from 1948 to 1952 was unique. "Usually," he pointed out, "you reorganize the Medical School . . . piecemeal." Georgetown was in the serendipitous position to do it "at one fell swoop" and bring in an array of specialists "all relatively the same age group [forties] . . . and each one . . . sold on . . . the curriculum and general educational philosophy."[47] "It was an exciting time," Charles Rath recalls. "We were young, and had all been recruited for a common purpose, which we enthusiastically supported. The spirit of cooperation was great. We each had definite responsibilities and a great amount of freedom to carry them out."[48]

Part of the goal of the revolution in faculty was to make research a central function of the school in its various departments. With the federal government and private foundations funding medical research in the postwar period at an unprecedented level, this concentration on research came at a very propitious moment. Between 1945 and 1950, the budget for the NIH, for instance, mushroomed from $3 to $52 million, much of it allocated to university research.[49] Georgetown received a growing proportion of funds from

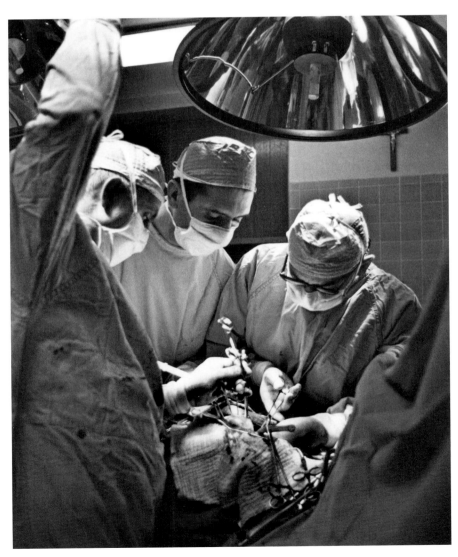

Charles Hufnagel, (*right*), professor of cardiovascular surgery. (Georgetown University Archives)

NIH and other agencies. The new Department of Oncology was one of the principal and earliest beneficiaries at Georgetown of this boom in funding. In 1948 it received a grant of $157,000 from the National Cancer Institute to conduct cancer research.[50]

Jeghers radically changed the curriculum. The teaching of the basic sciences was limited to the first year and a half of training. To prepare students for the clinical years, Jeghers introduced pathology, preventive medicine, and physical diagnoses into the fourth term. Virtually all teaching beyond second year was done in Georgetown Hospital and its affiliates, including new ones that Jeghers secured, with house staff, residents, and interns serving as clinical faculty. At Georgetown this required extensive structural changes in the new university hospital, which had been designed short-sightedly to be a community hospital, not a teaching one. Wards and other units were converted into research laboratories and classrooms. Air-conditioning was installed throughout the facility.[51] In addition, McNally raised the standards for admitting and grading students. Students now had to pass the first section of the national boards at the end of their basic training and the second section before their graduation. By 1950 Georgetown students took four out of the first seven places in the national boards. As Hunter Guthrie advised an alumnus who was complaining about Georgetown's rigid admission standards, thanks to "considerable housecleaning and a radical change in our admission policies," the school had climbed from last place in national ranking to one of "enviable distinction."[52] It was no surprise, but still highly gratifying and emblematic of the transformation that had occurred at Georgetown, when in 1949 the Council on Medical Education and Hospitals in its first postwar visit to the school removed it from the probation it had been on since 1938. The school was now not only fully accredited for the first time in a decade but on its way to becoming a first-rate medical center.

In recruiting new faculty for the revitalization of the medical center, McNally had implicitly departed from the decades-old policy of seeking Catholics for all possible positions. At the student level, however, he was determined to preserve Georgetown very much as a Catholic institution. As part of his reform, McNally wanted to establish an explicit mission of training Catholic doctors, with Catholics composing the main pool of applicants for admission, and other qualified applicants admitted only if space still remained. Catholics already formed the overwhelming majority of the student body—over four-fifths (306 of 369) in 1947–48. Nonetheless, the Catholic mission became the official policy in 1950, but there was so much protest from alumni and others about the policy that it was discontinued after barely one year.[53] In the meantime Georgetown Medical School admitted its first female students, the first being Sara Stewart in 1946 as a special student (Stewart, already the possessor of a PhD in microbiology, graduated in 1949 and went on to a distinguished career in cancer research at the National Institutes of Health and Georgetown and became one of the principal cancer researchers at the medical center). Six women were accepted in the regular admissions in 1947, including Sister Eileen Niedfield (MD 1951) who, as a missionary, became a hospital administrator and medical official in Bhutan.

The Other Sides of the Medical Center: Dentistry and Nursing

The Dental School, like the other schools of the university, experienced an enormous increase in enrollment following the war, from some 200 in 1944 to 361 by 1948; as in other schools, veterans dominated the student ranks. In the 1947–48 academic year they constituted 73 percent of dental students at Georgetown. Unlike the other schools, however, the Dental School did not experience an immediate surge in enrollment with the onset of peace. Enrollment rose only slightly during the first two years of the postwar period. This lag seems to have been the result of an official visit from its accrediting body, the Council on Dental Education, during the war, which produced an unfavorable report. What the visitors found, as they concluded euphemistically, was "not flattering." The admissions process was haphazard, more a thing of chance than of selection, which resulted in a student body that largely consisted of students who came to Georgetown for reasons of expediency—it was the one school that accepted them. The faculty was composed of too many part-timers, nearly 75 percent of the teaching staff. Its clinical faculty was woefully inadequate, "singularly lacking in vision and in knowledge of the trends in dentistry and in dental education." As for its financial condition, it was too heavily dependent on clinical income for its revenue (nearly half of its budget).[54] But the greatest weakness of the school, the team found, was its lack of "progressive, decisive and informed leadership." Georgetown badly needed a full-time dean who was qualified to lead it from what it was at present—at best "a trade-school"—to the level of university-grade dental education. "In short, there is perhaps no better location, background and environment anywhere in the United States for the development of an outstanding dental school. Heroic measures will have to be employed if this end is to be gained." The first step, they suggested, was to "search out the best qualified man in the country to lead the dental school."[55] In the meantime the school's official status would be "provisionally approved."

This report came as something of a shock to university officials. It had been barely a decade since the school had at long last received the A rating from the ADA. Regent McCauley felt that some aspects of the team's findings had been unjustified. They did not take into consideration the effect of losing fourteen faculty to war service upon overall teaching capability. Nor did they appreciate the strong but futile efforts the school had made earlier to recruit outstanding students from the District of Columbia through a generous scholarship program. With regard to the need for a full-time dean, McCauley could not have agreed more but did not think a national search was the way to secure one. There was already a man on the faculty, who had been at Georgetown for twenty-three years, who understood the school's problems, and who could "respond to the challenge of the report." John Burke (DDS 1921), a former president of the District of Columbia Dental Society, had the contacts and respect to attract a sufficient number of excellent dentists to the school's faculty. They would be part-time—school finances could not afford full-timers—but they would be perfectly capable of providing the kind of dental education sought by the ADA team.[56]

In the wake of this report, President Gorman appointed John Burke to be the first full-time dean of the school in the fall of 1944 as a first step toward correcting the school's deficiencies. Burke, who had been a member of the faculty since 1926, agreed to become dean, with the stipulations that he have full authority over faculty and students and that he and the executive faculty, not the regent, be the sole determiners of educational policy.[57] More change came in the latter years of the decade after the appointment of Edward Bunn, SJ, later president of the university, as regent of the Dental School (the previous regent of the Medical School had also served as regent for the Dental School) in 1948. Bunn's charge from President Gorman was to examine the organization and facilities of the school and to make the necessary changes to improve them.[58]

John P. Burke, dean of the Dental School, 1944–50.
(Georgetown University Archives)

Under Bunn's direction the school began an extensive renovation of the clinical facilities in the school: creating a children's clinic, a periodontal clinic, and a diagnostic department and enlarging the x-ray department and orthodontic laboratory. At the same time, the financing of the school was restructured to make it less dependent on clinical revenue. The administration made changes in key faculty staffing, such as the appointment of a new director of the Department of Oral Surgery. Enrollment grew to 362 by 1951, making Georgetown the ninth largest dental school in the nation, despite the raising of admission standards (fewer than 20% of applicants were accepted), and it was more diverse, although still heavily concentrated in the Middle Atlantic and New England areas. Minimal standards on a progressive basis were set for the promotion of students (a 1.5 GPA for sophomore year; 2.0 GPA for junior and senior years). Graduating students began consistently to pass the national board examinations.

In 1950 Dr. Clemens Rault, who had been chief of the Navy Bureau of Medicine and Surgery for Dentistry, succeeded John Burke as dean. Charles Murto became director of clinics. In that same year a team from the Council on Dental Education returned to Georgetown. They reported that, thanks to Dean Burke, "a great deal of progress and improvement" was clearly evident. The improvements and the new financial arrangement gave promise that Georgetown would continue to consolidate what was now "a good program of dental education." Accordingly, they gave the school an approved rating that removed it from probation.[59]

World War II, with its cadet nursing corps, had proved to be a boon to the Nursing School. But by the latter stages of the conflict, it became clear to university officials that the trend in nursing education was toward collegiate programs. From 1944 to 1950 the university struggled to convert nursing education at Georgetown from a traditional nondegree hospital training program to an academic school of nursing. Securing a qualified faculty was a first step toward fulfilling the requisites for admission into the Association of Collegiate Schools of Nursing. The Sisters of St. Francis, who had managed the training program since its inception in 1904, did not have the academic credentials to conduct a nursing school. In November 1944, the university brought in Anne Murphy as director of nursing education at Georgetown. Despite Murphy's qualifications and efforts, problems with Georgetown's training program continued. In 1945 barely half of the graduates of the diploma program passed the licensing examination.[60] Three years later, when the new hospital opened in 1947, the decision was made not to retain the Sisters of St. Francis as the managers of the hospital and, by extension, the nursing program. In their place, the Sisters of Charity of Nazareth, Kentucky, took over the management of the hospital as well as the Nursing School. Sister Agnes Miriam, SCN, succeeded Anne Murphy as director of nursing education.

In 1948, Edward Bunn, SJ, became regent of the Nursing School (as well as of the Dental School). Bunn, with advanced training in psychology, quickly addressed the question of what the educational character of the Nursing School at Georgetown should be. In 1949 he began to implement the steps needed to develop an academic nursing school with a degree program at its center. He named Sister Agnes Miriam dean of the school, and he created an executive council to devise standards and policies and to draw up a four-year curriculum. In 1950 a phasing out of both the three-year training program and the five-year degree program (which had drawn very few students during its decade of existence and produced even fewer degrees) was begun, and in 1951 a four-year program leading to the bachelor of science in nursing was made the standard at Georgetown. In that year the school was formally established as a professional educational body, separate from the university hospital.[61]

The Institute of Languages and Linguistics

In 1944 Edmund Walsh wrote to the provincial superior that he was devising a program for the postwar period that would focus on intensive training in various languages. The ASTP experience had persuaded him that a program fully utilizing modern technology for language instruction was crucial for the continued development of the School of Foreign Service as an educational resource for those intending to pursue careers in foreign service and international business. With the departure of the last ASTP cadets in June 1944, the time was opportune to make a beginning. Accordingly, in the summer of 1944 a spoken language program began, initially as a certificate program for those who wished to confine their studies wholly to languages. Courses were offered in French, German, Spanish, Russian, Portuguese, Chinese, and Japanese. Phonographic recordings, short-wave radio hookups, and a speech laboratory were all provided to facilitate the acquisition of languages. Demonstration of fluency in any particular language earned the student a certificate.[62] The program was open to women as well as men.[63]

After five years of operation Walsh moved to create an institute of languages and linguistics that would enable the school to utilize fully the new methods and technology that had been developed for language instruction, translation, and interpretation out of ASTP, the Nuremberg trials (where simultaneous translation in four languages had first been effectively used), and at the United Nations. As the provincial superior admitted when he sought permission from the superior general of the Society of Jesus in Rome to start the institute, "There is danger that the F[oreign] S[ervice] S[chool] may lose much of the good name and respect it has acquired in the educational world unless something is done at once to improve the language teaching, strengthen the faculty and experiment with the new methods of audio-visual presentation which recent experience has proved to be so valuable."[64] The institute was to have three goals: to give specialized training in languages, to conduct research in contemporary linguistics, and to improve the pedagogical resources for teaching languages. Language training would be offered in the Romance languages as well as in German, Slavic, Arabic, Chinese, and Japanese. Correlated courses in history, geography, and other area studies would be offered in the various languages of concentration. The institute would limit enrollment to those with two years of college who had language experience.[65] To earn a diploma, students would need to demonstrate proficiency in at least two languages.

In the summer of 1949 the university acquired the property of the former Academy of the Sacred Heart on Massachusetts Avenue as a home for the new institute. The International Business Machines Corporation agreed to furnish free to the institute—as a model program—phonographic instruments and simultaneous translation machines for instruction and laboratory work. Certain foundations made available funds for scholarships and professorships.[66] Leon Dostert, who had been responsible for developing the system of simultaneous language translation and interpretation, first at the Nuremberg trials and later at the United Nations, was named director. Twenty-one new faculty received appointments to the institute in 1949–50, including five women. Charles Ferguson and Ross MacDonald, PhDs from the University of Pennsylvania and Michigan, respectively, were two of the first faculty hired to teach linguistics. Stefan Ferdinand Horn, an Austrian émigré, was made head of the division of interpretation and translation. During its first year, Director Dostert inaugurated the Georgetown Round Table Meetings in Language and Linguistics, an annual symposium that over the next half century would become a major gathering for scholars from around the world in those fields and whose proceedings would form a perennial staple of the Georgetown University Press.

By its second year of operation, enrollment at the institute had reached nearly 250, with females accounting for about 40 percent of the students. The following year enrollment surpassed 300. By 1951 the number of languages offered by the institute had grown to thirty, including Pashto (language of Afghanistan), Romanian, Czech, Finnish, Turkish, Tagali, Bulgarian, and Afrikaans. The growing number of women, especially at the institute, along with a much smaller, but more visible, number within the School of Foreign Service (which, unlike the institute, was prominently on the main campus) was not a welcome development to certain officials of the university. The dean of the Graduate School, Gerard Yates, complained to President Guthrie in 1948 about the creeping presence of women students on campus. Yates claimed that both college students and faculty were complaining about the way "women students are coming to be a part of the undergraduate student body. While they are few in number, their presence is anomalous and indeed unwelcome."[67] Despite such resistance, the School of Foreign Service continued to maintain a coed presence of approximately fifty, and within a decade the institute had a student enrollment whose majority was female.

Georgetown, Edmund A. Walsh, and the Cold War

In the late winter of 1947, President Truman, in announcing that the world faced a choice between "two alternative ways of life," between free government and Communism, declared the existence of a cold war between the United States and the Soviet Union. In a March 1947 editorial, the *Hoya* discerned that the United States had arrived at a most critical point in its survival as a nation and as an international power. In the president's prom-

ulgation of what became known as the Truman Doctrine, or the commitment to use military means to defend free nations against Communist
expansion, as well as in a congressional attempt to outlaw the American
Communist Party, the paper perceived that the country was finally taking
decisive steps "to stop whistling in the dark, and to . . . say halt to the greedy
Russian Bear. . . . If Greece and Turkey are to be saved for the West, if all
Europe is to remain Christian and free, . . . Russia's subtly planned advances
and under-minings must be stopped."[68]

Edmund Walsh, who had been quietly critical of the Roosevelt administration's policy toward the Soviets, particularly in light of what he judged
disastrous consequences resulting from the Yalta and Potsdam agreements in
1945, rejoiced in this overdue determination of the Truman administration
to take the lead in combating the spread of world Communism. The School
of Foreign Service, along with its Institute of Languages and Linguistics, became a very conscious contributor to waging the ideological and geopolitical
conflict between the United States and the Soviet Union.[69] The institute offered specialized courses for air force officers in language translation and interpretation. Dostert served as a special consultant to the newly formed
Central Intelligence Agency in developing its language capabilities.

The school, along with the Graduate School, continued into the 1950s to
offer psychological warfare courses to air force personnel. In conjunction
with the State Department, the school began to offer intensive courses in
American history, international law, and foreign relations to Germans training to be diplomats, which led eventually to the establishment of formal
programs and lectureships at the university by the German Federal Republic.[70] Walsh continued to give regular lectures on the United States and the
Soviet Union to the War College. In his bestselling book, *Total Empire*, published in 1951, Walsh argued that only military power and the determination
to employ all of it aggressively, including a first-strike nuclear policy where
the circumstances warranted, could in the end ensure success for the United
States in combating the Soviet Union.[71]

When Senator Joseph McCarthy of Wisconsin inaugurated his campaign against domestic Communist subversion in February 1950, critics
quickly pointed to Edmund Walsh as the guiding spirit behind the senator's attacks. Drew Pearson, a nationally syndicated columnist, reported
that Walsh had had dinner with McCarthy at a local restaurant in January
1950, and, when in the course of their conversation McCarthy had indicated that he was looking for a good issue for his reelection campaign,
Walsh suggested that Communist subversion of government and other
United States organizations would be a very effective one. This story eventually became conventional wisdom about the origins of the McCarthy
reign of terror over the next five years. Walsh privately denied the charges
and offered to pay Pearson $1,000 if he could offer proof for the story. As
Donald Crosby, SJ, pointed out in his study of McCarthy and the Catholic

Church in 1978, the meeting certainly took place, but it was completely out of character for Walsh to raise the issue of domestic subversion as a fit campaign topic. His writings and speeches barely touched the subject; his overriding concern was the threat of external Communism and the measures the United States needed to take to defend itself and the Western world against this totalitarian menace. Other critics of the story have shown that McCarthy had engaged in antisubversive charges long before his dinner with Walsh.[72]

Meanwhile, Francis Heyden in 1946 had rebuilt the radio station in the basement of Copley and reestablished WGTB. Because the station's transmitter initially had a range scarcely beyond campus, Heyden began sending certain programs by wire to a local station in Arlington, Virginia. One of them was the *Georgetown Forum*, a weekly talk show of Georgetown faculty discussing the international issues of the day. The show became syndicated in 1950 through a national broadcast organization, the Liberty Network, to go out to more than 140 stations worldwide; by 1953 it was a regular feature on NBC television.[73] In the fall of 1951 the Liberty Network inaugurated a series, *Prologue*, produced by Georgetown college faculty, which consisted of programs on the lessons that American history provided for the current struggle against Communism.[74]

In the summer of 1947, the War Department asked the university to be the first institution of higher education to sponsor a reserve unit that would focus on strategic intelligence. To do so, the army director of intelligence wrote to President Gorman, "would be a valuable contribution to a program of importance to national security."[75] The 404th Strategic Intelligence Detachment, directed by government professor James Atkinson and staffed by Georgetown graduate students in area studies and languages, was shortly thereafter set up on campus and continued through the 1950s as a strategic intelligence research and analysis program.

Georgetown played a role in the establishment of one of the states that formed as a consequence of the early Cold War—the Federal Republic of Germany. Heinrich Kronstein, an émigré teaching comparative law at Georgetown, had close connections with the new German government, particularly with Konrad Adenauer's foreign policy advisor, Walter Hallstein, who had been a visiting professor at the law and foreign service schools during the academic year 1948–49. Early in the winter of 1951 Kronstein approached Brian McGrath, then dean of the college, and told him that a group from the provisional government of West Germany, the Committee on Foreign Affairs of the German Federal Parliament, was coming to the United States under the pretext of learning about the workings of American government. Its real purpose, Kronstein informed McGrath, was to represent the provisional government in securing from the United States an agreement that would serve as the substitute for a treaty of peace between the two countries and that would provide official U.S. recognition of

Konrad Adenauer, left, chancellor of West Germany, at his honorary degree ceremony in 1953 (Cardinal Patrick O'Boyle, center; Edward Bunn, SJ, right). (Georgetown University Archives. Photo by William Beanland.)

the fledgling German government and effective autonomy as a governing body. To keep these negotiations secret and to avoid the impression that the United States was orchestrating the matter, it was important that the meeting take place somewhere other than at the State Department or some other government facility. Kronstein asked if they could use McGrath's office for the get-together.

On a weekend in mid-February, a two-day meeting was held that became known as the Georgetown Conference on Germany. The six-member committee, comprising representatives from the government's major parties—the ruling Christian Democrats, their coalition partners, and the opposition Social Democrats—along with two members of the State Department, a member of the National Security Resources Board, and Kronstein, met for long sessions on Saturday and Sunday. The upshot of the discussions was an agreement that the German Federal Republic would have full authority over its own affairs, with the exception of security, which the Allies would provide, and certain limitations on foreign relations. In the course of the meeting, U.S. officials had assured the Germans that they were committed to defending them against any Soviet aggression and that such defense was feasible. Underlying the agreement was the commitment, even by the Social Democrats, that the Federal Republic of Germany's future lay with the West and not with the Soviets; for the immediate future, however, its contribution to Western defense should be financial. A few days later, the participating parties signed a formal contractual agreement at the State Department.[76]

"As a result of that [meeting]," McGrath observed decades later, "we were asked to cooperate in other ways" that promoted the status of West Germany as a European state. Through Hallstein, the university worked out an exchange program with the University of Frankfurt. In early 1953, Konrad Adenauer, through the influence of Kronstein, accepted Georgetown's offer of an honorary degree, the first to be given to him in the United States, and in April he came to Georgetown where, in an overflowing Gaston Hall, with reporters, cameramen, and film crews crowding the stage, Adenauer received his doctor of humane letters, honoris causa, and gave a brief but impressive address (in German, with a translator) to the assemblage.[77] That October in the same hall Walter Hallstein was given an honorary doctorate of laws before another large gathering of dignitaries and members of the Georgetown community, and he also delivered an address. These lectures became part of a series of formal talks given at Georgetown over the course of the next four years by European and American political leaders, including Giovanni Grochi, president of Italy; John A. Costello, the Irish prime minister; and John Foster Dulles, American secretary of state. The university published the speeches under the title *International Cooperation: Speeches by Distinguished Visitors at Georgetown University on Current Topics in International Relations, 1952–1956.*

"A Regime of Priestly, Scholarly, Fatherly University Administration"

In February 1949, despite Rome's hesitation about making the appointment, Hunter Guthrie, dean of the Graduate School, succeeded Laurence Gorman as the forty-second president of the university.[78] Guthrie, in his inaugural address, lamented that "man is floundering today because he has lost his ultimate orientations." Guthrie laid much of the blame for this loss of self-understanding at the feet of the modern university, "no longer the center for the communication of the totality of truth: religious, oral and intellectual." Under its aegis, man's normal aspirations for truth had been constricted to "the spawning of opinions" and the lack of any "plenary knowledge" or knowledge of ultimate causes. With the abandonment of revelation in university circles, the acquisition of certain knowledge, he told his audience, became an impossible task. The posturing of liberalism was the inevitable consequence. With the loss of certainty in knowledge came an abdication of authority and the advent of unqualified liberty. Nineteenth-century rugged individualism, laissez-faire, had been transplanted from the field of economics to the whole world of the intellect under the guise of academic freedom, "that Protean pulpit whereon may mount atheist and Catholic; fellow-traveler and capitalist; agnostic, liberal, [and] dogmatist." To this state of anarchy, Guthrie responded, "Truth is one, simple and integral."

In this conviction Georgetown and all schools in its tradition were recommitting themselves to classical education. As God had used Greece and Rome to predispose humankind intellectually and morally for his son's coming, so too did education need to recapitulate that process for the individual through an education that centered on the classics. Guthrie did concede that modernity had made one valuable contribution, the field of science, that Jesuit education had wisely incorporated within its curriculum as "a new factor of universal knowledge." But, in general, Georgetown's task in remaining a vital center of Jesuit liberal education was one of iconoclasm toward the larger culture. He told his audience, many of whom represented secular institutions devoted to modern intellectual idols, that he hoped Georgetown, "with God's help[,] will wield a heavier hammer in the future."[79]

International Cooperation and the *Congressional Record* reprinted Guthrie's speech. The Jesuit diarist was sure that the inauguration "left a lasting impression on all who attended. Rev. Fr. Rector's speech was indeed a masterpiece. The entire community looks forward to a regime of priestly, scholarly, fatherly University administration."[80] It is fair to say that Guthrie intended just that. He brought into office definite ideas of how the university needed to change and develop its administrative structure to become a modern university worthy of its size and importance. If tradition was the hallmark of Jesuit education vis-à-vis its curriculum, modernization was the necessary paradigm for its institutional structure. A year before he became president, Guthrie had written to the Jesuit supervisor of higher education in the region that "in a university of the size and importance of Georgetown, the office of Rector [religious superior] and the office of President should be divided. There should be a university senate. . . . To attract interest in the [university] there should be a Board of Trustees to maintain high academic standards." Also there should be a person charged with directing public relations. And economic consolidation was absolutely essential. "The University's funds should be drawn into one office, managed by a Treasurer . . . and a comptroller with expert financial training."[81]

The governing laws of the Society of Jesus prevented Guthrie from achieving a separation of the offices of president and rector, but he did manage, after repeated efforts over the course of two years, to persuade the Jesuit officials in Baltimore and Rome to create the position of superior of the Jesuit Community at Georgetown University, who would function as a delegate of the rector-president in governing the Jesuits in the university and free the president to concentrate on the administration of the university. Vincent Keelan, former provincial, became the first superior of the community in September 1951.[82]

One of Guthrie's first moves in April 1949 was to revive the board of regents, the lay advisory group that had been defunct since the middle 1930s, as the equivalent of a board of trustees for purposes of recognition, fund-raising, and overall advice. For some reason, that revival did not become a reality for three years, and then under a new name, the president's council, which Guthrie finally activated in the spring of 1952. The twenty-one-member council included, among others, Ambassador William Bullitt, William E. Leahy, John McShane, Thomas Leavey, and Raymond Reiss. At the first meeting of the council, Guthrie laid out the state of the university in order to enumerate the challenges and problems he wished the council to address.[83]

In the summer of 1949, he oversaw the incorporation of the Alumni Association as a permanent, independent organization. In the fall of 1951, he created an Office of University Development, with Charles Foley, SJ, as its first director. A public affairs office was set up under the development director. In the winter of 1951–52 plans were laid for the inauguration of an annual fund for alumni. Foley was also developing a long-range building program around which a capital fund-raising campaign could be built. Long-range planning had actually begun under Gorman in 1947, and Foley incorporated most of the earlier plans into the comprehensive one developed in 1952, which called for the conversion of Ryan Gymnasium into an administration building (to house university records, the treasurer, and development and public relations), a dining hall for undergraduates, a library, academic buildings to house the School of Foreign Service and Graduate School, a nurses' residence, new wings for the hospital and medical-dental schools, and endowments for chairs and scholarships. The projected cost was $15.8 million for these facilities and endowment, which were considered urgent needs. A fund-raising company was engaged to assess the climate for a capital campaign.[84]

The Korean War

Fewer than five years after the introduction of atomic weapons by the United States against Japan had brought World War II to a sudden end, the United States found itself at war in Asia again. The invasion of South Korea by armies of the Peoples' Republic of Korea on June 24, 1950, quickly brought American and other United Nations troops to the aid of South Korea. The Cold War was seemingly on the brink of becoming a hot one. Under the assumption (mistaken, as it turned out) that the North Koreans were surrogates for the Soviet Union in their latest drive to expand Communism, the specter of an accelerating nuclear conflict between the world's superpowers hung over the engagement on the Korean peninsula. From the dispatch of the first American forces from Japan to Korea in June, the expectation was that this conflict could easily escalate into World War III. A general mobilization of the nation seemed all too possibly imminent.

At Georgetown a string of emergency meetings of the board of directors and other administrative officials and faculty were held over the course of the summer months as the university attempted to plan for the impact of a general war that could become nuclear. The Graduate School devised special courses on language training, nuclear physics, and international relations, including an abbreviated version of the psychological warfare program, to attract military and government personnel. As a key member of the economics department, Joseph Solterer, urged during a special meeting in August, the Graduate School should prepare to be a "consulting and research institute" for the government in the case of global war. As for the undergraduate schools, with a general mobilization likely, a reinstitution of the ASTP seemed to be the best substitute for a student-depleted campus; preliminary steps for such a development were set in motion, which included an inventory of the facilities the university could offer the government for its use, and the appointment of a liaison between the university and the government.[85] As a safeguard against the disaster of a nuclear attack on Washington, officials made plans to microfilm student records and other documents for storage in the Jesuit novitiate in rural Pennsylvania. But what would actually happen was, as the vice rector admitted, "anyone's guess."[86]

By the time classes resumed in September, uncertainty still prevailed about the scope of the war and the government's response. The university expected, at the very least, that the government would insist that colleges implement a compulsory ROTC for all undergraduates. The board was prepared to institute such a requirement should that become necessary for the institution's survival.[87] In October, following the lead of the American Council on Education, the university reinstated the accelerated calendar that had just been terminated in 1949, since military authorities were strongly indicating that such a change was a minimal adjustment that schools should make in the national crisis.[88] In January 1951 Guthrie formed a university committee on mobilization to oversee the use of facilities by the government, should that develop, as well as the procurement of supplies during the national emergency.[89] But no general mobilization occurred, despite the sudden intervention of the Peoples' Republic of China in the conflict in November 1950.

A number of veterans who were on active reserve were recalled into service, particularly pilots and members of the navy and Marine Corps, such as James Fitzgerald (MD 1948), who had returned from the navy to Georgetown as an intern, only to be reactivated for the Korean crisis. Many underclassmen opted to stay in the army ROTC program for four years as a hedge against the draft. Others joined a navy ROTC program off campus.[90]

As it turned out, the draft remained a threat chiefly to students who were in academic difficulties. No SATC or V-12 programs were resurrected, but the air force joined the army in offering an ROTC program at Georgetown in 1951. The summer of 1951 came, but the accelerated schedule was not put into effect. By that time a stalemate had taken hold in Korea and truce talks had begun.

McDonough Memorial Gymnasium

For two decades Georgetown officials had been seeking to construct a new athletic facility to replace the antiquated Ryan Gymnasium. Initially, the Depression deferred any action. In 1938, in conjunction with the sesquicentennial of the university, a formal drive was begun among the alumni to raise $400,000 for a gymnasium, to be called Alumni Hall. The drive proved disappointing, to say the least. After a year's effort, only $35,000 had been raised, with an additional $80,000 in pledges.[91] The project was again put on hold when World War II intervened. In February 1948 the alumni campaign to raise funds for the facility, now to be named for Vincent McDonough, SJ, the longtime moderator of athletics, was renewed in Washington and eighty other cities, now with a goal of $800,000. Initial plans called for the gymnasium to be built out from the old one, with Ryan being remodeled for gymnastics, boxing, wrestling, and other individual sports. The new building, envisioned to house a five-thousand-seat arena for basketball, three squash courts, and a twenty-five-yard swimming pool, would be the largest arched-roof gymnasium in the country.[92] When it became obvious that the projected Ryan site was too small to house the complex, the planning committee in the winter of 1949–50 found an alternate in a ravine directly south of the observatory.[93] In Guthrie's first year in office, he finally made the commitment to construct the two-story facility to contain a basketball arena that could double as a convocation center with a built-in stage as well as bowling alleys and living quarters on the second floor. The projected cost was $861,000. Of this amount the Alumni Association had raised more than $500,000 toward its construction over the past decade of planning.[94]

Ground breaking took place in May 1950. A month later the Korean War broke out. Reinforced concrete replaced the unobtainable steel as roof support, which shrunk the intended size of the gymnasium considerably. The war also greatly increased the cost of materials and labor in general. The reduced size as well as the lack of adequate ventilation severely compromised its potential as a convocation and entertainment site. (The arena, intended to have a seating capacity of five thousand, ended up seating about half that number.) The original estimated cost of $861,000 escalated to more than $1.3 million, much of which the university had to borrow when alumni giving failed by far to meet the difference.[95] The McDonough Memorial Gymnasium formally opened in early December 1951 with a three-day celebration, featuring a basketball game with Fordham, a formal dedication ball, and a dedication concert by the National Symphony Orchestra, with Howard Mitchell conducting.[96]

"No More Football for Us"

The Korean War did provide the occasion for one significant change in the life of the university—the dropping of intercollegiate football. Football, resuming at the Hilltop in the fall of 1946, had all the potential of regaining the national stature it had acquired on the eve of World War II. The 1946 team, with Jack Hagerty back as coach, had a disappointing season, 5-3, with victories over Fordham and NYU being the only significant ones. The 1947 season proved to be worse as the team went 3-4-1. When the team repeated its previous year's record in 1948, including the first loss to George Washington in fifty-eight years, a general purge of the coaching staff and athletic department followed. The athletic director, Rome Schwagel, was forced to resign. Hagerty stepped in to take Schwagel's place. For the new coach, the university brought in from Yale Bob Margharita, twenty-eight, who had been an assistant coach under Hagerty. The moderator of athletics, Robert Parsons, SJ, saw the change as one indication that "big-time football is on its way out. . . . I definitely think it will happen in the East first."[97] That clearly was Guthrie's thinking in the summer of 1949. He wanted athletic scholarships for football sharply reduced from their current number of ninety and a schedule that would include only teams—traditional Catholic rivals, as well as Ivies and near-Ivies—that shared Georgetown's "scholastic approach to athletics." As he reminded the athletic moderator, "We are not in big time [football]."[98]

That may have been Guthrie and Parsons's thinking, but it was not that of Margharita or of the new athletic moderator, Neil Herlihy, SJ, who replaced Parsons in the summer of 1949. Scholarships for football did not decline. Herlihy attempted to camouflage their number by having athletes who were academically competitive counted as academic scholars rather than athletic ones. In place of Hagerty's two part-time coaches, Margharita brought in three full-time assistants and two freshmen coaches. Herlihy greatly increased the traveling budget to allow advanced scouting by coaches and better travel accommodations.

Margharita's first two months as head coach were a magic ride. Georgetown, with a sophomore-dominated squad led by quarterback Frank Mattingly, halfback Billy Conn, gargantuan (6' 4", 270 pounds) tackle James Ricca, and end Bob Noppinger, won its first five games, beating Holy Cross, Maryland, Wake Forest, NYU, and Boston College. The upset win over Boston College was the first in two decades over Georgetown's northern arch rival. Georgetown had given up only 65 points and was ranked third in the nation. The executives of the Sun Bowl wrote after the Boston College game to ask whether Georgetown would be interested in playing there on New Year's Day. The following week the magic carpet plummeted to earth as Fordham routed Georgetown, 42–0. Losses to Villanova, Denver, and George Washington followed. The regular season that had begun so marvelously ended 5-4. Amazingly, the Sun Bowl still wanted Georgetown. The surprised Guthrie readily accepted the bid. It would be, he reasoned, a good reward for the "excellent work" done by Margharita in his first season and a chance to strengthen ties with western alumni, many of whom were planning to attend the game.[99] On January 1, 1950, Georgetown played Texas Western in El Paso, Texas, before a crowd of fifteen thousand, losing a hard-fought game 33–20 to the Miners' superior ground attack.

If 1949 had been a semimagical season, 1950 was a disaster. The team won two of nine games. The victories against Holy Cross and Boston College were small consolation for the worst season since 1933, when Georgetown was in a period of de-emphasis. The fall of 1950 brought further bad news regarding football. The NCAA informed the university in September that it had been found in violation of the scholarship code for attempting to disguise athletic scholarships as academic ones and was facing censure at the upcoming plenary session of the NCAA in January.[100] Meanwhile, Guthrie was becoming more and more concerned about the financial drain of athletics, mainly football, on the university. The 1949–50 season revenues had fallen short of expenses by more than $74,000. Despite its Bowl appearance, football revenue had amounted to little more than $40,000. Adding in the cost of scholarships, the vast majority of which were for football, the total deficit was more than $290,000.[101] A significant part of the financial problem was the cost to rent Griffith Stadium and the meager receipts the university realized from the small crowds (an average of fewer than nine thousand) that the team drew for home games. In November 1950 university officials discussed plans to erect a five-thousand-seat stadium next to McDonough as a way to eliminate the rental costs.[102] At that same time, Guthrie took direct control of athletics, both to reduce costs and to ensure the subordination of athletic programs to academic priorities.[103]

That same fall Guthrie appointed a committee of the board of directors to examine the question of whether to drop football as an intercollegiate sport. The committee unanimously agreed that the university should discontinue football because of the expense involved and the serious inroads that practice and travel made into the academic lives of the players during the season.[104] In December, Guthrie, using the national state of emergency and the continuing uncertain future of collegiate education as a pretext, raised the question with his full board. Three months later they decided unanimously, both for financial reasons and because of the probable loss of

enrollment over the next year due to the draft, to drop football immediately.[105] Georgetown joined the ranks of fifteen other colleges who had
discontinued the sport since the close of the 1950 season. Still, as Arthur
Daley wrote in the *New York Times,* it was "a shock . . . when one of the
major teams announces that it has clipped off football" and ended sixty
years as a football power.[106]

In an article in the *Saturday Evening Post* the following October, Guthrie
explained why Georgetown had decided on "No More Football for Us!"
"Football is important," the president wrote.

We at Georgetown began to think it was too important. We wondered if it had not
soared completely out of the scale of educational values. Seventy-seven years is a
long life for a tail. In that time it can develop considerable wag—enough, perhaps, to
shake the purpose of an institution. We did not want that to happen. . . . So we
stopped the wag of football. . . . Educationally, in its present professionalized, specta-
tor-appeal form, it is indefensible. It has as much reason to subsist on the campus of
an educational institution as a night club or a macaroni factory.

As for the economics, dropping football meant eliminating the salaries of
coaches who made more than any chair of a department or internationally
recognized scholar. It meant eliminating a deficit that had cost the university
$1 million in a decade.[107]

Alumni reaction was mostly positive. "An astonishing number of alumni," Guthrie told the Association of American Colleges at their next annual
meeting, "did not care to see their alma mater operated as a minor league
farm for professional football."[108] Student reaction was more mixed, ranging
from consternation to stunned surprise to resignation that, as the *Hoya* put it,
"as long as the ruling has been made, we must seek out the good." Students
realized that reallocating the significant monies spent on this major sport
could enable the university to address long-standing academic and social
needs, such as a library or student union building.[109]

Football was not the only sport to be affected by the decision. Because so
many scholarship football players also played baseball, that sport, which,
along with track, had been the most successful of all of Georgetown's major
sports in the immediate postwar period, soon paid the price for its heavy
dependence on football scholarships. Joe Judge, the former Senators' first
baseman who as coach had made the Hoyas one of the top collegiate teams
in the East in the years immediately before the war, returned in 1948 to reestablish Georgetown baseball as an eastern power. In 1950 and 1951 the
Hoya baseball team, with Frank Mattingly its star pitcher, flirted with an
NCAA berth, as they went 12-8 and 13-4, respectively. It was the closest any
Georgetown baseball team would ever come to postseason play for more
than thirty years.

The track team of the late 1940s and early 1950s continued to excel in
the 1- and 2-mile relays, led by David Boland (BSS 1952), who helped set a

world indoor record for the 2-mile relay in 1951, and Charlie Capozzoli (BSBA 1953), one of the top milers in the country, who qualified for the 1956 Olympics in the 3,000 meters. Elmer Ripley returned in 1946, along with most of his 1943 NCAA runner-up basketball squad. In their first year back, playing their home games at Catholic University, they nearly equaled their 1943 record as they went 19-7. The following two years were much less successful, as the Hoyas failed to reach .500 in either season. Ripley resigned at the end of the 1950 season. His ten-year record at Georgetown was an impressive 133-82. Two new sports began in these postwar years: swimming and lacrosse. The first swim team was formed in 1949. Two years later Georgetown began to play intercollegiate lacrosse but discontinued it after three years, in 1954.

A "Loose Confederation"

There were various moves made toward the unification of the various schools and departments, from the symbolic—the switching of the Mass of the Holy Spirit as the inaugural event of the year for the college to that of the university as a whole—to the corporal, as with the establishment of a university health center for students of all schools in September 1950 and the creation of a central purchasing office in December 1949. In December 1949, Guthrie established an Office of Physical Plant, with Edward Powers, SJ, as superintendent of buildings and grounds, who was charged with establishing a personnel office for nonacademic staff. In January 1951 he ended the autonomy of the Athletic Association by putting control of its finances, hirings, and even scheduling within his own office. In May 1951 he established a university committee on rank, tenure, and salary to regulate and standardize hirings and promotions on the three campuses. The university acquired an official legal counsel from the firm of Chase and Williams in the fall of 1950. In that same period Guthrie increased the staff of his own office from one assistant to an executive assistant and four other assistants and secretaries. A special committee of the board of directors considered a retirement plan for all university faculty and professional staff.[110]

But it was the radical decentralized nature of Georgetown's schools that Guthrie most intended to change. Theoretically, the schools were under the direct control of the president through the leadership of Jesuit administrators, either as deans or regents (in those schools that had lay deans). In reality only the college and the Graduate School fit that pattern; the rest of the schools—especially law, medicine, and foreign service—operated like autonomous fiefdoms with Jesuit regent/deans controlling separate plants, faculty, and monies. The president had come into office with the provincial's charge to undertake a study of the institutional structure, and by midsummer Guthrie reported to the provincial that the most important reform in

Aerial view of campus, circa 1948. (Georgetown University Archives)

university structure that needed to be made was the "centralization of financial control." Georgetown, he was learning, had a modest endowment of $10 to $12 million (no one really knew what the total was), scattered by the comptrollers of the various schools in real estate, bonds, preferred stocks, common stocks, and cash, "without rhyme, reason or balance."[111] Most of it was in banks, drawing only 2 percent to 3 percent interest. If Georgetown was to develop, it was clear that a necessary precondition was a much fuller utilization of its financial resources than was provided by the present helter-skelter arrangement. "Georgetown has a great past," he wrote to the provincial superior, "and under God I think it has an even greater future. That future, however, depends in large part upon its clearing its financial decks for action."[112]

Guthrie appointed a committee on unification in 1950 to study the feasibility of such action, but the composition of the committee (Guthrie, James Wilkinson, SJ [the university treasurer], and two other supportive Jesuits) ensured that it would endorse Guthrie's plan. In December 1950, Guthrie laid out to the provincial the committee's rationale for economic and administrative unification. The "educational, economic and administrative benefits" to accrue from such unification was "beyond serious question," he was convinced. It would put Georgetown in line with ecclesiastical and corporate law as well as with the practice of the major educational institutions in the country. Then there were the prudential concerns: A committee of the Middle States Association was scheduled to visit the university in less than two months; there was clear warning that the inspection committee would look with disfavor on the segmented structure of Georgetown's finances and administration: "wasteful . . . duplication of effort, personnel, equipment, and records concerning payrolls, insurance matters, properties, holdings . . . separate bank accounts, and contracts entered into independently." Pending also was coverage of university employees by Social Security, which would be infinitely complicated by the present hydra-headed system. Unification would bring elimination of waste and increased economy in the use of resources and personnel. "Georgetown University," he concluded, "simply cannot afford an outmoded method of operation."[113]

In January 1951, at a special two-day meeting of the board of directors, Guthrie presented the committee's plan for unifying the university's finances, as well as maintenance, purchasing, and general services, to be put into operation by July 1951. He explained that the decision to unify had been neither his nor the committee's but the superior general's in Rome. As expected, the regents, Lucey and Walsh, had many objections to or concerns about the plan to switch from the "horizontal to the vertical arrangement," as it was delicately put—ranging from the timing to the lack of personnel to implement it and possible conflicts with the by-laws of the ABA. Guthrie had anticipated at least some of the regents' objections and presumably countered them during the meeting, but it would be another month before a resolution was introduced to the board to put the plan into effect.[114] It passed with unanimous support, even from the three regents. The arrival of the inspection committee of the Middle States Association of Universities and Colleges that same last day in February was likely the spur for the board's action.

As Guthrie had predicted, the Middle States committee looked askance at Georgetown's byzantine structure. In its report it concluded that the institution was too much of a "loose confederation" of essentially autonomous schools rather than interconnected components of a true university, with integration of governance, faculty, planning, resources, and finances. The isolated nature of these units was typified by each school's having its own faculty, admissions policy, budget and control of finances, library, and even its own bookstore. As the university was so radically decentralized at present, there was no effective central administration to promote and direct the pursuit of the common good. The report endorsed in the strongest language the plan of reorganization that Guthrie had introduced. Once that plan was carried out, "Georgetown should be operating effectively as a University."[115]

Two months later Guthrie engaged the services of the Chase National Bank to invest the university's assets—the $10 to $12 million—that were being collected from the various components of the institution as well as all future revenue. Guthrie could not restrain his elation. He wrote the provincial superior, "I honestly believe it means a great deal for the future security of Georgetown." From the experience of others he had consulted, he had confidence that, under Chase, Georgetown's portfolio would quickly grow over the next several years by as much as one-third or more, as others had done.[116]

A Sudden Exit

The Middle States committee, in its report on Georgetown, had praised Hunter Guthrie's ability "to give educational and administration leadership of high order to the University." It was crucial for the institution's continued progress that Guthrie be kept in office for an extended term, and it urged the superiors of the Jesuit order to make sure that Guthrie remained in office beyond the normal fixed term.[117] The normal term for Jesuit rector-presidents was a three-year term renewable once. In February 1952 Guthrie completed his first term and, without notice, began his second. As it turned out, it would be a very short one, less than six months. In early July he left the university, supposedly for some fund-raising and retreat in California and a vacation in New England. His vacation stretched into August, then September. In letters to his secretary, Guthrie indicated that he had been nearly worn out and needed a complete rest. How long that would be he seemed unable to predict. In late August he moved to his mother's summer cottage below Annapolis, then to Mercy Hospital in Charlotte, North Carolina, then to another Mercy Hospital in Baltimore in late September.[118] By that time the new school year had begun, and rumors were swirling regarding his whereabouts. He never returned. In early October he submitted by mail his resignation to the board of directors. In late October 1952, the announcement was made that the regent of the nursing and dental schools, Edward Bunn, SJ, had been named president of the university.

What had happened? According to one source, Guthrie decided that he could no longer continue as president, that his policies had alienated too many key persons at the university, that too many things were simply not working out. "Evidently . . . he made up his mind," recalled the then dean of the college, "that he had kicked things around so much, that he had lost the confidence of the community, and would rather go back to his [scholarly] work."[119] In his resignation note to the board of directors, Guthrie stated that in June—before he left Georgetown for California—he had written to the provincial asking permission to resign as president because of "the condition of my health."[120] Guthrie had been treated for tuberculo-sis—in Mercy Hospital in North Carolina fifteen years earlier—and he may have feared a recurrence. The provincial superior had apparently urged him to see what rest and a change of venue would do to improve his health, but by early August, with Guthrie reporting no change in his condition, the provincial acceded to his plea and began the process of submitting a terna (list of three nominees) to Rome for Guthrie's successor.[121] In late September the provincial superior summoned Bunn to Baltimore, where the provincial informed him that he had been named the new rector-president of Georgetown.

There is both written and oral evidence that bears out the explanation that more than concern for his health was behind Guthrie's sudden and highly secret resignation (there was never any public announcement of it; his successor was simply announced, as though Guthrie had disappeared). Guthrie felt that in the course of his three years as president he had still not won the active support of the major regents—Walsh, McNally, and Lucey. Their resistance to the unification plan ranged from McNally's stated coop-eration to Lucey's open opposition. Lucey's refusal to deal with the univer-sity treasurer, procurator, or physical plant director in administering the revenues and property of the Law School and his effective defiance of uni-fication (to the point of telling his faculty that Guthrie's plan had been re-scinded by Rome and the status quo ante restored) had led Guthrie in early April 1952 to request urgently that the provincial superior remove Lucey from Georgetown.[122]

Not only did Jesuit superiors fail to remove him (he would remain as regent for another decade), in June the superior general chastised Guthrie for his manner of governance that had hurt so many under him. Of par-ticular concern for the superior general was the way in which Guthrie had carried out the unification process ("too hurriedly, without sufficient con-sultation," with the false impression that the superior general had autho-rized the method and not merely the goal of unification). Had university officials been properly informed and involved in the process, the superior general admonished, those like Lucey would have fully cooperated. He advised Guthrie to be less critical of officials who were basically doing what former superiors had previously approved. Peace in the university and confidence in Guthrie would return, the superior general concluded, when the president changed his ways and repaired the damage done by his high-handed manner. In the same letter the superior general informed Guthrie that he was withholding approval for the construction of a dining hall, which was to have begun in July (and for which approval had been ex-pected).[123] Within a month after receiving this letter, Guthrie asked to be allowed to step down.

"He was disappointed in the way a lot of things were turning out and I believe that he thought everyone was blaming him (which they were),"

Heyden recalled from a conversation he had had with the president a few days before he left for California.[124] That the major breaking point for Guthrie was the opposition, covert or overt, of the "big three" regents, which Rome seemingly sanctioned, may be inferred from a comment Guthrie's successor made to him after Guthrie had sent his congratulations on Bunn's appointment. "I hope with God's help to build up on the firm foundation that you have made during your tenure here. My greatest consolation," the former regent of the Dental and Nursing Schools replied, "is the consciousness that I have tried throughout that period to give you wholehearted cooperation."[125] Now it was the new president's turn to attempt to expand that circle of cooperation.

CHAPTER 9

Edward Bunn and the Consolidation of the University, 1952–64

When [Father] Bunn came [in as president] he inherited a collection of colleges; when he left, he left a university.

GEORGE HOUSTON

"He Challenged Georgetown"

The surge in enrollment in American higher education that had occurred during the immediate postwar period persisted throughout the next decade. The rise in the percentage of Americans attending college was part of the socioeconomic mobility that greatly expanded the middle class in the country. American Catholics were fully involved in this educational leap in which sons and daughters of parents with high school diplomas or (frequently) less became holders of baccalaureate and graduate/professional degrees. By the 1960s, 45 percent of college-age Catholics were enrolled in higher education, which was higher than the national average. For some Catholic ethnic groups the figure was much higher, as it was for the Irish, with nearly 60 percent of the age cohort enrolled in institutions of higher education.[1]

Georgetown, with its predominantly Catholic population in both its undergraduate and graduate/professional schools, shared fully in this continu-

Edward Bunn, SJ, president of Georgetown, 1952–64.
(Georgetown University Archives)

ing growth. Enrollment in the College of Arts and Sciences increased from 1,209 to 1,547, a 28 percent increase. In the School of Foreign Service, the change was smaller, an 18 percent increase, but its two spin-offs, the Institute of Languages and Linguistics and the School of Business, grew by 53 percent and 57 percent, respectively. Nursing soared from 194 students in 1952 to nearly 300 in 1964, a 35 percent increase. The Graduate School experienced phenomenal growth during the period, from 691 to 1,284 (an increase of 85 percent). The Law School increased the size of its enrollment by more than one-third. The only schools to experience no change (dentistry) or a loss (medicine, 11 percent) were those that continued to maintain strict admission quotas. Overall, the student population of the university swelled from 3,539 in 1952 to 6,141 in 1964, a 74 percent overall increase.

Presiding over this boom period of a dozen years at Georgetown was Edward Bunn, SJ. No previous president had served such a long tenure. Bunn's longevity in office was partly a reflection of the growing autonomy of Jesuit institutions of higher education, particularly the universities. And partly it was a measure of his success in bringing Georgetown into the modern world of higher education through his completion of the unification of the authority structure and finances of the institution, which his predecessor had begun; his integration of the faculty within unified departments; his setting of standards for faculty; his establishment of provisions for health, educational, and retirement benefits for university employees; his institutionalization of fund-raising within the university; and the provision of facilities —academic, clinical, and residential—that contributed to the greatest physical expansion in the history of Georgetown to match the student population surge.

The fifty-six-year-old Bunn, a Baltimore native and third-generation German American, worked his way through Loyola College (his father had died when he was eighteen months old). When he was appointed president in the fall of 1952, he brought more administrative experience to Georgetown than had any previous head of the institution. From 1938 to 1944, as president of Loyola, he led his alma mater through a remarkable period of progress, as he launched the college's first development campaign, effectively cultivated community leaders as financial supporters, greatly expanded Loyola's facilities, and promoted faculty involvement in the network of national scholarly and professional organizations. In 1944 he became director of studies for the Maryland Province, a position he held for the next eight years, during which he made an intensive study of the province's four institutions of higher education, including Georgetown. In 1948, while still serving as director of studies, he was named regent of Georgetown's schools of dentistry and nursing, and he was charged to reorganize both schools. His leadership over the next four years brought about the Dental School's restoration of its accreditation and the Nursing School's emergence as an authentic academic enterprise separate from the university hospital.

"I think that the secret of [the success of] Doc was he was willing to listen and to learn," thought Bunn's chief academic assistant at Georgetown,
Brian McGrath, SJ.[2] When Bunn became president, one of the first things
he did was to interview each faculty member in his office to get to know
them and to seek their thoughts about their work and the university. It
startled Karl Cerny, then a recently appointed assistant professor of government, that a college president would seek out even untenured faculty,
and he marveled at the personal rapport Bunn quickly established between
himself and the faculty, a rapport that largely perdured over the next dozen
years.[3] Under Bunn's paternal leadership, the university community, particularly its faculty and administration, "was more like a big family," Annik
Buchanan, one of the first female professors in the college, recalled fondly.
"We knew each other quite well." Familiarity promoted attachment, which
promoted loyalty.[4]

When Bunn returned from attending the general congregation of the
Society of Jesus in early December 1957, faculty and administration greeted him as a body on the steps of Healy and escorted him to a surprise reception in his honor in the Hall of Cardinals.[5] He was seemingly forever
accessible—to students, faculty, alumni—a benevolent father figure despite
his diminutive stature (a somewhat stocky 5' 7"). On the occasion of completing his tenth year in office, the *Hoya* remarked that he was "the easiest
member of the Administration for a student to see," and someone who
impressed with "his wit, humanity . . . [and] genuine interest in talking to
students." What he most conveyed, they sensed, was "an inspired realism"
that was remarkably effective at "sell[ing] the future of Georgetown" as a
vastly better place and convincing others to join him in the effort of making
it so.[6] "He challenged Georgetown," McGrath later reflected, "to broader
educational objectives that demanded new financial goals—for buildings,
for faculty, for student aid. [And] he did the hard work of raising the funds
needed for those goals."[7]

Unification and Integration

This period marked the emergence of presidential ascendancy within the
Jesuit institutions of higher education, as strong-willed presidents such as
Michael Walsh at Boston College, Paul Reinert at Saint Louis University, and
Edward Bunn at Georgetown became increasingly independent of the restraint of provincials and of the supervision of the Jesuit Education Association. The process was very gradual, even subtle, but the trend toward
autonomy was real enough. In the end it provided Bunn and other Jesuit
presidents the freedom to make changes and institute policies that previously would have been impossible to make without explicit permission from
higher Jesuit authorities.

"When Bunn came [in as president]," one of his former students who later became a key administrator judged, "he inherited a collection of colleges; when he left, he left a university."[8] One reason that Bunn was able to succeed where Guthrie had failed in completing the unification and integration of the various components of the university was the change in the status of the "big three"—the regents who had ruled fiefdoms in the Medical School, Law School, and School of Foreign Service during the previous decade. In the first six months of Bunn's tenure, two of the three regents were incapacitated: Edmund Walsh from a catastrophic stroke in January 1953, and Paul McNally from a heart attack two months later. Only Francis Lucey remained a force in the governing councils of Georgetown, and his power became increasingly weakened and isolated as the decade wore on.

Integration began at the departmental level. During his first year in office, 1952–53, Bunn combined the graduate and college faculties in economics, history, physics, and political science that previously had existed separately. Shortly afterward, he integrated the faculty of the School of Foreign Service into the unified departments. In September 1963 he integrated all modern language departments in the university. Previously there had been distinct language faculties for the college, the School of Foreign Service, and the Institute of Languages and Linguistics. Now there was a single department of foreign languages within the institute, with university-wide divisions for each language.

At the school level, unification took place in academic administration, library management, record keeping, and admissions. As a result of a recommendation of the Middle States report in 1951 that had found too many academic people reporting to the president, the office of academic vice president was created in 1955, with authority over all schools on the main campus. Brian McGrath, SJ, then dean of the college, moved up to this new position. That same year the various school libraries on the main campus were put under the direction of James Horigan, SJ.[9] To centralize academic record keeping, in 1956 Bunn appointed Joseph G. Connor to the post of university registrar. Joseph Moffit, SJ, became the first dean of admissions, with control over all undergraduate applicants. In 1961 an orientation program was inaugurated to introduce new students in all the undergraduate schools to the academic and social life of the university.

Under Bunn the governance of the university became more multilayered and more democratic. He made full use of the president's council, which Hunter Guthrie had instituted in the spring of 1952 as an advisory body in the shaping of policy for the university as well as a fund-raising core. He inherited a trio of regents who were powerful figures, indeed the de facto chief executives of their schools—Edmund Walsh in the School of Foreign Service, Paul McNally in the Medical School, and Frank Lucey in the Law School. Within the first six months of Bunn's tenure, as men-

tioned earlier, Walsh and McNally were both incapacitated. Walsh's replacement, Frank Fadner, SJ, in the School of Foreign Service, tried to act as Walsh had, although with much less success. McNally's replacement, Thomas O'Donnell, was not made dean, as McNally had been, and in general he did not try to rule as one. Indeed, Bunn himself regarded the regent, at least in the Medical School, not as an executive officer but as a liaison between the center and the president.[10] He continued to appoint regents in the other schools that lacked Jesuit deans—dentistry, nursing, foreign service, language and linguistics, and business—but in practice the regents more or less operated as liaisons, with the exception of Lucey, who continued as the chief executive officer (CEO) of the Law School for the next decade.

In 1954, Bunn formed a council of academic deans as a consultative and information-providing body for the president. He also insisted at that time that each school develop an executive faculty, which by 1958 was made the policymaking body of the respective schools. In 1962 he was responsible for the establishment of advisory boards or boards of visitors for the individual

President's council and administrators, circa 1962. John Snyder, seated far right. *Standing:* Joseph Sweeney; Joseph Sellinger, SJ (third from left); Joseph Sebes, SJ; Charles Foley, SJ; and Mark Bauer, SJ. (Georgetown University Archives)

undergraduate schools. With regard to governance by the faculty as a whole, in the winter of 1960–61 the Georgetown chapter of the American Association of University Professors proposed as an organized body to the board of directors the notion of faculty representation. The board had difficulties with certain features of the formal proposal but agreed in principle to the formation of a faculty senate in March 1961.[11] It would be several years before the senate became a reality.

The Road to Modernity

By the early 1950s the nation's postsecondary academic institutions, including Georgetown, were in a financial crisis chiefly due to inflation; a burgeoning bureaucracy that offered an unprecedented variety of services; and the need for greater academic resources such as library holdings and pedagogical technology. During the postwar period, university expenses persistently outran income, despite the steep increase in revenue from the tuition of a rapidly expanding student population. By 1953 expenses had increased by 215 percent from what they had been in 1942, whereas income had increased only 190 percent. During that same period, tuition at Georgetown had risen by 60 percent, significantly lower than the national average increase of 71 percent.[12]

To address this imbalance between revenue and expenses, and, more generally, to exercise control over the state of the institution, Edward Bunn, immediately upon taking office, introduced planning as a mechanism, a tool of academic modernity for shaping the growth and development of the university and providing the financial and human means to attain it. At the same time, the Ford Foundation provided funding to study the organization and operation of the entire university.

President Bunn hired an outside firm to do the study. Their report stressed the importance of determining the desirable size of the various components of the university over the next ten years so that intelligent planning could follow to determine the facilities, faculty, and staff needed to accommodate them. They also recommended that uniform policies and standards be set for faculty regarding appointments, contracts, promotion, and general faculty development.[13] Bunn sat down with his top administrators to determine what the physical, academic, and personnel needs of the university were going to be over the next ten years; what the priorities regarding facilities, programs, and faculty should be; and how they could best finance those needs. Among the needed facilities identified were a library; homes for the School of Foreign Service, Institute of Languages and Linguistics, and the Nursing School; a science building; a dormitory; a cafeteria; and additions to both the hospital and the Medical-Dental Building.

Metropolitan Washington's population doubled in the two decades from 1950 to 1970, from 1,464,000 in 1950 to 2,861,000 in 1970.[14] Much of the increase was driven by the spiraling growth of the federal government. Housing was in high demand for the burgeoning federal workforce, as well as others whose business relations with the government drew them to Washington. Georgetown became a prime site for those seeking housing close to federal Washington. The movement of affluent whites into Georgetown had begun in the 1930s, with the great infusion of government personnel that the New Deal brought. The higher property values, higher taxes, and higher rents that followed forced many black property owners or renters to sell and/ or vacate their homes, particularly in the part of Georgetown east of Wisconsin Avenue.

By 1950 the black community of Georgetown had fallen from their traditional one-third of the population to about 10 percent.[15] The Old Georgetown Act of 1950, which set standards for the preservation of the historic houses in the area, in effect completed the gentrification process of dislodging black residents to make Georgetown a virtually all-white neighborhood. Zoning restrictions, which, among other things, now required all dwellings to be single-family units, together with still more rising property values and taxes, were extremely effective in ending black Georgetown as a community.[16]

The university, in contrast, benefited from this development by acquiring various properties west of 35th Street formerly owned or rented by blacks that became available. Thus, in the 1950s, university officials renewed the prewar intention of expanding the main campus eastward to 35th Street. The university continued to acquire properties as they became available in the area bounded by Prospect, 37th, P, and 35th streets. By 1959 the university owned approximately 70 percent of the houses in the quadrant between 36th and 37th streets. Two years later university planners were anticipating extending the campus to 35th Street by the year 2000. Within the expanded campus would be an administration building, a classroom and office structure, a library, and a research facility. A plaza would be at the center of the enlarged east campus, and the roads between P and Prospect streets west of 35th would be closed.[17]

Another Greater Georgetown Campaign

To realize these goals the university was going to need to raise monies on an unprecedented scale. Greater enrollment would provide greater revenue, but that increase in enrollment would require more facilities, faculty, staff, and other support that would far outstrip the additional income. The university thus turned to some traditional sources of fund-raising as well as some very new ones. In the fall of 1953 the university announced the Greater

Georgetown Development Campaign with the goal of raising $14 million. At the kickoff dinner in October, President Bunn explained to the gathered alumni and other potential donors that planning and fund-raising were correlated parts of the modern life of universities. In the current situation, where tuition and serendipitous gifts were no longer sufficient to meet the rising costs of education, fund-raising had become a staple for a university to meet its operational expenses and capital projects. The Greater Georgetown Campaign was now "a normal function of the University . . . a necessary part of the university's planning. You can't run a university these days without such planning."[18]

In the same year that the university announced the Greater Georgetown Development Campaign, another fund-raising idea became a regular part of Georgetown's development strategy. At the initiative of James Ruby, the executive secretary of the alumni association, and another alumnus, Thomas Dean, in the spring of 1953, the board of governors passed a resolution to begin an annual alumni fund, to which alumni would make annual contributions as their ongoing way of supporting their alma mater. A university property on the corner of 36th and O streets was renovated to house the fund director, his staff, and Ruby. Eugene McCahill agreed to head the fund during its initial year and volunteered six months of his time to accompany the president or any other university official he would designate on a tour of cities where Georgetown alumni were concentrated. By car, plane, or train, Bunn or his surrogate spent a week traveling around the country to meet with alumni at dinners and/or receptions. "We visited cities two a day," McCahill remembered. "Ten cities or something like that on a trip." McCahill was pleasantly surprised at how receptive people were to their pitch for Georgetown. "They had never been asked before. They felt nothing was needed."[19] The result of this national solicitation was nearly $108,000, which Georgetown officials considered to be an excellent start. Two years later Eugene Stewart, first as fund chair and then as alumni association president, took over McCahill's role in peripatetic fund-raising. The sum continued to rise over the next decade. By 1964, the fund raised more than $400,000, nearly four times what had been realized during the initial year's drive. Even so, the proportion of alumni who contributed to the fund remained below 20 percent.

Unfortunately, the two campaigns, the Greater Georgetown and the annual fund, tended to compete with one another, as there was no overall coordination of earmarking individuals for specific funds. The national chairman of the alumni fund in effect acted on his own, and the director of development, Charles Foley, SJ, had little or no knowledge, much less authority, over whom the chair was soliciting. President Bunn and the top administrators, at least during the first year of the Greater Georgetown Campaign, when they were barnstorming the country with Gene McCahill, in essence made pitches for both the general campaign and the annual fund. The Greater Georgetown Campaign seemed to come off the worse of the two. Foley, who would typically make the case for supporting the Greater Georgetown Campaign, was not the convivial, persuasive type that one expects to be a fund-raiser. Foley felt constrained by the lack of coordination in the university's fund-raising efforts—a lack that he attributed to the president's failure to support him as the chief fund-raiser for Georgetown—and thought the campaign's goal of raising $14 million for ten or so buildings was far too ambitious and unfocused. After four and a half years into the campaign, the university had raised only $1.3 million, largely from alumni (nearly 50%), parents, and other individuals. Foundations and corporations had given a mere $172,755.[20] In 1963, nine years after the start of the campaign, the total amounted to more than $4 million, far short of the $14 million goal they had originally envisioned reaching by 1963.[21]

In 1960, and again in 1962, Bunn belatedly brought in outside firms to assess the potential support that Georgetown could realize among alumni, other individuals, corporations, and foundations and how best to tap those potential sources of funds in realizing the university's immediate and long-range needs. In the spring of 1963, John Price Jones, the second firm to be utilized, recommended that Georgetown organize a ten-year development program that would have a goal of $50 million. Given the university's meager accomplishments in its Greater Georgetown Campaign, this seemed to most members of the board of directors and president's council to be a wildly unrealistic goal.[22] Most thought a new goal should be no higher than the unrealized $14 million of the old campaign. Two members of the president's council, O. Roy Chalk and Eugene Stewart, thought it should be nearly twice that—$25 million—and the two, particularly Stewart, persuaded their fellow members to approve that figure. Another recommendation that one of the firms had made was that the university have as its head of development someone who had broad experience in fund-raising and could coordinate and give direction to the various formal and informal fund-raising efforts going on within the various schools of the university.[23] In November 1963, Bunn replaced Foley with James W. Egan, who had previously directed fund-raising for the University of Notre Dame and the University of Denver.[24] In October 1964, eleven years after the inauguration of the Greater Georgetown Campaign, Bunn announced to his council that a new campaign was being launched, with a goal of $25.1 million. It would become public when $5 million was raised—something the university had not previously been able to do in almost a decade of effort.[25]

A New Benefactor Emerges

Fortunately for Georgetown as well as the rest of private higher education in the United States, the federal government had by the 1950s committed itself to being a permanent major provider for the research and development of colleges and universities. What had begun as emergency wartime measures, culminating in the GI Bill in 1944, had by the early 1950s become a major ongoing investment in the nation's institutions of higher education, initially as part of the nation's defense needs, but increasingly as a way of strengthening the general welfare of American society. "There can be no question," Brian McGrath said with assurance in 1963, "that the Federal government has committed itself to [being] a major part in the educational system of the United States," just as it had committed itself to developing an integrated highway system in the 1950s.[26] The government funded defense-related research in the natural and behavioral sciences as well as more broadly focused research by the social sciences and humanities; it established loan and fellowship programs for graduate and undergraduate students; it provided the capital for centers and institutes engaged in teaching languages and in area studies; and, through such special legislation as the Higher Education Facilities Act of 1963, it gave grants and loans to colleges and universities for the construction of academic and residential buildings.[27]

Georgetown officials were quick to grasp the possibilities of federal support for their building and programmatic needs. By the early 1950s they recognized that the federal government was now a major source of funding for higher education and that an institution had to be alert to the federal funding opportunities and aggressive in seeking to exploit them.[28] Georgetown was an early participant in the Higher Education Association (HEA), a group of representatives from the major private and public educational associations, as well as those from federal agencies, who met monthly in downtown Washington to discuss educational affairs and to serve as a clearinghouse for funding opportunities, both private and public. The HEA provided Georgetown's representatives the ongoing occasion for establishing contacts and rapport with key people in the departments of the government involved with funding higher education projects.[29]

But the person most responsible for Georgetown's success in obtaining federal funding was T. Byron Collins, SJ, who had joined the university in 1954 as physical plant administrator. As the head of the physical plant, the responsibility for new construction fell to him and, as events proved, its financing. In 1956, with the help of Speaker John McCormack and Senator Wayne Morse,

T. Byron Collins, SJ.
(Georgetown University Archives)

he secured from Congress a special bill that provided $2 million in grants for the construction of a diagnostic facility at the Medical School. It was the first of a long series of mostly successful lobbying efforts that Collins led over the next four decades, first as physical plant head and eventually as head of the Office of Federal Relations, that resulted in the appropriation of hundreds of millions of dollars in federal support for Georgetown.

Under Collins's leadership, Georgetown became a pioneer among institutions of higher education in securing legislation specifically shaped to meet its needs, often through experimental programs designed as national models or exemplars. Collins and his staff built up a remarkable network of friendly congressional members and staffers, many of whom were graduates of Georgetown or of other Jesuit institutions, to ensure the successful passage of legislation from conception to appropriations. Collins often wrote the legislation that friendly representatives and senators introduced and shepherded through the two houses to become earmarked legislation for Georgetown. So in 1961 he authored PL 90-457, a bill that eventually provided $40 million in grants and long-term, low-interest loans to construct medical and dental facilities at Georgetown. For the building projects completed between 1956 and 1962, the federal government provided $12.8 million in grants and long-term, low-interest (2.7%–2.8%) loans. Indeed, from the late 1950s to the 1990s, Collins and his assistants in the Office of Federal Relations became the chief fund-raisers for the university.

Despite the administrative control and the new sources of fund-raising, the university continued to experience budget deficits throughout the 1950s and early 1960s, as the budget soared from $7 million in 1952 to more than $29 million in 1964. For fiscal year 1959 the deficit was more than $300,000, of which about two-thirds originated from the hospital's operations. A year later the hospital substantially reduced its deficit, but the deficit for the university as a whole grew to nearly $600,000.[30] From 1954 to 1964, the tuition for undergraduates was raised from $550 to $1,200. By 1964 tuition for the Medical School stood at $1,450; tuition for the Dental School was $1,200; and tuition for the Law School was $1,050. To enhance revenue from students that could pay in part for new or expanded services, an activities fee was introduced in the mid-1950s to offset expenses in development, public relations, the library, the athletic department, and elsewhere. In 1962 the board of directors created a special finance committee, composed of top administrators, to monitor university spending and financial planning.[31] The increase in ordinary revenue and the new watchdog committee notwithstanding, by 1964 the university found itself so financially strapped that it had to adopt a "policy of frugality" that canceled any new academic, administrative, or staff positions that had previously been authorized and put tight limits on spending for travel and supplies for university personnel.[32]

Building and Keeping a Faculty

One of Bunn's early goals was to improve the quality of the academic programs and their faculty in all the schools and departments of the university.
As prefect of higher studies for the Maryland Province, Bunn had conducted
a comparative study of the academic programs of four universities of com-
parable size to Georgetown in the summer of 1951: Princeton, Fordham,
Yale, and Saint Louis. Georgetown did not fare well in the comparison. He
had particular concern about the state of the natural sciences at Georgetown, especially chemistry. Bunn was determined to bring in strong department heads who would build faculties proficient in research and teaching.
"He had a vision of putting Georgetown on the map in the physical sciences,"
one science chair later reflected.[33] It took him a decade before he realized
the sweeping change he sought. Eventually he brought in an outside scientist from the Massachusetts Institute of Technology (MIT) to be his special
advisor for the area of the natural sciences. President Bunn also charged
Jacinto Steinhardt with coordinating scientific research and acquiring funding to support research. Steinhardt recommended that all science departments add members (some, such as mathematics, needed a great increase);
that only those scientists be hired who were active researchers and capable
of securing grants for their work, if not already possessing them; that their

George Chapman, chair of
the Department of Biology.
(Georgetown University Archives)

teaching be reduced to two courses a semester, one undergraduate and one
graduate; and that their graduate programs concentrate on the quality, not
the quantity, of their students.

Through Steinhardt, George Chapman was brought
in from Princeton in June 1963 to chair the biology department; to hire five proven biologists for the coming
academic year, all of whom were to be given immediate
tenure; and to start a graduate program. Among those
Chapman recruited was Otto Landman, a microbiolo-
gist, who came to Georgetown from his position as chief
of the microbial genetics branch in the army biological
laboratories. As a pioneer in the emerging field of molecular biology, his research and teaching focused on
molecular genetics during his nearly quarter century at
Georgetown.

A year earlier Louis Baker, a University of Pennsylvania PhD, had been brought in from Boston University to
head the chemistry department, a position he would
hold for the next twenty-two years. Both Chapman and
Baker brought with them grant money and the connections to secure more. Earlier, William A. Zorbach had
been appointed to the chemistry department in 1952,
where over the next fifteen years he taught organic

chemistry and became a prolific publisher of his research on arthritis and metabolic diseases. Another notable addition to the department was Joseph Earley in 1958. By 1968 the chemistry department could report that during the previous five years they had dramatically changed the character of their graduate program. Where once there had been only 20 full-time students out of the 100 enrolled, now there were 75 full-time students out of 90. Applications for the graduate program had risen from 25 to 230 for some 16 to 20 positions with financial support.[34]

In physics Edward Finn joined the department very early in Bunn's tenure. In 1955 the president persuaded an accomplished former department member, Robert Mooney, to return. Two years later the department appointed Harry Jean Watters, a former director of MIT's Cyclotron Laboratory and then at the Office of Naval Research (ONR), to offer graduate courses on nuclear physics. Because of his connections with the Atomic Energy Commission, the ONR, and other federal agencies, Watters, it was hoped, could develop the necessary facilities at the university and get access to other ones in the Washington metropolitan area for faculty and student experimental research in nuclear physics.[35] Three years later, probably at Watters's suggestion, Bunn wrote to one of Watters's colleagues at the ONR, William Thaler, who was considered to be a rising star in space-age physics, to offer him a

Louis Baker, chair of the Department of Chemistry. (Georgetown University Archives)

position at Georgetown. Thaler initially turned down the offer but reconsidered three months later and joined the physics department for the fall semester of 1960.[36]

By 1965 one member of the chemistry department wrote in retrospect, "Georgetown was offering Ph.D. degrees in astronomy, biology, chemistry, physics and mathematics. . . . Graduate work in science was now on a full-time basis and B.S. curricula had been broadened away from the preprofessional model with greater emphasis on pure science and on involving faculty and undergraduate students in research. . . . [All] were expected to conduct research."[37]

Two weak departments among the humanities that Bunn wanted to strengthen were philosophy and theology, both heavily composed of Jesuits, with theology exclusively so. The manual scholasticism that still prevailed in the philosophy department at the beginning of the 1950s was seen as abstract, dry as dust, and unrelated to life or to the other disciplines that it was supposed to be integrating. During the decade a corps of lay faculty, including Wilfrid Desan, Louis Dupré, Germain Grisez, Jesse Mann, Thomas McTighe, Rocco Porreco, and George Farre, received appointments. Together they brought an orientation to scholarship and professionalism in shaping the department. They also introduced philosophical traditions other than the scholasticism that had reigned since the beginning of the century. That development clearly strengthened the quality and status of philosophy at Georgetown, but it did not make for the utilization of philosophy as a synthesizing force within the curriculum. The philosophy curriculum, historically a watered-down version of that which Jesuit scholastics were given in their training, changed dramatically in the 1960s.[38] By the early 1960s, although the titles of the courses still suggested the hegemony of scholastic philosophy, the content of those courses increasingly had little or nothing to do with it. With the demise of scholasticism, philosophy effectively abandoned its role as the integrating discipline, as the decreasing hours allotted to philosophy in the curriculum, from 25 in 1962 to 12 in 1967, clearly indicated. If it was no longer the synthesizing power within the curriculum, it could no longer dominate.[39]

Theology was not even a department when Bunn took over. Theology courses were generally regarded as jokes, taught by clerical faculty who too often found themselves teaching theology by default.

William Thaler, chair of the Department of Physics. (Georgetown University Archives)

By the late 1950s, there was a deliberate effort to make it an authentic academic discipline by hiring faculty who had more than the Jesuit course of training in their background. William McFadden was the first Jesuit to be appointed to the faculty with a doctoral degree in theology. A number of laypeople were added to the department, both men and women. In 1963, John Ryan, SJ, was named as the first chair of the department. At the first department meeting that he called, he issued a gentle manifesto of what theology at Georgetown should be: a free inquiry into the realm of religious ideas and an unfettered discussion of the possibility of appropriating them into one's life. He introduced a new foundational course, "The Problem of God," which presupposed no specific religious belief but focused on the phenomena of religion within human history and culture. It was a distinct step away from the catechetical pedagogy that theology courses traditionally adopted. Ryan developed a broad series of elective courses that utilized theological reflection, including the study of classic religious texts, to grapple with new questions. That rationale for theology at Georgetown would over the next decade shape the faculty and the curriculum of the department, but, like philosophy, it would not sustain theology as an integrating force within the curriculum.[40]

Achievement in and potential for scholarship became factors in the hiring of faculty in the late 1950s, particularly after Monsignor John Tracy Ellis's attack on Catholic institutions for not producing scholars.[41] Doctoral degrees became a virtual prerequisite for new appointments, with Jesuits being the major exception (a significant number of those teaching philosophy and classics were Jesuit scholastics who had not yet completed their formal education).

Bunn was particularly entrepreneurial in drawing faculty to Georgetown, both as visitors and as permanent members. Thus he persuaded Martin C. D'Arcy, SJ, a noted philosopher who held a lectureship at Oxford, to become a continuing lecturer at Georgetown from 1956 to 1960 and 1964; besides the seminars he offered to philosophy students, D'Arcy gave occasional public lectures. Bunn secured William Lynch, SJ, an English professor from the New York Province, to become a major participant in the honors program, from 1956 to 1965. From Canada, Bunn recruited the Jesuit economist Emile Bouvier, who taught and published at Georgetown for several years in the late 1950s. Bunn gained the permission of Jesuit officials in India to bring a young physicist with a specialization in solar physics, Matthew Tekaekara, who had just completed his PhD at Johns Hopkins, to Georgetown in 1957 to work in the physics department as well as at the observatory. Jules de Kort, a Dutch astronomer, was another Jesuit who was successfully recruited to Georgetown in 1958. After four years of lobbying, Bunn convinced Jesuit superiors in Rome to allow Joseph Sebes, who was completing a doctorate in Chinese history at Harvard, to come to Georgetown.[42] Erik Larsen was brought to

Ian Karski, professor of government. (Georgetown University Archives)

Irfan Shahid, professor of Arabic. (*Ye Domesday Booke,* 1990)

Georgetown in 1955 to chair the fine arts department and Rudolph Schork Jr. in 1960 to head up the classics department. Edward Bodnar, SJ (PhD, Princeton), became a fixture in that department from 1959 to 1991 and served as chair for most of that time.

Refugees and émigrés were also prominent among the faculty appointed under Bunn. The best known was Jan Karski, the former Polish diplomat, who, as a member of the Polish underground during World War II, had been sent on a mission to Great Britain and the United States in 1943 to reveal to officials of the Allied governments the horrors that the Polish people were enduring under Nazi occupation, including the systematic killing of its Jewish population. In Washington, among those he briefed on the genocide was Edmund Walsh. At the end of the war, when Karski refused to return to his native country, which was now occupied by the Soviets, Walsh offered him a fellowship to pursue a doctorate in political science at Georgetown. When he completed it in 1954, Walsh offered him a position in the School of Foreign Service.[43]

Cyril A. Zebot, an economist and Slovenian refugee who had authored books on the Italian and Soviet economies during the 1940s, joined the economics department in 1958. A year later Bunn persuaded Henry Briefs, the son of Goetz Briefs, to return to Georgetown, where he had earned his doctorate and had previously taught, to chair the department. Hans Werner Weigert, an émigré from Germany in 1941, joined the government department in 1957 to teach graduate courses on political geography. Another distinguished refugee political scientist to join the government department was Heinrich Rommen. Wilfrid Desan, a Belgian expert on Jean-Paul Sartre and existential philosophy, joined the philosophy department in 1957. The following year Louis Dupré, with a doctorate from the University of Louvain, joined that department, having already published two books on the philosophies of Marx and Kierkegaard. Irfan Shahid from Palestine received an appointment to the Arabic department in 1963, where he quickly established himself as one of the university's outstanding scholars. A fellow countryman and refugee, Hisham Sharabi, joined the history department in 1953, which became his home for the next forty-five years, during which Sharabi distinguished himself through his works on European intellectual history and Arab culture.

Other notable appointments in the period included Joseph Huthmacher and Richard Walsh in history; Howard R. Penniman in government; John McCall, Thomas Francis Walsh, Roger Slakey, and

Members of the History/Government Department *(seated from left to right):* Hisham Sharabi; James Horigan, SJ; Valerie Earle; Howard R. Penniman; Gerard Yates, SJ; Jan Karski; and James Atkinson. (*Ye Domesday Booke,* 1968)

Raymond Reno in English; Francis Dineen, SJ, in linguistics; Maria Isabel Abreu in Portuguese; and Dmitry Grigorieff in Russian. In 1954 Valerie Earle became the first female faculty member of the business division of the School of Foreign Service and one of the first women faculty on the main campus. In 1955 Vera Cooper Rubin joined the astronomy department.

The Emergence of Research and Publication

In 1953 Charles Tansill pointed out to President Bunn that he was "one of the very few professors in Georgetown who does any publishing." That was something of a self-serving overstatement (Tansill was seeking a higher salary) but reflected the truth that too many of Georgetown's faculty were not scholars and published little. Because of the new appointments, that picture began to change in the latter 1950s and early 1960s. Brian McGrath, the academic vice president, reported in 1962 that in the previous decade

Valerie Earle, professor of government. (*Ye Domesday Booke,* 1968)

the amount of research undertaken at the university had "substantially improved." In 1952 the budget for research had been $600,000. By 1962 grants of more than $3 million were supporting faculty research, much of that in the Medical Center.[44] By 1964 the budget for research was approximately $7 million.[45]

One new source of funding for research in the sciences was from the newly established National Science Foundation (NSF), an integral part of the new state science order that emerged during the early years of the Cold War to promote an effective collaboration among universities, the military, and other government agencies in advancing, through basic research and technological development, national security and prosperity.[46] As a consequence of the Sputnik shock in 1957 and the race to catch up scientifically, the budget of the NSF was more than tripled (from $40 million to $130 million) for fiscal year 1959, and by 1966 had reached $480 million. In 1962 the NSF inaugurated its University Science Development program to funnel funds to institutions that showed unusual promise in upgrading their science departments and their scientific research.[47] Georgetown shared significantly in that program.

In 1956 the university established an academic research fund to support faculty projects. In 1957, $10,000 was allocated to faculty from the fund. In that same year the university contributed more than $12,000 toward the publication of four books written by faculty. Significantly, the university issued in 1964 a booklet listing the main campus faculty publications over the last decade to document the progress. Members of the astronomy, economics, government, and history departments were particularly active in publishing. The astronomy department began a monograph series featuring the research of faculty and doctoral students. By 1960 they had published seventeen volumes. Members of the economics department published six books over the decade, including a textbook authored by Goetz Briefs and his son, Henry. Twenty-three members of the government department had books or articles published, led by Victor Ferkiss, William O'Brien, Howard Penniman (three textbooks between 1958 and 1962), and Stefan T. Possony. History, like government, counted a very large majority of its members as publishing scholars. Jules Davids, who replaced Tansill; Joseph Durkin, SJ; Joseph Huthmacher; Carroll Quigley; Joseph Sebes, SJ; Hisham Sharabi; and Richard Walsh all had major books and/or articles in print during the period.[48] In philosophy, Rudolf Allers, Martin C. D'Arcy, Wilfred Desan, and Louis K. Dupré were the publishing leaders, with ten books among them.

A sign of the growing involvement of the faculty in scholarship was the Guggenheim grant awarded to John F. Callahan of the philosophy department in 1958, apparently the first such award won by a Georgetown faculty member. By the early 1960s, the size and complexity of grants and individual or group research contracts had grown to such a scale that there was a clear need for some central control and management. In 1964 the administration established the Office for University Grants and Sponsored Research. The office had authority to negotiate, contract, accept, and supervise all grants and projects.[49]

One group research project led to the creation of Georgetown's first research center. In 1962 the Ford Foundation offered to give the university two dollars for every dollar that the university raised to fund a pilot study on population increase.[50] The university subsequently raised $75,000 and duly received $150,000 from the foundation. In 1963 a Center for Population Research was established on campus to carry out research and training in biological and sociological aspects of population problems. Among the initial projects of the center were a statistical study of menstrual cycles, studies of Catholic fertility patterns and planning, a joint study with two Catholic universities in the Philippines on Philippine population demographics, and an investigation of Puerto Rican migration patterns.[51]

Henry Briefs, professor of economics. (Georgetown University Archives)

Professionalization

During the decade the university instituted a professionalization of standards and procedures for faculty. In 1955 faculty were required to make annual reports on their teaching, scholarship, and service to the university and academic society. In that same year the university established a uniform system of faculty titles and a policy for the granting of tenure and promotion to qualified faculty members. Also in that year a university-wide committee on rank, tenure, and salary was formed.[52] In that same period, tenured faculty who had served at the university for at least six years became eligible for sabbaticals. In 1957 the first faculty handbook was published, listing the responsibilities, privileges, and procedures for securing tenure and promotion. The administration put regular annual contracts into effect. Also in 1957 it established rules that set limits for outside consulting or other remunerative employment by faculty members.[53]

University officials also deemed the raising of faculty salaries to be a high priority, not only to attract new faculty, but also to keep those who too often moved on because of the low salary scales. President Bunn put the limited university assets into raising faculty salaries as much as possible. The effect on individual salaries was a modest one, but the effort impressed the Ford Foundation, which, among the nation's philanthropic bodies, had become the chief benefactor of higher education by the 1950s. In 1955 Ford began a $560 million program to improve the quality of private higher education; one of the program's chief goals was to raise faculty salaries, especially by giving grants to universities and colleges who had made extraordinary efforts

Karl Cerny, professor of government. (Georgetown University Archives)

to better faculty salaries.[54] The foundation awarded Georgetown more than $1.5 million, most of it toward an endowment for increases in faculty salary. It also awarded $2 million to the Medical Center toward its endowment, as well as nearly $200,000 to the hospital for its needs.[55]

Karl Cerny of the government department was one of those young professors looking elsewhere to secure more of a living salary when the Ford grant changed the landscape for salary increases. "I stayed at Georgetown [because of the Ford grant]," Cerny remembered. "With that [raise] we got out of the $200 annual increases and I could look forward to economic survival."[56] He spoke for many on the main campus. Thanks in large part to assistance from the Ford Foundation, faculty salaries rose substantially from 1952 to 1964 but still fell short of the salary range in comparable institutions. On the main campus in 1953 salaries ranged from $3,000 for an instructor to $8,000 for a full professor; by 1964, the range was $6,000 to $14,700. The administration was all too aware of the continuing need to close the gap. "There is increasing pressure for better salaries," McGrath wrote, "and if we are to hold the excellent laymen we have in the non-medical areas, it will take careful shepherding of our resources to meet this challenge."[57]

During Guthrie's administration, at McGrath's behest, planning had begun to institute a pension plan for faculty (until 1951 they did not qualify for Social Security). The plan, operated by the university, finally went into effect for the 1954–55 academic year. Faculty and administrative staff contributed 2.5 percent of their salary each year to the fund, while the university contributed 7.5 percent for each faculty and staff member. At retirement (initially age 60 for women, and age 65 for men) employees would receive annually between 45 percent and 50 percent of the average of their highest salary over a period of five years.[58]

Uniform medical coverage was another benefit introduced for faculty and other university employees in the late 1950s. A group insurance program was begun in 1958 through the Travelers Insurance Company. While a university insurance committee studied the insurance needed for major medical coverage, the university adopted the temporary policy of paying the salary for two months for a faculty member who became ill, with senior members receiving longer-term support at the discretion of the academic vice president.[59]

Faculty Retention and the Kearns Case

By the early 1960s there were clear tensions between the (mostly Jesuit) administration and the (mostly lay) faculty. "When I arrived here 6 ½ years ago," Wilfred Desan wrote to the graduate dean, James Horigan, SJ, at the end of 1963, "I was very much struck by the profound split between the clerical part of the university and the non-clerical or lay element. . . . I cannot say that over the years this situation has improved. I would even be inclined to say that it has aggravated." The problem, Desan thought, was not that the administration had become more distrustful of the lay faculty; he thought the contrary true, but "the Catholic layman in America has become more and more aware of his position, and claims, with reason . . . that he should play a more important part in the administrative decisions of the University" to which he had given "so much time, energy, and devotion."[60] Another faculty member, informed in 1963 that his contract would not be renewed, despite a decade of service, castigated "the rigidity and aloofness with which the administration conducts its business," feelings, he claimed, that were shared by many other faculty, who kept their silence out of fear that any criticism of the administration might endanger their positions.[61]

Francis Kearns was one faculty member who felt he had paid the ultimate price for his criticism of the administration. In the spring of 1963, Kearns had written a piece for *Commonweal* magazine in which he had deplored the administration's response to a student sit-in at a segregated diner in nearby Virginia.[62] The following September, in another *Commonweal* article, the assistant professor criticized Georgetown for restricting its hiring of black applicants to jobs of maids and groundskeepers. When Kearns failed to receive a promised pay raise the following year, he felt it to be a direct reprisal for his published criticism. When Kearns warned the academic vice president that the only recourse he had was to place the matter before the AAUP, he learned—two weeks later—that a clerical error was responsible for his failure to receive the recommended increase and that it had been rectified.

Three months later he received a letter informing him that his contract for the academic year 1965–66 would be terminated because his position, in the eyes of his chair, the deans, and the academic vice president, did not meet "the future needs of the Department."[63] The following day John McCall and sixteen other colleagues of Kearns in the English department penned a letter of protest to McGrath: His dismissal, they contended, could not "be defended on normal academic grounds. He is a good teacher, a productive scholar and his Department needs him." His dismissal, they argued, would rightly be construed as an infringement "on his academic freedom and therefore on ours."[64] McGrath, in his reply to the protesters, claimed that Kearns's termination had nothing to do with his criticism of the university or of Catholic education but rather was because of the supernumerary character of his position in a department that already had an accomplished professor in the field of American literature.[65] Undeterred, the English faculty secured a meeting with the president, the academic vice president, and the executive vice president, Gerard Campbell, SJ, to plead Kearns's case in person. The administrators now contended that it had been Kearns's less-than-competent teaching that had caused his dismissal. The English faculty persuaded them to form a committee of tenured English faculty to examine Kearns's teaching. In October the committee filed a report with the administration in which they strongly defended his teaching ability, as well as his scholarship, and urged that Kearns be renewed for the next academic year.[66]

In the meantime Kearns had approached the American Civil Liberties Union (ACLU) about his termination. Shortly afterward, a story about the case appeared in the *Washington Post* in early December that quoted Kearns as saying that his critical articles had been the cause of his dismissal. With the case now public, a student-faculty committee to keep Kearns was formed. In two days it gathered 1,200 signatures on a petition that urged the administration to reexamine Kearns's appeal and presented it personally to Gerard Campbell, SJ, the new president. Kearns's divulgences to the ACLU and the *Post*, however, had apparently doomed any possibility of changing the minds of Georgetown officials. The administration never responded to the petition and did not reopen his case.[67] In late February 1965 the East Campus Student Council censured the administration for its dismissal of Kearns and authorized its president to call for a demonstration of students in the schools of foreign service, business, and languages and linguistics. A week later its college counterpart called upon McGrath to answer in public the many questions raised in the Kearns case.[68] The action of the student councils got no more response from the administration than the earlier petition had obtained. No student demonstration ensued. Kearns left the university at the end of the academic year. As John Leo noted in *Commonweal,* whether the university had terminated Kearns for "cracking sensibilities" or failing to measure up to Georgetown academic standards was open to dispute, although what was known seemed to point to the former. What Kearns's colleagues had predicted—that his dismissal would be interpreted as a defeat for academic freedom at Georgetown—proved to be the widespread perception.[69]

Six months after the termination of Francis Kearns, one of his faculty supporters, John P. McCall, the president of Georgetown's chapter of the AAUP, wrote to the new president, Gerard Campbell, that what the events of the past year had pointed up was the "benevolent authoritarianism and . . . feudal dependence that characterized Georgetown's administration and the rest of the university respectively."[70] A little more than a year later, McCall announced that he was leaving Georgetown to take a position elsewhere. Five other tenured professors, he claimed, were also leaving because of low salaries and dissatisfaction with the administration. There were indications, he added, that sixteen others were contemplating the same course.[71] Earlier in 1966, Rudolph Schork Jr., chair of the classics department, had advised the academic vice president that he was resigning to accept an appointment elsewhere. "The reasons for my resignation," he wrote McGrath, "are many and complex."[72] Joseph Huthmacher, a full professor and the most prominent of Georgetown's historians, also left the university after the 1965–66 academic year to take a chair at the University of Delaware. The academic vice president explained that a turnover of thirty plus faculty was typical in any given year. But that the exodus would have included so many established professors seemed unusual.

A Building Boom

The university had built no academic facility since 1931 (White-Gravenor) and no housing since 1928 (Copley). In the 1950s, Edward Bunn set out on a building program that over the next fifteen years constructed more buildings than the university had done in its previous 165 years.

Ryan Administration Building
One of the first steps Bunn took to meet the physical needs of the university was to renovate Ryan Gymnasium in order to provide a central facility for administrative offices that were then scattered about the campus. In 1953 he spent $213,000 to convert Ryan to house the offices of university records, development, treasurer, accounting, public relations, and placement.[73]

St. Mary's Hall

While he was regent of the School of Nursing, Bunn had applied to the Department of Public Health for a loan to construct a residence for nurses near the hospital. The loan of $950,000 was approved at the beginning of 1953 for a facility to provide housing for three hundred students as well as facilities for a dining hall and all-purpose room.[74] In June the university purchased from Georgetown Visitation Convent a five-acre site fronting on Reservoir Road.[75] By that time the estimated cost of the building had risen to $1,350,000, and eventually cost more than $2 million, a sum ultimately covered by an additional federal loan and a grant from the District Health Commissioners.[76] The architect, Leon Chetelain, who had also designed McDonough Gymnasium three years before, had little discretion in planning St. Mary's. The building was the first at Georgetown in the Hill-Burton style of architecture —rectangular, flat-roofed, brick boxes that could be found across the country in the late 1950s, wherever federal funding set the guidelines for college construction.[77] Other buildings in the Hill-Burton style followed later in the decade: Walsh, Kober-Cogan, and New South. St. Mary's provided the first air conditioning of any Georgetown building—in the dining room, chapel, and offices.

St. Mary's Hall in 1956.

(Georgetown University Archives)

Edmund A. Walsh Building

By the mid-1950s the permit for the use of the temporary buildings (the Annexes) that the School of Foreign Service had been occupying since 1946 was about to run out. A planning committee proposed the construction of a classroom building on the site of the present public school building, the interns' residence, and the Capital Transit building at the corner of 36th and Prospect streets. The former hospital adjacent to the property was to be renovated for the use of the Graduate School, the School of Business, and the Institute of Languages and Linguistics. In November 1956 the university received permission from Rome to spend $1.6 million for construction and renovation.[78] The George A. Fuller Construction Company completed the building for its dedication as the Edmund A. Walsh Building by President Dwight Eisenhower in September 1958. The four-story building contained offices, classrooms, language laboratories, a multipurpose auditorium, a lounge, and a reference library.

Kober-Cogan Building

There was a perceived need for on-campus housing for medical and dental students. Of the 700 or so nonlocal medical and dental students, many, it was

Dedication of Edmund A. Walsh Building by President Eisenhower in 1958.
(Georgetown University Archives)

thought, preferred on-campus housing.[79] The university in the late summer of 1956 applied for a federal loan to construct a dormitory of 200 beds for medical and dental students. When they subsequently received a loan of $600,000 at 2.78 percent interest, they were able to leverage that as matching funds for a grant under the Hill-Burton Act to construct the $1.2 million facility.[80] It was named Kober-Cogan in honor of the former deans of the medical and dental schools.

Gorman Building

Another planning committee had decided that more extensive facilities for diagnosis, treatment, and research were necessary for the medical center. Funds were available from the General Services Administration, the Public Health Service of the District of Columbia, the Geschickter Foundation, and the Ford Foundation. The president of Ireland, Sean O'Kelly, dedicated the $3 million facility, adjoining the south wing of the hospital, on March 19, 1959.[81] The four-story, concrete-and-brick building, named the Lawrence C. Gorman Diagnostic and Research Building after the former president of Georgetown, included sixty-seven beds, a three-hundred-seat auditorium, and housing for twelve departments, including physical medicine, health services, and outpatient services. It contained clinics, including the dental clinic, and research laboratories, many of which were under the direction of the Department of Pathology and its director, Charles Geschickter. The departments of hematology and biochemistry also had extensive facilities for their research.

Dormitories

The enormous increase of enrollment in the late 1940s had severely strained the housing capacity of the university, which forced many students to seek accommodations off campus. By the early 1950s it was the consensus of administrators that all undergraduates should be housed on campus. With a loan of $3 million from the federal government under Title IC of the Housing Act of 1950, the Volpe Company began construction of a 400-bed facility on the site of the tennis courts due south of the O'Gara Building in the fall of 1958.[82] A year later the first students occupied the five-story, red-brick, flat-roofed building that contained 208 rooms and a dining hall with a seating capacity of 1,500. Unlike St. Mary's, the entire building, named New South in reference to the original college building, was air conditioned.

With New South completed, the university still needed an additional 1,000 beds to meet its goal of housing all undergraduates on campus. University officials decided to construct two dormitories, a men's facility to accommodate at least 400 beds to be built northwest of New North, and a women's with at least 300, on grounds just southwest of St. Mary's. Again loans were provided by the Housing and Home Finance Administration for

$4,575,000 for the construction of the two buildings.[83] The two dormitories, both high-rises standing more than six stories, opened in the fall of 1964. The men's dormitory was named for George Harbin, longtime mathematics professor and benefactor who had recently died; the women's hall was named for John Carroll's mother, Eleanor Darnall.

Reiss Science Building

The university had been planning the construction of a science building since the 1920s as part of the White Quadrangle. The Depression had forced a scaling back of the quadrangle, and White-Gravenor, the last building erected before World War II, was built to accommodate the chemistry department in addition to the classrooms and academic offices it provided. The other sciences were scattered about campus in the basement of Healy and in temporary buildings. In 1954 the university inaugurated a science building fund program to finance the project. It was not, however, until the fall of 1956 that the administration decided on a site for the building, an area just northwest of the White-Gravenor Building. From the NIH and the NSF the university received grants of $600,000 for the project. President Bunn, in a

Raymond Reiss Science Building in 1962. (Georgetown University Archives)

small plane piloted by Henry J. Blommer, an alumnus and member of the president's council who had been promoting the necessity of a building that would bring together all of the sciences at Georgetown, visited alumni and other potential benefactors across the country. Through the president's personal contacts and the work of the development office, nearly $2 million was raised over the next six years.[84] One alumnus who responded with a particularly large gift was the New York businessman Raymond Reiss, a charter member of the council, and the building was subsequently named the Raymond H. Reiss Science Building. After a very formal groundbreaking in the fall of 1960 (including a black-tie dinner), the McShane Construction Company completed the facility two years later, at a cost of approximately $4,250,000.[85]

Graduate Education: Growth or Concentration

In 1948 John Baptist Janssens, the superior general of the Society of Jesus, in a letter to the regional provincials in the United States, deplored the growth and multiplication of graduate programs in Jesuit colleges and universities as uneconomical and counterproductive. He called upon the provinces to consolidate graduate programs by pooling their resources and concentrating particular programs in certain universities (e.g., history at Fordham, astronomy at Georgetown). The following year, the executive committee of the Jesuit Educational Association recommended a regional application of this charge by having the institutions of a particular province pool their manpower to strengthen the respective preeminent graduate departments among them.[86] This recommendation, if acted upon, would have significantly benefited Georgetown, which, among the four institutions of higher education in the Maryland Province, had at the time a virtual monopoly on education at the graduate level. But local demand, the lure of academic prestige, and the economic revenue that graduate programs promised, particularly those that could draw federal or private foundation funding, all worked against consolidation and selective concentration in the 1950s.[87]

In the spring of 1952, Edward Bunn, still wearing the hat of provincial prefect of studies, had decried the ill-coordinated, unplanned overdevelopment of the Graduate School at Georgetown. Some specialized programs, such as that of psychological warfare, were siphoning needed resources from traditional departmental programs. Other graduate programs, such as physics, were barely functioning with one or two faculty. Bunn called for a reorganization of the school that would utilize its resources more efficiently and concentrate on a limited number of fields in which graduate education at Georgetown could excel.[88] A year later the graduate dean, Gerard Yates, SJ, issued a similar report that called for reorganization and concentration on

Aerial view of campus circa 1959. (Georgetown University Archives. Photo by Ben Wells.)

certain disciplines that were Georgetown strengths. Yates had attempted to start the reorganization but had met resistance from the department chairs, who formed the board of graduate studies and resented any attempt to challenge their autonomy.[89]

Far from eliminating weak programs and concentrating resources on a relatively few that would capitalize on the university's assets, the school increased its programs during the 1950s as it instituted new ones (Latin American studies and Russian area studies in 1959; MS in foreign service in 1961) or revived old ones (an English MA in 1954; a PhD in mathematics in 1961). In 1952 the school's enrollment was 691, and most of them were part time and overwhelmingly male (89%). There were fewer than thirty fellowships or scholarships available to graduate students. By 1964 enrollment had doubled to 1,284, with more than one-third of them full time (mostly in the sciences) and 30 percent of them women. Fellowships and scholarships now numbered over 100, with about half that number funded by outside sources, particularly through the NDEA. Fewer than one in twelve had any support, much better than the 4 percent who had had support in 1952, but still far below the ideal of funding for a vast majority of graduate students, which Dean James Horigan, SJ, recognized as "essential" for any quality graduate program. Part-time students remained the norm. The 1951 Middle States report criticized the high ratio of admissions in the school. Dean Yates noted in his 1953 report that the growth of the Graduate School had "probably been too rapid" and that the admission and general academic standards needed to be improved, which, he warned, would inevitably make for a small enrollment.[90] Despite decanal admonitions to make admissions more selective, by the early 1960s the vast majority of applicants were still being admitted to programs, and the Graduate School was larger than it had ever been.

Astronomy became an integral part of graduate education at Georgetown in the postwar period. Arguably, the astronomy department had the most successful graduate program in the 1950s and beyond. By the early 1960s it had become the largest graduate department of astronomy in the world, with fifty-five degree students. Much of the students' actual training came in work and observations for various government bodies, including the Naval Observatory, the Air Force Chart Service, the Bureau of Standards, the Army Map Service, and the Army Signal Corps. A number of outstanding graduates came from the program, including John P. Hagen (PhD 1949), who later headed the Department of Radio Astronomy at the Naval Research Laboratory; Martin McCarthy (PhD 1951), who joined the staff of the Vatican Observatory; Vera Rubin (PhD 1954), who stayed on as a faculty member while joining the Carnegie Institution; and George Coyne, SJ (PhD 1957), who became director of the Vatican Observatory.

By the 1960s the faculty consisted of Heyden, Carl C. Kiess of the Bureau of Standards, Vera Hagen, Rubin, Jules de Kort, SJ, and two others. In both 1952 and 1954, Heyden, in projects sponsored by the U.S. Air Force, designed and built the equipment for, and participated in, expeditions to photograph total solar eclipses and directed the examination by Georgetown faculty and students of the observations. For the 1954 expedition Heyden was in charge of selecting observing groups from various universities and government facilities and directing the observations made by recording the fading light of the sun by means of a photoelectric cell. Cooperating with several other international teams, the group set up fifteen sites along the path of total eclipse stretching from Hudson Bay to Pakistan. As Heyden pointed out, sequential observations of an eclipse, a kind of astronomical surveying, was one of the best ways to measure accurately the distance among continents.[91]

Besides the two eclipse expeditions, the astronomy department had contracts from government and private sources for high-dispersion spectroscopy and the analysis of the atmospheres of the planets.[92] In the 1950s and into the 1960s, the observatory was a daily scene of students and faculty astronomers carrying out experiments and observation. One evening Heyden gave

Francis Heyden, SJ, chair of the Astronomy Department.

(Georgetown University Archives)

a tour of the facilities to two visiting English scientists. "That night," he recalled, "every single instrument was being used by students. [They were] taking spectra of astrophysical metals . . . tacking variable stars . . . measuring the photoelectric intensities of the stars. The English scientists went away saying they never saw such a busy place."[93] But there were problems. As early as 1952 Heyden was complaining that the Georgetown site for observations was becoming worse by the year; it had become a victim of the lights of urbanization. "We would like to find a small piece of ground," Heyden wrote in a paper about the needs of the department, "about forty miles from Washington, in about the wildest most desolate country at that distance where we could be sure that no civilization would want to come in the remote future." On that site he planned to move their telescope for clear observations in a sky undiminished by city lights.[94] It was a dream Heyden pursued for the next two decades.

Despite low admission standards and a largely part-time student body, many of whom were employed in government agencies or the military, graduate education professors then recall a relatively high-qualified graduate cohort, particularly those in the PhD programs in the disciplines of government and history. Notable graduates of the period were Walker Connor (government PhD 1962), who became a professor at Trinity College in Hartford, Connecticut; Benjamin H. Alexander (chemistry PhD 1957), one of the first African American graduate students at Georgetown, who became a top research official at the NIH before being named president of Chicago State University in 1975; Daniel Callahan (MA philosophy 1957), who became director of the Hastings Institute of Society, Ethics and Life Sciences; Stanley Falk (history PhD 1959), who became the chief historian of the U.S. Air Force; Walter Nugent (MA history 1961), who established himself as a leader in the field of American diplomatic history; and John D. Buenker (history PhD), who did the same in the field of U.S. political history at the University of Wisconsin, Parkside.[95]

The 1961 Middle States Association report on Georgetown warned that if Georgetown was truly to become a fine university it had to make serious improvements in its graduate education. There was a general lack of cohesiveness in Georgetown's offerings, it was woefully lacking in library resources needed for advanced programs, and its programs tended to outreach the current faculty that it had to staff them. The Graduate School, it concluded, was at an awkward juncture: It either had to expand the library, faculty, and physical facilities to support its ambitious programs or cut them back to concentrate its physical and human resources more realistically on programs that had the potential for excellence.[96] In the sciences, particularly, the university did dramatically expand the faculty, and it built a facility that provided housing for the four departments and provided space for a science library and sufficient laboratories that allowed all the departments to conduct credible graduate programs. But the larger question of whether to concentrate limited resources on those graduate programs that held out the promise of being competitive on a national playing field was deferred to some unstated point in the future.

Summer School Origins

Summer classes dated back to World War II, when the university was on an accelerated schedule. With the end of the war, summer sessions continued. Gradually, particularly as the veterans graduated, there were relatively few Georgetown students taking courses during the summer. By 1953 there were only 95 students from the college enrolled in them. In that year there was discussion about formally beginning a summer school that would not only offer regular courses but also host workshops, symposia, and colloquia, in part to increase revenue for the university as well as to provide faculty with the opportunity to gain additional compensation. The school would target Georgetown students and those attending school elsewhere. It would also aim to attract professionals as well as other adults to its special programs. In the fall of 1953 James F. Dougherty, SJ, was appointed director of the university summer school. Eventually Paul Sullivan succeeded him, first as director, then as dean. By 1960 there were a total of 1,560 undergraduates taking summer courses, and more than half were from other colleges and universities. In the early 1960s the school experienced a phenomenal growth. In 1962 there were more than 3,100 students enrolled in more than 300 courses during the two sessions. English as a Foreign Language was a major draw for international students, with nearly 300 enrolled during that summer. A Latin workshop for high school teachers of Latin was given by Neil Twombly, SJ, and Richard O'Brien, SJ. Two three-day colloquia on Africa and Latin America, respectively, drew hundreds to the presentations. And the Peace Corps project added 285 other students for language training, area studies, and other topics.

The Emergence of the Law Center

In August 1953, Regent Frank Lucey wrote to President Bunn of his plan to transform Georgetown Law School from an institution that simply prepared students for the legal profession into "a more ambitious institution of legal education, a law center." Georgetown's unique location, Lucey noted, on the doorstep of the federal government and near its agencies and courts, positioned it ideally to develop "one of the finest Law Centers in the United States."[97] Subsequently, the Georgetown University Law Center became the standard identification of the school. Lucey never clearly defined what that center was to be, but, as Law Center historian Dan Ernst points out, the expansiveness of the title was an asset, as it allowed for "a great deal of experimentation in the novel legal climate of postwar America."[98]

There was, for one, a new emphasis on continuing legal education. In 1956 the school established a Legal Aid Society and, beginning in 1957, several institutes. In that year, Professor Heinrich Kronstein founded the Institute for Foreign and International Law. The institute sponsored research and conferences, such as the one on the Extra-Territorial Effect of Trade Regulations in April 1962 held at the Brookings Institute and attended by representatives from other nations as well as experts from universities in the United States who heard addresses by the president of the European Common Market, the Swiss ambassador, and others. The Institute for Church-State Law originated from a $50,000 grant that Professor Chester Antieau obtained in March 1962. The two books and other writings published under its auspices set out a basis in constitutional law and history for the evenhanded distribution of public aid to religious groups to promote "the concurrent interests of government and religion." At the close of the 1964–65 school year, the school folded the institute into a

Paul Dean, dean of the
Law School, 1955–69.

(Georgetown University Archives)

new body, the Institute for Law, Human Rights and
Social Values, directed by Dexter L. Hanley, SJ (**L** 1956).
Hanley and Paul Dean saw the institute as a way to
fulfill Georgetown's "particular obligation to the profession," to conduct research in the areas of jurisprudence and philosophy as a law school within a unique
Catholic tradition. Hanley also envisioned the institute sponsoring research into city planning, racial discrimination, economic aid, and labor law and relations,
among other areas. Under Hanley and his assistant,
Sherman Cohn, the institute continued the tradition
of symposia established by the law and morals forum
and added a new lecture series, the Edward Douglass
White lectures.[99]

The autocratic governance of the regent, however, increasingly was seen as the barrier to the development of
the center. In 1951 the Middle States Association inspection team had strongly recommended that the full-time
faculty be made the policymaking body within the
school. The regent stood in the way of such a transformation of policymaking, and, unsurprisingly, no change
occurred. Hunter Guthrie, of course, had failed in his attempt to remove Lucey as regent. His successor, although apparently content
to leave Lucey alone, began to attend the executive faculty meetings. At his
first one, he noticed a woman seated by the side of the regent at the head of
the table. Bunn publicly asked who she was, and when told she was the
registrar, Bunn said she had no business being at the meeting. Amid the pal-
pable shock of those in the room, Marie Stoll departed. Some faculty thought
in retrospect that that was the beginning of the end of the regent's absolute
rule.[100] If it was, the new dean of the school, Paul Dean, played a crucial role
in the evolution of power. Under Lucey, the role of dean had been largely
one of counseling students on academic matters. He had no role in forming
the budget (the regent and registrar shaped it in secret; the registrar also admitted students and prepared the academic catalogues) or in shaping policy.
He did not even have a secretary. When Paul Dean succeeded Hugh Fegan in
1954, he quietly but quite effectively began to change the nature and scope
of the dean's position.

"Paul Dean first had to free himself from Fr. Lucey," one veteran faculty
member noted. "[Then] he (with the strong support of Fr. Bunn) began faculty governance. That was a minus as well as a plus. The minus was that the
poor were now governing. So Paul had to find the way to maneuver forward
without causing a schism that could tear the school apart. . . . He was a master at this task."[101]

His first move toward faculty governance was securing approval from the administration in 1956 to set up a budget committee, composed of Lucey, four faculty members, and himself. That brought the budget process out into the open and gave the faculty input into the formation of the budget. Dean also lobbied Bunn to secure new faculty, most of them alumni of the school and highly qualified and loyal to the dean. Two alumni, Joseph Snee, SJ, and Richard Gordon, were appointed in 1954, and two others were hired, Kenneth Pye and Edwin Bradley, along with Helen Steinbinder, the first female faculty member, in 1956. In 1960 the president appointed another Jesuit alumnus, Dexter Hanley. Three years earlier, the executive faculty had voted to reach outside the school's alumni to secure qualified candidates for faculty positions. Chester Antieau, a national authority on the law of municipal corporations, was brought in from the University of Detroit in 1958, together with Sidney Jacoby, a German refugee. Two years later Stanley Metzger, who had been an adjunct, was made full time.

In 1958 the dean brought more faculty into the policymaking process by creating a faculty committee to revise the school's curriculum.[102] The following year they introduced a new curriculum that was significantly more flexible than the one it replaced. It reduced the hours for certain required courses and made electives of others. Upper-class students could now choose from a wide range of electives. For the first time students in both the day and evening divisions followed the same curriculum, which required each student to take at least one seminar in the program of courses. As the committee pointed out, it was necessary to make this obligatory if Georgetown was to compete with the leading law schools.[103]

In 1959 the dean created an Office of Placement. In that year he also effected faculty control over admissions, an area badly in need of reform, by hiring Kenneth Pye as director of admissions for the school and removing the registrar from any decision-making role. Admission standards for the school were minimal throughout the 1950s. Applicants to the school had a better than 4 in 5 chance of being accepted into the LLB program. Nearly three-quarters of them were Catholics from a network of Catholic colleges that were the major feeders for the school. Many of them (17%) were from Georgetown undergraduate schools.[104] Jewish students constituted a significant minority of 12 percent. Females made up but 2.2 percent of the school (the first female had enrolled in the fall of 1951). There were a handful of foreign students and slightly more African Americans. If admission rates were very high, so was attrition, particularly during the first year of matriculation. In 1952–53, the mortality rate was nearly 24 percent, with most of those being dropped or withdrawing in their initial year.[105] All told, attrition rates ranged as high as 60 percent for classes during the decade. The lax admission standards of the 1950s bore their deadliest fruit in the bar examination performances by graduates. Indeed, performances by Georgetown graduates worsened in the course of the decade. Of those Georgetown alumni who took the D.C. bar exam in 1950, 85 percent passed in June, and 80 percent passed in December. By 1952 the percentage of those passing dropped to 69 percent; by 1957 it fell to 54 percent.

In 1958 enrollment peaked for the school at 1,338. The next year it dropped sharply to 1,162, a consequence largely due to the introduction of more rigorous admissions standards by the new director of admissions. It was also the result of the unprecedented competition in securing the best graduates from Catholic colleges (many were now opting for Ivy League law schools or their equivalent). By 1962 the decision was made to recruit heavily in "new markets," the Ivy League schools as well as eastern and midwestern independents.[106] By 1964 admission rates had fallen dramatically to 54 percent, a respectable ratio among leading law schools.[107] Under the new guidelines for admission, total enrollment had continued to fall, reaching a low of 980 in 1961, but gradually recovered as Georgetown began casting its recruiting net beyond the traditional, largely Catholic, feeder schools.

Kenneth Pye and Richard Gordon visited some 55 colleges and universities during the 1962–63 academic year; they gave particular attention to recruiting from women's and historically black colleges.[108] Median LSATs rose sharply from 490 in 1959 to 559 in 1963, putting the school in twelfth place in that category among law schools. The number of Georgetown graduates in the school declined sharply. By 1961 only eight of the top seventeen feeder schools were Catholic. Ivy League graduates now constituted 10 percent of the school's enrollment. As diversity increased in the makeup of the student population, so did the numbers. By 1964 the school population stood at 1,220, an increase of 36 percent from 1952. Not only was the quality of the students sharply improved, but the school was now the fourth largest in the country. Catholics now were but a bare majority in the school. Jewish enrollment had risen to nearly 20 percent. Females were still an exotic presence at 3 percent of enrollment. Students from the Northeast now made up nearly half of the population (48%). Local students had declined to only 17 percent of the school. Foreign students were more numerous than they had been in 1952 but were still barely 1 percent of enrollment. One factor that continued to hurt Georgetown's ability to recruit was the lack of scholarships. The number of scholarships available increased from 27 to 54 from 1954 to 1963, but they were dwarfed by those that other schools could offer (e.g., Harvard 414, Yale 216). Georgetown's financial aid of $71,507 was barely discernable next to Harvard's $391,817 or Yale's $201,306.[109]

One area in which Georgetown students did remarkably well in the 1950s was in the National Moot Court Competition. Georgetown teams qualified for the nationals every year during the decade. Georgetown's first four teams reached the finals of the national competition. In 1950, Georgetown, represented by Everett Olinder, Vincent Pepper, and Gil Zimmerman, with Paul Dean as moderator, bested teams from Northeastern, Yale, Albany, and Kansas City to win the national title. Olinder was voted best advocate. Two years later the team, composed of Richard Alan Gordon, John D. Spellman, and A. Kenneth Pye, all of the class of 1953, won a second title as they defeated the University of Chicago in the final. This time Gordon was chosen best advocate.[110] The next year Georgetown returned to the finals with a team of Charles Whelan, SJ; Raymond W. Began; and Rex A. Jeminson but surrendered the title to the University of Nebraska in a controversial decision, despite winning the prize for best brief. Their extraordinary success confirmed Georgetown officials' confidence in the outstanding courtroom advocates that their brand of legal education was producing.[111] As their moderator, Paul Dean, noted years later, "They set a standard of excellence that continues to guide Georgetown as it trains advocates for all stages of the administrative and judicial process."[112] By the 1960s, however, their record began to decline. In 1962, when the Georgetown team was eliminated in the first round of the nationals, Dean suggested that it might be better, for the future, to concentrate on the in-house Moot Court Competition rather than on the national competition. The former, which involved many students, had tended to suffer over the past decade from the stress put on the preparation of a foursome to carry Georgetown's name to the national stage of moot competition.[113]

Two other student-run organizations within the school won national recognition in this period. The student bar association, which had been founded in 1950 to conduct special educational and social functions, including guest lectures, was ranked the top student bar association in the nation by the American Law Student Association in 1958. Four years later, the Law School newspaper, *Res Ipsa Loquitur,* was named the outstanding student newspaper of the major law schools in the United States.[114] The *Georgetown Law Journal* continued to enjoy a high reputation as one of the best law school periodicals in the country.

A number of graduates distinguished themselves in the academy of legal education. Richard L. Braun (1953), became dean of the University of Detroit Law School, then dean at the law school of the University of Dayton; A. Kenneth Pye (1953) left the faculty at Georgetown to join the law faculty at Duke before becoming president of Southern Methodist University; Francis J. Conklin, SJ (1961), became dean of the Gonzaga University Law School; Charles Whelan, SJ (1954), joined the faculty at Fordham Law School; Joseph B. Kelly (1960) became a professor at Dickinson School of Law; and Norman Lefstein (1964) was a professor of law at the University of North Carolina when he was named dean of the Indiana University School of Law in 1987.

Among those who obtained federal and state judgeships were James T. Barker (1953) for the National Labor Relations Board; Sylvia Bacon (1959), associate judge of the District of Columbia Superior Court; Rose Murphy McBrien (1959), judge of Family Court in New York State; Mark N. McCormick (1960), a justice of the Supreme Court of Iowa; and Norma Holloway Johnson (1962), a judge of the Superior Court of D.C. Several graduates subsequently served in the Congress of the United States: George J. Mitchell (1960), as Democratic senator from Maine; Patrick Leahy (1964), as Democratic senator from Vermont; John Durkin (1965), as Democratic senator from New Hampshire; Angelo D. Roncallo (1953), as Republican representative from the Third District in New York; Michael Castle (1964), as Republican representative from Delaware; James Robert Jones, as Democratic representative from Oklahoma; Frank Wolfe (1965), as Republican representative from Northern Virginia since 1981; and Herbert Bateman (1956), who represented the First District in the Northern Neck of Virginia from 1983 to 2000. Among those to make careers in the government were Grace Nolan Broderick (1956) in the Department of the Interior; Russell A. Rourke (1959), who served in the Defense Department before becoming secretary of the air force in 1985; Mary Lawton (1960), who became the highest-ranking woman in the Department of Justice; Richard E. Wiley (1962), who chaired the Federal Communications Commission in the 1970s; and S. John Byington (1963), who chaired the United States Consumer Product Safety Commission in the Carter administration.

By 1960 President Bunn became convinced that he had to strip Lucey of his executive power. Unlike Guthrie, he did not try to appeal to the provincial superior but took action himself through a more democratic process. On Ascension Thursday in 1960, Bunn invited members of the executive faculty of the Law School, but apparently not Lucey, to a luncheon. During the luncheon Bunn sought their advice on possible changes in the administrative structure of the school. In particular Bunn wanted to know what they thought of making the regent fundamentally a consultor within the school's administration.[115] In June 1960 Joseph Snee, SJ, a graduate of the school and a member of its faculty, wrote the president that it was urgent that he take steps to change Lucey's position at the Law Center. The problem, Snee observed, was that the regent was, in practice, the chief administrator of the school, despite the faculty handbook's clear statement that the dean was to be the "sole administration head of each school." With the impending visit of the Middle States team in October, it was vital that Bunn take active measures by restricting the responsibilities of the regent to being a representative of the school to the board of directors, with no administrative authority in the law center. Unless such steps were taken voluntarily, he warned, the university risked being forced to do the same by outside evaluators.[116]

Not until mid-August did the executive faculty respond to Bunn's request. They completely concurred with his idea of making the regent a consultative position. They also recommended that the position of the school's registrar be "downgraded considerably" to that of a subordinate to an assistant to the dean and Marie Stoll herself made registrar emerita.[117]

That fall Bunn appointed a committee charged with revising the school's constitution. The committee reported in March 1961 an emendation that named the regent as "university representative" who had no administrative authority in the Law School. A month later the Middle States team issued its report, which, among other things, recommended that the law faculty be given greater authority, that the registrar's office be reorganized, and that the dean be given more control over finances. "It would seem that at least one top-flight law school should be located in Washington," they concluded. "There is none now. The Georgetown Law Center has age and prestige. If adequate resources were provided it could match the performance of the best schools in other parts of the country."[118]

In June the provincial superior, John Daley, the former dean of the Georgetown Graduate School, wrote Lucey that his golden jubilee as a Jesuit was an appropriate time for him to step down as regent. At a meeting of the executive faculty on June 30, Bunn announced that Lucey had been made regent emeritus, that Frank Dugan was stepping down as dean of graduate programs, and that A. Kenneth Pye and Richard Alan Gordon, members of Paul Dean's second championship moot court team, had been appointed to the respective offices of associate and assistant deans. That same day, Bunn dismissed Marie Stoll, who had remained at her post despite requests for her resignation.[119] Brian McGrath was made the new regent. Lucey continued to teach jurisprudence at the school until January 1970.

In 1964 full-time faculty had grown to twenty-six, a 65 percent increase since 1952. The faculty-student ratio, one to forty-seven, was far better than the minimal one to seventy-five that the AALS required, but still the same as it had been a dozen years before. In his 1962 report, Dean pointed out that the school needed more professors to lower the student-faculty ratio as well as to allow for sabbaticals that were a sine qua non for cultivating research among the faculty. He also noted that salaries were not competitive (Georgetown's salary scale ranked thirty-second among law schools, far below that of the leading ones). At that level, Dean maintained, the school could attract neither persons in private practice nor in government agencies, the two major markets Georgetown had in which to recruit.[120]

Dean slowly but steadily built a faculty of value. Gradually he built up the salaries. He inaugurated summer research grants to enable faculty to pursue scholarship. He hired a faculty secretary to assist, among other things, with the typing of manuscripts for journal articles and books. In 1962 he made two appointments of note: Paul Kaskell, a Harvard Law graduate, and Bernard Burrus, who had practiced in a prominent Wall Street firm. It was a signal that Georgetown could compete in hiring graduates of the top law schools and attorneys from the best firms. It also set the pattern for the school's hires thereafter: graduates of Harvard and Yale, as well as some of its own outstanding alumni, including Sherman Cohn (1957), whom Dean brought in from the Justice Department in 1964.

From the time he became dean, Paul Dean concentrated efforts on improving the school's library. He made the librarian's position full time and gave him assistants to staff the library. Holdings grew from 49,419 in 1955 to 82,019 in 1959; periodicals nearly doubled from 3,740 to 6,190. Student usage also nearly quadrupled from 1951 to 1959. By 1963 the holdings of the library topped 130,000 volumes. The budget for library acquisitions had risen from $10,000 in 1954, when Dean took office, to a high of $48,000 in 1958.[121] Still, the library ranked but twenty-second among major law schools. The library badly needed to expand its housing capacity and reading areas. Lack of space, indeed of a separate facility, was the paramount problem. Every major law school had its library in a separate building.

Dean was also responsible for the development of what became Georgetown Law's greatest strength in legal education in the final three decades of the twentieth century—its clinical programs. The wave for establishing such programs was beginning to crest in the latter 1950s with the creation of the National Council on Legal Clinics under the leadership of William Pincus, which established programs that brought together the legal academy and legal profession in an effort to improve the American legal system.[122] It was a movement that got little or no traction in the leading law schools, who feared that such programs would introduce a trade school element into legal education. Those schools who had clinical programs, such as Duke and the University of Southern California, utilized them as extracurricular activities. Georgetown, by contrast, made its program an integral part of the curriculum. By embracing the concept, Dean, one faculty member judged, "put us in the forefront [of legal education] when the Harvards of this world were looking down on clinical and practical education. That was a tremendous gamble . . . but it paid off."[123]

Georgetown's first legal clinic had a very local origin. When a U.S. attorney for the District of Columbia urged the city's law schools to establish legal aid clinics for indigent criminal defendants, Dean and some Georgetown faculty saw the opportunity to take advantage of the school's reputation for producing trial lawyers, secured funding from an outside source, and set up the E. Barrett Prettyman Program in 1960, named for an alumnus of the school who was then chief judge of the U.S. Court of Appeals in the District. Kenneth Pye became its first director. His goal was to create, over time, a cadre of persons who could return to their communities to begin clinics there.[124] Six Prettyman fellows, graduate students seeking a master of trial advocacy degree, began their one-year program in Washington's criminal courts in the fall of 1960.[125] Eventually Georgetown undergraduates began to participate in the program as well, with internships offered by the U.S. Attorney's Office. In 1963 the Ford Foundation began to support the program, which enabled Pye to increase the fellowships from six to eleven and to extend them from one year to two years. It also allowed the program to expand its indigent representation to include civil as well as criminal cases.[126]

Another clinical program related to the D.C. courts was the Georgetown Bail Project, which originated from another grant from the Ford Foundation in 1963 to do a three-year study of the bail system in the District's courts and to make recommendations, on the basis of their findings, on releasing without bail specific defendants who had a certain level of ties with the community. David McCarthy, another outstanding graduate (1960), was hired to direct the project. A criminologist and law students from Georgetown and other area schools made up the project staff. Within the first two years of the project, 1,324 persons had been released without bond. Ninety-seven percent showed for their trials.[127] By the time the grant expired in 1966, the project had succeeded in releasing more than two thousand defendants and had inspired similar programs in more than fifty cities across the country.[128] The project was also the catalyst for two bills enacted by Congress (written by the project staff) for the District of Columbia. The laws gave legal sanction to the rationale for releasing accused criminals without bail that the Georgetown Bail Project had employed. They also set up a permanent agency to carry on the project's work. McCarthy and Paul Dean were at the White House for President Johnson's signing of the Bail Reform Act of 1966.[129]

In January 1967, *Time* magazine, in an article on law schools, singled out Georgetown as a leader in providing in-court training for its students. It quoted U.S. Judge J. Skelly Wright as praising the school for providing "probably the most systematic and thorough training in trial advocacy offered anywhere in the country." By that time Georgetown students had defended nearly 2,500 clients through the program. Many of the graduates of the Prettyman program, *Time* noted, went into public legal service as a career.[130]

The Prettyman program was a centerpiece of graduate education at Georgetown, which was the fastest growing sector of the school. By 1960 students in graduate programs represented about 15 percent of enrollment, more than double what it had been eight years earlier. The heaviest graduate enrollment was in the Continuing Legal Education Institute, which by 1960 counted 160 students. The institute continued to offer courses for lawyers and other specialists on trial preparation and strategy, taxation, estate planning, trade regulation, and other topics of interest. Under the direction of Frank Joseph Dugan (1938), who oversaw the graduate programs from 1954 to 1960, there was a change in emphasis from "skills" programs, such as those offered by the institute, to degree programs in patent law or some other specialty of two years' duration, which involved examinations and research. A visiting committee of the American Association of Law Schools in 1963 found the change in the character of graduate programs to be a large step toward putting graduate education on the same academic level as its undergraduate counterpart at the school.[131]

Dean's highest priority when he became the chief academic officer of the center in 1961 was a new home, something the Middle States team had found to be the university's most critical need during its visit in the fall of 1960. "We desperately need a new building," Dean reported in 1962. "The failure to have an acceptable building," he reported, "has placed us at a competitive disadvantage. Unquestionably our building is the least adequate of any of the major law schools in the country."[132] The law center, Professor Richard Gordon reported to the president's council in 1964, was losing many superb applicants from the finest colleges in the East who, when visiting the center, were put off "by the warehouse character of the exterior and the wholly inadequate and unattractive facilities within." At a time when other law schools had recently built new facilities, the contrast between what prospective students encountered at those places and what they saw at Georgetown put the latter as a severe disadvantage.[133] Six years earlier Dean had told the president's council that the law center was facing the predicament of expanding its facilities or losing the reputation it was gaining as a leading center of law. Added to the challenge was the knowledge that they had committed themselves to increasing the enrollment substantially by 1964. Among the specific needs were classrooms, a library, student housing, and administrative and faculty offices.[134]

The long-range plan of the university was to move the school to the main campus. In 1959 the consulting firm of Cresap, McCormick & Paget was brought in to make a study of whether it was better to build anew at their present, downtown location or construct a law facility on the main campus. On the basis of the firm's study over several months, including interviews with administration, faculty, students, and alumni, it issued its report in March 1960, which concluded that, although it was feasible to locate the school either downtown or on the main campus, the former location had far greater advantages, with its proximity to courts, legal libraries, and administrative agencies. Given the increasing emphasis on clinical legal education, such proximity seemed to make it imperative that the downtown site be chosen. Moreover, their interviews discovered that faculty and students both overwhelmingly favored the downtown location. Clinching the matter was the fact that the main campus lacked the space (estimated at a block and a half) that would be needed to accommodate the school.[135]

Deliberation over various possible sites continued into 1965. Finally, in the spring of that year, the decision was made to purchase a site of some 83,212 square feet, located between First, Second, F, and H streets northwest, more than enough to accommodate the 60,000-foot building then planned.[136] Paul Dean immediately began a fund-raising effort to make the building a reality within the next five years.

By the mid-1960s the law center, under Paul Dean's leadership, was a school very much on the rise among the legal education establishment. A later dean claimed that "none has a stronger claim to the title [Founder of the Modern Law School than Paul Dean, particularly in his commitment] to hiring faculty 'who are better than we are,' who shared his vision, who brought prominence to the institution, and who were open to change."[137] He was setting it on a path to break through the ceiling separating the elite law schools from the rest.

The Medical School: Growing a Reputation

In March 1953 a heart attack hospitalized Paul McNally, SJ, who had played such a key role (some thought the top role) in the remarkable progress of the medical center over the past decades. Four months later, because of continuing poor health, he stepped down, at Bunn's insistence, as regent and dean of the Medical School. Significantly, President Bunn did not replace him with a Jesuit who would act as both regent and dean but rather divided the two offices. He appointed Thomas O'Donnell, SJ, as regent and Francis M. Forster, MD, chair of the Department of Neurology, as dean. Bunn clearly did not regard the office of regent as one of administrative authority. As he explained to Foster, "I consider the Regent to be the liaison officer between the Medical School, the Hospital, and my office."[138] Unfortunately, the clarification was not made public, and confusion remained about the relationship between dean and regent.

In 1957 the university created two new positions in the administration of the medical center: an associate dean in charge of the hospital and clinical areas and an assistant dean for research. The increasingly complex operations of the hospital called for the first appointment, which went to Dr. Charles D. Shields. The proliferating research programs and the grants that funded them called for the second. Dr. Walter C. Hess, chair of the Department of Biochemistry, became the first assistant dean for research.

Harold Jeghers, who as the head of medicine had brought so many new faculty to the school, much preferred the building of a faculty to managing it. When given the opportunity to assist with the inauguration of the Seton Hall Medical School, Jeghers left at the end of the 1955–56 school year.[139] By the time he departed, the Medical School faculty had grown enormously. Where there had been only 1 full-time faculty member in the clinical sciences in 1946, there were now 38. The preclinical departments had not experienced the same dramatic increase, but there had been a steady rise in numbers of full-time members to reach 50 by the 1957–58 academic year. All told there were 567 staff faculty members and 123 residents engaged in teaching. And the sharp growth continued into the 1960s. Full-time faculty increased by 120 percent from 1957 to 1963, from 90 to 198.[140]

John Stapleton, **M** 1946, chair
and professor of medicine.
(*Georgetown Medical Bulletin*, vol.
28, no. 3)

Theodore Koppanyi continued to chair the Department of Pharmacology, which he had done since 1930. Under Koppanyi's long tenure, the department was one of the leaders in the science of pharmacology. Valuable contributions were made at Georgetown to many areas of the science, especially those related to metabolism, central nervous system depressants and stimulants, and autonomic pharmacology. In the latter 1950s Koppanyi was the coinventor of an ion exchange resin kidney. By the 1960s many members of the department were doing research in neuropharmacology, while others concentrated on cardiovascular, cellular, and behavioral pharmacology, as well as on drug metabolism.[141]

John F. Stapleton, a Georgetown graduate, joined the Department of Medicine in 1952. He later became the medical director of the Georgetown Hospital. George Elmer Schreiner, another alumnus, had joined the department a year earlier. In 1955 he performed the first kidney transplant from a cadaver to a fifteen-year-old boy. Bruce I. Schnider, still another graduate of the school (1948), was appointed to the Department of Medicine in 1953.

Hubert V. Pipberger joined the division of cardiology in 1956. In a project cosponsored by the school and by the Bureau of Standards and the Veterans Administration, he developed a method of analyzing electrocardiograms by means of electronic computers, for which he won the William S. Middleton Award for Outstanding Research Achievement in 1961. Another exceptional cardiologist to join the division in 1957 was Joseph K. Perloff, who continued to publish widely in his field, most notably *The Clinical Recognition of Congenital Heart Disease.*

In the Division of Endocrinology, Laurence Kyle, chair of medicine, and John Canary, head of the division, made notable advances in the diagnosis of primary hyperparathyroidism, the secretion of excessive hormone in one's system. Their success attracted hundreds of patients with the disease to Georgetown in the 1950s and 1960s for diagnosis and treatment.[142]

By the early 1960s, Charles Hufnagel, with major assistance from John Gillespie and Peter Conrad, had gained world renown for Georgetown's cardiac surgery. The trio teamed to develop new techniques and mechanisms for treating cardiac disease: the replacement of a defective aortic heart valve with an artificial ball-valve in 1952, the grafting of segments of animal arteries onto those of humans in 1953, the implantation of the first synthetic (orlon) aorta in 1954, the development of a freeze-dry technique for storing an arterial graft in 1955, the invention of a pneumatic heart pump in 1957, the making of a heat exchanger for cooling and heating blood in 1958, the development of a technique for creating hypothermia to suspend respiration and circulation in order to repair a diseased valve directly in 1961, the manufacture of a mechanical heart massager and respirator in 1962, and the first successful kidney transplant in the

Washington area in 1965. Patients were now coming to Georgetown from around the world to seek treatment for many heart ailments that were hitherto mortal.[143]

In September 1959 two Georgetown surgeons, William T. Spence and Alfred J. Luessenhop, performed pathbreaking brain surgery on a woman who had suffered a cerebral hemorrhage. By inserting tiny plastic pellets into a neck artery, they were able to dam off life-threatening blood ways into her brain, and the patient recovered without any paralysis or impairment. By utilizing the arteries as a surgical channel, Luessenhop performed the world's first embolization.[144]

Roger Carroll Baker Jr. joined the surgery department from the University of Chicago in 1953. He brought with him a reputation for pioneering research in kidney disease and quickly became the leading urologist in the Washington area. In the 1960s he developed a method for opening the kidney to perform repairs and then resew it; in that same decade, in a joint effort with doctors in Canada and Spain, Baker invented a new procedure for removing a cancerous bladder and replacing it with one made from a piece of the patient's bowel. In 1959 Peter W. Conrad, a Georgetown graduate (1954), brought his specialization in cardiovascular surgery to the department. In 1960 Robert Coffey, the chair of surgery, created a new division of surgical oncology and appointed John F. Potter (1949), then a research fellow at the National Cancer Institute, to head it.

A sign of the extraordinary caliber of the surgery department was the election in 1956 of both Coffey and Hufnagel to the elite 250-member American Surgical Association. Coffey and Hufnagel also illustrated the division of labor that was taking place in virtually all medical departments between the chair and other members of the department. Coffey was the manager, recruiter, promoter, and fund-raiser, and Hufnagel was the researcher and experimenter. Coffey gave the department visibility among both those in the medical academy and the general medical profession by attending and participating in regional and national meetings. He also was very active in recruiting full-time members for the department. By the latter 1960s there were thirty-five full-time members in the Department of Surgery.[145]

A new division in surgery that was created during the period was ophthalmology. James F. O'Rourke (1949), while a research fellow at the Wills Eye Hospital, earned an MS degree in ophthalmology at the University of Pennsylvania. As a research associate at the NIH, O'Rourke conceived the idea of establishing an ophthalmology residency program at Georgetown that would train residents at District of Columbia General Hospital and other health facilities in the area during a three- or four-year plan that combined basic science, research, and clinical experience. In 1956 he got a training grant from the NIH to do so, and the program began under O'Rourke's direction a year later. In 1958, Peter Y. Evans was appointed teaching fellow in ophthalmology to assist O'Rourke. Evans took charge of the District of Columbia General Hospital Eye Service as the major clinical base of the program. By 1958 four residents were involved with the program. Two years later the number of residents grew to twelve. In 1961, O'Rourke became director of the division of ophthalmology.

Roy Eliot Ritts Jr., who was appointed assistant professor of medicine and associate professor of microbiology in 1958, a year later became chair of the Department of Microbiology and carried out a successful campaign of recruiting outstanding microbiologists to a department that had been understaffed. The department soon flourished in its research and grant support.[146]

John Philip Utz, appointed professor of immunology in 1952, became a leading publisher in that field. Desmond O'Doherty joined the Neurology Department in 1952 and became chair in 1958 when Frank Forster left to move to the University of Wisconsin Medical School. Margaret M. Kenrick, one of the first women appointed to the school, joined the Department of Physical Medicine and Rehabilitation in 1956 and later chaired it.

In the Department of Psychiatry, Murray Bowen came from the National Institute of Mental Health to Georgetown in 1959. Bowen, who had performed psychiatric training at the Menninger Clinic, had developed the theory of family therapy in the treatment of psychiatric problems. George N. Raines, the chairman of the department, assured him that he could freely pursue the testing of his theory about the social context of mental health.[147] In 1960 the center established in-patient psychiatric service.[148] Thomas E. Macnamara joined the Department of Anesthesiology in 1957. After a brief stint on the staff of the Massachusetts General Hospital in Boston, he returned to Georgetown in 1962 to head the department.

The faculty for the basic sciences, the weak link in the school, was gradually strengthened by new hires and chair appointments. Faculty with PhDs became more and more prominent in the basic science departments. In 1955, Lawrence L. Lilienfield (MD 1949, MS 1954, PhD 1956) joined the Department of Physiology and Biophysics. John Rose (MD 1950) became chair of physiology in 1958. The two of them revitalized the teaching of the department and built up a strong research program. Lilienfield published widely in his area of kidney function. In the 1960s he succeeded Rose as chair and helped establish exchange and language programs for medical schools in Saigon and Tel Aviv. In 1956, Estelle Ramey, who had a doctorate in endocrinology, joined the department from the University of Chicago. At Georgetown she became a prolific publisher in her field and gained wide recognition for her science-based advocacy of women's rights. Another new appointee to physiology was Peter Aloysius Kot in 1960, who in 1964 was awarded an Established Investigatorship by the American Heart Association to do full-time basic research on cardiovascular disease.

Above: Lawrence L. Lilienfield, **M** 1949, professor of physiology. (Georgetown University Archives)

Right: John Rose, **M** 1950, professor of physiology and dean of the Medical School, 1963–74.

The 1950s and 1960s became the "golden era" of medical research, fueled in large part by the massive injection of funding from the federal government.[149] By 1966 the federal government expended $1.4 billion on medical research (in 1947 the total had been $27 million).[150] Foundations, which had been the principal source of medical research funding before World War II, now became supporters of special medical experiments, such as the reform of medical education. In particular, grants from the NIH could be used to supplement salaries as well as fund research projects. By the mid-1960s the NIH had become "the NSF for the basic biological sciences," and most of its funding went to medical schools.[151] Indeed, the infusion of federal grants allowed medical centers to increase their faculty, particularly in the clinical sciences, a trend that benefited Georgetown as well.[152]

Initially there was considerable reluctance among administrators and faculty at Georgetown to seek federal funding out of fear that federal money would be linked with federal control or regulation. In fact, the government had adopted an implicit policy, based on its remarkably fruitful collaboration with university and medical scientists during World War II, of sponsoring and funding research in independent institutions without government control.[153] Thanks to the persistence and energetic pursuit of federal funding by Dean Frank Forster and the appointment of grant-conscious faculty, the medical center from the late 1950s into the early 1960s received a steady growth of grants. In 1958–59 grants had totaled $1.5 million. By 1961–62 grants covered 251 research projects totaling some $2.5 million. By 1963–64, the total had risen to $3.7 million in grant money.[154] As medical research merged with theoretical biology, much of the research in the basic science divisions settled in the area now called "biomedical." In clinical areas, research became increasingly specialized and often centered in the region of applied biochemistry.[155] By one barometer of research activity, Georgetown stood sixth among medical centers by the mid-1960s in the number of research abstracts submitted to *Clinical Research*, a major lister of clinical investigations.[156] In 1963 the Department of Medicine alone housed 131 research projects, and its faculty produced 137 publications and gave 80 papers or presentations at academic meetings.[157] One sign of the expanding nature of medical research at Georgetown was the addition to the Animal House Research Building in 1957, which enabled the facility to house 500 dogs for research, rather than the 200 the original building accommodated.

In 1955 the John A. Hartford Foundation awarded $105,000 to the school for the development and evaluation of a renal service as well as to fund research on abnormal metabolism.[158] It was the beginning of a long-term relationship between the Foundation and the school for renal research and related areas.

In 1961, as a result of its growing reputation for research, the school received $300,000 from the NIH to establish a clinical research study unit for general research of a broad spectrum of diseases. Georgetown became one of thirty-two medical centers in the United States that set aside a certain portion of their hospital beds for testing and treating patients with various diseases. George Schreiner was made director of the operation, which was housed in the west wing of the second floor of the hospital. The unit acted as a magnet for medical fellows seeking rotations at Georgetown.[159]

Given the fundamental changes occurring in the world of medical knowledge and practice in mid-twentieth-century America, it was natural that curriculum revision became an ongoing concern within the medical academy. Another force driving this curricular examination was the emergence of the National Board of Medical Examiners test as the norm for securing a medical license. The test actually comprised three parts extending over four years, including the examination on basic sciences at the end of the second year of medical school, the examination on the clinical areas at the end of senior year, and a comprehensive exam at the end of one's internship. Medical curriculum evolved throughout the period to keep pace with the changing medical world. In 1956 Georgetown received $2 million from the Ford Foundation, the interest of which was to be used for medical education over the next ten years; after that, the school was free to use the capital as it saw best.

Concern about the current curriculum led to the creation of a committee on medical education in 1956, which was charged to evaluate both preclinical and clinical instruction in the school and to design an ideal curriculum schedule and methodology. In 1957 the school applied to the Commonwealth Fund for a grant to revise its curriculum. It subsequently received $100,000, with the promise of an additional $200,000 if the university provided matching funds.[160] It did so. The medical education committee, under John Rose, found that too much of the education, particularly in the first and second years of training, was didactic and classroom related and was not clinical enough or patient based. At the same time, so many clinical specialties had developed within the school that it was no longer possible to do clerkships within all of them.[161] The result was an extensive restructuring of the curriculum in 1958. It represented an interdisciplinary and integrated approach to the teaching of the medical sciences. In the portion of the curriculum that dealt with the basic sciences, there was a thorough elimination of instruction that merely duplicated an area covered in another course, a serious reduction of lecture courses for sophomores, and the removal of such courses for juniors, with lectures being replaced by seminars and conferences for both sophomores and juniors in which faculty from several departments participated. The new curriculum broadened the elective system for seniors in choosing clerkships in various specialties. For seniors there was a rationalization of the internship process in the 1950s with the establishment of the national intern matching plan by the AAMC, the AMA, and the hospital associations, in which Georgetown students participated.

A lingering ghetto mentality, with its wish to provide Catholics with the opportunity for a medical education, even as conditions changed in the larger medical world, continued into the 1950s to maintain the training of Catholic doctors as the school's chief mission. As the school administration reported to a foundation it was hoping to secure funding from, Catholics, whether male or female, were given preference, but there were no quotas or restrictions for any other class of applicants. The reality was that Catholics made up the vast majority of the applicants. And the Catholics almost universally came from Catholic colleges. In the first-year class of 1955, for instance, twenty were from Georgetown, thirteen from Holy Cross, and eleven from Notre Dame. Only 21 of the 115 (18%) in the class came from colleges other than Catholic institutions. By the fall of 1962 those from Catholic colleges still made up nearly three-quarters of the first-year class. The admissions rate was an impressively low one: 20 percent in the mid-1950s; 15.5 percent by 1963–64. The school invited selected applicants to campus for interviews by the regent, a preclinical department head, and a clinical department head. Out of 290 or so interviewed, they would admit 200. The acceptance rate was normally better than 55 percent.

In 1952 enrollment was 440. About a sixth (15.2%) were local. Nearly three-quarters (72.7%) were from the Northeast. About a third (34.5%)

were veterans. Females made up 6 percent of enrollment. Twelve years later enrollment had declined to 393, down 10.6 percent. Over that period there had been declining interest nationally in medicine as a career, a trend that continued into the early 1960s. Georgetown's shrinking enrollment reflected that trend. But if the medical student body was smaller, it was more diverse. Catholics now made up slightly more than three-quarters of the enrollment. Jews were a rapidly growing presence at 15.7 percent of the student body. Only three medical students had been in the armed services. There were now also fewer females, 18 (4.5%), probably a reflection of the adverse reaction that women professionals had experienced in the postwar period.

A number of graduates made careers in medical education, a trend that had become very prominent for medical school graduates throughout the country in the 1950s and early 1960s. "The best students chose these careers," John Rose thought. "We began to encourage first-year medical students to spend their first summer doing bio-medical research." That evidently set a course for many of them that carried them into the medical academy as teachers and researchers.[162] Andrew P. Ferry (1954) became professor of ophthalmology at the Mount Sinai Medical School of the City University of New York before becoming chair of the ophthalmology department at the Medical College of Virginia. William P. Nelson (1956) became a professor of medicine, in the division of cardiovascular diseases, at the University of Kansas. Paul R. Torrens (1958) became a professor at the School of Public Health of the University of California at Los Angeles. Paul Corcoran (**C** 1955, **M** 1959) chaired departments of physical medicine at Tufts and Harvard, respectively. Thomas Andreoli (1960) became the chair of the Department of Internal Medicine at the University of Arkansas for Medical Sciences where his research in the field of kidney and urological diseases won wide recognition. Murray Joseph Casey (1962) became a professor of obstetrics and gynecology at the University of Wisconsin Medical School. Albert F. LoBuglio (1962) became a professor of oncology at the University of Alabama and director of its Comprehensive Cancer Center. Carla Elizabeth Goepp (1964) joined the faculty at the Jefferson Medical College in Philadelphia. Two graduates became medical missionaries: Sister Patricia M. Fitzmaurice (1958), who practiced surgery in Hong Kong, and Sister Fernande Pelletier (1959), who for many years practiced field medicine in Ghana.

Hospital

The 1950s saw the emergence of the hospital as the center of clinical teaching and as a valuable research component for the medical center. Hospital administration, particularly that of a teaching hospital, had become an enormously complex business. Dealing with the plethora of insurance payers, regulatory matters, huge staff, and related financial dealings all required a professional administrator. Tellingly, in 1957, the Organization of University

Health Administrators had been established in recognition of the changing nature of hospital administration. At Georgetown the professionalization of hospital administration came in 1961, when Bunn and Maloney became convinced that the current nun administrator was not up to the task. The two drew up a job description entailing the professional qualifications that an administrator should have. Bunn went to visit the mother superior of the order in Kentucky and explained to her that her own nuns at Georgetown wanted the administrator replaced. When he showed her the job description for the position, she replied that she had no nuns with such credentials and offered to withdraw all of her sisters.[163] In July 1961 the Sisters of Charity of Nazareth, who had had charge of the hospital since it opened in 1947, left Georgetown. The Sisters of Saint Joseph took their place in staffing and administering certain operations of the hospital.

With the loss of the sister administrator of the hospital due to the departure of the Sisters of Charity, President Bunn saw the opportunity to reorganize and professionalize its administration. Given the large, complex operation that the Georgetown Hospital had become by the 1960s, Bunn thought that the top administrator should be a physician with considerable experience in the management of medical facilities. He appointed Charles Shields of the Department of Physical Medicine and Rehabilitation, who in his army service during World War II had been chief of hospitals and medical care in the North African and Italian theaters. The medical director became the CEO of the hospital, the responsibilities of which had previously had been held by the medical dean.

In postwar America, public usage of hospitals increased dramatically as prosperity and the establishment of private medical insurance in many industries and businesses enabled millions of Americans to utilize to an unprecedented degree medical care in general and hospitals in particular. Private patients came to greatly outnumber indigent ones, and private and semiprivate rooms replaced the wards that traditionally had dominated hospital care sites.[164] Attending physicians for the private patients posed a threat to residents in the control of medical care and the opportunity for education. In the late 1950s at Georgetown, the head of medicine, Laurence Kyle, worked out a modus operandi between admitting doctors and residents that assured house officers sufficient responsibility for the care of private patients.[165] Georgetown shared in the rapidly growing market of patients and soon found its 1947 hospital too outmoded and inadequate to meet the demands upon it. In 1955 the university received a grant of $1,147,000 from the U.S. government under PL 221 (the Hill-Burton Act) to expand and remodel the hospital. Together with a grant of nearly $200,000 from the Ford Foundation, these funds provided about half of what was needed to expand to add outpatient facilities and increase the bed capacity from 367 to 432. The new wing was planned also to provide teaching space, faculty offices, and research laboratories.[166]

Internships and Affiliations

The explosion and fragmentation of knowledge in medicine, as in other disciplines, led to an accelerating trend toward specialization in the postwar world. More and more medical students, after completing their internships, sought residencies, or additional periods of training, at teaching hospitals where they could pursue specialties.[167] The number of residents at Georgetown, as elsewhere, grew immensely in the 1950s and 1960s as the rising interest in residencies among medical graduates was matched by a growing demand for clinical services that had been created by the modern medical culture of more numerous, more transient, and sicker patients, coupled with exploding technology. As a result, residents began to outnumber interns. By 1960 there were ten interns and eighteen residents at Georgetown Hospital. Graduate medical education became a major academic program at Georgetown.[168] To accommodate the numbers seeking residencies, teaching hospitals began to establish affiliations with veterans' or community hospitals for their graduate medical students.

Georgetown established affiliations with a variety of government and community hospitals, including a number of distant ones. From his experience in Boston, Harold Jeghers knew the value of affiliations with community hospitals for educating one's teaching medical staff and providing patients for the teaching of medical care. In 1948 he negotiated an agreement with Arlington Hospital in Virginia to provide a site for student clerkships as well as residents. A similar affiliation was worked out with Prince George's General Hospital in Maryland the following year.[169] His vision of utilizing community hospitals as important places for medical education and research enabled him to include hospitals that were remote from medical centers. In the early 1950s, Jeghers started an experimental program of affiliation with four community hospitals in Massachusetts and New York. At each of these, a full-time director of medical education was established who would supervise interns and residents. The Georgetown faculty would visit these hospitals on a regular rotating basis and spend a day or two conducting ward rounds and giving conferences to the attending physicians and house staff. Students would be sent to the affiliates for clerkships.[170] By 1964 Georgetown had affiliations with St. Vincent Hospital, in Worcester, Massachusetts; Mercy Hospital in Buffalo, New York; Kenmore Mercy Hospital, in New York City; and St. Mary's Hospital, in Rochester, New York.[171]

When Jeghers returned to the Medical Center for a visit at the end of 1961, he was struck by how much it had improved since he had left five years earlier. That impression resonated with what he had been picking up among his broad contacts within medical academia, "that Georgetown is now [regarded] as one of the progressive, vigorous, forward-looking medical schools. . . . The secret and vitalizing element responsible for all this," he felt, no doubt with some pride, "is . . . the many talented faculty members of Georgetown. . . .

That this 'rubs off' on the students" was quite evident by the many "very top internship positions" Georgetown graduates were securing. Another key indicator of the school's coming-of-age was the number of graduates, such as John Rose and Lawrence Lilienfield, who were becoming research scientists of national stature. The school had achieved a national reputation in several areas: aortic valve surgery, the use of the artificial kidney, clinical cardiology teaching techniques, and research in antihypertensive drugs. In general, he found, "you have achieved an unusually favorable balance for research, clinical patient care, and teaching."[172] But such success could not breed complacency. "Now is the time to really push," he concluded, "so these accomplishments will be the foundation for a tremendous future growth. One senses that this is now a realizable possibility."[173]

In 1958 a team representing the Council on Medical Education and Hospitals of the AMA as well as the AAMC visited the medical center. They found a serious deficiency in the administrative structure of the school and hospital. The dean, whom they considered should be the top executive of the center, was in fact not so. A large part of the problem was the ambiguous relationship between the dean and the regent. "[The] regent," they found, "is at the same time in a position above and below that of the Dean." The dean, they insisted, should be responsible for admissions, research, conduct of the clinical departments, and finances, as well as the administration of the hospital, which fundamentally existed to provide a clinical laboratory for the Medical School. But, in fact, the dean operated as the head of the faculty without control over admissions (the regent was still the major gatekeeper in practice), the academic operations of the hospital, or the clinical budget for the center. There were other complaints beyond the administrative structure, including an overly didactic curriculum, a "grossly inadequate library," and insufficient faculty supervision of student internships. Its criticism extended to all departments except the Department of Medicine. The survey group felt it had no choice but to recommend that Georgetown be placed on confidential probation until the leadership structure and the other problem areas were addressed.[174]

Dean Forster, who had never, as he admitted, liked "deaning," used the occasion to resign and return to the Neurology Department. Hugh Hussey, who had succeeded Jeghers as head of medicine, was named dean. Hussey had a national presence as chairman of the Council on Clinical Cardiology of the American Heart Association, as chairman of the board of the AMA, and later as editor of the *Journal of the American Medical Association.*

Less than two years later the council sent another survey team to evaluate the center. Despite finding persistent deficiencies in several departments, the team recommended that the school's accreditation be restored. The quality of at least some of the basic science departments had certainly improved in the interim. Another factor that might well have played into the council's decision was the pending change in the administrative structure that had drawn such criticism in 1958. In November 1960, President Bunn created the position of vice president for medical center affairs, which eliminated the regent's position and subordinated the dean of the Medical School to the vice president. This position had evolved in the administration of medical education for many universities, and the move was a reflection of that. For the first time, ultimate authority for the center resided in one person. The move was a reflection of the growing importance of the medical center and the complexity of the university. Bunn in effect was saying that he could no longer function as the formal CEO of the medical center, with the deans and hospital administrator reporting to him, but that someone in the medical center itself had to do so.

In November 1960 he named William Maloney, SJ, who a year before had been appointed regent of the Dental and Nursing Schools.[175] Maloney held the position until 1962 when he became president of St. Joseph's College in Philadelphia. Joseph F. Cohalan, SJ, then treasurer of the university, succeeded him briefly until his sudden death in May 1963. Mark H. Bauer, SJ, a member of the biology department, was named the new vice president for medical center affairs shortly afterward.

Georgetown officials were all too conscious of their shortfalls in facilities that would enable them to become a first-rate medical center: a library (their holdings of slightly more than 32,000 volumes was far below the 55,000 minimum for an academic medical library), teaching auditorium, and modern clinical facilities, including a critical care unit. The need for additional facilities was an urgent one, not only because of the growth in the undergraduate and graduate programs and the increased research by faculty, but also because the very ability to retain and attract faculty members increasingly depended on the availability of space and the quality of facilities.[176] The additional facilities were badly needed to sustain the reputation that the center had been acquiring over the past decade.

The Dental School

Through the 1950s and into the 1960s the school benefited from the strong leadership of its dean, Clemens Rault. The Middle States evaluating team in 1961 found him to be "an exceptionally competent and thorough administrator" who had sound control of the school's programs and the high respect of his faculty.[177] In 1963 the American Association of Dental Schools recognized his leadership by electing him president at their annual meeting.

The Middle States committee found many features of the school's academic programs to be "outstanding": its experimental teaching in the basic sciences, its oral surgery program at both the graduate and undergraduate levels, and the teacher-training program for graduate students. The enthusiasm of the faculty for the overall academic program and their commitment to it impressed the team. Among the faculty were Harry B. Sheldon, chair of the Department of Operative Dentistry; E. Reed Smith (1947), who returned from service in the Korean War to head the Department of Periodontics; Everett N. Cobb (1958), who joined the Department of Operative Dentistry after graduation; Mary Christine De Risi, who became the first woman member of the faculty in 1952 as professor of prosthodontics; and Gustave O. Kruger, George E. Morin, and Ernest Bouchard. In 1956 the latter three became the first dental faculty allowed to participate in the Intramural Private Dental Service at the school whereby full-time faculty members were able to supplement their teaching salary by treating private patients on-site, with half their fees going to the school. The introduction of the dental service was both a strategy for retaining as well as recruiting full-time faculty, and also a means of increasing the revenue of the school. The number of full-time faculty participating in the service gradually increased; by 1959 the service occupied a wing of the Gorman Building.[178]

Clemens V. Rault, dean of the Dental School, 1950–66. (Georgetown University Archives)

By the middle 1950s the faculty were involved in research to an unprecedented degree. In 1957 the school's full-time faculty were engaged in forty research projects. Collectively they had produced forty-six articles in professional journals. By 1962, by the gauge of scholarly output, the school's faculty ranked eighth among their counterparts in forty-eight schools of dentistry in the country. It enjoyed the same ranking in grants received, receiving $357,123 in 1961–62 alone.[179]

Enrollment began a slow decline in the early 1950s that continued into the early 1960s. In 1952 enrollment in the school was 368. Like the Medical School's, it was heavily Catholic (83.6%). Regionally, 16 percent were local; 70 percent were from the Northeast. There were no females. But 43 percent were veterans, and nearly one-third were married. Two-thirds had a bachelor's degree. (Georgetown was hardly unique among dental schools in the 1950s in not making possession of the baccalaureate a prerequisite; indeed, the proportion of its students who had degrees was well above the national average. Only 43% of dental students across the nation had bachelor's degrees.) After bottoming out at 317 in 1961, enrollment recovered by 1964 to reach its 1952 mark. Catholics now comprised 63 percent of dental students. There were a handful of female students. Locals now made up one-fifth of the school, but the Northeast was still the dominant region of origin at 62 percent. Married students still made up about one-third of those enrolled, but there were now only thirteen veterans.

Everett N. Cobb, **D** 1958, Dental School faculty.

(*Apollonian* 1958)

Like the Medical School, the Dental School saw its mission primarily colored by religion: the training of Catholic dentists. Its stated admissions policy was, first, the selection of the best qualified applicants from Jesuit colleges; second, from non-Jesuit Catholic colleges; and third, from other colleges and universities. As late as 1962 the school continued to accept applicants who lacked the baccalaureate. By now a minimum of two years of college was required, including thirty-two credit hours in the sciences. Approximately half the applicants were accepted in 1952. In the fall of 1953 the first female entered the school. There was a very high attrition rate of more than 20 percent per year, about ten times the national average, mostly due to scholastic deficiencies.[180] By 1955 the dean was complaining about the difficulty of securing qualified applicants. The number of applicants declined in the mid-1950s as the national pool shrank.[181] In 1957, despite planning for an incoming class of 100, only 81 of the 389 applicants were accepted and enrolled. The dean made a plea for alumni to recruit qualified applicants, particularly females (who were considered an untapped market—only 1 percent of dentists in the country were female).[182] In 1959 letters publicizing the school were sent to student counselors in all Catholic high schools, colleges, and universities.[183]

President Bunn acknowledged to an official of the ADA that the quality of dental students did not match that of students in Georgetown's other schools, either undergraduate or professional, a phenomenon that he regarded as one not peculiar to Georgetown. "As a rule," he wrote, "the better students do not tend to the Dental Profession." Dean Rault cited the competition of natural sciences, the high cost of dental education, and the difficulty in establishing a financially remunerative practice as the main factors that worked against gravitating young men and women to a career in dentistry.[184] Although Georgetown's tuition at $700 was lower than most private dental schools in the country, school officials were reluctant to increase it, even though the school was encountering a deficit (by 1961 more than $100,000), for fear that it would discourage applicants and cause those already enrolled to drop out.[185] By 1960 faculty members were complaining about the Catch-22 situation in which it found itself: having difficulty recruiting a sufficient number of qualified applicants, subsequently gaining a poor reputation for being forced to dismiss too many failing students, which then made their ability to recruit all the harder.[186]

The growth of the national pool and stepped-up recruiting efforts produced a favorable change in the quality and quantity of applicants to the school by the early 1960s. For the entering class of 1963, there were 756 applicants, of whom 104 were enrolled. The next year there were even more applicants, and for the first time the school stopped accepting applications after April. Despite the focus on attracting female applicants, the percentage of females remained minimal through the mid-1960s, far below the 7 percent of the national female dental student enrollment. Nonetheless, Dean Rault felt confident overall that they had survived a difficult period in student admissions and that prospects for the future were bright.[187]

In 1954 the school was the twelfth largest dental school in the nation. It had outgrown its facilities, which themselves were outmoded, having been basically unaltered since they had opened a quarter century earlier. "The increased number of students," Dean Rault commented in 1957, "together with the greatly expanded research programs [in both the medical and dental schools] require that more space be provided."[188] After their visit in the fall of 1960, the Middle States team cited the school's facilities as its most glaring weakness. The clinics, lecture rooms, laboratories, and library all needed updating and expansion. The library's holdings of something more than 35,000 volumes was judged inadequate for the size of the school and the scope of its programs. The team's report indicated that the state of the facilities would have presented a problem for the school in maintaining its accreditation had Rault not assured them that a "complete rehabilitation" of the facilities, including the laboratories, was scheduled for the immediate future. A committee had for more than three years been making detailed plans for an addition to the Medical-Dental Building that would provide the urgently needed facilities. Supportive congressmen had introduced a bill in Congress to secure the funding for the addition. But two years later, in 1962, when the Council on Dental Education visited the school, the renovations had still not occurred. Despite criticism of the inadequacy of the facilities, which echoed the earlier evaluation team, the council reaccredited the school anyway.[189]

Third- and fourth-year students continued to treat patients in the dental clinic. By 1962 they were seeing approximately six thousand patients a year, a number smaller than the clinic could accommodate, but the maximum given the number of dental students available.[190] Students also continued to publish the Georgetown University *Dental Journal* twice a year.

Among the class of 1958 was the first woman to graduate from the school, Sister Martha Mary Mehrl. A member of the Medical Mission Sisters, the Dubuque, Iowa, native, after graduating from Georgetown, was sent to Pakistan to set up a clinic in Rawalpindi; she later worked in Uganda as the lone dentist among a population of more than one million.[191] Other graduates from the 1950s included Joseph M. Kelly (AB 1951, DDS 1953), who became an oral surgeon in Worcester, Massachusetts, and president of the Massachusetts Dental Society; Joseph R. Salcetti (1953), who became chair of the Council on Federal Dental Service as well as a member of the faculty at Georgetown; and Col. Alfred A. Villacara Jr. (1959), who made a career in the dental corps of the U.S. Army.

Graduate education in oral surgery, dental materials, oral pathology, and physiology showed a strong growth by the early 1960s, thanks in large part to affiliations with the Naval Dental School and the Army Dental Corps that allowed their members to earn master's degrees at Georgetown. A few graduate students pursued doctorates under the Georgetown faculty. By 1963 total enrollment in graduate programs reached seventy-nine, with more than half being naval or army officers.

In 1960 the school received a $100,000 grant from the National Institute of Dental Research to fund a teaching-research program for graduate students. Dr. Baldev Raj Bhussry, who had been appointed director of graduate studies in 1957, was named director of the program. The grant provided stipends for students who were planning a career in dental teaching or research. Students spent from three to five years in the program, dividing their time between teaching, taking courses, and research.[192]

During the 1950s the increase in the number of dentists nationwide did not keep pace with the increase in general population. At the same time, the growing national prosperity and concern about dental health resulted in twice as many people seeking dental care than had sought it a decade earlier. This situation prompted many dentists in the District of Columbia metropolitan area to seek trained dental assistants to enable them to treat more patients. At the request of many local dentists (51% of whom were alumni of Georgetown Dental School), school authorities began to consider establishing a course for oral hygienists in 1950. As noted earlier, the school had had such a program during the 1930s. When nothing resulted from this latest consideration, the District of Columbia Dental Society passed a resolution in 1958 that urged the school to reestablish the dental hygiene program. In the fall of 1960, the school, in conjunction with Marymount College in Arlington, Virginia, and Montgomery Junior College in Maryland, began to offer a two-year course for dental assistants that led to an associate of arts degree. Nine women were enrolled in the original class and worked each afternoon with senior dental students in caring for patients.[193]

The Making of a University

The Middle States Association visited Georgetown in late October 1960 for its decennial evaluation. Its major finding was that, thanks to Bunn's leadership, "Georgetown has really made itself a university, not just an overgrown college or collection of colleges." It applauded the moves the university had taken to create "a democratic educational community" within its necessarily hierarchical framework, but noted that there was still a distance to go before the results were "altogether satisfactory." "Georgetown," it concluded, "has brought into being a harmonious, well articulated educational society." But it thought that the faculty across the campuses needed to be given "a still greater role in shaping the University's future." In general, the university was still falling short in utilizing the valuable resources that lay faculty and administrators represented at Georgetown.

CHAPTER 10

Toward the Fulfillment of a Vision

As an educator he has brought Georgetown from the past and focused her on the future, giving her a spirit and direction. . . . This Anniversary Year has been . . . a monument to Father Bunn as well as to Georgetown.

HOYA, December 11, 1964

College of Arts and Sciences:
More than a Channel to Medicine and Law

In 1952 Georgetown College was a regional Catholic school, with 80 percent of its students coming from the Northeast, especially the Middle Atlantic states, including the District of Columbia. Ninety-five percent of them were Catholic. Graduates of Gonzaga College High School in the District continued to receive half scholarships to Georgetown. In 1953, 112 of the 166 academic scholarships in the college were held by Gonzaga graduates. One in 12 students in the college was the son of an alumnus. There were few foreign students, between 1 and 2 percent of enrollment, and these were mostly from Central America, the Caribbean, but especially from Puerto Rico. The proportion of veterans had shrunk to 3 percent of the college's population. The college, one alumnus of the period observed, "was very heavily identified with immigrant families, largely Irish and Italian. Middle and upper-middle class. Very often the first generation to go to higher education."[1] Unsurprisingly, relatively few worked while in school—about 14 percent. Admissions standards were average—about two-thirds of applicants were admitted. (In 1963, for instance, Harvard and Princeton were exceptional in having admission rates of 30% and 33%, respectively. More typical was Amherst, which had an admission rate of 60%.)

But if admission was relatively easy, persevering until graduation was not. In 1958 the attrition rate for college students between admission and graduation was approximately 30 percent. Five years later, 35 percent of the freshman class failed to survive the first year at Georgetown, half of whom left the college because of academic failure.[2] Between 1952 and 1964, enrollment increased by nearly a quarter, but student demographics changed little. The middle- to upper-middle-class, northeastern Catholic population persisted. The most perceptible changes were in the decline of the proportion of students from the metropolitan Washington area, from 27 to 13 percent (probably attributed in large part by the ending of the Gonzaga scholarships), and in the emergence of other regions as significant sources of students (the Midwest 15%, the South 12%, and the West 6%). Those from the Middle Atlantic and New England states had become an even more dominant portion of college students, representing 58 percent of enrollment. Veterans had virtually disappeared; there were only three in the entire college in 1964.

A majority of students in the college were preparing for careers in law and medicine. Majors reflected this pattern. Biology majors, overwhelmingly

College students on a social outing with friends circa 1963. (*Ye Domesday Booke,* 1963)

premeds, accounted for 28 percent of majors; English, history, and government majors—heavily populated with those seeking to go on to law school—comprised 27 percent.[3] The Jesuit provincial prefect of studies warned in 1957 that the college urgently needed to take steps to change the outside perception that it was "merely a channel into the medical and legal professions."[4] As late as 1963, 60 percent of college students were planning to study law, medicine, or dentistry after their undergraduate years.[5] Relatively few were in the traditional bachelor of arts program, which still included Latin as a prerequisite. In 1963, only 158 of 1,336 (11.8%) college students were in the AB program. Four hundred and eighty three, mostly in biology, were working toward a bachelor of science degree. A slight majority (50.1%) were in the bachelor of science in social science program, which included majors in history, government, and economics.

In 1955, Joseph Sellinger, SJ, became associate dean in 1955 when Brian McGrath was named academic vice president while retaining the title of dean. Two years later Sellinger was given the title as well as the responsibilities, which he had assumed in 1955. Once he officially became dean, Sellinger moved to implement an honors program for the top twenty nonscience sophomores who had had an outstanding academic record in their first year. "I felt we were not challenging the best students," Sellinger later observed. "Plus . . . we were getting all the rejects from the Ivies. . . . Students would tell me, well I don't want to be here anyway. So I thought we needed to do something to change that."[6] The honors program was the result. A corps of faculty, including William Lynch, SJ, Louis Dupré, Joseph Durkin, SJ, Jesse Mann, Raymond Reno, and Hisham Sharabi, directed the three-year pro-

Joseph Sellinger, SJ, dean of the College of Arts and Sciences, 1957–64. (Georgetown University Archives. Photo by Bob Young.)

gram. It was the catalyst for the founding of the scholarly journal *Viewpoint*, which had issues, spanning the lifetime of the honors program (1961–65), that were heavily made up of essays and papers that had originated in the courses of the program.

The graduates of the program, in large part, formed a cohort that breached the top professional and graduate schools. Thus Cornelius Moynihan (1961), the founding editor of *Viewpoint*, went on to Harvard Law School; John Brian Oak (1962) became one of the first Georgetown graduates to enter Yale Medical School. David Harnett (PhD 1962, Harvard) held important administrative positions at several universities; Paul Mattingly (PhD 1962, Wisconsin) became a professor of history at NYU and for many years edited the *History of Education Quarterly*; James Scanlon (PhD 1962, Virginia) became a professor of history at Randolph-Macon College; Philip Quinn (1962) became a professor of philosophy at Brown and then Notre Dame; Nicholas Kilmer (MA

1962, Harvard) became an artist and author; James Wiseman, OSB (1963), held a chair in theology at the Catholic University of America.

Throughout Georgetown's history, the classical languages had been considered integral to a liberal arts education and a synthesizing force within the curriculum. It had been a prerequisite for the bachelor of arts degree. In the early twentieth century, however, philosophy had in practice become the center of the curriculum, as the credit hours devoted to the various branches of philosophy indicated (twenty-five, as opposed to sixteen for Latin). Even after authorities dropped Greek early in the twentieth century as a requirement for the bachelor of arts, more and more students arrived at Georgetown with no background in classical languages, either Greek or Latin, and thus opted to take the non-Latin academic program that led to the bachelor of science in social sciences. As early as 1941 the college awarded more BSSS degrees than ABs. By the late 1950s, as noted, only a very small percentage of students in the college were earning the bachelor of arts degree (41 awarded in 1958, compared to 167 BSSS degrees), resulting in the anomaly that the College of Arts and Sciences, which considered itself the heart of liberal education at Georgetown, was awarding the signature degree of a liberal arts education to only one in ten of its students.

Recognizing this discrepancy, Sellinger secured permission from Rome (such a change had to be authorized by the superior general of the Jesuits) to grant the AB degree without Latin under certain conditions.[7] The dean interpreted that permission as broadly as possible so that the alternate degree, the BSSS, was for all intents and purposes eliminated by 1962, and the AB became the standard degree for nonscience majors in the college. Latin courses quickly became a virtual preserve of classics majors and those considering that field as a concentration.

In 1958 the curriculum committee of the college executive council recommended that the curriculum for the first two years needed serious revision. What needed to be implemented into the education of the Georgetown college freshman and sophomore, they urged, was a curriculum that would truly provide a broad education that supplied to all students "a unified body of knowledge and a common acquaintance with our culture" as a preparation for the specialized, indeed preprofessional curriculum of the last two years of college. The school acted on the committee's recommendation, and subsequently each student in the college was required to choose from a set of courses in the humanities, the social sciences, math and the natural sciences, and modern language, respectively, during the freshman and sophomore year. In addition, the student would take theology each semester from first year through senior year, and philosophy each semester from sophomore year on. Besides philosophy and theology, each student in junior and senior years would take three electives per semester, mostly in the student's major. In 1962 the college introduced the requirement of oral comprehensives in their respective major fields for all students.

By and large, graduates of the college during this period unsurprisingly pursued the careers that had shaped their choice of majors at Georgetown. Among the class of 1960, 50 of the 235 graduates entered law school, and 42 others began medical or dental school. Twenty-seven graduates went on to graduate school. Four entered the seminary. Thirty-five began duty in the air force or army.

Outstanding graduates who made law their career included Peter Ortiz (1956), who became a justice of the Supreme Court in Puerto Rico; Richard Coleman (1957, **L** 1961), who became a prominent lawyer in California and the president of the Los Angeles Bar Association; James R. Zazzali (1958, **L** 1962), who became attorney general for the state of New Jersey and later an associate justice on the state's supreme court; Neil F. Hartigan (1959), who in the 1980s became attorney general and later lieutenant governor of Illinois; Edward E. Sherman (1959), who became a professor of law at Indiana University and the University of Texas as well as an author of books on civil procedure; Thomas F. Hogan (1960, **L** 1966), who was named by President Ronald Reagan to be United States district judge in the District of Columbia; Robert S. Bennett (1961, **L** 1964), who became a prominent lawyer in the District, among whose famous clients were Clark Clifford and William Jefferson Clinton; and Thomas Hale Boggs Jr. (1961), who became a highly successful lawyer-lobbyist in Washington from the 1970s on. Antonin Scalia (1957) made a career as a legal counsel in the federal government before President Reagan appointed him to the United States Supreme Court, the second Georgetown alumnus to serve on the court.

Among those who went into the medical profession were Peter Cyrus Rizzo III (1953), who became a noted orthopedic surgeon and member of the Medical Review Board in New York City. Carlos Garcia (1954, **M** 1958), Donald F. Leon (1954, **M** 1957), and William Ayers (1957, **M** 1961) all made careers in academic medicine, Garcia as head of the cardiovascular department at the Paitilla Medical Center in Panama, Leon as dean of the University of Pittsburgh School of Medicine, and Ayers as associate dean of Georgetown's Medical School and as professor of pediatrics. Richard M. Sarles (1957) became a professor of psychiatry and pediatrics at the University of Maryland School of Medicine; Michael Dunn (1958, **M** 1962) chaired the Department of Ophthalmology at the New York Eye and Ear Infirmary in New York City; Frederick K. Goodwin (1958) became a director of research at the National Institute of Mental Health in Bethesda; Adolph Hutter (1959) became a professor at the Harvard Medical School; Arthur Hull Hayes Jr. (1961) headed the division of clinical pharmacology at the Hershey Medical Center of Pennsylvania State University; Vincent Dennis (1962, **M** 1966) became professor of medicine and chief of the division of nephrology at Duke University; Brian Conway (1964, **M** 1968) taught retinal surgery at the Johns Hopkins University and later chaired the Department of Ophthalmology at the University of Virginia School of Medicine;

and James H. Schully (1965) held a chair in neuropsychiatry at the University of South Carolina School of Medicine.

Despite the absence of a business major, a significant portion of graduates had success as business executives. Bill Bidwell (1953) inherited from his father the National Football League's franchise in St. Louis and then moved the franchise to Phoenix. Barry Sullivan (1953) made a career in banking, becoming CEO of the First Chicago Corporation, one of the nation's largest bank holding companies; Thomas J. Stanton Jr. (1954) also became a CEO of a major bank, First Jersey National Bank in the 1980s; Robert Kaiser (1956) became a top official of the Export-Import Bank of the United States, while serving as an adjunct professor of international business diplomacy at Georgetown; John W. Sullivan (1956) became a leading developer in Philadelphia as president of the Reading Company; Peter V. Hall (1957) became a major executive for the Bank of America; Laurence McGivney (1959) became a top stockbroker in the investment firm of Alex Brown & Sons in New York; Peter Tanous (1960) had a successful career in investment banking while writing novels about the financial world; William Moore (1961) received the *Dallas/Fort Worth Journal*'s Executive of the Year Award in 1985 for his success in reviving the fortunes of a high-technology corporation; Charles H. Ross Jr. (1961) became the president of Merrill-Lynch & Company; Charles Rossotti (1962) became a leader in the computer technology and consulting industry; Paul Tagliabue (1962) became a lawyer and, in 1989, commissioner of the National Football League, where his astute leadership in securing lucrative television contracts and effective cooperation between union and management brought the league unprecedented prosperity and popularity; Daniel Altobello (1963), after holding several top administrative positions at Georgetown, became the president of the Marriott Corporation's airport operations division.

With the draft in effect during the 1950s and 1960s, a small proportion of graduates extended their service beyond the required two years to make a career in the military. P. Roland Politano (1953) became a Green Beret in the U.S. Army (and, after retirement, a prize-winning author in the 1990s); Richard A. Stratton (1955) became a navy pilot who was shot down over North Vietnam and spent six and a half years in prison camps there; Michael C. Kerby (1958) became a wing commander in the United States Air Force; John A. Leide (1958) became a major officer for military intelligence for the U.S. Army; George E. Deliduka (1959), as a major in the U.S. Air Force, won multiple Distinguished Flying Crosses for his service in Vietnam; and Francis J. West Jr. (1961) also served in Vietnam as a naval intelligence officer and later was director of strategic research at the Naval War College.

Each year several graduates entered the seminary to study for the priesthood. Among them were Louis Gigante (**C** 1954), the captain of the basketball team in 1953–54 who became a priest in the Archdiocese of New York. Charles Gonzalez and Leo O'Donovan, both of the class of 1956, entered the

Jesuits and eventually became, respectively, rector and president of the university; David Toolan (1957) entered the Jesuits and became a literary editor for both *America* and *Commonweal;* Gaspar Lobiondo (1958) entered the Jesuits in 1956, served as a missionary in Chile and then headed the Woodstock Theological Center at Georgetown; Thomas Gleason (1958) became president of the Jesuit School of Theology at Berkeley; Brian McDermott (x 1958) also became a Jesuit and taught at Weston Theological Seminary and Georgetown; and Thomas Stahel (1959), among other positions, served as provincial superior of the New Orleans Province of the Society of Jesus.

If emulation is the sincerest form of flattery, then the significant minority of graduates who made careers in the academy was a testament to the pedagogical effectiveness of the college faculty. Besides the alumni of the honors program already noted, other career academics included Bernard J. Lammers (1954), professor of public law and government at St. Lawrence University for nearly forty years; Richard Shelly Hartigan (1958), a professor of political science and classics at Loyola University of Chicago and the author of several books on politics, war, and the law; John Gerin (1959), professor of microbiology at the Georgetown University School of Medicine; Solomon Snyder (1959, **M** 1962), professor of neuroscience at the Johns Hopkins University; Philip L. Quinn (1962), professor of philosophy at the University of Notre Dame; Merritt Roe Smith (1963), professor of the history of technology at the Massachusetts Institute of Technology who won a Guggenheim Fellowship in 1983; John Brough (1963), professor of philosophy at his alma mater; Thomas Scheye (1963), academic vice president at Loyola College in Maryland; and John Glavin (1964) and John Pfordresher (1965), both of whom returned to Georgetown to join the Department of English.

John Guare (1960) became a noted playwright and screenplay writer. Michael J. Leahy (1961) became an editor at the *New York Times.* Paul Janensch (1960) became editor of the *Louisville Courier Journal.* Patrick J. Buchanan (1961) became a political writer and commentator as well as a presidential candidate of the Reform Party in 2000.

The School of Foreign Service: In Search of an Identity

From the time of Father Walsh's stroke in November 1952 to his death nearly four years later, the administration of the School of Foreign Service was in a caretaker mode. Walsh, as regent, had been the actual chief executive officer of the school. With his incapacitation, no one was really in charge. Authority was split among the executive assistant to the regent (Frank Fadner, SJ), the dean (John Parr), the chairs of the departments of economics, government, and history (all still distinct from their counterparts in the College of Arts and Sciences and the Graduate School), and the school secretary, Jit Trainor, who perhaps was the most influential in setting policy.

Even before Walsh's death in October 1956, the school was in a crisis of identity. Brian McGrath, SJ, then dean of the college, pointed out to President Bunn in 1953 that the school was concentrating on short-term special programs at the expense of the undergraduate program, which should be central to the school's mission. There was no cohesion in the curriculum because each of the three departments set out its own requirements with no attempt to coordinate them as a whole. The school, he concluded, needed a dean who would set and implement policy and programs.[8] In the spring of that year Bunn had created a committee to make a study of the organization and operations of the school. John Waldron, a faculty member of the English department of the school since 1921, chaired the committee. In December 1953 he reported to the president for the committee that many of the problems of the school derived from its origin as a unique school.[9] It had consequently developed sui generis under Walsh's direction. Unfortunately, Walsh himself was absent for long stretches of time, including the period immediately following the end of World War II when the school grew enormously and forced the staff to cope with the increasingly complex operation that the school became by the early 1950s. As a result, nonacademic persons assumed responsibility for setting the academic course of the school, which had produced the admission of too many unqualified students and the institution of programs that conflicted with the major business of the school—the education of undergraduates. The main recommendation of the report was that the undergraduate curriculum be lengthened to five years, including internships, to fulfill the original intention of Constantine McGuire and Walsh of establishing a school of "higher studies in languages and foreign relations" for persons who already had experience in government or private business.[10]

Subsequent attempts to reorganize the school led to separating the Division of Business Administration (1957) and the Institute of Languages and Linguistics (1959) into separate schools. Neither of these reorganizations addressed the identity problem that continued to plague the School of Foreign Service. The integration of the previously separate departments of economics, government, and history with those of the Graduate School and college aggravated the problem by denying the school its own faculty. In 1960 Bunn appointed another committee, three faculty members closely associated with the school, to study its needs. This committee subsequently reported that the two paramount needs of the school were a clear identity or understanding of its mission as well as a dean who could "give it leadership, inspiration, tone and professional direction." This leader would need to firmly implement the school's mission and enhance the school's reputation through effective representation of it in educational and governmental circles and by strengthening its resources through successful fund-raising. They suggested some suitable potential candidates for the position, including George Kennan, Hans Morgenthau, Paul Nitze, and Henry Kissinger.[11]

The following year the Middle States Association's evaluation of the school provided a coda to the internal criticism of the past decade. "The most troublesome question," the team concluded, "is whether this unit is really a school at all; or whether it is a kind of social science major that in most cases spans three departments." Despite its national and international reputation, the School of Foreign Service seemed to be failing in its mission of providing the education needed for those in modern foreign service. "The visitors sense a drifting about," they added. If the school was to regain its former prestige, it needed a dean who would give it direction by clarifying its purpose, developing its curriculum, establishing a rigorous admissions policy, and promoting its public relations.[12]

A consequence of the Middle States report was the naming in 1962 of a new regent, Joseph Sebes, SJ, and a new dean, William Moran, a former federal lawyer whose government experience was in foreign aid, with the apparent understanding that the latter would be the chief administrative officer in the school. Moran began yet another review of the curriculum and aims of the school. This exercise resulted in the initiation of a BSFS/MSFS five-year program, as an apparent attempt to boost the numbers of those working toward the recently established MSFS degree. The school eliminated two majors (foreign trade and international transportation) because they were considered too vocational, and a new major in international economic affairs was put in their place.[13] The administration introduced new courses related to international affairs since World War II.[14] It tightened admission standards, which decreased the size of the incoming class. At the same time, it admitted far more transfer students than it had previously so that the size of the school continued to grow. But tensions remained, as well as differences about the objectives of the school, between the dean and regent, on the one hand, and the executive faculty of the school, on the other.

In 1952 enrollment in the school numbered 885; in 1964, 967, an increase of less than 9 percent, but if one subtracts the approximately 50 percent of the schools' students who were in a business administration program, the gain in enrollment is substantial: 54 percent. Locals accounted for 30 percent of the school's population in 1952; 15.2 percent twelve years later. That no doubt reflected the discontinuation of evening classes in 1964. Like the college, there was a significant increase in the proportion of students coming from the Northeast (31.1% in 1952, 40.5% in 1964). Also there was a gain in the percentage of students coming from the Midwest and West (8.9% to 12.2%, and 6.3% to 8%, respectively). Only the South remained unchanged in the proportion of students it sent to Georgetown (at nearly 16 percent). Catholics were not as dominant in the school as they were in the college but were still a very large majority: 68 percent in 1952 and 71.5 percent in 1964.

Females made up 6 percent of the school in 1952, when they were limited to the evening division. Allowed into the day division beginning in 1953, albeit in very small numbers, females by 1964 made up 15 percent of enrollment. Curiously, foreign nationals declined as a proportion of the school from their 9 percent presence in 1952 to 6.5 percent in 1964. In 1952 nearly half of the School of Foreign Service students worked (47.4%); twelve years later, fewer than one-quarter of them (22.3%) did. Again the discontinuation of evening classes was very likely the largest factor in that change. In 1952 veterans were still a very large presence in the school (37%); by 1964, as in the college, they had virtually disappeared (3.3%). The absence of veterans would also explain the decline in the percentage of those married—from more than one-fifth in 1952 to one-twentieth in 1964. And few School of Foreign Service students during this period had previous ties to Georgetown; sons of alumni accounted for but 2 percent of enrollment, in both 1952 and 1964.

Admissions standards were minimal in the school, at least until the university unified the admissions process for all undergraduate schools in 1959. In 1953, for instance, the acceptance rate was 94 percent. But there was a very high attrition rate. In 1955, 245 of 1,155 students (21%) either withdrew or failed out, far more than the number of graduates (145). By 1957 the admissions rate had dropped to 66 percent, which matched that of the college.

At the beginning of the 1957–58 academic year, the name of the school was changed—to honor the man who had guided it during its first four decades—to the Edmund A. Walsh School of Foreign Service. Notable graduates who entered the foreign service during this period included Melissa Foelsch Wells and Allan C. Davis of the class of 1956; three members of the class of 1957 (Edward C. Bittner, Edward P. Gallagher, and John W. Shirley); Arthur Reichenbach (1959); three members of the class of 1960 (Edward Peter Djerejian, Alphonse La Porta, and Frederick W. Schiek); Gregory L. Mattson and Gerald Scott, both of the class of 1962; and Carol Lancaster (1964), who was deputy assistant secretary of state for Africa during the Carter administration. Faradj Panahy (1960) and H. E. Alan Sullivan (1961) became career officers in the Iranian and Canadian foreign service, respectively. Simcha Dinitz (1953) joined the Israeli foreign service and was ambassador to the United States in the 1970s.

Several made careers in the academy, including William Gillette (1955) in political science at Rutgers; Walter O. Weyrach (1955), who taught family law at the University of Florida; John W. Dardess (1958) in Chinese history at the University of Kansas; Michael J. Horan (1960) in political science at the University of Wyoming; Carmen Brissette Grayson (1962) in history at Hampton College; and Jane Walsh Mattingly (1962), who directed special education programs in New Jersey. Thomas J. Dodd (1957) taught Latin American history at his alma mater for a quarter of a century before serving as ambassador to Uruguay and Costa Rica in the Clinton administration.

Vince Carlin (1954) became chief news editor for television of the Canadian Broadcasting Company. Michael Ryan (1953) became a professional actor in theater, television, and films. Paul Erdman (1956) became a novelist of the banking world, and John L. Fugh (1957) became judge advocate general in the army. Anthony D. Thomopoulos (1959) became president of ABC Entertainment.

In the political world, three school graduates of the period made a mark. Vincent F. Callahan Jr. (1957) became the perennial Republican representative of his district in Fairfax County, Virginia. Philip Sharp (1959) served several terms as a Democratic congressional representative from Indiana. Antonio Anaya (1964) became a lawyer and the governor of New Mexico.

Languages and Linguistics: Becoming More Than an Institute

During the first decade of the Institute of Languages and Linguistics, the focus was on the teaching of languages, including English, and linguistics to special students, many of them government personnel, both military and civilian. Those in degree programs were in a small minority. The number of languages taught—thirty-two at one point in the 1950s—reflected the ad hoc nature of most of the academic activity in the institute. Most faculty were part-time and brought in to teach a specific course, in what was often an esoteric language, for one or two semesters. A minority that included Bernard Choseed, Paul Garvin, Michael Krupensky, Pierre Maubrey, Hugo Mueller, and Michael Zarechnak gradually formed the nucleus of a permanent faculty.

Special events, such as the annual Round Table Meetings in Language and Linguistics, which began in 1950, and special projects were integral to the academic life of the institute in its first decade. An early project that became an important part of the institute's contribution to linguistic development was one involving machine translation. Leon Dostert was the originator of the attempt to make machine translation a reality, having been motivated to build a practical translation machine at a conference on machine translation theory that he had attended at Harvard in the fall of 1952. Dostert subsequently persuaded IBM to provide the necessary equipment, and, under the direction of Paul Garvin, the first practical machine translation of language, later to be known as the Georgetown-IBM experiment, was performed successfully in January 1954. That initial demonstration engendered much national publicity but no funding to support further development, until the Soviet Union, impressed by the results at Georgetown, announced its intention of pursuing the practical ends of machine translation. That threat unlocked government coffers, and Georgetown became a major beneficiary. In the fall of 1956 Dostert established a Machine Translation Research Center at the institute.

The center's research became a major activity of the institute as well as the primary recipient of outside funding.[15] Another project that the institute promoted during its first decade was one in spoken Latin. Professor Waldo Sweet at the University of Michigan had pioneered the structural linguistic teaching of Latin, and Georgetown faculty and officials at the institute felt compelled to take up the challenge of further developing the teaching of Latin through a descriptive linguistic methodology. Dostert hoped to get the project underway in 1956, but the lack of qualified faculty postponed its beginnings until 1958 when Neil Twombley, SJ, joined the institute as professor of Latin. Two years later, Richard O'Brien, SJ, a linguist trained at the University of Michigan, became Twombley's collaborator in the project.[16] The pair taught the first summer session of spoken Latin in 1961 to high school and college teachers. At the same time, they worked together in preparing textbooks on oral Latin. From 1961 to 1967, they published ten volumes for use in high school and college courses across the country.

In the 1952–53 academic year, the university approved the creation of a bachelor's program in linguistics. The following year the institute inaugurated graduate education with the introduction of master of science programs in languages and linguistics. Both programs quickly attracted candidates. There were initially 22 degree candidates in 1954, but by 1963 there were nearly 200. Dostert also proposed to establish a doctoral program in linguistics in the mid-1950s, but a lack of faculty as well as funding to support fellowships forced him to defer it.

In 1959 Robert Lado joined the institute as professor of linguistics. The forty-five-year-old Lado had received his PhD at Michigan in 1950 and had been director of the English Language Institute at Michigan when he accepted the appointment to Georgetown. During his initial year at Georgetown he was named director of the institute, as Dostert stepped down to become director of research in mechanical translation and special projects. In 1962 Lado's title was changed from director to dean as the institute became a school within the university—the School of Languages and Linguistics, although the formal name change did not occur until 1967.

The school that Lado inherited was, in general, in very good shape. The Middle States team had found it to be one of the strongest academic components of the university, if not the strongest; its overall performance was excellent, and it had an effective curriculum that interwove language training with the study of cultures and a faculty whose research achievements were outstanding and could well support doctoral programs.[17] From the outset, Lado meant to build on this strength; indeed, he had ambitious plans for his school. Taped to his desk was a paper on which he had written his agenda:

Robert Lado, director of the Institute of Languages and Linguistics, 1960–62; dean of the Institue of Languages and Linguistics, 1962–74. (Georgetown University Archives. Photo by Bob Young.)

1. Establish a Ph.D. program in Languages and Linguistics.
2. Obtain Ford Foundation support for this program.
3. Seek permanence and national visibility for the faculty.
4. Try to establish the top language program in the nation.
5. Seek an enrollment of 500. . . . Make it a special school. Cut down on special students and concentrate on degree candidates.
6. Bring the American Language Institute to Georgetown.
7. Establish Latin American University connections.
8. Balance the budget.
9. Set up a Publications Department that will pay for itself.
10. Build a G[eorgetown] Languages of the World Building.[18]

Lado was remarkably successful in achieving most of his goals. In 1961 he was able to put in place the PhD program in linguistics that Dostert had failed to implement. Since the middle 1950s, several important additions had been made to the linguistics faculty, including Richard S. Harrell (PhD, Harvard), Robert J. DiPietro (PhD, Cornell), Harvey Sobelman (PhD, Harvard), Francis P. Dineen, SJ (PhD, London), and F. J. Bosco (PhD, Michigan). Charles Kreidler, also with a doctorate from the University of Michigan, was due to join the institute in 1963. Other significant faculty appointments that undergirded these doctoral programs included Robert William Lowe (PhD, Paris), as professor of French in 1958; Marianna A. Poltoratzky (PhD, Graz-Austria), as professor of Russian in 1957; Margareta Brosch Bowen (PhD, Vienna), in translation and interpretation in 1955 (she would join the faculty as a permanent member in 1971); and Alfred Obernberger (PhD, Marburg), as assistant professor of German in 1963. Also there was now money available from the federal government as well as private foundations for fellowships. The National Defense Education Act of 1958 (NDEA) proved to be a boon for the school. The act established a program that provided long-term, low-interest loans to students in institutions of higher education, as well as fellowships for those preparing for careers in the academy and funding for institutions to establish centers for teaching modern foreign languages and related area studies. The school benefited from all three aspects of NDEA.[19] Lado was particularly successfully in securing for the school a disproportionate share of doctoral fellowships available through the NDEA.

In the 1961–62 academic year, doctoral programs began in theoretical linguistics, linguistics applied to English as a second language, and linguistics combined with French, Spanish, German, or Russian (later the program was expanded to include Arabic, Chinese, Japanese, or

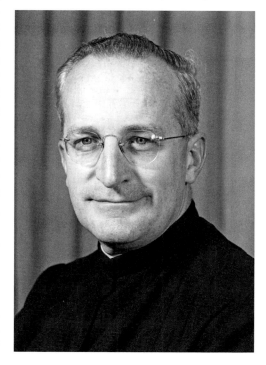

Francis Dineen, SJ, professor of linguistics. (Georgetown University Archives. Photo by Bob Young.)

A group of institute students in language lab. (Photo provided by Gretchen Van Tassel-Shaw)

Portuguese as concentrations). Through (eventually) an eight-year grant from the Ford Foundation, Lado secured the necessary support for the program. He brought in additional faculty that not only provided the critical mass to start the doctorate program but, as a group, greatly strengthened the prestige and visibility of the school.[20] And the undergraduate curriculum was recast much more on a liberal arts foundation. The graduate programs expanded as well. By 1964 there were ninety-six MS candidates and forty-one PhD candidates in linguistics alone.

During his first year as director, Lado managed to add the American Language Institute (ALI) to the school. The ALI had originated in 1942 as an orientation center and provider of an introduction to English for immigrants and refugees at the Webster Americanization School in Washington. By the 1950s its main purpose was to introduce English to foreign students. In 1961 it was teaching English as a Second Language to more than 1,000 students a year from fifty or so countries who were sponsored by the Agency for International Development, the International Cooperation Administration, and the Department of State for Higher Education in the United States. Once at

Georgetown, the ALI increased its student capacity to 1,500 a year in six-week training sessions.[21] David Harris (Ph.D. Michigan) accompanied the ALI as its director.

The institute more than doubled its enrollment from 306 in 1952 to 770 in 1964. In truth, the growth was more than it appeared. In 1953, of 367 students, only 54 were in degree programs. As late as 1956 there were but fourteen students who earned bachelor of science degrees at commencement. An overwhelming number of students in the institute through the 1950s were special students, many of them from the armed services. Males dominated enrollment, with 88 percent of the institute's student population. By 1962, not only had the population of the institute, now school, more than doubled (690), but full-time students in degree programs now made up the vast majority of those enrolled.(71.3%). Student demographics had changed as well. Catholics made up 41.8 percent of the institute in 1952; in 1964, they made up 64.2 percent. The dominant male majority of 1952 became a modest minority in 1964 (36.1%). In 1952, 58.8 percent were working; in 1964 only 22.5 percent were working. Foreigners had made up less than one-fifth of the enrollment in 1952; by 1964 they made up nearly one-third (30.3%). Veterans comprised 29 percent of the institute in 1952, and they made up 3.3 percent in 1964; in 1952, 23.8 percent were married, in 1964 10.3 percent were married. The ninety-one bachelor's degrees in linguistics or languages that the school awarded in 1966 reflected the great change in academic programs over the past ten years, as bachelor's programs became the major academic concentration.

The feminization of the institute was not by design. By 1964 school officials were concerned about the female dominance within the student body. The dean, Robert Lado, admitted that the school would profit from better gender balance in its enrollment and that the admission committee was alive to the need to promote balanced enrollment, even though the incoming class in the fall of 1964 was the strongest academically in school history.[22] Over the next several years, while male enrollment remained steady, female enrollment declined somewhat, so that by 1967 males made up 37.7 percent of enrollment, probably the result of a negative action admission program for women.

Among early graduates who had distinctive careers were Muriel Vasconcellos (1958, PhD 1985), who, as an undergraduate student, was involved with the beginnings of machine translation at Georgetown and later became chief of the Terminology and Machine Translation Program of the Pan-American Health Organization; Robert Meskill (1959), who earned a doctorate in linguistics and became professor of cognitive and linguistic science at Brown University; and Howard Simons (1959), who became managing editor of the *Washington Post* in the 1970s.

The grants that the school received in the 1960s, along with the sharp increase in enrollment, enabled the School of Languages and Linguistics to balance its budget after nearly a decade of running a deficit. Lado also formally institutionalized the Georgetown University Press as the publication arm of the school. Richard O'Brien, SJ, became the first director. By 1963 there were sixteen volumes in the monograph series in languages and linguistics, which had begun in 1950. The press also began its long-standing contributions of publishing reference grammars and dictionaries in various Arabic languages.

From the early 1950s, institute officials talked of constructing new facilities. In 1952, Dostert was looking to construct an eight-story wing to the building they occupied on Massachusetts Avenue. He envisioned the institute's location in the middle of Embassy Row and close-by federal Washington to be a distinct advantage, given the attraction of their special programs to embassy and government personnel.[23] He fought in vain the decision to relocate the institute to the east campus in the Nevils Building in 1956. By the time Lado became director in 1960, the institute had long since become part of the lower campus.

In 1962, Lado summed up the reasons for the school's success. "The pioneering nature of the work in the Institute at a time when the international interest in foreign languages and linguistics is at an all-time high is partially responsible for our reputation." The annual Round Table gave the school regular exposure to the international academic community. Special projects such as the one in machine translation had commanded wide attention and influence. "Our faculty in linguistics has been full of stars." The securing of the Ford Foundation grant for the PhD program and the acquisition of the ALI with its AID contract were recognitions of the school's emergence as a major player in language education.[24]

Business School: A Rocky First Decade

Since 1936 the Division of Business Administration had been a major part of the School of Foreign Service and accounted for one-third of the degrees awarded before World War II. For a great many students among the enormous influx after the war, many of them returning veterans, a business major became the prime magnet for their concentration. By 1951 nearly one-half of the degrees from the school were in business administration. In his examination of the school as provincial prefect of studies in 1951, Edward Bunn saw the weight of the Division of Business Administration as a threat to the identity of the school itself. "I feared that if this situation continued," he later wrote, "the Foreign Service School would soon lose its identity."[25] When Bunn became president, he began to take steps to separate the division from the school. He asked a member of the president's council, M. S. Syzmczak, then head of the board of governors of the Federal Reserve System, to do a feasibility study of the faculty, facilities, courses, and other things needed to implement such a change.[26] Syzmczak did the study and solicited funding from the local business community in order to implement the start-up of a new school. The study convinced university officials that there was a growing market for education in the fields of business and public management that the new school could tap.[27] Meanwhile, a committee under the leadership of Henry M. Cunningham, the assistant director of business administration in the School of Foreign Service, was appointed to do general planning for the new school, including its size, curriculum, housing, and other matters. Two new programs, public administration and banking, were added to the existing majors of accounting and business management. An enrollment goal of eight hundred was established (a goal that would be realized only two decades later).

The purpose of the school, as described in the university catalogue, was "to impart a balanced education consisting of liberal arts and professional courses, integrated to prepare the student to assume positions of responsibility in business, finance and government." With two administrative offices in the ground floor of Healy, three full-time faculty, and classes in the Annex, the school began operations in September 1957, offering both day and evening programs. Cunningham became the school's first director, a position he held until 1960, when he was succeeded by Raymond Pelissier, one of the three original, full-time faculty. In the following year, Joseph Sebes, SJ, replaced Frank Fadner, SJ, as regent of the school.

The Middle States report of 1960 found the Business School to be the weakest school in the university. The very nature of the school seemed to the committee to be unclear: was it a professional school or a liberal arts one with a business concentration? Whatever the case, the committee found the curriculum of the school to be too highly specialized. Accounting had far too large a place in the curriculum. Students took too many courses in their area of concentration. More science, both physical and behavioral; mathematics; and liberal arts in general were needed in the curriculum, particularly in freshman and sophomore years. As for the faculty, too few were full time, too many lacked terminal degrees, and they did very little research. Finally, the library holdings were woefully inadequate.[28]

In the light of that critical report, the school revised the curriculum along the lines the Middle States Association had recommended. Pelissier and Sebes proceeded to introduce more liberal arts courses into the required curriculum and cut down on the preprofessional courses, particularly in accounting. More full-time faculty were brought on, including Othmar Winkler (statistics) and George McMammon (management). Pelissier was also determined to improve the quality of students in the school. "At present," he wrote in the fall of 1960, "students in Business Administration are generally less able than those in the CAS and SFS."[29] The dean managed to bring business faculty into the admissions process to reduce, if not prevent, the dumping of weak applicants to the college and School of Foreign Service into the Business School.

Othmar Winkler, professor of statistics. (Georgetown University Archives)

Accepting women on an unrestricted basis was one sure way to improve student quality. The prevailing policy was to admit only those women to the Business School who were local, Catholic, and unable to attend an out-of-town Catholic institution where they could receive an education in business administration. In arguing for the admission of women without restriction, Pelissier noted that the current cadre of women in the school, although only 5 percent of total enrollment, constituted about one-half of the academic top tenth there. His plea failed to change the policy.[30] When the school faculty was again removed from the admission process in 1963, the school resumed its role as "the Graveyard of Georgetown," as one faculty member recalled, to which unqualified candidates for the college or School of Foreign Service could be diverted in order to meet the enrollment quota assigned to the Business School.[31]

In 1957–58 business students totaled 378, 20 (5.2%) of whom were women. More than four-fifths were Catholic. Nearly half were employed (45%). Foreign students made up 13.4 percent of enrollment. Seven percent were children of alumni. One-quarter of them were married. In 1964–65, just seven years later, the school had grown by one-third to a population of 567, of whom 30 (5.2%) were females and 68 (11.9%) were foreign. Catholic representation was even higher than at the beginning of the school, at nearly 90 percent. Those working had dropped to fewer than one-quarter of the total. And those married now made up only 7 percent of business students. Seven percent were children of alumni. In 1957, 33.5 percent were local, 23 percent were from the Northeast, 8.2 percent from the North-central region, 17.4 percent from the South, and 1 percent from the West. In 1964–65, 19.9 percent were local, 42.6 percent from the Northeast, 9.8 percent from the North-central region, 15.5 percent from the South, and 3 percent from the West. In their demographics regarding religion, work, foreign origin, regional distribution, and marriage, the Business School closely resembled the School of Foreign Service from which it had sprung. Only in terms of alumni relations did the school compare most closely to the college.

Among the graduates in the first decade of the school were Saul S. Gefter (1960), who made a career in foreign service; George Houston (1961), who became a faculty member of the school and a vice president for finance for the university; Patricia McShane (1962), who became an examiner for the Federal Reserve Board; Paul Anthony Ritacco (1964), who became a well-known figure in public television in the D.C. area; and Teresa Turner Iannaconi (1965), who became an administrator for the Securities and Exchange Commission.

Even before it became a separate school, the Division of Business Administration had inaugurated in 1954 a biennial forum for investment bankers as a way of building rapport between the local financial community and business administration at Georgetown. Every other October a two-day forum was held on campus devoted to a particular topic, such as international trade and finance, which was the theme of the 1964 forum. Director Cunningham, who had been responsible for the establishment of the forum, saw its major effect at sustaining interest among local bankers in the banking program, in particular, and business administration at Georgetown, in general, and ensuring their continuing support.[32]

Pelissier, during his tenure as director, also endeavored to establish graduate education within the school. If Georgetown truly strove to be the leading Catholic university in the country, he argued, graduate business education should be part of its academic profile. As the tenth largest and one of the fastest-growing metropolitan regions in country, there was a distinct need for advanced business training in Washington. Such graduate programs would also strengthen the school by attracting high-quality faculty, something the school had difficulty doing with only an undergraduate curriculum.[33] But the university was not yet ready to commit itself to graduate education in business. It first had to decide whether to continue with the school itself or to collapse business into departments within the college and School of Foreign Service.

There had been doubt about the where and how of the Business School at its creation in 1957, reflected in the title given to the school's head—director rather than dean. In light of the Middle States Association's critical observations about the school, as well as recent reports of the Carnegie and Ford foundations about the problems of undergraduate business education, in March 1962, President Bunn appointed a committee headed by Vice President McGrath to consider whether the Business School should be phased out. Eight months later the committee recommended that the school be gradually discontinued, with new majors in foreign business management and business administration created in the School of Foreign Service and the College of Arts and Sciences, respectively.[34]

Not until a year later, at a special three-day meeting to do general planning, did the board of directors take up the committee's recommendation. Sebes successfully pleaded that, before any decision was made, an outside group be brought in to evaluate the whole matter of business education at Georgetown.[35] The three-man committee examined the school in a three-day visit in late March 1964 and recommended that the school not be phased out but rather fully established as a separate body within the university. It found that the school badly needed strong leadership; it recommended that a new head of the school be appointed, presumably someone outside of Georgetown, and given the title of dean. The curriculum should be pared down (five fields of concentration were too many) and admission standards raised to the level of the college. The evening division needed to have the same curriculum and standards for admission as the day division. Once the new dean had gotten the undergraduate program on a strong foundation, they should seriously consider introducing a graduate program. In April 1964 the board acted on the committee's recommendation by committing itself to the school as a permanent unit of the university. Pelissier was terminated as director of the school, and Sebes was made acting head until a permanent dean could be found.

Nursing School: Finding a Place

In 1953 eight seniors became the first to graduate from the baccalaureate program of the Nursing School. The commitment to a baccalaureate program proved to be a felicitous one for the school. Between 1952 and 1964 enrollment increased by 35 percent, from 212 students to 327. By 1954 the school stood third among 41 Catholic nursing schools in the United States in enrollment.[36] Indeed, by the early 1960s, the school was receiving far more applications than its facilities could accommodate.[37] Catholics continued to dominate nursing enrollment, with 92 percent of the student nurses being of that faith in 1964 (93.8% of them in 1952), but regional demographics changed significantly as the school shifted from a diploma program to a degree one. The percentage of local students declined from more than one-quarter of the population in 1952 to about one-fifth (21.7%) in 1964. There was also a decline in the number of those from the Northeast, which in 1952 supplied a majority of those enrolled (53.3% in 1952) but accounted for only 38.2 percent in 1964. At the same time, there were increases in those from other sections, particularly the Midwest, which by 1964 was the home region of nearly 10 percent of Georgetown nursing students. Representation from the South and West also increased to 9 percent and 4 percent, respectively. In 1952 just three students were married, and those were enrolled by special permission; by 1964 there were twenty students (6%) with husbands, although nursing students were still prohibited from marrying.

The upgrading of nursing education from a diploma program to a bachelor of science in nursing implicitly required a more qualified faculty, whose tenuring and promotion, at least theoretically, would be determined by how well they met the general standards set for faculty within the university. In 1954, of twelve, full-time faculty in the school, a slight majority (seven) held a master's degree, six others had a bachelor's degree, and one no degree.

There was virtually no research or publication among them. And turnover was high. In 1954 half of the faculty were new, and five of them were replacements for those who had resigned positions at the close of the previous academic year. By 1960, of twenty-four, full-time members, only three had been at Georgetown more than five years; one-quarter of the faculty had been there less than a year. And the proportion of faculty with advanced degrees had actually declined from the early 1950s. Only four of the permanent faculty had master's degrees. One of them, Ann Douglas, was in the process of obtaining a doctorate, but she was the exception. The revolving door pattern continued into the 1960s. In 1961 there were three resignations; in 1963, there were eight.[38] In the early 1950s, Dean Angela Marie attributed the high turnover rate to a variety of factors, including marriage, pregnancy, the transfer of a husband's job to a different location, and the pressure involved in adjusting to a new academic program and the heightened standards for faculty that it entailed.[39] One mechanism promoting faculty stability was the five-year training grant that the school received in 1957 from the National Institute of Mental Health, which enabled the school to bring in Dr. Elizabeth Smith to integrate mental health education into clinical experiments.

The curriculum was daunting: Courses and clinical practice totaled 151 credits over four calendar years, of which 80 were in nursing, 22 in biology, 8 in chemistry, 12 in philosophy, 11 in English, 6 in theology, and 12 in social science. Ninety-eight of the credits had to be completed within the first two years, including summers. In their first semester alone, students carried the equivalent of 25 credit hours, although they received credit for only 19. This moved the regent, L. C. McHugh, SJ, to question in 1954 whether the curriculum, as constructed, was appropriate for an academic program.[40] By 1957 curriculum credit hours had been reduced to 140, with clinical practice hours particularly decreased.

The change in the academic program also affected relations between the school and the hospital. The administrator of the hospital and nurse supervisors seemed not to appreciate that nursing students now were primarily students and not nursing assistants and that their service in the hospital now had to take second place behind their formal education in the classroom and lab. Conditions improved with the appointment of Stella Warfield, who had been on the faculty since 1948, as the first clinical coordinator between the hospital and the school. The launching of the newsletter *Nursing Progress* in 1954, a joint publication of the school and hospital, was another effort to build common ground between these two medical center components.

If student achievement in national and state board examinations served as barometers of the quality of the curriculum, the verdict was a very positive one, as graduates did very well in the national examinations, from the mid-1950s into the mid-1960s. Outstanding graduates during the first decade of the program included Helen Creighton (1956), who became the first

First graduates of degree program from the School of Nursing, 1953, with Angela Marie, SCN, dean of nursing. (*Caduceus*, 1953)

woman to be named Distinguished Professor at the University of Wisconsin-Milwaukee; Mary Lee Biegler Lynch (1958), who earned an MS in psychiatric nursing and worked in that field; Martha Louise Mitchell (1960), who became director of nursing for the Connecticut Mental Health Center and a faculty member of the Yale University School of Nursing; Angela Barron McBride (1962), who earned a doctorate in developmental psychology and became dean of the Indiana University School of Nursing; and Margaret Hayes Jordan (1964), the first African American graduate of the school, who became president and chief executive officer of Texas Medical Resources, a consortium of Dallas-area hospital and medical research centers.

Along with the four-year baccalaureate program, there was also a supplemental program, or graduate nurses program, that offered a BSN to nurses who had graduated from a diploma program but lacked the academic degree. To those who qualified for the program, the school awarded a two-year tuition fellowship of $3,000. In return, the graduate nurses had to work in the hospital twenty hours per week during the academic year and full time in the summer. Their curriculum, like the undergraduate one, combined general education courses with nursing courses, plus specialized offerings, such as public health nursing, advanced medical and surgical nursing, and mental hygiene. Five years after it instituted the program, the nursing faculty decided to suspend the program because, with the great growth in the undergraduate program, they simply lacked the faculty resources to staff the specific courses that the graduate nurses program required.[41] For five years the program was not offered, but it was begun again in 1962, when additional faculty had been acquired (there were now twenty-three, full-time members). Twenty-five nurses from Georgetown Hospital entered the revived program.

In the early summer of 1952, Angela Marie, SCN, a member of the faculty, was appointed dean of the school, the second Sister of Charity of Nazareth to hold that position. A few months later L. C. McHugh, SJ, was made regent of the school by President Bunn. It quickly became evident that the pairing was an impossible one for the administration of the school. The dean for her part was sure that the regent, far from supporting her, was actively working against her and fomenting opposition among students and faculty. She threatened to resign if nothing changed.[42] McHugh, for his part, found that the dean was preventing him from having any meaningful participation in the administration. McHugh pleaded with Bunn to tell Angela Marie that he was now the official regent and what his duties were. As it was, the dean acted as though Bunn himself was still regent as well as president.[43] McHugh was convinced that the school needed a new dean, that Angela Marie, although hardworking, intelligent, and devoted to the school, lacked the temperament needed for her post. She was "arbitrary, unfair, impulsive, suspicious, [and] threatening" in her dealings with others; she could not delegate authority and had utterly alienated her faculty.[44] McHugh's plea for a change in administration or at least a clarification of his authority as regent apparently brought no response from the president.

The following year McHugh took the initiative on one of the matters that had concerned him in his report to Bunn: the academic image of the school. McHugh had suggested at that time that "the Georgetown Collegiate School of Nursing" would be a more appropriate name than "School of Nursing" and that prizes should be established for nursing graduates just as they were for students in the other schools of the university. The following year McHugh proceeded to pursue these changes. Apparently without consulting the dean, in March 1954 he sought approval for the "Nursing College" to have its own Tropaia, or awards, exercise. Bunn agreed to establish a Nursing School class day exercises during the coming commencement.[45] McHugh then issued a directive that the name to be used in the future was College of Nursing. The dean immediately informed Bunn and appealed to him not to allow such a change in title to occur, listing all the practical reasons why it would be both costly and confusing.[46] Bunn sided with the dean, and the board of directors subsequently declared that the name of the school was hereafter to be the Georgetown University School of Nursing.

For overstepping his authority, McHugh was removed as regent; the position went unfilled for more than two years, at which point Bunn appointed Thomas O'Donnell, SJ, who was already regent of the Medical School, to be regent of the Nursing School as well, with the vague charge of coordinating all activities within the medical center.[47] Despite some continuing faculty criticism of her administrative manner, Angela Marie remained in office until 1958 when she was transferred by her order to a hospital in her native Kentucky. The president remained strongly supportive of her, no doubt appreciating the gains in enrollment and student achievement that had taken place during her tenure as dean.

Her successor, also a Sister of Charity of Nazareth, Kathleen Mary Bohan, SCN, had earned bachelor's and master's degrees in nursing at the Catholic University of America. When informed that she was to be the new dean of nursing at Georgetown, the thirty-two-year-old wondered whether she had enough experience to take on the responsibilities. "No one told me anything," she later recalled. "I was just told to go up there, do what the Jesuits wanted, and let [the order] know how it was going."[48] She did more than that. She and Dean Sellinger of the college decided that nursing students should take general education classes with college students, something that the university board of directors had previously forbidden, but which both outside evaluators and nursing students themselves had called for as a means of improving and enhancing their general education courses.[49] She adopted a collegial relationship with her faculty as well and relaxed the rules that her predecessor had tended to apply inflexibly. Under her administration the faculty grew in numbers and qualifications. Ann Douglas, who joined the faculty in 1959, became the first faculty member to earn her doctorate in 1961 at the Catholic University of America.

Ann Douglas, dean of the Nursing School, 1963–67. (*Caduceus*, 1964)

When the Middle States Association evaluated the school in the fall of 1960, its committee found it "young and vigorous" and commended the school for its progress over the previous decade. The committee judged the faculty to be competent but in need of development in order to meet the academic standards expected of university faculty in the areas of degrees held and of research and publication.

International Programs

In the academic year 1953–54, Georgetown counted 275 foreign students, 199 of them undergraduates. By 1956 they numbered nearly 400, and a faculty member was assigned to advise them.[50] In the following year 9 scholarships were established, one by each school in the university, for Catholic Hungarian refugees.[51] By 1964 there were 608 foreign students, including 384 undergraduates. Of the graduate students, 193 were in the Graduate School.

In 1955 Georgetown began its first study abroad program. Twenty juniors in the college, together with the program's director, Gerard Yates, SJ, sailed in September for the Catholic University of Fribourg in Switzerland, where they spent the year. By 1964, Georgetown was conducting two junior year abroad programs, including the one in Fribourg, plus several summer school sessions in European countries. Gerard Yates, now chair of the committee on foreign students, thought that the time had come for the oversight of foreign students, the maintenance of the programs abroad, and the selection of students for Fulbrights and other scholarships to be integrated into one Office of International Student Programs with a full-time director.[52]

In the summer of 1961, Bunn brought to Georgetown another Jesuit, Californian and historian George Dunne. Bunn had originally wanted Dunne to become dean of the School of Foreign Service. By the time Dunne was available, that post had been filled, so Bunn made him his assistant for international programs. When, however, he began to survey the actual international programs that Georgetown had in operation, he discovered that each was being run by a Jesuit "who regarded it as his special domain." So Dunne went looking for an international program that he could start at Georgetown. A Peace Corps training program seemed a natural for the university, given that so much of the Peace Corps training consisted of language preparation, certainly one of Georgetown's strongest academic assets. That argument persuaded the director of the Peace Corps, Sargent Shriver, to make Georgetown the center of a consortium of area universities (American, Catholic, George Washington, Johns Hopkins, Howard, and Maryland) that would be training sites for various Peace Corps projects. Georgetown received the largest project, the training of three hundred volunteers for service in Ethiopia. Unfortunately, no institution in the United States, including Georgetown, taught Amharic, the official language of Ethiopia, so Dunne had to recruit twenty-five Ethiopians studying in the United States as his language "faculty." That random recruitment turned out to produce a very uneven range of instructional effectiveness, but the overall program proved successful enough for the Peace Corps program to continue at Georgetown, as it did for the next five years.[53]

A Rhodes and Phi Beta Kappa

In 1959 Georgetown had two of its students, George Giard Jr. and Walter Niegorski, reach the finals of the Rhodes competition. Giard (**C** 1960) became the first Georgetown student to win a Rhodes Scholarship. "G's showing in the recent Rhodes Scholarship competition should remove finally and forever any lingering vestige of the group inferiority complex which has seemed at times to infect a good segment of the student body," the *Hoya* editorialized. The paper thought it more than coincidence that Giard's award came in the year that graduated the first group in the honors program. Giard himself was one of twenty-nine honors graduates.

Four years later the university gained an even more important honor. As early as 1933, probably at Coleman Nevils's initiation, the university had applied for a chapter of Phi Beta Kappa (PBK) without success. Even without a formal visit from the United Chapters, PBK officials informed the university that it was deemed "not yet ready for a chapter." Two years later a new president submitted an application that drew a positive response from the United Chapters—that its president would personally visit the campus for an examination. Georgetown officials thereupon had second thoughts about their prospects; among other things, the presence of faculty members who were PBK—a key criterion for securing a chapter—was virtually nonexistent at Georgetown: only one. The university consequently withdrew its application.

As noted in chapter 8, in 1948 university officials had established a Gold Key Society, composed of certain professors and graduate students as well as a few undergraduates, as a way of preparing the ground for a PBK chapter. Initially there were five faculty and nine students. During the first decade, the college contributed the most members (sixty-seven), followed by the

Joseph A. Panuska, SJ, and James Lambert, fellow Delta chapter members of Phi Beta Kappa, at induction ceremony in mid-1960s. (Georgetown University Archives)

School of Foreign Service (fifty-eight) and the Graduate School (fifty-three). Annual dinners and sponsored lectures were the main activities of the group.[54] Four years after the formation of the Gold Key Society, Georgetown submitted its third application to the United Chapters, this time through fifteen faculty members, led by Franklin B. Williams Jr., who were members of PBK. To Williams's shock, the United Chapters informed him in late December 1952 that the committee on qualifications did not find them among the ten best applicants warranting an official inspection.[55] Nearly a decade passed before the faculty group of PBKs, now numbering at least fifty-six, made a fourth application in 1961 that proved successful. Georgetown was not chosen to be visited, but the subsequent self-evaluation report that the university prepared for the United Chapters and the PBK team that visited the campus in the spring of 1963 resulted in Georgetown's admission as a chapter (Delta of D.C.) in September 1964.[56]

Student Life: Between the 1950s and 1960s

When Joseph Rock, SJ, took over as prefect of discipline in 1951, he had been given a new title, director of student personnel, and told by then president Hunter Guthrie "to take the policeman's big stick out of that job." The previous prefect had focused heavily on catching students who were violating curfew (e.g., sneaking back onto campus after lights-out) or some other restriction on student behavior (e.g., having lights on after the prescribed bedtime). Rock conscientiously worked to broaden the functions of the office to include strengthening the ways in which student life outside the classroom could function more as a part of the educational process and less as a series of hoops to jump through or cleverly bypass.

But almost six years later, Rock, in his departing report to the president on the state of student life at Georgetown, expressed some frustration that his efforts had fallen short of his reach. He noted that students resented the still too repressive discipline. The drinking policy of total abstinence on campus, outside of certain social events, had to be liberalized and made less draconian. Room checks at regular times were a necessary means of supervising students, but they should not be carried out in a manner more appropriate of "a reign of terror." "At present," he continued, "the student spirit is strained and nasty." He proposed a structural reorganization in order to change the culture of repression and inflexible enforcement of rules. He called for the creation of a director of student affairs at the vice presidential level, with deans of men and women, the health administrator, the director of psychological services, chaplains, and the heads of placement and student activities being accountable to him.[57]

Five weeks after Rock submitted his report, the *Hoya*, in an editorial, called for a "liberalization" of the academic and disciplinary rules then in operation, which would involve delegating greater responsibility to the student. "Would a relaxation of certain regulations increase student responsibility? We think so. Would increased assumption of responsibility by the students be a boon to the University? We are sure it would."[58] Despite Rock's urging, the structure of student personnel was not changed, nor was there any immediate change in discipline. Over the next several years, however, there was a relaxation of rules and, in some cases, a rescission. Thus, in 1961–62, the practice of requiring resident students to attend two weekday masses was abolished. There was also the gradual abandonment of curfews for upperclass men as well as nightly room checks.

Hazing remained an initiation ritual for freshmen, albeit in somewhat token form by the early 1950s. The *Hoya,* in an editorial titled "Is Hazing Outmoded?" noted that the new orientation program for freshmen at the beginning of the year in large part was fulfilling the function that hazing had served in the past. But it concluded that hazing still had its value and called upon the sophomores to carry out their traditional role of enforcers of hazing.[59] Four years later, in March 1958, the paper had a change of heart and came out for the abolition of compulsory hazing.[60] The sentiments of the newspaper did not prevail. Hazing greeted the freshmen the following fall, but the freshmen rebelled and refused to cooperate with tradition. University authorities then banned one of the staples of the hazing process: the annual challenge between freshman and sophomores.[61] The combination of freshman resistance and administration order effectively ended the initiation rites that had begun in the 1920s.

By the 1959–60 academic year, in an attempt to both control and promote responsible drinking, the board of directors weighed the feasibility of a rathskeller on campus for undergraduates. Richard McCooey (**C** 1952) secured approval for the construction of both an inn and a rathskeller on a site owned by the university on the east campus. McCooey's inspiration was Mory's at Yale; he wanted to provide an alternative to cafeteria food for students, as well as provide a reputable watering hole. The Federal-style building was completed in May 1962. The Tombs, a subterranean, low-ceilinged bar and grill, with booths topped by checkered tablecloths and walls filled with World War I posters and Georgetown athletic memorabilia, opened in the spring of 1962. There was one table permanently reserved for the Chimes. On the upper floor was the decidedly upscale 1789 Restaurant, featuring French cuisine, in dining rooms furnished in eighteenth-century tidewater manorial style.

On the night of May 15, 1963, just before the start of final exams, several hundred students stormed from their dormitories to gather in Healy Circle to voice an olio of grievances including administrative secrecy regarding the use of fees and tuition, the mediocre quality of theology courses, the lingering disciplinary measures that they regarded as oppressive, and the miserable quality of the cafeteria food (there had been an earlier food fight in the cafeteria to demonstrate the limited usefulness of the cuisine). Vocal protest soon turned to vicarious violence as firecrackers were set off, then to the displaced charivari of a panty raid on the girls' dormitory beyond the wall at the Georgetown Visitation Convent. At this point metropolitan police arrived with dogs who dispersed the crowd and arrested nine students. The following evening the head of student personnel, John Devine, ordered the students to assemble in the cafeteria in New South. While he was reading the riot act to them, someone set fire to the Annex, a World War II surplus building on 37th Street that had been used as a classroom but was now slated for demolition. Before District firemen could contain it, the wooden structure quickly burned to the ground as students cheered the conflagration.[62] Police took two juniors into custody on suspicion of setting the fire but later released them when they passed a lie detector test.[63]

The upshot of the "riot" was a letter from the archbishop of Washington and the formation of a faculty-student grievance committee. The archbishop warned that trespassing by a male on cloistered property such as the Visitation Convent, for any reason, including a "panty raid," was cause for excommunication for any Catholic.[64] The president of the Yard, Nick Nastasi, sent out a letter to college students on May 18 in which he advised that the protests, mass demonstrations, and destructive actions had reached the point of being counterproductive. As a well-intentioned step toward achieving some positive response from the administration, he announced that the college student council was setting up a sixteen-member, student-faculty grievance board to serve as a forum for student complaints. The faculty-student committee held hearings that following fall during which students testified about their academic and disciplinary concerns, but nothing apparently came of this investigation, and the committee soon became moribund.[65]

Ironically, at a meeting of the college's advisory committee a few days after the "riot," several members urged that the university rid itself of the paternalistic character that governed its relationship with undergraduates and instead focus on a policy of expanding the area of student responsibility as they matured from freshmen to seniors.[66] In fact, what occurred in rather rapid fashion over the next few years was the collapse of the rationale of in loco parentis that governed administrative control of student behavior. The requirement, for instance, that students attend all classes except for a certain minimum number in each course that they were allowed to "cut" was finally ended. The mandatory dress code of coat and tie for males and dresses for females was abolished in 1965.

Three traditional student activities continued strongly during the period. The glee club, under the direction of Paul Hume, in November 1952 performed with the National Symphony Orchestra in McDonough Hall. In January 1953, it twice gave performances in New York City. Three years later, in April 1956, the glee club sang to a nationwide audience on *The Ed Sullivan*

Paul Hume, professor of Fine Arts and the Glee Club.

(Georgetown University Archives)

Show, the invitation coming in return for Father Bunn's baptizing the granddaughter of the television host.[67] The club continued annually to give performances both on campus as well as in cities where there was a large concentration of Georgetown alumni, such as a midwestern tour of Pittsburgh, Detroit, and Chicago in 1962 and in St. Louis in 1964. An attempt by the Nursing School administration to introduce women to the club in 1960 failed; as a result, school officials formed the nursing school glee club, which existed for several years thereafter.

Mask and Bauble, the student theater group, received a new faculty director, Donn Murphy, who had joined the English faculty in 1954. When Murphy became director, the Mask and Bauble was quartered in one of the military surplus buildings on the corner of 37th and O streets. In 1958 the society moved its productions to Trinity's auditorium. A chance meeting of Murphy with then senator John Kennedy and his wife, Jacqueline, outside Mask and Bauble's home on 37th Street led years later to an invitation from the White House to stage a series of arts performances in the East Room following state dinners and the like that Mrs. Kennedy had planned. In the end, Murphy and members of Mask and Bauble arranged twenty-one programs at the White House for the Kennedy and Johnson administrations. The programs featured major artists including Pablo Casals, Grace Bumbry, Leontyne Price, André Watts, and prominent ballet companies.[68]

In April 1953 the senior musical, *Two for the Nose,* ran for three nights at Trinity Theater. Seven years later the annual spring offering became known as "Calliope." John Guare, future Tony-winning playwright, wrote the score and libretto for Calliope I, *The Thirties Girl.*

In debating, a new era of success began with the arrival of William M. Reynolds as coach in 1960. He organized the members of the Philodemic Debating Society into research teams on the national topic and used intramural debates as preparation for tournaments. The result was that Georgetown debaters won 80 percent of their intercollegiate competitions during the decade. In 1962 the quartet of John Brough, Richard Hayes, Terrence Goggin, and John Hempelmann won the Cherry Blossom Tournament. Georgetown, which had started the tournament in 1949, had never taken top honors during the first twelve tournaments. In April 1962, Georgetown finished fifth in the national championship, the National Intercollegiate Tournament at West Point. The following academic year, with Hayes, Goggin, and Hempelmann now joined by Bob Shrum,

Donn Murphy, professor of Fine Arts and director of Mask and Bauble, in Riggs Library. (Georgetown University Archives)

Georgetown won or placed second at several prestigious tournaments, such as the Harvard Invitational. After this highly successful season, President Bunn wrote Reynolds that he had "added an outstanding page to the [proud] history of the Philodemic."[69]

A new form of organized extracurricular intellectual activity was the Georgetown college quiz bowl team, which debuted in 1954 on NBC radio's *College Quiz Bowl* program. In January 1954 the Georgetown quartet of Leo O'Donovan, Paul Maloy, Laszlo Hadik, and Paul Troy made an impressive first showing but lost out to a co-ed team from Brown-Pembroke. Five years later the Hoyas became quiz bowl champions when they defeated Northwestern, then the holders of the title. The Georgetown foursome of Michael M. Hughes, Thomas Anderson, Dennis Duffy, and Timothy J. Murphy reigned for five weeks, fending off challenges from Princeton and Tulane. The program had by then moved from radio to television. Georgetown defended its title three times in McDonough Gym, where hundreds

William A. Reynolds and debate team, 1962–63. (Georgetown University Archives. Photo by Bob Young.)

Program for the third production of "Calliope," 1962. (Georgetown University Archives)

of enthusiastic students cheered on the Hoya team. In their third defense, Georgetown lost in a very closely contested knowledge battle to the University of Notre Dame. "College bowl fever," which swept through campus for more than a month in the late winter of 1959, subsided as quickly as it had sprung up.

Two new clubs on campus were political ones: the Young Democrats and the Young Republicans. During the 1960 presidential campaign, both were very active, bringing speakers to campus and circulating information about the various issues of the campaign.

From the beginning of the 1960s, the *Hoya* grew in size as well as in its coverage of events within the university and beyond. In 1963–64 the *Hoya* declared itself to be no longer the publication solely of the College of Arts and Sciences but a university-wide newspaper. As a consequence, it resigned its seat on the college council. It had begun thinking of itself as the university paper as early as 1958, although its financial support continued to come from the college, and membership on the staff was restricted to college students.[70] In 1963 the paper opened its staff to those from schools within the university other than the college. It saw this change as part of the unification movement that had been going on within the university over the past decade.[71] Two years earlier, the *Georgetown College Journal,* in response to the same trend, had opened its pages to students from all schools of the university.

In February 1960 the board of directors approved Frank Heyden's proposal to secure the license for and to construct a 250-watt, noncommercial, educational, frequency modulated broadcast station. When the license followed in 1961 and WGTB-FM went on the air, President Bunn reflected, "It is obvious that the FM Radio Station has great potential value, and should be used for the training of students in all schools of the university. It is of the utmost necessity since the station now covers a large area in Washington, Maryland, and Virginia, that the programs be of the highest quality."[72] Both the judgment and charge would be tested in the station's stormy history during the next decade.

Sports minus Intercollegiate Football

Sports at Georgetown, stripped of intercollegiate football, was a decidedly modest operation. The entire athletic budget for the 1956–57 academic year was $189,000. Despite football's absence as a varsity sport, a new football field, between the observatory and the hospital, was added in 1954, named Kehoe Field in honor of the former moderator of athletics.

Hunter Guthrie's decree of "no more football for us" proved not to be absolutely true. Georgetown discontinued intercollegiate football after the 1951 season, but interclass tackle football, with teams representing the four undergraduate classes, took its place. Teams played a five-game schedule against the other classes. Former varsity coaches Jack Haggerty, George Murtaugh, and Pops Sweetman initially served as coaches. There were cheerleaders, including women from the Nursing School, by 1962. But interclass competition proved to be no substitute for rivalries with Fordham or Boston College. By 1957 the athletic moderator reported that students were showing little interest in the intramural version. Players tended to tire of the daily practices the coaches insisted upon.[73] Still, interclass football survived for thirteen years, but student pressure to restore the sport at the intercollegiate level became a formidable force by 1963, when a sophomore, Rory Quirk (1965), led a student petition drive for the resumption of intercollegiate football on a non-scholarship basis. Administrators agreed to allow a single game to be played against another school, following the completion of the intramural season. A team composed of players selected from the four class teams was chosen to play against Frostburg State College at Kehoe Field on November 23, 1963. John F. Kennedy's assassination the day before the scheduled contest forced a cancellation. A year later, Georgetown defeated an old foe from the 1930s, NYU, 28–6, before an on-campus record crowd of eight thousand at Kehoe Field. Quarterback Rory Quirk and fullback John Drury were the stars for the resurrected Hoyas.

In basketball, now the university's major sport, Georgetown teams during the period generally ranged from good to poor. From 1952 to 1956, Harry "Buddy" Jeannette, a former National Basketball Association star, was the coach. During his tenure the Hoyas twice qualified for the New York–based National Invitational Tournament, which at the time was a more prestigious postseason competition than its NCAA counterpart. But Jeannette's overall

Paul Tagliabue scoring against New York University in McDonough, 1962.

(*Ye Domesday Booke*, 1962)

record was a mediocre 50-49. His successors fared even worse: The 1956–57 season was a particular disaster. The following years saw some improvement, with the team of 1959–60 nearly avoiding a losing season at 11-12, with key victories being over Maryland and George Washington. The following year, a Georgetown alumnus, Tommy O'Keefe, who had starred on the teams of the late 1940s, became coach. Paul Tagliabue, the leading rebounder of the previous year, had returned, joined now by Bob Sharpenter, Tom Coleman, and Tom Matan. They finished the year 11-10, with major victories over George Washington, Boston College, and NYU. It marked the first winning season for Georgetown basketball since 1955.

Buoyed by this success, in the fall of 1961 a group of students started the student athletic committee to publicize games and provide cheerleaders (nursing students) and a mascot. The mascot was a bulldog, whose name happened to be Jack, the first of many bulldogs to come. With very high expectations (Tagliabue and Sharpenter were back, plus Vince Wolfington, Ed Lopata, and Jim Cristy), the team began the 1961–62 season with victories over American University and the University of Maryland. During the holidays the team won the Richmond Invitational Tournament, beating the University of Richmond and Virginia Military Academy. Then a string of losses followed in January, and more in February. Still, they finished the season 14-9, the best record since 1953.

The following year, 1962–63, with Christy and Lopata as cocaptains, the team got off to an even better start than the year before, beating Maryland, Boston College, Holy Cross, and American, among others. The high point of the season was the defeat of top-ranked Loyola of Chicago at the Palestra in Philadelphia during a holiday tournament. A series of losses on the road in February ruined any chance for a postseason invitation. The team finished 13-12. In the 1963–64 season, the team sharply improved its record to 15-10. Jim Christy led the way to two victories over Maryland in home and home contests. At Cole Field House, Christy scored 44 points in March against Maryland to break Jim Barry's scoring record. But a disastrous trip north ensured that the team would again sit out the postseason tournaments.

Track was the sport in which Georgetown enjoyed its greatest success in the period from 1952 to 1964. Elmer "Hap" Hardell, who had coached track at Georgetown from 1939 to 1949, returned in 1955 and headed the track and cross-country programs before retiring in 1961. Georgetown's strengths continued to be in the relays and distance running. There was a perennial lack of quality field events participants, which severely limited Georgetown's success in dual meets in the spring.

Hardell's successor, Steve Benedek, had come to Georgetown in 1957 as assistant professor of physical education after being involved in the Hungarian revolution. A national pentathlon champion of Hungary in 1951 and 1952, Benedek had taught track and cross-country at the university level in Hungary before the aborted revolution made him an émigré. In February 1962, John Reilly won the AAU indoor championship in the 1,000-yard at Madison Square Garden. That June, Reilly ran third in the 880-yard run in the AAU outdoor championships in California. The following fall the cross-country team went undefeated (8-0). In February 1963 the 2-mile relay team (Charlie McGovern, Ed Schmitt, Ed Duchini, and Reilly) set a world record with a time of 7:29 at the Mason-Dixon Games in Louisville. The team finished sixth in the IC4A Indoor Championships at Madison Square Garden. That fall the cross-country team went 6-2. The following autumn the cross-country team went undefeated for the second time in three years and capped their success by winning the IC4A championship. Joe Lynch was the top runner.

Four new sports in the era were hockey, polo, lacrosse, and soccer. The first began as a club sport in the winter of 1963–64. Polo also started as a club in 1955. In 1960–61 it gained varsity recognition. In that split season the chuckers, led by Carlos Uhart, José Rodriquez, and Frank Schiffino, beat Pennsylvania, Yale, and Virginia in fall competition, their only loss coming to the national champion Cornell. In the spring Georgetown beat Virginia for a second time but lost again to Cornell. The following fall season, they were undefeated. But again they lost to Cornell in the spring. In the fall of 1963, they finally bested Cornell; by the spring season they were 5-0, which earned them an invitation to the NCAA tournament in New York City. They played Yale, whom they had beaten in the fall, in the semifinals, but this time Yale won by a large margin, 14–6.

Lacrosse returned as a club sport in the spring of 1963. Tom Daley, a law student, was coach for the first game against Villanova. In its second season the club went 3-4, avenging the loss to Villanova by beating them in Philadelphia 10–9. Hopes for a .500 season were dashed when Villanova canceled the rematch at Georgetown.

The soccer team, established in 1952, lost its first contest to Howard, 4–1. It played a regional schedule. Regular opponents were the University of Maryland, Loyola, Mount St. Mary's, Howard, and the University of Virginia. By 1959–60, the team enjoyed two winning seasons with Steve Benedek as coach. In 1963 the team beat Loyola for its best win of the season. Peter Amene and Nik Kamil starred. The team finished 4-4 for the year.

Don Cadle, coach of crew.

(Georgetown University Archives)

Two spring water sports were among the most successful of the university's teams in the early 1960s. Sailing, with ten boats for competition, ranked in the top five in the Middle Atlantic district during the 1962–63 season. Crew, the oldest varsity sport at Georgetown, was revived in 1957. A major development for the crew was the advent of Don Cadle as coach in 1960. Cadle, a former Oxford rower, had previously coached at Yale before coming to Georgetown. Under Cadle the team became a national power by the early 1960s. In his second year, Georgetown went undefeated in regattas before the small college rowing championships in Philadelphia, the Dad Vails, where the crew finished third among twenty-five varsity crews. The following year, 1962, the crew again entered the Dad Vails undefeated. This time proved the charm, as Georgetown won its first Dad Vails championship. In 1963 the Hoyas had lost only one race before heading to Philadelphia for the championships as favorites to repeat. And they came close, losing by one length to Marietta College, whom they had bested in a regatta several weeks earlier. The next year was a different story. Despite a mixed record in regattas and dual races, the varsity heavyweight eight won the Dad Vails for the second time in three years.

Baseball, with Tom Nolan managing, continued to struggle as a nonscholarship sport. In 1959 and 1960 the team managed to win a total of four games while losing twenty-nine. The season of 1963 was a high-water mark for the team. Led by Marty Vickers, Mike Funck, and Bob McCarthy, the team finished 8-7, its first winning season in a decade.

Women began intercollegiate competition in basketball during the 1951–52 season. The team, composed largely of nursing students, played a four-game schedule against local colleges. Kathleen White (1957) of the sailing team was the first Georgetown woman to win a varsity letter. In 1960, basketball, field hockey, and tennis were officially established as intercollegiate sports for Georgetown women. Two years later Nathalie Paramskas was appointed instructor in physical training for women. Paramskas headed the Women's Athletic Association until its merger into the Department of Athletics in 1974.

The University and the Community

Georgetown was one of the prime movers in establishing educational television in the Washington area. Daniel Power, SJ, of the university joined with representatives from George Washington, Howard, and other local institutions to sponsor a series of meetings involving people in regional educational and cultural activities to discuss the prospects for integrating education into the new medium. As a result, the group, with financing from the universities and the public school systems of Montgomery County, Maryland, and Arlington County, Virginia, in 1953 formed the Washington Educational Television Association, with Power as its vice president, and applied for a television license. Channel 26, WETA, began operations in 1956. Frank Heyden gave one of the first experimental teaching programs, a lecture on astronomy.[74]

Edward Bunn was one of the founders of the Consortium of Universities of the Washington Metropolitan Area. This educational corporation grew out of an effort to coordinate and rationalize graduate education in the region. In June 1962 representatives of the five local universities, including Georgetown, established an exploratory committee. Discussion and planning gradually led to a broader mission than just graduate education. When it was finally incorporated in 1967, its charter called for the "improvement of educational, scientific and literary facilities and programs," the availability of courses in the five schools to all undergraduates and graduates of the member institutions, the promotion of joint research, the common establishment of major research and other educational facilities, and the coordination of graduate academic programs, including the elimination of duplicate programs. The five charter members were American, Catholic, George Washington, Georgetown, and Howard.

Georgetown, Integration, and the Civil Rights Struggle

Edward Bunn had been born and grew up in Baltimore, a segregated southern city. Like most southern whites, he was reared in the culture of the Lost Cause. That two great-uncles had died in the service of the Confederacy only strengthened the "mystic chords of memory" that tied him to region and race. As a Jesuit friend wrote, "Doc Bunn freely admitted that he had such [racist] feelings." But, the friend went on, "he did not succumb to these feelings. . . . It was Doc Bunn [who ended segregation at Georgetown]."[75] In fact, the record was more mixed than the friend's recollection.

Edward Bunn headed Georgetown during the years that Washington was becoming the first major city in the nation to have a majority black population (1957) and as the civil rights movement for the full inclusion of blacks within American society reached its apogee.[76] Integration at Georgetown antedated President Bunn. The foreign service, law, and graduate schools had all integrated in the late 1940s and continued to have African Americans on their rolls. During Bunn's twelve-year tenure, two more schools admitted black students, Patricia Brauer to nursing in the fall of 1952 and Harry Thomas Campbell to the college in 1962. Black enrollment in the university in general continued to be minimal, averaging fewer than fifteen into the middle 1960s. The hospital continued to be segregated by race, and the dental clinic would not treat nonwhites. When Brauer attempted to get dental treatment at the clinic in early 1953, she was refused, despite being a student in the university. L. C. McHugh, then regent of the school, wrote letters to Bunn in which he urged him to right the injustice that had been done to Brauer. After the second letter, the president assured the regent that he would have the dean of the Dental School, Dr. Rault, institute a new policy that would allow nonwhite students to get treatment at the clinic. Several weeks later McHugh asked Bunn what had come of the new policy. The president responded that he had "discussed the matter" with the dean "about ten days ago" and asked him to study what arrangements could be worked out. "Nothing has been done yet," a frustrated McHugh noted in an internal memo still later in the semester. "Doc is in no hurry," he recorded. "My bet is that by the time Rault has worked out a plan, she will not need our services."[77] Indeed, Patricia Brauer apparently dropped out of school after that semester.

The policy of treating black students at the clinic eventually went into effect, but the exclusion of other blacks continued into the 1960s. In 1956 a mother attempted to make an appointment at the clinic for her nine-year-old son. The receptionist at the clinic told her that they did not treat nonwhites and suggested that she take him to Howard. The woman's husband wrote an irate letter to Bunn: "We are Catholics and feel as if we have the right to use facilities owned by the Church without being insulted because God made us brown."[78] Nearly a month later the president informed him in a contradictory manner that the clinic would shortly be closing for the summer and could accept no further patients at this time, but gratuitously added that the clinic had such a backlog that the waiting time was running up to two years, besides mentioning that the policy of the school was to "accept non-white patients who are associated with the School or the faculty."[79] Two years later the clinic rejected another black Catholic, a government worker, on the grounds that it only treated Georgetown students. Since the rejectee's superintendent was a client of the clinic, she knew this to be false. "I called my pastor," she wrote Father Bunn, "and he was shocked to know that a Catholic dental school refused Catholic patronage."[80] The reply was nearly identical to that which the complainant two years earlier had received, but added, "Since . . . the dental clinic is a purely private clinic, receiving no public support, the authorities reserve the right to accept or not accept patients at their discretion. Students are naturally given priority, since dental care is included in the student health program."[81]

Racism became an issue touching the faculty as well. Charles Callan Tansill was, during his dozen years in the history department at Georgetown, not only the university's most prolific scholar (as an author of fourteen books) but its most controversial. The diminutive, mustachioed, Texas-born Tansill had reputedly been dismissed from American University in 1937 for his outspoken defense of Adolf Hitler and his Nazi regime. A decade later he charged that Abraham Lincoln had deliberately "tricked" the South into starting the

Civil War. In 1952, in *Back Door to War: The Roosevelt Foreign Policy, 1933–1941*, he argued that Franklin Roosevelt secretly led the nation into war to save Great Britain by maneuvering Japan into attacking the United States. Three years later, in a talk to the Defenders of State Sovereignty and Individual Liberty in Arlington, Virginia, Tansill, himself a division commander of the Sons of the Confederacy, denounced the *Brown v. Board of Education* decision of the Supreme Court for "using [integration] as a pretext to invade states' rights." According to an eyewitness, he went on to predict that integrated schools would lower educational standards and that claims about the equal intelligence of blacks and whites were "sheer bunk."

The outcry over Tansill's remarks was instantaneous. An African American Catholic physician wrote President Bunn that "it is unbelievable that a great institution like Georgetown would condone the beliefs of bigotry" and urged that stern measures be taken against Tansill.[82] The president told the Arlington paper that Tansill's alleged remarks were "contrary to the policy and teaching of Georgetown University."[83] Later, a Washington newspaper quoted Tansill as advising the southern states to "defend themselves with the state militias" against the enforcement of *Brown*.[84] The following spring the graduate dean, John Daley, SJ, informed Tansill that the university had decided to invoke its retirement policy in his case (the historian was then sixty-five) and offered him emeritus status for 1956–57 with full pay. When Tansill protested that he knew that retirement was not automatic at sixty-five in cases where the university wanted to retain a professor and warned that they could not replace him in the field of diplomatic history, Bunn told him that his regular appointment would expire at the end of the academic year.[85] His emeritus status continued until 1958.

In 1961 Laurian Cardinal Rugambwa of Tanganyika became the first African or person of African ancestry to receive an honorary degree from the university. At the reception afterward for the cardinal, Bunn introduced individually to the cardinal the black staff members, all of whom had been invited to the event.[86]

Under the title "Stop the World—We Want to Get Off!" the *Hoya* editors in the early fall of 1962 reflected on President Kennedy's dispatch of federal troops to Mississippi to enforce integration at the university there. They admitted that Georgetown students "to a man, either support or accept as inevitable the fact of integration." But, they went on, "if integration is to work forever, it must gain popular support." Laws, they implied, should not be enforced on a local people against their will. In the centenary of the Civil War, the editors felt a kinship with those students who had left Georgetown in 1861 out of their conviction about states' rights. "The recent situation in Mississippi," they thought, "is practically analogous; and perhaps our decisions should be also analogous. . . . [W]e cannot afford to be cowed by executive orders, bands of federal troops, and . . . incomplete presidential logic."[87]

On February 12, 1963, three Georgetown students, one of them black, were refused service in an Arlington, Virginia, diner. A day later, they returned, with a dozen other students, and again attempted to get served. Within five minutes, local police arrested them. The student personnel office at Georgetown issued a statement that the individuals had been acting on their own, not as representatives of the university. Two months later, as discussed in the last chapter, a junior faculty member of the English department, Francis E. Kearns, in the pages of the Catholic journal of opinion, *Commonweal,* criticized the Georgetown community in general—administration, faculty, and students—for the "casual indifference" with which they had reacted to the sit-in and for their failure to give moral support to these witnesses for racial justice.[88] Prodded by Kearns's indictment, the college student council passed unanimously a resolution of support for integration, commendation for the students who participated in the sit-in, and criticism of the administration for its "equivocal" press release.[89]

In late August 1963, two alumni, working on campus as teaching assistants for the Peace Corps program, appealed in vain to several top administrators, including President Bunn, to have the university sponsor a Georgetown delegation to the March on Washington, which Dr. Martin Luther King Jr. was leading. The administration, consistent with the position it had taken the previous February, did not wish to be identified with the civil rights movement. Any delegation of Georgetown-connected people would be marching on their own. So David Hartnett and Paul Mattingly put up signs across campus, advertising the march, and on Wednesday, August 28, about fifty to seventy-five marchers, made up primarily of Peace Corps trainees along with some other students and Jesuit scholastics, proceeded out of Healy gate at noon and made their way on foot along the two-mile route to meet up with the other quarter-million marchers at the Lincoln Memorial.[90]

Student initiative eventually pulled the university into the movement's orbit. That November the student council and the Washington Club, in an effort to broaden understanding of the civil rights movement, sponsored a Washington intercollegiate workshop in the Hall of Nations on the topic "Can Integration Come too Fast?" Spokespersons for the Congress for Racial Equality (CORE), the Urban League, and the National Association for the Advancement of Colored People (NAACP) responded to questions posed by students from George Washington, Georgetown, Howard, and Trinity. A month later about ninety students marched from the main campus to Capitol Hill to petition for the civil rights bill. On the Hill, they joined about three hundred other students from Howard, Trinity, and American to lobby their representatives. The following April the university hosted a prayer meeting in McDonough for the pending civil rights legislation in Congress. Despite the foul weather and threats of violence, more than six thousand packed the gymnasium for the event, which came off peacefully.[91] In January of the next year, Georgetown provided housing for the biracial Mississippi Democratic Freedom delegation when they came to Washington to contest the seating of the five Mississippi congressmen who had won offices in an election virtually closed to blacks. The university had, however reluctantly, indeed come a long way from Patricia Brauer's experience with the dental clinic.

Its support of civil rights, however, proved all too vulnerable to challenge. In the spring of 1964, the director of nursing service, a Sister of Saint Joseph, sent a notice to the hospital's nurses that the American Nursing Association was looking for nurses to be available in the Senate gallery as the civil rights bill was being filibustered by southern senators. Sister Francesca informed those nurses who supported the bill and could volunteer their time that they would be permitted to do so. That occasioned a letter from Congressman Joel Broyhill of Virginia, protesting the use of what he deemed economic pressure to compel employees to support a political position of those in authority. He warned that such action might well imperil the federal funds that the hospital was receiving (funds that Broyhill had been instrumental in procuring), if it appeared that they were being used "to promote political activities." The hospital director, Charles Shields, replied to Broyhill that Sister Francesca's notice had not been intended to "establish policy in the area of civil rights for our Hospital" and that he had instructed her to remove the notices.[92] Shields's expedient action satisfied Broyhill, and the congressman continued to be one of the university's best channels for securing federal assistance on the Hill.

Georgetown, Political Washington, and the Cold War

At a banquet held at the Mayflower Hotel in November 1952 to honor his Golden Jubilee as a Jesuit, Edmund Walsh in his prepared remarks to the large gathering recalled the day forty years earlier when Chief Justice White had spoken at the dedication of the John Carroll statue. White, Walsh remembered, had talked about the synergistic relationship between university and government, that the fate of each in truth hung upon the other and that each had to serve the other. In that mutual dependence, Walsh went on, the present threat of Communism posed the greatest challenge ever to both the academy and the state; like it or not, they were both "cast into that epoch" in which the Russian Revolution had been transformed into "a Messianic drive for world domination."[93] Walsh suffered a massive stroke at the conclusion of that speech and until his death four years later was a shell of himself. His days as a major voice of the anti-Communist crusade were past. But the university that Walsh had played a major part in shaping during the first half of the twentieth century continued its role of service to the nation, not least in aiding the government in the ongoing Cold War.

One of the ways in which Edmund Walsh saw that Georgetown could very practically assist the nation in the Cold War was to train individuals for positions in a military government that the United States might well need to establish in countries that might be occupied as a result of war, much as it had found it necessary to set up military governments in Germany and Japan after World War II. Any future war with the Soviet Union and/or its satellites would be an ideological conflict in which the goal would inevitably be the destruction of the enemy's government. Into that vacuum the United States would need to implant a military government as the first step toward reconstruction of the civil society. In 1948 he had arranged for Charles Kraus, a colonel in the United States Army whom Walsh had met in Germany, to teach in the School of Foreign Service a group of courses involving the principles and processes involved in the formation of government in an alien environment. Later, when the government made the decision to establish military government reserve units at selected universities in the country, Kraus, at Vice President McGrath's urging, had applied to the government for authorization to establish a military government reserve unit at Georgetown.

In April 1951, the Judge Advocate's Office approved the formation of a reserve unit at Georgetown for one hundred students chosen from the college and the School of Foreign Service.[94] Georgetown was one of three schools to be chosen in February 1951 to prepare officers for top positions in any future military government that was projected to have jurisdiction over as many as 20 million people. Georgetown, the army felt, was uniquely qualified for such a program, given its medical school, hospital, School of Foreign Service, and strength in political science, area studies, and international law.[95] The 352nd Military Government Area Reserve Unit was inaugurated at Georgetown in 1951.

The army intended the unit to be the nucleus for a much larger program involving the training of a minimum of six hundred military personnel on campus for military government, should "M-day" (presumably actual war with the Soviets) ever arrive. At that point, the program would encompass much of the campus and a large portion of the faculty.[96] As it turned out, Georgetown was the only institution of higher education to have a type A military government headquarters reserve unit.[97]

At the request, and with the support, of the federal government, the university, through the Institute of Languages and Linguistics, developed language training programs in two countries critical to U.S. interests in the Cold War. The Yugoslavian training program grew out of the recommendation of a Yugoslav air force officer who had studied English at the institute. The Yugoslav government in turn sought the State Department's assistance in 1952 to establish a program at Georgetown for teaching English to Yugoslav technicians. Subsequently, in the fall of 1952, the Institute of Languages and Linguistics agreed to train Yugoslavs in the methods and techniques of the institute, as well as teaching them English. But Dostert convinced the U.S. government officials that it would be far more economical to send a small team of English teachers, with language laboratory equipment, to the Balkan country itself as a form of assistance to this breakaway from the Soviet

Union.[98] The program began in the fall of 1952 at the Universities of Belgrade and Zagreb; by 1954 it had expanded to six university sites in Yugoslavia.[99]

The establishment of the Yugoslav project in 1952 led the Turkish government to request that the United States sponsor a similar project in its country. In December 1953 the institute signed a contract with the Office of International Economic Cooperation (OIEC) to provide a staff and establish a formal training program at Ankara, which became the Georgetown English Language Program (GELP). In announcing the program, the university made clear its Cold War connection. The technical knowledge and linguistic ability the trainees would receive, the Georgetown News Service reported, "will strengthen Turkish defenses against Communist aggression."[100] The program, with a faculty of seven, began in Ankara in 1953 to train high school and university faculty in teaching English. At the conclusion of their training in Ankara, some of the participants came to Georgetown for further training in teaching methodologies and linguistics. In the fall of 1955 the first group of Turks arrived at Georgetown, a pattern that continued into the 1960s. At the height of the program, three hundred Turkish teachers were being trained in a year.[101] GELP also developed a series of textbooks for the teaching of English in Turkish high schools. A third activity was a literacy program for Turkish soldiers in reading Turkish, which reportedly enabled more than a half-million Turks to become literate.[102] The program continued until 1965.

The Cold War provided a catalyst for the establishment within the university of two think tanks, one very short lived and one that proved long lasting, devoted to strategic and geopolitical studies. The short-lived one was the Ethnic Institute, which was the outgrowth of a research project for a congressional select committee on Communist aggression in 1954. In June, Wisconsin congressman Charles Kersten, chair of the committee, had asked the university to help organize and present their reports on Communist aggression. Georgetown eventually agreed to provide both academic and technical assistance to the committee. With financing by the Central Intelligence Agency (CIA) and the Committee for Free Europe, the project began in September 1954 in offices in White-Gravenor. Fourteen experts on Eastern and Central Europe were engaged to review and summarize the material that the Committee for Free Europe had collected. Historian Tibor Kerekes was operational director of the project, with James Atkinson, Roman Debicki, Lev Dobriansky, Jan Karski, Olgerd Sherbowitz-Wetzor, Cyril Toumanoff, and Walter Wilkinson as faculty assistants. In January 1955 Kerekes proposed that Georgetown establish an Ethnic Institute for research projects not only for the select committee but for other branches of the government as well as for private groups.[103] The university approved the proposal, and the institute began sometime during the 1955–56 academic year. By 1961 the university considered the institute a financial burden, although it was receiving just under $10,000 a year. However, the institute had failed to generate significant outside support. Kersten had been defeated for reelection in 1954, and his select committee was terminated. Kerekes had retired from the faculty although he was still the director. The board of directors voted to close the institute as of June 1962.[104]

The Center for Strategic Studies was another product of the Cold War. Indeed, the original proposed title for the institute was the Research Center for National Survival. Its founding grew out of discussions among William Baroody, head of the American Enterprise Institute (AEI); David Abshire, who had earned a PhD in government at Georgetown and was then the director of special projects at the AEI; retired admiral Arleigh Burke; and James Horigan, SJ, who had been Abshire's mentor at Georgetown. The four shared the view that a tunnel vision in which military force, especially nuclear weapons, dominated the field of focus was blinkering American strategic thinking. They wanted to establish a center where the political, social, and economic forces could be weighed as closely as the military forces in shaping strategy.[105] In the fall of 1961, Horigan brought the proposal for the center before the Georgetown board of directors. It was to be a research organization, patterned after the Institute for Strategic Studies in London, concerned with the study of foreign affairs, particularly those affecting the interests of the United States. It would be self-financing. The university would only be responsible for certain overhead costs. In return, the center would generate a number of fellowships for graduate students and significant remuneration for ordinary Georgetown faculty who participated in the center's projects and programs. The board agreed to establish the center under the university's aegis, and the Georgetown Center for Strategic Studies opened in September 1962 in a university-owned townhouse on 36th Street.[106] Burke was the first director; Abshire was the executive secretary; and Richard Allen, later Ronald Reagan's national security adviser, was the first professional staff member.

Early on, a number of Georgetown faculty were actively engaged at the center in working groups that addressed strategic issues in various parts of the world, notably Karl Cerny, William O'Brien, and Eleanor Lansing Dulles (the sister of John Foster Dulles) of the government department; Henry Briefs of the economics department; and Jules Davids and Hisham Sharabi of the history department. The center also periodically hosted conferences on international issues. The first one, held at Georgetown in the Hall of Nations in January 1963, might possibly have been the most important, with the participants, who included Henry Kissinger, Herman Kahn, Edward Teller, Stefan Possony, James Schlesinger, and Murray Weidenbaum, underscoring in differing ways the underlying rationale of the center: the connections between economic issues and strategy. The center later in the year published the papers and discussions of the conference under the title *National Security: Political, Military and Economic Strategies in the Decade Ahead.* It served to provide the center's research agenda for the rest of the 1960s.[107]

At the departmental level, Georgetown developed several classified research projects for the army and defense agencies in the 1950s. The chemistry department had a contract with the Chemical Warfare Service to do research in chemical weapons. Two large research projects involving a staff of more than sixty persons were funded by the army: the Geography Survey, begun in 1948, and the Economic Survey, starting in 1951.[108] Through the two projects, the dean of the Graduate School reported in 1953, "we have established excellent relations with the Army authorities, rendering a necessary patriotic service, producing highly commendable work, and gaining prestige thereby." In addition, the Army Transportation Corps, impressed by the work produced at Georgetown in the Geography Survey, had commissioned a secret exploration on the Greenland ice cap, which a Georgetown team had carried out in the summer of 1952.[109]

Hans Weigert, the Department of Government research professor who directed the Economic Survey (apparently an intelligence investigation of the political economy of the Soviet Union and its satellites), sensitive to criticism that such government projects were a threat to the independent nature of academic research, admitted that it was not easy to assess the impact of the project upon the university but thought it was positive to the extent that it had made possible a new and valuable research activity for the Graduate School; that its annual budget in excess of $140,000 meant a net income of some $40,000 for the school; that it provided money and valuable research experience, in the field of psychological warfare among others, for some of the school's outstanding graduate students; and that it generated immense goodwill on the army's part that might well translate into important government-sponsored projects in any future national emergency.[110] Indeed, the major general of the army who oversaw the project wrote to the graduate dean in May 1953 that "by your splendid work you are contributing substantially to the National Defense effort. . . . Our association with your great institution has been of inestimable value in the carrying out of our intelligence mission, and I sincerely hope that this association will continue for many years."[111]

In fact, it continued for the rest of the decade. The Geography Survey (later known as the Transportation Research Project) had an even larger budget of $190,000, which produced income of $70,000 for the school. In 1956 the Economic Survey completed its intelligence studies of the Soviet Union and its satellites and received a new contract from the Office of Special Warfare for the Department of the Army, which covered the Asian Communist areas. This led to an enlargement of the staff, with academics brought in with specializations on China.

Lev E. Dobriansky, associate professor of economics, was particularly active among the faculty in anti-Soviet activity. As president of the Ukrainian Congress Committee of America, he was a frequent testifier before congressional committees about the plight of the "captive nations" in Eastern Europe under Soviet domination. He was a contributor to publications by both the House Un-American Activities Committee as well as the House Select Committee on Communist Aggression.

In 1953, he made a plea before the House Committee on Foreign Affairs to have it support a resolution that he had helped frame that called for the establishment of diplomatic relations with the Soviet republics of Ukraine and Belarussia, if only as part of a strategy of assuring the anti-Communist people in those two nations of the United States's willingness to assist them in their struggle against Communist imperialism.[112] Earlier in that year, he had proposed that Georgetown establish a Center for Space Studies, with funding from the federal government and/or the Ford Foundation. The university, he asserted, was an ideal place for such a center, the "logical development of Georgetown's long-term interest in geopolitics," as the conquest of space by the United States would enable it to establish in space a station or satellite, armed with nuclear weapons, that would serve as a modern "portable Gibraltar commanding the world" and "almost guarantee the end of Soviet aggression." It would, he estimated, cost some $10 billion to bring about, but that was far cheaper than the containment policy ("Operation Rathole," he called it) that the United States had already thrown $100 billion into, with sickening results. "Here," he pronounced, "is the road map of the future—indeed world domination and Western survival—perched in a space platform that we had best be the first to build."[113] Dobriansky's Doctor Strangelove-ish plea garnered no support from university officials or anyone else in a position to make it happen.

The threat of internal subversion by Communists or leftist sympathizers became a prominent issue for anti-Communist forces during the Cold War. University professors were considered particularly dangerous sources of subversion, and a concerted campaign against faculty who had been Communists or were suspected of being so led to a new purge of leftist professors at institutions of higher education across the country. In 1952, Senator Pat McCarran, chair of the Senate's Judiciary Committee on Internal Security, claimed (without noticeable evidence) that the Communist Party in the United States could count on the active support "of at least 3,500 professors—many of them as dues-paying members, many others as fellow travelers, some as out-and-out espionage agents."[114] Despite the AAUP's position that the Communist Party was a legal political body in the United States, and hence affiliation of any sort with it was not cause for expulsion from an academic institution, in practice many universities fired or forced out professors who were Communists, were suspected of being members of the party, or had refused to confirm that they were or were not in testimony before Congress or other political bodies. When Senator Joseph McCarthy announced his intention to begin his own probe of the professorate at the beginning of 1953, Presidents Lloyd Marvin of George Washington and Hurst Anderson of American both voiced their concern about the threat to academic freedom such an investigation implied. Edward Bunn, on the contrary, welcomed it. It was good, he observed, to have the opportunity to show the public "the caliber and quality of your instruction."[115]

McCarthy's investigation never reached Georgetown, but within the next year the university did its own policing of at least one suspect faculty member. In the spring of 1954, a student in the Institute of Languages and Linguistics informed a Georgetown Jesuit that the institute was employing two faculty, George L. Trager and Moukhtar Ani, who had been dismissed from the State Department because they were considered security risks. Upon investigation, Georgetown officials found out that Trager, a professor of Chinese, had already testified before the McCarran committee, that he had admitted that he been "been associated with Communists for a period of years during the Thirties," but had denied under oath that he was now a Communist. On the strength of that admission, administrators in the Institute of Languages and Linguistics ruled his classes off-limits to their students, ensuring that Trager would have virtually no one in his classes for the 1953–54 academic year. The board of directors then decided to ask for his resignation. It made no judgment, it noted, about "his association with Communists," but his lack of students prevented the university from appointing him as full professor, as the university had originally intended to do after he served two years as visiting professor. Trager subsequently resigned, clearly forced out because of his Communist past. Ani's contract was also apparently not renewed.[116]

However, there proved to be distinct limits that the administration placed upon any anti-Communist activism of its students. When Hungarians, many of them students, attempted in the fall of 1956 a peaceful revolution against their Communist government that ultimately turned violent and brought a brutally crushing response from Soviet troops called in to quell the uprising, Georgetown students, like most of the rest of the Western world, misreading the internal Hungarian struggle between differing Communist factions as a revolt of anti-Communists against Soviet domination, were stirred to take action in sympathy with their Hungarian counterparts. The student council of the School of Foreign Service passed a resolution, fifty-four to four, for Georgetown students, in league with students from other local schools, to parade down Pennsylvania Avenue to the White House, where they would demonstrate in protest of the Eisenhower administration's failure, despite its earlier promise to "liberate the captive nations" and roll back Communism, to come to the aid of the revolutionaries in Eastern Europe.

"This is a dangerous situation," Stephen X. Winters, SJ, special assistant to President Bunn, wrote him on October 30, 1956. "There is to be a meeting on Campus tonight . . . of various area universities." Most of the top administrators, Winters told him, opposed the idea of the march out of fear that it would lead to disturbances and "bring opprobrium on the University."[117] President Bunn forbade Georgetown students from participating in the demonstration and urged them instead to set aside November 1 and 2, All Saints and All Souls days, as a special time of prayer for the Hungarian students, including those who had died during the uprising.[118]

Prayer prevailed over protest, but at least some student leaders at Georgetown felt that force was the only logical response to the growing horror that Hungarians were experiencing. "Today," the *Hoya* in a hyperbolic editorial in mid-November told its readers, "we see before us what is slowly amounting to the greatest act of genocide ever perpetrated upon any nation. . . . The issue seems to be clearly joined: Can we sit back and watch a nation die, or are we prepared to accept the only alternative open to us, namely total war?" The decision had to be made, the editors concluded, and Georgetown's students should use their small influence to make the right choice happen.[119]

In 1958 the Philodemic Society wished to invite debaters from Moscow University to participate in their Cherry Blossom Debate Tournament, whose topic was to be "That the Future Development of Nuclear Weapons Should Be Prohibited by International Agreement." The board of directors refused to allow the invitation to any students in Communist countries on the grounds that they likely would not be authentic students, but older men who would by age and experience have an unfair advantage over Georgetown or other American college students and who would hardly have the academic freedom to speak openly. Ironically, the directors also worried that the topic itself might disturb the State Department, and the United States government in general.[120] Four years later the dean of the College of Arts and Sciences, acting on the understanding that it was general university policy, refused to allow the International Relations Club to invite any speakers from Communist countries.[121]

In late October 1962, a sudden crisis atmosphere swept the nation and campus when President Kennedy warned the nation in a televised address that Russia had begun placing nuclear missiles in Cuba and that the United States was imposing with its naval forces a quarantine on any further Russian supply of missiles by sea. For the next week, the school, like the country, lived under the imminent threat of a nuclear apocalypse. "Confessions were continuous for several days" after Kennedy's announcement, the official Jesuit diarist reported.[122] On the second day of the crisis, the *Hoya* ominously noted, "Either our sober threats will have helped to alleviate the obnoxious situation in Cuba or they will have brought it to a logical if horrendous fruition. Whatever the alternative, the crisis has certainly allowed the President and, under his leadership, the country to show its true mettle. If there had been any doubt about our will to sacrifice our comfort, our personal futures, our lives, in the interest of worldwide liberty, there should be no longer."[123]

Outside the White House on Sunday, October 25, a group of seventy-five Georgetown students picketed a student group from the National Student Peace Union protesting the Kennedy administration's quarantine. "We are confident," the Georgetown contingent stated in a flyer announcing the counterprotest, "that the vast majority of students support the position taken by the U.S. government."[124] Finally, after several days of tense standoff at sea, the Soviet vessels turned back, the United States and the Soviet Union reached an informal agreement that removed the Russian missiles from Cuba and U.S. missiles from Turkey, and the crisis passed.

Thirteen months later on a Friday in November the main campus was keenly anticipating the football game scheduled for the next day against Frostburg State University, marking a return to intercollegiate play for Georgetown. As it happened, they had to wait another year for the revival of football at Georgetown. President Kennedy's assassination that day canceled all weekend activities, including the football game. Within an hour of the announcement of the president's death, a mass was offered for Kennedy and the nation in the Quadrangle overflowing with students, faculty, and staff. "An air of gloom & deep sorrow prevailed over the Campus," the Jesuit diarist recorded. An eerily quiet mourning continued through Monday, with classes canceled for the funeral of the president. Father Gerard Campbell, in black vestments, celebrated a Solemn Requiem Mass in McDonough for the Georgetown community; Father Bunn was an invited guest at the Funeral Mass in St. Matthew's Cathedral.

Mass in Dahlgren Quadrangle following the assassination of President Kennedy, 1963. (Georgetown University Archives. Photo by Bob Young.)

Remembrance and Aspirations

For the 175th anniversary of Georgetown, planners decided to commemorate the milestone year, not for three days, as previous anniversaries had been celebrated, but for more than a full year, in order to get the full publicity and recognition that such an occasion warranted. George Dunne, SJ, the assistant to the president for international programs, was named the primary director of the 175th anniversary and was given a budget of $250,000. The celebration officially began in late September 1963, the Feast of the (Jesuit) North American Martyrs, with the Mass of the Holy Spirit, the event that traditionally opened the academic year. Before the beginning of the mass, Pope Pius VI appeared on a giant screen in the gymnasium to extend via Telstar his personal greetings and blessings on Georgetown's celebration to the assembled three thousand students, faculty, and guests.

During the next fifteen months there was a 175th anniversary lecture series, including Barbara Ward; Franz Cardinal Koenig, Leo Cardinal Suenens, and Bernard Cardinal Alfrink, three prelates who had gained renown during the Vatican Council; California governor Edward "Pat" Brown; and Robert M. Hutchins, among others. There were also symposia on "The Relevance of Edmund Burke" and "Poverty in Plenty." For the latter, Dunne secured Michael Harrington, whose book *The Other America* had inspired the symposium, as well as Gunnar Myrdal, the noted Swedish sociologist. The poverty symposium attracted particularly wide interest in Washington. Gaston Hall was filled to capacity throughout the daylong panel presentations. Dunne thought the attention that the conference generated was partly responsible for the Johnson administration's later war on poverty.[125] Papers from the symposia were published by P. J. Kenedy & Sons under those respective titles as part of a Wisdom and Discovery Book series. There were conferences on labor management, business administration, and foreign affairs. For the occasion, Joseph Durkin, SJ, published *Georgetown: The Middle Years, 1840–1900*. A film about the history and character of the university was also produced for the celebration. The National Symphony and the Georgetown Glee Club performed a concerto composed in celebration of Georgetown's anniversary.

Dunne had intended to conclude the anniversary in early December 1964 with a three-day symposium involving some of the world's most distinguished theologians on the subject of "Man and Freedom" and a closing convocation with a speech on freedom by President Kennedy, who would be given an honorary degree by the university. The president had agreed to give the speech. When Kennedy was assassinated, President Johnson agreed to speak in his predecessor's place. Dunne secured Karl Rahner, Hans Küng, and John Courtney Murray as the theologian participants. To Dunne's amazement, interest in the theologians and the topic forced him to reschedule the symposium from the simultaneous translation room of the School of Foreign Service (Rahner was to speak in German) to McDonough Gymna-

President Lyndon Johnson addressing the convocation that closed the 175th year celebration, 1964. (City News Bureau, Washington, DC)

sium and install a giant screen in Gaston Hall that would televise the proceedings to hundreds who could not be accommodated in McDonough. "It must have been," Dunne later reflected, "the largest audience ever to turn out in the United States to listen to theologians."[126]

At the convocation, Eunice Kennedy Shriver, the late president's sister, accepted the posthumous honorary degree in her brother's name. The convocation, attended by several hundred delegates from academic institutions around the world, as well as the various elements of the Georgetown community, was followed by a Solemn High Mass, after which many of the crowd journeyed to the Sheraton for a banquet, which brought the yearlong celebration to a close.[127]

As the *Hoya* commented the following week, the convocation not only brought the anniversary year to an end but also marked the end of an era— the twelve years that Edward Bunn had been president of Georgetown University. The paper tallied the physical accomplishments of this master builder but cautioned that they were secondary to Bunn's paramount achievements as president. "As an educator," they wrote, "he has brought Georgetown from the past and focused her on the future, giving her a spirit and direction that no building can impart. This Anniversary Year has been . . . a monument to Father Bunn as well as to Georgetown."[128]

Chasing a Vision

John Carroll had set out with extremely modest resources to realize the audacious aim of establishing a school that would rank with any to be found in the young Republic. The trio of Irish Americans—Thomas Mulledy, William McSherry, and James Ryder—who led Georgetown during most of the antebellum period adumbrated the idea of making Georgetown the university that it legally was, but it was Patrick Healy in the 1870s who pursued the idea of making Georgetown a university. Healy revived and refined Carroll's vision by giving the institution a radically new sense of itself as a Catholic university that could be a peer to any institution of higher learning in the nation, an ideal that his chief accomplishment, the Healy Building, proclaimed in stone to the capital city it faced. Healy placed the college at the center of the university, while integrating the professional schools within the administration and mission of the institution. Healy's protégé, Joseph Havens Richards, pursued a more developed notion of what constituted a modern university and managed to put in place the beginnings of a community of intellectual specialists and researchers, as well as the facilities to support them and the graduate and professional education that Richards saw at the core of the contemporary academy. Unfortunately, the failure of Richards's immediate successors to share his goal and, more important, the decision of Jesuit regional and general superiors to concentrate their higher education resources on other universities, meant that Georgetown did not make meaningful progress toward becoming a real university during the next two decades.

John Creeden's Greater Georgetown Plan in the aftermath of World War I represented an attempt to develop and consolidate the elements of the university, but it was virtually stillborn, to be revived with more lasting, if limited, results by Coleman Nevils at the end of the 1920s. Only with Hunter Guthrie's ascent to the presidency in the post–World War II era did Georgetown recover the Healy-Richards idea of a Catholic university, but his tenure proved too short to accomplish much of what he saw necessary for Georgetown to make itself a true university. Edward Bunn had the time, the determination, and the means to make that happen.

As several persons commented about the significance of the yearlong celebration of the university's 175th year, the intellectual and cultural substance of the various programs and productions in commemoration of Georgetown's anniversary had set a high image for the university to live up to. That it had come this far, they agreed, was the best testament to what

Bunn had wrought during his dozen years at Georgetown's helm. In the course of his presidency he had acquired sufficient autonomy to distance the university from the higher Jesuit authorities, who too often in the past had acted as an inhibitor of the institution's progress. Others had planned before him, but none had been granted the time that Bunn had been given to implement the plans.

His unprecedented length of tenure had provided him with the ability to provide continuity to realize the physical, financial, and academic development that he set out for the university. He constructed eight buildings and renovated another. He had made fund-raising an institutional part of the university's life and had capitalized on the new federal source of funding to secure support for capital improvements on a scale the university had never before known. He oversaw the professionalization of standards and procedures for faculty. He took vital steps to center within the faculty policymaking at the school and department levels, a change that proved to be particularly beneficial to the emergence of the Law Center as a leader in legal education. With limited resources, he had made significant gains to make faculty salaries more competitive. Under Bunn, there was an emphasis on faculty research on the main campus and on the institutional support to foster it. He had not only unified the institution, making it an actual university rather than a collection of schools, but, more than anyone, given it a vision of what Georgetown could be—the premier Catholic university in the nation—and had begun the movement to fulfill that vision.[129]

Riggs Library served as the main university library from 1890 to 1971. It has been named as one of the ten most beautiful libraries in the world.

APPENDICES

APPENDIX A

Student Enrollments, 1889–1965

ACADEMIC YEAR	COLLEGE	MEDICAL	LAW	DENTAL	NURSING	SFS	SLL	SBA	GRAD
1889–90	83	124	253						
1890–91	85	114	268						
1891–92	105	126	227						
1892–93	110	135	267						58
1893–94	141	125	304						
1894–95	130	82	288						
1895–96	122	86	274						18
1896–97	123	94	308						34
1897–98	106	86	280						41
1898–99	121	104	253						27
1899–1900	142	123	276						25
1900–1901	122	120	288						24
1901–2	92	143	275	29					14
1902–3	92	141	286	27					10
1903–4	84	133	299	18					7
1904–5	87	92	342	28					14
1905–6	77	78	409	24					16
1906–7	110	77	459	23					7
1907–8	101	82	495	14					0
1908–9	109	117	614	54	17				0
1909–10	147	131	730	83	26				0
1910–11	171	159	889	116	33				0
1911–12	189	129	986	125	31				0
1912–13	191	99	1,023	153	44				0
1913–14	194	81	912	145	41				0
1914–15	209	54	924	145					6
1915–16	236	60	851	118					4
1916–17	241	71	690	133					4
1917–18	252	73	781	80					4
1918–19	351	120	1,052	91					0
1919–20	447	172	1,153	114					8

Student Enrollments, 1889–1965 (*continued*)

ACADEMIC YEAR	COLLEGE	MEDICAL	LAW	DENTAL	NURSING	SFS	SLL	SBA	GRAD
1920–21	445		1,079	163		250			10
1921–22	536		1,252			350			
1922–23	536		1,238	156		440			
1923–24	538	292	1,150		44	505			15
1924–25	626		990			558			10
1925–26	712		620			567			14
1926–27	874	344	489	129		572			7
1927–28	1,055	418	573	149		547			12
1928–29	973		453		74	538			12
1929–30	955	519	478	147		485			28
1930–31	962	567	493	208	70	451			29
1931–32	831	598	436	232	78	396			32
1932–33	612	588	461	276	73	373			33
1933–34	526	550	476	225	68	313			67
1934–35	556	507	518	207	93	297			30
1935–36	532	475	787	165	94	404			20
1936–37	578	414	723	125	94	440			28
1937–38	642	368	660	154	86	436			54
1938–39	678	337	650	166	88	492			68
1939–40	690	326	593	165	109	534			128
1940–41	703	308	584	183	80	628			119
1941–42	713	299	533	201	81	623			101
1942–43	652	298	208	198	92	604			87
1943–44	1,055	318	130	206	97	582			53
1944–45	268	368	151	202	151	237			122
1945–46	346	355	206	160	161	326			167
1946–47	1,464	364	766	200	152	1,099			325
1947–48	1,660	369	915	233	121	1,716			468
1948–49	1,731	389	917	278	136	1,753			573
1949–50	1,553	414	919	319	184	1,517			658
1950–51	1,475	431	903	338	213	1,111	259		637
1951–52	1,248	428	808	360	209	893	244		701
1952–53	1,218	440	801	361	212	885	306		691
1953–54	1,190	455	891	368	197	941	367		647
1954–55	1,304	447	949	362	194	992	321		713
1955–56	1,336	442	1,060	367	185	1,155	375		790
1956–57	1,312	424	1,133	382	191	791	355	387	795
1957–58	1,252	407	1,238	359	213	715	385	378	810
1958–59	1,240	404	1,338	356	209	694	380	406	908
1959–60	1,342	396	1,162	339	220	858	504	455	874
1960–61	1,423	398	989	335	217	853	486	504	860
1961–62	1,438	394	980	317	230	935	561	550	864
1962–63	1,500	386	1,097	332	261	970	690	557	998
1963–64	1,531	423	1,160	368	271	916	748	557	1,168
1964–65	1,564	393	1,220	369	327	967	770	567	1,284

APPENDIX B

Presidents of the University, 1888–1964

Joseph Havens Richards, SJ, 1888–98

John D. Whitney, SJ, 1898–1901

Jerome Daugherty, SJ, 1901–5

David Hillhouse Buel, SJ, 1905–8

Joseph J. Himmel, SJ, 1908–12

Alphonsus J. Donlon, SJ, 1912–18

John B. Creeden, SJ, 1918–24

Charles W. Lyons, SJ, 1924–28

W. Coleman Nevils, SJ, 1928–35

Arthur A. O'Leary, SJ, 1935–42

Lawrence C. Gorman, SJ, 1942–49

J. Hunter Guthrie, SJ, 1949–52

Edward B. Bunn, SJ, 1952–64

APPENDIX C

Prefects of Studies/Deans of the College of Arts and Sciences, 1889–1964

Prefects of Studies

Joseph Havens Richards, SJ, 1889–98

James P. Fagan, SJ, 1898–1901

John A. Conway, SJ, 1901–3

W. G. Read Mullan, SJ, 1903–5

Charles Macksey, SJ, 1905–9

John B. Creeden, SJ, 1909–18

Edmund Walsh, SJ, 1918

W. Coleman Nevils, SJ, 1918–22

William T. Tallon, SJ, 1922–24

Louis J. Gallagher, SJ, 1924–26

Robert A. Parsons, SJ, 1926–28

R. Rush Rankin, SJ, 1928–31

Deans

John J. McLaughlin, SJ, 1931–32

Vincent J. Hart, SJ, 1932–33

George F. Strohaver, SJ, 1933–34

John E. Grattan, SJ, 1934–42

Stephen F. McNamee, SJ, 1942–46

Charles L. Coolahan, SJ, 1946–49

Edward G. Jacklin, SJ, 1949–51

Brian A. McGrath, SJ, 1951–57

Joseph A. Sellinger, SJ, 1957–64

APPENDIX D

Deans of the Graduate School, 1900–1967

Henry J. Shandelle, SJ, 1900–1906

Charles Macksey, SJ, 1906–7

Thomas I. Gasson, SJ, 1914–23

John H. Fasy, SJ, 1923–25

Louis J. Gallagher, SJ, 1925–26

Robert A. Parsons, SJ, 1926–27

Arthur A. O'Leary, SJ, 1927–28

R. Rush Rankin, SJ, 1928–31

John J. McLaughlin, SJ, 1931–32

Miles J. O'Mailia, SJ, 1932–34

Frederick W. Sohon, SJ, 1934–36

Aloysius J. Hogan, SJ, 1936–38

Wilfrid Parsons, SJ, 1938–40

Edward C. Phillips, SJ, 1940–42

Hunter Guthrie, SJ, 1942–49

Gerard Yates, SJ, 1949–55

John M. Daley, SJ, 1955–60

James B. Horigan, SJ, 1960–67

APPENDIX E

Deans of the Medical School, 1889–1974

G. Lloyd McGruder, 1889–1901

George M. Kober, 1901–28

John A. Foote, 1929–31

William Gerry Morgan, 1931–35

David V. McCauley, SJ, 1935–46

Paul A. McNally, SJ, 1946–53

Francis M. Forster, 1953–58

Hugh H. Hussey, 1958–63

John C. Rose, 1963–74

APPENDIX F

Deans of the Law School, 1889–1969

Martin Morris, 1889–1900

George E. Hamilton, 1900–1903

Harry M. Clabaugh, 1903–14

George E. Hamilton, 1914–41

Hugh J. Fegan, 1941–55

Paul R. Dean, 1955–69

APPENDIX G

Deans of the Dental School, 1901–66

William N. Cogan, 1901–13

Shirley W. Bowles, 1913–19

Bruce L. Taylor, 1919–22

W. B. Hoofnagle, 1922–26

William N. Cogan, 1926–38

Joseph L. B. Murray, 1938–44

John P. Burke, 1944–50

Clemens V. Rault, 1950–66

APPENDIX H

Superintendents/Principals/Deans of the School of Nursing, 1903–67

Superintendents

Sister Geraldine, OSF, 1903–8

Sister Rodriquez, OSF, 1908–26

Sister Joanilla, OSF, 1926–29

Principals

Sister Mary Euphrasia, OSF, 1929–39

Sister Mechtilda, OSF, 1939–40

Sister Joanilla, OSF, 1940–45

Director of Nursing Education

Anne Mary Murphy, 1945–47

Deans

Sister Agnes Miriam, SCN, 1947–52

Sister Angela Marie, SCN, 1952–58

Sister Kathleen Mary, SCN, 1958–63

Ann Douglas, 1963–67

APPENDIX I

Deans of the School of Foreign Service, 1919–66

Edmund A. Walsh, SJ, 1919–21

Roy S. MacElwee, 1921–23

W. F. Notz, 1923–35

Thomas H. Healy, 1935–43

Edmund A. Walsh, SJ, 1945–50 (*Acting*)

Frank L. Fadner, SJ, 1950–58 (*Acting*)

John F. Parr, 1958–62

William E. Moran Jr., 1962–66

Directors of the Institute of Languages and Linguistics/Deans of the School of Languages and Linguistics, 1949–74

Directors

Leon Dostert, 1949–60

Robert Lado, 1960–62

Deans

Robert Lado, 1962–74

Francis P. Dineen, SJ, 1967–69 (*Acting*)

APPENDIX K

Directors/Deans of the School of Business Administration, 1957–65

Directors

Henry M. Cunningham, 1957–60

Raymond Pelissier, 1960–64

Dean

Joseph S. Sebes, SJ, 1964–65 (*Acting*)

Directors/Deans of the School of Summer and Continuing Education (School of Continuing Education), 1953–67

Director

James F. Dougherty, SJ, 1953–54

Deans

Paul Sullivan, 1954–63

Rocco E. Porreco, 1963–67

Academic Vice President, 1955–67

Academic Vice President

Brian A. McGrath, SJ, 1955–67

Executive Vice Presidents for Medical Center Affairs, 1960–68

Executive Vice Presidents for Medical Center Affairs

William Maloney, SJ, 1960–62

Joseph F. Cohalan, SJ, 1962–63

Mark H. Bauer, SJ, 1963–68

APPENDIX O

Regents of the Law, Medical, Dental, Nursing, Foreign Service, Languages and Linguistics, and Business Schools, 1920–68

Regents of the Law School

Thomas Chetwood, SJ, 1928–30

Francis Lucey, SJ, 1930–61

Brian A. McGrath, 1961–68

Regents of the Medical School

Walter Summers, SJ, 1924–29

John Gipprich, SJ, 1929–34

David V. McCauley, SJ, 1934–46

Paul McNally, SJ, 1946–53

Thomas O'Donnell, SJ, 1953–59

William Maloney, SJ, 1959–62

Regents of the Dental School

Walter Summers, SJ, 1924–29

John Gipprich, SJ, 1929–34

David V. McCauley, SJ, 1934–46

Paul McNalley, SJ, 1946–48

Edward Bunn, SJ, 1948–52

Thomas O'Donnell, SJ, 1953–59

William Maloney, SJ, 1959–62

Regents of the Nursing School

Edward B. Bunn, SJ, 1948–52

William F. Maloney, SJ, 1952–53

Lawrence C. McHugh, SJ, 1953–54

Thomas O'Donnell, SJ, 1956–59

William Maloney, SJ, 1959–62

Regents of the School of Foreign Service

Edmund A. Walsh, SJ, 1920–56

Frank Fadner, SJ, 1956–62

Joseph Sebes, SJ, 1962–66

Regents of the School of Languages and Linguistics

Frank Fadner, SJ, 1962–68

Regents of the Business Schools

Frank Fadner, SJ, 1957–61

Joseph Sebes, SJ, 1961–68

Georgetown University Buildings by Construction Date, 1890–1962

Main Campus

1890	Riggs Library
1893	Dahlgren Chapel of the Sacred Heart
1904	Ryan Hall
1906	Ryan Gymnasium (Ryan Administration Building after 1953)
1926	New North Building
1931	Copley Hall
1933	White-Gravenor Building
1946	Barracks
1946	Annex I and II (razed in 1963 and 1971, respectively)
1947	Poulton Hall
1951	McDonough Gym
1958	Walsh Building
1959	New South Hall
1962	Raymond Reiss Science Building

Medical Center

1893	Medical School wing
1898	Georgetown University Hospital (Old)
1898	Medical Interns' Residence (Ryder Hall after 1949)
1901	Dental Department Building
1904	Hospital addition
1908	Nurses quarters
1908	Hospital addition (Lisner)
1912	Hospital addition (Riggs)
1913	Kober-LeClerc Memorial Wing
1919	Hospital addition (Jung)
1920	Nurses quarters addition
1927	Hospital addition (35th and Prospect streets)
1930	Medical-Dental Building
1944	St. Mary's Hall (Xavier Hall after 1956)
1947	Georgetown University Hospital (New)
1956	Hospital wing
1956	St. Mary's Hall
1959	Gorman Diagnostic Clinic
1959	Kober-Cogan Building

Law Center

1891	Georgetown Law Department Building
1911	Law Department wing

About the Author

Robert Emmett Curran is professor emeritus of history at Georgetown University. He was born in Baltimore, Maryland, and attended the College of Holy Cross, where he received a BA with honors in history. He later received an MA in history from Fordham University before earning a PhD in history from Yale University. In addition to writing numerous journal articles and chapters and reviews, Curran has published three books: *Michael Augustine Corrigan and the Shaping of Conservative Catholicism in America, 1878–1902*; *American Jesuit Spirituality: The Maryland Tradition, 1634–1900*; and *The Bicentennial History of Georgetown University, 1789–1889*. After teaching at Georgetown for more than thirty years, he now lives with his wife, Eileen, in Richmond, Kentucky, where his nonacademic interests include running, playing the banjo, and choral singing.

Notes

CHAPTER 1

1. Joseph Havens Richards, "Address of Welcome to Bishop John J. Keane," Other Colleges Files, box 1, folder CUA 1890–99, GUA.
2. Ibid.
3. C. Joseph Nuesse, *The Catholic University of America: A Centennial History* (Washington, DC: Catholic University of America Press, 1990), 62–70.
4. Joseph Havens Richards to William Doherty, SJ, January 23, 1897, 996–98, Joseph Havens Richards Letterbooks, vol. 12, GUA (hereafter Richards Letterbooks).
5. Martín to Purbrick, Rome, March 28, 1898, Liber Litterarum Generalis (hereafter Liber), Marylandia (hereafter MD), 1886–1900, Archivum Romanum Societatis Jesu (hereafter ARSI).
6. Richards to H. T. B. Tarr, January 11, 1890, 175–78, Richards Letterbooks, vol. 5.
7. Richards to General Lefevre, September 21, 1894, 717–20, Richards Letterbooks, vol. 9.
8. Richards to E. Francis Riggs, November 2, 1888, 24, Richards Letterbooks, vol. 2.
9. *Georgetown College Journal* (hereafter *CJ*) 19 (June 1891); Lawrence Carleton Chamberlain, "Georgetown University Library, 1789–1937," MSLS thesis, Catholic University of America, 1962, 67–72.
10. Richards to Anna Smith, October 24, 1888, 188–91, Richards Letterbooks, vol. 2.
11. *CJ* 25 (April 1897); Richards to J. W. Dunphy, August 26, 1896, 199–200, Richards Letterbooks, vol. 12.
12. Richards to Thomas A. E. Weadeck, October 28, 1893, 734, Richards Letterbooks, vol. 8; Chamberlain, "Georgetown University Library," 85–86.
13. Minutes of the Province Consultors, 1888–1912, November 3, 1891, Maryland Province Archives at Roland Park (hereafter MPARP); Richards to John Gilmary Shea, May 11, 1889, 44–48, Richards Letterbooks, vol. 4; Richards to John Gilmary Shea, August 18, 1891, 230–32, and Richards to John Dahlgren, December 18, 1891, 344–47, Richards Letterbooks, vol. 6; Diary of the Administrator of the Jesuit Community (hereafter House Diary), 1890–93, 505–14, Georgetown University Special Collections (hereafter GUSC).
14. *CJ* 24 (December 1895).
15. *CJ* 23 (October 1894).
16. Visitation of W. O. Pardow, February 7, 1896, Memorials of Provincial Visitations, 1831–1956, Georgetown Jesuit Community Archives.
17. Richards to Thomas Campbell, SJ, May 6, 1889, 82–86, Joseph Havens Richards Letterbooks, vol. 1, Society of Jesus, GUA.
18. The five, all Jesuits, were John Hagen (astronomy), Edward Hoker Welch (philosophy), John Murphy (philosophy), James Dawson (physics), and Cornelius Clifford (rhetoric).

19. Campbell to Richards, New York, May 9, 1889, Richards Papers, box 2, folder 7.
20. Richards to Father Meyer, February 11, 1895, 400–410, Richards Letterbooks, vol. 2, Society of Jesus.
21. Richards to Anderledy, Georgetown, September 1, 1888, MD 12-X-1, ARSI.
22. Richards to John Hagen, SJ, October 17, 1888, 118, Richards Letterbooks, vol. 2, Society of Jesus.
23. Richards to James Doonan, SJ, October 28, 1888, 215, Richards Letterbooks, vol. 2, Society of Jesus.
24. Francis A. Tondorf, SJ, "Fr. John G. Hagen, S.J.," *CJ* 55 (April 1927): 313; J. Stein, SJ, "Johann Georg Hagen, S.J.," *Astronomische Nachrichten,* Band 240, no. 5744. col. 131–36.
25. Richards to William Pardow, March 9, 1894, 253–57, Richards Letterbooks, vol. 2, Society of Jesus.
26. Richards to James Doonan, April 18, 1890, 592–95, Richards Letterbooks, vol. 5.
27. Richards to Francis Barnum, March 1, 1897, 191–93, Richards Letterbooks, vol. 13.
28. Ibid.
29. William F. Rigge, SJ, *Jesuit Astronomy,* part 2, *The Restored Society, 1814–1904* (Northfield, MN: n.p., 1904), 37.
30. J. Marra, SJ to Richards, Pueblo [Co.], August 15, 1895, Richards Papers. For Forstall's service, Richards paid the California Province $600 annually, enough to support the education of two California scholastics.
31. Richards to Shandelle, July 12, 1896, 79–82, Richards Letterbooks, vol. 3, Society of Jesus.
32. "University Notes," *CJ* 22 (December 3, 1893): 51.
33. J. Havens Richards, SJ, "An Explanation in Reply to Some Recent Strictures," *Woodstock Letters* (hereafter *WL*) 26 (1897): 148.
34. Richards to Am. Mandalari, SJ, November 2, 1896, 683, Richards Letterbooks, vol. 12.
35. Chamberlain, "Georgetown University Library," 82.
36. Under Richards, Georgetown discontinued the practice of awarding master's degrees for those graduate alumni who had established themselves in some profession.
37. Minutes, November 9, 1896, Minutes of the Directors, 1797–1989, GUA.
38. Minutes, May 17, 1897, Minutes of the Directors, 1797–1989, GUA.
39. Purbrick to Martín, New York, January 10, 1899, MD 13-I-34, ARSI.
40. Richards to Henry Shandelle, July 12, 1896, 79–82, Richards Letterbooks, vol. 3, Society of Jesus.
41. Martín to Richards, Fiesole, July 20, 1896, Richards Papers.
42. Richards to Patrick Healy, March 6, 1896, 724–26, Richards Letterbooks, vol. 11; Richards to Pardow, August 29, 1896, 92–96, Richards Letterbooks, vol. 3, Society of Jesus.
43. Richards to Cowardine, May 14, 1890, 703–6, Richards Letterbooks, vol. 5.
44. John B. Whitney to Miss Baer, August 22, 1898, John B. Whitney Letterbooks, vol. 1.
45. Patrick Healy to Richards, December 3, 1897, Richards Papers, box 2, folder 2.
46. Frisbee to Meyer, Woodstock, March 23, 1897, MD 12-III-58, ARSI.
47. Martín to Richards, Rome, April 16, 1897, 370–71, Liber, MD, 1886–1900, ARSI; Martín to Pardow, Rome, February 2, 1897, 355, Liber, MD, 1886–90, ARSI.
48. Martín to Pardow, Rome, June 3, 1895, 283–86, Liber, MD, 1886–90, ARSI.
49. Patrick Henry Ahern, *The Catholic University of America, 1887–1896: The Rectorship of John Keane* (Washington, DC: Catholic University of America Press, 1948), 100–103.
50. Richards to Father Provincial, November 24, 1893, 177–82, Richards Letterbooks, vol. 2, Society of Jesus.
51. Father Meyer, March 3, 1894, 247–51, Richards Letterbooks, vol. 2, Society of Jesus.
52. Father Provincial, May 9, 1894, 297–301, Richards Letterbooks, vol. 2, Society of Jesus.

53. Martín to Pardow, Rome, September 5, 1895, 297–98, Liber, MD, 1886–90, ARSI.

54. Minutes, March 17, 1897, Minutes of the Directors, 1797–1989, GUA.

55. Richards, "Explanation in Reply to Some Recent Strictures," 149.

56. Campbell to Anderledy, Georgetown, March 15, 1889, MD 12-XXIV-2, ARSI.

57. Campbell to Anderledy, Georgetown, March 15, 1889, MD 12-XXIV-2, ARSI.

58. Anderledy to Richards, Fiesole, May 20, 1890, Liber, MD, 1886–1900, ARSI.

59. Boursaud to Anderledy, New York, April 28, 1891, MD 12-XXIV-19, ARSI.

60. Campbell to Anderledy, Frederick, June 3, 1890, MD 12-XXIX-18, ARSI.

61. Richards to Anderledy, Georgetown, March 16, 1890, MD 12-XXIV-3, ARSI.

62. Richards to to [?], [1891], MD 12-XXIV-26, ARSI.

63. Richards to Martín, Georgetown, January 12, 1896, MD 12-X-44, ARSI.

64. Purbrick to Martín, New York, March 11, 1899, MD 13-I-36, ARSI.

65. Minutes of the Province Consultors, May 5, 1889, MPARP; Richards to Thomas Campbell, January 12, 1889, 47–49, Richards Letterbooks, vol. 3.

66. Richards to Doonan, August 24, 1889, 460–62, Richards Letterbooks, vol. 4.

67. Campbell to Whitty, New York, June 5, 1891, MD 11-III-8, ARSI; Thomas Hughes to Whitty, New York, June 2, 1891, MD 11-III-6, ARSI; Campbell to Anderledy, New York, August 17, 1891, MD 11-III-12, ARSI; Minutes of the Province Consultors, November 10, 1891, MPARP; Campbell to Anderledy, New York, November 11, 1891, MD 11-III-17; Whitty to Richards, Fiesole, December 30, 1891, Law 1889–91, GUA.

68. *CJ* 19 (October 1890): 8–9.

69. Richards to Rev. S. Henrionet, New Orleans, Louisiana, August 15, 1895, 134, Richards Letterbooks, vol. 11; Richards to P. F. Collier, June 27, 1896, 58–60, Richards Letterbooks, vol. 12. Richards was intent on separating, if not eliminating, the preparatory school, even though a large percentage of students continued to fall into that category.

70. Richards to J. P. Alexander, City, September 2, 1895, 184–85, Richards Letterbooks, vol. 11.

71. Richards to J. W. Coveney, April 11, 1894, 74, Richards Letterbooks, vol. 9.

72. Richards to Frederick S. Leland, October 23, 1888, 187, Richards Letterbooks, vol. 2.

73. By 1890 the terms "freshman," "sophomore," "junior," and "senior" had entered the college's lexicon, at first used interchangeably with the old designations of "first grammar," "poetry," "rhetoric," and "philosophy," and by 1896 had replaced the traditional terms for classes.

74. Richards to Brosnahan, November 9, 1896, 729–31, Richards Letterbooks, vol. 12.

75. *WL* 26 (1897): 153. Richards thought there were more than four hundred Catholic students at Harvard alone. Richards to James A. Conway, April 26, 1897, 443–46, Richards Letterbooks, vol. 13. Jeffrey Wills, in *The Catholics of Harvard Square*, estimates that there were eighty or so Catholic undergraduates at Harvard in the 1890s, but many more Catholics in the law school, the largest in the nation. Wills, ed., *The Catholics of Harvard Square* (Petersham, MA: Saint Bede's, 1993), 77.

76. Austin O'Malley, "Catholic Collegiate Education in the United States," *Catholic World* 67 (1898): 289–304, cited in Kathleen Mahoney, "*Fin-de-Siècle* Catholics: Insiders and Outsiders at Harvard," *U.S. Catholic Historian* 13 (Fall 1995): 19–48.

77. E. L. Keyes to Richards, Newport, July 8, 1889; E. L. Keyes to Richards, New York, July 22, 1889; Edward L. Keyes Jr. to Richards, August 3, [1889], Alumni Files, GUA.

78. Richards to Presidents of Jesuit and Catholic Colleges, April 7, 1897, 399–402, Richards Letterbooks, vol. 13.

79. Richards to Rev. James J. Chittick, February 21, 1896, 684–85, Richards Letterbooks, vol. 11.

80. Eliot to Richards, North-East Harbor, Maine, August 4, 1893, Timothy Brosnahan Papers, box 8, folder 155, GUA. Boston College and Holy Cross were subsequently added to the list as well. Georgetown sent several graduates to the Harvard Law School over the rest of the decade. For the Harvard Law School controversy in

general, see Mahoney, "*Fin-de-Siècle* Catholics," 19–48, as well as her *Catholic Education in Protestant America: The Jesuits and Harvard in the Age of the University* (Baltimore: Johns Hopkins University Press, 2003).

81. Richards to Timothy Brosnahan, March 18, 1898, 750–51, Richards Letterbooks, vol. 14.

82. Richards to Prendergast, July 1890, 889–92, Richards Letterbooks, vol. 5.

83. Richards to Charles E. Gorman, June 11, 1896, 12, Richards Letterbooks, vol. 12.

84. David E. Cannella, "The Philodemic Debating Society: The Pursuit of Eloquence and Truth from 1894 to 1939," in *Swift Potomac's Lovely Daughter: Two Centuries at Georgetown through Students' Eyes,* ed. Joseph Durkin, SJ (Washington, DC: Georgetown University Press, 1990), 123–24.

85. Richards to Jerry [?], April 17, 1894, 180, Richards Letterbooks, vol. 9; Richards to Timothy Brosnahan, SJ, January 3, 1895, 172, Richards Letterbooks, vol. 10; Richards to Honorable Charles E. Gorman, April 11, 1895, 511, Richards Letterbooks, vol. 10.

86. May 2, 1895, House Diary, 550-16, GUA.

87. Richards to Patrick Healy, October 4, 1888, Richards Letterbooks, vol. 2; Agreement between the Medical and Academic departments, cited in George Hamilton and Martín Morris to Richards, July 1, 1891, Richards Papers, GUA.

88. May 15, 1893; March 19, 1894, Medical Faculty Minutes, GUA.

89. January 9, 1894, Medical Faculty Minutes, 1890–96, GUA.

90. Richards to W. O'B. Pardow, SJ, April 11, 1895, 512–15, Richards Letterbooks, vol. 10.

91. Richards to Pardow, October 12, 1895, 487–88, Richards Letterbooks, vol. 2, Society of Jesus. A survey of the students had revealed that nearly one-half of them were attending full time. Richards, "Address at the Opening of Day Classes at the Medical Department of Georgetown University, Monday, September 30, 1895," Medical School Files, GUA.

92. *Washington Post,* October 2, 1900.

93. Richards to Cowardin, May 14, 1890, Richards Letterbooks.

94. Paul Starr, *The Social Transformation of American Medicine* (New York: Basic Books, 1982), 145–48.

95. Comments of Richards in *CJ* 48 (March 1920): n.p.

96. March 11, 1896, Medical Faculty Minutes, GUA.

97. As Paul Starr notes, with the advent in the 1890s both of sophisticated diagnostic tools, especially X rays, and of the sterile conditions that hospitals could best offer, most surgeries began to take place in the hospital rather than the physician's office. Starr, *Social Transformation of American Medicine,* 155–57.

98. April 15, 1896, Medical Faculty Minutes, GUA; Richards to Meyer, May 14, 1896, 55–62, Richards Letterbooks, vol. 3, Society of Jesus.

99. *Annuae Litterae, Collegii Georgiop.,* 1898, 43–44, ARSI.

100. Richards, "Explanation in Reply to Some Recent Strictures," 148.

101. Patricia Barry, *Surgeons at Georgetown: Surgery and Medical Education in the Nation's Capital, 1849–1969* (Franklin, TN: Hillsboro Press, 2001), 85, 112–13.

102. Ibid., 88.

103. *CJ* 56 (April 1928).

104. September 26, 1894, Medical Faculty Minutes, GUA.

105. May 20, 1891, Medical Faculty Minutes, GUA.

106. November 8, 1894, Medical Faculty Minutes, GUA.

107. April 9, 1895, Medical Faculty Minutes, GUA.

108. July 13, 1896; June 5, 1897; September 14, 1899, Medical Faculty Minutes, GUA.

109. October 11, 1892, Medical Faculty Minutes, GUA.

110. Richards to Robert N. Wood, June 13, 1893, Richards Letterbooks, vol. 8.

111. Starr, *Social Transformation of American Medicine,* 17.

112. Richards to Mandalari, January 7, 1890, 150, Richards Letterbooks, vol. 5.

113. Medical School Files, Records of the Association of Medical Students of Georgetown University, 1890–91, GUA.

114. *National Cyclopedia of American Biography* (New York: J. T. White, 1930–), vol. A, 29–30 (hereafter cited as CYC); Lewis J. Amster, "Bailey Ashford: 'Prophet of Tropical Medicine,'" *Hospital Practice*, [April 15, 1985], 139–50.

115. See Robert Stevens, *Law School: Legal Education in America from the 1850s to the 1980s* (Chapel Hill: University of North Carolina, 1982), chap. 5.

116. James Therry, "A Partial History of Georgetown University Law School" (unpublished typescript, n.d.), 19, Law School, GUA.

117. Richards to Pardow, April 5, 1892; and Richards to C.C. Shriver, July 1, 1891, Richards Letterbooks, vol. 6. J. F. Denson was the architect. See *CJ* 19 (February 1891).

118. *CJ* 19 (May 1891).

119. Therry, "Partial History," 29.

120. Richards to Holaind, December 8, 1890, 74–75, Richards Letterbooks, vol. 6.

121. Catalogue, 1896, GUA.

122. Therry, "Partial History," 31.

123. Harvard and Columbia, the two schools larger than Georgetown, both had more than four hundred students by the mid-1890s.

124. By 1902 only twelve of ninety-two law schools in the country were using the case method. Five years later that number had risen to thirty. Stevens, *Law School*, chap. 6.

125. Ibid., 96.

126. Morris to Richards, July 12, 1895, Law School, GUA; Richards to Pardow, May 9, 1897, 203–6, Richards Letterbooks, vol. 3, Society of Jesus. Harvard did not make a three-year program a necessity until 1899. Stevens, *Law School*, 37.

127. *CYC*, 39:581.

128. Richards to Patrick Healy, Washington, October 4, 1888, Richards Letterbooks, vol. 2, 37–38. The debt in 1888 was $94,000. By 1892 it had risen only marginally to $97,500. Richards to Whitley, January 30, 1892, 410–12, Richards Letterbooks, Society of Jesus, vol. 1. That did not include the $48,000 owed on the new law building. Richards to C. C. Shriver, July 1, 1891, 192–95, Richards Letterbooks, vol. 6.

129. September 12, 1894, House Diary, 550-16, GUA.

130. Mrs. Horace R. Kelly, New York, to Richards, September 6, 1893; and Mrs. Horace R. Kelly, New York, to Richards, March 25, 1894, Alumni Files, GUA.

131. February 8, 1898, Medical Faculty Minutes, 1897–1901, GUA.

132. Richards to George Hamilton, May 5, 1897, 525–26, GUA, Richards Letterbooks, vol. 13. Professors in the Law School regularly received $1,000 per year before the reductions, half of what the Columbian School, for instance, was paying.

133. Richards to James Fairfax McLaughlin, January 4, 1898, 603, Richards Letterbooks, vol. 14.

134. Roger Geiger, *To Advance Knowledge: The Growth of American Research Universities, 1900–1940* (New York: Oxford University Press, 1986), 276–77.

135. Richards to H. T. B. Tarr, January 11, 1890, 175–78, Richards Letterbooks, vol. 5.

136. *CJ* 25 (April 1897): 86.

137. Richards to W. G. Eliot, March 21, 1894, 121, Richards Letterbooks, vol. 9.

138. Richards to Henry V. Turner, [March 1889], 595–98, Richards Letterbooks, vol. 3.

139. Richards to Eiling, February 19, 1895, 395–96, Richards Letterbooks, vol. 10; Richards to Thomas Walsh, December 8, 1896, 859–62; and Richards to R. H. Clarke, December 21, 1896, 917–18; and Richards to James A. Grant, November 16, 1897, 365, Richards Letterbooks, vol. 12.

140. Geiger, *To Advance Knowledge*, 49.

141. *CJ* 19 (May 1891): 148.

142. "Donations listed by Fr. Richard," [sic], Los Gatos, Cal., October 18, 1900, Richards Papers, box 2, folder 12, GUA.

143. Richards to Charles B. Kenny, December 10, 1897, 489–91, Richards Letterbooks, vol. 14.

144. Richards to William T. Connolly, January 15, 1895, 207, Richards Letterbooks, vol. 10.
145. Richards to Pardow, August 29, 1896, 92–96, Richards Letterbooks, vol. 3, Society of Jesus.
146. The first one had been a room in the original building. In 1833 a separate floor of the new student center, the South (Mulledy) Building, was set aside as the chapel. Until the 1830s Georgetown students regularly attended Mass and other liturgies at Trinity. With the addition of the South Building chapel, the center of student religious life shifted to campus, if very inconspicuously.
147. July 28–30, 1891, House Diary, 550-16, GUA; Richards to Thomas Campbell, November 22, 1891, 378–79; and Richards to Whitley, January 30, 1892, 402–12, Richards Letterbooks, vol. 1, Society of Jesus.
148. Richards to Whitley, January 30, 1892, 402–12, Richards Letterbooks, vol. 1, Society of Jesus.
149. *CJ* 22 (October 1893).
150. Richards to Mrs. Mary J. McDermott, June 12, 1896, 17, Richards Letterbooks, vol. 12; June 5, 8, 13, 1896, House Diary, 550-16, GUA.
151. Mary Mitchell, *Chronicles of Georgetown Life, 1865–1900* (Cabin John, MD: Seven Locks Press, 1986), 92–93.
152. Richards to George E. Hamilton, November 2, 1890, 55, Richards Letterbooks, vol. 6.
153. Richards to Secretary of Agriculture, November 5, 1895, 416, Richards Letterbooks, vol. 11.
154. Richards to Doonan, April 18, 1890, 592–95, Richards Letterbooks, vol. 5.
155. May 28, 1894, Minutes of the Directors, 1797–1989, GUA; Richards to Commissioners of the District of Columbia, August 13, 1894, 504, Richards Letterbooks, vol. 9.
156. October 22, 1894, Minutes of the Rector's Consultations, 531-1, GUA (hereafter cited as Consultors' Minutes); June 22, 1895, Minutes of the Directors, 1797–1989, GUA; August 5, 1895, Consultors' Minutes, 531-1, GUA; August 5, 1895, Minutes of the Directors, 1797–1989, GUA; August 5–6, 1895, House Diary, 550-16, GUA.
157. *Washington Evening Star,* February 25, 1898, sec. 2, p. 4.
158. February 25–26, 1898, House Diary, 550-16, GUA.
159. March 1, 1898, House Diary, 550-16, GUA.
160. Richards to Meyer, February 11, 1895, 402; and Richards to Pardow, February 19, 1895, 414–16, Richards Letterbooks, vol. 2, Society of Jesus.
161. *WL* 53 (1924): 269.
162. Richards to Pardow, August 29, 1896, 95–96, Richards Letterbooks, vol. 3, Society of Jesus.
163. Purbrick to Martín, New York, January 9, 1898, MD 13-I-6, ARSI.
164. March 22–24, 26, April 12, May 22–23, 25, 1898, House Diary, 550-16, GUA.
165. *Annuae Litterae, Collegii Georgiop.,* 1898, 43–44, ARSI. Richards, then forty-six years old, spent the next decade serving as a spiritual counselor at Boston College and the novitiate in Frederick. By 1909 his health had improved to the point that he could return to administration in secondary and higher education in New York City and Buffalo, respectively. He died at Holy Cross College in 1923.

CHAPTER 2

1. "Father John Dunning Whitney," *WL* 47 (1918): 88–93.
2. Purbrick to Martín, New York, January 10, 1899, MD 13-I-34, ARSI.
3. Martín to Whitney, Rome, May 22, 1900, Whitney Papers, box 2, folder 6.
4. Whitney to J. Havens Richards, March 11, 1901, 277, Whitney Letterbooks, vol. 2.
5. Martín to Purbrick, May 9, 1900, Liber, MD, 1886–1900, ARSI.
6. Gannon to Martín, New York, August 6, 1906, MD 13-II-40, ARSI.
7. Court of Appeals of the District of Columbia, no. 48367, MD 13-XIII-14, ARSI.

8. Sydney Mudd to Buel, Washington, April 27, 1906, David Hillhouse Buel Papers, GUA.

9. Hanselman to Wernz, June 26, 1908, MD 14-II-2, ARSI.

10. Hanselman to Wernz, June 26, 1908, MD 14-II-2, ARSI.

11. Wernz to Hanselmnan, Rome, July 12, 1908, Liber, MD, 1900–1911, ARSI. Four years later Buel left the Society of Jesus and married. He taught at various New England preparatory schools before becoming an Episcopal priest in 1922. He died a year later. *New York Times*, January 22–23, 1913; May 26, 1922; May 24, 1923.

12. August 28, 1908, Minutes of the Directors, 1797–1989, GUA.

13. "Reverend Joseph Himmel, S.J.," n.d., Joseph Himmel Papers, 169-1, GUA.

14. "Father Joseph J. Himmel, S.J.," Himmel Papers, 169-1.

15. Richards to Himmel, New York, January 21, 1910, Himmel Papers, 169-2.

16. Himmel to Wernz, Washington, July 17, 1910, MD 15-X-8b, ARSI.

17. Hanselman to Wernz, New York, November 7, 1911, MD 14-V-35, ARSI; Wernz to Hanselman, Rome, December 28, 1911, Liber, MD, V, ARSI.

18. "Father Alphonsus J. Donlon," *WL* 55 (1926): 449.

19. Donlon to Maas, Washington, March 21, 1914, MD 16-XII-11, ARSI.

20. Whitney to John J. Creeden, SJ, October 6, 1900, 895, Whitney Letterbooks, vol. 1.

21. Whitney to Commissioner of Education, San Juan, Porto Rico [*sic*], September 15, 1900, Whitney Letterbooks, vol. 1.

22. *CJ* 43 (October 1914): 52.

23. June 23, 1905, House Diary, 550-17, GUA; November 6, 1905, Consultors' Minutes, 1896–1907, 531-1, GUA.

24. *Annuae Litterae, Collegii Georgiop.,* 1904, ARSI 1503.

25. Wernz to Hanselman, Rome, March 8, 1908, 243, Liber, MD, 1900–1911, ARSI.

26. "The Regents of the University and Our colleges," *WL* 25 (1896): 133, cited in Miguel Anselmo Bernad, SJ, "The Faculty of Arts in the Jesuit Colleges in the Eastern Part of the United States: Theory and Practice" (diss., Yale University, 1951), 316.

27. Philip Gleason, *Contending with Modernity: Catholic Higher Education in the Twentieth Century* (New York: Oxford University Press, 1995), 32–36. The New England Association for Colleges and Secondary Schools had been established in 1885; the Middle Atlantic Association formed in 1892.

28. "Schedula Nova, College Course," [1900], MD 13-III-4, ARSI.

29. Martín to Gannon, Rome, April 25, 1905, Liber, MD, 1900–1911, ARSI.

30. Hanselman to Buel, New York, January 1, 1908, Buel Papers, 159-3, GUA.

31. *Schedule of Studies for the Colleges of the Maryland–New York Province, 1910, accompanied by explanatory remarks and letter of Rev. Father Provincial,* cited in Bernad, "Faculty of Arts," 370–78.

32. For a study of this development, see Jon H. Roberts and James Turner, *The Sacred and the Secular University* (Princeton, NJ: Princeton University Press, 2000), chap. 6.

33. John B. Brough, "Philosophy at Georgetown University," in *Georgetown at Two Hundred: Faculty Reflections on the University's Future,* ed. William C. McFadden (Washington, DC: Georgetown University Press, 1990), 116–17. Kathleen Mahoney argues that this reform of 1910 proved unworkable in fitting the *Ratio* to the new academic order that had emerged in American higher education, and by the 1920s, Jesuit colleges, by their adoption of standard methods for measuring curricular fulfillment, by the introduction of majors, and by the elimination of Greek as a requirement for the AB degree, had effectively abandoned the coherent curriculum the *Ratio* had called for in order to conform to American academic conditions. It seems to me that, while admitting the special place that the classics and philosophy continued to hold in Jesuit higher education, she misses the new role of philosophy as the basic provider of coherence within the revised Jesuit educational schema. See Mahoney, *Catholic Education in Protestant America,* 235–37.

34. Creeden to Herman Walmesley, Washington, November 4, 1913, MD 16-I-30, ARSI.

35. Donlon to Wernz, Washington, October 1914, MD 16-XII-10, ARSI.

36. Donlon to Wernz, Washington, November 3, 1913, MD 16-XII-6, ARSI.

37. Meeting of Provincials, April 23–24, 1913, MD 16-I-10, ARSI; Wernz to Maas, Rome, November 24, 1913, 128–29; and Wernz to Maas, Rome, January 20, 1914, 136, Liber, MD, V.

38. Donlon to Vicar-General, Washington, October 1914, MD 16-XII-10, ARSI.

39. Vicar General to Maas, Rome, January 29, 1915, Liber, MD, V, ARSI.

40. Donlon to Ledochowski, Washington, October 29, 1915, MD 16-XII-14, ARSI.

41. Gannon to Martín, New York, December 10, 1905, MD 13-II-88, ARSI.

42. Buel to Martín, Washington, May 5, 1907, MD 13-X-3, ARSI.

43. Wernz to Maas, Rome, June 28, 1914, Epistolae, ARSI.

44. Mahoney, *Catholic Higher Education in America*, 215.

45. *CJ* 44 (November 1915): 125.

46. David L. Waldron, "Immigration," *CJ* 40 (October 1911): 6–11.

47. *CJ* 44 (November 1915): 126.

48. *CJ* 39 (October 1910): 39–40.

49. *CJ* 44 (November 1915): 78.

50. *CJ* 46 (December 1917): 184.

51. *CJ* 42 (March 1914): 329.

52. *CJ* 31 (May 1903): 408–9.

53. Martín to Whitney, Rome, November 22, 1898, Whitney Papers, box 2, folder 6.

54. Purbrick to Martín, New York, January 10, 1899, MD 13-I-34, ARSI.

55. Gannon to Daugherty, New York, September 12, 1901, Graduate School Files, box 1, folder 1901–27, GUA.

56. Fagan to Martín, New York, September 8, 1902, MD 13-III-9, ARSI.

57. January 19, 1907, Consultors' Minutes, 1896–1907, 531-1, GUA.

58. May 12, 1907, Consultors' Minutes, 1896–1907, 531-1, GUA.

59. Wernz to John Wynne, Mondragone, August 12, 1907, *Responsa*, MD, 1900–1911, ARSI.

60. Hanselman to Wernz, New York, July 20, 1910, MD 14-IV-17, ARSI.

61. Agustin Udias and William Stauder, "Jesuit Geophysical Observatories," *Eos, Transactions, American Geophysical Union* 72 (April 16, 1991): 188.

62. *WL* 54 (1925): 109.

63. *CJ* 47 (November 1918): 86.

64. *CJ* 41 (May 15, 1913): 570.

65. *CJ* 47 (October 1918): 44.

66. Stevens, *Law School*, 96.

67. October 15, 1905, Consultors' Minutes, 531-1, GUA.

68. Therry, "Partial History," 15–16; Hanselman to Wernz, New York, March 21, 1912, MD 14-VI-5, ARSI.

69. Dan Ernst et al., *The First One Hundred and Twenty-five Years: An Illustrated History of the Georgetown University Law Center* (Washington, DC: Georgetown University Law Center, 1995), 54–56.

70. *CJ* 39 (May 1911): 408–9; *CJ* 45 (October 1916): 31; *CJ* 45 (November 1916): 85–86; *CJ* 45 (December 1916): 149.

71. Cited in Ernst et al., *First One Hundred and Twenty-five Years*, 37–39.

72. George Kober to David H. Buel, SJ, Washington, October 17, 1905, Medical School Files, GUA.

73. May 28, 1900, Medical Faculty Minutes, GUA.

74. His books included *Essentials of Materia Medica and Therapeutics* (1910), *Safeguarding Children's Nerves* (with James J. Walsh, 1924), *Diseases of the New-Born* (1925), and *Diseases of Bones and Joints in Childhood* (1926). Michael E. Lynott to Whitney, August 10, 1900, Faculty File, GUA; *National Cyclopedia of American Biography,* 39:249–50.

75. March 12, 1908, Medical Faculty Minutes, GUA.

76. April 11, 1912, Medical Faculty Minutes, GUA.

77. George Rosen, "From Frontier Surgeon to Industrial Hygienist: The Strange Career of George M. Kober," *American Journal of Preventive Health* 65 (June 1975): 638–43.
78. *New York Times,* April 25, 1931.
79. Barry, *Surgeons at Georgetown,* 73.
80. *Washington Star,* March 13, 1936; December 20, 1933.
81. February 11, 1904, Medical Faculty Minutes, GUA.
82. March 10, 1908, Minutes of the Directors, 1797–1989, GUA; April 9, 1908, Medical Faculty Minutes, GUA; *Annuae Litterae, Collegeii Georgiop.* 1908, ARSI 1503, 49–50.
83. June 7, 1911, Medical Faculty Minutes, GUA; Himmel to Wernz, Washington, April 17, 1911, MD 15-X-10, ARSI.
84. Donlon to Wernz, Washington, July 23, 1912, MD 15-X-13, ARSI.
85. Kober quoted in Barry, *Surgeons at Georgetown,* 70.
86. John F. Stapleton, *Upward Journey: The Story of Internal Medicine at Georgetown, 1851–1981* (Washington, DC: Georgetown University Printing and Graphics Department, 1996), 42.
87. February 6, 1905, Medical Faculty Minutes, GUA.
88. Ibid.
89. November 11, 1909, Medical Faculty Minutes, GUA.
90. See October 8, 1908, Medical Faculty Minutes, GUA, urging faculty to send patients to Georgetown hospital rather than elsewhere.
91. William G. Rothstein, *American Medical Schools and the Practice of Medicine: A History* (New York: Oxford University Press, 1987), 144.
92. November 8, 1906, Medical Faculty Minutes, GUA.
93. Donlon to Wernz, Washington, July 23, 1912, MD 15-X-13, ARSI.
94. Abraham Flexner, *Medical Education in the United States and Canada: A Report to the Carnegie Foundation for the Advancement of Teaching* (New York: Carnegie Foundation for the Advancement of Teaching, 1910), 203.
95. Starr, *Social Transformation of American Medicine,* 117–21; Barry, *Surgeons at Georgetown,* 78.
96. Barry, *Surgeons at Georgetown,* 80.
97. March 10, 1912, Medical Faculty, Minutes GUA.
98. Murray Galt Motter, professor of physiology, to the faculty of the Medical School, March 14, 1903, Medical School Files, GUA.
99. April 14, 1910, Medical Faculty Minutes, GUA.
100. May 12, 1910, Medical Faculty Minutes, GUA.
101. June 15, 1910, Medical Faculty Minutes, GUA.
102. Donlon to Wernz, Washington, January 18, 1913, MD 16-XII-3, ARSI.
103. October 8, 1914, Medical Faculty Minutes, GUA.
104. September 20, 1911, Medical Faculty Minutes, GUA.
105. October 12, 1911, Medical Faculty Minutes, GUA.
106. December 14, 1911, Medical Faculty Minutes, GUA. That same month the AMA's Council for Medical Education recommended the same minimum standard of full-time faculty, which all but guaranteed that other states would follow New York's lead. Barry, *Surgeons at Georgetown,* 79.
107. N. P. Colwell, to George Kober, July 19, 1912, Medical School Files, GUA.
108. N. P. Colwell to George M. Kober, August 5, 1912, Medical School Files, GUA.
109. Kober to Colwell, August 14, 1912, Medical School Files, GUA.
110. Colwell to Kober, September 5, 1912, Medical School Files, GUA.
111. Inspection, November 15, 1912, Medical School Files, GUA.
112. *By-Laws of the Medical Faculty of Georgetown University* (Washington, DC, 1912), Medical School Files, GUA.
113. Stapleton, *Upward Journey,* 42.
114. Richards to Dr. W. W. Evans, January 6, 1891, 87, Richards Letterbooks, vol. 6.
115. Richards to W. W. Evans, December 18, 1896, 903, Richards Letterbooks, vol. 12; February 1, 1897, Consultors' Minutes, 531-1, GUA; Richards to W. W. Evans, February 4, 1897, 53, GUA, Richards Letterbooks, vol. 13; March 17, 1897,

Minutes of the Directors, 1797–1989, GUA; Richards to Provincial [Purbrick], September 23, 1897, 305–7, Richards Letterbooks, vol. 3, Society of Jesus; Purbrick to Richards, New York, September 28, 1897, Dental School Files, 1897–1905, GUA; October 4, 1897, Consultors' Minutes, 531-1, GUA.

116. April 11, May 7, 1901, Medical Faculty Minutes, GUA.

117. Whitney to G. L. Magruder, April 26, 1901, 368; and Whitney to Joseph Tabor Johnson, May 12, 1901, 398–99, Whitney Letterbooks, vol. 2; May 13, 1901, Medical Faculty Minutes, GUA; M. J. Cobert [of Hamilton and Colbert] to Daugherty, July 24, 1901, Jerome Daugherty Papers, GUA; Articles of Agreement, entered into this third day of August, A.D., 1901, between W. N. Coogan, C. E. E. Ferguson, Jesse Ramsburgh, M. Griffith and Edwin R. Hodge, all of the City of Washington, District of Columbia, . . . and the President and Directors of Georgetown College, Dental School Files, 1891–1905, GUA.

118. Special Meeting of the Medical Faculty, July 5, 1901, Dental School Files, 1897–1905, GUA; December 14, 1901, Medical Faculty Minutes, GUA.

119. Judith F. Giuliani, "History of the Georgetown University Dental School" (unpublished manuscript, 1990), 3.

120. Report of Tabulation Committee, National Association of Dental Examiners, Dental School Files, 1906–21, GUA.

121. Kober to Rector, June 18, 1903, Dental School Files, 1897–1905, GUA.

122. February 20, May 21, and September 12, 1908, Minutes of the Regular Faculty Meeting, Dental Faculty Minutes, Dental School Files, GUA.

123. Giuliani, "History of the Georgetown University Dental School," 6; September 23, 1907, Minutes of the Directors, GUA.

124. August 26, 1913, Minutes of a Special Faculty Meeting; and Minutes of the Regular Faculty Meeting, April 15, 1915; May 21, and October 19, 1916, Dental Faculty Minutes, Dental School Files, GUA.

125. December 21, 1916, Minutes of the Regular Faculty Meeting, Dental Faculty Minutes, Dental School Files, GUA.

126. June 13, 1906, House Diary, 550-18, GUA.

127. Memorandum of Edward Devitt, SJ, Georgetown, November 16, 1905, Executive Vice President for Financial Affairs, folder 202, 56N7, GUA.

128. Financial statements of Georgetown College, D.C., 1898–1918, Executive Vice President for Financial Affairs, GUA. Representative endowments at small, prestigious colleges in the East during the second decade of the century were $1 million at Swarthmore, $800,000 at Bucknell, and $550,000 at Franklin and Marshall. W. Bruce Leslie, *Gentlemen and Scholars: College and Community in the "Age of the University," 1865–1917* (University Park: Pennsylvania State University Press, 1992), 244.

129. Anthony Maas to Ledochowski, New York, September 20, 1915, MD 16-XII-13, ARSI.

130. Alumni Advisory Committee Files, 272-5, GUA.

131. June 1, 4, November 20, 1907; March 10, 1908, Minutes of the Directors, 1797–1989, GUA; June 4, 1908, House Diary, 550-18, GUA; Clarence E. Fitzpatrick to Buel, Boston, March 3, 1908; Clarence E. Fitzpatrick to Buel, May 8, 1908; Clarence E. Fitzpatrick to Buel, June 8, 1908; Fitzpatrick to Himmel, Boston, November 5, 1908, Alumni Advisory Committee Files, 272-5, GUA.

132. Anthony Maas to Wernz, New York, November 30, 1913, MD 16-I-31, ARSI; November 17, 1913, Consultors' Minutes, 531-1, GUA; February 28, 1914 Minutes of the Directors, 1797–1989, GUA; [Board of Regents' By-Laws], H-1, MPARP.

133. *CJ* 40 (May 1912): n.p.

134. Donlon to Wernz, Washington, July 23, 1912, MD 15-X-73, ARSI.

135. June 13–16, 1914, House Diary, 550-19, GUA.

CHAPTER 3

1. *CJ* 47 (January 1919): 210–14.
2. *CJ* 43 (February 1915): 296–97.
3. *CJ* 44 (November 1915): 126.
4. For the academy's rabid response to the call to arms, see Carol S. Gruber, *Mars and Minerva: World War I and the Uses of the Higher Learning in America* (Baton Rouge: Louisiana State University Press, 1975), 81–102.
5. April 18, 1917, House Diary, 550-19, GUA.
6. April 19, 1917, House Diary, 550-19, GUA.
7. *CJ* 45 (April 1917): 427.
8. Shandelle to Himmel, Georgetown, [May 10,] 1917, Himmel Papers, folder 169-03.
9. Donlon to Ledochowski, Washington, April 30, 1917, MD 16-XII-22, ARSI.
10. *CJ* 46 (November 1917): 134; *CJ* 46 (February 1918): 345–46; *WL* 46, no. 2 (1917): 400.
11. *WL* 47, no. 1 (1918): 117; *CJ* 46 (December 1917): 179.
12. Lynn D. Gordon, *Gender and Higher Education in the Progressive Era* (New Haven, CT, 1990), 81–82, cited in John R. Thelin, *A History of American Higher Education* (Baltimore: Johns Hopkins University Press, 2004), 199.
13. *CJ* 46 (December 1917): 179–80.
14. Stapleton, *Upward Journey,* 44.
15. Donlon to Provincial, Washington, November 27, 1917, H-1, MPARP.
16. Provincial to Donlon, Baltimore, November 1917, H-1, MPARP.
17. Gruber, *Mars and Minerva,* 99, citing the quote in Parke R. Kolbe, *The Colleges in War Time and After* (New York, 1919), 27.
18. January 4, 1917, Medical Faculty Minutes, GUA.
19. April 12, 1917, Medical Faculty Minutes, GUA.
20. George Tully Vaughan, *Papers on Surgery and Other Subjects,* 387–88, cited in Barry, *Surgeons at Georgetown,* 174.
21. Barry, *Surgeons at Georgetown,* 175.
22. April 6, 14, 1917, Minutes of a Special Faculty Meeting, Dental School Files, GUA.
23. *Hoya,* February 26, 1920.
24. In the late spring of 1917, for instance, a mathematics professor was called to the War Department to assist in designing a fair system of drafting through a lottery in order to avoid the widespread criticism that had greeted the last draft during the Civil War. The professor provided a simple but equitable method that the department adopted. *WL* 47, no. 1 (1918): 122.
25. Curtis G. Breant to Anthony J. Maas, Washington, January 10, 1918, Alphonsus J. Donlon Papers, 159-5, GUA.
26. December 9, 1917, House Diary, 550-19, GUA; *WL* 47, no. 1 (1918): 119.
27. *WL* 47, no. 2 (1918): 254.
28. Gruber, *Mars and Minerva,* 163.
29. "Report of Committee on Academic Freedom in Wartime," February–March 1918, *AAUP Bulletin,* 34–35, cited in Gruber, *Mars and Minerva,* 167.
30. Cited in Gruber, *Mars and Minerva,* 206.
31. *New York Times,* April 19, 1918, sec. 6, p. 4.
32. *United States Reports, 247, October Term, 1917. Cases Adjudged in the Supreme Court at October Term, 1917* (New York, 1918), 3–7, cited in Therry, "Partial History," 52.
33. May 13, 18, 1918, Minutes of the Executive Committee; and Hugh Fegan to George Hamilton, July 1, 1918, Law 1912–19, GUA.
34. Donlon to Ledochowski, Washington, February 22, 1918, MD 16-XII-26, ARSI.
35. *CJ* 46 (February 1918): 345–46.
36. "Georgetown and the War," *CJ* 47 (October 1918): 53.
37. Ibid., 52.
38. "Georgetown and the War," *CJ* 47 (December 1918): 154.
39. Maj. Gen. J. T. Dickman, USA, to Chief of Staff, GH/Q, Am.E.F., December 28, 1918, Alumni Files, 390.12, GUA.

40. "Georgetown and the War," *CJ* 47 (January 1919): 215.

41. "Georgetown and the War," *CJ* 47 (November 1918): 99.

42. Jonathan Frankel, "The Ivory Boot Camp," *Harvard Magazine* 94 (September–October 1991), 71–74, cited in Thelin, *History of American Higher Education,* 200.

43. Varia 62-11, GUA.

44. *WL* 48, no. 1 (1919): 114.

45. *CJ* 47 (October 1918): 37.

46. Old Archives, "1915–1918," College Files, GUA.

47. *CJ* 47 (October 1918): 31–33.

48. "Dad Said Go," in *On the Hilltop: Reflections and Reminiscences by Georgetown Alumni* (Washington, DC: Georgetown University Press, 1966), 35.

49. *WL* 47, no. 3 (1918): 403.

50. Gina Kolata, *Flu: The Story of the Great Influenza Pandemic of 1918 and the Search for the Virus That Caused It* (New York: Farrar, Straus and Giroux, 1999), 6–7.

51. In Washington, DC, more than 70 percent of naval personnel were stricken. A. A. Hoehling, *The Great Epidemic* (Boston: Little, Brown, 1961), 90.

52. October 10, 1918, House Diary, 550-19, GUA.

53. Statement of Lt. Francis M. Munson, USN, "Influenza at Georgetown University during the Pandemic of 1918," House Diary, 550-19, GUA.

54. *CJ* 47 (June 1919): 505.

55. "Cohonguroton (River of Swans)" was understood to be the Indian name for the Potomac. *CJ* 47 (June 1919): 482.

56. Donlon to Ledochowski, Washington, July 11, 1918, MD 16-XII-23, ARSI.

57. "Opening Address of Rev. John B. Creeden, S.J.," *CJ* 47 (June 1919): 517.

58. Gleason, *Contending with Modernity,* 46–56.

59. Donlon to Provincial, n.d., H-1, MPARP.

60. Georgetown educators also attributed the poor quality of their preparatory students to the integrated structure. "Parents now want a separate school for their boys and one removed from the City, so we are not getting the best class of students," Donlon explained to the superior general in 1916. Donlon to Ledochowski, Washington, [January 1916], MD 16-XII-15, ARSI.

61. Whitney to Joseph H. McGuire, June 15, 1901, 461–62; and Whitney to M. F. Morris, June 22, 1901, 482, Whitney Letterbook, vol. 2, GUA.

62. October 14, 1912, Consultors' Minutes, 531-1, GUA. One additional reason that impelled Georgetown authorities to act was the fear that the Catholic University was about to sponsor a prep school within the city, thereby competing with Georgetown for funds to support it. Donlon to Wernz, Washington, January 18, 1913, MD 16-XII-3, ARSI.

63. William S. Abell, *Fifty Years at Garrett Park, 1919–1969: A History of the New Georgetown Preparatory School* (Garrett Park, MD: Georgetown Preparatory School, 1970), 14–16.

64. May 2, 1916, Consultors' Minutes, 531-1, GUA. The total cost of the building was $230,000. Besides the benefaction of $80,000 from Walters, the university raised nearly $100,000. It finally transferred $47,000 from hospital funds to meet the balance of the costs of the new school. March 13, 1917, Consultors' Minutes, 531-1, GUA; Donlon to Ledochowski, Washington, July 11, 1917, MD 16-XII-23, ARSI.

65. Abell, *Fifty Years at Garrett Park,* 17.

66. Rockwell to "Father Rector," New York, December 14, 1918, John Creeden Papers, 159-5, GUA.

67. *CJ* 47 (June 1919): 517–18.

68. *CJ* 47 (March 1919): 320.

69. Donlon to Wernz, Washington [April 1913], MD 16-XII-4, ARSI; April 30, 1913, Consultors' Minutes, 531-1, GUA.

70. Creeden to Rockwell, n.d. [but likely December 1918], H-1, MPARP.

71. Constantine E. McGuire to Richard Tierney, SJ, May 16, 1918, School of Foreign Service (hereafter SFS), 1918–31, GUA; J. de S. Coutinho, "In the Halls of George-

town University: Some Events in the School of Foreign Service, 1919–1960," n.d., Frank Fadner Papers, GUSC.

72. Memorandum on a School for the Diplomatic and Consular Service, unidentified material, SFS, 1918–31, GUA.

73. Coutinho Memoirs, Fadner Papers, GUA.

74. Draft of a circular by the Provisional Committee for the Organization of the Georgetown University School of Foreign Service, n.d., unidentified material, SFS, 1919–31, GUA.

75. Coutinho memoirs, Fadner Papers.

76. Address delivered at Annual Convention of American Manufactures Export Association, Waldorf-Astoria Hotel, October 17, 1919, Edmund Walsh Papers, GUSC.

77. *Catholic Standard* (May 17, 1919).

78. *CJ* 49 (October 1920): 33.

79. Coutinho memoirs, Fadner Papers.

80. Creeden to Rockwell, Washington, July 28, 1919, H-1, MPARP; Seth Tillman, *Georgetown's School of Foreign Service: The First Seventy-five Years* (Washington, DC: Edmund A. Walsh School of Foreign Service, 1994), 4–5; *CJ* 49 (October 1920): 33.

81. Creeden to Rockwell, Washington, January 25, 1919, H-1, MPARP; *WL* 48, no. 1 (1919): 114.

82. Tillman, *Georgetown's School of Foreign Service,* 10.

83. "The Georgetown University Plan of Education for Foreign Trade," *CJ* 49 (March 1921): 288–92.

84. *CJ* 49 (June 1921): 488. Seventeen of the eighteen graduates also took the examinations for trade commissioner. Fifteen passed.

85. "Widening the Sphere," *CJ* 53 (April 1925): 356.

86. Edmund Walsh, "Welcoming Address at Honorary Degree Ceremony for the Minister of Foreign Relations of Venezuela," *CJ* 49 (May 1921): 380–82.

87. Tillman, *Georgetown's School of Foreign Service,* 13.

88. Walsh published two geopolitical works, *Total Power* (1948) and *Total Empire* (1951).

89. Christopher J. Lucas, *American Higher Education: A History* (New York: St. Martin's Press, 1994), 204.

90. Creeden to General, [1921], copy, Creeden Papers, folder 454-6.

91. Coleman Nevils Papers, box 11, folder 109, GUA.

92. "Needs of Georgetown University," [1922], Dental School Files, 1897–1905.

93. May 25, 1923, Minutes of the Directors, 1797–1989, GUA.

94. February 3, 1926, Minutes of the Directors, GUA; December 3, 1928, Consultors' Minutes, 531-1, GUA.

95. *Hoya,* February 19, 1920.

96. October 27, November 21, 1919, Consultors' Minutes, 531-1, GUA.

97. "Georgetown Endowment Association," [1922], folder 203, item 56R6, MPA.

98. April 10, 1919, Medical Faculty Minutes, GUA.

99. Creeden to Superior General, n.d., copy, Creeden Papers, folder 454-6.

100. Creeden to Lawrence Kelly, Washington, April 4, 1924, MPARP. Ernest LaPlace was the regent who proposed that the university gradually centralize all of its schools.

101. Circular, n.d., MPARP.

102. Paul Venable Turner, *Campus: An American Planning Tradition* (Cambridge, MA: MIT Press, 1984), 215–40.

103. *CJ* 52 (October 1923): 24.

104. "Georgetown University: The School of Medicine, The School of Dental Surgery, The Hospital [1921]," Medical School Files, GUA.

105. Memorandum from the Executive Committee of the Georgetown Endowment Association, n.d., Dental School Files, 1897–1925, GUA.

106. Creeden to Ledochowski, [1923], folder 454-6, Creeden Papers.

107. Creeden to Ledochowski, n.d., copy, folder 454-6, Creeden Papers.

108. April 17, 1924, Consultors' Minutes, 531-1, GUA.

109. His dean, Robert Parsons, found his three-hour workday and his ignorance about matters related to the university appalling. "The university is very badly in need of money and there doesn't seem to be much constructive thought about the means of obtaining it. . . . Perhaps much more could be done for the university if the Rev. Rector would do more work." Robert A. Parsons to Provincial, Washington, December 31, 1927, H-1, MPARP.
110. June 8, 1924, Minutes of the Board of Regents, 272-6, GUA.
111. November 17, 1924, Consultors' Minutes, 531-1, GUA. The total cost for the construction of the building was $341,453.
112. *CJ* 55 (November 1926): 46.
113. Georgetown's three chief Jesuit competitors in the area—Fordham, Holy Cross, and Boston College—also experienced sharp increases in enrollment during the period, but they all tended to draw much more heavily from the upper working and lower-middle classes.
114. December 10, 1926, Minutes of the Directors, 1797–1989, GUA.
115. *WL* 50 (1921): 240.
116. Folder 454-6, Creeden Papers, n.d.
117. *Hoya,* September 30, 1920.
118. Joseph Rockwell to Creeden, New York, September 14, 1920, folder 454-6, Creeden Papers.
119. April 21, 1923, Consultors' Minutes, 531-1, GUA.
120. Creeden to General, [1921], folder 454-6, Creeden Papers.
121. *CJ* 49 (October 1920): 27–28.
122. January 28, 31, 1922, House Diary, 550-20, GUA.
123. *Library Associates Newsletter,* 1990, GUA.
124. March 13, 1925; December 13, 1928, House Diary, 550-20, GUA; Lyons to Provincial, Washington, March 12, 1925, H-1, MPARP.
125. The ABA's Root Committee on Legal Education in 1920 had concluded that among the prerequisites for a recognized law school were two years of college education for admission and a four-year program of study for evening schools, such as Georgetown. The following year the ABA approved both requirements as part of its recommended standards for law schools. Stevens, *Law School.*
126. Joseph F. Hanselman, SJ, to Creeden, Rome, June 7, 1921, folder 413-6, Creeden Papers.
127. June 3, 12, 19, 1920, Consultors' Minutes, 531-1, GUA; June 19, 1920, Minutes of the Directors, 1797–1989, GUA; "Georgetown University—School of Law Constitution," Law School Files, GUA.
128. September 8, 1920, Minutes of the Directors, 1797–1989, GUA. Supposedly the board of regents was concerned about rationalizing and integrating, under the university, the administrative structure of all the schools, in light of the growth of individual schools and the creation of a new one (SFS), but it is significant that only the Law School was reorganized.
129. *On the Hilltop,* 70–71.
130. Fagan to Hamilton, July 1, 1920, Law School Files, 1912–19, GUA.
131. Creeden was also attempting to move the school toward a goal of gradually eliminating part-time faculty. Since the faculty to this point consisted entirely of part-time staff, Creeden saw little movement toward reaching the goal beyond the core faculty created for the day division. Meeting of Executive Faculty, December 17, 1920, Law School Files, 1920, GUA.
132. Resolution adopted by Board at meeting of July 1, 1921, copy, Law School Files, GUA; Therry, "Partial History," IV, 12.
133. Ernst et al., *First One Hundred and Twenty-five Years,* 83.
134. Therry, "Partial History," IV, 18–19.
135. George E. Hamilton to Father John B. Creeden, SJ, September 29, 1921, cited in Therry, "Partial History," IV, 21.
136. Memoranda Re: Law School, Law School Files, 1923–24, GUA.
137. *Hoya,* June 7, 1926.

138. Therry, "Partial History," IV, 18.

139. Creeden to Ledochowski, n.d., copy, folder 454-6, Creeden Papers.

140. Indeed, according to President Lyons in a response to a Vatican questionnaire in 1917, the university had adopted and "is applying its policy of substituting Catholics for non-Catholics." Questionnaire, March 1927, Charles W. Lyons Papers, GUA.

141. Secretary [Fegan] to Hamilton, July 1, 1921, Law School Files, 1920–21, 111-3; Fegan to Hamilton, July 1, 1929, Law School Files, 1928–31.

142. The chair had been established at $75,000, with $60,000 raised by alumni and $15,000 raised from faculty members. *Hoya,* June 1, 1923; Hamilton to Frank D. Cronin, Washington, October 27, 1926, Law School Files, 1925–28; Therry, "Partial History," IV, 20.

143. September 18, 1919, Medical Faculty Minutes, GUA.

144. Circa Creeden, "Recollections of A.J. Bouwhuis, S.J," November 29, 1962, 413–16, 187-12, Creeden Papers.

145. Barry, *Surgeons at Georgetown,* 181.

146. Clarence J. Schwikhardt, "Did You Have Tondy for Physiology?" *On the Hilltop,* 140.

147. Kober to Lyons, Washington, May 19, 1925, H-1, MPARP.

148. W. G. Summers to Kelly, Washington, July 6, 1926; and W. G. Summers to Kelly, Washington, July 15, 1926, H-1, MPARP.

149. Petitio ad A.R.P. Generalem Mittenda pro Extensione Nosocomii Georgiopolitani in Urbe Washington, July 31, 1926, H-1, MPARP.

150. *Hoya,* October 14, 1926; Pamela Ginsbach, "A History of the Georgetown University Medical School" (unpublished manuscript), 4, 17.

151. June 3, 1920, Consultors' Minutes, 531-1, GUA.

152. March 20, 1920, Consultors' Minutes, 531-1, GUA.

153. Barry, *Surgeons at Georgetown,* 183–85.

154. April 18, May 16, 1918; and February 19, 1920, Minutes of the Regular Meeting of the Faculty, Dental Faculty Minutes, Dental School Files, GUA.

155. George B. Ellis to John Creeden, Washington, January 6, 1922, Creeden Papers.

156. Albert L. Midgley, to Ellis, May 13, 1924, Dental School Files, 1922–26, GUA.

157. Giuliani, "History of the Georgetown University Dental School."

158. Of forty-one dental schools rated, twenty-six were placed in the A category; thirteen, including Georgetown, in the B; and two in the C. Georgetown was the only one of six Jesuit schools not to have an A rating. Classification of the Dental Schools of the United States, by the Dental Educational Council of America, August 1, 1926, attached to letter from Albert I. Midgley to Creeden, August 10, 1926, Dental School Files, GUA.

159. C. W. Lyons to Thomas J. Barrett, President, Dental Educational Council of America, November 6, 1924; Summers to William J. Gies, Carnegie Foundation, New York City, July 28, 1926; and Lyons to Gies, July 29, 1926, Dental School Files, 1922–26, GUA.

160. "Classification of the Dental Schools of the United States by the Dental Educational Council of America," August 1, 1926, Dental School Files, GUA.

161. May 22, 1926, Dental Faculty Minutes, Dental School Files, GUA.

162. Summers to Kelly, Washington, July 6, 1926, H-1, MPARP.

CHAPTER 4

1. Ronald A. Smith, *Sports and Freedom: The Rise of Big-Time College Athletics* (New York: Oxford University Press, 1988), 83–95, 119–39. See also Clifford Putney, *Muscular Christianity: Manhood and Sports in Protestant America, 1880–1920* (Cambridge, MA: Harvard University Press, 2001).

2. October 12, 1891; September 19, October 22, 1894, Consultors' Minutes, 531-1, GUA.

3. Richards agreed to provide an additional scholarship for the baseball team if the students hired a coach. October 27, 1891, House Diary, 550-15, GUA; *Washington Star,* March 27, 1897; Richards memo to Fr. Minister, Georgetown, January 15, 1897, Richards Papers, box 2, folder 12.

4. Jon Reynolds, "It's Been So Long since Last We Met . . . Lie Down, Virginia Lie Down," *Georgetown Magazine,* November–December 1982, 14–15.

5. *CJ* 23 (March 1895): 65.

6. Richards to Thomas Harlin, SJ, Washington, April 26, 1895, 566, Richards Letterbooks, vol. 10; February 22, 1898, Consultors' Minutes, 531-1, GUA; March 7, 1898, House Diary, 550-16, GUA.

7. Richards to Gen. Lefevre, September 21, 1894, 717-20, Richards Letterbooks, vol. 9.

8. Richards to Mrs. Walsh, December 4, 1895, 484–87, Richards Letterbooks, vol. 11.

9. January 16, February 4, 1896, House Diary, GUA.

10. "Athletic Notes," *CJ* 19 (December 3, 1890): 55.

11. November 24, 1892, House Diary, 550-16, GUA.

12. William McFadden, "What the Hell *Is* a Hoya?" *Georgetown Magazine,* Spring–Summer 1992, 20–23.

13. "Notes on the Music," program for the inauguration of John Joseph DeGioia as forty-eighth president of Georgetown University, October 13, 2001, DAR Constitution Hall.

14. Smith, *Sports and Freedom,* 88–95.

15. Richards to Outerbridge Horsey Jr., July 5, 1894, 468–69; and Richards to Condé Nast, August 28, 1894, 583–88, Richards Letterbooks, vol. 9.

16. *Washington Post,* November 30, 1894.

17. Bahen was the point man in the "human catapult" play that Georgetown had designed as a sure ground gainer in an era where a first down's requirement was only five yards. Bahen, carrying the ball, would jump into the joined hands of two crouching teammates and be propelled into the air and across the opposing line. Ironically, he suffered a head injury from one such catapult but refused to leave the game only to be fatally struck down a few plays later. Morris A. Bealle, *The Georgetown Hoyas: The Story of a Rambunctious Football Team* (Washington, DC: n.p., 1947), 33–35.

18. December 4, 1894, Minutes of the Directors, 1797–1989, GUA.

19. Richards to Rev. B. W. S. Bishop, December 14, 1894, 34, Richards Letterbooks, vol. 10.

20. June 6, 1893, House Diary, 550-16, GUA.

21. Richards to Martín, February 11, 1895, Richards Letterbooks, Society of Jesus, vol. 2.

22. Martín to Pardow, February 24, 1896, Liber, MD, 1886–1900, ARSI.

23. Washington Post, May 12, 1895; *Washington Times,* May 12, 1895. The song was sung to the popular tune "Nancy."

24. *Washington Post,* June 2, 1895. Six of the eleven top players were from the graduate, law, and medical departments. The average age of the players was twenty-two, and three of them were twenty-four.

25. Jon Reynolds, "Greased Pigs and Other Sports," *Georgetown Magazine,* Fall 1993, 12.

26. November 9, 1895, House Diary, 550-16, GUA.

27. May 29, 1896, House Diary, 550-16, GUA.

28. *New York World,* May 31, 1896.

29. *Washington Times,* April 8, 1896.

30. Martín to Purbrick, Rome, November 27, 1899, MPA, box 123, folder 2.

31. "De Abusibus," an eighty-two-page typewritten Latin copy of a memorial to Wlodimir Ledochowski, SJ, July 4, 1930, 44, 77, Thomas Hughes Papers, GUA.

32. *CJ* 29 10 (July 1901): n.p.

33. *Canton Repository,* March 11, 1900.

34. Lawrence H. Cooke, "The History of the Georgetown Crew: Guardian of the Blue and Gray," in *Swift Potomac's Lovely Daughter: Two Centuries at Georgetown through*

Students' Eyes, ed. Joseph Durkin, SJ (Washington, DC: Georgetown University Press, 1989), 332–33.

35. *Boston Herald,* June 1899.
36. *New York Times,* June 1899.
37. *Washington Times,* June 1, 1999.
38. [John Conway?] to Walter Camp, January 21, 1897, Sports Archives Files, box 1, AA 1897–99, GUA.
39. Richards to John B. Ryan, Washington, August 28, 1893, 535–39, Richards Letterbooks, vol. 8.
40. Richards to Mrs. Mary Wefers, Washington, September 6, 1897, 105–7, Richards Letterbooks, vol. 14; Richards's note, Alumni Files, GUA.
41. October 13, 1898, Medical Faculty Minutes, GUA.
42. April 30, 1898, Medical Faculty Minutes, GUA.
43. October 12, 1899, Medical Faculty Minutes, GUA; Report of students holding scholarships in the School of Medicine—Georgetown University, for the Session of 1899–1900, Medical School Files, GUA.
44. Richards to J. W. Wadsworth, Genesee, N.Y., July 18, 1896, 115–17, Richards Letterbooks, vol. 12.
45. Richards had heard that athletes from Princeton and other leading schools were playing in the summer leagues with impunity. Richards to J. W. Wadsworth, Genesee, N.Y., July 18, 1896, 117; and Richards to A. F. West, Princeton, July 18, 1896, 122–24, Richards Letterbooks, vol. 12.
46. June 22, 1895, Consultors' Minutes, 1893–95, 531-1, GUA.
47. October 4, 1897, Consultors' Minutes, 531-1, GUA. In that same year (1897), Georgetown was one of the institutions polled by Walter Camp about their athletic polices and standards. The Jesuit president of the Athletic Association replied, "A study of athletics as they are carried on at Georgetown will disclose many features *peculiar* to this University which serve to place Georgetown in a unique position at this time when so much that is faulty—is manifest in College athletics—We have ever encouraged athletic sport for sport's sake only—and anything hostile to the true spirit of clean athletics or opposed to the best interests of the student has been carefully avoided and wherever manifested quickly condemned." Only amateur athletes were allowed to represent Georgetown, he insisted, and they were all legitimate students in good standing. The athletic world, he suggested, seemed unwilling to admit that tiny Georgetown could have accomplished the remarkable record it had compiled in baseball, track, and other sports, save by resorting to professionals posing as students. Among the larger universities (Yale, Harvard, Pennsylvania, Princeton, Cornell, and Columbia), he concluded, "Georgetown has in recent years won a high rank—we do not understand why she is not honored accordingly by the writers of athletic annals." Conway to Camp, January 21, 1897, Sports Archives Files, box 1, AA 1897–99, GUA.
48. *Washington Times,* April 10, 1904.
49. *CJ* 33 (May 1905): 414–15.
50. "An Open Letter to the Student Body of Georgetown University," May 22, 1905, Sports Archives Files, box 1, AA 1900–1910, GUA.
51. May 26, 1905, House Diary, 550-16, GUA.
52. Jerome Daugherty to Public, July 12, 1905, Sports Archives File, box 1, AA 1900–1910, GUA.
53. Ibid.
54. November 6, 1905, Consultors' Minutes, 531-1, GUA; John S. Watterson III, "The Football Crisis of 1909–1910: The Response of the Eastern 'Big Three,'" *Journal of Sport History* 8 (Spring 1981): 35–36.
55. Smith, *Sports and Freedom,* 198–206.
56. April 12, 1907, Consultors' Minutes, 1896–1907, 531-1, GUA.
57. John Sayle Watterson, *College Football: History, Spectacle, Controversy* (Baltimore: Johns Hopkins University Press, 2000), 112.

58. *Annuae Litterae, Collegii Georgiop.,* 1909, 51–52, ARSI 1503; Wernz to Hanselman, Rome, February 14, 1910, 393, Liber, MD, 1900–1911, ARSI.

59. Watterson, *College Football,* 136–37.

60. February 18, 1906, House Diary, 550-18, GUA.

61. Buel to Maurice J. Joyce, September 26, 1906, Buel Papers. In comparison, the intercollegiate coaches, even in 1908, were receiving considerably less: crew: $1,000, football: $800, baseball: $600, and track: $300. Statement of Joseph Himmel, SJ, n.d., Sports Archives Files, box 1, AA 1900–1910, GUA.

62. Reynolds, "It's Been So Long since Last We Met," 14–15.

63. By 1916 the graduate manager was claiming a net of $2,273 for the sport. But this did not include the costs of the scholarships for the players. *CJ* 45 (June 1917).

64. Donlon to Maas, Washington, December 10, 1913, MD 16-I-53, ARSI.

65. Hugh J. Golden, "Georgetown Football: A Complete History (1874–1987)" (unpublished paper), 13.

66. *Washington Times,* October 24, 1914.

67. *CJ* 45 (April 1917).

68. Report of the Athletic Association for 1927, MPARP, H-1. This led the university to resort to seeking "contributions" from the various schools for the support of athletics. In 1924, for instance, the Law School contributed more than $3,000 to the athletic department to meet their expenses. Hugh Fegan to Creeden, June 17, 1924, Law School Files, 1923–24, GUA.

69. Parsons to Provincial, August 1, 1927, H-1, MPARP. A number of prominent athletes, such as Jack Hagerty and Claude Grigsby, captain of the football team in 1927, did seem to move back and forth between different schools, especially the Law School and the School of Foreign Service, during the decade.

70. *Hoya,* April 30, 1925.

71. Edward McHugh, "Georgetown Track and Baseball," in *Swift Potomac's Lovely Daughter: Two Centuries at Georgetown through Students' Eyes,* ed. Joseph Durkin, SJ (Washington, DC: Georgetown University Press, 1989), 342–43.

72. *Hoya,* February 16, 1928.

73. *CJ* 54 (December 1925): 128.

74. Rory Quirk, "Georgetown Lou," *Georgetown Magazine,* November–December 1979, 22–25.

75. Little to Nevils, Washington, May 4, 1929; and "Summary of Figures," Football File, Sports Archives Files, GUA.

76. Quirk, "Georgetown Lou," 25.

77. Recommendation for Fr. Dineen, SJ, "Football 1931," Sports Archives Files, GUA.

78. Lou Little denied both charges, despite clear evidence to the contrary. "There is no such thing as an athletic scholarship at Georgetown," Little told a reporter in reaction to the report. *Washington Post,* October 24, 1929. Three years after Little's denial, Nevils made his own regarding athletic scholarships: "There are no athletic scholarships at Georgetown nor were there long before the Carnegie Committee investigation frowned upon this method of securing athletes," this at the very time the president was announcing internally that they were adopting a no-scholarship policy. *Washington Star,* May 13, 1932. For a discussion of the context and implications of the report, see John R. Thelin, *Games Colleges Play: Scandal and Reform in Intercollegiate Athletics* (Baltimore: Johns Hopkins University Press, 1994).

79. *Washington Star,* May 11, 1932.

80. *Hoya,* October 31, 1934.

81. March 26, 1933, Minutes of the Board of Regents, 272-6, GUA; Ralph P. McCarthy, Director, to Nevils, June 3, 1932, "Georgetown University Athletic Association, 1929–1939," Sports Archives Files, GUA.

82. *Hoya,* October 11, 1933.

CHAPTER 5

1. *New York Times,* October 28, 1928; Nevils to Wlodimir Ledochowski, January 12, 1929, copy, Nevils Papers, box 1, folder 2.
2. In "Inaugurations" box, "Georgetown University Presidents' Inaugurations" folder, GUA.
3. "Addresses on the Occasion of the Inauguration of W. Coleman Nevils, S.J., D.D. as President of Georgetown University," Nevils Papers, box 1, folder 3.
4. *CJ* 57 (December 1928): 111–12.
5. William G. McDevitt, *The Hilltop Remembered* (Washington, DC: Georgetown University Press, 1982), 61.
6. *Baltimore Sun,* April 8, 1934.
7. March 25, 1930, House Diary, 550-20, GUA.
8. *CJ* 58 (April 1930): 414.
9. April 9, 1934, House Diary, GUA; *CJ* 62 (April 1934): 455. Genevieve Garvan Brady, the widow of the New York financier, Nicholas Brady, was, together with her husband, a major benefactor of Catholic charities and works of the Society of Jesus in the Northeast.
10. *CJ* 61 (November 1932).
11. August 27, 1928, Minutes of the Directors, GUA.
12. March 14, 1930, Minutes of the Directors, GUA; Financial Statement, May 30, 1930, H-1, MPARP.
13. Edward Phillips to Nevils, New York, September 14, 1929, Nevils Papers, box 1, folder 5; Phillips to Nevils, September 19, 1929, H-1, MPARP; Consultors' Minutes, 531-1, GUA; Nevils to Provincial, September 17, 1929, H-1, MPARP; February 20, 1930, Minutes of the Directors, GUA; Phillips to Nevils, March 22, 1930, H-1, MPARP.
14. March 1, 1930, Minutes of the Directors, GUA.
15. Nevils to J. Neal Power, Washington, May 16, 1930, Nevils Papers; Farrell to Nevils, Washington, May 30, 1930, H-1, MPARP; October 20, 1930, Consultors' Minutes, 531-1, GUA.
16. The chapel was named the Cowardin Chapel of St. William, in memory of William Reynolds Cowardin, SJ (xC 1871), who had been a professor and counselor at the college in the late nineteenth century.
17. February 16, 1931, House Diary, 550-20, GUA; *CJ* 61 (November 1932).
18. March 9, 1932, Consultors' Minutes, 531-1, GUA.
19. Nevils to Phillips, n.d., H-1, MPARP. Once more the contractor had made a contribution of $5,000 to reduce the total cost.
20. March 26, 1933, Minutes of the Board of Regents, 272-6, GUA.
21. *CJ* 61 (March 1933).
22. *American Business Journal,* January 1, 1933, quoted in *CJ* 61 (February 1933): 297.
23. With seven hundred boarders, the president estimated an annual income of some $60,000, enough to provide the core of an endowment for the Medical School.
24. February 20, 1931; September 8, 1934, Consultors' Minutes, 531-1, GUA.
25. February 27, 1939, Consultors' Minutes, 531-1, GUA.
26. Constance McLoughlin Green, *Washington: Capital City, 1878–1950* (Princeton, NJ: Princeton University Press, 1963), 377–78.
27. *CJ* 59 (December 1930): 144.
28. *Hoya,* April 13, 1932.
29. Ibid.
30. *Hoya,* April 27, 1932.
31. *Hoya,* October 12, 1932.
32. *CJ* 61 (November 1932): 66.
33. *Hoya,* February 8, 1933; *CJ* 61 (December 1932): 118.
34. *Hoya,* March 1, 1933.
35. *CJ* 61 (March 1933): 354–55.
36. March 6, 1933, House Diary, 550-20, GUA.

37. Green, *Washington,* 392; Carl Abbott, *Political Terrain: Washington, D.C., from Tidewater Town to Global Metropolis* (Chapel Hill: University of North Carolina Press, 1999), 102, 120.
38. *Hoya,* March 29, 1933.
39. *Hoya,* November 15, 1933.
40. *Hoya,* April 11, 1934.
41. *Hoya,* November 11, 1936.
42. McDevitt, *Hilltop Remembered,* 51.
43. June 11, 1934, Minutes of the Board of Regents, 272-6, GUA.
44. April 27, 1933, Minutes of the Directors, GUA.
45. GULS Reports, 1933–34, Law School Files, GUA.
46. Joseph A. Farrell to Phillips, September 2, 1935, H-1, MPARP.
47. June 9, 1935, Minutes of the Board of Regents, 272-6, GUA.
48. June 6, 1932, Minutes of the Board of Regents, 272-6, GUA.
49. June 6, 1936; February 13, 1937, Minutes of the Board of Regents, 272-6, GUA.
50. Audit of finances, 1937–38, H-1, MPARP.
51. October 21, 1933, Consultors' Minutes, 531-1, GUA.
52. March 19, 1940, Consultors' Minutes, 531-1, GUA.
53. Inaugural Address, November 23, 1935, Arthur A. O'Leary Papers, GUA.
54. *CJ* 67 (February 1939): 263.
55. William C. McFadden, SJ, "'Catechism at 4 for All the Schools': Religious Instruction at Georgetown," *Georgetown at Two Hundred: Faculty Reflections on the University's Future* (Washington, DC: Georgetown University Press, 1990), 150–53.
56. *Hoya,* December 11, 1929.
57. February 12, 1936, House Diary, GUA.
58. April 15, 1937, House Diary, 550-21, GUA.
59. *CJ* 60 (February 1932): 273.
60. *CJ* 61 (May 1933): 543–44.
61. *CJ* 65 (November 1936): 7.
62. John G. Bowen, "Hoya, Saxa, Cardinal Pacelli!" in *On the Hilltop,* 25; October 22, 1936 House Diary, 550-21, GUA.
63. Jack Spalding, "Make Haste Slowly," *On the Hilltop,* 163.
64. Raymond Reiss interview, June 6, 1983.
65. *Washington Post,* March 16, 1938.
66. March 16, September 14, 18, 1938, House Diary, GUA.
67. Barry, *Surgeons at Georgetown,* 190.
68. Ibid., 195; Stapleton, *Upward Journey,* 55.
69. Rothstein, *American Medical Schools and the Practice of Medicine,* 162–64.
70. *WL* 54 (1925): 110.
71. *Hoya,* February 25, 1925; March 15, 1928; *CJ* 59 (March 1931): 410; Coyle to Phillips, Washington, November 10, 1931, H-1, MPARP.
72. *CJ* 60 (February 1932): 269.
73. Kenneth M. Ludmerer, *Learning to Heal: The Development of American Medical Education* (Baltimore: Johns Hopkins University Press, 1985), 208–10.
74. Edward Parker Luongo, *A Biography of Wallace Mason Yater, M.D.* (Washington, DC: privately published, n.d.), 54.
75. Stapleton, *Upward Journey,* 56.
76. Barry, *Surgeons at Georgetown,* 201.
77. Stapleton, *Upward Journey,* 56.
78. Report of Harold Rypins, MD, to Harlan H. Horner, Asst. Commissioner for Higher Education in New York, April 16, 1934, H-1, MPARP.
79. Phillips to Nevils, November 6, 1928, H-1, MPARP.
80. Nevils to Phillips, Washington, August 14, 1933, H-1, MPARP.
81. January 30, 1933, Consultors' Minutes, 531-1, GUA.
82. Martin J. Nolan to Gipprich, Washington, May 12, 1932; and Officer of National Federation of Women's Clubs to Phillips, July 15, 1934, H-1, MPARP.
83. [Unsigned report on Medical School], October 10, 1934, H-1, MPARP.

84. Meeting of the Executive Faculty, 1934, Medical School Files, 1932–37.
85. Nevils to Phillips, n.d., H-1, MPARP.
86. Nevils to Phillips, Washington, August 30, 1931, H-1, MPARP.
87. March 23, 1928, Consultors' Minutes, 531-1, GUA; Summers to Provincial, March 2, 1928, H-1, MPARP.
88. Summers to [Phillips], June 4, 1929, H-1, MPARP.
89. June 2, 1929, Consultors' Minutes, 531-1, GUA.
90. "Report of Father Provincial on the transfer of Father Walter G. Summers from Georgetown," July 1929, H-1, MPARP.
91. June 13, 1931, Consultors' Minutes, 531-1, GUA.
92. Nevils to Reverend Hunter Guthrie, July 9, 1949, W. G. Morgan Faculty File, cited in Barry, *Surgeons at Georgetown*, 205–6.
93. Nevils to Phillips, Washington, July 22, 1932, H-1, MPARP.
94. Ibid.
95. Luongo, *Biography of Wallace Mason Yater*, 67–68; Barry, *Surgeons at Georgetown*, 202–3.
96. Prentiss Willson to Nevils, March 23, 1931, Medical School Files, 1929–31, GUA.
97. Phillips to Nevils, July 20, 1932, H-1, MPARP.
98. James A. Gannon to Phillips, Washington, August 10, 1933, H-1, MPARP; Barry, *Surgeons at Georgetown*, 194, citing Edmund Walsh to Madigan, August 1, 1932, Medical School Files and Alumni Files, GUA; Gipprich and Morgan to Nevils, September 12, 1932, Correspondence, Medical School Files, GUA.
99. Barry, *Surgeons at Georgetown*, 194; Gannon to Nevils, July 31, 1933; and Gannon to Phillips, August 10, 1933, H-1, MPARP.
100. Phillips to Nevils, August 11, 1933, H-1, MPARP.
101. Nevils to Phillips, Washington, August 14, 1933, H-1, MPARP.
102. Phillips to Nevils, July 27, 1934, H-1, MPARP. With Gipprich's departure, Bennett left as well.
103. Phillips to Arthur O'Leary, December 11, 1934, H-1, MPARP.
104. Luongo, *Biography of Wallace Mason Yater*, 62; Barry, *Surgeons at Georgetown*, 213.
105. H. G. Weiskotten to McCauley, September 26, 1935, H-1, MPARP.
106. Barry, *Surgeons at Georgetown*, 213; Phillips to O'Leary, July 9, 1935, H-1, MPARP.
107. Report of Inspection [of Association of American Medical Colleges], April 3–6, 1938, H-1, MPARP.
108. November 22, 1938, Minutes of the Board of Regents, 272-6, GUA.
109. Executive Faculty of Medical School to President and Board of Directors, November 17, 1938, H-1, MPARP.
110. Ibid.
111. December 5, 1938, Consultors' Minutes, 531-1, GUA.
112. March 9, April 28, 1939, Minutes of the Directors, GUA.
113. "Report of Re-inspection of Georgetown University School of Medicine," Medical School Files, 1938–40, GUA; Fred C. Zapffe to McCauley, January 30, 1940, H-1, MPARP.
114. Student Body to Gipprich, July 14, 1930, Medical School Files, 1929–31, GUA.
115. Gipprich to Nevils, July 14, 1930, Nevils Papers.
116. C. V. Vignes, DDS, Dean School of Dentistry, Loyola University, New Orleans, to Nevils, April 15, 1931; and Nevils to Vignes, April 20, 1931, Dental School Files, GUA.
117. Nevils to Phillips, February 9, 1932, H-1, MPARP; 1932, Consultors' Minutes, 531-1, GUA.
118. Phillips to Nevils, February 14, 1932, H-1, MPARP.
119. The required college course work consisted of eight hours each of biology, inorganic chemistry, and organic chemistry, along with six hours each in physics and English.
120. Nevils to Phillips, Washington, August 12, 1933, H-1, MPARP.
121. Nevils to Phillips, February 9, 1932, H-1, MPARP; 1932, Consultors' Minutes, 531-1, GUA.

122. *CJ* 63 (November 1934): 114.
123. Giuliani, "History of the Georgetown University Dental School," 25.
124. Anna Keeton Wiley to Nevils, August 30, 1932; and Nevils to Wiley, September 1, 1932, Dental School Files, GUA.
125. Among the signees were James A. Farrell, George E. Hamilton, and Raymond H. Reiss. Undersigned to Edward C. Phillips, SJ, June 11, 1934, Nevils Papers, box 4, folder 35.
126. Ibid.
127. Nevils to Phillips, June 3, 1935, H-1, MPARP.

CHAPTER 6

1. *Washington Post,* July 3, 1935.
2. Inaugural address, November 23, 1935, O'Leary Papers.
3. Brian McGrath, SJ, interview, August 2, 1983.
4. Chamberlain, "Georgetown University Library," 95–96.
5. Brian McGrath to Bellwoar, September 7, 1962, O'Leary Papers, folder 84-5.
6. *Hoya,* October 20, 1937; *Washington Herald,* October 17, 1937.
7. George Bull, SJ, "The Function of the Catholic Graduate School," *Thought,* September 1938, quoted in Michael V. Gannon, "Before and After Modernism: The Intellectual Isolation of the American Priest," in *The Catholic Priest in the United States: Historical Investigations,* ed. John Tracy Ellis (Collegeville, MN: St. John's University Press, 1971), 359.
8. Paul A. Fitzgerald, SJ, *The Governance of Jesuit Colleges in the United States, 1920–1970* (Notre Dame, IN: University of Notre Dame Press, 1984), 25–35.
9. Ibid., 38.
10. April 25, 1932, Consultors' Minutes, 531-1, GUA.
11. "Some General Observations on Post Graduate Work at Georgetown University," November 16, 1932, Reports, Graduate School Files, GUA (hereafter "General Observations"). This is an unsigned document, but internal evidence strongly indicates Healy as the author.
12. "General Observations," 1.
13. Ibid., 2.
14. Ibid., 3.
15. Ibid., 16.
16. Georgetown had, since 1924, been an associate member of the AAU.
17. "'Directions' of the Reverend Father Commisarius of Studies," [January 1935], Graduate School Files, GUA.
18. Aloysius Hogan, "Report on Present Conditions," September 24, 1936, Reports, Graduate School Files, GUA.
19. Aloysius Hogan, handwritten note attached to "Report on Present Conditions," March 6, 1937, Graduate School Files, GUA.
20. Henry W. Briefs, "Goetz Briefs on Capitalism and Democracy: An Introduction," *Review of Social Economy* [1983]: 212–13.
21. "Statistics of Divisions, 1934–37," FCI, Registrar Files, GUA.
22. McGrath interview, August 2, 1983.
23. Copy of notes made by Edward Phillips, SJ, "Report on the State of the Georgetown Astronomical Observatory," [1925]; and Phillips to Provincial, December 22, 1925; and McNally to Provincial, Washington, March 31, 1929, H-1, MPARP.
24. Francis J. Heyden, SJ, *The Beginning and End of a Jesuit Observatory (1841–1972)* (Qauezon City, Philippines, n.d.), 12.
25. October 31, 1939, Consultors' Minutes, 531-1, GUA.
26. H. W. Arant, "Report of Visitation of American Association of Law Schools," [1937], Law School Files, GUA.
27. January 22, 1932, Minutes of Executive Faculty Meeting, Law School Files, GUA, cited in Therry, "Partial History," V, 7.

28. "Memorandum," November 14, 1932, Law School Files, GUA, cited in Therry, "Partial History," V, 9.
29. "Memorandum to Faculty," May 19, 1932, GUA, cited in Therry, "Partial History," V, 10.
30. June 6, 1936, Minutes of the Board of Regents, 272-6, GUA.
31. Arant, "Report of Visitation."
32. Francis Lucey, "History of the Georgetown University Law School," 5, cited in Therry, "Partial History," V, 17–18.
33. June 5, 1932, Minutes of the Board of Regents, 272-6, GUA.
34. December 17, 1936, Executive Faculty Minutes, Law School Miscellaneous Files, GUA.
35. *Washington Post,* February 20, 1936.
36. October 26, 1933, Minutes of the Executive Faculty, Law School Files, GUA, cited in Therry, "Partial History," V, 49.
37. Therry, "Partial History," V, 18–19.
38. Ibid., V, 6.
39. Ibid., V, 32.
40. Nevils to Provincial, July 12, 1933, H-1, MPARP.
41. Nevils to Ledochowski, January 14, 1929, Nevils Papers, box 1, folder 2; Thomas F. Healy to Nevils, February 14, 1931, SFS Files, GUA.
42. *CJ* 64 (January 1936): 252; *CJ* 65 (October 1936): 50.
43. *Hoya,* November 9, 1938.
44. Ibid.
45. McCauley to O'Leary, December 5, 1935, GUA, cited in Alma S. Woolley, *Learning, Faith, and Caring: History of the Georgetown University School of Nursing, 1903–2000* (Washington, DC: Georgetown University School of Nursing, 2001), 35.
46. Woolley, *Learning, Faith, and Caring,* 35.
47. James B. Sweeney to O'Leary, October 12, 1939, Nursing School, 1906–46, GUA, cited in Woolley, *Learning, Faith, and Caring,* 36.
48. "An Alumni Bureau?" *Hoya,* December 7, 1932; "An Alumni Secretary," *Hoya,* January 23, 1935.
49. June 11, 1934, Minutes of the Board of Regents, 272-6, GUA; "Alumni Organization," *Hoya,* April 3, 1935; *CJ* 63 (April 7, 1935): 472.
50. *Washington Herald,* July 3, 1935.
51. Walsh to Provincial, August 12, 1937, H-1, MPARP; "Statistics of Divisions, 1934–37," FCI, Registrar Files, GUA.
52. April 10, May 2, June 25, 1938, House Diary, GUA.
53. October 18, 1938, Consultors' Minutes, 531-1, GUA.
54. McGrath interview, August 2, 1983; Ruby to Vincent I. Bellwoard, SJ, August 31, 1962, O'Leary Papers, folder 84-5; Ruby to George N. Butler, President's Office, memo, January 6, 1950, Hunter Guthrie Papers, GUA.
55. *Washington Post,* November 1, 1932.
56. Ibid., January 1, 1934.
57. August 9, 1933, Minutes of the Directors, GUA. A board composed of the president, Kehoe, and another member was to determine the number of scholarships and the individuals that would receive them.
58. July 18, 1938, Consultors' Minutes, 531-1, GUA; McGrath interview, August 2, 1983; Jack Hagerty, "Four Great Men," *On the Hilltop,* 88–91. There were three minor sports—tennis, golf, and sailing—that received no scholarships.
59. *Washington Herald,* October 15, 1934.
60. Ibid.
61. The first use of the nickname in public print was in the *Washington Star* on December 11, 1927. The sports editor of the *Star* had grown frustrated in trying to squeeze "Georgetown" or "Hilltoppers" into headlines. He demanded that someone on the sports staff come up with a shorter reference. "Hoyas"—the best-known Georgetown cheer, or perhaps the team mascot—was the nickname of choice. *Washington Star,* November 20, 1940.

62. *Washington Star,* October 11, 1937.

63. GUA, 550-20, House Diary, November 19, 1938, House Diary, 550-20, GUA.

64. *Washington Star,* November 17, 1940.

65. *Washington Times Herald,* November 18, 1940.

66. Edmund Walsh to Provincial, August 12, 1937, H-1, MPARP; Ruby to Bellwoar, O'Leary Papers.

67. Walsh to Provincial, August 12, 1937, H-1, MPARP; *Washington Evening Star,* [1937].

68. Release of April 22, 1939, Sesquicentennial Files, folder 2, GUA.

69. *CJ* 67 (May 1939): 504–5.

70. Robert Cohen, *When the Old Left Was Young: Student Radicals and America's First Mass Student Movement, 1929–1941* (New York: Oxford University Press, 1993).

71. *New York Times,* May 19, 1935.

72. October 21, 1933, Consultors' Minutes, 531-1.

73. O'Leary to Provincial, February 23, 1937, H-1, MPARP; February 22, 1937, Consultors' Minutes, 531-1, GUA.

74. Aaron Goldman, "Georgetown Revisited with Pride," *On the Hilltop,* 86.

75. *Hoya,* May 4, 1932.

76. *Hoya,* February 22, 1933.

77. *Hoya,* May 2, 10, 1934; *CJ* 63 (October 1934): 28.

78. *Hoya,* "Discrimination," January 20, 1937.

79. *Hoya,* "The Color Line," March 1, 1939.

80. February 27, 1939, Consultors' Minutes, 531-1, GUA.

81. *Hoya,* March 27, 1935.

82. *Hoya,* April 10, 1935.

83. *Hoya,* April 17, 1935.

84. *Hoya,* April 28, 1937.

85. E. James Hickey to Catholic deans, April 9, 1938, H-1, MPARP.

86. April 26, 1938, House Diary, GUA.

87. *CJ* 66 (May 1938): 485.

88. *Hoya,* May 4, 1949.

89. Cohen, *When the Old Left Was Young,* 155–56, 165.

90. *CJ* 65 (November 1936): 125.

91. Arthur O'Leary, "Talk to Law Alumni," October 3, 1935, Law School Files, GUA.

92. *Hoya,* November 4, 1936. The paper noted that one-sixth that number of Communists in Russia—the party's size in 1917—had been sufficient to engineer the revolution.

93. *Hoya,* October 28, 1936.

94. *Hoya,* February 23, 1939.

95. *CJ* 67 (February 1939): 309–10.

96. *Hoya,* March 22, 1939.

97. *Hoya,* March 29, 1939.

98. *Hoya,* October 16, 1940; Cohen, *When the Old Left Was Young,* 311–12.

99. *Hoya,* October 18, 1939.

100. *Hoya,* May 22, 1940.

101. *Hoya,* October 30, November 13, 1940; *CJ* 69 (October 1940): 7.

102. *Hoya,* November 5, 1941.

103. *Hoya,* May 21, 1941.

104. *CJ* 70 (April 1942): 10; David Brinkley, *Washington Goes to War* (New York: Knopf, 1988).

105. GUA, House Diary, December 7, 1941, House Diary, GUA.

CHAPTER 7

1. December 15, 1941, Minutes of the Directors, GUA. The directors exhibited a somewhat selective memory in touting the university community's unflagging "patriotism" in every previous national crisis, inasmuch as the community had

been gravely divided during the Civil War, with a large majority of alumni who served in that war wearing the uniform of the Confederacy.

2. Jay Rosenstein, "A 'Rousing Hoya' for the War Effort," *Georgetown Today,* January 1977, 13–14.

3. "Keeping at It," *Hoya,* December 17, 1941.

4. December 14, 1941, House Diary, GUA.

5. *CJ* 71 (November 1942): 29, 34.

6. *Hoya,* August 4, 1943.

7. *CJ* 70 (April 1942): 25.

8. V. R. Cardozier, *Colleges and Universities in World War II* (Westport, CT: Praeger, 1993), 6.

9. January 5, 7, 1942, Minutes of the Directors, GUA; January 20, 1942, House Diary, GUA; John E. Grattan, SJ, to parents, February 14, 1942, H-1, MPARP.

10. Royden Davis, SJ, interview, March 24, 1986.

11. William Reardon, "G.U. at War," *CJ* 72 (September 1943): 15.

12. Davis interview, March 24, 1986.

13. April 21, 1942, Consultors' Minutes, 531-1, GUA.

14. *Hoya,* December 9, 1942.

15. October 8, 1942; April 15, 1943, Minutes of Executive Faculty, Law School Files, GUA.

16. January 4, 1943, Minutes of the Directors, GUA.

17. October 8, 1942, Executive Faculty Minutes, Law School Files, GUA.

18. Evan Thomas, *The Man to See: Edward Bennett Williams, Ultimate Insider; Legendary Trial Lawyer* (New York: Simon & Schuster, 1991), 40–41.

19. Philip Feldman interview, October 2, 1983.

20. *CJ* 73 (August 1945): 22.

21. March 15, 1942, Consultors' Minutes, 531-1, GUA.

22. Cardozier, *Colleges and Universities in World War II,* 7.

23. Ibid., 19–22; Louis E. Keefer, "Birth and Death of the Army Specialized Training Program," *Army History* (Winter 1995): 1–2.

24. Cardozier, *Colleges and Universities in World War II,* 26.

25. Woolley, *Learning, Faith, and Caring,* 44.

26. November 30, 1943, Consultors' Minutes, 531-1, GUA.

27. "I decided if I ever had the opportunity to help these people," he later wrote, "I would take it." The chance finally came in 1958 when President Dwight Eisenhower appointed him to chair an international committee on medicine and health that Walsh utilized to deploy medical personnel to countries throughout the world to teach hygiene and train native people in health care. *Georgetown Magazine,* Fall 1987, 43.

28. January 11, 18, 1943, Minutes of the Directors, GUA; February 1943, Consultors' Minutes, 531-1, GUA; *Washington Star,* August 22, 1943, cited in *CJ* 72 (September 1, 1943): 27.

29. *CJ* 71 (April 1943): 33.

30. September 3, 1943, House Diary, GUA.

31. Gleason, *Contending with Modernity,* 213.

32. Davis interview, March 24, 1986; James A. Nash, "The Battle of the University," *CJ* 72 (September 1943): 30.

33. "Military Training," *CJ* 72 (January 1944): 19.

34. Accompanying Giraud was Leon Dostert, a member of his staff, on leave from the School of Foreign Service. July 10, 1943, House Diary, GUA.

35. Edmund Walsh to James E. Walsh, December 3, 1943, Walsh Papers.

36. Stephen F. McNamee to Edward Coffey, SJ, October 5, 1943, H-1, MPARP.

37. GUA, House Diary, September 10, 1943, House Diary, GUA.

38. Annual Report [of Treasurer], 1942–43, H-1, MPARP; September 11, 1943; January 7, 1944, House Diary, GUA.

39. Memorandum by Eugene L. Stewart, secretary to the president, August 28, 1947, Statistics, 1944–48, Registrar Files, FCI, GUA. The university charged the army

approximately $1,660 (the regular student rate) for each soldier student for tuition, room, and board. January 20, 1942, Minutes of the Directors, GUA.

40. *Georgetown Magazine,* September 2002, 17.
41. Keefer, "Birth and Death of the Army Specialized Training Program," 5.
42. Discipline Office Newsletter (hereafter DON) 13 (April 1945): 7, GUA.
43. DON 13 (April 23, 1945).
44. June 23, 1945, House Diary, GUA.
45. May 8, 1945, House Diary, GUA.
46. DON 16 (September 11, 1945).
47. *CJ* 74 (September 1945): 11.
48. DON 7 (July 26, 1944): 2.
49. *New England Journal of Medicine* (March 17, 1955): 454–55.
50. DON 10.
51. Paul Lambert to Ray Spratt, n.d., http://spratt.org/blozis.html.
52. *Hoya,* May 25, 1945.
53. DON 14 (June 15, 1945).
54. Thelin, *History of American Higher Education,* 259.
55. Roger L. Geiger, *Research and Relevant Knowledge: American Research Universities since World War II* (New York: Oxford University Press, 1993), 13.

CHAPTER 8

1. Thelin, *History of American Higher Education,* 261.
2. Keith W. Olson, *The G.I. Bill, the Veterans, and the Colleges* (Lexington: University of Kentucky Press, 1974), 23–24; Elizabeth A. Edmondson, "Without Comment or Controversy: The G.I. Bill and Catholic Colleges," *Church History* (December 2002): 822; Thelin, *History of American Higher Education,* 263.
3. Olson, G.I. Bill, 31, 43, 45. Olson estimates that nearly 450,000 veterans, who would have otherwise not attended college, took advantage of the bill (48).
4. Registration statistics, 1946–47 folders, SFS Files, GUA. By 1948, Catholics constituted a minority within the school, albeit a very large minority (49%).
5. GUA, Financial Report, 1947.
6. Davis interview, March 24, 1986.
7. Daniel Degnan, SJ, interview, July 30, 1987.
8. James Shannon interview, June 9, 1983.
9. David Nugent, SJ, to Gorman, May 31, 1947, "1947," Medical School Files, 1938–49, GUA; Paul A. McNally, SJ, to Gorman, June 18, 1947, H-1, MPARP.
10. Francis K. Drolet, SJ. "Negro Students in Jesuit Schools and Colleges: A Statistical Interpretation," *WL* 76 (1947): 308, cited in Albert Sidney Foley, SJ, "The Catholic Church and the Washington Negro" (PhD diss., University of North Carolina, 1950), 200–201.
11. May 22, 1948, Consultors' Minutes, 531-1, GUA.
12. The first African American law students were Winston A. Douglas, Elmer W. Henderson, William D. Martin, and Lutrelle F. Parker. All four graduated in 1952.
13. William A. Ryan, SJ, to Rosemary Seeger, July 20, 1950, Lawrence C. Gorman Papers, box 4, GUA; Foley, "Catholic Church and the Washington Negro," 201.
14. Oscar Morrison was a transfer student from Howard who was married and held down two jobs, one as a government clerk, another as a cab driver. When he attempted to get dental care on campus, he was directed to go to the Howard University Dental School for treatment. Morrison eventually transferred to George Washington, when Georgetown raised its tuition. He looked back with fondness on Frank and Jesse Mann, Jules Davids, Carroll Quigley, Edmund Walsh, Frank Fadner, "and a few others" who had "helped pave the way for Georgetown University's changing [racial] image." Oscar F. Morrison, letter to the editor, *Georgetown Today,* May 1973, 34–35.
15. Degnan interview.

16. Dean's Report, 1949–50 and 1951–52, College Files, GUA.
17. Gerard Yates, SJ, to Edward Bunn, May 27, 1949, Graduate School Files, box 1, 1949, GUA.
18. Shannon interview; Degnan interview.
19. *Washington Times-Herald,* February 1, 1950; *Washington Star,* February 1, 1950.
20. Stephen F. Alleva, "'A Lasting, Lifetime, Loving Singing Group': The Georgetown Chimes as an Ideal Institution" (thesis, Georgetown University, 2005), 1–32.
21. Donald Walsh interview, December 14, 1983.
22. McGrath to Guthrie, March 16, 1951, H-1, MPARP.
23. Francis Burch, SJ, "Joseph Hunter Guthrie," in *American National Biography* 9, 742–43.
24. Guthrie to Edward Bunn, SJ, March 25, 1948, Graduate School Files, box 1, 1948, GUA.
25. Ibid.
26. Guthrie to Bunn, July 31, 1964, GUA, 405-2, Bunn Papers.
27. Ibid.
28. Report of the Inspection of Georgetown University, Washington, D.C., by the Commission on Institutions of Higher Education of the Middle States Association of Colleges and Secondary Schools, February 28–March 3, 1951, M1–M11, Academic Vice President Files, GUA (hereafter Middle States Report).
29. Geiger, *Research and Relevant Knowledge,* 21–24, 59.
30. Lucas, *American Higher Education,* 232–33; Hugh Davis Graham and Nancy Diamond, *The Rise of American Research Universities: Elites and Challengers in the Postwar Era* (Baltimore: Johns Hopkins University Press, 1997), 30–32.
31. Minutes of War Emergency Meeting of Graduate Faculty, August 2, 1950, War Emergency Plans, 80, GUA.
32. Francis Heyden, SJ, interview, November 27, 1984. The air force would later honor him with the Air War University Award in 1958 for his service to the department.
33. Gerard Yates to Charles Foley, SJ, March 20, 1952, Development Files, box 1, 1947–57, folder 148-4, GUA.
34. Royce Moch, Dept. of State to Thomas F. Daly Jr., June 16, 1949, copy, Varia Files, box 21, folder 353-1, GUA. Daly was an editor of *Vital Speeches.*
35. November 9, 1942, Consultors' Minutes, 531-1, GUA.
36. The final cost of the building was $3.6 million, of which the government funded $2,850,000.
37. One of the largest contributors was the Congress of Industrial Organizations (CIO), which gave $55,000 to the university for the project. January 5, 1947, Minutes of the Directors, GUA; James E. Colliflower, Bulletin 15, September 18, 1945, MPARP, H-3; McNally to Keelan, August 24, 1945, H-1, MPARP.
38. Stapleton, *Upward Journey,* 68–69.
39. Luongo, *Biography of Wallace Mason Yater,* 123–29.
40. Barry, *Surgeons at Georgetown,* 226.
41. Hugh Hussey was the chief faculty person who pressed Jeghers as a candidate with the dean, Father McCauley, and the executive faculty. Hussey had learned of Jeghers through George Schreiner, a recent Georgetown graduate interning at Boston City Hospital. Stapleton, *Upward Journey,* 94.
42. Barry, *Surgeons at Georgetown,* 228.
43. Harold Jeghers interview, June 9, 1983.
44. John Rose interview, December 11, 1986; James Fitzgerald interview, January 31, 1986.
45. Stapleton, *Upward Journey,* 99–100.
46. Ibid., 104.
47. Jeghers interview.
48. Quoted in Stapleton, *Upward Journey,* 102.
49. Graham and Diamond, *Rise of American Research Universities,* 31.
50. *Washington Post,* September 25, 1948.

51. Jeghers interview.

52. Guthrie to Seward Anthony Schroder Jr., June 15, 1950, H-1, MPARP.

53. As James Ruby, director of the Alumni Association, explained to a Jewish alumnus, in attempting to defend the policy, "There is no quota system; . . . in any one year if there should be less than 120 qualified Catholic candidates, the remaining places are assigned strictly on an academic basis." Ruby had to concede that there was little chance that this would actually happen, given the large number of Catholic applicants. Ruby to Albert L. Cohn, December 11, 1951, Medical School Files, 1952, GUA.

54. Gorman to Keelan, September 30, 1944, H-1, MPARP; Giuliani, "History of the Georgetown University Dental School," 38.

55. Council on Dental Education—American Dental Association—Survey of Dental Schools, 1942–43, Report on the School of Dentistry of Georgetown University, Dental School Files, GUA.

56. As McCauley observed to President Gorman, the ability to recruit a qualified, though part-time, faculty was "most important in view of our financial structure, because a dean from out of town would undoubtedly be forced to fill Faculty vacancies with full-time men." David V. McCauley, SJ, to Gorman, September 29, 1944, Gorman Papers.

57. Burke to McCauley, August 1, 1944, Dental School Files, GUA.

58. Edward Bunn, SJ, to Gorman, Report on the Dental School [1949], Dental School Files, GUA.

59. Shailer Peterson, Secretary of the Council on Dental Education, to Guthrie, February 7, 1950; and Dean's Report, 1950–51, Dental School Files, GUA.

60. Woolley, *Learning, Faith, and Caring,* 51.

61. Ibid., 68.

62. Walsh to Keelan, June 21, 1944, H-1, MPARP.

63. [Announcement of] Spoken Language Program, H-1, MPARP.

64. Nugent to John B. Janssens, SJ, August 3, 1949, H-1, MPARP.

65. This original provision, which lasted fewer than three years, apparently reflected Walsh's original intention about the nature of the School of Foreign Service. As he explained in 1941, his original purpose in setting up the school had not been to create a comprehensive division that would include basic liberal arts education, but rather a specialized school that would accept candidates who already had two years of college. He claimed that the idea of a change to a four-year program came in the early 1920s when he was in the Soviet Union and university officials bowed to the pressure of parents and others looking for the school to provide a complete college education. As of 1941, Walsh intended to return to the original policy, "as soon as this can be prudently done." Memorandum communicated orally to Father Phillips, Dean of the Graduate School by Walsh, March 14, 1941, Graduate School Files, box 1, 1940–41, GUA.

66. Guthrie to Nugent, July 26, 1949, H-1, MPARP.

67. Memorandum of Yates to Guthrie, Graduate School Files, folder 1, 1948, GUA.

68. *Hoya,* March 14, 1947.

69. School officials were embarrassed in 1950 when a member of the institute, John De Francis, published a book, *Nationalism and Language Reform in China* (Princeton, NJ: Princeton University Press, 1950), in which he praised the language reforms that the Chinese Communists, whom De Francis considered "federal nationalists," were carrying out as one instrument toward the creation of nationalism. John Hadley Cox to [Dostert], n.d., School of Languages and Linguistics (hereafter SLL) Files, 1950, GUA. De Francis's contract was not renewed at the school.

70. Walsh to Justice Robert Jackson, November 3, 1950, in "Walsh" file, box 21, Robert H. Jackson Papers, Manuscript Division, Library of Congress, as cited in Patrick J. McNamara, "Edmund A. Walsh, SJ, and Catholic Anticommunism in the United States, 1917–1952" (PhD diss., Catholic University of America, 2003), 253.

71. Edmund A. Walsh, *Total Empire,* 253, 258–59, as cited in McNamara, "Edmund A. Walsh and Catholic Anticommunism in the United States," 264–65.

72. Donald F. Crosby, SJ, *God, Church, and Flag: Senator Joseph R. McCarthy and the Catholic Church, 1950–1957* (Chapel Hill: University of North Carolina Press, 1978), 47–52; McNamara, "Edmund A. Walsh and Catholic Anticommunism in the United States," 270–72.

73. Frank Blair, the NBC commentator, was the impetus for the creation of the forum. Blair, then an announcer for WARL, the local northern Virginia station, walked into Heyden's radio studio one day in 1946 to ask about the prospect of Georgetown's producing certain shows for his station. When Heyden asked what kind of programs he had in mind, Blair mentioned a discussion program on current affairs as one possibility. Heyden interview. Blair subsequently became vice president of the Liberty Broadcasting System. October 11, 1950, Minutes of the Directors, GUA.

74. October 28, 1951, House Diary, GUA.

75. Chamberlin to Gorman, July 18, 1947, Graduate School Files, box 1, SJ, GUA.

76. Heinrich Kronstein, "Discussion with the Members of the Foreign Relations Committee of the German Federal Parliament," February 12, 1951; and McGrath, memorandum, February 14, 1951, Brian A. McGrath Papers, GUSC.

77. McGrath interview, August 8, 1983; "Discussion with the Members of the Foreign Relations Committee of the German Federal Parliament," draft, n.d., McGrath Papers; and House Diary, April 7, 1953.

78. September 14, October 29, December 7, 1948, Consultors' Minutes, MPARP.

79. "Presidential Address, May 1, 1949," in *Tradition and Prospect: The Inauguration of the Very Reverend Hunter Guthrie, SJ, as Thirty-fifth President of Georgetown University, April 30 and May 1, 1949* (Washington, DC: Georgetown University, 1949), 70–74.

80. May 1, 1949, House Diary, 550-20, GUA.

81. Guthrie to Edward Bunn, SJ, March 25, 1948, Graduate School Files, box 1, 1948, GUA.

82. November 30, 1949, Consultors' Minutes, 531-1, GUA; Guthrie to Nugent, January 30, 1951, H-1, MPARP; September 12, 1951, House Diary, GUA.

83. Thomas A. Dean to Guthrie, May 7, 1952, copy, H-1, MPARP.

84. Memorandum of Donald T. Sheehan to Gorman, October 15, 1947; and "Report on New Construction," [1951], Development Files, box 1, 1947–57, folder 148-4, GUA.

85. Ryan to Bunn, July 21, 1950, Dental School Files, GUA.

86. July 18, 1950, Minutes of the Directors, GUA; Minutes of Special Meeting in Copley Lounge, August 11, 1950, Graduate School Files, box 1, GUA.

87. September 23, October 11, 1950, Minutes of the Directors, GUA.

88. Guthrie to Nugent, October 20, 1950, H-1, MPARP.

89. January 18, 1951, Minutes of the Directors, GUA.

90. Walsh interview.

91. James Ruby to Vincent I. Bellwoar, SJ, August 31, 1962, O'Leary Papers, folder 84-5; June 12, 1939, Consultors' Minutes, 531-1, GUA.

92. *Washington Star,* February 9, 1948.

93. Degnan interview.

94. Guthrie to Nugent April 22, 1950, H-1, MPARP.

95. McGrath interview, August 4, 1983. The largest contribution, in fact, was given, not by an alumnus, but by the parent of a student. Charles Finn Williams of Cincinnati gave $75,000 toward the construction, for which he was awarded an honorary degree by the university in 1950. Charles Mathews Williams, Alumni Files, GUA.

96. December 7–9, 1951, House Diary, GUA.

97. *Washington Post,* December 22, 1948.

98. Guthrie to Herlihy, July 18, 1949; and Guthrie to Herlihy, December 16, 1949, Sports Archives Files, AA, GUA.

99. Guthrie to Nugent, November 21, 1949, H-1, MPARP.

100. September 16, 1950, Consultors' Minutes, 531-1, GUA.

101. 1950, Finances, AA, GUA.

102. Guthrie to Nugent, November 15, 1950, H-1, MPARP.
103. Memorandum, Guthrie to McGrath, January 24, 1951, "1951," AA, GUA.
104. McGrath interview, August 4, 1983.
105. December 16, 1950, Consultors' Minutes, 531-1, GUA; March 21, 1951, Minutes of the Directors, GUA.
106. *New York Times,* March 28, 1951.
107. *Saturday Evening Post,* October 13, 1951.
108. Address reported in Washington *Catholic Standard,* January 4, 1952.
109. *Hoya,* April 11, 1951.
110. October 11, 1950, Minutes of the Directors, GUA.
111. Guthrie to Nugent, May 4, 1951, H-1, MPARP.
112. Guthrie to Nugent, July 12, 1949, H-1, MPARP.
113. Guthrie to Nugent, December 30, 1950, H-1, MPARP.
114. In the summer of 1950, Guthrie had had his assistant, George Butler, do research on the effect that diversion of Law School funds to the coffers of the university would have on its accreditation. Butler reported that nothing in the ABA's constitution, by-laws, or standards for law schools prohibited the use of school income for larger university purposes. George N. Butler to Guthrie, July 31, 1950, Law School Files, GUA; January 26, 29, 1951, House Diary, GUA; January 25, 26, February 28, 1951, Minutes of the Directors, GUA.
115. The committee also questioned the soundness of having effectively divided authority between regent and dean in several of the schools (Foreign Service, Law). And it criticized inbreeding of faculty in the college, law, and dental schools. It also pointed out the paucity of scholarship among faculty in the undergraduate and professional schools. It thought that an integration of the separate faculties of the college, Graduate School, and School of Foreign Service was a logical step that should be pursued. Middle States Report, B-3.
116. Guthrie to Nugent, May 4, 1951, H-1, MPARP.
117. Middle States Report, B-3.
118. Guthrie to Margaret Sweetman, July 28, 1952; Sweetman to Guthrie, July 30, 1952; Guthrie to Sweetman, August 11, 1952; Sweetman to Guthrie, September 2, 1952; Sweetman to Guthrie, September 16, 1952, Guthrie Papers, varia, 405-2.
119. McGrath interview, August 5, 1983.
120. Ibid.; Handwritten note from Guthrie, September 22, 1952, Minutes of the Directors, GUA.
121. August 5, 1952, Consultors' Minutes, MPARP. By this time Guthrie was talking about the "things my successor should get on to." Hunter to Keelan, August 11, 1952, Bunn Papers.
122. Guthrie to Nugent, Holy Saturday [April 12, 1952], H-1, MPARP.
123. Excerpts of letter of General Janssens to Guthrie, n.d., but internal evidence strongly suggests the late spring or early summer of 1952, H-1, MPARP.
124. Heyden interview; Heyden to Vince [Beatty], September 28, 1952, Guthrie Papers, varia, 405-2.
125. Bunn to Guthrie, October 21, 1952, Guthrie Papers, varia, 405-2.

CHAPTER 9

1. William P. Leahy, SJ, *Adapting to America: Catholics, Jesuits, and Higher Education in the Twentieth Century* (Washington, DC: Georgetown University Press, 1991), 125–27.
2. McGrath interview, August 5, 1983.
3. Karl Cerny interview, February 26, 1987.
4. Annik Buchanan Interview, April 14, 1986.
5. December 5, 1957, House Diary, GUA.
6. "Reflections on a Tenth Anniversary," *Hoya,* October 25, 1962.
7. Brian McGrath, Eulogy, June 22, 1972, Holy Trinity Church, printed in *Georgetown Today,* July 1972, 11.

8. George Houston interview, January 23, 1985.

9. Memorandum, Bunn to Leon E. Dostert, December 10, 1954, "1954," SLL, GUA.

10. Bunn to Forster, June 29, 1955, 1955–58, Medical School Files, GUA.

11. GUA, Minutes of the Directors, February 3, 1960; GUA 550 5B, Minutes of the Directors, March 16, 1961.

12. Bunn to Rault, June 25, 1953, Dental School Files, GUA.

13. McGrath interview, September 14, 1983; Bunn to Maloney, March 23, 1953, Bunn Papers.

14. Abbott, *Political Terrain,* 121.

15. Kathleen M. Lesko et al., *Black Georgetown Remembered: A History of Its Black Community from the Founding "The Town of George" in 1751 to the Present Day* (Washington, DC: Georgetown University Press, 1991), 89–95.

16. Ibid., 95–97.

17. *Courier,* November 1961, 7.

18. President's Address: Greater Georgetown Development Campaign Initiation Dinner, October 24, 1953, Bunn Papers, box 1, folder 1953.

19. McGrath interview, August 5, 1983; Eugene McCahill interview, May 30, 1986.

20. May 6, 1958, President's Council, GUA.

21. October 13–14, 1962, President's Council, GUA. The two major gifts to the university during this period came from legacies, both in 1964. John Vinton Dahlgren left to Georgetown in his will $1.7 million, to be used to build a new chapel, not among the university's planned additions. The other legacy was given by a local woman, Mrs. Flather, a gift of $260,672, which was put into the endowment fund for the hospital. February 20, 1964, House Diary, GUA; February 28, 1964, Board of Directors, 550 5A, GUA.

22. April 27–28, 1963, President's Council, 221-4, GUA.

23. Georgetown University Survey Report, [1960], President's Office Files, GUA.

24. November 1–3, 1963, President's Council, 221-4, GUA.

25. October 11–13, 1964, Minutes of the President's Council, 221-5, GUA.

26. "Address to Workshop on Selected Problems in Administration of American Higher Education," delivered at the Catholic University of America, June 24, 1963; and Speech to the Jesuit Research Council of America, Saint Louis University, January 7, 1967, McGrath Papers.

27. Graham and Diamond, *Rise of American Research Universities,* 41–43.

28. McGrath interview, September 14, 1983.

29. Ibid.

30. Byron Collins to Daley, January 14, 1960; and Byron Collins to Daley, January 11, 1961, MPARP, H-2.

31. September 21, 1962, Minutes of the Directors, 550 5B, GUA.

32. Ibid., May 22, 1964.

33. George Chapman interview, January 7, 1987.

34. "Preliminary Proposal: Advanced Academic Program in the Crime Laboratory Disciplines," August 1, 1968, Law School Files, box 3, GUA.

35. Mooney to Daley, September 21, 1956, Graduate School Files, GUA.

36. October 2, 1960, News Service Files, GUA; typed note, October 3, 1960, Faculty Files, GUA.

37. Joseph E. Earley, "Science and Story at Georgetown," in *Georgetown at Two Hundred,* ed. William C. McFadden, 188–89 (Washington, DC: Georgetown University Press, 1990).

38. Brough, "Philosophy at Georgetown University," 118.

39. Ibid., 119–20.

40. McFadden, *Georgetown at Two Hundred,* 155–57.

41. As Bunn noted much later about the impact of Ellis's jeremiad on Georgetown, "We became concerned with the goal of excellence in the quality of education. . . . This has brought us closer and closer in quality to the secular institutions of higher education." That applied to the quality of faculty as well as to that of the education

offered. "Implications of the Changes in Higher Education for Jesuit Institutions of Higher Learning," 1968, Chancellor Bunn's Papers, box 5, folder T, GUA.

42. Stephen F. McNamee, SJ, to Bunn, September 28, 1954, SLL, GUA; Dostert to Bunn, December 13, 1954, H-1, MPARP.

43. Maura Griffin, "Notes from the Underground," *Georgetown Magazine,* Spring 1989, 8–11.

44. McGrath to Daley, February 20, 1962, MPARP, H-2.

45. "Remarks of Very Rev. Edward B. Bunn, SJ," Bunn Papers, Misc., box 3, 1964.

46. For the evolution of this state science in the post–World War II period, see Patrick J. McGrath, *Scientists, Business, and the State, 1890–1960* (Chapel Hill: University of North Carolina Press, 2002).

47. Geiger, *Research and Relevant Knowledge,* 174–77.

48. Davids's *America and the World of Our Time: U.S. Diplomacy in the Twentieth Century* (1960) was judged by the *New York Times* to be one of the best books published on world affairs in that year. Davids had earlier been involved in the writing of a more noted book, for which he received virtually no credit. In 1954, Jacqueline Kennedy took an American history course that Davids was teaching. One of his lectures was about the political courage that Andrew Johnson had shown in confronting Reconstruction. Mrs. Kennedy apparently discussed the lecture with her husband, because at the next class she asked if Professor Davids could supply for Senator Kennedy a list of those who qualified as examples of outstanding political courage. Sometime afterward, Davids received a call from Kennedy's assistant, Theodore Sorenson, who asked if he would look at a rough draft of *Profiles of Courage.* Davids provided a long critique of the draft, and, as a result, Sorenson asked if he would care to write chapters about four individuals: Daniel Webster, Samuel Houston, Lucius Q. C. Lamar, and George W. Norris. Davids wrote those chapters; Sorenson apparently wrote the rest. Kennedy then reworked the whole book and wrote, so Davids believed, the opening chapter about "Courage and Politics." When *Profiles in Courage* was published in 1957, Kennedy alone was listed as the author. In December of that year, Drew Pearson on *ABC News* charged that the book had actually been ghostwritten. Kennedy, who had already won a Pulitzer Prize for the work, felt he could not let the charge go unchallenged, for fear not only that the prize would be withdrawn but also that the accusation could ruin his chances of running for president. Kennedy and Sorenson eventually persuaded ABC News and Pearson that the book was fundamentally his. The still somewhat skeptical Pearson later wrote in his diary that Kennedy had admitted that Sorenson had done "an awful lot of work." Lost in all of this was Davids, who received $700 from Kennedy for his work, plus a promise that the senator was interested in doing a sequel on great duels in American history for which Davids would be a coauthor and share fully in the royalties. That project, alas, never even had a beginning. Davids to McGrath, August 5, 1957, GUA; *New York Times,* October 18, 1997; *Washington Post,* December 11, 1996; Clark Clifford, *New Yorker,* April 1, 1991; Davids, interview with author.

49. November 19, 1964, Minutes of the Directors, GUA.

50. November 30, 1962, Minutes of the Directors, GUA.

51. Bunn to Oscar Harkavy, Ford Foundation, July 22, 1964, Bunn Papers.

52. Minutes of the Meeting of the Council of Academic Deans, cited in Minutes of the Executive Faculty of the School of Dentistry, January 5, 1955.

53. March 29, 1957, Minutes of the Directors, 550-5A, GUA.

54. McGrath interview, September 14, 1983; Thelin, *History of American Higher Education,* 283.

55. Bunn to W. Griffin, July 5, 1957, Bunn Papers.

56. Cerny interview.

57. McGrath to Daley, February 20, 1962, MPARP, H-2.

58. November 21, 1952; February 27, April 24, December 11, 1953; January 22, November 5, 1954, Minutes of the Directors, GUA.

59. November 14, 1958; December 11, 1959, Minutes of the Directors, 550-5A, GUA.

60. Desan to Horigan, December 3, 1963, Graduate School Files, GUA.
61. Weigert to McGrath, January 28, 1963, Academic Vice President Files (hereafter AVP), GUA.
62. Francis Kearns, "Sit-In," *Commonweal,* April 19, 1963, 100–102.
63. Francis Kearns, "Social Consciousness and Academic Freedom in Catholic Higher Education," *The Shape of Catholic Higher Education,* ed. Robert Hassenger (Chicago: University of Chicago Press, 1967), 223–29.
64. John P. McCall et al. to McGrath, June 18, 1964, AVP, GUA; John Leo, "The Kearns Case," *Commonweal,* January 29, 1965.
65. McGrath to McCall, June 22, 1964, AVP, GUA. That response appeared to avoid the question of why, this being the case, he had been appointed in the first place. In fact, the department had been searching for two *additional* Americanists that semester.
66. Leo, "Kearns Case," 563.
67. *Hoya,* January 15, 1965.
68. *Hoya,* March 4, 1965.
69. Leo, "Kearns Case," 566. Kearns later obtained a position in the English department at Lehman College of the City University of New York, which he held for the next four decades.
70. McCall to Campbell, December 15, 1964, Gerard Campbell Papers, GUA.
71. *National Catholic Register,* March 9, 1966.
72. Schork to McGrath, February 21, 1966, AVP, GUA.
73. October 25–26, 1952, President's Council, GUA; February 27, 1953, Minutes of the Directors; Maloney to Bunn, Baltimore, June 10, 1953, MPARP, H-2; December 10, 1953, House Diary, GUA; "Report on the Development Program," President's Council Meeting, April 24, 1954, H-1, MPARP.
74. November 21, 1952; February 27, 1953, Minutes of the Directors.
75. Bunn to Maloney, June 22, 1953, H-1, MPARP.
76. Charles J. Foley to EBB, May 20, 1953, MPARP, H 1-7; August 11, 1955, Minutes of the Directors, GUA.
77. The Hospital Survey and Construction Act of 1946, which provided construction funds for community hospitals, became known as the Hill-Burton Act, for its sponsors in the Senate, Lister Hill and Harold H. Burton. The act set rather rigid guidelines for the architecture of such buildings, and that architectural style also came to be known as Hill-Burton. Subsequent university construction with federal funding and accompanying architectural restraints came to be known generically as Hill-Burton.
78. Maloney to Bunn, November 5, 1956, H-1, MPARP. The constitutions of the Society of Jesus required that local institutions of the order secure permission from the headquarters (curia) in Rome for any major construction.
79. Bunn to Maloney, April 2, 1957, MPARP, H 1-6.
80. Bunn to Maloney, April 2, 1957, MPARP, H 1-6.
81. In his honor, a medical scholarship for Irish students was established by the university. March 19, 1959, House Diary, 550-24, GUA.
82. October 6–7, 1956, President's Council Files, GUA; August 10, 1956; November 14, 1958, Minutes of the Directors, GUA.
83. October 13–14, 1962; April 27–28, 1963, President's Council Files, GUA; September 17, 1963, Minutes of the Directors, GUA.
84. "Georgetown University, Survey Report, A Confidential Report Prepared by Community Counseling Service, Inc., Empire State Building, New York, N.Y.," [1960], President's Office Files, GUA; October 8–9, 1960, President's Council Files, 221-3, GUA.
85. Minutes of the President's Council, May 5–6, 1962, President's Council Files, 221-4, GUA.
86. Fitzgerald, *Governance of Jesuit Colleges,* 132.
87. Leahy, *Adapting to America,* 132–33.

88. Bunn, "GU Graduate School," February 1952, Graduate School Files, box 1, 1952, GUA.
89. Graduate School Files, box 1, 1953, GUA.
90. Dean's Report, 1952–53, Graduate School Files, box 1, 1953, GUA.
91. Heyden, "Progress Report for 1952–53," Graduate School Files, box 1, 1953, GUA; Heyden, Memorandum on the June 30, 1954, Eclipse Expedition, H-1, MPARP.
92. Heyden, *Beginning and End of a Jesuit Observatory.*
93. Thomas Derry, "The Georgetown Observatory: A Room with a View," *Georgetown Magazine,* Fall 1987, 16–17.
94. Heyden, "Needs of Department of Astronomy," April 2, 1952, Graduate School Files, box 1, 1952, GUA.
95. Alexander originally had come to Washington in 1954 to do his doctoral studies at Howard, but when he discovered that Georgetown was accepting blacks for graduate programs, he applied to Georgetown.
96. Middle States Report, October 1960.
97. Annual Law School Report for the Year 1952–53, Law School Files, GUA.
98. Ernst et al., *First One Hundred and Twenty-five Years,* 123.
99. Ibid., 148.
100. Sherman Cohn interview, November 17, 2005.
101. Cohn interview.
102. Ernst et al., *First One Hundred and Twenty-five Years,* 134.
103. Stevens, *Law School;* "Faculty Meeting, January 21 and January 28, 1959," Law School Files, GUA; Minutes of the President's Council, May 5–6, 1962, President's Council, 221-4, GUA; Annual Report, 1959, Law School Files, GUA.
104. In 1959, of the twenty-three top schools supplying students to the Law School, fifteen were Catholic.
105. Those dropped for academic reasons made up but one-quarter of those leaving. However, as the regent explained in his annual report, many of those leaving because of financial reasons or the draft also had poor academic records. Annual Report, 1953, Law School Files, GUA.
106. Dean's Report to President's Council, May 1962, Law School Files, GUA.
107. Michigan, for instance, had an acceptance rate of 46 percent, Harvard 41percent, Yale 33 percent, and Virginia 49 percent.
108. Ernst et al., *First One Hundred and Twenty-five Years,* 145.
109. Dean's Council, February 15, 1963, Law School Files, 1963, GUA.
110. Ernst et al., *First One Hundred and Twenty-five Years,* 130.
111. Ibid., 124.
112. Ibid., 135.
113. Dean's Report, May 1962, Law School Files, GUA.
114. Ernst et al., *First One Hundred and Twenty-five Years,* 123.
115. Executive Faculty to Bunn, August 15, 1960, Law School Files, 1960, GUA.
116. Memo from Joseph M. Snee, SJ, to Bunn, June 10, 1960, Law School Files, 1960, GUA.
117. Executive Faculty to Bunn, August 15, 1960, Law School Files, 1960, GUA.
118. Middle States Report, cited in Ernst et al., *First One Hundred and Twenty-five Years,* 138.
119. Ernst et al., *First One Hundred and Twenty-five Years,* 138.
120. Dean's Report to President's Council, May 1962, Law School Files, GUA.
121. Dean's Council, February 15, 1963, Law School Files, 1963, GUA.
122. Wallace J. Mylniec, "The Intersection of Three Visions—Ken Pye, Bill Pincus, and Bill Greenhalgh—and the Development of Clinical Teaching Fellowships," *Tennessee Law Review* 64 (Summer 1997): 964–65.
123. Cohn interview.
124. Wallace Mylniec interview, April 12, 2006.
125. Ernst et al., *First One Hundred and Twenty-five Years,* 128–29.
126. GU News Service, September 18, 1966, "Ford Foundation Grant Extends Georgetown Law Center's Legal Internship Program," Law School Files, 1966, GUA.

127. "District Bail Bond Project to Wind Up as Grant Ends," *Washington Star,* March 15, 1966.

128. *Georgetown Record,* August 1966.

129. Ibid.

130. *Time,* January 27, 1967.

131. AALS [Walter Gellhorn], Special Committee of Graduate Study, Report on Georgetown University, May 8, 1963, draft, Law School Files, 1963, GUA.

132. Dean's Report to President's Council, May 1962, Law School Files, GUA; Dean's Report, May 1962, Law School Files, GUA.

133. December 4, 1964, Minutes of the President's Council, 221-5, GUA.

134. May 6, 1958, Minutes of the President's Council, GUA.

135. "Location of the Law Center," March 1960, Law School Files, box 2, GUA.

136. The cost of acquiring the site was $2.3 million. May 1–2, 1965, Minutes of the President's Council, 221-5, GUA.

137. Dean David McCarthy, cited in Ernst et al., *First One Hundred and Twenty-five Years,* 146.

138. Bunn to Dean of the Medical School and Administrator of the Hospital, June 29, 1955, Medical School Files, 1955–58, GUA.

139. Stapleton, *Upward Journey,* 117.

140. Application for Commonwealth Fund, January–March 1957; and Dean's Report, May 1964, Medical School Files, GUA.

141. *Georgetown University News,* October 21, 1970; Description of Department of Pharmacology, n.d. [c. 1970], Medical School Files, GUA.

142. Barry, *Surgeons at Georgetown,* 279–80.

143. Ibid., 148–49; *Washington Post,* February 24, 1963.

144. *Washington Post,* March 1960; Barry, *Surgeons at Georgetown,* 259–60.

145. Barry, *Surgeons at Georgetown,* 253–55.

146. Clemens V. Rault and Hugh H. Hussey to McGrath, September 20, 1960, Medical School Files, GUA.

147. Michael E. Kerr, "Darwin to Freud to Bowen: Toward a Natural Systems Theory of Human Behavior," *Georgetown Magazine,* Spring 1989, 16–19, 44–45.

148. February 19, 1960, Minutes of the Directors, 550-5A, GUA.

149. Kenneth M. Ludmerer, *Time to Heal: American Medical Education from the Turn of the Century to the Era of Managed Care* (New York: Oxford University Press, 1999), 139.

150. Ibid., 142.

151. Geiger, *Research and Relevant Knowledge,* 181–85.

152. Ludmerer, *Time to Heal,* 143–44.

153. Starr, *Social Transformation of American Medicine,* 338–44.

154. Dean's Report, May 1965, Medical School Files, GUA.

155. Ludmerer, *Time to Heal,* 150.

156. "From the Dean," *Georgetown Medical Bulletin,* August 1966, 3.

157. Stapleton, *Upward Journey,* 144.

158. August 18, 1955, Minutes of the Directors, GUA.

159. Stapleton, *Upward Journey,* 141.

160. October 12, 1958, Minutes of the President's Council, 221-3, GUA.

161. Rothstein, *American Medical Schools and the Practice of Medicine,* 296–311.

162. John Rose interview with Pam Ginsbach, n.d.

163. John Stapleton interview, August 24, 1994.

164. Ludmerer, *Time to Heal,* 163–65.

165. Stapleton, *Upward Journey,* 141.

166. Bunn to Maloney, December 21, 1955, MPARP, H 1-6.

167. Ludmerer, *Time to Heal,* 181–83.

168. By 1965, Ludmerer observes, 63 percent of the doctors in the country classified themselves as specialists. Of the 37 percent who admitted to being generalists, half were over sixty-five years old. Ludmerer, *Time to Heal,* 187.

169. Stapleton, *Upward Journey,* 129–31.

170. John C. Rose, "A System of Continuing Medical Education," *Medical Annals of D.C.* (September 1967): 510–13; Stapleton, *Upward Journey,* 133–34; William Ayers interview, December 10, 1986.
171. *Georgetown Medical Bulletin,* May 1965, 241–42.
172. A survey of eighty-seven medical schools in 1961–62 ranked Georgetown thirty-first in the ratio between full-time students and full-time faculty and thirty-third in sponsored research. Bauer to Campbell, September 21, 1964, Executive Vice President, Medical School Files, GUA.
173. Jeghers to Hugh Hussey, February 3, 1962, Medical School Files, GUA.
174. Report of Survey Group, [1958], Medical School Files, GUA.
175. Bunn to Rault, November 3, 1960, Dental School Files, GUA; Rose interview with Ginsbach.
176. Ludmerer, *Time to Heal,* 160.
177. Middle States Report, 1961.
178. Rault to Bunn, July 23, 1956, "1957"; Bunn to Rault, September 17, 1956, "1956"; and Dean's Report, 1963–64, Dental School Files, GUA.
179. Minutes of Dean's Advisory Council, March 2, 1962, Dental School Files, GUA; May 5–6, 1962, Minutes of the President's Council, 221-4, GUA.
180. Executive Faculty Meeting, October 10, 1956, Dental School Files, GUA.
181. Minutes of the Executive Faculty Meeting, April 4, 1956, Dental School Files, GUA.
182. Dean's Report, 1957–58, 7–8, Dental School Files, GUA.
183. Dean's Report, 1958–59, 11, Dental School Files, GUA.
184. Bunn to Dr. John A. Perkins, Chair, Commission on the Survey of Dentistry, February 16, 1959, Dental School Files, 1959, GUA; May 5–6, 1962, Minutes of the President's Council, 221-4, GUA.
185. March 5, 1958, Minutes of the Executive Faculty Meeting; and Dean's Report, 1961–62, 34–35, Dental School Files, GUA.
186. Report of C. V. Rault to Georgetown University Alumni Association Members, September 9, 1961, Dental School Files, 1961, GUA.
187. Dean's Report, 1961–62, 9; and Rault to Bauer, May 12, 1964, "1964," Dental School Files, GUA.
188. Dean's Report, 1956–57, 27–28, Dental School Files, GUA.
189. Dean Rault to Alumni, November 13, 1962, Dental School Files, 1962, GUA.
190. May 5–6, 1962, Minutes of the President's Council, 221-4, GUA.
191. Joyce Shelby, "One Dentist for a Million People," *Georgetown Magazine,* January 1975, 30.
192. *Washington Star,* February 7, 1960.
193. Dean's Report, 1960–61, 9, Dental School Files, GUA; Judith Martin, "Hand-to-Mouth Existence," *Washington Post,* April 15, 1962.

CHAPTER 10

1. Ayers interview.
2. Advisory Council meeting, May 18–19, 1963, College of Arts and Sciences Files (hereafter CAS), GUA.
3. 1958–59 statistics, Registrar Files, GUA.
4. Joseph K. Drane to Maloney, May 13, 1957, H 1-3, MPARP.
5. Advisory Council meeting, October 18–19, 1963, CAS, GUA.
6. Joseph Sellinger interview, January 27, 1989.
7. Maloney to Bunn, October 30, 1958, H-1, MPARP.
8. McGrath to Bunn, October 13, 1953, SFS, GUA.
9. Waldron to Bunn, December 23, 1953, "1953"; and Fadner to Bunn, March 24, 1954, "1954," SFS, GUA.
10. John Waldron to Bunn, December 28, 1953, SFS, 1954, GUA.
11. William O'Brien, Chair (the other two members were Jules Davids and Stephen Gilbert), "Report No. 1 of the University Liaison Committee for SFS," n.d., SFS, GUA.

12. "The Competence of Georgetown University 'to unite the means of communicating Science with an effectual provision for guarding and preserving the Morals of Youth,' as appraised by an Evaluation Team Representing the Middle States Association of Colleges and Secondary Schools, which Visited the University on October 23–27, 1960," AVP, Reports of Inspections by Middle States Association, GUA.

13. William E. Moran Jr. to Bunn, "Annual Report for the Academic Year 1962–63," June 1963, SFS, 1963, GUA.

14. May 5–6, 1962, Minutes of the President's Council, 221-4, GUA; Moran to McGrath, November 29, 1963, SFS, GUA; Tillman, *Georgetown's School of Foreign Service*, 40–41.

15. Georgetown University School of Languages and Linguistics, *The Lado Years* (Washington, DC: Georgetown University Press, 1973), 5–6 (hereafter *Lado Years*).

16. Lado to Robert F. Harvanek, July 26, 1960, SLL, GUA.

17. Middle States Report, October 1960, iv.

18. *Lado Years,* 7.

19. In the 1961–62 academic year, Georgetown students received approximately $200,000 in National Defense loans, many of which went to SLL students. After 1958 the school regularly became one of the largest beneficiaries of NDEA fellowships for its languages and linguistics graduate students. With NDEA funding the SLL also began in 1960 a summer institute for training in various languages for elementary and secondary schoolteachers.

20. *Lado Years,* 8.

21. Bunn to James E. Victory, director, Office of Participant Training, ICA, November 30, 1960; Director's Report, 1961; and GU News Service, November 12, 1961, SLL, GUA.

22. Minutes of Advisory Council Meeting, October 5, 1964; and Lado to Bunn, October 23, 1964, SLL, GUA.

23. "Development Plan," December, 1952, SLL, GUA.

24. Survey of Opinions and Attitudes of Dr. Robert Lado, SLL, GUA.

25. Bunn to Sebes, March 12, 1962, School of Business Administration Files (hereafter SBA), 1962, GUA.

26. Henry Cunningham to Syzmczak, December 20, 1954, SBA, 1937–54, GUA.

27. Memo, Cunningham to Bunn, November 1955, SBA, 1955, GUA.

28. Middle States Report, October 1960.

29. Pelissier to Bunn, September 13, 1960, SBA, 1960, GUA.

30. November 28, 1961, Minutes of the Directors, 550-5B, GUA; Pelissier to Bunn, November 28, 1961, "1961"; and Bunn to Pelissier, December 3, 1962, "1962," SBA, GUA.

31. Ottmar Winkler interview, September 26, 1986.

32. Cunningham to Bunn, June 15, 1959, SBA, 1959, GUA.

33. Pelissier, [November] 1961, Report on Graduate Education, SBA, GUA.

34. Haller to Bunn, November 27, 1962, SBA, GUA.

35. December 2–4, 1963, Board of Directors, SBA, GUA.

36. Dean's Annual Report, 1953–54, Nursing School Files, 1953–54, GUA.

37. May 5–6, 1962, Minutes of the President's Council, 221-4, GUA.

38. Dean's Report, 1963, Nursing School Files, GUA.

39. Dean's Annual Report, 1953–54, Nursing School Files, 1954, GUA.

40. Executive Faculty Committee meeting minutes, April 23, 1954, OP, Nursing School, January–August 1954, GUA, cited in Woolley, *Learning, Faith, and Caring,* 72.

41. Angela Marie to Bunn, February 13, 1957; and Alice Higgins to Angela Marie, [February 1957], Nursing School Files, GUA.

42. Maloney to Bunn, Baltimore, February 19, 1953, Georgetown Jesuit Community Archives.

43. McHugh to Maloney, May 22, 1953, Nursing School Files, GUA.

44. L. C. McHugh to Bunn, "Schematic Report of Observations on the Administration of the Nursing School, February–July 1953," July 23, 1953, Nursing School Files, 1953, GUA.

45. McHugh to Bunn, March 12, 1954, Nursing, GUA, cited in Woolley, *Learning, Faith, and Caring*, 76.

46. Angela Marie to Bunn, April 5, 1954, Nursing School Files, GUA.

47. GU News release, September 28, 1956, cited in Woolley, *Learning, Faith, and Caring*, 76.

48. Woolley, interview with Sister Kathleen Mary, July 8, 1995, cited in Woolley, *Learning, Faith, and Caring*, 89.

49. Ibid.

50. Memo, Paul Locher to McGrath, February 14, 1956, Academic Vice President Files, GUA.

51. January 31, 1957, Minutes of the Directors, 550-5A, GUA.

52. Yates to Campbell, January 22, 1965, Campbell Papers.

53. George Dunne, SJ, *King's Pawn: The Memoirs of George H. Dunne, S.J. (1905–1989)* (Chicago: Loyola University Press, 1990), 265–67.

54. Franklin B. Williams Jr., "Delta of D.C.: The Early Years, 1965–1980," President's Office Files, 940419, GUA; Yates Memorandum, "A Note on the Gold Key Society," [1958], GUA.

55. Carl Billman to Williams, December 19, 1952, CAS, GUA.

56. Williams, "Delta," 4–6.

57. Joseph Rock to Bunn, April 8, 1957, H 1-3, MPARP.

58. *Hoya*, May 16, 1957.

59. *Hoya*, October 15, 1953.

60. *Hoya*, March 20, 1958.

61. *Hoya*, October 2, 1958.

62. *Washington Post*, May 18–19, 1963; Rose Marie L. Audette, "Everything in Moderation: Social Activism and University Reform, Georgetown University, 1960–1970" (honors thesis, Georgetown University, 1981), 26.

63. Daniel Altobello interview, February 26, 1987; *Washington Post*, May 19, 1963.

64. O'Boyle to Students of Georgetown, May 20, 1963, GUA, cited in Craig Goldblatt, "Look beyond the Campus, to America Itself: Student Activism at Georgetown University during the 1960s and the Founding of *The Georgetown Voice*" (unpublished paper, Georgetown University, 1988), 8.

65. Nastasi to Gentlemen of Georgetown, May 18, 1963, Students Files, GUA; Kearns, "Social Consciousness," 226–27.

66. Advisory Council Meeting, May 18–19, 1963, CAS, GUA.

67. Bunn to Maloney, November 15, 1955; House Diary, April 1, 1956, H-1, MPARP.

68. Carolyn Stevens, "Donn B. Murphy: Bringing Up the Lights for Three Decades of Students," *Georgetown Magazine*, September–October 1984, 12–13.

69. Bunn to Reynolds, May 31, 1963, Bunn Papers.

70. *Hoya*, January 16, 1958.

71. *Hoya*, February 13, 1964.

72. January 16, 1961, Minutes of the Directors, 1956–61, 550-5A, GUA.

73. "Athletic Program at GU," Fred A. Brew, SJ, March 12, 1957, H-103, MPARP.

74. "Remarks," November 20, 1977, McGrath Papers.

75. Dunne, King's Pawn, 264–65.

76. Howard Gillette Jr., *Between Justice and Beauty: Race, Planning, and the Failure of Urban Policy in Washington, D.C.* (Baltimore: Johns Hopkins University Press, 1995), 154.

77. [McHugh], "Gripe Record," Nursing School Files, 1953, GUA

78. R. B. Deyo to Bunn, May 31, 1956, Dental School Files, GUA.

79. Bunn to R. B. Deyo, June 19, 1956, Dental School Files, GUA.

80. Mrs. Ivy C. Matthews, to Bunn, April 15, 1958, Dental School Files, GUA.

81. Bunn to Matthews, April 24. 1956, copy, Dental School Files, GUA.

82. Harold M. Johnson to Bunn, October 12, 1955, Tansill Faculty File, GUA.

83. Bunn to R. D. Sparks, Managing Editor, *Daily Sun*, October 18, 1955, Bunn Papers.

84. *Washington Daily News,* n.d.

85. Tansill to Bunn, April 5, 1956; and Bunn to Tansill, July 13, 1956, copy, Bunn Papers.

86. June 19, 1961, House Diary, GUA.

87. *Hoya,* October 4, 1962.

88. Kearns, "Sit-In," 94–102.

89. *Hoya,* May 2, 1963.

90. Paul Mattingly, e-mails to the author, January 8, 2007; August 28, 1963, House Diary, GUA.

91. April 28, 1964, House Diary, GUA.

92. Sister M. Francesca to All Nursing Units, March 30, 1964, Nursing, 1964, GUA, cited in Woolley, *Learning, Faith, and Caring,* 105; Unknown to Joel Broyhill, May 11, 1964, copy sent to Charles Shields, 1964; and Shields to Broyhill, May 13, 1964, copy, Nursing School Files, GUA.

93. "Speeches and Remarks made at the Jubilee Dinner honoring Edmund A. Walsh, SJ, on his Fiftieth Anniversary as a Member of the Society of Jesus," Mayflower Hotel, Washington, DC, November 15, 1952, GUA.

94. McGrath to Guthrie, April 12, 1951, Kraus Faculty File, 1054, GUA.

95. McGrath to Guthrie, November 13, 1951, Kraus Faculty File, 1054, GUA.

96. McGrath to Guthrie, November 13, 1951, Kraus Faculty File, 1054, GUA.

97. April 6, 1952, News Service, GUA.

98. October 17, 1952, Minutes of the Directors, GUA; *Lado Years,* 4.

99. Report on Academic Developments, 1952–53, SLL, 1953, GUA.

100. GU News Service, March 16, 1954, SLL, GUA.

101. "Technical Assistance Project History and Analysis Report of the Georgetown Participant Language Training . . . under the sponsorship of the Government of the Republic of Turkey and the Agency for International Development," SLL, GUA; GU News Service, March 16, 1954, SFF, GUA; Lado Years, 5.

102. Richard J. O'Brien, SJ, ed., *Georgetown University Round Table on Languages and Linguistics* (Washington, DC: Georgetown University Press, 1971), v–vi.

103. September 24, 1954, Minutes of the Directors, GUA; Minutes of Meeting on the Kersten Project, January 3, 1955, Graduate School Files, box 1, 1955, GUA.

104. October 4, 1961 Minutes of the Directors, 550-5B, GUA.

105. James Allen Smith, *Strategic Calling: The Center for Strategic and International Studies, 1962–1992* (Washington, DC: Center for Strategic and International Studies, 1993), 3.

106. November 28, 1961, Minutes of the Directors, 550-5B, GUA.

107. Smith, *Strategic Calling,* 22–24.

108. "Summary Report on the Graduate School," Graduate School Files, 1953, GUA.

109. Dean's Report, 1952–53, Graduate School Files, box 1, 1955, GUA.

110. Weigert to Yates, November 17, 1954; "Security Policy for Clearance of Personnel to Be Employed by Georgetown University and Assigned to the Research Project," January 14, 1954; Weigert to Daley, January 14, 1954, Graduate School Files, box 1, 1954, GUA.

111. R. C. Partridge to Yates, May 4,1953, Graduate School Files, box 1, 1955, GUA.

112. *Hoya,* October 8, 1953.

113. *Hoya,* February 26, 1953.

114. Lucas, *American Higher Education,* 225.

115. *Washington Evening Star,* January 1, 1953.

116. Anonymous memorandum, "Towards a Georgetown Institute of Interpretation, Languages, & Linguistics"; and confidential memorandum to Bunn, April 5, 1954, SLL, 1954, GUA; May 21, 1954, Minutes of the Directors, GUA; Bunn to Maloney, August 19, 1954, H 1-4, MPARP.

117. Winters to Bunn, October 30, 1956, SFS, 1956, GUA.

118. Bunn to Rev. Francis L. Rozsaly, OP, November 21, 1956, Other Colleges Files, 154-1, box 1, folder CUA, GUA.

119. "Hungary: The Alternatives," *Hoya,* November 15, 1956.

120. November 21, 1958, Minutes of the Directors, 550-5B, GUA.

121. January 22, 1962, Minutes of the Directors, 550-5B, GUA.

122. October 22, 1962, House Diary, GUA.

123. *Hoya,* October 25, 1962.

124. Students Files, 1960–66, GUA.

125. Dunne, *King's Pawn,* 282–83.

126. Ibid., 285–87.

127. Ibid., 287–90.

128. *Hoya,* December 11, 1964.

129. Thomas Fitzgerald interview, April 1984; Royden Davis interview, March 24, 1986.

Selected Bibliography

PRIMARY SOURCES

Archives

Archives of the Archdiocese of Baltimore
Archivum Romanum Societatis Jesu
  Epistolae Vicarum Generalium in Russia, 1809–14
  Liber Litterarum Generalis (Register of the Letters of the General of the
      Society of Jesus)
  Litterae Annuales Provinciae Marylandiae
  Marylandia
Georgetown Jesuit Community Archives
  Memorials of Provincial Visitations
Georgetown University Special Collections
  Alphonsus J. Donlon Papers
  Brian A. McGrath, SJ, Papers
  Diary of the Administrator of the Jesuit Community (House Diary)
  Edmund Walsh, SJ, Papers
  Frank Fadner, SJ, Papers
  Georgetown University Archives
    Academic Vice President/Provost
      Reports of the Inspections of Georgetown University by the Middle States
          Association of Colleges and Secondary Schools
    Alumni
    Alumni Advisory Committee
    Arthur A. O'Leary, SJ, Papers
    Catalogues (University, Undergraduate Schools, Graduate School, Law School,
        Medical School, Dental School)
    Chancellor Bunn Papers
    Charles W. Lyons, SJ, Papers
    Coleman Nevils, SJ, Papers
    College, Old Archives
    College of Arts and Sciences
      Dean
    David Hillhouse Buel, SJ, Papers
    Dental School
      Dental Faculty Minutes
      Judith F. Giuliani. "History of the Georgetown University Dental School."
          Unpublished typescript, 1990.

Development
Discipline Office Newsletters
Edward Bunn, SJ, Papers
Executive Vice President for Financial Affairs
Faculty
Financial Record Series
Gerard Campbell, SJ, Papers
Graduate School
   Dean
   Reports
Hunter Guthrie, SJ, Papers
Jerome Daugherty, SJ, Papers
John B. Whitney, SJ, Letterbooks, 2 vols., 1898–1901
John B. Whitney, SJ, Papers
John Creeden, SJ, Papers
Joseph Havens Richards, SJ, Letterbooks, 14 vols., 1888–98
Joseph Havens Richards, SJ, Letterbooks, Society of Jesus, 3 vols.
Joseph Havens Richards, SJ, Papers
Joseph Himmel, SJ, Papers
Lawrence C. Gorman, SJ, Papers
Law School
   Executive Faculty Minutes
   James Therry. "A Partial History of the Georgetown University Law School."
      Unpublished typescript, n.d.
   Reports
Maryland Province Archives at Roland Park
  Minutes of the Province Consultors
   Medical School
     Correspondence
     Executive Faculty Minutes
     Medical Faculty Minutes
     Pamela Ginsbach. "A History of the Georgetown University Medical School."
       Unpublished manuscript.
     Records of the Association of Medical Students of Georgetown University
   Minutes of the Board of Regents
   Minutes of the Directors, 1797–1989
   Minutes of the President's Council
   Minutes of the Rector's Consultations
   News Service
   Other Colleges
   President's Office
   Registrar
   School of Business Administration
   School of Foreign Service
   School of Languages and Linguistics
   Sesquicentennial
   Sports Archives
   Students
   Thomas Hughes, SJ, Papers
   Timothy Brosnahan, SJ, Papers
   Varia
   War Emergency Plans

Newspapers

Baltimore Sun
Boston Herald
Canton Repository
Hoya

National Catholic Register
New York Times
New York World
Washington Catholic Standard
Washington Daily News
Washington Evening Star
Washington Herald
Washington Post
Washington Star
Washington Times
Washington Times Herald

Magazines and Bulletins

Commonweal
Georgetown College Journal
[Georgetown] *Courier*
Georgetown Magazine
Georgetown Medical Bulletin
Georgetown Record
Georgetown Today
[Georgetown University] *Library Associates Newsletter*
Georgetown University News
Time
Woodstock Letters

Books

Ashford, Bailey Kelly. *A Soldier of Science*. New York: W. Morrow and Co., 1934.

Busey, S. C. *Personal Reminiscences and Recollections of Forty-Six Years of Membership in the Medical Society of the District of Columbia*. Washington, DC: Medical Society of the District of Columbia, 1895.

Casper, Donald. *"Doc" Bunn: A Remembering*. Washington, DC: Georgetown University, 1975.

Dunne, George, SJ. *King's Pawn: The Memoirs of George Dunne, S.J. (1905–1989)*. Chicago: Loyola University Press, 1990.

Flexner, Abraham. *Medical Education in the United States and Canada: A Report to the Carnegie Foundation for the Advancement of Teaching*. New York: Carnegie Foundation for the Advancement of Teaching, 1910.

McDevitt, William G. *The Hilltop Remembered*. Washington, DC: Georgetown University Press, 1982.

McLaughlin, J. Fairfax. *College Days at Georgetown and Other Papers*. Philadelphia: J. P. Lippincott Co., 1899.

National Cyclopedia of American Biography. New York: J. T. White, 1930–.

O'Brien, Richard J., SJ, ed. *Georgetown University Round Table on Languages and Linguistics*. Washington, DC: Georgetown University Press, 1971.

On the Hilltop: Reflections and Reminiscences by Georgetown Alumni. Washington, DC: Georgetown University, 1966.

Richards, J. Havens. *A Loyal Life: A Biography of Henry Livingston Richards*. St. Louis, MO: Herder, 1913.

Tradition and Prospect: The Inauguration of the Very Reverend Hunter Guthrie, SJ as Thirty-Fifth President of Georgetown University, April 30 and May 1, 1949. Washington, DC: Georgetown University, 1949.

Articles

"Notes on the Music." Program for the Inauguration of John Joseph DeGioia as Forty-eighth President of Georgetown University, October 13, 2001. DAR Constitution Hall.

Richards, J. Havens, SJ. "An Explanation in Reply to Some Recent Strictures," *WL* 26 (1897).

Interviews

(Unless otherwise noted, all interviews are by the author)

Altobello, Daniel. February 26, 1987.
Ayers, William. December 10, 1986.
Buchanan, Annik. April 1986.
Cerny, Karl. February 26, 1987.
Chapman, George. January 7, 1987.
Coffey, Robert. July 23, 1993.
Cohn, Sherman. November 17, 2005.
Collins, T. Byron, SJ. September 26–27, October 6, 1972 (Interview by Joseph Durkin, SJ.)
Davis, Royden, SJ. March 24, 1986
Degnan, Daniel, SJ. July 30, 1987.
Doan, Thomas. May 30, 1986.
Dumm, Rosalin. n.d. (Interviewed by Pam Ginsbach.)
Durkin, Joseph, SJ. November 8, 1995.
Feldman, Philip. October 2, 1983.
Fitzgerald, James. January 31, 1986.
Fitzgerald, Thomas, SJ. April 1984.
Heyden, Francis, SJ. November 27, 1984.
Houston, George. January 23, 1985.
Jeghers, Harold. June 9, 1983.
McBride, Nevins. May 30, 1986.
McCahill, Eugene. May 30, 1986.
McGarrity, Rose. November 30, 1988.
McGrath, Brian, SJ. August 2, 4, 5, 8, 1983; September 14, 1983.
Millwater, Charles. January 29, 1991.
Mlyniec, Wallace. April 12, 2006.
Penn, Donald. February 20, 1991.
Power, Daniel, SJ. October 5, 1972 (Interview by Joseph Durkin, SJ.)
Price, Marie. June 15, 1983.
Reiss, Raymond. June 6, 1983.
Rose, John. December 11, 18, 1986.
Rose, John. n.d. [interview by Pam Ginsbach].
Sellinger, Joseph, SJ. January 27, 1989.
Shannon, James. June 9, 1983.
Stapleton, John. August 24, 1994.
Walsh, Donald. December 14, 1983.
Winkler, Ottmar. September 26, 1986.

SECONDARY SOURCES

Books and Articles

GENERAL

Abbott, Carl, "Dimensions of Regional Change in Washington, D.C." *American Historical Review* (December 1990): 1367–93.
———. *Political Terrain: Washington, D.C., from Tidewater Town to Global Metropolis.* Chapel Hill: University of North Carolina Press, 1999.
Amster, Lewis J. "Bailey Ashford: 'Prophet of Tropical Medicine.'" *Hospital Practice,* [April 15, 1985], 139–50.
Barrows, Clyde W. *Universities and the Capitalist State: Corporate Liberalism and the Reconstruction of American Higher Education, 1894–1918.* Madison: University of Wisconsin Press, 1990.
Bender, Thomas, et al. "Institutionalization and Education in the Nineteenth and Twentieth Centuries." *History of Education Quarterly* (Winter 1980): 449–72.

Bledstein, Burton J. *The Culture of Professionalism: The Middle Class and the Development of Higher Education in America.* New York: Oxford University Press, 1976.

Brinkley, David. *Washington Goes to War.* New York: Knopf, 1988.

Cardozier, V. R. *Colleges and Universities in World War II.* Westport, CT: Praeger, 1993.

Cohen, Robert. *When the Old Left Was Young: Student Radicals and America's First Mass Student Movement, 1929–1941.* New York: Oxford University Press, 1993.

Cremin, Lawrence A. *American Education: The Metropolitan Experience, 1876–1980.* New York: Harper & Row, 1988.

Diamond, Sigmund. *Compromised Campus: The Collaboration of Universities with the Intelligence Community: 1945–1955.* New York: Oxford University Press, 1992.

Geiger, Roger. *To Advance Knowledge: The Growth of American Research Universities, 1900–1940.* New York: Oxford University Press, 1986.

Geiger, Roger L. *Research and Relevant Knowledge: American Research Universities since World War II.* New York: Oxford University Press, 1993.

Gillette, Howard, Jr. *Between Justice and Beauty: Race, Planning and the Failure of Urban Policy in Washington, D.C.* Baltimore: Johns Hopkins University Press, 1995.

Graham, Hugh D. *The Uncertain Triumph: Federal Education Policy in the Kennedy and Johnson Years.* Chapel Hill: University of North Carolina Press, 1984.

Graham, Hugh David, and Nancy Diamond. *The Rise of American Research Universities: Elites and Challengers in the Postwar Era.* Baltimore: Johns Hopkins University Press, 1997.

Green, Constance McLaughlin. *Washington: Capital City, 1878–1950.* Princeton, NJ: Princeton University Press, 1963.

Gruber, Carol S. *Mars and Minerva: World War I and the Uses of the Higher Learning in America.* Baton Rouge: Louisiana State University Press, 1976.

Hoehling, A. A. *The Great Epidemic.* Boston: Little, Brown, 1961.

Horowitz, Helen Lefkowitz. *Campus Life: Undergraduate Cultures from the End of the Eighteenth Century to the Present.* Chicago: University of Chicago Press, 1987.

Keefer, Louis E. "Birth and Death of the Army Specialized Training Program." *Army History* (Winter 1995): 1–7.

———. *Scholars in Foxholes: The Story of the Army Specialized Training Program in World War II.* Jefferson, NC: McFarland & Co., 1988.

Keyser, Elmer Louis. *A Medical Center: The Institutional Development of Medical Education in George Washington University.* Washington, DC: 1973.

Kolata, Gina. *Flu: The Story of the Great Influenza Pandemic of 1918 and the Search for the Virus That Caused It.* New York: Farrar, Straus and Giroux, 1999.

Lamb, D. S., et al. *History of the Medical Society of the District of Columbia, 1817–1909.* Washington, DC: 1909.

LaPiana, William P. *Logic and Experience: The Origin of Modern American Legal Education.* New York: Oxford University Press, 1994.

Lesko, Kathleen M., et al. *Black Georgetown Remembered: A History of Its Black Community from the Founding of "The Town of George" in 1751 to the Present Day.* Washington, DC: Georgetown University Press, 1991.

Leslie, W. Bruce. *Gentlemen and Scholars: College and Community in the "Age of the University," 1865–1917.* University Park: Pennsylvania State University Press, 1992.

Levine, David O. *The American College and the Culture of Aspiration, 1915–1940.* Ithaca, NY: Cornell University Press, 1986.

Lucas, Christopher J. *American Higher Education: A History.* New York: St. Martin's, 1994.

Ludmerer, Kenneth M. *Learning to Heal: The Development of American Medical Education.* Baltimore: Johns Hopkins University Press, 1985.

———. *Time to Heal: American Medical Education from the Turn of the Century to the Era of Managed Care.* New York: Oxford University Press, 1999.

Martin, Judith. "Hand-to-Mouth Existence." *Washington Post,* April 15, 1962.

McGrath, Patrick J. *Scientists, Business and the State, 1890–1960.* Chapel Hill: University of North Carolina Press, 2002.

Nichols, John Benjamin, et al. *History of the Medical Society of the District of Columbia.* Part II. Washington, DC: n.p., 1947.

Oakes, Guy. *The Imaginary War: Civil Defense and American Cold War Culture.* New York: Oxford University Press, 1994.

Olson, Keith W. "The G.I. Bill and Higher Education: Success and Surprise." *American Quarterly* (December 1973): 596–610.

———. *The G.I. Bill, the Veterans, and the Colleges.* Lexington: University of Kentucky Press, 1974.

Putney, Clifford. *Muscular Christianity: Manhood and Sports in Protestant America, 1880–1920.* Cambridge, MA: Harvard University Press, 2001.

Roberts, Jon H., and James Turner. *The Sacred and the Secular University.* Princeton, NJ: Princeton University Press, 2000.

Robin, Ron. *The Making of the Cold War Enemy: Culture and Politics in the Military-Intellectual Complex.* Princeton, NJ: Princeton University Press, 2001.

Rothstein, William G. *American Medical Schools and the Practice of Medicine: A History.* New York: Oxford University Press, 1987.

Rudolph, Frederick. *The American College and University: A History.* New York: Random House, 1962.

———. *Curriculum: A History of the American Undergraduate Course of Study since 1636.* San Francisco: Jossey-Bass, 1977.

Saunders, Francis. *The Cultural Cold War: The CIA and the World of Arts and Letters.* New York: New Press, 2000.

Schrecker, Ellen W. *No Ivory Tower: McCarthyism and the Universities.* New York: Oxford University Press, 1986.

Simpson, Christopher, ed. *Universities and Empire: Money and Politics in the Social Sciences during the Cold War.* New York: New Press, 1998.

Smith, Ronald A. *Sports and Freedom: The Rise of Big-Time College Athletics.* New York: Oxford University Press, 1988.

Starr, Paul. *The Social Transformation of American Medicine.* New York: Basic Books, 1982.

Steinberg, Stephen. *The Academic Melting Pot: Catholics and Jews in American Higher Education.* New York: McGraw-Hill, 1974.

Stevens, Robert. *Law School: Legal Education in America from the 1850s to the 1980s.* Chapel Hill: University of North Carolina Press, 1983.

Stevens, Rosemary. *In Sickness and in Wealth: American Hospitals in the Twentieth Century.* New York: Basic Books, 1989.

Thelin, John R. *Games Colleges Play: Scandal and Reform in Intercollegiate Athletics.* Baltimore: Johns Hopkins University Press, 1994.

———. *A History of American Higher Education,* Baltimore: Johns Hopkins University Press, 2004.

Turner, Paul Venable. *Campus: An American Planning Tradition.* Cambridge, MA: MIT Press, 1984.

Vesey, Lawrence R. *The Emergence of the American University.* Chicago: University of Chicago Press, 1965.

Wang, Jessica. *American Science in an Age of Anxiety: Scientists, Anticommunism, and the Cold War.* Chapel Hill: University of North Carolina Press, 1999.

Watterson, John S., III. "The Football Crisis of 1909–1910: The Response of the Eastern 'Big Three.'" *Journal of Sport History* 8 (Spring 1981): 33–49.

Watterson, John Sayle. *College Football: History, Spectacle, Controversy.* Baltimore: Johns Hopkins University Press, 2000.

Winks, Robin W. *Cloak and Gown: Scholars in the Secret War, 1939–1961.* New Haven, CT: Yale University Press, 1987.

GEORGETOWN UNIVERSITY HISTORY AND RELATED DOCUMENTS

Abell, William S. Fifty *Years at Garrett Park, 1919–1969: A History of the New Georgetown Preparatory School.* Garrett Park, MD: Georgetown Preparatory School, 1970.

Alleva, Stephen F. "'A Lasting Lifetime, Loving Singing Group': The Georgetown Chimes as an Ideal Institution." Thesis, Georgetown University, 2005.

Amster, Lewis J. "Bailey Ashford: Prophet of Tropical Medicine." *Hospital Practice* (April 15, 1985): 139–50.

Audette, Rose Marie L. "Everything in Moderation: Social Activism and University Reform, Georgetown University, 1960–1970." Honors thesis, Georgetown University, 1981.

Barry, Patricia. *Surgeons at Georgetown: Surgery and Medical Education in the Nation's Capital, 1849–1969.* Franklin, TN: Hillsboro Press, 2001.

Bealle, Morris A. *The Georgetown Hoyas: The Story of a Rambunctious Football Team.* Washington, DC: Columbia Publishing Co., 1947.

Bernad, Miguel Anselmo, SJ. "The Faculty of Arts in the Jesuit Colleges in the Eastern Part of the United States: Theory and Practice." PhD dissertation, Yale University, 1951.

Brauer, Car. M. *The Man Who Built Washington: A Life of John McShain.* Philadelphia: Hagley Museum, 1996.

Briefs, Henry. "Goetz Briefs on Capitalism and Democracy: An Introduction." *Review of Social Economy* 41 (1983): 212–27.

Brough, John B. "Philosophy at Georgetown University." In *Georgetown at Two Hundred: Faculty Reflections on the University's Future,* ed. William C. McFadden, 109–41. Washington, DC: Georgetown University Press, 1990.

Cannella, David E. "The Philodemic Debating Society: The Pursuit of Eloquence and Truth from 1894 to 1939." In *Swift Potomac's Lovely Daughter,* ed. Joseph Durkin, SJ, 121–34. Washington, DC: Georgetown University Press, 1990.

Chamberlain, Lawrence Carleton. "Georgetown University Library, 1789–1937." MSLS thesis, Catholic University of America, 1962.

Cooke, Lawrence H. "The History of the Georgetown Crew: Guardian of the Blue and Gray." In *Swift Potomac's Lovely Daughter,* ed. Joseph Durkin, SJ, 321–39. Washington, DC: Georgetown University Press, 1990.

Crosby, Donald F., SJ. *God, Church, and Flag: Senator Joseph R. McCarthy and the Catholic Church, 1950–1957.* Chapel Hill: University of North Carolina Press, 1978.

Derry, Thomas. "The Georgetown Observatory: A Room with a View." *Georgetown Magazine,* Fall 1987, 16–17.

Earley, Joseph E. "Science and Story at Georgetown." In *Georgetown at Two Hundred: Faculty Reflections on the University's Future,* ed. William C. McFadden, 185–99. Washington, DC: Georgetown University Press, 1990.

Ernst, Dan, et al. *The First One Hundred and Twenty-five Years: An Illustrated History of the Georgetown University Law Center.* Washington, DC: Georgetown University Law Center, 1995.

Foley, Albert Sidney, SJ. "The Catholic Church and the Washington Negro." PhD dissertation, University of North Carolina, 1950.

Georgetown University School of Languages and Linguistics. *The Lado Years.* Washington, DC: Georgetown University Press, 1973.

Goldblatt, Craig, "Look beyond the Campus, to America Itself: Student Activism at Georgetown University during the 1960s and the Founding of *The Georgetown Voice.* Unpublished paper, Georgetown University, 1988.

Golden, Hugh J. "Georgetown Football: A Complete History (1874–1987)." Unpublished paper.

Gorman, Vincent J. "Georgetown University: The Early Relationship with the Catholic University of America, 1884–1907," *Records of the American Catholic Historical Society of Philadelphia* (Fall 1991): 13–31.

Griffin, Maura. "Notes from the Underground." *Georgetown Magazine,* Spring 1989, 8–11.

Hanley, Thomas O'Brien, SJ, ed. *The John Carroll Papers.* 3 volumes. Notre Dame, IN: University of Notre Dame Press, 1976.

Hess, Walter C. "The History of the Georgetown University School of Medicine, 1930–1964." *Georgetown Medical Bulletin* (August 1964): 48–59.

Heyden, Francis J., SJ. *The Beginning and End of a Jesuit Observatory (1841–1972).* Quezon City, Philippines, n.d.

Kearns, Francis. "Sit-In." *Commonweal,* April 19, 1963, 100–102.

———. "Social Consciousness and Academic Freedom in Catholic Higher Education." In *The Shape of Catholic Higher Education, ed. Robert Hassenger.* Chicago: University of Chicago Press, 1967.

Keeler, Virginia M. "The Search for Freedom and Freedom Found: The Life and Art of Brother Francis C. Schroen, S.J." Master's thesis, Georgetown University, 1989.

Kerr, Michael E. "Darwin to Freud to Bowen: Toward a Natural Systems Theory of Human Behavior." *Georgetown Magazine,* Spring 1989, 16–19.

Leo, John. "The Kearns Case." *Commonweal,* January 29, 1965.

Luongo, Edward Parker. *A Biography of Wallace Mason Yater, M.D.* Washington, DC: privately published, n.d.

McFadden, William. "'Catechism at 4 for All the Schools': Religious Instruction at Georgetown." In *Georgetown at Two Hundred: Faculty Reflections on the University's Future,* ed. William C. McFadden, 143–68. Washington, DC: Georgetown University Press, 1990.

———. "What the Hell Is a Hoya?" *Georgetown Magazine,* Spring–Summer 1992, 20–23.

McFadden, William C., SJ, ed. *Georgetown at Two Hundred: Faculty Reflections on the University's Future.* Washington, DC: Georgetown University Press, 1990.

McHugh, Edward F. "Georgetown Track and Baseball." In *Swift Potomac's Lovely Daughter,* ed. Joseph Durkin, SJ, 341–46. Washington, DC: Georgetown University Press, 1990.

McNamara, Patrick J. "Edmund A. Walsh, SJ, and Catholic Anticommunism in the United States, 1917–1952." PhD dissertation, Catholic University of America, 2003.

Meagher, Timothy. "The Irish-American at Georgetown and Holy Cross, 1870–1917." Senior thesis, Georgetown University, 1971.

Mitchell, Mary. *Chronicles of Georgetown Life, 1865–1900.* Cabin John, MD: Seven Locks Press, 1986.

Mlyniec, Wallace. "The Intersection of Three Visions—Ken Pye, Bill Pincus, and Bill Greenhalgh—and the Development of Clinical Teaching Fellowships." *Tennessee Law Review* 64 (Summer 1997).

———. "The Georgetown University Law Center, 1967–1972." Unpublished paper delivered at the Georgetown University Law Faculty Retreat, 1991.

Nash, James A. "The Battle of the University." *CJ* 72 (September 1943): 30.

Quirk, Rory. "Georgetown Lou." *Georgetown Magazine,* November–December 1979, 22–25.

Quirk, Rory F. *Hoya Saxa: Georgetown Football, 1874–1978.* Washington, DC: n.p., 1979.

Reardon, William. "G.U. at War." *CJ* 72 (September 1943): 15.

Reynolds, Jon. "It's Been So Long since Last We Met . . . Lie Down, Virginia Lie Down." *Georgetown Magazine,* November–December 1982, 14–15.

Rigge, William F., SJ. *Jesuit Astronomy. Part 2, The Restored Society, 1814–1904.* Northfield, MN: n.p., 1904.

Rose, John C. "A System of Continuing Medical Education." *Medical Annals of D.C.* (September 1967): 510–13.

Rosen, George. "From Frontier Surgeon to Industrial Hygienist: The Strange Career of George M. Kober." *American Journal of Public Health* 65 (June 1975): 638–43.

Rosenstein, Jay. "A 'Rousing Hoya' for the War Effort." *Georgetown Today,* January 1977, 13–14.

Shea, John Gilmary. *Memorial of the First Centenary of Georgetown College, D.C. Comprising a History of Georgetown University.* Washington, DC: P. F. Collier, 1891.

Shelby, Joyce. "One Dentist for a Million People." *Georgetown Magazine,* January 1975, 30.

Smith, James Allen. *Strategic Calling: The Center for Strategic and International Studies, 1962–1992.* Washington, DC: Center for Strategic and International Studies, 1993.

Stapleton, John F. *Upward Journey: The Story of Internal Medicine at Georgetown, 1851–1981.* Washington, DC: Georgetown University Medical Center, 1996.

Stein, J., SJ. "Johann Georg Hagen, S.J." *Astronomische Nachrichten,* Band 240, no. 5744, col. 131–36.

Stevens, Carolyn. "Donn B. Murphy: Bringing Up the Lights for Three Decades of Students." *Georgetown Magazine,* September–October 1984, 12–13.

Stone, Lawrence. "Prosopography." *Daedalus* 100 (Winter 1971): 46–49.

Thomas, Evan. *The Man to See: Edward Bennett Williams, Ultimate Insider; Legendary Trial Lawyer.* New York: Simon & Schuster, 1991.

Tillman, Seth P. *Georgetown's School of Foreign Service: The First Seventy-five Years.* Washington, DC: Edmund A. Walsh School of Foreign Service, 1994.

Tondorf, Francis A., SJ. "Fr. John G. Hagen, S.J." *CJ* 55 (April 1927): 313.

Udias, Agustin, and William Stauder. "Jesuit Geophysical Observatories." *Eos, Transactions, American Geophysical Union* 72 (April 16, 1991): 188.

Waldron, David L. "Immigration." *CJ* 40 (October 1911): 6–11.

Walsh, Edmund. "Welcoming Address at Honorary Degree Ceremony for the Minister of Foreign Relations of Venezuela." *CJ* 49 (May 1921): 380–82.

Woolley, Alma S. *Learning, Faith, and Caring: History of the Georgetown University School of Nursing, 1903–2000.* Washington, DC: Georgetown University School of Nursing, 2001.

JESUIT AND CATHOLIC EDUCATIONAL HISTORY

Ahern, Patrick Henry. *The Catholic University of America, 1887–1896: The Rectorship of John J. Keane.* Washington, DC: Catholic University of America Press, 1948.

Edmondson, Elizabeth A. "Without Comment or Controversy: The G.I. Bill and Catholic Colleges." *Church History* (December 2002): 820–47.

Fitzgerald, Paul A., SJ. *The Governance of Jesuit Colleges in the United States, 1920–1970.* Notre Dame, IN: University of Notre Dame Press, 1984.

Gannon, Michael V. "Before and After Modernism: The Intellectual Isolation of the American Priest." In *The Catholic Priest in the United States: Historical Investigations,* ed. John Tracy Ellis, 359. Collegeville, MN: St. John's University Press, 1971.

Gleason, Philip. *Contending with Modernity: Catholic Higher Education in the Twentieth Century.* New York: Oxford University Press, 1995.

Hassenger, Robert, ed. *The Shape of Catholic Higher Education.* Chicago: University of Chicago Press, 1967.

Hennesey, James, SJ. "Jesuit Higher Education." *History of Education Quarterly* (Autumn 1985): 391–97.

Leahy, William P., SJ. *Adapting to America: Catholics, Jesuits, and Higher Education in the Twentieth Century.* Washington, DC: Georgetown University Press, 1991.

———. "The Rise of the Laity in American Catholic Higher Education." *Records of the American Catholic Historical Society of Philadelphia* (Fall 1990): 17–32.

Mahoney, Kathleen. *Catholic Higher Education in Protestant America: The Jesuits and Harvard in the Age of the University.* Baltimore: Johns Hopkins University Press, 2003.

———. "Fin-de-Siècle Catholics: Insiders and Outsiders at Harvard." *U.S. Catholic Historian* 13 (Fall 1995): 19–48.

Neusse, C. Joseph. *The Catholic University of America: A Centennial History.* Washington, DC: Catholic University of America Press, 1990.

Power, Edward J. *A History of Catholic Higher Education in the United States.* Milwaukee: Bruce, 1958.

Rury, John L. "The Urban Catholic University in the Early Twentieth Century." *History of Higher Education Annual* (1997): 5–32.

Stamm, Martin J. "Laicization of Corporate Governance of Twentieth Century American Catholic Higher Education." *Records of the American Catholic Historical Society of Philadelphia* (March–December 1983): 81–99.

Wills, Jeffrey, ed. *The Catholics of Harvard Square.* Petersham, MA: Saint Bede's, 1993.

Index